COFFEE

COFFEE

MARY BANKS, CHRISTINE MCFADDEN, CATHERINE ATKINSON

HERMES HOUSE

This edition is published by Hermes House

Hermes House is an imprint of Anness Publishing Ltd
Hermes House, 88–89 Blackfriars Road, London SE1 8HA
tel. 020 7401 2077; fax 020 7633 9499; info@anness.com

© Anness Publishing Ltd 1999, 2002

Published in the USA by Hermes House, Anness Publishing Inc.
27 West 20th Street, New York, NY 10011; fax 212 807 6813

A CIP catalogue record for this book is available from the British Library.

Publisher: Joanna Lorenz
Editor: Margaret Malone
Designer: Ian Hunt (reference) and Jane Felstead (recipes and jacket)
Photography: William Lingwood (recipes), Louisa Dare (steps and equipment)
and Janine Hosegood (coffee bean samples)
Food for Photography: Carol Tennant (recipes)
Styling: Helen Trent (recipes)
Editorial Reader: Hayley Kerr
Production Controller: Don Campaniello

Previously published as *The World Encyclopedia of Coffee*

Printed and bound in China

1 3 5 7 9 10 8 6 4 2

NOTES

For all recipes, quantities are given in both metric and imperial measures and, where
appropriate, measures are also given in standard cups and spoons. Follow one set, but
not a mixture because they are not interchangeable.

Standard spoon and cup measures are level.
1 tsp = 5ml, 1 tbsp = 15ml, 1 cup = 250ml/8fl oz

Australian standard tablespoons are 20ml. Australian readers should use 3 tsp in place
of 1 tbsp for measuring small quantities of gelatine, cornflour, salt etc.

Medium eggs are used unless otherwise stated.

Contents

THE WORLD
OF COFFEE

Everything you ever wanted to know about coffee is contained within this fascinating and beautiful book. Intended as a definitive guide to coffee, the reference section explores the history and cultural, political and economic impact of coffee across the world plus examines on a country-by-country basis the tastes and characteristics of coffee produced today. It also explains how to grind, brew and make the perfect cup of coffee.

In the second half of the book, there are over 70 recipes demonstrating the wonderful versatility of coffee in the kitchen, with delicious souffles and meringues, puddings, fruit and frozen desserts, and enticing cakes, pastries and breads.

THE HISTORY
OF COFFEE

This section traces the mysterious and conflict-ridden journey of
the coffee bean from its Ethiopian birthplace, through Arabia
and the Middle East, and on to Europe and the New World.
The crucial role of the beverage in shaping the spiritual and
social life of medieval Arabia and Turkey is examined, as is
how, later, it became irrevocably entrenched in Western cultures.
The vital role of the coffee house in the political, economic and
cultural life across the world is covered, both historically and up
to the present day. There is also a section devoted to the myriad
methods of early coffee brewing and a discussion on
coffee-drinking and coffee products.

THE GENESIS OF THE BEAN

Ever since its migration from north-east Africa to Arabia many hundreds of years ago, this vital bean has played a multifaceted role in moulding history. That short hop across the Red Sea helped alter social, political and economic life not only in Africa and the Middle East, but in mainland Europe, Britain and the Americas too. Coffee has made the fortunes and misfortunes of many, oiled the wheels of communication, inspired creative minds, stimulated the tired, and, for countless imbibers the world over, become a daily necessity.

Myths and Mysteries

So great was the mystique ascribed to coffee, that conjecture over the who, how and when of the invention of the beverage and the discovery of its properties was intense. Doctors, lawyers, poets and philosophers all had their pet theories and great kudos was linked to association with the so-called "discovery". As a result, in medieval Arabia and later in 17th-century Europe, stories and legends were rife.

Parched Corn or Black Broth

Those with a historical bent and a lively imagination traced the bean back to Old Testament tales, claiming that it was the same "parched corn" that Abigail gave to David, and Boaz to Ruth. Many were convinced it was the "black broth" of the Lacedaemonians, as the Spartans were then called. Petrus de Valle, a well-known Italian traveller, believed that coffee dated as far back as the Trojan war, suggesting that "the fair Helen with other ladies of Priamus's Court, used sometimes to drown the Thoughts of the Calamities she had brought upon her Family and Country, in a Pot of Coffee". Others thought that, in Homer's *Odyssey*, the substance called "nepenthes", which Helen mixed with wine and which "banishes sadness and wrath from the heart" was coffee.

Banesius, a late 18th-century writer, theorized in a treatise on coffee that since it was a medicine and most medicines were discovered by chance, the discovery of "this Liquor was as much a proof of fortuitous Experience as any of those (other medicines)".

Following this line of thought, Banesius went on to recount the ubiquitous fable of the dancing goats, in which an Arab or Ethiopian goatherd complained to the Imam of a neighbouring monastery that his flock "two or three times a week not only kept awake all night long but spent it frisking and dancing in an unusual manner". The Imam, concluding that the animals may have eaten something that was causing the reaction, went to the pasture where they danced. Here he found berries growing on shrubs, and he decided to try them himself.

Having boiled the berries in water and drunk the resulting brew, the Imam found that he was able to stay awake at night without any ill effects. Encouraged by what had been an enjoyable experience, he "enjoin'd the daily Use of it to his Monks, which, by keeping them from Sleep, made them more readily and surely attend the Devotions they were obliged to perform at Night time... It continued to keep them in perfect Health; and by this means it came to be in request throughout that whole Kingdom".

Dr James Douglas, in his scholarly work *Yemensis fructum Café ferens; or, a description and history of the Coffee tree* (1727), somewhat scathingly dismisses Banesius's story as having "too great an Air of Fable to be in the least depended on", stating that "those who are acquainted with the Nature of Vulgar Traditions, especially those of Eastern nations, will understand its thin credibility".

One of the many variations of the tale – this one by Sir Thomas Pope Blount – tells of how the Imam tried the coffee experiment upon "another sort of Beast, a sleepy Heavy-headed Monk". In a short time, the story goes, it had such a wonderful effect on him, that it "quite alter'd his Constitution, and hereafterwards became more quick, brisk, and airy than generally that sort of Cattle are".

Left: "Ruth on the Field of Boaz", wood engraving, from The Bible in Pictures, Leipzig, 1860 by Julius Schnorr von Carolsfeld (1794–1874).

Basic botany

Coffee comes from the fruit of an evergreen shrub, or tree, which flourishes in tropical and subtropical regions around the world. The trees produce delicate clusters of jasmine-scented blossoms, and fruit known as "cherries". Cocooned in each cherry, protected by pulp and parchment, are two coffee beans. Since approximately four thousand beans are needed to produce one pound of roasted coffee, few commodities require so much in terms of human effort.

Right: **Coffea arabica,** *botanical magazine, London, 1810.*

The Muslim View

The Muslims had another story which Dr Douglas describes as "still more wonderful, but equally groundless". The Muslims claimed that because of their special relationship with "Providence", and so that they would gain from so "beneficial a Liquor", the archangel Gabriel was sent to reveal to the prophet Mohammed "the Virtues and manner of preparing it" (coffee).

Yet another legend tells of the dervish Omar, known for his ability to heal the sick by prayer. Exiled from his home town of Mocha to a cave in the desert and nearing starvation, Omar chewed berries from shrubs growing nearby. Finding the berries too bitter, he roasted them, hoping to improve the flavour. Obviously a man

of refined palate (and surprisingly well equipped with the necessary utensils), he decided the berries now needed boiling to soften them. He drank the resulting fragrant brew and was instantly revitalized, remaining in this state for several days.

A picturesque variation of the same tale states how Omar saw a bird of marvellous plumage in a tree, where it sang an exquisitely harmonious song. When he reached out for the bird, Omar found only flowers and fruit in its place. He filled his basket with these and returned to the cave, intending to boil a few meagre herbs for dinner. However, he boiled the fruit instead and created a savoury and perfumed brown drink.

Eventually – and both variations concur with this – patients from Mocha came to the cave for medical advice. They, too, were given the drink and, since this is a legend, they were of course cured. When news of the "miracle cure" reached Mocha, Omar was invited to return in triumph and was subsequently made the patron saint of the city.

Despite the vast literature assembled by many historians, no one has ever been able to say positively how and when the plant was discovered. Its origins therefore remain shrouded in legend in which truth and imagination are inexorably entwined.

Below: 1950s British advertisement referring to the story of the discovery of coffee's properties by goats eating the berries of a certain tree.

ODYSSEY FROM AFRICA

The coffee plant found its way from Ethiopia to Arabia sometime between AD 575 and AD 850. How it got there is not clear, but one possibility is that seeds were brought by African tribes-people as they migrated northwards from Kenya and Ethiopia to the Arabian peninsular. They were eventually driven back by spear-throwing Persians but they left behind coffee trees growing in what is now the Yemen.

Myths and Legends

Another possibility is that Arab slave traders brought the seeds back from their raids on Ethiopia; or, as is more likely, the responsibility lay with the Sufis – a mystical Islamic sect best-known for their "whirling dervishes". Classical Arabic literature endorses this, suggesting that it was a Sufi grand master, Ali ben Omar al Shadili, who brought coffee seeds to Arabia. Al Shadili had lived for a while in Ethiopia before founding a monastery in the Yemenite port of Mocha (Al Mukha). Since he later became known as the Saint of Mocha, he appears to be the same legendary Omar who discovered coffee berries while exiled in the desert, though the stories do not quite tie up.

   According to Dr Douglas, a reasonably reliable account was unearthed in a collection of original manuscripts by Monsieur de Nointel, Louis IV's ambassador at the Arab ports. Written by an Arab in 1587, the document gives what was believed at the time to be the earliest account of the use of coffee and its subsequent spread through the Middle East. The author tells how the Mufti of Aden, while travelling through Persia in the mid-15th century, came upon some of his compatriots enjoying coffee. Returning to Aden in poor health, he remembered this liquor and thought it might help him recover. He sent for some, and found that it not only prevented sleep without any ill effects, but also "dissipated all manner of Heaviness and Drowsiness, and made him more bright and gay than he was wont to be".

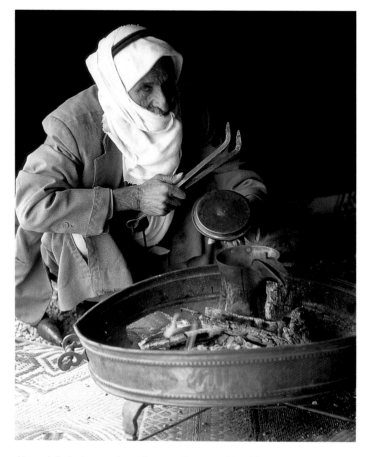

Above: A Bedouin preparing coffee according to traditional Arabic methods.

Wishing to share the benefits with his dervishes, the Mufti gave them coffee before they embarked on their night-long prayers. He found that they, too, were able to perform "all their Exercises of religion with great Alacrity and Freedom of Mind".

   Whatever the route and circumstances, there is firm evidence that the first cultivated coffee trees grew in monastery gardens in the Yemen, and most Arab authorities agree that the Sufi community was in one way or another responsible.

From Food to Beverage

As with the discovery of the plant and its journey to Arabia, the process of development from food to hot beverage is also a matter of historical speculation.

   The comments of the early European explorers and botanists indicate that the Ethiopians chewed raw coffee beans – obviously appreciative of their stimulating effect. They also pounded ripe coffee cherries, mixed them with animal fat and moulded the resulting paste into pellets. This powerful cocktail of fat, caffeine and meat protein was a vital source of concentrated energy, particularly valuable in times of tribal conflict when warriors were required to give their all. The cherries were probably eaten as a ripe fruit, too, since the pulp is sweet and contains caffeine.

Early records also show that a wine was made from the fermented juice of the ripe cherries. The wine was called *qahwah*, meaning "that which excites and causes the spirits to rise", a term which was eventually used for both wine and coffee. Since wine was prohibited by Mohammed, coffee was nicknamed "the wine of Araby".

It seems possible that coffee was treated as a food in Arabia, too, and only later mixed with water to make a drink. The earliest version of the beverage was probably a liquid produced by steeping a few whole hulls in cold water. Later, the hulls were roasted over an open fire, and then boiled in water for about thirty minutes until a pale yellow liquid was produced.

By about AD 1000, the drink was still a relatively crude decoction made with green coffee beans and their hulls. It was probably not until around the

Right: Illustration showing the early Arabic method of brewing coffee over an open fire.

13th century that the beans were dried before use. They were laid out in the sun, and once dry, could be stored for longer periods. After that, it was a small step to roast them over a charcoal fire.

Early Uses

Initially, coffee was consumed only as part of a religious ceremony or on the advice of a physician. Once the medical men had observed coffee's beneficial effects, more and more of them started to prescribe it. Coffee was used to treat an astounding variety of ailments, including kidney stones, gout, smallpox, measles and coughs. A late 17th-century treatise on coffee and its uses quotes the work of Prosper Alpinus, a botanist. In his book on the medicines and plants of Egypt, Alpinus writes: "It is an excellent Remedy against the stoppage of Women's Courses, and they make often use thereof, when they don't flow so fast as they desire...it is a quick and certain remedy for those Women, who not having their courses are troubled with violent pains."

He goes on to describe how coffee was made: "This Decoction they make two ways: the one with the skin or the outside of the aforesaid Grain, and the other with the very substance of the Bean. That which is made with the skin is of more force then the other...

The Grain...is put into an Iron Instrument firmly shut together with the coverlid, through this Instrument they thrust a Spit, by the means thereof they turn it before the Fire, till it shall be well roasted; after which having beaten it into a very fine Powder, you may make use thereof, in an equal proportion according to the number of people that will drink it: Viz the third part of a spoonful for each person, and put it into a glass of boyling Water, putting a little Sugar thereto: And after having let it boyl a small time, you must pour it into little dishes of porcelain or any other sort, and so let it be drunk by little and little, as hot as it can be possibly indur'd".

Bun and bunchum

The African word for the coffee plant was *bun*, which then became the Arabic *bunn*, meaning both the plant and the berry. Rhazes (AD 850–922), a doctor who lived in Persian Iraq, and a follower of Galen and Hippocrates, compiled a medical encyclopedia in which he refers to the bean as *bunchum*. His discussion of its healing properties no doubt led to the belief that coffee was known as a medicine over a thousand years ago. Similar references appear in the writings of Avicenna (AD 980–1037), another distinguished Muslim physician and philosopher.

The word "coffee", meaning the drink, is a modified form of the Turkish word *kahveh* which, in turn, is derived from the Arabic *kahwa* (or *qahwah*).

Above: Portrait of Avicenna, Muslim physician, painting c. 17th century.

THE WINE OF ARABY

Above: On the steps of a Turkish coffee house, illustration, early 19th century.

Coffee Takes a Hold

The new drink quickly spread from Aden to neighbouring towns, and by about the end of the 15th century had reached the holy city of Mecca. Here, as in Aden, coffee-drinking at first centred around the dervish community at the mosque.

Before long, the citizens were also regularly drinking coffee at home and in public areas set apart for the purpose. They did so with obvious enjoyment as an Arab historian reports: "Thither Crowds of People resorted at all Hours of the Day, to enjoy the pleasure of Conversation, play at Chess and other games, dance, sing, and divert themselves all manner of ways, under the pretence of drinking Coffee".

As the centre of the Muslim world, Mecca's social and cultural practices were inevitably copied by Muslims in other major cities. Within a relatively short time, therefore, coffee-drinking took hold throughout much of Arabia, spreading west to Egypt, and north through Syria. The coffee habit was also established further by the Muslim armies who, at that time, were advancing through southern Europe, Spain and North Africa, and east to India. Wherever they went, they took coffee with them.

Coffee thus became an integral part of Middle Eastern life. So crucial was the drink to the smooth-running of society that, in many areas, marriage contracts stipulated that a husband should allow his wife as much coffee as she wanted. Failure to do so was grounds for a woman to sue for divorce.

Coffee in Persia

The coffee habit perhaps took root in Persia even before it came to Arabia. Persian warriors were said to have driven back the Ethiopians when they tried to settle in the Yemen. The Persians would have undoubtedly found to their liking the coffee cherries growing on the trees planted by the Ethiopians, and taken them back to their own country. The story of the Mufti of Aden also refers to coffee-drinking in Persia in the mid-15th century.

Following the example of the Mufti of Aden and his monks, religious communities throughout Arabia took up the practice of drinking coffee. Little by little, however, its use spread beyond religious confines. Aden's citizens were among the first to take up the habit. Since the Mufti was a respected authority on Muslim law and presumably would not knowingly consume an illegal substance himself, they were keen to follow his example and try this new drink themselves.

Coffee-drinking took place in the mosque where, after the monks had had their fill, the Imam offered it to others who happened to be present. Served in this ceremonious manner against a background of devout chanting, coffee-drinking was seen as a wholesome and pious activity. However, everyone who tasted coffee liked it and wanted more, and it was not long before word spread of the rewards to be reaped from visiting the mosque.

Anxious to quell the trend, religious authorities tried in vain to restrict coffee consumption. Imams and monks were allowed to imbibe, but only in conjunction with their nightly prayers; physicians were also allowed to prescribe small quantities. However, as the less spiritually inclined continued to make late-night appearances at the mosque, and doctors increasingly began to prescribe coffee for all manner of ills, it was hard to curtail its use.

Recipients in the mosque found coffee a pleasant stimulant and conducive to sociability. Before long, the beverage was sold openly in the area, attracting a motley crowd of law students, night workers and travellers. Eventually, the whole city took up the practice, not just at night but round-the-clock and in the home too. Not surprisingly, the hot, strong coffee was particularly popular during Ramadan, when fasting is obligatory from sunrise to sunset.

Coffee and religious devotion

The Muslims were convinced that the drink was a gift from Allah and were almost fanatical in their enthusiasm, as the following eulogy – or tirade – shows. Translated from the Arabic and printed, curiously, in the Transylvanian Journal of Medicine in the early part of the 19th century, the original is said to be the work of Sheik Abdal-Kader Anasari Djezeri Haubuli, son of Mohammed:

"O COFFEE! thou dispellest the cares of the great: thou bringest back those who wander from the paths of knowledge. Coffee is the beverage of the people of God, and the cordial of his servants who thirst for wisdom...
...Every care vanishes when the cup bearer present thee the delicious chalice. It will circulate fleetly through thy veins, and will not rankle there: if thou doubtest this, contemplate the youth and beauty of those who drink it...
...Coffee is the drink of God's people; in it is health...Whoever has seen the blissful chalice, will scorn the wine cup. Glorious drink! thy colour is the seal of purity, and reason proclaims it genuine. Drink with confidence, and regard not the prattle of fools, who condemn without foundation..."

From very early on, most major Persian cities boasted stylish and spacious coffee houses situated in the best parts of town. These establish-ments had a reputation for serving coffee quickly, efficiently, and "with abundance of Respect". As a rule, the political discussions and resulting disturbances usually associated with the coffee house scene were kept low-key; it seems the clientele were more interested in hedonistic pursuits. Persian coffee houses developed a reputation for talking, music, dancing and "other things of that kind", and there are even several reports of how the government was obliged to put a stop to "the infamous practices committed there".

An English traveller tells the tale of how the wife of the Shah tactfully appointed a mullah – an expert in legal and ecclesiastical matters – to make a daily visit to a particularly crowded and popular coffee house. His job was to sit there and entertain the patrons with civilized discussion of poetry, history and law. A man of discretion, he avoided controversial political issues, and disturbances were therefore rare. The mullah became a welcome visitor.

Having seen that the scheme was a success, other coffee houses soon followed suit and employed their own mullahs and story-tellers. These newfound entertainers sat in a centrally placed high chair "from whence they make speeches and tell satirical stories, playing in the meantime with a little stick and using the same gestures as our jugglers...do in England".

Coffee in Turkey

Despite having reached neighbouring Syria, coffee-drinking was relatively slow to spread to Turkey. However, following the expansion of the Ottoman Empire and the subsequent conquest of Arab Muslims, the Turks finally took to coffee drinking with a vengeance, as an English doctor writing from Constantinople confirms: "When a Turk is sick he fasts and takes Coffa, and if that will not do, he makes his will, and thinks of no other Phisick".

New watering holes According to a 16th-century Arab writer, the first two coffee houses in Constantinople were set up in 1554 by a couple of Syrian entrepreneurs quick to spot a trend. Their premises were impressively furnished with "very neat couches and carpets, on which they received their company, which first consisted mostly of studious persons, lovers of chess, trictrac, and other sedentary Diversions". Other equally opulent coffee shops quickly opened, sometimes to the dismay of the more pious Muslims. They were richly decorated and the clientele reclined on luxurious cushions while they were entertained with stories and poetry as well as singing and dancing by professional performers.

Despite the ever-increasing number of new establishments, the coffee houses were always crowded with people. Historians disagree as to the social standing of the clientele, some saying the coffee houses were frequented almost exclusively by "the lower orders", others claiming that they

Right: A Turkish domestic servant preparing coffee in the home.

appealed to all levels of society. As Hattox states in *The Social Life of the Coffeehouse*: "From the assumption that all classes went to coffee houses it does not of necessity follow that all classes went to the same coffee house."

The legal profession obviously found the coffee houses a useful place for networking, since the patrons of one establishment were said to consist mainly of travelling *cadhis* (judges) who were in Constantinople looking for work;

the professors of law or other sciences, as well as students coming up for graduation and eager to secure a prestigious job. Even the chief officer of the Sultan's palace and other high-ranking members were seen to drop by.

The travelling English – writers, botanists, doctors – had never seen anything like the coffee houses and wrote extensively about them. Henry Blunt in his *Voyage to the Levant* recounted with amazement: "for there upon Scaffolds half a yard high and covered with Mats, they sit crosse-legg'd after the Turkish manner, many times two or three hundred together, talking, and likely with some poor Musick passing up and down".

Sir George Sandys wrote somewhat disapprovingly: "there sit they chatting most of the day, and sip of a Drink called Coffa...in little China Dishes, as hot as they can suffer it, black it is as soot, tasting not much unlike it...which helpeth, as they say, Digestion, and procureth Alacrity. Many of the Coffa-men keeping beautiful Boys, who serve...to procure them Customers".

Coffee at home The Turks drank as much coffee at home as they consumed at the coffee house. A French traveller observed: "as much money must be spent in the private families of Constantinople for coffee as for wine at Paris". Sir Henry Blunt wrote in a letter to a friend: "for besides the innumerable store of Coffa-houses, there is not a private fire without it all day long".

Blunt went further, extolling the many therapeutic benefits of drinking coffee: "they (the Turks) all acknowledge how it freeth them from Crudities caused by ill Diet, or moist Lodging, insomuch as they using Coffa Morning and Evening, have no Consumptions which ever come of Moisture; no Lethargies in aged People; or Rickets in Children, and but few Qualms in Women with Child: But especially they hold it of singular prevention against the Stone and Gout."

Left: Large numbers gathered in the coffee houses to gossip and sip coffee.

CUSTOM AND RITUAL

Once coffee had started to lose its religious associations, coffee houses, or *qahveh khaneh*, sprang up all over the Middle East. There were also hole-in-the-wall coffee shops, and strolling vendors who heated coffee over small spirit lamps and filled the dishes of passers-by.

At the same time, coffee-drinking had become equally well established in the home. No social interaction was complete without it. Coffee was served by barbers before haircuts, by merchants before and after bargaining, at chance meetings between friends and at the most formal of banquets. European travel writers were astounded by the level of consumption. One wrote: "They drink coffee not only in their houses, but even in the publick streets as they go about their business, and sometimes three or four people, by turns, out of the same cup".

A Better Brew

By the early 16th century, whole coffee beans were roasted on special stone trays, and later on metal plates. Once roasted, the beans were boiled for thirty minutes or more, producing a strong dark liquor which was stored in vats until needed. As demand increased, however, preparation and brewing techniques improved. Coffee was freshly made with pulverized beans and boiling water. Sugar and delicious spices, such as cardamom, cinnamon and cloves, were added to improve the flavour. Although the use of roasted beans had become common practice, coffee made with the lightly roasted cherries (with the bean removed) was still highly prized in the Yemen where the coffee trees grew. Known as "Sultan's coffee", it was drunk mainly by those of the highest rank, or by visitors to whom it was served as a testimony of respect and honour.

Café à la Sultane

"*The manner of making the* Café à la Sultane *is this. They take the husks of perfectly ripe fruit, beat them, and put them in an earthen Pan over a Charcoal-Fire, keeping them constantly in motion, and only toast them until they change Colour a little. At the same time Water is set to boil in a Coffee-Pot, and when the Husks are ready, they throw in both the outer and inner Shells separately, about three times as many of the first as of the last; then boil them up in the same manner as common Coffee. The Colour of the Liquor is pretty much like that of best English Beer. The Husks must be kept in dry Places till they are used; for the least Moisture spoils the Taste of them.*"
Dr James Douglas, 1727.

Above: A strolling street vendor of coffee, Istanbul, early 18th century.

Life in the Coffee House

As the coffee houses proliferated, so did competition for customers. The coffee house masters tried to attract clientele "not only by the goodness of their Liquor, neatness and dexterity of their Servants" but also by sumptuous surroundings and entertainment. Musicians, jugglers and dancers were employed, and puppet shows were provided as well.

When customers grew bored with what the house had to offer, and conversation began to flag, they would make their own entertainment. Poets would be asked to recite, or, if a dervish was present, he would be invited to deliver a light-hearted sermon.

Backgammon, chess and various card games were also popular. Gambling almost certainly took place, as did drug use. Coffee had become popular with opium users, and there were always two or three *narghiles* (water pipes) available for the leisurely smoking of hashish or tobacco while customers waited to be served.

The British ritual of buying rounds of drinks in pubs undoubtedly has its roots in the Turkish coffee house. If a customer saw someone he knew about to order a coffee, he would shout a single word *caba*, meaning "gratis", which indicated to the proprietor that he was not to take the man's money. The newcomer, in turn, would individually greet all those already present before taking his seat. If an older man arrived, everyone would rise in respect and the best seat would be vacated for him.

It was customary to drink coffee as hot as the mouth could bear, so it was sipped, or more probably slurped, from a small china dish – handles were to come later. Early English travellers were probably amused, or even repelled, by this strange, rather exotic habit. One wrote: "they are sometimes near an hour on one dish...and it is none of the least diversions which strangers find among them, to hear this Sipping-Musick in a publick Coffee House, where perhaps some hundreds are drinking at a time".

Above: Turkish coffee house, lithograph, 1855.

Coffee Drinking in the Home

In 16th-century Constantinople, there was no house, rich or poor, Turkish or Jewish, Greek or Armenian, where coffee was not drunk at least twice a day, and usually more often – twenty dishes a day was not uncommon. It became a custom in every home, no matter how humble, to offer coffee to visitors and it was considered unspeakably ill-mannered to refuse it. At formal banquets, guests were offered coffee immediately upon arrival, and they were plied with it continually for the duration of the feast, which could have lasted as long as eight hours.

Though coffee-drinking had become an accepted part of everyday life, it nevertheless continued to maintain its magic. The way in which coffee was served in the home was always ceremonious. There was a requisite exchange of courteous greetings, enquiries after health and family, the praising of God, and elaborate rituals, similar in complexity to those of the Japanese tea ceremony. Melon seeds and dates might be served alongside the coffee to add to the enjoyment.

Most well-to-do households kept coffee stewards, whose sole responsibility was to attend to the preparation and serving of coffee. The chief steward, known as the *Kahveghi*, had the privilege of an "apartment" – probably little more than a cupboard – situated next to the coffee hall where visitors were received. The hall was decorated with richly coloured rugs and cushions, and gleaming ornamental coffee pots. Coffee was served with great decorum on silver or painted wooden trays large enough to hold up to twenty porcelain coffee dishes. These were always half-filled, not only to prevent spillage, but so that the dish could be held with the thumb below and two fingers on the upper edge.

Very grand households also kept pages, or *Itchoglans*, who, at a nod from the head of the household, took the coffee from the stewards and, with impressive dexterity, handed it to visitors without either touching the rim, burning themselves or spilling a drop.

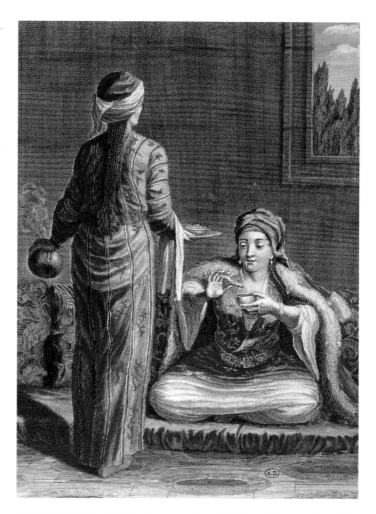

Above: Wealthy households had servants whose sole duty was to prepare the coffee.

Lord Byron on coffee

The Victorian poet's view of Turkish coffee comes across in this poem:
And Mocha's berry, from Arabia pure,
In small fine china cups, came in at last;
Gold cups of filigree, made to secure
the hand from burning, underneath them placed.
Cloves, cinnamon, and saffron, too, were boiled
up with the Coffee, which, I think, they spoiled.

COFFEE AND CONFLICT

When a seemingly exclusive group of people are seen to be enjoying themselves and getting a little lively, especially at night, other groups tend to feel threatened. So it was in 16th-century Arabia when the political and religious leaders could not fail to ignore the good times being had in the coffee house. As Hattox states in *The Social Life of the Coffeehouse*, the relaxed clubby atmosphere inevitably led to caffeine-induced airing of news, views and grievances concerning the state. Even worse, attendance at the mosque was in decline now that coffee could be obtained elsewhere.

The first place to experience the crackdown was the holy city of Mecca, where an assembly of muftis, lawyers and physicians declared that coffee-drinking was not only contrary to religious law but caused physical harm. The level of argument that went on demonstrates the passion which coffee aroused and the conflict it provoked amongst those anxious to be seen to be taking the politically correct line.

The Suppression of Coffee Drinking

The story goes that the Governor of Mecca was scandalized by the behaviour of a group of coffee-drinkers in the mosque who were legitimately preparing themselves for a long night of prayer. At first the Governor thought they were drinking wine, which was of course forbidden by Muslim law. Even when assured otherwise, the Governor concluded that coffee made people drunk or at least prone to acts of civil disorder, and he decided to prohibit its use. However, he first summoned a group of experts and asked for their considered opinion.

The legal experts stated that coffee houses were indeed in need of some reform, but that there was a fine line as to whether coffee beverages themselves were genuinely physically harmful, or whether they were simply a catalyst that adversely affected people's behaviour. Not wishing to take final responsibility for such a serious and delicate issue, they declared that the decision should rest with the physicians.

Two Persian brothers – practising physicians in Mecca – were summoned; it was no accident that one of them had written a book discouraging the use of coffee. Medical practice in those days was based on the concept of bodily humours, and the brothers accordingly declared that *bunn*, from which coffee was usually made, was "cold and dry" and therefore harmful to health. Another doctor present argued that *bunn* "scorched and consum'd the Phlegm", and could not possibly have the qualities attributed to it by the Persian brothers.

After protracted debate, everyone decided to play safe, and agreed that it would be prudent to declare coffee an illegal substance – as the Governor had intended all along. As a result, many of the assembled company eagerly confirmed that coffee had indeed "disordered their senses". One man inadvertently declared that when he drank coffee he experienced the same effects as wine produced – a laughter-provoking comment since he would have had to break Muslim law in order to know. When questioned, he imprudently acknowledged he had drunk wine and was duly punished.

Right: As coffee houses grew in popularity, it was not long before the relaxed behaviour of the coffee drinkers attracted the notice of religious and political leaders.

The Mufti of Mecca, a holy man and a lawyer by profession, heatedly opposed the decision but was alone in defending the drink. Ignoring the Mufti, the Governor signed a declaration outlawing the selling or drinking of coffee both in public and in private. All stores of the seditious berry were burnt; the coffee houses were shut down and their owners pelted with the fragments of broken pots and cups.

The declaration was sent to the Sultan of Egypt, who, much to the Governor's embarrassment, was astonished to hear of the condemnation of a beverage which the whole of Cairo found wholesome and beneficial. Moreover, Cairo's doctors of law, who had much greater status than those at Mecca, found nothing illegal in the use of it. The Governor was duly reprimanded and told he could use his authority only to prevent disorders that might take place in the coffee house. Coffee-drinking, which in any case had been going on behind closed doors, was restored. A year later, the Sultan condemned the Governor to death for his crime against coffee; the two Persian physicians subsequently met the same fate.

Arguing the finer points of Islamic law in relation to coffee became increasingly bizarre and esoteric. In Constantinople, for example, religious zealots claimed vehemently that the process of roasting reduced coffee to charcoal, and to use such a base article at the table, was grossly impious. The Mufti agreed and declared that coffee was illegal.

As usual, the ban was never entirely followed. People gradually reinstated coffee-drinking at home, and, having given up hope of enforcement, the officers of the law started to grant permission for coffee to be sold in private. Eventually, a less scrupulous Mufti was appointed and the coffee houses were opened again.

Next, a tax was introduced forcing Constantinople's coffee-house owners to pay an amount proportionate to business done. Despite this hefty contribution to government coffers, the

Above: The ritual of coffee drinking encompassed grinding, brewing and serving.

price of a cup of coffee remained as low as ever – a sure indication of the vast amount served.

In the years to follow, repeated attempts at suppression were made throughout the Middle East by political and religious leaders. Each time the usual string of complaints met with the usual anarchistic resistance. Lacking popular support and faced with divided opinion among the lawyers, physicians and religious experts, the attempts consistently failed. By the end of the century, coffee-drinking was a deeply rooted habit throughout the Middle East that no level of prohibition could budge.

MIGRATION OF THE TREE

Towards the end of the 16th century, reports from travellers and botanists of a strange new plant and drink began to reach Europe from the Middle East. As the reports grew in number and frequency, European merchants started to realize the potential of the new commodity. Already involved with Middle Eastern trade, the Venetians were quick to exploit this opportunity, and the first bags of coffee beans arrived in Venice from Mecca in the early 1600s.

The Arab Monopoly

Supplying coffee to the Venetians was the start of a lucrative export business for the Arabs, and one which they guarded jealously for almost a century. Great lengths were taken to ensure that no bean capable of germination left the country; beans were either boiled or parched, and visitors were kept well away from the coffee plantations. Until about the end of the 17th century, the Yemen was the only centre of supply for the European coffee trade.

Dutch Enterprise

Around the time that the Venetians took delivery of their first consignment of beans, Dutch merchants began to examine the possibility of coffee cultivation and trading. They already had a considerable amount of information from the botanists, and the merchants saw no reason why the Arabs should maintain their monopoly. At the time, the Dutch were probably Europe's most proactive traders and in possession of the best merchant ships. It comes as no surprise, therefore, to learn that a Dutch merchant managed to steal a coffee plant from Mocha and bring it unharmed back to Europe.

By the middle of the century, cultivation trials had been set up in the East Indian Dutch colony of Java – hence the well-known Mocha-Java blend of bean – and by the 1690s plantations had been established in rapid succession in the neighbouring island colonies of Sumatra, Timor, Bali and Celebes. The enterprising Dutch East India Company had also begun

large-scale cultivation in Ceylon, where the plant had already been introduced by the Arabs.

The Universal Coffee Nursery

In 1706, Dutch growers in Java sent home the first crop of beans and a coffee plant, which was carefully transplanted in the Amsterdam Botanical Garden. This consignment, though small, was to play a key role in the annals of the coffee trade. Amsterdam became the trading centre for coffee grown in the Dutch colonies, and the plant produced berries from which seedlings were later taken to the New World. Dr James Douglas, an 18th century scientist, regarded these plants as the ancestors of coffee plantations in the West, and named the Amsterdam Botanical Garden "the universal coffee nursery".

The Tree for the King

In 1714, the burgomaster of Amsterdam presented the King of France, Louis XIV, with a healthy five-foot coffee tree

COFFEE MERCHANTS.

Above: Arab merchants strictly controlled the trade of Mocha coffee produced in Yemen.

Above: Once Dutch traders broke the Arabian monopoly, coffee soon spread to all parts of the world. Painting by H Vroom, 1640.

grown in the Botanical Garden. The French had not been blind to the commercial success of the Dutch, and had in fact smuggled seed from Mocha to Réunion Island off Madagascar. They had been less successful with propagation at home, however, so "The Tree", as this specimen from Amsterdam became known, was received with the utmost gratitude and respect. It was planted in the Jardin des Plantes where a greenhouse had been especially built, and entrusted to the care of the Royal Botanist.

It was Louis XIV's secret ambition that the seeds from The Tree would be the progenitors of future coffee plantations throughout the French colonies. His wish came true, for The Tree flowered, bore fruit, and became the ancestor of most of the coffee trees presently growing in Central and South America.

Cultivation in the New World

The question as to whether it was the Dutch or the French who first introduced coffee cultivation to the New World has long been a matter of dispute. In the year following delivery of The Tree to the French, the Dutch sent coffee plants from the Amsterdam Botanical Garden to their territories in Guiana in northern South America. A short time later – the date is not certain – a French naval officer, Gabriel Mathieu de Clieu, determined to bring coffee cultivation to the New World, procured with great difficulty one or more coffee seedlings from the Jardin des Plantes. Historians disagree as to whether it was a single plant or several.

De Clieu set sail with his precious cargo to the island of Martinique, north of Guiana. The journey was long and arduous. Not only did a fellow passenger repeatedly try to destroy the

seedlings, even managing to rip off some of the leaves, but the voyage itself was fraught with danger and difficulty. There were terrifying storms, attacks by pirates, and finally the ship was becalmed for days on end. Though the water supply had almost run out, de Clieu shared his scanty ration with his precious plant. Miraculously, both survived, and the seedling was transplanted in the officer's garden. Kept under armed guard, the tree flourished and grew to maturity, and de Clieu was rewarded with his first harvest in 1726.

Fifty years later, there were nearly nineteen million coffee trees in Martinique and de Clieu's dream was well on the way to fulfilment. From the two coffee-growing centres of Martinique and Dutch Guiana, cultivation radiated throughout the West Indies and Central and South America.

ESTABLISHING PLANTATIONS

Wherever the European colonists went, they took coffee with them, though the Catholic missionaries and religious communities undoubtedly played a key role in its migration too. With their natural interest in botany, monks were curious about the plant, and, as in the early days in the Yemen, coffee trees were often nurtured and studied in monastery gardens.

Initially, France was Europe's major supplier of coffee. The French took the plant from Martinique to the islands of Guadeloupe and Saint Domingue (now Haiti), and from 1730 onwards, cultivation spread rapidly throughout the French Antilles.

Meanwhile, coffee production had advanced into a large number of other countries. The Spanish took it to Puerto Rico and Cuba, and later to Colombia, Venezuela and westwards to the Philippines. From Dutch Guiana (now Surinam), cultivation spread to French Guiana, and from there in 1727 the Portuguese introduced it to Brazil, destined later to become the world's largest producer. In 1730, the British introduced coffee to Jamaica where the highly prized Blue Mountain beans are still produced.

By around 1830, the Dutch colonies of Java and Sumatra were the chief suppliers of coffee to Europe. Financed by the British, India and Ceylon tried to compete, but could not budge the Dutch. In the mid 1800s, a coffee blight called *Hemileia vastatrix* swept through the whole of Asia and wiped out the supply, giving Brazil a long-awaited opportunity. Within a few years Brazil had become the world's leading coffee supplier, a position it still holds today.

The Final Stage of the Journey

By the end of the 19th century, coffee had spread both east and west in a belt lying roughly equidistant between the Tropics of Cancer and Capricorn. The Dutch, French, English, Spanish and Portuguese had between them managed to establish thriving coffee plantations in all their territories which lay within the zone.

The final stage in coffee's journey took place in the early 1900s in German East Africa (now Kenya and Tanzania). German settlers planted coffee on the slopes of Mount Kenya and Kilimanjaro – ironically only a few hundred miles from coffee's original home in Ethiopia. Coffee had completed its nine-century circumnavigation of the world.

The effect of the slave trade

The Portuguese and Dutch imported massive numbers of African slaves to Brazil and Java. Coffee production more than doubled, while it fell in other areas.

	in £m 1832	1849
Brazil	80.6	180.0
Java	40.3	100.0
French and Dutch West Indies	17.9	6.0
Venezuela	13.4	20.0

From *Coffee As It Is, and As It Ought To Be*. P.L. Simmonds, 1850

Above: Workers on a South American coffee plantation. 19th-century engraving by F. M. Reynolds.

PLANTATIONS IN BRAZIL

In the early 1700s, Brazil had yet to start growing coffee. In 1727, when invited to help settle a boundary dispute between Dutch and French Guiana, the Brazilians were glad to mediate since it gave them a potential opportunity to procure some of Guiana's closely-guarded coffee seedlings.

The story goes – and there are several versions – that Francisco de Mallo Palheta, a dashing army captain and well-known womanizer, was despatched to Guiana to arbitrate. Once there, he proceeded to ingratiate himself both with the Governor and his wife, with whom he had a brief affair. The boundary dispute resolved, the time came for Palheta to leave. The Governor's wife presented him with a bouquet as a token of thanks for his services, both political and amorous. Hidden among the flowers were cuttings of a coffee plant. Here the versions vary; some say he was openly presented with a thousand seeds and five living plants. Whatever the truth, Palheta returned to Brazil with the cuttings, seeds or plants.

Cultivation started on a small scale, mainly for local consumption. However, the plant adapted itself so well to the local topography, soil and climate that cultivation grew to an intensive scale. By 1765 the first shipments of beans had been exported to Lisbon.

Pioneer Planters

The first planters had to hack away areas of mosquito-infested jungle in sweltering heat. They not only had to plant the coffee seedlings, but, more importantly, food for themselves. Next, they had to get a roof over the heads of their family, slaves, machinery and harvests. Since the forest encroached on all sides, they were completely isolated, so the early *fazendas*, or estates, were the nuclei of human life in the rainforest.

As the taste for coffee spread among Europe's and America's expanding urban populations, the planters grew more wealthy, the *fazendas* larger and life became more comfortable. It was a time of unprecedented prosperity.

As Stanley Stein points out in *Vassouras, a Brazilian Coffee County, 1850–1900*, coffee cultivation in Brazil had a colossal impact on economic and social life. From an economic view, coffee cultivation created an unhealthy dependence on a staple crop subject to the fluctuations of a world market. The crop was also subject to the vagaries of the weather. Cold winds blowing in from the Andes brought severe frosts, and on several occasions the plantations were nearly destroyed.

Socially, coffee cultivation sired a new aristocracy – the coffee barons with their massive *fazendas* and autocratic lifestyle. It also resulted in an unprecedented influx of African slaves, which not only stratified society but also changed forever the ethnic makeup of central Brazil. However, it can be argued that the ultimate cause of these devastating changes was not the cultivation of the plant itself but the insatiable demand from Europe for the drink.

Coffee and slavery

The *haciendas* and *fazendas* – the massive estates of the Spanish and Portuguese colonies – grew on the back of slave labour. Between 1840 and 1850, more than 370,000 African slaves were openly smuggled into Brazil. Slavery was abolished in Spanish-speaking colonies by the 1850s, though it continued through to 1888 in Brazil.

Above: Coffee bean collection, painted by Francisco Miranda, 1750-1816.

THE COFFEE TRADE

Despite the Arab monopoly, coffee beans began to infiltrate Britain and mainland Europe from very early on via the botanists' pockets. By the early 17th century, coffee beans could be found in the cabinets of interested botanists throughout the continent. Small sacks of beans were also brought in by private individuals already familiar with the drink – merchants, diplomats, business people and travel writers, for example, but it was not long before coffee attracted the attention of merchants.

The First Shipments

Since Venetian merchants had long sailed the waters of the East, and were doing much business in Constantinople, it is widely accepted that they were the first to import coffee to Europe. The precise date is not known, but the first shipment of beans must have arrived in Venice around the early 1600s.

Hot on the heels of the Venetians, the Dutch started shipping coffee; trade records mention coffee beans from Mocha as early as 1616, though it seems they confined shipments to their colonies in Asia and the New World, since it was not until 1661 that the Netherlands received its first substantial consignment of beans. Coffee was also introduced very early on into Austria and Hungary, making an overland entrance via the northern extremities of the Turkish Ottoman Empire.

Following the shipping routes, coffee reached all the major European ports – Marseilles, Hamburg, Amsterdam and London – by around the middle of the 17th century, though it was some time before regular lines of supply were firmly established. It arrived in the 1660s in North America, probably via Dutch colonists in New Amsterdam (renamed New York after the British took control in 1664). A century later, coffee made the reverse journey across the Atlantic when Brazil started shipping it to Lisbon.

The Coffee Trade Evolves

In its journey from plantation to cup, coffee inevitably passed through the hands of the brokers and merchants. Coffee-trading attracted speculators and entrepreneurs right from the start, though it was a precarious business subject to cycles of boom and bust.

In the early days, supplies were often erratic due to adverse weather conditions which affected both the crop itself and the means of transport. The arrival of the next shipment was always uncertain, and when it did arrive, the merchants were forced to pay whatever the ship masters demanded. The artificial price manipulation combined with erratic supply, forced coffee into the status of a luxury.

By post-Industrial Revolution days, shipping and the machinery associated with coffee grew more sophisticated.

Above: In some cases, merchants instructed workers to throw the coffee beans into the sea to avoid the lowering of coffee prices. Illustration, Brazil, 1932.

Telecommunications came into being, enabling crop forecasts to be sent by cable. As supply and distribution systems developed, more and more traders entered the market. Many of them formed syndicates which attempted to corner sections of the market and force prices up, and from the 1860s onwards, organized Coffee Exchanges were set up in major coffee-trading centres such as New York and Le Havre.

Coffee Auctions

Shapiro tells us in *The Story of Coffee*, that bags of coffee were sold in London at what were known as candle auctions. Bids were accepted for lots as long as a lighted candle set up in front of the auctioneer continued to flicker. Once the candle went out, the lot went to the last bidder. In the United States, before the New York Coffee and Sugar Exchange was set up, coffee merchants would roam the streets in particular areas, taking bids and then selling the bags to the highest bidder at the end of the day.

Coffee merchants could be formidable figures. A young American, entering the trade, described them thus: "I ask you to picture those silk-hatted, frock-coated, bewhiskered and highly dignified gentlemen, whom one approached with awe and trembling knees, (they) were the importers and jobbers of coffee who carried large and assorted stocks of East Indian, Central and South American growths for sale to the wholesale grocers, and to the large traders".

Processing the Product

In 17th-century Europe and North America, coffee beans were at first sold unroasted and unground. American consumers bought green coffee by the bag or half bag, and roasted it on a pie plate in the oven, or in a frying pan over the fire. The British appeared to be fussier; one former planter stated that "the care of roasting the beans and grinding is thought by many masters of families too delicate and important a task to be entrusted... to any servant".

The invention of the coffee mill in 1687 contributed to the beverage's widespread use, but brought with it the problem of adulteration. Because of the colour and powerful aroma of ground coffee, it was easy for unscrupulous vendors to "take it down". Among the substances used were roasted rye, grated burnt crusts, roasted acorns, sand, clay and sawdust. Even worse were the East London "liver-bakers". The same British planter complained: "They take the livers of oxen and horses, bake them and grind them into a powder, which they sell to the low-priced coffee-shopkeepers. Horse's liver coffee bears highest price". He pointed out that it could be identified by allowing coffee to cool. A thick skin then formed on the top.

Above: Roasting imported coffee beans in an English factory, black and white engraving, 1870.

COFFEE AS MEDICINE

Once in Europe, coffee beans moved first from individual botanists' cabinets to the apothecaries' shops, where they became a vital part of the pharmacopoeia used by 17th-century doctors, chemists, herbalists and even midwives.

Coffee was looked on as a medicine not only because of its high price, but perhaps because of its strong taste – a "black, nasty Hel-burnt Liquor" as one person wrote. Hahnemann, founder of homeopathy, stated firmly: "Coffee is strictly a medicinal substance...No one has failed to be disgusted for the first time he smoked tobacco. No healthy palate ever found strong coffee, without sugar, palatable on the first trial".

The doctrine of bodily humours taught by the herbalist Galen (AD 131-200) continued to dominate European as much as Islamic medicine. The theory stated that the four humours – yellow bile, black bile, phlegm and blood – were reflected in a person's physical makeup. If the humours became too unbalanced, illness would result. In turn, each humour was linked to two physical qualities – heat, cold, moistness or dryness. Food, drink and medicines were thought to possess these qualities, and were administered to correct imbalances.

As is generally the case with coffee, there was disagreement. Some physicians claimed its qualities were cold and dry, others that they were hot and dry. Still others argued that the qualities of the coffee husks were different from those of the bean. This confusion is evident when we see the variety of ailments for which coffee was prescribed.

A somewhat tongue-in-cheek booklet, written in 1663, gives examples of "Persons, and Places of their Abode, who were cured (by coffee) when left off by the Physitians". These included "Benjamin Bad-cock (who) drank Coffee in Layden, and his Wife... remained barren four years, after which he left drinking Coffee, and in three quarters of a Year she had a goodly chopping Boy", and "Anne Marine of Rotterdam...troubled with a Corn on her upper Lip, the more it was cut, the bigger it grew, so that she at last drank Coffee, and the Corn dropt into the Dish as she held it to her Mouth".

On a more serious note, a French doctor, having collaborated with colleagues, asserted that among its many therapeutic effects coffee counteracted drunkenness and nausea, promoted the flow of urine and relieved dropsy, smallpox and gout. The French Larousse encyclopedia stated that coffee was particularly indicated for all men of letters, soldiers, sailors and workers who were staying in hot surroundings, and, strangely, for the inhabitants of countries where cretinism was rife.

Coffee and creativity

Still more enthusiastically, Balzac in his *Treatise on Modern Stimulants* writes: "The coffee falls into your stomach, and straightaway there is a general commotion. Ideas begin to move like the battalions of the Grand Army on the battlefield when the battle takes place. Things remembered arrive at full gallop, ensign to the wind."

Above: Honore de Balzac, French author. Painting by L. Boulanger, 1809-1867.

Coffee as a Stimulant

Certain after-effects of caffeine did not go unnoticed. One respected medical man wrote: "When I awake I have the intelligence and activity of an oyster. Immediately after our coffee, the stores of memory leap, so to speak, to our tongues; and talkativeness, haste, and the letting slip something we should not have mentioned, are often the consequence. Moderation and prudence are wholly wanting".

More positively, a Dr Thornton asserted: "A cup of Coffee strengthens and exhilarates our mental and bodily faculties; and nothing can be more refreshing either to the studious or the laborious".

Other eminent writers also wrote appreciatively of coffee's power to stimulate creativity. Balzac, Zola, Baudelaire, Victor Hugo, Molière and Voltaire were among its most ardent imbibers. Both Voltaire and Molière are quoted as replying to the remark that coffee was a slow poison: "I have drunk it upwards of fifty years, and unless it were very slow indeed, I would certainly have been dead long ago".

The effects of over-indulgence gave rise to considerable medical comment. Hahnemann refers to the "coffee disease" which results in "an unpleasant feeling of existence, a lower degree of vitality, a kind of paralysis". Other negative effects were reputedly melancholia, piles, headaches and a reduced libido.

There was concern, too, about the harmful effect coffee might have on children and nursing mothers. It was thought to be a major cause of tooth decay and rickets in children, and "a rattling of the breast" in nursing mothers.

Amongst coffee's opponents was Sinibaldi, an eminent Italian medical writer. He stated: "The commerce which we have opened with Asia and the new world, in addition to the smallpox and other diseases, has brought a new drink, which has contributed most shockingly to the destruction of our constitutions...it produces debility, alters gastric juice, disorders digestion, and often produces convulsions, palsy of the limbs and vertigo."

Above: The stimulating and invigorating properties of coffee are shown in a positive light in this advertisement from the Pan-American coffee bureau in the 1950s.

The medical debate was to continue for many years, as doctors, pursuing new avenues of insight, argued the pros and cons of coffee, claiming it to be alternatively therapeutic and detrimental to the body and mind. This debate still continues today.

Coffee and healthy skin

As a country where green tea has been the national beverage for nearly 1,000 years, Japan was understandably slow to take up coffee drinking. It was not introduced until the 19th century and even today is still a relatively undeveloped market.

Apart from drinking coffee, however, Japan is home to the slightly unusual practice of lying in the roasted coffee beans. It is thought that the coffee contains elements beneficial to healthy skin.

Right: Absorbing coffee's nutrients via the skin.

COFFEE CONSUMPTION DEVELOPS

Having escaped the confines of medicine and developed into a social activity, coffee-drinking spread through Europe during the first half of the 17th century. However, it was not until about 1650 onwards that we begin to hear more of when, how and by whom coffee was sold and drunk.

The people largely responsible for its growth were not necessarily the merchants, the aristocracy or well-healed professional travellers. As Shapiro states in *The Story of Coffee,* it was the "countless unnamed peddlers who spread through the streets of

Europe carrying on their backs the gleaming tools of their trade – coffeepots, trays, cups, spoons and sugar. These men bore the steaming, potent gospel of coffee beyond the boundaries of the East to the as yet uninitiated West".

At first, however, the new beverage fell under harsh criticism from the Catholic church. Fanatical priests claimed – with somewhat hazy logic – that if Muslims were forbidden wine, which was sanctified by Christ, then coffee must be a substitute invented by the devil. Pope Clement VIII in the 16th

century eventually brought the dispute to an end by sampling coffee for himself and declaring it a truly Christian beverage. Once word of papal approval became known, coffee-drinking flourished freely throughout Europe.

Social Change and the Birth of the Coffee House

The reasons for coffee's swift and almost universal popularity were more complex than papal approval or mere availability. In *Drugs and Narcotics in History*, Porter and Teich suggest that the timing was also important. The period between the 17th and 19th centuries was one of profound social, cultural and intellectual change. Coffee was simply a timely adjunct; people took to it because they were ready for it.

Firstly, there was an urge to establish some sort of private life outside the constraints of the family, and new gathering places were therefore needed. For the aristocracy the cultural life of the courts was gradually declining and this created another need for a new type of venue.

Secondly, the period was a time of progressive ideas – the age of Enlightenment in France, and later, the rise of the libertarian Risorgimento movement in Italy. (In hindsight, for such a time of enlightenment, the huge rise in slave labour needed to work on the coffee plantations in Brazil and the Dutch East Indies, is an uncomfortable parallel development.) However, public meetings, harangues, resolutions and "the rest of the machinery of agitation" were not part of the culture. Coffee houses became the chief outlet through which public opinion could vent itself.

Thirdly, developing alongside these changes was a growing criticism of the unwelcome effects of wine and beer. Coffee was obviously the perfect alternative since it provided a means of socializing without fear of intoxication.

In Europe, as in Turkey, the coffee house attracted clientele from all walks of life; professional and political mingled with commercial, creative and commoner. New forms of social interaction developed. Merchants

Above: Coffee vendor, Paris. Illustration by M. Engelbrecht, c. 1735.

Above: "Blowing a cloud at Offley's", Interior of Offley's coffee house, c. 1820, scene of much animated discussion.

seeking an alternative to the ale-house needed a place where they could transact their business, as did the emerging financial and insurance communities. The coffee houses were also the type of place where artists and writers working in isolation could make contact with each other and the world.

When the coffee houses first opened, communication and information services – newspapers, telephones, directories and street maps, for example – were non-existent. The owner or head waiter of a coffee house therefore fulfilled yet another need by taking on the multifarious role of social arbiter, diplomat, matchmaker and message-taker. As George Mikes says in *Coffee Houses of Europe*: "(the head waiter) shared your secrets and knew them if you didn't want to share them, lent you money and lied for you when pursued by persistent creditor, kept letters for you especially those not meant for wife's eyes. Not everyone knew your private address but everyone knew which coffee house you went to".

Taxation and Duty

Aware of the potential income from mass consumption, revenue-hungry governments tried to stimulate demand by abandoning their former policy of prohibition and concentrating on taxation instead.

The English government in 1663 was quick to license coffee houses and levy an excise duty on coffee sold. Even so, compared to alcohol, coffee remained a bargain. The English coffee houses enticed huge numbers of working men

from the ale-houses – a trend deemed beneficial by both wives, in the early days at least, and Government, though not by the breweries. Realizing that further taxation would reverse the trend, the Government progressively reduced the duty – each reduction marked by huge increase in consumption.

In complete contrast, Frederick the Great of Prussia, in support of the barley growers and breweries, banned the working classes from drinking coffee and insisted they revert to drinking beer.

Coffee consumption

The figures demonstrate the rapid growth of coffee consumption in the 19th century particularly in the United States where no import duty was charged.

	weight in millions of pounds 1832	1849
Holland and Netherlands	90.7	125.0
Germany and North of Europe	71.7	100.0
France and South of Europe	78.4	95.0
Great Britain	23.5	40.0
United States and British North American Provinces	45.9	120.0 (US) and 15.0 (BNAP)

THE COFFEE CONSUMERS

Coffee is universally popular, but there are some countries where it seems much more than just a drink. How coffee is drunk, and by whom, is part of its continuing appeal and mystique.

ITALY

Italy was the first country in Europe to import coffee commercially. The first shipments arrived in Venice in the 1600s just after citrus fruits had been introduced from the East. Vendors roamed the streets selling beverages such as lemonade, orangeade, chocolate and herbal infusions. Once coffee was available in reasonable quantities, the vendors added it to their wares, though they were still referred to as *limonáji* (lemonade sellers) rather than *caffetiéri* (coffee sellers). Coffee was immediately accepted by the Italians and became a familiar and widely used beverage.

As coffee flourished as a drink, so did the coffee houses. One of the earliest on record, situated in Leghorn (Livorno), dates back to 1651. It was mentioned by an English traveller who was intrigued by the roasting of coffee beans. He surmised "that roasting was by chance or perhaps from a debauch'd palate, as some with us love the burnt parts of broil'd meat", which also indicates that the barbecue may have had its devotees from very early on.

By the end of the century, Venice boasted several coffee houses situated around the Piazza di San Marco.

Florian's, said to be Europe's most celebrated coffee house, was opened in 1720. Venetians and the international elite flocked there to enjoy the gossip and the music from the orchestra playing on the terrace. It was patronized by famous artists and writers including Byron, Goethe and Rousseau. Perhaps because Florian's was the first coffee house to admit women, Casanova was a regular patron too.

In Padua, a former lemonade seller opened Pedrocchi's – one of the most beautiful and flamboyantly kitsch coffee houses ever to be seen. Caffè Greco in Rome, named after its Greek owner, was patronized by the international music set – Mendelssohn, Rosetti, Liszt and Toscanini were regular visitors.

Above: "Cafe Greco in Rome", painting by Ludwig Passini, 1832-1903.

Above: Drinking coffee on the steps of the Cafe Florian, early 19th century drawing.

FRANCE

Coffee was reputedly brought to France in 1644, but it was almost fifteen years later before the beverage became popular. Consumption was at first centred around Marseilles, where it was introduced by traders who had grown used to drinking it in the Middle East.

Meanwhile, in Paris, in 1669, the Turkish ambassador Suleiman Aga brought coffee to the court of Louis XIV. The most extravagant coffee parties were held in opulent castles hired especially for the purpose. Isaac D'Israeli gives a graphic description: "On bended knee, the black slaves of the Ambassador, arrayed in the most gorgeous costumes, served the choicest Mocha coffee in tiny cups of eggshell porcelain, hot, strong and fragrant, poured out into saucers of gold and silver, placed on embroidered silk doylies, fringed with gold bullion, to the grand dames, who fluttered their fans with many grimaces, bending their piquant faces – berouged, bepowdered and bepatched – over the new and steaming beverage."

Though many of the aristocracy were quick to adopt coffee, there were some who found it distasteful. The German wife of Louis XIV's brother compared it to the Archbishop of Paris's breath; Madame de Sévigné, after an initial flirtation, rejected it as violently as she had chocolate; another nobleman would use it only as an enema, though he remarked that it did the job very well.

The Rise of the Café

The first coffee house opened in 1672 but it was little more than a bar in which sales of cognac exceeded those of coffee. Coffee houses really came into their own in 1686 when an Italian, Francisco Procopio dei Coltelli, an ambitious and astute waiter, opened Procope's. Wisely marketing itself a lemonade shop, Procope's sumptuous decor and air of sophistication attracted a clientele keen to distance itself from the more loutish elements of the day. It was only when coffee began to outsell other beverages that the name *café* was given to the whole establishment.

Though not all the coffee houses were as elegant as Florian's – some were little more than dimly lit back rooms – they were a melting pot of intellectual, creative and political ideas. Throughout the 18th and early 19th centuries, coffee houses opened one after the other in most major cities. By the end of the century the *bottega del caffè* had become an indispensable part of life. They were the centre of information, conversation, entertainment, and even education, for all levels of society – professional, artisan, trades-people, ladies and gentlemen of the leisured classes, intellectuals and political activists.

Coffee and the Spanish

The 17th-century Spaniards were committed chocolate drinkers since it was their conquistadors who had 'discovered' the cocoa bean in Central America. It was not until as late as the 19th century that coffee house culture began to take hold. By the early 20th century, artists and writers were frequenting coffee houses in Barcelona, Granada and Madrid. Even so, for many years chocolate still remained the drink of the traditionalists.

Procope's quickly became a literary salon frequented by eminent poets, playrights, actors and musicians. Rousseau, Diderot and Voltaire, among others, drank excessive amounts of coffee there. Later, during the French Revolution, the young Napoleon Bonaparte was also a patron.

The opening of Procope's marked the beginning of serious coffee drinking in Paris. Other coffee houses soon opened and they were not short of customers. Aux Deux Magots was another favourite haunt of the literary set; Verlaine and Rimbaud were among its patrons. Artists and intellectuals flocked to the Café de Flore nearby. The Café de la Paix was a monument to ostentatious display, attracting clientele which included royalty and poets. It was a competitive business, just as it had

been for Turkish proprietors a century earlier. The owners of the newer establishments had to be resourceful in attracting customers. Entertainment was laid on – poetry reading, plays, songs and dances – and eventually food was served too.

The objectors naturally started to make themselves heard. Feeling threatened, the wine makers, in a burst of patriotism, claimed that coffee was an enemy of France. They were joined by doctors, who up until then had shown neither misgivings nor enthusiasm about coffee. They argued that it was the fruit of a tree desired only by goats and animals, and that drinking it burned the blood, weakened

Above: French breakfast coffee, in its traditional large bowl, and croissant.

Above: Entertainment and coffee at the Café de la Paix, engraving from Parisian Life by David Carey, 1822.

the spleen and produced leanness, palsies, impotence, quiverings and distempers. Needless to say, their warnings fell mostly on deaf ears.

At home, the French were somewhat avant-garde in their coffee-drinking. They were probably unique in serving coffee not only in large bowls in which the breakfast baguette was dipped, but also *au lait* (with milk). They were the first to initiate the after-dinner coffee, which they served strong and black in tiny cups (*demi-tasse*), usually with a liqueur to aid digestion. Mrs Anne Roe, an English traveller and author, wrote around 1777: "Coffee is so much the fashion in France, especially in genteel houses, that one can scarcely finish their dinner before coffee is introduced, and they drink it scalding hot; all which conspire utterly to destroy the coats of the stomach".

Coffee and the French are beautifully summed up in this esoteric description by a 19th-century English journalist: "Coffee is to the Frenchman what tea is to the Englishman, beer to the German, *eau de vie* to the Russian, opium to the Turk, or chocolate to the

Above: Still an institution, the Café de la Paix as seen by night, 1938.

Impressions of coffee

"Black as the devil, hot as hell, pure as an angel, sweet as love." Prince Talleyrand (1754-1839), French diplomat and wit, on the ideal cup of coffee.

"The history of coffee houses, ere the invention of clubs, was that of manners, the morals and the politics of a people." Isaac D'Israeli.

"Strong coffee, and plenty, awakens me. It gives me warmth, an unusual force, a pain that is not without pleasure. I would rather suffer than be senseless." Napoleon Bonaparte, French emperor. *Painting, left, by Gérard von François, 1770-1837.*

Spaniard... The *garçon*, at your call for *demi-tasse*, has placed before you a snowy cup and saucer, three lumps of sugar, and a *petit verre*. He ventured the *petit verre*, inferring, from your ruddy English face, that you liked liqueur. Another *garçon* now appears; in his right hand is a huge silver pot, and in his left, another of the same material, uncovered: the former contains coffee – the latter, cream. You reject cream, and thereupon the *garçon* pours out the former until your cup – aye, and almost the saucer – actually overflows. There is hardly space for the three lumps, and yet you must contrive, somehow, to insert them...*Café noir*... pleases all the gustatory nerves, its savour ascends to rejoice the olfactory, and even your eye is delighted with those dark, transparent, and sparkling hues, through which your silver spoon perpetually shines. You pronounce French coffee the only coffee."

AUSTRIA

Records show that the Viennese were drinking coffee at home in the mid-1660s, though the coffee houses themselves did not open until the 1680s. The Viennese predilection for coffee was undoubtedly inspired by the Ottoman Ambassador, who set up residence for several months, bringing with him a vast retinue of servants and, of course, coffee. Coffee was served to Viennese guests, who took to the strange new drink with enthusiasm – so much so that a formal complaint was lodged by the city treasurer about the amount of wood being used for the fires needed to prepare the brew. By the time the Ambassador came to leave, the Viennese were buying beans from a trading company in the Orient and brewing coffee for themselves.

About 20 years later, in 1683, Vienna was under siege by the Turks. A Polish immigrant, Franz Kolschitzky, having something of a Turkish appearance, bravely slipped through enemy lines to carry messages between a waiting Austrian relief army and the besieged Viennese. Thanks to his heroism, the Turks were defeated and they fled in confusion, leaving behind a variety of exotic equipment. Amongst the loot were sacks of green beans which Kolschitzky claimed for himself.

In recognition of his bravery, the city elders awarded Kolschitzky a house in which he is reputed to have opened the first of the city's many coffee houses. According to some versions of the tale he first started selling coffee beans door-to-door and then demanded the house; still other variations indicate that the honour of opening the first coffee house went to an Armenian. Whatever the truth, coffee had arrived in Vienna.

The city's coffee houses were an institution – not just a place but more a way of life. They served excellent coffee (a legendary twenty-eight different types) and provided newspapers and journals in abundance. Unique to the Viennese style were the wooden

Above: Cafe Sperl, Vienna, 1910.

newspaper poles, marble-topped tables and bentwood chairs that later became the hallmark of coffee houses throughout Europe.

Viennese patrons – male, naturally – were as unique as the coffee houses. As one writer put it, they shared a *Weltanschauung* – a way of looking at the world by those who do not want to look at the world at all. Another wrote

Above: Karlsplatz – the café booth built by Otto Wagner during his Secessionist period in Vienna.

Right: "The coffee boiler"
Viennese coffee house
scene with chess players,
a smoking Armenian,
and a newspaper
reader,
c. 1840.

Der Kaffeesieder
Zuckerbaeker, Mandolleti,Liqueur Fabr u. Brandweinbrener

that a hatred of fresh air and exercise was an almost universal trait, and that they were no great lovers of home life either. Many dropped by their favourite coffee house several times a day – in the morning and afternoon for a quiet read of the papers, in the evening for games or intellectual discussion.

The most famous coffee houses, such as the Griensteidl, and the Sperl, had an erudite clientele of writers, political activists and artists. Many became a stronghold of extreme views – the Griensteidl, for example, was opposed to women's emancipation. But there were also other establishments for "textile merchants, dentists, horse dealers, politicians and pickpockets".

Chicory

Although the Dutch had access to some of the best coffee in the world, they were curiously partial to chicory – the roasted and ground root of the wild endive. An English coffee planter complained it had "no other virtue than that of colouring...the water in which it is boiled or infused". Since good quality coffee was cheap, a possible reason for its use was that it tamed the effect of caffeine. Chicory later became popular in northern France, Germany and Scandinavia.

Coffee houses continued to proliferate not just in Vienna, but all over the Austrian Habsburg dominions. Those in Prague, Krakow and Budapest were as popular as any in Vienna. However, Vienna remained the "mother of coffee houses". By 1840 there were over 80 in the city, and by the end of the century the total came to an unbelievable 600.

THE NETHERLANDS

As one of the major coffee-trading nations, it is hardly surprising that the Dutch were free of the usual conflict surrounding the use of coffee. Consumption began in the home at the turn of the 16th century. By the time the first coffee houses opened in the mid-1660s, there was "hardly a house of standing where coffee is not drunk every morning". Not only the middle and upper classes, but even their servants had acquired a taste for coffee.

The coffee houses had their own unique style. Though elaborately furnished, their dark panelled walls and gleaming copperware gave them a particularly cosy atmosphere. Many were located in the financial areas, where merchants and administrators gathered to conduct business.

In some Dutch cities the coffee houses were situated in beautiful gardens. Here, patrons could enjoy a coffee under the shade of a tree while looking out onto a magnificent view. The garden cafés were particularly popular in spring when the gardens were ablaze with fruit blossoms and tulips.

SCANDINAVIA

Although the Finns now hold the world record for coffee consumption, paradoxically, Scandinavia was slow to take it up. Introduced in the 1680s, probably by the Dutch, coffee aroused hostility from early on. By 1746, a royal edict had been issued against coffee- and tea-drinking. The following year, those who continued to indulge had to pay a hefty tax, or suffer the indignity of having their crockery confiscated. Coffee-drinking was completely prohibited in 1756, though the ban was eventually lifted and huge taxes imposed instead. Sporadic attempts at suppression continued until the 1820s when the government simply gave up.

Not much has been written about the early coffee houses, but it seems they lacked the opulence of their southern counterparts. In Oslo, they were Spartan

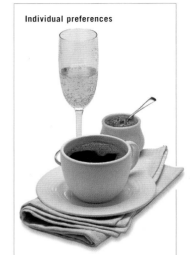

Individual preferences

Frederick the Great of Prussia was said to take "only seven or eight cups in the morning, and a pot of coffee in the afternoon". Made with champagne, the coffee was occasionally flavoured with a spoonful of mustard.

single-room establishments, popular with students, serving not only coffee but food to go with it – bowls of porridge, for example.

Middle-class Finns did better at home, holding large and elaborate coffee parties at which guests would drink up to five cups.

GERMANY

Coffee was introduced in 1675 to the court at Brandenburg in northern Germany by a Dutch physician. He was encouraged by Frederick William, a ruler known for his Calvinistic attitudes and temperate habits. Around the same time, the first coffee houses opened in Bremen, Hanover and Hamburg. Other cities rapidly followed suit and by the early 18th century, there were eight in Leipzig and ten or more in Berlin alone.

Coffee remained a drink of the aristocratic classes for some time. The middle and lower classes did not take to it until the early 18th century and it was even later before coffee was drunk at home.

Above: Drinking coffee in a German café, for female patrons only. Illustration 1880.

Above: A coffee house for the European wealthy classes. Print by Von August Hermann Knopp, 1856.

Since the coffee houses were a male stronghold, middle-class women set up *Kaffeekränzschen* (coffee clubs) – referred to by their uneasy husbands as *Kaffeeklatch* (coffee gossip).

In 1777, in an ill-concealed attempt to protect the breweries and to stem the flow of income to foreign dealers, Frederick the Great, rather hypocritically, issued a manifesto, part of which reads: "It is disgusting to notice the increase in the quantity of coffee used by my subjects...My people must drink beer...Many battles have been fought and won by soldiers nourished on beer; and the King does not believe that coffee-drinking soldiers can be depended upon to endure hardship or to beat his enemies..."

Coffee was prohibited from the working classes on the grounds that it caused sterility, but this simply gave rise to a lively black market trade. The king finally outlawed the roasting of beans in private homes, even appointing "coffee sniffers" to track down illicit aromas to their source. This ludicrous state of affairs was short-lived, though, and by the beginning of the 19th century, coffee had been reinstated.

Germany now took the lead in European coffee consumption. Coffee was served at mealtimes, at the *Kaffeekränzschen*, and at family get-togethers on Sunday afternoons. Coffee houses nevertheless remained no-go areas to respectable women. However, in public parks there were pavilions and special tents (*Zelte*) to which families could bring their own pre-ground coffee, and the patron simply provided hot water. The turn of the century saw the rise of another family-style institution – the Café – which sold cakes as well as hot drinks. At first these *Konditorein* were used as an alternative to the coffee houses, but eventually they took over and the old-style coffee house gradually disappeared.

Coffee and music

Bach's *Coffee Cantata* (1734) was a satirical operetta which provides an insight into bourgeois attitudes. It tells of the efforts of a stern father to check his daughter's propensity for coffee-drinking by threatening to make her choose between a husband and coffee. Unperturbed, the daughter sings an aria beginning, "Ah, how sweet coffee tastes – lovelier than a thousand kisses, sweeter far than muscatel wine".

GREAT BRITAIN

The early history of coffee in Britain is substantially different from that of mainland Europe and North America. Firstly, the coffee house era in Britain was intense but short-lived. Secondly, coffee-drinking at home was not a common feature. The majority of the British public, it seems, found the intricacies of roasting, grinding and brewing beyond them; pouring boiling water on tea leaves was more to their liking. That said, Britain was one of the first countries to start importing coffee.

John Evelyn's diary provides the first reliable reference in 1637, when a Turkish refugee brought coffee to

Right: English coffee party relaxing after parade at military station in India, c. 1850.

Above: English coffee house, anonymous artist, 1668.

Oxford. The beverage became popular with students and dons, who sooner or later discovered that its stimulating properties were beneficial to prolonged or nocturnal study. The Oxford Coffee Club was eventually formed – later to become the Royal Society. Around 1650, a Jew named Jacob opened the first coffee house, called the Angel. Another soon appeared in London, in St Michael's Alley, Cornhill, set up by a Greek named Pasqua Rosée.

The new beverage had its opponents as well as advocates. A disgusted 17th-century commentator complained that it was "made of Old Crusts, and shreds of Leather burnt and beaten to a Powder"; another described it as "Syrup of soot and essence of old shoes". William Cobbett (1762–1835), politician, reformer and economist, was one of the few within his peer group to denounce coffee as "slops".

Coffee Houses Become Established

Nevertheless, by 1660 the London coffee houses were a deeply entrenched institution and were to remain so for the next fifty years. Even disasters such as the Great Plague (1665) and the Great Fire (1666) failed to stop their rapid spread across the city. Coffee houses became vital to the lives of anyone involved in business – meetings took place in them, deals were done, contracts signed and information exchanged. They were the birthplace of modern institutional monoliths such as The Stock Exchange, the Baltic and Lloyds Insurance. The coffee houses also provided a watering hole for artists, poets and writers, lawyers and politicians, philosophers and sages, who all had their favourite haunts. In his diary, Samuel Pepys (1633–1703) makes countless references to visits paid to this or that coffee house throughout London.

Some establishments charged an admission fee of one penny and, in return, visitors were offered the opportunity to debate current issues. These became known as "penny universities" and were centres of political and literary influence.

The coffee houses were also the strongholds of the gossipmongers, as this extract from a verbal attack on "Newsmongers' Hall" shows:
"There they can tell you what the Turk Last Sunday had to dinner;

Who last did cut De Ruyter's corns, Amongst his jovial crew... You shall know there what fashions are, How periwigs are curled; And for a penny you shall hear All novells in the world..."

Above: Rowdy behaviour in an English coffee house, c. late 17th century.

The Prohibition of Coffee Drinking

In 1675, fearing potential political unrest, Charles II issued a proclamation closing down the coffee houses. He already had the support of the women of London who, in a strongly worded and somewhat lewd petition, expressed their concern about the "Excessive Use of that Drying, Enfeebling LIQUOR". Claiming that it made men sexually inactive, the women, who were not allowed in the coffee houses, complained that their husbands spent idle time and money away from the home, as a result of which the "entire race was in danger of extinction". The men responded with equal vigour, stating that it was not the coffee that made them "less active in the Sports of Venus", but the "insufferable Din of your ever active Tongues".

Despite the women's support, prohibition of the coffee houses was short-lived. After vigorous petitioning by merchants and retailers, they were reopened on condition that the proprietors should prevent the "reading of all scandalous papers and books and libels; and hinder every person

Above: The Great Subscription Room at Brook's Club, St James's Street, London. Painting by Rowlandson and Pugin, 1809.

Above: An English outdoor coffee stall, c. 1860. Painting by C. Hunt, 1881.

from declaring, uttering or divulging all manner of false and scandalous reports against government or ministers". The absurdity of the stipulation was obvious, and it was soon withdrawn. Coffee houses continued to operate as usual and no more was heard of suppression.

Along with the rise in coffee's popularity, the temperance movement was starting to gain hold. Under its influence, many of the working class were starting to exchange the fireside of the ale house for that of the coffee house. Since coffee houses were now frequented by all levels of society, there was anxiety – in some circles at least – about improper or unwelcome behaviour. Printed regulations were hung in conspicuous places (*see box*).

The Decline of Coffee Drinking

By the early 18th century, no matter how conspicuous the regulations, the atmosphere of the coffee houses changed. Many of them started to serve alcohol and attracted a different sort of clientele. As a result, the intelligentsia moved on to form literary clubs, while "gentlemen" retreated to the safety of their own exclusive clubs in Pall Mall and St James's. Commercial and financial groups found it more practical and convenient to operate from offices or from new types of premises set up for professional associations. Another factor was the growth of circulating libraries in the latter half of the 18th century. Up until then, the coffee houses had been the sole supplier of newspapers and pamphlets, but now the libraries not only made available literature of all types, but also supplied English and foreign newspapers. Patrons who had once enjoyed a quiet read of the papers in the coffee house, now preferred to do it elsewhere.

Although the upper and middle classes had adopted coffee-drinking, tea was rapidly gaining in popularity. Other cafés emerged, selling other types of non-alcoholic drink, and food. By the end of the century, coffee was on the way out. Coffee's popularity would not soar again until the late 20th century.

> **The rules and orders of the coffee house**
> "First, gentry, tradesman, all are welcome thither,
> And may without affront sit down together:
> Pre-eminence of place none here should mind,
> But take the next fit seat that he can find...
> Let noise of loud disputes be quite forborne,
> Nor maudlin lovers here in corners mourn,
> But all be brisk, and talk, but not too much;
> Of sacred things, let none presume to touch...
> To keep the house more quiet and from blame,
> We banish then cards, dice and every game..."

Above: A group of people enjoying cups of coffee and tea from a late-night stall at Blackfriars, London, England, 1923.

Below: The sumptuous interior of the Army and Navy Club House, London. Painting by R. K. Thomas.

NORTH AMERICA

Coffee was probably drunk from early on by the Dutch colonists in New Amsterdam (renamed New York in 1664), but the first reliable reference to its entry into North America occurs in 1668. Two years later, a license to sell coffee was issued to Dorothy Jones in Boston, and coffee houses soon opened throughout the eastern colonies.

In those hard-working days, coffee house management was looked on as women's work, though respectable women would not actually have been patrons. In complete contrast to European attitudes, the concept of whiling away idle hours in the coffee house was anathema. The coffee houses themselves lacked the clubby atmosphere of their European counterparts – the majority were closer to taverns which offered rooms to travelling workers and soldiers, and they attracted a correspondingly rowdy clientele. One of the more respectable was Boston's celebrated Green Dragon, headquarters of Revolution-plotting colonists, and in that sense did not differ greatly from coffee houses the world over.

The Boston Tea Party

Symbol of protest at the British tax on tea, the Boston Tea Party (1773), marked the acceptance of coffee as America's national beverage. Thereafter, coffee houses continued to spring up in major cities, some playing a vital role in the shaping of American history. Merchants Coffee House in New York was the scene of endless political discussion, declarations and strategic planning. Its famous rival, the Tontine, jointly owned by over 150 New York businessmen, served as a Stock Exchange, as well as occasional banqueting rooms and a record office for the arrival and departure of ships.

Like their English counterparts, habitués of the American coffee house eventually took their custom elsewhere as other social institutions evolved: business associations, gentlemen's clubs, banks and stock exchanges. The coffee house itself started to merge with taverns, hotels and restaurants.

Though the coffee house failed to maintain a stronghold, coffee itself became increasingly popular. The influx of European immigrants undoubtedly helped. The annexation of territories

such as Florida and the French-speaking regions along the Mississippi, further expanded the market.

Coffee kept the pioneering spirit going – when the covered wagons set out for the west, coffee went too. It was even drunk by Native Americans, and legend has it that land was swopped for tools, rifles and bags of Java beans.

For the soldiers fighting the Mexican War and the Civil War, coffee was an essential part of their rations. They liked their coffee "hot, black and strong enough to walk by itself". It was so highly prized that the soldiers went to amazing lengths to make sure it was shared out equally. Identical piles of coffee were apparently spread out on a mat and the sergeant, with his back turned on the soldiers, would call out names at random.

By the mid-19th century coffee was firmly embedded in the lives of Americans. They were consuming a staggering $8\frac{1}{2}$ pounds of coffee per head every year, compared to a European intake of $1\frac{1}{2}$ pounds. Coffee was drunk in town and country, by all, regardless of social standing. Coffee had become the national beverage.

Above: Colonials dressed as Indians throw British tea into Boston Harbour, heralding a rise in coffee drinking lithograph, 1846.

COFFEE SOCIETY TODAY

By the 1900s, coffee was still the beverage of choice in Europe and coffee house culture was firmly entrenched. Intellectuals and artists frequented the cafés in large numbers, particularly in Germany and Eastern Europe.

Coffee Drinking in Europe

In Germany, Berlin, for example, was rapidly becoming an international metropolis. Coffee houses such as the *Nollendortplatz* were regular meeting places for droves of enthusiastic young Germans, Scandinavians, Russian and Jewish émigrés who flocked there to read their plays and poems out loud. The scene attracted more and more people who simply wanted to be part of what was going on – including "young girls who style themselves as sculptresses and art experts", as one scathing male author wrote.

The coffee house scene in Vienna was equally cosmopolitan. By 1910, the city was home to countless immigrants from neighbouring Danube countries and beyond. With the exception of Paris, few European cities formed the cultural focal point for such a wide area. The coffee houses were allowed to stay open for as long as they had customers. For writers or students living in cramped and noisy lodgings, the coffee house became a second home. For the price of a cup of coffee, they could sit and read or write all day in comfort and warmth. There was no shortage of reading matter. Even in the 1900s, a licence was needed to sell newspapers in the street, so they were not so easy to come by. The coffee house, however, had most newspapers and magazines delivered directly, and thus provided a service similar to the modern public library reading room.

Budapest and Prague also boasted countless coffee houses which, in one way or another, were key to the development and growth of important artistic and literary movements. In Budapest, the Café Vigadó – though some say it was the New York – was the meeting place for the editorial board of a now-famous magazine *Nyugat* (West); Café Gresham was the haunt of a famous group of artists, dealers and experts, known in art history as the Gresham Circle. The reading of the first draft of Kafka's *Metamorphoses* took place in a back room of the Café Central in Prague.

Changes to coffee houses Though they fulfilled a vital social and cultural function, the economics of city life made it impossible for the coffee houses to continue in this way. Rising rents are not paid by allowing a person to "occupy a whole table by himself, stay there for hours for the price of a cup of coffee, insist on getting glasses of water and all the newspapers and magazines of Europe". Many of these delightful places became café-restaurants where the unique atmosphere became a thing of the past. In those that remain, the price of a cup of coffee reflects economic reality.

Above: A coffee house between the two World Wars.

Coffee in Britain

By the 1900s, the British taste for coffee had all but disappeared and tea-drinking had taken its place. Encouraged by the government, the British East India Company was importing more and more tea from Asia, and as a result, tea had become fashionable among all levels of society.

There was something of a revival of coffee house culture with the advent of grand establishments such as the Café Royal in London. Run by French proprietors, the Café Royal attracted a sophisticated clique of artists, poets and writers, including Oscar Wilde and Aubrey Beardsley, but it was a mockery of café life in Paris. People were thrown out for not being smartly dressed, and the "art" promoted was "homogenized for Mayfair drawing rooms".

With these magnificent cafés came the phenomenon of "café society" with its overtones of glamour and wealth. As American comedian Bob Hope said: "Café society is where they have mink for breakfast".

In complete contrast, coffee – if it can be called that – was also sold in dreary railway refreshment rooms and "cafés", along with sandwiches curling at the edges and ageing, stale cakes.

The Festival of Britain, in 1951, marked the end of post-war parsimony, and the start of a celebration of the bright new world of contemporary British culture. In keeping with the spirit of the times, The Coffee House opened near London's Trafalgar Square with the aim of providing not only a meeting place where coffee and light meals could be had in pleasant surroundings, but also lending wall-space to up-and-coming young artists. The Coffee House was soon followed by another establishment in nearby Haymarket. This was a gleaming shrine to contemporary design, notable for its striking ceiling-high edifice of coloured glass panels over which trickled a stream of water. Though both establishments in their intent and purpose attempted to replicate the early coffee houses, they differed wildly from their prototypes in terms of atmosphere and decor.

Above: Though the inspiration behind the revival of coffee drinking in Britain was the traditional Parisian pavement café, below, most of the new coffee bars, such as this one in Coventry Street, London, above, soon developed their own particular style.

Above: The 1950s in Britain saw the rise of coffee bars open to men and women.

Gone was the warm fug of dark wood-panelled rooms; the modern coffee house was a "shining thing of chromium and plated glass; brilliant colour and contemporary design". This was to set the style for the years to come.

The coffee bar The end of the 1950s saw the emergence of the coffee bar, with its hissing espresso machine and youthful clientele. The first to open in London's Soho included The Moka Bar, Act One Scene One, The Two I's, Heaven and Hell and the Macabre – the latter painted entirely in black with coffins as tables. The names of these places went down in history for people

growing up in the early 1960s, for they were the birthplace of the music industry as we know it today. Music singers and groups such as Lonnie Donegan played live, and pop singer Tommy Steele began his show business career in The Two I's. Juke boxes were installed playing the latest hits.

Just like their 17th-century counterparts, these establishments provoked the same vociferous debate. It was the era of the teenager and teenage gangs, and there were invariably some caffeine-induced disturbances. While reviled by some critics, the music played was looked on

by others as an "emotional stabilizer". A rather patronizing article in a contemporary catering magazine stated: "Juke boxes have proven their worth by keeping young people off the streets and out of the pubs, drinking coffee and soft drinks instead of spirits. Most coffee bars have found the younger customers well behaved...more often than not they are content with talking, listening, humming or tapping their fingers...rather than getting up and 'jiving' about."

Coffee bars spread rapidly to the provinces. By 1960 there were over 2,000 of them, and at least 200 in London's West End. They were not only popular with teenagers, but also with patrons wanting light refreshment while shopping, or before and after the theatre, and, unlike their 17th-century predecessors, they were popular with most women.

Despite their lively atmosphere, the coffee bars of the 1950s and 60s gradually faded from view. Again, many became restaurants and others started selling alcohol. Eventually they had also to compete with the wine bars of the 1970s.

The 90s revival The 1990s saw something of a coffee house revival, though. The ubiquitous spread of the Internet brought with it the cybercafé, equipped with computers and coffee, where those so inclined may sit and surf the web. These places attract a particular clientele, but, just like their forebears, they fulfil a need by providing a meeting place for like-minded souls and for those who might otherwise spend their days in isolation in front of a computer screen.

The 1990s also saw the development of speciality coffee shops, selling fine single-estate beans, often equal in quality to the finest of wines, and treated as seriously. Developing alongside came a rash of modern coffee houses – the antithesis of the 50s coffee bar – styled on minimalist lines and selling a bewildering choice of coffee from around the world. The British public have come full circle in their coffee drinking.

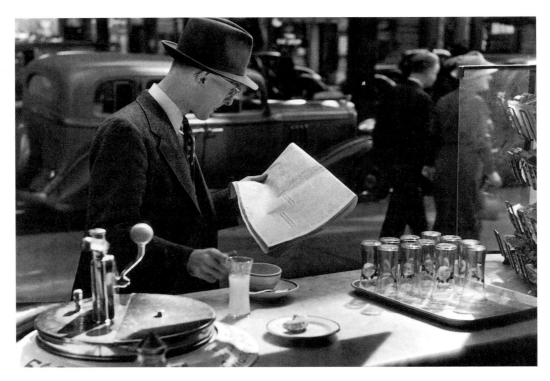

Above: Breakfast USA-style – coffee and a fruit juice while reading the paper at a roadside coffee stall, c. 1949.

Coffee Drinking in the United States

The habits of coffee drinkers in America developed quite differently from those in Europe and Britain, and the tastes and coffee drinking establishments often differed. For Americans travelling abroad in the late 19th and early 20th centuries, European coffee simply did not measure up to their home-brewed coffee. In *A Tramp Abroad*, Mark Twain declares: "You can get what the European hotel keeper thinks is coffee, but it resembles the real thing as hypocrisy resembles holiness. It is a feeble, characterless, uninspiring sort of stuff, and almost as undrinkable as if it had been made in an American hotel".

Conversely, Europeans travelling in America bemoaned the lack of congenial coffee houses in which to while away the hours.

By the early 20th century, coffee imports to the United States had tripled, and annual consumption was up to 11 pounds per head. Consumption peaked after World War II in 1946 at 20 pounds a head.

The 1920s saw a number of coffee houses established in New York's Greenwich Village, the artists' traditional quarter. They became known as "Java spots" and were popular with American writers, film-makers, singers and actors, and with the many new emigrant writers and artists.

During the 1960s these coffee houses had become popular with the young. The legendary musician Bob Dylan is said to have arrived from the West at the Cafe Wha in Greenwich Village, and asked the manager if he could sing a few songs.

Since these decades, coffee consumption in the US has dropped from 60-70 per cent of the population to around 50 per cent. This is partly due to increased competition from other beverages and partly due to increased health consciousness, particularly among women.

Coffee in the 1990s Though the majority of Americans do their coffee-drinking at home, the 90s saw the rise in popularity of outlets such as Starbucks, selling speciality coffees. These include gourmet or single-estate coffees as well as various kinds of cappuccino, espressos and flavoured coffees. As in the United Kingdom, there is also an increasing number of cybercafés and drive-throughs, as well as coffee shops in upmarket fast-food outlets, convenience stores and bookshops.

THE ART OF BREWING COFFEE

From the moment coffee-drinking took hold, an enormous amount of ingenuity and effort went into perfecting the art of brewing. Not content with the simple act of pouring hot water over grounds and letting it sit, inventive minds in Europe and the United States managed to produce an astonishing variety of equipment – drips, filters, percolators and pressure machines, to name but a few. Edward Bramah states in his classic *Tea and Coffee*: "Between 1789 and 1921 the United States Patent Office alone recorded more than 800 devices for brewing coffee, not to mention 185 for grinders, 312 for roasters and 175 miscellaneous inventions with some bearing on coffee". Automatic vending machines were later added to the list.

The Cafetière

One of the earliest devices was the cafetière, which made its debut in France around 1685. Its use became widespread throughout the reign of Louis XV. It was no more than a simple jug (carafe) with a heating plate warmed by a spirit lamp below. It was superseded in about 1800 by the first percolator, invented by Jean Baptiste de Belloy, the Archbishop of Paris. In Belloy's cafetière, the ground coffee was held in a perforated container at the top of the pot and hot water was poured over it. The water passed through the small holes in the container and into the pot below.

Unusual Early Inventions

A few years later after the invention of the cafetière, a formidable American named Benjamin Thompson, also known as Count Rumford, moved to Britain. Dissatisfied with the standard of coffee served – in those days it was subjected to lengthy boiling – he set about inventing a coffee-maker and eventually came up with the ominous-sounding Rumford Percolator. It was a great success, instantly finding a place in the annals of coffee-making history.

Just before 1820, the coffee biggin – the predecessor of the filter – became popular in England. In this device, ground coffee was placed in a flannel or muslin bag suspended from the rim of an earthenware pot. Hot water was poured over but, because of the bag, the water remained in contact with the coffee for longer, producing a different type of brew.

Brewing Coffee on a Large Scale

Up until the Industrial Revolution, there was no real need to make coffee in large quantities. However, with the growth of workshops and factories, combined with long working hours, some form of liquid refreshment was needed. Rail travel was becoming established, and with it, the evolution

Above: Early inventions in the development of coffee brewing techniques, from the late 18th century.

Above: The Parisian Grill, London, with an Italian espresso machine, instrumental in the transformation of British drinking habits.

of the station buffet. At the same time, coffee houses, and later on hotels and restaurants, needed to find a way of producing a continuous supply of the beverage in a quick and efficient manner. We thus have the start of the development of catering equipment.

Around 1840, a Heath Robinson-like piece of apparatus appeared in Britain, invented by Robert Napier, a well-known Scottish marine engineer. The machine worked on a vacuum principle in which coffee was siphoned from a heated container through a filter and into a receiving vessel. Though not very efficient, it was to provide inspiration for later inventions capable of producing coffee in industrial quantities.

Coffee was made on a larger scale in France in a monstrous contraption which Isabella Beeton in *Modern Household Cookery* refers to as

"Loysel's hydrostatic urn". Invented in 1843 by Edward Loysel de Santais, the device worked on the principle of hydrostatic pressure in which the build-up of steam forces hot water through a valve and then down through the coffee grounds. It was a sensation at the Paris Exposition of 1855, where it supposedly produced two thousand cups of coffee an hour – presumably in small cups.

The Cona

The Cona (vacuum pot) was a rather unique system that became widespread in the late 1930s. This consisted of two interconnecting toughened glass containers placed on top of each other and heated by a spirit lamp or gas or electric heater. The water in the lower container was forced into the top and drained through the coffee grounds back into the lower container.

The Espresso Machine

Perfecting Loysel's system from the previous century, the Italians went on to produce the revolutionary espresso machine which was to become so integral to Italian life. It was invented in 1948 by Achille Gaggia from Milan. These shiny hissing monsters were feared for their temperamental natures and billowing clouds of steam, but the dark, rich espresso coffee they produced was worth the time and trouble. The machines were also unique in producing a steaming hot foam of milk which transformed an espresso into a cappuccino – so called because its colour was reminiscent of the pale brown robes of the Capuchin monks. The classic cappuccino is traditionally a double espresso crowned with frothed milk and sometimes sprinkled with a powdering of rich, dark chocolate.

IN SEARCH OF THE IDEAL BREW

The majority of early coffee-drinkers in Europe made the beverage in much the same way as the Turks. Boiling water was poured on to finely ground coffee in the cup, resulting in a thick and potent brew. As coffee-brewing equipment proliferated, however, so did the nuances of national styles. Various individuals, too, had their own somewhat eccentric methods.

French Perfection

Coffee as perfected by the French was generally acknowledged among connoisseurs to be the best. Cast-iron coffee roasters and wooden coffee grinders were *de rigueur* in every household. Instead of boiling the beverage for hours, the French generally favoured the infusion method at first, before moving on to the drip-filter coffee pot and, later, the more sophisticated percolator.

Napoleon Bonaparte had his own way of brewing the perfect cup, and favoured the use of cold water. A connoisseur at the time wrote: "Put about two ounces of ground coffee for each person into a Percolator Coffee-Pot, pressing down with a ramrod, withdraw this and put on the tin covering for spreading the water over the coffee. Pour on the coffee clear cold water, and when a sufficient quantity has filtered through, plunge the jug containing the liquor into boiling water just before taking it to the table."

Some of the 19th-century coffee houses served specialities such as *mazagran*, an Algerian-style coffee extract diluted with cold water and served in a special stemmed glass. The practice of spiking coffee with alcohol also developed. William Ukers describes a unique iced coffee served in Normandy: "The man...takes half a cup of coffee, and fills the cup with Calvados, sweetened with sugar, and drinks it with seeming relish. Ice-cold coffee will almost sizzle when Calvados is poured into it. It tastes like a corkscrew, and one drink has the same effect as a crack on the head with a hammer".

Left: A classic combination – coffee with a dash of liqueur.

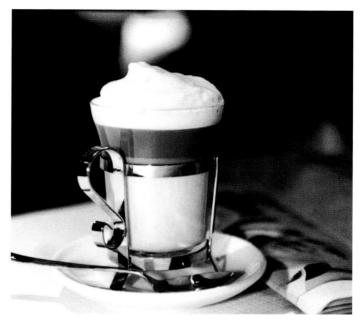

Above: Coffee and cream, which was a speciality of Austrian coffee houses.

Cream Lovers

Austrian coffee-drinkers favoured the French-style drip method or a pumping percolator device called the Vienna coffee machine. They were among the first to serve coffee with a cloud-like topping of whipped cream.

On entering an Austrian coffee house, it was an absurd request to simply ask for a coffee. As George Mikes points out, there was a rich choice to be had: "strong, weak, short, long, large, medium, small, in a glass, copper pot, light brown, with milk, whipped cream, espresso...Turkish – gold, nut gold, nut brown, Kapuziner (dark) or Franciscans (lighter), with rum, whisky, with egg".

Northern Europe and Scandinavia shared the Austrian weakness for cream, though the Danes preferred their coffee black. The Dutch were particularly civilized in their manner of serving – good quality coffee was served in a pot on a tray accompanied by a pitcher of cream, a glass of water and a tiny plate with three sugar cubes.

In Scandinavia, the more sophisticated European brewing methods and manner of serving did not catch on. Coffee was generally boiled or stewed in a kettle and then brought to the table in a pot, or even poured straight from the kettle. The Finns were reputed to use fish skins to settle coffee grounds and clarify the brew.

Unusual Brewing Methods

British coffee in the 19th century was not always universally recommended. Despairing of procuring a good cup of coffee in Britain, one former planter concluded: "coffee is spoiled in the burning, and sufficient care is not taken in preparing it for the table".

He goes on to deplore the "antediluvian method" of frying coffee beans with butter, declaring: "In private families, where this beverage is taken once a day, a coffee-roaster must be provided...Those who have not the facilities for roasting the berries themselves, should employ one or other of the leading coffee-roasters...who may be safely entrusted with the...berry".

Slow and steady Dr William Gregory of Aberdeen, England swore by lengthy cold water percolation requiring a laboratory-like arrangement of glass cylinders, funnels and bottles. The process took three or four days which, as he himself acknowledged, was a little tedious, stating: "it is necessary, as soon as the first portion is exhausted, to see a second in operation. In this way a supply is always to hand".

American eccentricities The Americans were particularly esoteric in their coffee-brewing habits. Boiling was the preferred technique, for ten minutes or even up to several hours. Some early recipes advised adding the white, yolk and even the crushed shell of an egg to provide richness of colour when milk was added. If fresh eggs were in short supply, an uncooked square of codfish skin was sometimes recommended. These curious techniques were reputedly popular with many American coffee lovers as late as 1880.

"Why do they always put mud in the coffee on paddle steamers?" *William Thackeray, writer and traveller, 1850.*

Advice from a 19th-century epicure

"Beat up an egg – two for a large pot – and mix it well with the coffee, till you have formed it into a ball; fill the pot with cold water, allowing room enough to put in the ingredients; let it simmer very gently for an hour, but do not think of stirring it, on any account; just before it is required, put the pot on the fire and warm it well; but as you value the true aroma, take care that it does not boil. Pour it off gently, and you will have as pure and strong an extract of the Indian berry as you desire. Use white sugar-candy in powder in preference to sugar; cream, if attainable; if not, boiled milk." Benson Hill writing in *Epicure's Almanac.*

Left: Despite the basic simplicity of the coffee-brewing procedure, variations on coffee-brewing technique are endless and ingenious. Everyone has a particular method which works best for them, as this 19th-century method for brewing coffee with eggs demonstrates.

Variations on a Theme

Coffee essence The famous Camp liquid coffee essence, in its tall square bottle, came on the market at the start of the century, and is still on sale today. It was popular during both World Wars when coffee was rationed. The chicory-based essence is pre-sweetened and is traditionally made by diluting it with hot milk.

Instant coffee In 1901, the first soluble dried coffee extract was invented by Japanese-American scientist Satori Kato of Chicago. It was quick to prepare, produced no tiresome grounds to dispose of, and the flavour never varied. Among the first to use it were members of an expedition to the Arctic. With the ease of preparation, soluble coffee found a ready market during World War I when it was widely used by American forces serving in England.

Following a request to find a long-term solution to Brazil's coffee surpluses, Nestlé introduced "Nescafé" into Switzerland in 1938. It came on the market a year later in Britain, managing to rekindle the coffee habit there, albeit in a weakened form.

Below: Just some of the many syrups, essences and flavourings, such as vanilla and cinnamon, that are available today for adding to coffee.

Above: Advertisement for Paterson's "Camp Coffee", 1890.

Decaff In 1903, a German coffee importer named Ludwig Roselius, having received a shipment of seawater-soaked beans, gave the beans to researchers. Using a combination of steam extraction and chlorine-based solvents, they perfected a way of removing the caffeine without changing the flavour. Roselius patented the process in 1905 and began marketing caffeine-free coffee under the name Kaffee Hag. The product was introduced in the United States in 1923 as Sanka, a contraction of the French *sans caffeine*, and found a ready market of coffee drinkers anxious to limit the effects of caffeine.

Flavoured coffee In the 1970s, small coffee-roasting companies in the United States started to introduce flavoured coffee. Initially, flavourings were developed to replace those containing alcohol – Irish Cream and amaretto, for example. However, a more recent trend has been for sweeter tastes, aimed at young or first-time coffee drinkers. As a result, flavours such as tiramisu, vanilla and toffee are becoming popular. Spicy flavours – not so dissimilar from those used in 16th-century Turkey – and fruit flavours are also gaining ground. Spices such as cardamom, cinnamon, orange zest and roasted fig are among those commonly used.

Canned coffee Ready-to-drink canned coffee was first launched by the Japanese in 1969. This was partly due to the popularity of vending machines in Japan. Not surprisingly, uptake in Europe and America has been slow, but it is popular throughout Asia where cold drinks are perhaps more welcome.

Below: Coffee in a can from Japan.

rainfall is unpredictable or even scanty. Similarly, it survives when equatorial temperatures soar, although it's happiest at an average temperature somewhere between 24–30°C/75–86°F.

Robusta trees flower rather irregularly, and take 10–11 months to go from blossom to mature cherry. The ripe cherries are generally picked by hand, except in Brazil where the flat terrain and vast spaces allow machine harvesting. Robusta is processed mostly by the "unwashed", or dry method, and the beans are smaller and more hump-backed than those of arabica; they are also often distinguished by small points at either end of the central "crack" on the bean. Robusta trees produce a slightly higher yield per hectare than do arabica trees. The most common varieties of robusta are *conilon* from Brazil, the *Java-Ineac, Nana, Kouilou* and *congensis*.

Other cultivars Hybridization has produced other cultivars which are propagated from cuttings rather than seeds, such as the more successful *arabusta*, developed by the French Coffee and Cocoa Institute in the 1960s and exported to many parts of the world from the Ivory Coast. The goal of most hybridization is to combine the best qualities of arabica, robusta, and perhaps of some of the better natural mutants, with the hope of possibly improving all. The natural *hibrido de Timor*, the dwarf *Ruiru Eleven* from Kenya, the rust-resistant *catimor*, and the *icatu* hybrids are names of some strains involved in, or resulting from, experiments in hybridization.

There are many reasons why the development of new coffee hybrids is the object of so much activity around the globe. In various cases, these efforts have pursued higher crop yields, larger beans or uniformity in bean size, better cup flavours, drought-resistant trees, adaptability to specific soil, and variants in caffeine content, to name but a few sought-after results. Almost no factors, however, present a greater challenge to coffee researchers than the two biggest enemies of the coffee plant: insects and diseases.

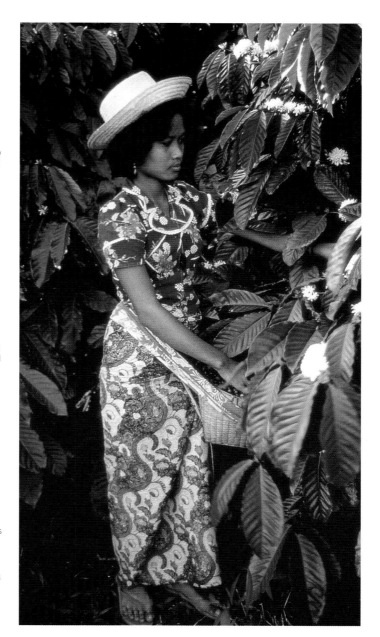

Above: A Javanese woman searches for the ripe fruit among the coffee tree leaves.

PESTS AND PROBLEMS

There are countless pests and diseases that regularly wreak great damage on coffee crops every year around the world. Perhaps one of the most surprising things about the fact that coffee production is the second largest in the world after oil, is that it is an industry subject to such a great number of natural disasters, in the form of pests, diseases and weather patterns.

Pests

It has been estimated that there are at least 850 species of insects that regularly book tables at their favourite coffee plantations. There are those who enjoy a salad of tender green leaves, such as various leaf-miners; leaf-cutting ants; leaf-skeletonizers; thrips; countless caterpillars; and nutrition-sucking scale, which come in shades of green, white and brown, and are such messy eaters that the mucus they leave behind breeds a fungus disease called "soot". There are many mealy bugs and numerous nematodes, whose secret binges on coffee roots go unnoticed until the plants appear to suffer from nutritional problems, while stem and twig borers prefer a liquid lunch straight from the tap. The antestia bug, whose first choice is green cherries, but who will settle for buds or even twigs, is like an elegant vampire; no one knows he has supped until the pulping process exposes the darkly stained zebra-striped parchment coatings, and the beans within, shrivelled and black, decayed with the fungus which often accompanies him. The Mediterranean fruit fly does her damage by laying her eggs in the pulp of the coffee fruit, which then becomes an all-you-can-eat buffet for the young maggots. The yellow tea mite may find itself in the wrong venue, but it stays nevertheless.

By far the most serious coffee pest is the dreaded coffee berry borer, the *broca del cafeto*, a tiny black female beetle that bores into a coffee cherry, going through the fruit pulp and penetrating the coffee bean itself, where she lays her eggs. If the bean is not totally destroyed by the voracious tunnel-making larvae, it will succumb

Above: It may look harmless, but the grasshopper is a prey on the coffee tree.

to the secondary rot fungus carried by the borer. Coffee berry borers were first noted in Africa in 1867, since which time they have infested every coffee-growing continent around the world, causing billions of dollars' worth of damage and devastation.

Global trends in pest control management are attempting to reduce, and hopefully ultimately replace, the use of chemical pesticides by the introduction and encouragement of natural predators and parasites of the coffee-preying pests. For example, a current International Coffee Organization project, funded by the United Nations' Common Fund for Commodities, hopes to control the coffee berry borer in at least seven member coffee-producing countries, by releasing certain wasps which prey on the borer beetles.

Diseases

Unfortunately, coffee diseases have no natural predators, and although fewer in number than the hordes of coffee pests, coffee diseases are still largely chemically controlled. Although fungicides are not as ecologically harmful as pesticides and herbicides, all chemical treatments are expensive. The best control of coffee plant diseases is careful quarantine, but

that is not easy to enforce, especially given the extent of international travel. One of the worst coffee plant diseases is leaf rust (*Hemileia vastatrix*). First reported in 1861 in Africa, by 1870 it had completely wiped out the coffee industry of Ceylon, which resorted to tea-growing. The virulent leaf rust quickly spread to every continent in the

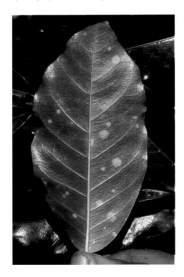

Above: Leaf rust.

coffee-growing world, although some countries have thus far been spared. It is thought that leaf rust is spread by spores being carried on the clothes of travellers from one country to another, particularly by people working in the coffee trade. It is lethal for arabica trees, but robusta is resistant to it.

A soil-inhabiting fungus causes another devastating coffee disease, tracheomycosis, also known as vascular fungus, or coffee wilt disease, to which robusta is more susceptible than arabica. In fact, it was this disease that almost totally destroyed the Ivory Coast's original coffee plantations of liberica trees in the 1940s, after which time the Ivory Coast became a large grower of robusta and the developer of arabusta. In the Democratic Republic of Congo, coffee production has fallen consistently since 1994, due to this disease and internal tribal warfare affecting the same regions.

Another very serious disease affecting arabica trees is coffee berry disease (*colletotrichum coffeanum*). Also called brown blight and red blister, coffee berry disease is a fungus, first identified in Kenya in the 1920s, which may attack a coffee tree in the wake of its carrier, the antestia bug. Rain splashes can also spread residues of the disease, even those from a previous crop. The disease attacks the coffee cherries, causing maximum damage to green cherries, turning them dark with decay. Fungicidal sprays are successful in controlling coffee berry disease only to some extent, and therefore this disease is the subject of much hybridization research.

Hybridization can certainly offer hope for conquering many coffee enemies, as one variety, susceptible to a particular pest or disease, is crossed with another variety which is naturally resistant. Although crossbreeding may eventually see the disappearance of some coffee diseases (thus far what is seen is more the disappearance of flavour), there is a category of coffee enemy to which all varieties are vulnerable: these are the natural disasters that plague many coffee-growing regions.

Natural Disasters

Because of the particular climate and soil required for growing coffee, plantations are sometimes located in rather precarious positions on the slopes of volcanoes. Active or not, volcanoes exist in areas of seismic instability, as evidenced by the terrible earthquake of January 1999, which struck the Colombian coffee-growing centre of Armenia, a victim of similar devastation in only 1988. Indeed, since 1972, Mexico, the Philippines, Panama, Costa Rica, Guatemala and Nicaragua have all suffered earthquake damage.

Hurricanes are endemic to the tropics, and although little coffee is grown in coastal areas, almost all tropical islands and the countries of the narrow isthmus of Central America are subject to serious tropical storms. Out of Nicaragua's 30 per cent crop loss due to Hurricane Mitch in 1998, only ten per cent consisted of destroyed trees, mostly by mudslides; the rest was cherries going rotten because the roads to processing mills were impassable. Tidal waves are more infrequent than hurricanes, but can be equally devastating, as witnessed by the massive force of the wave that hit Papua New Guinea in 1998.

Less dramatic, but seemingly always present *somewhere* in countries heavily dependent on coffee crops, are more universal disasters such as droughts, famine, bad weather (such as the freak hailstorm of October 1998, in the Brazilian state of São Paulo, which went largely unnoticed by the rest of world because it destroyed *only* an estimated 100,000 bags of coffee), political disturbances if not actual revolutions, and of course, the coffee enemy that causes chaos in coffee prices for the entire world: frost.

Frost is the bane of the Brazilian coffee crop, but it can occur in any country where the best coffee is grown in higher altitudes near the extremities of the tropical belt. Although a mild frost can sometimes be alleviated slightly with hot air machines, even one night of freezing temperatures can certainly do enormous damage to a coffee crop; a truly hard frost will completely kill the trees. Considering the years of labour and cost invested in a plantation of mature coffee trees, it must be heartbreaking to see it all come to nothing in just a few hours of cold weather.

Below: Frost destroys a Brazilian crop.

HARVESTING AND PROCESSING

Far more is done on a coffee plantation than just growing and harvesting the fruit. When coffee cherries ripen, they must be picked almost immediately, not an easy thing to time when a single tree's fruit is in various stages of maturity simultaneously. In most arabica-growing areas the ripe cherries will be carefully hand-picked and dropped into the picker's basket, the weight of which determines the picker's pay and, in areas of smoother terrain and shorter trees, can be as heavy as 100kg/220lb by the end of the day. The same tree will be visited on several different days as more cherries ripen.

A harvester will "strip-pick" the entire tree when the majority of its cherries are ripe, by sliding his or her fingers down the branches, causing all the cherries, ripe or not, to fall to the ground. Alternatively, a large vehicle will be driven slowly down the row of coffee trees, and its revolving arms will knock the looser, and hopefully riper, fruit to

Below: Hand-pickers head out for a day's work in the mountainous regions of Java, where they use ladders to reach the tops of the trees.

Above: The process of winnowing requires the use of a large sieve-like hoop for tossing everything into the air and retaining only the cherries.

Left: A Brazilian winnower tossing the machine harvest into the air, hoping to lose all but the coffee cherries.

the ground. Harvesting machines are used primarily in Brazil, where the immense, flat terrain of the large *fazendas* (estates) allows the trees to be planted in even, widely spaced rows.

If the fruit is on the ground, it must be raked up and "winnowed" by workers who, using large meshed hoops, fling the sweepings into the air several times; twigs, leaves, cherries and dust are tossed up high, and the worker, like a juggler, catches the cherries as the lighter weight materials are blown aside. A major problem with the hand-stripping and machine methods of harvesting is that many cherries are included which are not at a point of perfect ripeness; these under- or overripe cherries must be removed by extra sorting or else they will lower the grading quality. All quality arabicas will be sorted several times, beginning with hand-sorting the cherries. This initial task of hand-sorting is often done by women and children.

The Coffee Cherry

The coffee fruit is called a cherry primarily because it is about the same size, shape and colour as an actual cherry. Beneath the bright red skin is the pulp, a sweet, sticky yellow substance, which becomes slimy mucilage towards the centre of the fruit, where it surrounds the coffee beans, which are actually the seeds. There are normally two beans per cherry, facing each other's flat side, like peanut halves. On the surface of the beans is a very thin, diaphanous membrane, called the silver skin. Each bean (and its silver skin) is encased in a tough, cream-coloured, protective bean-shaped shell, or jacket, called parchment, or pergamino, which serves to keep the bean separate from the mucilage. Beans destined to be seed beans for growing new coffee plants must remain in their parchment if they are to sprout.

Left: Hand-sorting in Indonesia.

Above: Coffee cherries set out in the Kenyan sun to dry.

Normal coffee trees sometimes produce a few smaller-than-average cherries in which only one bean forms. This single bean, called variously a peaberry, perla or caracol, will not have a flat side; rather, it will be small and almost completely round. Sorted out and collected together, peaberries sell at a slightly higher price than do normal coffee beans from the same trees. Many people swear that the peaberry flavour is better, although it may just be that, because of the special sorting, few, if any, defective beans are able to slip through.

Processing the Cherry

The next step after harvesting is to remove the beans from the surrounding fruit pulp, which is done by either the washed (wet process), or the unwashed (dry process). The latter, dry processing, is the separation method, used where there is a shortage of water or equipment, or both. Because most robusta and much low-quality arabica coffee is dry-processed, many people,

experts included, wrongly assume that any dry-processed or "natural" coffee, must be inferior. On the contrary, most of Ethiopia's wonderful varied arabicas are dry-processed, and some of these are world class coffees; almost all Brazilian arabicas are naturals, or unwashed, and there are some superbly smooth, sweet and full-bodied Santos beans.

Dry processing In spite of its description, dry processing begins with the washing of the newly harvested cherries, not only to clean the cherries but to implement another sorting procedure, as the floaters – defective beans due primarily to insect infestation or over-ripeness – are easily picked out at this stage. The cherries are then spread out to sun-dry; if on patios they are raked, and if they have been placed on matting stretched across trestles, or on some other raised platform, they are hand-turned, for about three weeks. They are protectively covered from any night condensation or rain – the unwashed process tends to be used in

drier regions anyway – and the drying process may be finished with hot-air machines. When only about 12 per cent of their moisture content remains, they are either stored in silos or are sent on for final processing at a mill or factory, which may be under government control. Here they undergo hulling, which in one operation removes all of the dried skin, pulp, and parchment from the beans.

From this point the procedures are the same for both washed and unwashed beans: they are polished, screened and sorted, processes usually done with more sophisticated equipment, including electronic sorting machines; and then graded and bagged. After this the bags of green (still unroasted) beans may go into storage or they may be exported.

Wet processing This system is much more expensive, due to far greater requirements of equipment, labour, time and water. Before any fermentation can begin in the freshly picked cherries, they are immediately washed in large

Right: Pushing the pulped beans through the system of channels, which sorts them by size and weight.

tanks from which the water carries them into a system of channels. Staying in contact with the fresh-flowing water helps to loosen the outer skin, while the cherries are carried towards a depulping machine. Here they lose their skin and some of the pulp, but the flowing water takes the beans, still wearing their parchment covering and a lot of the sticky mucilage, through various screens, sieves and sluices, which further sort the beans by size and weight.

At last the beans arrive in a fermentation tank, where any remaining mucilage is broken down by natural enzymes during a 36-hour soak. The fermentation is monitored and controlled, as it must only remove the mucilage and not develop off-flavours in the beans themselves. The parchment beans, once clear of mucilage, are rinsed, drained and spread out on patios or wire-mesh platforms, and left to dry in the sun.

As in the dry method, the parchment beans are turned and raked for between one and two weeks, or they may go into low-temperature drying machines, until their moisture content is about 11–12 percent: the last stages are critical because over-drying makes them brittle and they can lose quality; under-drying means vulnerability to unwanted fermentation, fungi and bacteria or bruising during subsequent hulling. Parchment beans are stored for about a month, and can be stored for several months in a controlled atmosphere. When exportation is imminent, the beans are taken to the curing mill where the parchment is removed by hulling, and the washed beans undergo the same processes as do the dry-processed beans.

Right: Once through the various stages of soaking and pulping, parchment beans are rinsed, drained and spread out to dry on large, flat patios or wire-mesh platforms.

SORTING AND GRADING

Governments of countries which export coffee usually operate or advise a department or agency which establishes a standard, regulates and monitors the coffee trade, and assesses bean quality through quality control inspectors. In many countries the administrator is a coffee board authority; in others it is an institute, possibly under the control of the ministry of agriculture or of trade and industry.

Grading Coffee

Unfortunately, there is no international standardization of coffee quality, as coffee is graded by a set of characteristics peculiar to each producing country. A sample of beans is taken from a bag, judged according to that country's standards, and the sack of beans from which the sample was taken is given a quality rating, good or bad, depending on the outcome of the assessment. The characteristics by which most coffee is graded are appearance (bean size, uniformity, colour); number of defective beans per sample; cup quality, which of course includes flavour and body; and whether the beans roast well and evenly. Because the classifications of grades and the descriptive terminology differ from country to country, and the standards of quality are only relevant within that country's range of coffees, it is not easy to interpret a coffee's true quality without some familiarization of the particular country of origin's grading system. There is at least one constant, uniform reference from country to country: all countries determine bean size with standardized screens, so the buyer doesn't have to guess how large is large or how small is small from the producer's relative point of view.

A coffee may bear an exotic regional name, and/or may be classified by the processing (washed or unwashed). It may have a descriptive title, or just an alphabetical letter or two, possibly followed by a number. For example, in certain countries where the coffee industry has been nationalized, the grading system may seem to be rather

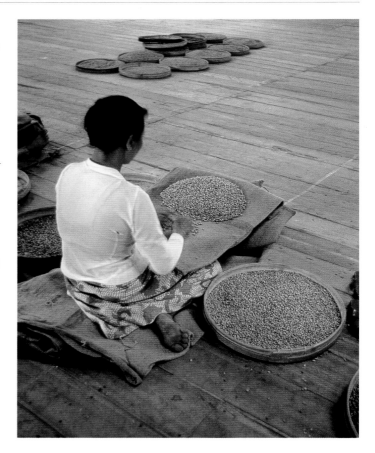

Above: The task of sorting through the wet-processed beans is a methodical one.

uninspiring, as in Kenya, where a bag of coffee may be a washed "AA", with a number to denote one of ten cup-quality classes; yet this ordinary-sounding coffee is acknowledged by most experts to be consistently one of the world's best coffees. In India, however, a Plantation A – assume "washed" because an unwashed is designated "cherry" – was one of the highest qualities available, but was not in the same league as the Kenyan. India, however, has recently changed to a free market, so it remains to be seen what grading system will be used.

Most Caribbean and Central American countries indicate quality by words denoting altitude: Costa Rica's eastern regions produce LGA (low grown Atlantic), MGA (medium grown Atlantic), and HGA (high grown Atlantic), while the western slopes grow HB (hard bean), MHB (medium hard bean), GHB (good hard bean) and SHB (strictly hard bean); the harder the bean, the higher the altitude and the price! The best plantations of Costa Rica can label their own bags as well as denote the altitude, and both Costa Rica and Nicaragua also use exotic regional names. Nicaragua also indicates classifications of quality and altitude with titles like Central Bueno Lavado (MG), Central Altura for high grown, and Central Estrictamente Altura (SHG). Guatemala is a bit more obscure with its altitude designations, since the adjectives, which sound purely descriptive, indicate altitudes beginning at 700m/2,296ft and rising to 1,700m/5,577ft: Good Washed, Extra Good Washed, Prime Washed, Extra Prime Washed, Semi Hard Bean (SH), Hard Bean (HB), Fancy Hard Bean and Strictly Hard Bean (SHB).

National systems for grading Countries that have unique ways of designating different qualities of coffee include Brazil, which classifies each bag by the species of coffee, the port from which the coffee is exported (Santos, Parana, etc), and then by a defective bean qualification, for example: NY (meaning "we are counting the defective beans the way the Americans understand it") and Standard 3 (which means an average sample of 300 grams would have 12 defective beans). The defects also include points for stones and twigs. Brazil's grading also includes bean size, colour, density, shape, roast potential, cup quality, processing method, crop year and lot number.

Modest Ethiopia, with some truly aristocratic world-class coffees, is content to denote simply the processing, the name of the region of production, and a grade number between 1 and 8, each of which indicates a certain number of defects. Colombia's grading is even simpler: each bag has the name of the region, and sorts by size, e.g. Excelso beans are smaller versions of the Supremo.

Indonesia has recently changed from its old Dutch system of grading. Now, R=Robusta, A=Arabica, WP=wet processed, DP=dry processed; six quality grade numbers, with 1&2 High, 3&4 Medium, 5&6 Lower grades; AP after the grade number means After Polished, and L, M and S stand for bean sizes large, medium and small. For example, R/DP Grade 2L would be a dry processed large-bean robusta of very high quality; A/WP Grade 3/AP would denote a medium-quality polished washed arabica.

The glossary overleaf lists some terms used by the coffee trade to describe particular coffee beans and their attributes. In some cases several explanations are given because, in general, there is no standardization of terms; interpretations may therefore vary or even seem to be contradictory.

Above: Professional sorters grade coffee beans by size, by painstakingly putting the beans into corresponding holes.

Grading Terminology

While the following terms may vary slightly from country to country, these are the generally accepted definitions and will give you an excellent idea of how one sample of coffee beans is differentiated from another.

Above: Black bean.

Black bean Insect-damaged; dead cherry fallen from tree pre-harvest; decomposed bean; overripe; metal contamination.

Bold bean The size falling between medium and large.

Broken Over-dried brittle beans, easily broken into pieces during hulling.

Brown bean In arabica, a colour denoting overripeness; over-fermentation; under-fermentation (brownish tinge); or soiled, lack of pre-washing.

Discoloured bean Any bean outside the range of normal (green/blue in arabica, khaki/brownish/yellowish in robusta) colour, indicating poor processing, with possible defective flavour.

Elephant ear Malformed cherry containing one large bean partly encircling a smaller; the two interlocking parts can separate in roast, but flavour is not impaired (East Africa).

Elephant bean Slang name for Maragogype variety, world's largest coffee beans; generally prized for appearance, good roast, smooth flavour; gradually dying out as financially unprofitable. Not to be confused with the malformed elephant/elephant ear bean.

Floater Under-ripe, or overripe bean, or brown bean that surfaces in washing – lacks density.

Foxy Off-flavour from beans either with red tinge, perhaps overripe; over-fermented (delay in pulping); yellow cherry; frost.

Hard bean Fairly mediocre arabica beans, indicates lower altitudes in countries where "strictly hard bean" is the best quality; not to be confused, however, with "hard" flavour.

Hull coffee Dry-processed beans before hulling has removed the surrounding dried cherries.

M'buni East African word for dry-processed (sun-dried) cherry. Also over-fruity, tart, sour flavour.

Natural bean Denotes dry-processed coffee bean.

Above: Insect-damaged beans.

Pale Yellow in colour, from immature cherries or drought-affected; will not darken satisfactorily in roast; unpleasant nutty flavour of several can spoil batch (*see* Quaker).

Parchment Protective covering or jacket (endocarp) encasing bean within the cherry, which must be intact if bean is to germinate; also "pergamino".

Left: Over-fermented beans.

Parchment coffee Wet-processed beans before hulling has removed their parchment coverings.

Peaberry Also, perle, perla, caracol; small rounded bean (malformation) produced singly in a small cherry; sorted together they command a higher price than normal beans, even ones from the same trees.

Pod Beans still encased in the dried cherry after hulling, constitutes defect in sample.

Above: Pulper-nipped beans.

Pulper-nipped Bean damaged during pulping; subsequent appearance can lower quality assessment.

Quaker Similar to Pale, but not caused by immaturity, although terms are sometimes used interchangeably (*see* Pale).

Ragged Bean not fully developed due to drought.

Stinker Overripe cherry; or over-fermentation; insect- or microbe-damaged bean; bean flavour is powerfully pervasive and rotten, sour odour when crushed; undetectable by human eye, glows under ultraviolet light of electric sorting machines; contaminates entire batch.

Strictly hard bean (SHB) Quality arabicas grown at highest altitudes, where density of bean concentrates flavour.

Strictly high grown (SHG) Different grading terminology for basically the same conditions as strictly hard bean.

Triage Lowest grade of coffee, never exported; left-overs; figurative factory floor sweepings.

Unwashed Dry-processed beans.

Washed Wet-processed beans.

Yellow bean In arabica, bean colour caused by over-drying.

COFFEE TASTING

Coffee tasting, also called "cupping", is the sensory evaluation of coffee, which assesses more than just taste; the senses of smell, taste and "feel" are all involved. Smell and taste are very dependent on each other, and difficult to separate in assessment; of course, there are some coffees that will not taste as they smell, but in general the attribute of flavour can be interpreted almost as much an aroma as a taste, and an aroma is a very good indication of the taste to follow. There are four basic tastes – salt, sweet, acid and bitter – and most specific tastes fall into one of these categories. The sense of feel involved in assessing coffee evaluates the coffee's body – its weight, fullness and texture in the mouth.

Coffee beans are regularly tasted all along the market route, though the really serious tasting is done when the coffee is graded, in its country of origin, and at a second stage when it is sold to the importing country.

Evaluating the Flavour

First, prepare the samples and equipment needed: identical cups (ideally) for each coffee to be tasted; the coffee samples and a coffee measure; another empty cup; a spoon (silver is traditional) about the size and shape of a soup spoon, or shallower; a glass of water in which to rinse the spoon between coffees; a glass of room-temperature water (or a water biscuit or cracker) for clearing the palate; a jug (pitcher) or spittoon (garboon is the specialist term); and a kettle of very hot water, just under boiling point.
• Plan to taste at least two coffees, as a frame of reference.
• Grind should be medium ("cafetière/ percolator" grind). If the coffees are ground in succession in the same grinder, start with a clean grinder and wipe out the grinder between samples.
• If the tasting is a true comparison, the degree of roast should be as much the same for all samples as possible; if tasting is simply to choose a preferred coffee, taste every coffee in whatever style or roast it comes supplied. The lighter the roast, the more the true

unique flavour of the coffee is exposed; the darker the roast, the more all coffees begin to taste the same, and the easier it is to hide the flaws. In a darker roast, the coffee tastes less acidic, but since acidity is the main indicator of altitude, quality and price, it is a shame if the expensive acidity disappears in the roaster.
• Measure out the same amount of dry coffee into each cup, about 8g/ 1 heaped tbsp to 150ml/5fl oz/²⁄₃ cup of water. Sniff the dry coffees. Write down any noteworthy observation about the dry smell. It is always advisable to arrange the coffees in an orderly row for tasting, placing those which may be the strongest – particularly if any robustas are to be tasted – at the end.
• Pour water just off the boil to the same level in each cup. Do not stir. Wait a couple of minutes, then bend over each cup and smell the surface, which is a mass of floating grounds.
• Break the crust (the grounds floating on the surface of the cup), by inserting the tasting spoon through the surface flotsam, again while bending over the cup and inhaling the aroma at very

close range. You could spoon up and smell some of the grounds and liquid from the bottom of the cup – this action will probably help to settle the grounds as much as anything.
• With the spoon, lightly skim any remaining grounds off the coffee's surface, and sling them into the extra empty cup. (Dipping the tasting spoon into the glass of rinsing water will get rid of any grounds left on it.)
• Get a medium-full spoonful of coffee, place it against the lips and virtually inhale it, with plenty of air and into the mouth, slurping noisily, attempting to get some of it all the way to the back of the mouth immediately. Swish it around the mouth, and after a few seconds, spit the liquid out. Make some notes for later comparison, rinse the spoon and go on to the next coffee.
• Try to taste all the coffees at the same temperature and in close conjunction with each other. As the coffees cool, go back and taste them again, as the flavours may change slightly.

Below: A professional coffee taster with the samples of brewed coffee.

Coffee Tasters' Terminology

This list may seem a little daunting, but remember that what you are looking for in a good cup of coffee is essentially body, aroma and flavour. Choose a coffee that you like and see what you can detect. Alternatively, try coffee where the taste is not as it should be, and compare it with a good brew to try to see where the differences lie.

Acidic Very desirable coffee quality, sharpness detected towards front of mouth; denotes quality and altitude; can be fruity (citrusy, lemony, berry-like, etc) or a pure tongue-tip numbing sensation (Costa Rica, Kenya, Mexico offer good examples).

Aftertaste/finish Flavour/mouthfeel remaining after coffee has left the mouth, sometimes surprisingly different from actual coffee taste.

Aromatic Coffee with intensive pleasant fragrance (for example Hawaii, Colombia, Jamaica, Sumatra).

Ashy Coffee with flavour/aroma of cold fireplace ashes.

Astringent Mouthfeel characteristic that "draws" the tongue and tissues, often apparent as after-taste.

Bitter Basic flavour sensation detected at the back of the mouth and soft-palate, often as after-taste, sometimes desirable to a limited degree (as in dark-roast, espresso). Not to be confused with acidity.

Above: The basic taste of coffee is made up of body, aroma and flavour.

Blackcurrant Flavour reminiscent of blackcurrant or berries; some acidity but with stronger undertones not found in citrusy, highly acidic coffees; not a negative term.

Body Signifies the perception of texture or weight of liquid in the mouth; thin or light body can feel watery (a few high-grown arabicas); full-bodied means heavy liquor, as in Sumatra, Java, and most robustas.

Broth-like Pleasant flavour in some lighter East African coffees similar to clear soup, like bouillon, often accompanies slightly citrusy flavour.

Burnt Carbon-type flavour and aroma, as in burnt toast; over-roasted.

Caramel Sweet flavour reminiscent of caramelized sugar, or, slightly different: candy floss (cotton candy).

Cerealy Flavour like unsweetened grain or oatmeal, sometimes found in under-roasted robusta coffee, bland and not particularly pleasant.

Cheesy Rather pungent flavour/aroma of slightly sour, curdled milk or cheese.

Chemical/medicinal Coffee with unnatural off-flavours, real or reminiscent of tainting.

Right: Where it all starts – with the whole roasted coffee beans.

Chocolatey Flavour reminiscent of chocolate which can be found in various crops (some Australian, New Guinean and Ethiopian, for example).

Citrus Flavour reminiscent of citrus fruits due to high acidity; very desirable, denotes quality and high-altitude growth.

Clean Pure coffee flavour, no twists or changes in the mouth, no different after-taste (Costa Rica sometimes provides good examples).

Dirty Coffee tasting as if the beans have been rolled in dirt or soiled.

Dry A certain type of acidity and/or mouthfeel, but not, as in wine, the opposite of sweet; often accompanies light, or even delicate coffees, such as Mexican, Ethiopian and Yemeni.

Dusty Dry-earth taste and smell, exactly like dust, though not the same as dirty or earthy.

Earthy Aroma/flavour reminiscent of damp black earth, organic, mushroomy, cellar-like (can be found, for example, in some Javan or Sumatran coffees "gone wrong").

Floral Coffee beans having a very fresh, floral, heady aroma, like that of floral-scented perfume.

Fruity Flavour/aroma often found in good arabica coffees, reminiscent of a wide range of fruits: citrus, berries, currants, etc, always accompanied by some degree of acidity; this is usually positive, but can indicate overripeness or over-fermentation.

Gamey Unusual and interesting flavour, often found in dry-processed East African coffees (such as Ethiopian Djimmah), reminiscent of cheesy, but not sour or negative.

Grassy Green and astringent aroma with an accompanying taste like a new-mown lawn, sometimes found in coffees from Malawi and Rwanda.

Green Aroma/taste of unripe fruit or plants, as when green stems or leaves are crushed or broken; can denote under-roasting.

Hard Flavour, not to be confused with hard bean. In terms of flavour, hard signifies a brew lacking sweetness and softness.

Harsh Strong, unpleasant, sharp or "edgy" flavour; also used to describe Rio-y, iodine-like flavour.

Hidey Aroma/taste like animal hides, uncured leather, or, at best, new leather shoes.

Lemony Flavour very like mild lemon found in very acidic coffee, such as that from Kenya.

Light, mild Light-bodied coffee, pleasant low-to-medium acidity. Some Mexican, Honduran and Santo Domingan coffees exhibit these characteristics.

Malty Coffee flavour very like malted barley, sometimes in combination with chocolatey, sometimes alone.

Mellow Soft, with pleasant low-acidity.

Metallic Sharpness, acidity slightly gone wrong. Some Nicaraguan coffee, for example, can be overly metallic.

Mocha, mokka Arabica coffee originally named for the old port of Yemen, now also associated with Ethiopian Harrar coffee. Nothing to do with chocolate, although coffee drinks with mocha imply chocolate with coffee.

Musty Flavour of improper drying, mildew, generally undesirable.

Neutral Bland coffee, very low acidity, not derogatory, as implies no off-tastes; good for blending (often describes many ordinary Brazilian arabicas).

Nutty Pleasant flavour reminiscent of nuts, often peanuts (some Jamaican).

Papery A taste/aroma exactly like dry paper, slightly similar to dusty.

Phenolic Flavour/aroma so medicinal as to cause olfactory sensation reminiscent of phenol.

Rancid/rotten The flavour of a spoiled oily product, as in rancid nuts or rancid olive oil; fairly disgusting; can cause involuntary gagging.

Rio-y Iodine, inky flavour from microbe-tainted beans. Prized for traditional brewing in Turkey, Greece, Middle East.

Rounded Cup balance with no overpowering characteristic, well-balanced; can also mean pleasantly smooth, without being sharp.

Rubber Aroma/taste reminiscent of tyres, garages, often detected in certain robustas, for example.

Sacky Coffee tainted by improper storage, flavour/aroma of hemp, possibly damp.

Salty One of four basic tasting categories, occurs occasionally in coffee; also can denote presence of chicory in coffee blend.

Smoky Aromatic flavour of woodsmoke, very pleasant attribute sometimes found in certain coffees such as some from Guatemala and also occasionally some Indonesian arabicas.

Smooth Mouthfeel not sharp or astringent, pleasant, sometimes combines with winey flavour.

Soft/strictly soft Coffee with low acidity, mellow sweetness, pleasant roof-of-the-mouth easiness (possibly similar to the feel of Italian red Lambrusco wine); some Brazilian Santos for example.

Sour Undesirable "dirty socks" flavour of over-fermentation.

Spicy Aroma/taste of spice, perhaps sweetish or peppery, found in certain coffees, such as those from Java, Zimbabwe, Guatemala; or the more erratic Yemen and Ethiopian coffees.

Stalky This gives a flavour reminiscent of dry vegetable matter or other plant material stalks.

Stinky Rotten flavour indicating possible contamination by "stinker" bean.

Sweet Pleasant, mellow, agreeable; sometimes used to describe soft coffees, but also can be found in highly acidic coffees.

Thin Term when coffee's body does not equal acidity or flavour; out-of-balance, watery, wishy-washy in mouthfeel.

Tobacco-y Aroma/flavour characteristic of unsmoked plug (chewing) tobacco.

Turpentine-y Smell or taste reminiscent of chemical, possibly phenolic-like substance.

Well-rounded, well-balanced Cup giving impression of good mix of flavour, acidity, body, and perhaps aroma.

Wild Term describing certain Ethiopian/Yemeni coffees – suggesting unusual, inconsistent, and interesting; sometimes used with spicy; also exotic, tangy, complex.

Winey Combination of slightly fruity flavour, very smooth mouthfeel and texture reminiscent of wine. Term should not be used indiscriminately to denote acidity; better reserved for coffees with genuine feel (more than taste) of wine, slightly rare but unmistakable (in some Kenyan as after-taste; found in some Ethiopian Harrars, Yemeni, and various others).

Woody Flavour peculiar to either dead (indicating old crop, coffee stored too long) or green wood flavour found in certain coffees, like fresh saw-dust; neither very pleasant.

Yeasty/toasty Flavour reminiscent of either yeasty (unbaked) bread, or bread lightly toasted.

Left: Roasting coffee darker can hide the less desirable characteristics of a coffee sample which may not be of the highest quality.

COFFEE-PRODUCING COUNTRIES

Today, because of increased communication and improved transportation, the world now appears very small, and almost anything is accessible to those who want it. It is, therefore, remarkable how much the coffee trade seems still to follow the old colonial routes. The explanation for this is to be found in the national coffee taste preferences established during periods when European powers supported, or exploited, their own colonies, either by using the plants indigenous to the colony, or by introducing certain crops desirable or profitable for the mother country.

If coffee, an extremely lucrative and sought-after commodity, was not native to a colony, its cultivation was often quickly encouraged and nurtured. For example, much of the coffee consumed in France today contains a surprisingly large amount of robusta, the coffee variety produced in those West African countries which made up much of France's empire and were, geographically, – important in the days of shipping – France's nearest colonies.

Because of the activities of the British East India Company, which traded coffee among Eastern countries, but introduced tea to India and Britain, Britain drank far more tea than coffee from the mid-1700s. The British colonial acquisitions during the late 1800s and after World War I were primarily concentrated in East Africa, all arabica-growing regions; and, along with that from Jamaica, the coffee Britain consumed was primarily arabica. Even today, although many British coffee companies import robusta, they will seldom admit to doing so, as the overall preferred taste in Britain is for arabica.

Portugal, the great power in early exploration and colonization, did not retain many of its early colonies, although today it is still the main buyer for its last coffee-growing colonies, Angola and Cape Verde, which it gave up in 1975; Mozambique, also lost that year, basically stopped growing coffee when the Portuguese colonists pulled out. Portugal lost Brazil quite early on when the colony became independent in 1822, as an indirect result of Napoleon's invasion of Portugal.

North America, made up of colonies itself and a melting pot of all nations, is also a melting pot of coffee, with a wide range of coffee preferences, and accommodating virtually all tastes.

Production figures used in the following coffee-producing country profiles are based on information received at the time of publication.

Right: One of the best ways to familiarize yourself with the many different types of coffee available is to think about the countries that grow coffee, and to sort them into a few main coffee-growing regions. This book has grouped coffee growers into four principal regions: Africa; Central America and the Caribbean; South America; and the South Pacific and South-east Asia.

The map opposite shows all of the countries covered in the following pages, highlighting the main types of coffee grown there: arabica, robusta, a combination of these two, and the new hybridizations.

In some cases the estimated statistics given in the country profiles may differ from the information given at the back of the book, which represent the latest total figures for the 1998/99 crop year. Coffee bag figures represent a unit of 60kg/132lb of green coffee, no matter what size bag is actually used in any particular country. Also, exportable production figures may differ from those of actual exports, as green coffee can be stored for some time before shipment. The ICO expects the 1998/99 global coffee crop to be a very good harvest of about 105,241,000 bags. The statistics of coffee-producing countries who either are not members of the International Coffee Organization, are not included in this figure.

Right: Every year nearly 80 million bags of coffee are exported around the world.

AFRICA

As the birth place of coffee, it is fitting that the continent of Africa produces some of the world's finest coffees. In many countries, however, social, political and economic problems make the production of coffee a difficult task.

Angola

In the 18th century Portuguese colonists began coffee cultivation in what is now the People's Republic of Angola. Although robusta is not generally a word associated with high quality, that is exactly what differentiates the best of Angola's robusta (Ambriz and Amboin) from that of other countries. The beans are uniform in size and colour, cleanly processed (mostly by the dry method), sorted and carefully graded. The robusta is grown on shaded trees in the northern plains, approaching the delta of the Congo River. Angola's inland plateau has a far more temperate climate than the plains, and an altitude of 1,800m/5,905ft allows some cultivation of arabica coffee, which is mild, unassumingly neutral, and in blending could easily substitute for an average-quality Brazilian Santos. Since the devastation of the civil war, however, it is very scarce; before the 1994 peace treaty, production sank to 33,000 bags, compared to 3.5 million bags in 1973.

Benin (formerly Dahomey)

Shaped a bit like a vertical house key, Benin can really only grow coffee in the south, its least arid zone, where many small-holders intersperse the coffee trees with palms. Although Benin's coffee – robusta and some arabusta – is too small a crop to list as a percentage of world production, it still probably exports more coffee than it grows, due to smuggling activities with Nigeria.

Burundi

Coffee brings far more income to this small land-locked African country than any other commodity. Indeed, its citizens, while appreciating the very good washed arabica, of which Burundi grows more than robusta, will consume less than one per cent, preferring the

earnings from exporting the rest, which is good quality, clean, well-graded, and has both good acidic flavour and body. However, there is some concern over future production of coffee due to tribal unrest.

Above: Burundi superior full wash, top quality green beans.

Cameroon

Cameroon is known as a producer of robusta coffee, although about one-third of its crop is the Blue Mountain variety of arabica, which is grown in the western volcanic regions. Primarily wet-processed, at one time the arabica coffees produced on the European plantations equalled the high-quality coffees of Central America. The robusta growths, first brought from Zaire, are grown now in all the provinces except in the extreme north.

Cape Verde

Cape Verde, the Windward and Leeward Islands off the extreme west coast of Africa, is not a member of the International Coffee Organization, so

no statistics are available on its current coffee production. The Portuguese, who dominated these islands from the 15th century until 1975, first planted arabica trees in 1790. The gradual transformation of the islands to desert, due to severe droughts, has reduced coffee growing in the volcanic soil from various heights to only the higher mountainsides, at altitudes between 500–900m/1,500–2,700ft.

There is no hydroelectric power, and no irrigation is possible, so water is precious and scarce, but the humidity from the fog generated by the north-west trade winds sustains the few remaining coffee trees, which also serve as windbreaks and soil-erosion deterrents. In a good year the dry-processed coffee yield may be sufficient to export, mostly to Portugal, but the islanders, coffee-drinkers themselves, actually have to resort to importing coffee, mostly from Angola, to satisfy local demand.

Central African Republic

The Central African Republic, which used to be part of French Equatorial Africa, still sells most of its coffee, a very important cash crop for the country, to France. Italy is its other main buyer. The robusta varieties are the usual canephora and the more interesting Nana robusta, first discovered growing wild on the banks of the Nana River in the extreme western region. The coffee is carefully classified, and consistent in quality and

Above: Cameroon robusta green beans.

roast, but because the country is land-locked, any problems in steady availability are due to transportation difficulties. The debilitating coffee disease tracheomycosis originated here.

Comoros

Between the Mozambique coast and the island of Madagascar lie four small islands which were under French control for many years. Today they

make up the Federal and Islamic Republic of the Comoros, although one of them, Mayotte, opted to remain under French territorial administration. Coffee, mostly robusta, is grown on Mayotte and Mohéli islands, shaded by banana and coconut trees. The quality of the hand-picked dry-processed beans is not bad, and about two-thirds of the small crop (often less than 1,000 bags) is exported. The remainder satisfies the high consumption demands of the local population, about 700,000 people.

Congo

This country of nine provinces includes a small section of Atlantic coastline, and was once the middle part of French Equatorial Africa. The equator runs across the top third of the country, and its climate is basically the non-varying heat and humidity of equatorial regions. The all-robusta crop produced by the republic seems to be increasing. Unusually, the average-to-good coffee is not graded by size, as the beans are generally uniform, but rather by number of defective beans, of which the top grade Extra Prima has none. The cup quality is that of an average-to-good robusta, neutral and clean.

Democratic Republic of Congo

The former country of Zaire grows robusta, mostly of the Marchand type, but far more interesting to the specialist coffee trade is the arabica crop, which makes up less than 20 per cent of the harvest. These trees are grown at a very high altitude in the mountainous plateau regions of Kivu province, where the land rises towards the volcanic mountains marking the edge of the Great Rift Valley, and the lake-studded borders shared with Tanzania, Burundi, Rwanda and Uganda.

Most of the wet-processed arabicas, of good, bright blue or blue-green colour and consistent appearance, have remarkably few defects. At best the Kivu arabicas can be described as a fine,

Left: Cash cropping. In many countries the exportation of coffee provides most of the income from foreign sources.

perfect balance of good body and acidity, and the Maragogype is an extremely pleasant soft coffee.

Unfortunately, the coffee crop of the Democratic Republic of Congo has been decreasing gradually over the past decade. The larger plantations are poorly maintained, and the finest coffees, grown in a region rife with tribal warfare and tracheomycosis, must be transported through other countries on the land-locked eastern border before exportation from the Indian Ocean ports. The Kivu arabicas are thus extremely rare to find. The new Kabila regime intends to rebuild a free market economy, hopefully supportive of greater coffee production.

Equatorial Guinea

Coffee is second only to cocoa in importance for this beautiful country, which consists of five islands and a bit of continental West Africa. The coffee is mostly robusta and liberica, but arabica is grown. Independence in 1968 after 190 years of Spanish rule led only to disastrous dictatorships, and today, in spite of its fertile, rich soil, Equatorial Guinea's reduced production of coffee (and cocoa) has not recovered. The country has resumed relations with Spain, buyer of almost its entire crop.

Ethiopia

The earliest accounts of coffee all refer to its being a native of this region of old Abyssinia; indeed, the coffee processed

Right: Kivu arabica beans from the Democratic Republic of Congo.

today by many Ethiopian villagers is simply picked off untended, wild bushes. Although an extremely poor country, suffering from an infrastructure destroyed by civil war, and racked by periodic serious droughts, Ethiopia is a significant producer of coffee, both in quantity and quality, still managing to export some of the world's finest and most individual coffees, some of which have a very low natural caffeine content. The regions growing the best coffees are generally the Sidamo, Kaffa, Harrar and Wellega, but within each region some coffees are traditionally unwashed (naturals) and some are washed. In general, the unwashed coffees may be described as wild or gamey in flavour, not a taste to everyone's liking, but extremely interesting, if variable. At times, other terms, such as lemony, delicate, winey, floral and soft may be applied to certain Ethiopian coffees. In appearance, the beans are not only unimpressive, but may be downright off-putting, and in some cases the processing is a bit haphazard, if not careless, resulting in a maddening unpredictability. Nevertheless, these coffees are not run-of-the-mill, and may represent the epitome – in other words,

Above: Ethiopian Sidamo grade 2 washed medium-roasted beans.

as good as it gets – of coffee-tasting. Some of the best-known Ethiopian coffees are Djimmah, Ghimbi, Lekempti, Harrar (both long berry and short berry, known for their soft, winey Mocha flavour – a name stolen from the old Yemeni port of Mokka), Limu, and Yergacheffe.

Due to the unique, wonderfully delicate flavours, it is never a wise thing to dark-roast Ethiopian beans. In fact, to come across these beans dark-roasted might suggest an inferior crop for that year's production.

Gabon

The former French colony still sells much of its crop of decent, neutral robusta to France, and the rest to the Netherlands. Interestingly, much of Gabon's coffee is grown in the north, and as it occasionally seems to export more than it grows, there is a strong possibility that the more enterprising Equatorial Guineans, on the north-west border, smuggle beans into Gabon, where the small, mostly urban population enjoys relative prosperity due to oil-rich natural resources.

Below: Ethiopian Djimmah roasted beans.

Ghana

Formerly the "Gold Coast" British colony, Ghana provides 15 per cent of the world's cocoa, which is cheaper to grow than coffee. In areas where the soil is not favourable for cocoa, however, the government encourages coffee cultivation. Although the coffee is rather nondescript robusta, it is bought mainly by Britain, Germany and the Netherlands.

Above: Ghanaian robusta medium roast.

Guinea

In 1895, the French introduced arabica from Tonkin to their colony, but the yield was poor; the climate and soil of this republic (since 1958) however, grows good "neutral" robusta in its forest shades. Unfortunately, 25 years of Marxist dictatorial rule broke many trade connections between Guinea and Western countries, and today rivalry between ethnic groups, questionable legislative elections, as well as crippling world debts, have not been conducive to re-establishing the stable trade needed to improve coffee quality or quantity. Some Guinean coffee finds its way into the Ivory Coast, its neighbour to the east.

Ivory Coast (Côte d'Ivoire)

The Ivory Coast is usually Africa's second-largest coffee producer. Thirty three years of a stable one-man presidency, with a relatively smooth transition to another seemingly stable leader, plus monetary and defence aid from its former ruler, France, have helped to provide the stability that a long-

term, labour-intensive industry such as coffee requires. The rather average quality and its consistent and reliable supply, make Ivory Coast robusta attractive to many coffee blenders throughout the world, although France and Italy buy much of the crop (which may include beans smuggled in from its neighbours, poor, land-locked Mali to the north, and Guinea to the west). An agricultural research centre near Abidjan recently developed arabusta, the most successful coffee hybrid yet produced.

Kenya

For quality rather than quantity, Kenya's high-grown, wet-processed arabica is one of the world's great growths. The fairly narrow range of flavours is good and consistent, probably because the Kenyan industry is strictly regulated by the Coffee Board of Kenya (Nairobi), which determines the grading of each bag of green beans, at times even blending together green beans from different plantations under the House Blend label. Those bags marked "AA" are the top quality and are sought-after by the gourmet coffee trade. Kenyan coffee is noted for its sharp, fruity, sometimes even lemony or citrus flavours, due to high acidity, and for the consistent (small, round and deep greeny-blue) appearance of the beans, be they AA, the more commonly exported "AB", or the celebrated and expensive Kenyan peaberries.

Above: Kenyan peaberry green beans.

Liberia

What can be said about a country that in 1980 had 165,000 bags – though not all of it traceable to its own coffee plantations – of exportable coffee, and now produces less than 5,000? Though the quality was never particularly good, the robusta was usable – the USA bought most of it – which is more than could be said for the native liberica. There were high hopes for the arabusta possibilities, and a soluble-coffee factory was planned. Unfortunately, warring factions and corruption of power have led to a total economic collapse in recent years.

Madagascar

Coffee is Madagascar's most important export, although the island is the leading world producer of vanilla. A French colony until 1960, Madagascar, after 18 years of radical socialism, is now a multi-party democracy trying to re-establish its ties with Western trade and rebuild its agricultural programmes. The larger robusta growth is ranged along the slopes of the long eastern coastline, while the arabica regions are on the central plateau. Generally, the coffee, much of which is bought by France, is excellent, and there are plans to

Above: Ivory Coast robusta grade 2.

develop more plantations, especially as the more-than-14-million residents are enthusiastic drinkers.

Part of any future plans for coffee expansion, however, is the desire to preserve the forests, home to unique species of flora and fauna.

Malawi

When Malawi (formerly Nyasaland) became independent from British rule in 1964, it spent nearly thirty years under the rule of one despot, Banda. Now, under stable multi-party rule, poverty is still endemic, but human rights, education and literacy are increasing; all conducive to the labour-intensive business of growing coffee. The arabica coffee is grown mostly on small-holdings and processed locally in the mountainous plateaux at the extreme ends of this long, narrow country. Drought eclipses all other problems, but it is hoped that more of this excellent coffee, reminiscent of an average Kenyan, will be available for world consumption in the near future.

Above: Malawian medium-roast beans.

Mozambique

Portugal used this colony to grow tea, while its coffee-growing colony was Angola. Consequently, the arabica (Blue Mountain variety) grown here, supplemented by the wild *racemosa*, meets only local demands. After independence in 1975 and a 15-year civil war, Mozambique is one of the poorest countries in the world. Now, with a fragile democracy and many millions in aid pledges, there is a remote possibility that someday Mozambique could be an exporter of good coffee once again, as it has not only the climate and soil, but also the second-largest harbour in Africa.

Nigeria

Unfortunately, there is little positive to say about this country's coffee. The mostly robusta crop is of poor and inconsistent quality, although Britain is one of the main buyers of its former colony's crop. Smuggling, corruption, crime, debt, pollution, and aid-stopping human rights violations have helped to shrink the economy since the oil-rich boom of the 1970s, which the various military regimes sadly allowed to totally eclipse the more long-term government agricultural support.

La Réunion

Today, the main crop of this small volcanic island 805km/500 miles east of Madagascar is sugarcane. How very different from the days when coffee planting was mandatory of all free citizens, when destroying a tree exacted the death penalty, and when the monetary currency was backed by coffee! The island of Bourbon, as the French colony was then named, gave its name to the oldest, and still best, variety of arabica coffee, and it was from two trees brought here from Yemen in 1715 that many of the world's coffee plantations originated.

Rwanda

German and Belgian colonizers reinforced Tutsi domination here, and since a Hutu government achieved independence in 1962, there has been violent, if at times intermittent, tribal warfare. The arabica coffee quality is generally good, although it could be said it almost suffers from excess; the extremely rich soil, abundant rainfall, strong sun and quick growth may be the collective cause of a peculiar grassy taste sometimes found in all but the superior grade. Coffee is still very much Rwanda's primary source of income, and in spite of the warfare and pest infestations, its production is increasing. The Rwanda Coffee Board currently plans to rehabilitate 76 of the 140

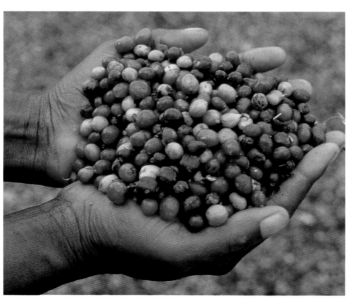

Above: Freshly picked cherries show a mix of both ripe and immature fruit.

coffee-growing communes by providing fertilisers, pesticides and new high-yielding plants.

St. Helena

This South Atlantic island, the only dependency still receiving British budgetary aid, was annexed by the East India Company in 1659 and began growing coffee when seeds were brought from Yemen in 1732. At some point the cultivation was abandoned, and the only remaining trees were wild.

Although at present the island's main economic activities cannot support the population, an enterprising coffee roaster in the 1980s began the revitalization of a tiny coffee industry which may soon become noted for hand-produced, totally organic, good-acidity and balanced, quality coffee.

São Tomé & Príncipe

Although cocoa brings in 90 per cent of São Tomé's export earnings, it still produces coffee, most of which is a reputedly lovely arabica, grown in the rich soil sloping up to the island's volcano. Since the Marxist regime, which greatly reduced coffee-growing, was replaced by a democratic constitution in 1990, the islands are seeking closer relations with various Western countries, in particular their old colonizer, Portugal, and the United States, so perhaps more of this coffee will become available on world markets.

Sierra Leone

Another sad story of a country decimated by military coups and civil war. Until as late as 1985, the robusta grown in this former British colony of freed slaves was some of the best of African blending coffee – FAQ (Fair Average Quality) and neutral (an important term for robusta) in the cup.

South Africa

For a long time South Africa has grown some good quality arabica coffee, cultivated from plants of the Bourbon and Blue Mountain variety, originally brought from Kenya. The region of growth is mostly that of Kwa-Zulu Natal, which, with Southern Brazil, is one of the few regions which dares to grow coffee outside of the tropical zone. There are many reasons, however to doubt that much of the coffee grown here will ever reach the world market; the 1996 constitution is decidedly fragile, and racial tensions and personal dangers run high; the country is heavily populated and, indeed has to import much of the coffee it consumes; and because much of the international trading is based on lucrative mineral and mining resources. The labour-intensive coffee production and accompanying slow profit turnover do not seem encouraging to those lovers of good coffee around the world.

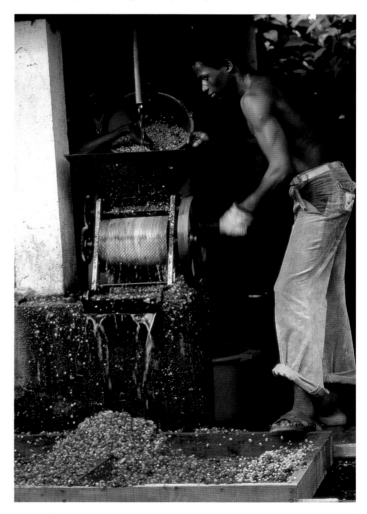

Above: Picked coffee cherries lose skin and pulp in wet-process pulping machines.

Above: Drying coffee cherries must be raked and turned to dry evenly and thoroughly before hulling.

Sudan

This country is blessed with high altitudes, and wild coffee, probably spread by bird and beast from Ethiopia, already grows there. Ambitious plans, however, of a few years past to grow more of this excellent arabica, have sadly come to little. A series of problems, from civil wars, droughts, disease and starvation, through to international isolation due to concerns for human rights and terrorism have resulted in the decimation of any coffee industry whatsoever.

Tanzania

Although Tanzania is still a very poor country, in almost every area of activity it is improving. An economic reform programme has helped to cut inflation and the budget deficit, and IMF-backed aid is helping to reorganise the agricultural sector. Coffee is Tanzania's number one crop, but where previously most of the arabica coffee was produced on large estates, leaving robusta production to the small-holders, today many small-holders with access to the equipment of a co-operative are able to grow arabica coffee. The washed

coffee is excellent, reminiscent of Kenyan coffee, but the acidity is less intense and the overall feel slightly milder and lighter; also the quality is not quite as consistent as that of Kenyan beans. The older bourbon variety still produces the best flavour, aroma and body. Moshi, near Mount Kilimanjaro, is a main coffee-marketing centre in an area where many small-holders grow a combined crop of coffee shaded by banana trees.

Togo

Togo's coffee story is happily different from many other former colonies in Africa. The democratic government and efficient civil service encourage and help the cultivation of the rather ordinary, but well-graded, dry-processed neutral robusta. It produces a fairly large harvest, considering that Togo is a very small country. Its own domestic coffee consumption is low,

Right: Tanzanian Chagga.

so it can export most of what it grows and it is happy to diversify its market, selling its coffee to various European buyers, including its former colonizer France, although the Dutch often take the bulk of the crop.

Togo maintains a good road system, and its capital is a coastal port, which can make a real difference to the success of a coffee crop. Although the country has few natural resources, its citizens, particularly the market-women of Lomé, who basically control the country's retail trade, are enterprising.

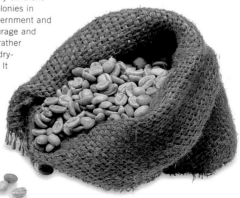

Uganda

Since 1986, President Museveni's "no-party democracy" has thus far saved Uganda from the ethnic tensions which have destroyed the economies of neighbours Rwanda and Sudan, from which thousands of refugees have poured into Uganda. Economic liberalizations have attracted aid receipts and private sector investments; the road system is under repair, and coffee production, mostly robusta, is high. Financial experts know that one crop providing 93 per cent of a country's export earnings is not always healthy. However, it is great news for coffee lovers, as a small percentage of tea-drinking Uganda's coffee is very good washed arabica, grown mostly in the Bugisu region adjoining the border with Kenya (whose coffee is very similar). Indeed, before privatization, some arabica beans were smuggled into Kenya for its better, unregulated prices; since privatisation some arabica is now smuggled to avoid the Ugandan government's tax.

Above: Uganda arabica Bugisu AA green beans.

Yemen

As Arabia (Arabia Felix to the Romans), this small country gave its name to arabica coffee, which was introduced to the world through its ports. Lying on the eastern shores of the Red Sea, geographically it is Asian, but in reality the general coffee character is closer to those of its nearest coffee-growing neighbour, Ethiopia.

Mocha coffee Yemeni coffees are the original Mocha, taken from the name of the old port, today's Al Mukha. "Mocha"

Above: Yemeni roasted mocha "31".

coffees grown in Ethiopia (notably Harrar and Djimmah), are the impostors, although the tastes, like those of unwashed arabicas, may be similar to the Yemeni flavours: wild, gamey, winey, dry, delicate, varied and unpredictable, possibly with some chocolate over-tones. They are, however, different coffees; the Ethiopian mochas will be cheaper, as the true Yemeni beans, even the most common (Sanani, from San`a, and Matari, from the province of Bany Matar) are quite scarce.

After Yemen sided with Iraq in the Gulf War, Saudi Arabia expelled a million Yemeni workers, whose return so burdened the government that it stopped many farm subsidies, and farmers began growing the more profitable narcotic *qat* plants. Also, the political instability which resulted in a civil war in 1994 is still disruptive to the Yemen economy.

Zambia

Unlike some other African countries, Zambia's problems do not seem to be political (other than the one of bureaucratic corruption) or racial; its weakness is the fact that it is dependent

Above: Zambia green beans.

on copper for 90 per cent of its export earnings, and copper prices have fallen and Zambia's reserves are declining. Perhaps because it is land-locked and lacks a good road network, Zambia's arable land is under-utilized. At any rate, the government seems committed to market reforms, and certainly its encouragement of more cultivation of the excellent Zambian coffees is resulting in greater crops. Zambian coffee is similar in flavour to other East African arabicas; its lightness is particularly reminiscent of coffee from Tanzania, with whom it shares its Northern border near the coffee-growing Muchinga Mountains.

Above: Zimbabwe dark-roasted beans.

Zimbabwe

Although much of land-locked Zimbabwe is a high-altitude country, rainfall is erratic and drought common, except in the mountains of the eastern region near the Mozambique border, where most of its fine washed arabica coffee is grown. Coffee from Zimbabwe, the best of which is found near the town of Chipinge, may not be as famous as Kenyan, but it shares many of the same cup characteristics: it is generally free from off-tastes, and has fruity acidity and good aroma; it may also have a slightly peppery flavour not found in coffee from Kenya.

Like Malawian coffee, it is sometimes recognised as a gourmet coffee by the speciality coffee trade, depending on the particular crop. Whether the government's repeated declarations to nationalise farms and plantations will ultimately affect coffee production, remains to be seen.

CENTRAL AMERICA AND CARIBBEAN

The coffees from Central America are justly renowned for their completeness in terms of body, flavour and aroma.

Costa Rica

Many people hope to go to Heaven when they die; coffee lovers hope to go to Costa Rica. This little Central American republic enjoys the best possible conditions for growing superb coffee: a high-altitude central plateau (the Meseta Central) basking in a mild, temperate climate with good moisture and cool nights, and covering about 2,000 square miles; rich volcanic-based soil; ports on two oceans; and a stable, organized, commercially-oriented government. Of course, Costa Rica is not problem-free: the inaccessibility of the highest altitudes makes coffee transportation difficult and expensive, and there is always the worry of volcanic activity and the devastating

Above: A traditional Costa Rican painted cart carries the fruit picked on the plateau.

Above: Tuj San Marcos de Tarrazu green beans.

tropical storms which plague Central American existence. Costa Rica, unlike its neighbours, lost only about 90,000 bags of coffee to Hurricane Mitch.

The coffee, Costa Rica's agricultural mainstay, is all washed arabica – it is socially unacceptable even to mention the word robusta – and natives enjoy a high standard of consumption; in fact, Costa Ricans drink more than twice the amount of coffee consumed in Italy.

Quality coffee The best coffees are generally those from around the capital city of San José, and the nearby towns of Heredia and Alajuela. The Tarrazu region to the south of San José produces some superb coffees of exquisite acidity and "clean" cup liquor. Bags of beans may be labelled by the area, such as Tarrazu's Tres Rios, Dota, and San Marcos, or by owner/estate names, such as FJO Sarchi company, located on the slopes of the Poas volcano. La Minita, Windmill, Henri Tournon (HT) – whose green beans are really turquoise – are names indicative of high altitude and a sharp, tangy acidity, perhaps the most desirable attribute in a cup of coffee. Some experts shriek at the idea of drinking Costa Rican coffee any way but black; however, the sharpest acidity gives a wonderful mild flavour when the coffee is drunk with a little milk or cream.

Costa Rican coffee is almost always very fragrant, and the cup flavour is "clean" and pure. Occasionally, the body in a cup of Costa Rican coffee may err to the thin side, but the flavour is so exquisite, that a thinner liquor can be excused. Sometimes one hears of Costa Rican coffee being dark-roasted. Unless the coffee is below the usual standards or somehow defective, such a practice should be avoided at all costs, as a darker roast destroys the lovely acidity, and the flavour loses the desired distinctive (and expensive-tasting) qualities.

Right: A dark roast spoils the acidity of Costa Rican beans.

Cuba

Since the collapse of the USSR, Cuba's mainstay in export trade, Cuba's economy has been in recession. Desperate to attract foreign capital, Cuba is allowing some outside investments in the hotel and tourist industry, a showplace for its arabica coffees, which are increasing in production, although sugar, of course, is still the main export crop. Cuban coffee, which has been grown since the mid-1700s, is clean and flavourful, and carefully processed and graded; it is marketed under exotic names, which in reality indicate only particular bean-size averages, the largest being Extra Turquino. Cuban coffee is lower in acidity than that of most other Caribbean coffees due to Cuba's lack of high altitudes. It is, however, pleasant in the cup and is best dark-roasted.

Below: Cuban Extra Turquino.

average beans. Dark-roasting accents the lovely, mellow sweetness of the Cibao, Bani and Ocoa coffee beans.

Dominican Republic

When Hispaniola was partitioned in 1697 between France and Spain, Spain's share was the eastern two-thirds of the island. Coffee, which has been grown here since the early 1700s, and is still traded under the Santo Domingo name, is not a major crop, but the washed arabicas are good. The best coffee, grown in the south western Barahona region, is known for its acidity and full body. Slightly less acidic but very satisfying in the cup are the soft, full-bodied Bani and Ocoa coffees, from the slopes of the southern end of the central *cordillera*. Cibao are the rather

El Salvador

This poor country, small and densely populated, precariously nested on top of a seismic zone with 20 volcanoes, possesses no natural resources. Its infrastructure (roads, bridges and electricity), destroyed by eleven years of civil war, hangs on to its fragile existence by two thin strings: coffee and international aid. With little chance to diversify, the country has relied on its wet-processed arabica to bring in 90 per cent of its export earnings in spite of serious attacks of rust and pests.

In October 1998, Hurricane Mitch's torrential rains figuratively washed away at least 150,000 bags of coffee, and probably more was ruined by humidity-induced fungus after the floods abated. Salvador coffee (its trade name) is grown at various levels of altitude, all of it rather high, and is graded accordingly; the blue-green SHG is the best, with its acidy flavour, medium-to-full body and sweet overtones. "Pipil" is the brand name of a reputedly excellent organic coffee.

Guadeloupe

This little island at the northern end of the Caribbean Windward Islands is caught between wanting complete autonomy from France's Overseas Department while being almost completely dependent on French aid. In 1995, its unemployment was 26 per cent. Because banana prices are extremely unstable, it is now seeking to expand sugar production. Yet, it still grows tiny amounts of what must have been a world-class coffee, described by Philippe Jobin as "one of the best 'crus' of the world...hard to replace for lovers of high class coffee". The climate, soil, workforce, expertise and resources are available, so perhaps the gourmet coffee trade could encourage Guadeloupe to bring this coffee back from virtual extinction.

Guatemala

Coffee is the first crop of Central America's largest economy, where 90 per cent of the population still live below the poverty line. The extreme inequalities in wealth and land distribution limit modernization. Coffee is grown on very large, wealthy *haciendas* (estates), and on a few thousand *fincas*, or farms, all owned mostly by *ladinos* (non-Indians), as well as on many thousand subsistence small-holdings worked by poor Indians, mostly in the highlands. Guatemala has not yet

Left: Salvador high-grown coffee, classified according to superior European Preparation standards.

*Right: Guatemalan
Huehuetenango green beans.*

succumbed to the temptation to
replace old varieties of trees, such as
Bourbon, with high-yield, low-taste
varieties, although the low yield per
hectare is costly. There are sponsored
programmes to help small-holders to
minimise their costs, enabling them
to continue with high-quality, low-yield
trees for the gourmet market.

*Above: Guatemalan genuine Antigua
green beans.*

Types of coffee Guatemalan coffee is
rated by many experts as one of the
best growths in the world. Unlike the
Costa Rican coffees, Guatemalans vary
more from region to region, although
the general flavour profile of "medium-
to-full-bodied liquor, perfectly balanced
with good acidity and complex smoky,
spicy and chocolate tones" would fit
many, if not most. Near the capital city
is the famous Guatemala Antigua, the
old city founded by the conquistadors
and destroyed by an earthquake in
1773, which gives its name to one of
Guatemala's finest coffees. Towards the
north is Cobán, another city whose
name represents high altitude resulting
in high-quality acidity. There are
numerous other regions of superb
Guatemalan coffees, but
Huehuetenango, in an isolated
western area, is a name
increasingly noted for fine acidity
and unique flavours in coffees grown
mostly on small-holdings.

Haiti

In the 1697 partition of Hispaniola,
France received Haiti, the western third
of the island. Aided by Toussaint
L'Ouverture's rebellion, Haiti was free by
1804, and thus began what will soon
be two hundred years of political
instability. This poorest of countries,
where many houses are windowless
earthen huts, depends very much on
coffee for much of its income.

Unfortunately, the coffee grading and
classification is a confused process,
and the simplest explanation is that
coffee samples are graded by size of
bean, altitude, cup quality, defective
beans and number of stones included.
The old trees, growing nearly wild, still
produce lovely large bluish beans of the
typica variety, heavy with humidity,
which are often dry-processed, mostly
by peasants. Sweet and mellow, these
full-bodied coffees with lowish acidity –
particularly the rich, winey, washed SHG
beans – can be excellent, but not
reliably so; they are perhaps at
their best roasted
medium-dark.

Most Haitian coffee is biologically pure
simply because fertilizers, pesticides
and fungicides are too expensive for the
average Haitian grower.

Honduras

Like most other Central American
countries, Honduras markets its
coffees by designation of altitude.
Honduras produces washed
arabicas, clean with good acidity
and flavour, possibly lacking only
slightly in body – overall, a high-
quality coffee, perhaps not in a gourmet
class, but a worthy contributor to a
blend. Hurricane Mitch caused direct
losses of nearly 500,000 bags of
Honduran coffee, but future production
may also be affected, depending on
transportation, infrastructure damage
and time required for repair.

Jamaica

Few coffee-drinkers realize that
Jamaica earns most of its money from,
and is the world's third-largest producer
of, bauxite, and that, in fact, its famous
Blue Mountain coffee grows only on the
eastern tip of the island, in a small area
extending no further west than
Kingston. The production is shared by
only three parishes: St. Andrew, where
coffee was originally planted in 1728
by Sir Nicholas Lawes; Portland, on
the northern slopes of the
mountains; and the parish

*Left:
Honduran
green beans.*

of St. Thomas on
the south side. Other
coffee-growing parts of
Jamaica, which collectively would
occupy an area twice the size of the
Blue Mountain coffee estates and
farms, actually grow about 75 per cent
of Jamaica's coffee.

These other regions sell coffee bags
labelled High Mountain Supreme and
Prime Washed Jamaica, names

*Right:
Jamaica
Blue
Mountain
roasted beans.*

perfectly innocent on their own,
but dangerously close to Jamaica
Blue Mountain in all but quality. In fact,
although we speak in "bags", the real
Jamaica Blue Mountain comes in
barrels, and anyway, all exported
Jamaican coffee is certified by the
Coffee Industry Board. Even so, the
unwary would-be JBM consumer is
seldom safe, as when buying 200 grams
of roasted beans (which is about all
anybody can afford), they might not
actually see the container the beans
were shipped in. Also there are many
countries who grow the Blue Mountain
variety of arabica, and a few even have
a Blue Mountain range of hills.

As more Jamaica Blue Mountain
coffee is sold than that small area could
possibly produce, remember Davy
Crockett's motto, "Be sure you're right,
then go ahead": buy 100 per cent pure
Jamaica Blue Mountain Coffee only
from a reputable source.
Aroma and balance Jamaica Blue
Mountain is only a high-quality
Caribbean coffee, and as such, is
subject to much the same vagaries that
Mother Nature inflicts on other
Caribbean coffees. A good crop will
produce a cup that is an exquisite
balance of nutty aroma; bright, but
not overwhelming acidity; delicate
sweetness; and a clean but
nectar-like finish. The body
may be slightly lacking in
fullness, and someone
who likes a hearty cup
of coffee may need to
use more than normal
to brew a satisfying
cup – another
consideration
when getting out
your wallet at the
cash till. An inferior crop,
especially possible with recent
years of over-production leading to
possibly less careful processing, may be
disappointingly mediocre, and could
be easily outclassed by a Costa Rican,
Guatamalan, or even Cuban.

One possibility for change in the
Jamaican Blue Mountain market is that
while Japan has for nearly thirty years
been its major purchaser, with the rest
of the world scrambling to pay princely
sums for the remnants, Asia's economic
crisis has plunged Japan into a terrible
recession, and this could alter
somewhat the distribution of the world's
most expensive coffee.

Martinique

This tiny island in the middle of the
Lesser Antilles, described by Columbus
as "the most beautiful country in the
world", was where Capt. Gabriel
Mathieu de Clieu, in the 1720s, decided
to plant the coffee tree "stolen" from
Louis XIV's royal greenhouse. The first
coffee specimen to enter the Western
Hemisphere, it flourished in the rich
volcanic soil of Mt. Pelée's slopes, and
became the progenitor of the millions of
coffee trees grown throughout the New
World in the early colonial period.

After a hundred years of success,
Martinique's coffee plantations
declined, greatly hindered by the
natural disasters that seem to strike
Martinique, situated in "Hurricane
Alley", about every five years. Today,
Martinique's citizens, like those of

*Above: Jamaica
Blue Mountain
green beans.*

Above: The first stage of processing the cherries is rinsing in water.

Right: Mexican roasted beans.

are very individual and never boring.

Like many Central American countries, Mexico is subject to earthquakes, particularly in the mountainous regions where the better coffees are grown. Due to its size and location, however, Mexico is not always affected simultaneously by the same problems as other Central American producers. While Honduras, El Salvador, Nicaragua, Guatemala, and Panama were all plagued by floods, rain, or heavy humidity caused by Hurricane Mitch, Mexico was in the throes of a severe six-month drought, that eventually caused the loss of about 400,000 bags.

Guadeloupe, receive French subsidies for their high levels of unemployment. Coffee production seems a thing of the past. The few remaining ageing trees are sporadically attended to, but as Martinique has the climate, the soil, workforce, etc., one can only hope the situation will improve.

Mexico

Mexico, which grows some fairly average, mostly washed arabica coffees, classifies its crop by altitude-denoting terms similar to those of Nicaragua. Although many regions of southern Mexico grow coffee, there are some coffees which rise above the average, not only literally in altitude, but in interesting, hard-to-describe and sometimes unpredictable flavours.

In the state of Veracruz on the Gulf of Mexico, the mountainous region near Coatepec produces an excellent "altura", characterized by a light body, but with a slightly sharp, dry acidity, which sometimes has nutty or chocolate hints. The alturas of nearby Huatusco and further inland Orizaba are also fine coffees. Oaxaca, the more remote south-western state, gives its name to good coffees, including Oaxaca Pluma. Chiapas, adjoining the southern border with Guatemala, grows large amounts of arabica marketed under the name of Tapachula. Flavourful and particularly aromatic, and occasionally bordering on the "sour", Mexico's alturas and SHG's are not to everybody's taste, but they

Nicaragua

The very poor country of Nicaragua, for which coffee is the main export crop, reported crop losses of up to 30 per cent of its more than 1-million-bag-average crop after it was hit by Hurricane Mitch in October 1998. Thankfully, 20 per cent of the devastation was due to impassable roads preventing the crop reaching the processing mills, and therefore was not permanent damage. The remaining 10 per cent of the loss was direct damage when a massive mudslide from the Casita volcano destroyed entire coffee fields in the region of Matagalpa. All Nicaraguan coffees are wet-processed arabicas grown in fertile volcanic-based soil.

Under normal conditions, Matagalpa and the neighbouring town of Jinotega produce the best Nicaraguan coffee, of which the SHG is known for its large beans, slightly salty acidity, and

medium-to-full body and good aroma. The Nicaraguan version of the Maragogype variety represents the world's largest coffee beans, although the flavour is generally not quite as universally appreciated as that of the

Above: Nicaraguan SHG medium roast.

Guatemalan Maragogype.

Panama

Panama's main coffees grow in the far western region nearest the Costa Rican border in the high-altitude slopes around the Barú volcano, where the regional names are David and Boquete; the district of Chiriquí, and slightly to the east, Tole, produce notable high-grown washed arabicas. Café Volcán Barú is a newer gourmet coffee from the same region. The SHB Panamanian

Below: Nicaraguan Maravilla roasted coffee beans.

Above: Medium-roasted beans from Boquete, in north-western Panama.

coffees are known for their deep green colour, light body, bright but not sharp acidity, and pleasant, sweet taste; major buyers of Panama coffee are the French and the Scandinavians. The damage sustained by Panama's coffee crop from the heavy rains brought by Hurricane Mitch was about one-fifth of the 1998/1999 crop, or about 45,000 bags.

Puerto Rico

What a nice change to read about a Caribbean island revitalizing a dying coffee trade, which is exactly what Puerto Rico has been doing. Always reckoned to have been one of the world's best growths, Puerto Rico is supplier to the Vatican. A few years ago it grew less coffee as it drank more, and in 1968 stopped exporting coffee completely, as it was importing far more than it grew.

At the same time, the US minimum wage law, effective in the Associate State of Puerto Rico, ensured the Puerto Rican workforce a far higher standard of living than that enjoyed by any other Caribbean population, while attracting US industry to its "cheap" labour. As almost no struggling coffee plantations could afford to pay US minimum wages, coffee-growing was nearly a thing of the past, except for a few thousand small-holders, grouped into local cooperatives. Now, at least two of these cooperatives, Yauco, (whose "Yauco Selecto" is simply superb) and Lares, have revived coffee production by producing, in the wake of the US's demand for "specialty" (sic) coffees, high-quality beans of the grand

old varieties, carefully picked and graded. The gourmet coffees are expensive to produce, but they exact high prices, which quality-seeking buyers from several foreign countries are willing to pay.

The Puerto Rican *crus*, which could be called the world's most "powerful" coffees, were always known for their intense aroma and deep, rich, and amazingly sweet flavours, fully balanced by a heavy liquor; how wonderful to have them back again.

Trinidad & Tobago

These two islands, 14km/9 miles off the coast of Venezuela, grow what is called "small amounts" of robusta coffee, mostly for instant coffee processing; in fact, these "small amounts" make up a crop that annually exceeds the combined harvests of Liberia, Gabon, Equatorial Guinea and Benin. But

"small" is relative to the matter of income: after gaining independence from Britain in 1962, the oil-rich islands enjoyed a high level of prosperity – Trinidadians for several years had the reputation of importing more Scotch whiskey per capita than any other country – while constantly increasing its oil production and refinery.

In recent years, however, world oil price movements have highlighted a need to diversify. Tobago is finally developing its tourism, as not only its beaches but also its butterfly species attract tourists. Behind the all-is-well façade, the interior of Trinidad is home to dissatisfied poverty-stricken farmers; unemployment, crime, drugs-related problems, and oil-spills are a constant threat. The day may yet come when the demanding, but satisfying, business of growing more coffee may offer an alternative to the tourist trade.

Above: Coffee tree with ripe cherries ready for picking.

SOUTH AMERICA

Brazil, as the world's largest coffee producer dominates this region, but there are a number of countries producing superb beans worth trying.

Argentina

Argentina grows so little coffee that its production figures are difficult to obtain. The Tropic of Capricorn runs across the extreme north of the country, and the two general areas where coffee can be grown are the moderately humid and tropical north-east, where it was introduced by the Jesuits in 1729 in Misiones, and the north-west Andean provinces around Tucumán. Because of their exclusion from the tropical zone, the Argentine coffee trees, which are arabica, are subject to the periodic ravages of frost.

Bolivia

The Bolivian coffee crop is hand-picked, mainly washed arabica. Although most of it is of exportable quality, Bolivia is land-locked, and the problem is one of supply. Coffee is cultivated on about 30,000 acres, many in areas so remote that there is practically no way to transport the beans out during certain seasons. Also, as is the case with several South American countries, the temptation to produce coca is often too much for the inhabitants of poorer regions to resist. Bolivian coffees tend to be slightly bitter, but, based on figures of the last several years, the coffee crop is improving in both quantity and quality, as older trees are being replaced. Perhaps Bolivia will soon be able to provide more accessible, available beans for the world market.

Brazil

Just how much is "an awful lot"? Although the quantity may vary from year to year, there is simply no other way to describe the Brazilian coffee crop, which can usually claim one-third of total global production. Unlike many other coffee-producing countries, however, who may export all of the good coffee and drink very little at home, Brazilians in one year will consume about 12 million bags, much of it in the form of the much-beloved *cafèzinho*, the tiny cup of usually good-quality black coffee drunk by most Brazilians several times a day.

It is interesting to note that in Brazil the word for "breakfast" is *café da manhã* (morning coffee), whereas in Portugal, which in theory speaks the same language, "breakfast" is the rather less descriptive *primeiro almoço* or *pequeno almoço* (as in the French "little lunch" definition of breakfast).

Types of coffee Brazil grows both arabica and robusta, but the crop is primarily arabica, mostly dry-processed. With both the Equator and the Tropic of Capricorn passing through it, the bulk of Brazil lies in the tropical zone, and around eight million acres of Brazilian land is dedicated to coffee-growing. Towards the northern part of the country, where the climate is hotter and the terrain flatter, is where the robusta (conilon variety) is grown, shaded from the more direct rays of the sun.

The coffee improves towards the south of the country, where the best arabica is grown in higher terrain, but these plateau regions are very close to the bottom edge of the tropical zone, and frost is frequently a problem, if not a major disaster. When frost warnings are reported in southern Brazil,

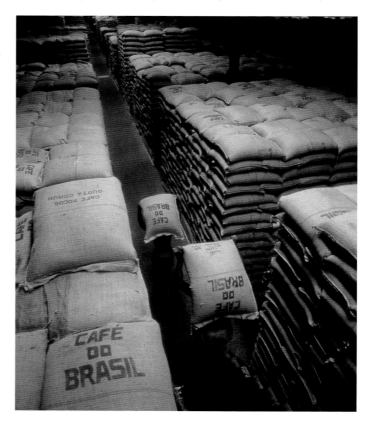

Above: Each bag in this Brazilian warehouse contains the annual harvest of 60 trees.

Above: Aerial view of one of the many large coffee-growing plantations in Brazil. The flat terrain suggests robusta cultivation.

Above: Brazilian Santos green beans.

international trade coffee prices immediately jump in anticipation of a possible shortage.

Seventeen Brazilian states grow many varieties of coffee, but there are four or five regions which dominate the exportable coffee cultivation. Brazilian beans are identified, categorized and graded by many different criteria, the first of which is the port of export. The more northerly state of Bahia, which produces some good washed arabica among its generally average dry-processed coffees, and small amounts of Maragogype, exports its coffee through the port of Salvador de Bahia. The smaller state of Espírito Santo ships its rather average beans from Vitória; the large state of Minas Gerais (Sul de Minas is an excellent coffee), uses both the ports of Rio de Janeiro and the more southerly port of Santos, which is also the port for the various coffees produced in the state of São Paulo. Santos exports the "flat bean" Santos and the superior Bourbon Santos. The southern-most Brazilian coffee port is Paranagua, from which the state of Paraná ships its coffees.

Quantity or quality Brazilian arabicas are not usually included in the ranks of gourmet or speciality coffees. Indeed, pushed to a general description of these enormously-varying growths, most experts would say that Brazil coffee is poor-to-average quality, low-to-moderate acidity and neutral or bland in flavour, a fairly accurate profile of most of the millions of bags exported by Brazil. Part of the problem with the quality is the fact that the sheer space in Brazil

Left: Brazilian Sul de Minas medium roasted beans.

allows the operations of huge plantations, where the picking is not picking at all; it may be "stripping" or even machine-harvesting. In either case, the mix of fruit will include coffee cherries at wide ranges of maturation, and the odds are that no amount of later sorting will

The cup quality classifications can be mystifying, since, besides rather obvious terms such as "full body", "bad cup", "fair cup", and "fine cup" among others, there are more elusive terms used to describe Brazilian coffees, such as "strictly soft" and "Rio-y" (pronounced with a long "i", despite the fact that it comes from the state of Rio).

The term "hard" in Brazilian coffee means, as might be expected, the opposite of "soft". "Rio-y" coffee is easier to explain: this is the coffee which gives Middle Eastern coffee blends their distinctive flavour. On its own, "rio-y" coffee tastes medicinal, harsh, inky or iodine-y. The flavour is thought to be the result of certain micro-organisms and is not always present every year in crops from the same soil, although the geographic areas in which it is found have increased considerably. Shunned by most countries for being strongly defective, rio-y coffee is avidly sought by Turkey, Greece, Cyprus and most Middle Eastern countries, as well as by Denmark. Blended with Ethiopian coffee, the rio-y flavour seems to benefit from the Middle Eastern practice of boiling the coffee with sugar.

There was a time when Brazilian coffees made up 60 per cent of the world crop, and they were the standard "extenders" for almost every blend in the world; their unobtrusive character, generally good body and plenteous supply ensured that Brazilian coffee was the basis for most of the world's blended brands. It is interesting to note that the International Coffee Organization's preliminary statistics for the 1998 crop list the average "unit value" of Brazilian exports at 110.95 US cents per pound, which is extremely close to the prices of all the world's coffees averaged together: 110.05 US cents per pound. These figures mean that if a blender, when considering what beans to buy in order to produce a decent flavour in an average-priced blend, must bulk out his blend with something cheaper than the average Brazilian coffee, to offset the higher prices of coffees used for better flavour.

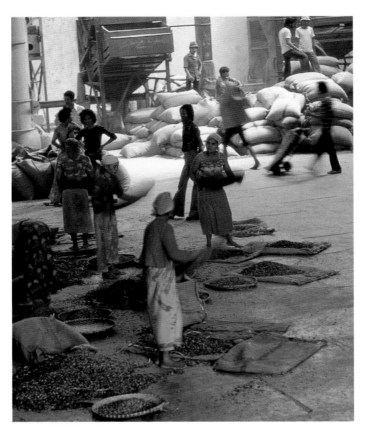

Above: Graded and sorted coffee beans are bagged, to be made ready for export.

produce a truly homogeneous yield. Hypothetically, even the most meticulous harvesting could not make up for the lack of any really high altitudes in Brazil's topography; without the altitude there is little acidity, and the result is the bland character attributed to most of Brazil's coffees.

Of course, there are exceptions to every rule, and those who automatically dismiss Brazil from the list of the world's "gourmet" coffee producers probably have never been privy to some of the best Brazilian Santos coffees, which may not be common or easily obtainable, but do exist.

There are estates in southern Brazil where high quality is pursued intensely, and careful tending and detailed experimentation in processing have led to the production of some truly wonderful coffee – smooth, well-balanced and mellow. The best Brazilian coffee comes from young trees of the bourbon variety, whose small, rounded beans produce excellent cup qualities, fine acidity and sweetness. After the Brazilian bourbon trees have produced a few crops, the beans become larger and lose a bit of their flavour; the coffee is then described as "flat bean Santos".

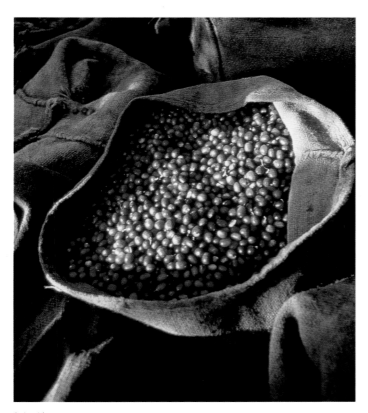

extremely difficult to harvest it any other way, given that the slopes are steep in the mountainous terrain – and the trees are usually shaded by interspersed banana trees. The climate provides plenty of moisture, so there is no irrigation or mulching required.

Above: Colombian Popayán excelso dark-roasted beans.

Colombia

Unfortunately, the rich soil which produces Colombia's best coffees is the result of past volcanic activity in an area of continuing subterranean instability. Although the massive earthquake which tore through the heart of Colombia's largest coffee-growing region in January 1999 miraculously did little damage to the trees themselves, farming infrastructure suffered 65 per cent damage, which could cause a drop in quality as farmers economize for necessary repairs. Whatever the outcome, Colombia will still hold its position at second place in the global statistics for coffee-growing, as its nearest rival is Vietnam, whose production of robusta, though increasing, is less than half Colombia's.

Coffee-growing areas Colombia's three mountain ranges, or *cordilleras*, are really lines of Andean foothills which run from north to south, and it is on their slopes that the arabica coffee of Colombia is grown in altitudes ranging from 800–1900m/2,624–6,233 ft. The coffee is all hand-picked – it would be

Above: Colombian "supremo" medium-roast beans.

The central *cordillera* is the most productive region both in quantity and quality, particularly as it contains the well-known name of Medellín, one of the best-balanced coffees of Colombia, combining full-bodied heaviness with good flavour and medium acidity. Manizales, another town of the central zone, and Armenia, whose coffees are less acidic, but winey in texture with excellent aroma, in the western *cordillera*, together with Medellín, form the MAM acronym under which the majority of bags from Colombia are exported. Another central zone favourite is coffee from Libano, which in the "supremo" form is a visual delight, as its large beans roast smoothly and evenly. Popayán and San Agustín are notable coffees from the southern part of the central *cordillera*, as is coffee from the district of Nariño, very near the Ecuador border. Nariño has the reputation of producing the cup preferred by the Vatican, (a distinction claimed equally by the island of Puerto Rico), and Starbucks, the chain of coffee speciality shops, also allegedly holds exclusive rights to the supremo beans from Nariño.

Colombia's eastern coffee region produces another half-dozen or so commercial coffees, of which two are better known for excellent quality: Bogotá, from the area around the capital city, is a fine coffee with a slightly lower acidity than those of the central zone. Bucamaranga, from the more northerly part of the eastern *cordillera*, has the low acid and mellow, rounded flavour of a "soft" coffee.

Flavour and aroma The old arabica cultivars are gradually being replaced with other more productive varieties, such as the cost-efficient "variedad Colombia", as the aged trees are removed. Developed in Colombia, this arabica strain is also being planted in other countries, much to the dismay of

Above: Colombian San Agustín medium-roasted beans.

discerning tasters, who find the flavour of the new variety disappointing, especially in comparison to the bourbon beans, which can be a felicitous combination of flavour, aroma, body and a golden colour when milk or cream is

added. The acidity of Colombian coffees seldom matches that of certain Kenyans and Costa Ricans, but in general Colombia produces a more balanced cup, particularly in coffees of slightly heavier body.

Colombia enjoys one advantage over all other South American countries: it can export coffee through ports on either ocean. The export crop is fairly evenly divided between the ports of Buenaventura on the Pacific, and Cartagena, Barranquilla, and Santa Marta on the Atlantic. Such easy access from the plantations to international trade routes, coupled with the world-wide promotional work done by the Federation Nacional de Cafeteros de Colombia, has ensured a strong market for Colombian coffee in both North America and Europe.

Colombia also exports the highest volume of soluble (instant) coffee in the world, the expected 1998/99 figure of which is a whopping 659,000 bags' worth, mostly freeze-dried.

Ecuador

Ecuador, like Brazil, grows arabica as well as robusta; the robustas are unwashed, and the arabicas are wet- or dry-processed. The large (gigante or Galapagos classifications) arabica beans are heavy with humidity, but produce a thin-bodied liquor, and a slightly woody and mediocre flavour, although the aroma is good. The trees are interspersed with banana and cocoa trees for shading.

French Guiana

South America's last "colony" – a French Overseas Department – once famous for the notorious offshore penal colony of Devil's Island, is composed mostly of equatorial jungle and species-rich rainforest. The only coffee grown here now is from robusta trees in domestic gardens, but French Guiana had its moment of coffee glory when, through a romance of illicit passion and deception in the early 18th century, the little colony was the gateway through which the all-conquering bean first reached Brazil.

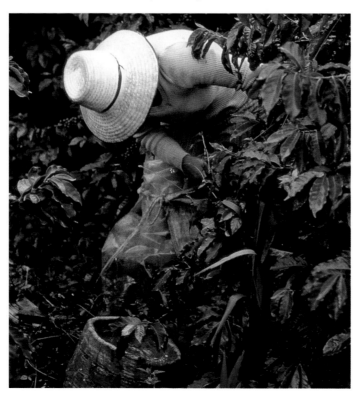

Above: Hand-picking coffee in Colombia: not an easy job in mountainous terrain.

Galapagos Islands

Gourmet coffee lovers might want to keep a look out for a coffee grown in very high altitudes on the small island of San Cristóbal. The coffee estate was established long before the islands became a national park, which banned any further agricultural development and any use of chemicals. The organically-produced coffee is said to be superb, and there is scope for the production on this family-run plantation to increase.

Guyana

The Dutch founded three colonies here, Berbice, Demerara and Essequibo, which passed to Britain in 1814 and became British Guiana. Independent since 1966, Guyana produces bauxite, gold, rice, sugar and diamonds, but it still grows some coffee, primarily low-quality liberica, most of which is consumed locally, but may be shipped to the US for instant processing before re-importation into Guyana.

Paraguay

This country has been attempting to increase its arabica coffee crop for some time. As a country with no minerals, land-locked and remote, it must depend on its own agriculture for general subsistence, and hope that its neighbours stay financially healthy, as its biggest exports are electricity (for which Brazil's "standing charges" sometimes represent 25 per cent of the total Paraguayan national budget), and contraband. The coffees are unwashed arabicas, cultivated mostly towards the eastern border where the altitude is highest, and the cup quality is unsurprisingly similar to the rather nondescript arabicas grown in Paraná, across the Brazilian border. All of the coffee must be taken overland through seasonally impassable terrain for shipping from the ports of Brazil, Argentina and Chile.

Peru

Coffee is one of Peru's main crops, and it provides a living for many poor families who work small-holdings in the Andean foothills. Punto, on Lake Titicaca, Cuzco and the Urubamba and Chanchamayo Valleys, and the northern provinces of Piura, San Martin, Cajamarca and Lambayeque, are producing some good quality coffees, certified as organically grown and are all areas where quality is important and improving. In general, Peruvian coffees are excellent blending coffees, as they are mild, pleasant and sweet, and occasionally some really top quality Peruvians are beginning to appear.

Suriname

Suriname was Dutch-owned from 1667, when the British swapped it for New

Above: Venezuela has been producing beans like these since 1730.

Left: Peru exports most of its washed arabicas, keeping the unwashed for internal consumption.

Amsterdam (New York), until its independence in 1975. It was through Dutch Guiana, as it was called in 1714, that coffee-growing came to South America. Today it grows only small amounts of wild-tasting liberica, sold to Norway.

Venezuela

The best coffees produced in this oil-rich country are those grown practically on the spine of the Andean *cordillera de Mérida*, which collectively are known as Maracaibos, as they are shipped from the port of that name. Several names of good Maracaibos include the word Táchira, the far western state; and the regions of Mérida, Trujillo and the town of Cúcuta (which is so far west it appears to be in Colombia!) also give their names to fine coffees. Other coffees are shipped under the names of the *haciendas* where they are grown. Coffee from the eastern mountains is designated as Caracas, for the proximity to the capital.

The coffee industry, having lapsed into mediocrity under government nationalization in the 1970s, is now pulling itself out of the decline, no doubt encouraged by the growing gourmet coffee market. Some of the old haciendas are once more the source of some lovely, if slightly unusual coffees. Venezuelan coffees, unlike other South American growths, tend to be delicately light, if not actually thin; slightly winey, and of only moderate acidity, with a rather appealing individual aroma and flavour.

SOUTH PACIFIC AND SOUTH-EAST ASIA

This area contains some of the most enterprising coffee producing countries.

Australia

Nearly 40 per cent of Australia lies above the Tropic of Capricorn, but much of the area in this tropical zone is not suitable for coffee cultivation: the rainfall, if adequate at all, is very variable, and the altitude conducive to producing good arabica is limited. Even so, at least since the 1970s arabica coffee has been grown in Queensland, some on a rather experimental basis; one in particular, "Skybury", hit the world stage in the early 1980s and has not looked back. Grown from the same Blue Mountain variety as the celebrated New Guinea Sigri, Skybury has received great commendations by many experts. At least its price will ensure that it doesn't suffer the same fate as that of other well-meaning Australian coffees of the 1980s: because Australians consume far more coffee than the farmers can hope to grow, any average Australian product that acquires favour with the home market will probably at some point have to be extended with imported coffee, particularly that from Papua New Guinea.

Cambodia

About forty years ago, commercial coffee plantation in Cambodia began. Soon coffee, mostly robusta, but a little arabica as well, was grown in at least five different regions of Cambodia. After the terrible events that befell Cambodia in successive years, it is difficult now to guess the state of the plantations. It is worth hoping, however, that Cambodia, like Vietnam, may have a future as a coffee-producing country once again.

China

It is known that arabica coffee is grown and processed in China's south-west province of Yunnan, where a mountainous region is crossed by the Tropic of Cancer, the northern edge of the tropical belt. Here the summer temperatures are modified by higher altitudes and good rainfall, and the mild, dry winters enjoy a temperature

Left: Australian "Skybury" green beans.

range of 8-20°C/46-68°F. The Chinese government releases no figures on its coffee production, however, and because certain countries, especially Tanzania, repay debts to China in coffee beans, there is no assurance that any coffee exported from China was actually grown there. The International Coffee Organization is actively encouraging more coffee consumption in China, of which a by-product could be greater production of coffee, as the necessary growing conditions are present.

Fiji

After twenty-seven years of independence from Britain, Fiji has just rejoined the Commonwealth, having replaced its constitution with one more acceptable to the international community. At one time Fiji grew a small crop of robusta, which it processed by the washed method, and which was sold primarily to New Zealand. It also imported coffee for its own consumption.

The island of Vitu Levu consists of mainly mountainous terrain, including Mount Victoria (1,324m/4,344ft) and some higher places on the other smaller islands. As Fiji is attempting to further diversify its income perhaps it will be encouraged to grow more coffee.

French Polynesia

This French Overseas Territory is really a combination of 130 islands spread out over a Pacific area the size of Europe. The bourbon arabica is grown on various islands, each of which carries

out its own wet processing, and the coffee is then sent to Papeete, Tahiti, for hulling and grading. The islands tend to consume all that they grow and process. The large-bean coffee has been described as pleasantly mild rather than acidic, with good strength and aroma, and is therefore a well-rounded satisfying cup. Tahiti Arabica is the commercial name, but it is seldom found outside the islands which grow it.

Hawaii

Hawaii has been growing coffee since 1818, and today both the island of Kauai and the big island of Hawaii grow it, although it is the latter's coffee from the slopes of the Mauna Loa volcano in the western Kona zone that gives its name to the only coffee grown in the United States. Expert opinions on Kona coffee vary; certainly in several ways it can be compared to Jamaica Blue Mountain: although the climate and soil are ideal, the growing area is limited, the processing is extremely careful and the appearance of the beans impeccable; it is a natural product and some crops are better than others. It is scarce and expensive, and many blends

Above: Hawaiian Kona medium-roast coffee beans.

Above: A coffee plantation in the flat terrain of Kauai, Hawaii.

are sold as "Kona" which may contain five per cent of the genuine coffee. (The blends may, of course, be excellent, depending on the other coffees, which are likely to be superior, but more affordable, Latin Americans.) The Hawaiian coffee industry must compete with the tourist trade for its workers, and therefore wages are extremely high, compared to those of other countries.

Flavour and aroma Hawaiian Kona differs from Jamaica Blue Mountain in many ways, although both are known for a mild, "fair" acidity, medium body and fine aroma; also, the descriptor "nutty" is sometimes applied to the flavour profiles of both. Some experts detect in Kona a spicy, cinnamon-like flavour, a quality not found in Jamaican coffee, while other experts have difficulty detecting much flavour at all.

In sheer bountiful yield, no other coffee trees on earth can vie with the volume of fruit taken from Kona trees. The best, and surest, way to drink Hawaiian Kona is to sip it with the locals, as the best quality is kept at home. Tourists are willing to pay the normal "high dollar" price, which really is at a premium, as there are none of the normal shipping costs involved.

India

The entire economy of India is undergoing a radical change, as the government is shifting from a position of protectionism to the encouragement of totally free, global marketing. The coffee industry, which had been nationalized some time back, did little to encourage growers to improve their quality or produce coffee with individual character; same-grade beans from all regions were "blended" by the Indian Coffee Board under a uniform grading system, producing simply "Plantation A", "Plantation B", etc. As of December 16, 1998, the Indian parliament finalised a decision to allow coffee growers to sell 100 per cent of the produce on the open market. It can only be assumed that the old romantic coffee names will have true significance once more, particularly for the 40 per cent of India's crop that is arabica.

Above: Indian Plantation A medium-roast beans.

Coffee growing areas The arabica coffee-growing region of India is basically three states in the Southwest. Mysore, which accounts for most of the arabica, is that grown in what is now the state of Karnataka. Mysore can be described very generally as having good body, low acidity, mellow sweetness and a well-balanced strong flavour; however, it sometimes can be described as neutral, which probably reflects on those Kent-variety arabicas, which generally have less distinctive flavour than the older classics like bourbon. The state of Tamil Nadu produces good arabica; one in particular is grown in the high altitude of the Nilgiri region in the state's west.

Above: Green beans from Mysore, India.

The most interesting arabica of India in both name and taste is the unwashed "Monsooned Malabar". The Malabar coast is the western shore of the entire state of Kerala. In the days of sailing, when coffee took months to reach Europe, it developed a particular taste during the voyage because of exposure to sea-air and humidity; the colour also changed from green to a rather strange yellow. European consumers became fond of the enhanced body and enriched, if slightly peculiar, flavour, so when steamers shortened the sailing time, India began to "artificially" reproduce the flavour by exposing coffee for about six weeks to the humid south-west monsoon winds that begin in May or June.

These unusual coffees are not dissimilar to other "aged" coffees, such as those of Sulawesi, Java and Sumatra, and they are generally cheaper and easier to obtain.

Above: Indian Monsooned Malabar medium-roast beans.

Above: Sumatran Lintong Grade 2 roasted beans.

Indonesia

The coffee industry provides a livelihood for around five million people in Indonesia, and currently vies with Vietnam as the third most prolific coffee producer, and 90 per cent of its crop is ordinary robusta. The arabicas, however, are another story, and the word "ordinary" doesn't come into it; Indonesia, as the world's largest archipelago, sprawls across 5,000km/3,107 miles, and its 13,677 islands lie in three different time zones. It is therefore not surprising that its arabicas, which have far more scope for individuality than robustas, cover an amazing range of sometimes quirky but always interesting differences. A general description of most of the Indonesian arabicas would contain the words rich, full-bodied, lowish-acidity, and a prolonged aftertaste, in addition to terms more specific to the individual coffees.

Sumatra There are three main islands and one or two smaller ones which together produce very nearly 100 per cent of all Indonesian coffees, arabica and robusta; Sumatra, the western-most

Above: Sumatran Mandheling grade 2 green beans.

large island, grows 68 per cent. Much of the arabica is sold simply as Sumatran or Blue Sumatran; many of the Sumatran trees are newly planted in virgin, highly organic, volcanic soil, which is very fertile, and the coffees, which are only partly wet-processed, are strong and assertive.

One of the few washed coffees is the gourmet-quality Gayo Mountain, sweetly spicy and exotically herbal in character, named for its area of origin in the extreme north-western province of Aceh. Linthong, or Lintong, from North Sumatra, is similar to, but generally not quite as consistently good as, Mandheling, from the north and the west-central regions.

Mandheling, with the deep, rich flavour and smoothness of a low-acidity coffee, merits the title "world's heaviest coffee", according to many experts. Ankola, also from the west-central region near the port of Padang, may not have quite the body of a Mandheling, but it is regarded by some connoisseurs as the world's finest unwashed arabica.

Above: Indonesian washed Java Jampit green beans.

Java The island of Java, which grows about 12 per cent of Indonesia's coffee, was where the Dutch began the first coffee-growing outside of Islam. About 300 years of intensive cultivation has left Java's soil a bit depleted. After the *hemileia vastatrix* (leaf rust), infestation of the late 19th century, only the highest-grown arabicas survived, and those scarce growths have recently been replaced with more productive arabica varieties, to the detriment of the flavour. "Estate Java"

is now a wet-processed coffee, with more acidity, and less body, flavour and finish than the original Java arabicas, which had been known for rich smoothness, heavy body, and an earthy, mushroomy sort of flavour obtained only in unwashed coffees. There were five government-owned estates, including Jampit, Blawan and Pankur.

Above: Indonesian Sulawesi Kalossi Toraja roasted beans.

Sulawesi The third main island of arabica production is Sulawesi, which grows 9 per cent of all Indonesian coffee; under the Dutch, the island was called Celebes, the name under which much of the arabica coffee is today exported from the port of Ujung Pandang. The unwashed Kalossi coffees from the south-western region of Toraja are the true aristocrats of all Indonesian coffees. They have the heavy body and smooth texture associated with Indonesian coffees, as well as the deep earthy, mushroomy, sweetness; there is, as well, because of slightly increased acidity, a hint of fruit.

Overall, the best and most distinctive range of Indonesian coffees are those which have been aged. The coffees may be sold as "Old Government", "Old Brown" or "Old Java". Or they may simply be designated "aged" coffees, and may come from Java, Sulawesi or Sumatra. The ageing process carried out in the damp, warm climate – not the same as simply lengthy warehousing in another part of the world – lowers what acidity there may have been, enhances the sweetness and gives the already smooth, dense liquid an even heavier body. Other descriptors spring

Above: Indonesian "Old Brown" Javanese green beans.

to mind, like soft, velvety, golden and warm. In fact, an interesting suggestion is to replace the after-dinner liqueur with a small black cup of an "aged" Indonesian, particularly a Celebes Kalossi, as its concentrated, sweet, syrupy consistency is virtually liqueur without the alcohol. (And the cost is probably about the same!)

Other coffee growing areas Other arabica coffees known to be excellent are those grown on Bali, Flores and Timor, although Timor stopped growing coffee after annexation by Indonesia; one can hope production will resume again soon, as it seems Indonesia is in the process of reversing the annexation of the former Portuguese colony.

There is one more type of coffee obtainable from Indonesia, which is *kopi luak*. "Kopi" is the word for "coffee", and the luak is a small weasel-like animal particularly fond of coffee cherries. Villagers collect the animals' "droppings" and remove the hard coffee beans, which are then washed and further processed by less natural means. The flavour is exceptional, and the beans command a high price.

Laos

In recent years, the strongly communist Laos People's Democratic Republic has opened up to foreign investment, as well as receiving international aid and subsidies to encourage farmers to substitute cash crops for opium poppies. Laos' most important agricultural resources are currently listed as timber and coffee. Information on the type and quality of the coffee

grown, and the regions of cultivation is not readily available, but in the past, the Laotian climate, soil and topography allowed the production of arabica, robusta and excelsa, which, during the 1970s, fell to amounts that could only sustain local consumption.

Malaysia

Although Malaysia grows arabica, robusta and excelsa, its main coffee crop is the higher-yielding and highly unpalatable liberica species, grown mostly in Western Malaya. Western Malaya is also the site of a small area of arabica trees, which is located in the higher altitudes of the Cameron Highlands. Because of the large population of the country, local consumption generally consumes all the coffee that can be grown. Malaysia is very

concerned with economic success, and as coffee is not as lucrative a crop as some others, such as palm oil, rubber, timber and, of course, oil and gas, it is not usually seen to be a priority crop for cultivation.

New Caledonia

This small group of islands, called Kanaky by the natives, lying 1,497km/930 miles north-east of Australia, is still a French Overseas Territory, although independence seems possible. The windward (eastern)

Below: "Kopi Luak" comes from droppings of the luak animal, containing undigested coffee beans. The beans are collected, washed and processed – the resulting coffee is considered a rare delicacy by coffee lovers.

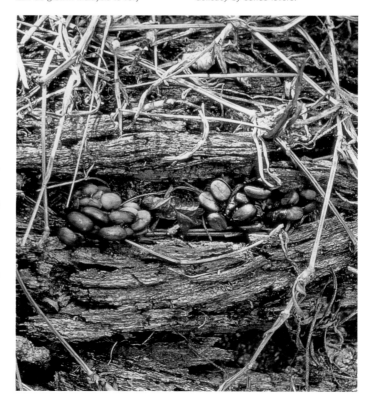

coast has the distinction of growing the world's best robusta, while the little arabica still grown comes from the western side of the island. The robusta is unusual for its type, as it is described as delicate, although the flavour of both coffees, known commercially as "Nouméa", is said to be aromatic and rich. The arabica is seldom exported, as the islands prefer to save the best for themselves, which they can afford to do, since New Caledonia has large deposits of nickel, accounting for 25 per cent of the world's supply.

Above: New Guinean "Y" grade roasted beans.

Papua New Guinea

It was probably extremely fortunate for all coffee lovers that coffee-growing came late to Papua New Guinea. Otherwise, the disastrous plague of *hemileia vastatrix* (leaf rust) that wiped out arabica plantations throughout South-east Asia and Oceania in the late 1800s, would have ensured that today Papua New Guinea would be growing mostly robusta, like so many other countries who replanted with resistant species at the cost of good flavour.

Much of New Guinea's arabica is grown, washed and further processed in varying degrees by natives of rural, and sometimes isolated, villages located in the high-altitude mountainous region which occupies so much of Papua New Guinea's landmass. These coffees are an extremely important source of revenue for Papua New Guinea, providing a living for hundreds of thousands of people, and the government provides encouragement and support by announcing, at the start of each year's crop, an ensured

minimum price it will pay for the coffee, in the event that the market price should fall unexpectedly.

Gourmet quality coffee New Guinea coffee was cultivated from Blue Mountain variety stock, and the results make the New Guinea washed arabicas rather different from other coffees from this part of the world. Although New Guineas have good body and sweetness, as do many Indonesians, they also have a higher acidity closer in style to Central Americans. In short, a good New Guinea coffee can stand on its own, or be a terrific contribution to any high-quality blend, since it has literally everything to offer.

The sorting and grading, after some inconsistencies, is now regular and stringent. The top AA grade is very scarce, while about 60 per cent of beans make up the ordinary, decent "Y" grade. Quality names to look out for include Arona, Okapa and Sigri.

Philippines

The world's second-largest archipelago has everything it takes to grow good quality coffee in large amounts. In fact, it already grows all four of the main commercial species, robusta, liberica, excelsa and arabica, and is experimenting with hybrids. The small crop of good arabica, known for its full, slightly spicy flavour, is concentrated on the southern island of Mindanao.

At one time the Philippines were in fourth place for world coffee production, but that was before the terrible rust infestation that wiped out most of the arabica growths of South-east Asia, the Philippines included, in the late 1800s.

Above: Philippino arabica green coffee beans.

Above: Vietnamese robusta medium-roasted coffee beans.

As the arabica is not very acidic, and the flavour is fairly strong, this coffee works well where a darker roast is appreciated, as in after-dinner or espresso blends.

Sri Lanka

The world's greatest tea exporter, this island, which Tamils and Sinalese have cohabited in conflict for 14 centuries, grew a lot of good arabica coffee, until almost the entire crop was destroyed by *hemileia vastatrix* (leaf rust) in 1870. Although tea-growing basically replaced coffee cultivation, the British colonists introduced robusta, which still accounts for the majority of the generally poor-quality coffee, which is sold under the name Sinhala.

Taiwan

Taiwan is known for its consumerism, and coffee is no exception. Trendy gourmet coffee houses vie for high-street prominence in Taipei. The small good-quality well-processed arabica crop, grown in the mountain region which dominates the island, is all consumed locally.

Thailand

Thailand's current coffee crop of about only a million bags is mostly robusta, grown primarily in the Malay Peninsula; some arabica is grown in the highlands of the north and north west. Recently Thailand seems to be eager to increase its coffee cultivation, which may be due to several reasons. Any increase will help to satisfy the consumption demands of its 58.8 million population, and at the same time utilize the potentially abundant workforce of hundreds of thousands of indigenous hill people and refugees from Laos and Cambodia in virtually all rural regions of the country. It will also help to redistribute the country's wealth and population from Bangkok, one of the world's most congested cities, by developing commercial interests in more remote provinces, and help to replace the growth of opium poppies in the Golden Triangle. There is one major problem for increased coffee production, as well as for other crops: there is a major national water shortage exacerbated by a lack of water storage facilities; deforestation has contributed to both flooding and droughts; and the massive amounts of water required to maintain numerous golf courses designed to improve the tourist industry adds to the problem.

Vanuatu

Previously the New Hebrides, this Pacific archipelago became independent from joint French and British rule in 1980. Copra and cocoa are the main exports, although coffee-growing had been introduced to the islands at the same time by the Europeans. Today, while Vanuatu, frightened by declining copra and cocoa prices, explores the possibilities of other export crops, cattle roam around the several hundred remaining robusta trees, which are basically untended except when the cherries are picked. The small crop is dry-processed completely by hand, loaded in 60 kg/ 132lb bags and sent to France. Although ungraded, it is described as fairly homogeneous and good.

Vietnam

As usual, the French first introduced coffee-growing to their colonies of Indo-China, but when most of the arabica succumbed to rust, it was replaced with robusta, the quality of which is fairly ordinary. What is not ordinary is the incredible growth in the Vietnamese coffee industry. After the devastation of the war, the remains of the French colonists' coffee estates were turned

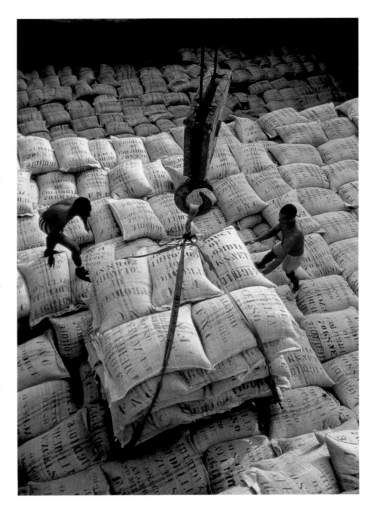

into state collectives. In 1980 Vietnam was 42nd in world coffee production. In 1982 it exported 67,000 bags.

In 1988, with the imminent break-up of the Soviet Union, the Vietnamese government encouraged private enterprise, and by 1993 it exported over three million bags of robusta, a figure which the 1997 crop saw more than doubled to 6.893 million bags, putting it third in world production behind Brazil and Colombia, with Indonesia

Above: Though Colombia's coffee production outnumbers that of Vietnam by nearly two to one, Vietnam's rise from 42nd to 3rd place in world production rankings has been meteoric.

close behind. And, while the coffee crop was burgeoning, so was the rice, as Vietnam became the third largest exporter after the US and Thailand. No wonder Vietnam is being billed as the next Asian "tiger".

ROASTING

Of all the processes involved with coffee, the quickest and most critical is roasting. Roasting coffee is a terrible responsibility, because, in a few minutes, beans that cost hundreds of people time, effort and money can be completely ruined by ignorance or carelessness. Roasting coffee is an art, and like all true art, it takes years of practice before one becomes a master roaster; also, roasting is learned only by trial-and-error experience, and the errors may ruin many beans.

Above: These two samples of the same Ugandan Bugisu arabica bean show the differences that occur during roasting, not only in colour, but also size and shape.

The main reason that roasting is difficult is that virtually every batch of beans is different from every other.

In factories, a small sample of every shipment is "batch" roasted to anticipate every potential problem

that could arise in a commercial-size roast of perhaps 114kg/250lb of beans. A bright rather than a dull roast is desired, as dullness can indicate over-drying or poor processing; also, a good quality sample of beans will appear even, since a variety of colours, particularly "pales", among the coffee beans can indicate immature picking, poor sorting of cherries, and varying degrees of fermentation and drying on the plantation. Misshapen beans, broken beans, or simply an overly wide variety in bean sizes constitutes a "ragged" roast, as different-sized beans roast to different colours in the same roast.

The physical changes that occur to beans during roasting are many; the obvious changes are that the beans get bigger, gaining up to a third more of their former "green" size; this is because the decomposing carbohydrates create carbon dioxide, which literally causes the cells of the bean to expand. Meanwhile, most of the moisture remaining in the green beans after the plantation depulping, drying, storing and shipping, will be evaporated by the heat of roasting, and the beans will thus lose weight. Although moisture content can account for up to 23 per cent of green bean density, dehydration during roasting is usually kept to a maximum of about 15 per cent of the beans' weight, lest they become tasteless, brittle objects that reduce to powder at the first touch of a grinder's blade. The other very obvious physical change is that beans change colour during roasting.

Above: Sacks of different coffee samples, ready for roasting.

The Roasting Process

The most important effect of roasting beans is that the flavour is developed through the complex chemical changes caused by heat, which is the process of pyrolysis. It is estimated that a coffee bean contains more than 2,000 chemical substances, which may be broken down or changed during roasting into hundreds of "volatile aroma compounds". Various acids, oils, proteins, vitamins, sugars, starches, and caffeine are altered; some are enhanced and some are diminished. In certain cases, some substances are both developed and then burned away if the roasting time is extended.

A light roast is seldom used commercially, as it shows up all the flaws inherent in beans, many of which will disappear, or at least be hidden by other flavours, in a dark roast. For example, if a coffee has the distinctive, sometimes unusual, pleasant and expensively-acidic qualities of a high-grown arabica, it is better for it not to be dark-roasted. The darker the roast, the more uniform all coffees taste, as a truly dark roast will overwhelm the taste-buds, allowing them to perceive nothing of the coffee itself. A darker roast may sweeten some coffees, but only to a point; past a certain degree of roast all coffee becomes bitter. Also, the darker the roast, the greater the loss of acidity, that most sought-after quality.

Coffee roasters all vary in size and capacity, but the roasting process changes little from one size to another. All equipment should be pre-heated to a roasting temperature some minutes before the green beans are added, so all surfaces are uniformly hot. Many roasters are equipped with a revolving drum, often lined internally with curved metal strips which constantly toss the beans towards the centre of the drum. Above all, beans must be kept moving if they are to roast evenly, without burning. In fact, if a drum stops revolving while the heat is still on and the beans are hot, there is a danger of instant combustion within the drum. (The saying goes, "You're not a coffee roaster 'til you've had your first fire!")

Fine Tuning

The actual roast is a balancing act. Depending on the condition of the beans and the desired degree of roast, the beans are roasted at temperatures between about 200-240°C/392-464°F, give or take about 20°C/68°F on either side. Many roasters have devices for air ventilation, which, like fan-assisted ovens, cause the beans to cook faster. As the roast goes on (in total the process will take between about 8 and 14 minutes in a conventional-heat roaster), the beans retain more heat, and start to turn first yellow-green, then gold and into shades of brown. (All but the smallest drum roasters have devices allowing samples to be manually taken and returned to the drum.) The critical decision-making time is when the beans start to make popping sounds, as within seconds of this they turn dark very quickly. The drier the beans, the sooner the "popping" of pyrolysis begins; therefore, beans which are less green when unroasted, such as robusta, roast much quicker. Moisture-laden high-grown arabicas will take a bit longer to reach the same degree of roast.

The problem is deciding at what degree of roast each coffee tastes best, and the same coffee, roasted to

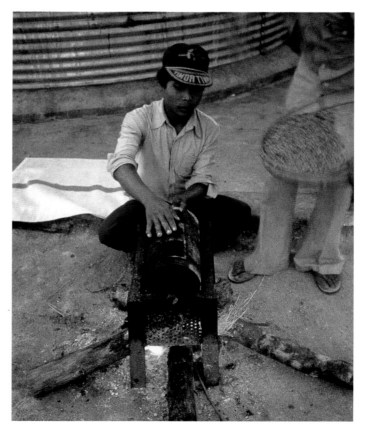

Above: Home roasting with a revolving drum over an outdoor fire.

different colours, will taste different. Even more complicated is the fact that the same coffee roasted to the same colour at a higher temperature for a shorter time, will taste different if roasted at a lower temperature for a longer time. With extremes of either time or temperature, the same colour roast can produce coffee that tastes under-cooked internally – cerealy or even green, or over-cooked – dried out, brittle when ground, or even burnt.

The last maddening fact of roasting is that the beans really need to be removed from the roaster immediately before the optimum colour is obtained, as they will darken in spite of cooling devices, such as revolving air-cooled trays outside the front of a drum roaster, or even the quick burst of water (quenching) of larger commercial machines, designed to stop the beans' continued cooking after they have left the drum. In later stages of roasting, beans release oils. Sometimes, even if a darker "oily" roast is not intended, the beans, if left in the roaster a fraction too long, will develop oil on their surfaces while in the cooling tray.

Types of Coffee Roasters

There are many sizes and types of coffee roasters available, ranging from factory machines, helped by sophisticated quenching-devices and automatic timers, with the capacity to roast hundreds of pounds of beans, down to tiny "professional" batch roasters which roast no more than a couple of hundred grams. Some companies use "high-yield" roasters, developed in the 1970s, which "roast" beans in relatively small amounts, but in a matter of precisely-timed seconds, perhaps up to two minutes, on fluidised "beds" of hot air rather than with the directly-transferred heat of metal drums. Called high-yield because the beans' surface areas expand so much as to produce more coffee when ground, these roasters are not favoured by many experts, who feel that the high-yield flavour is not as fully developed and round as that produced in conventional roasters.

There are small table-top roasters for the domestic market, but they can be hard to find, and expensive when located. Many people find it a joy to

Above: Roasted coffee beans spill out of the drum into the cooling tray below.

roast small amounts of coffee in frying pans over a cooker-burner (on the stove). (Oven-roasting is not recommended namely because it is not possible to keep the beans moving, and the roast is therefore usually very uneven and uncontrollable.) To roast coffee beans correctly, use a heavy, possibly cast-iron, frying pan, which has been warmed up. Add a single layer of beans over a low heat, increasing the heat to high as they roast, stirring constantly with a wooden spatula. In some Middle-Eastern countries whole spices such as cloves, cinnamon, cardamom, ginger, or fennel may be added, to be ground with them later. Other countries actually roast the beans in small amounts of butter or sugar, depending on the desired flavour.

When the beans are roasted to the desired colour, they must be cooled immediately, perhaps by putting them into a pre-chilled container, or onto a very cold surface. It is not advisable to grind beans for brewing immediately after roasting as the flavour will be sharp, green and sour. To achieve the desired mellowness of a good brew, do not grind until the coffee beans have had time to de-gas, preferably for a minimum of 12 hours.

Above: Checking the beans after the roasting is completed.

Degrees of Roast

As in tasters' terminology, there is no standardized definition of different degrees of roast. "Light", "medium" and "dark" are the most-used terms, but coffees are seldom truly light-roasted, and there are many perceived degrees of medium and dark. (Also, it should be noted that Turkish coffee is not dark-roasted.) A combination of various opinions results in the following possibilities:

Light This roast is used only for extremely good-quality delicate or high-grown arabicas. Ideal for breakfast coffees when acidic coffees are mellowed by the addition of milk or cream. The American version of this roast, "Cinnamon", is so called because of the colour of cinnamon bark. It is high in acidity and low in body. Also sometimes called "half-city" or "New England" roast.

Medium "American roast"; or possibly "city" if slightly darker than medium. Also called "regular", "brown"; as dark as possible with no oily surfaces.

Viennese American term meaning slightly darker than medium roast. This roast is speckled with dark-brown spots, and a bit of oil on surface; also "light French", or "full city".

Dark "Spanish"; "Cuban"; there may be some oil on bean surface, "deep brown"; French roast.

Continental Can also be referred to as "Double roast"; "High"; in America, "French roast", "New Orleans roast" and "European". With a nearly bitter-chocolate colouring, this roast is variously described as very dark; dark French, heavy and Italian.

Italian In America, darker than in Italy; may be called "espresso" roasts (or may not!); almost black and very oily; the predominant taste is the roast rather than the coffee. Coffee beans should never be burned black.

Even if there were universal agreement on the meaning of the above roasting terms, there would not be general consensus as to how dark certain coffees should or should not be roasted. In America, all roasts are becoming darker, probably because of the emphasis on espresso and espresso-based drinks, which are seen to be the height of sophistication. In fact, in many other countries as well, there are those who think the goal of all roasting is to make the coffee taste pleasant and balanced even if this involves suppressing the more unique and unusual flavours. It must be remembered that dark roasts were originally designed to hide the flaws of inferior coffees, and to bring out the best in cheap blends loaded with inferior-tasting robusta. Surely true sophistication is to approach every coffee with an open mind, prepared to judge it on its own merits.

Light-roasted beans

Medium-roasted beans

Dark-roasted beans

Above: A very enjoyable facet of coffee is the fact that there are enormous differences, which can be appreciated only when each coffee is treated to its own best roast, even if its more unusual attributes are, if not shocking, at least outside the normal range of coffee tastes.

BLENDING

An ideal cup of coffee should have good aroma, good colour (if milk or cream is to be added), good body, and good tastes for whichever way the coffee will be roasted, brewed and served at any intended time of day. Out of the millions of bags of coffee processed every year, relatively few can provide the "ideal cup" criteria without a little help from their friends, the other coffees with whom they will be blended. Regarding the few that can stand alone, they will probably not provide an all-round, perfect, well-balanced cup; rather, they will have one or two particularly fine points which more than compensate for falling short on another aspect or two.

Balancing Flavours

Each coffee used in a blend should make its own contribution. Dark roasting hides the not-so-desirable flavours of robustas, and of other coffees which may happen to have lower acidity, but usually have good body, which is only enhanced by the dark roast. Conversely, many high-grown arabicas, while producing a sharp flavour that can dominate the overall tastes of other less acidic coffees, are "thin-in-the-cup", and lack body. With these watery arabicas, the solution is not to roast darker, as roasting burns off the acids that contribute to the sharp, "expensive" taste. Other coffees may be pleasantly acceptable, having no particularly distinctive quality either to recommend or condemn them; these neutrals are ideal for bulking out a blend, as their flavours are not obtrusive, nor are they lacking in body.

There are no rules or taboos in blending coffees, but the idea is to combine coffees that complement each other, not those that are similar. A good starting point, therefore, for a middle-of-the-road, any-time-of-day well-rounded cup of coffee, would be a blend of perhaps 35 per cent high-grown arabica to provide the dominant flavour, 15 per cent darker-roasted robusta or heavier-bodied, lower-acidity coffee to provide the body, and 50 per cent of a more neutral and possibly more affordable

Above: Few coffees, on their own, can provide the perfect combination of good aroma, colour, body and taste. Blending seeks to achieve this in a consistent form.

coffee, like an average Brazilian Santos, or one of the slightly lower quality and less expensive Central American coffees. The character of this blend could be changed considerably just by altering the proportions. Also, lowering the proportions of each would allow for the addition of a small amount of a different, fourth, coffee, perhaps an unwashed arabica, as most "natural" arabicas are known for their sweetness.

All blends should be worked out in percentage weights with a taste or style in mind, whether the overall blend is to be, for example, a "fruity" blend; a "mild" breakfast coffee; a deep, rich, syrupy after-dinner indulgence; a naturally low-caffeine blend; a high-caffeine "pick-me-up" with lots of caffeine-rich robusta; or perhaps simply a strongish-flavoured coffee to provide the basis of an alcoholic coffee cocktail. If a blend is to be used often and remain consistent, the availability and affordability of each particular coffee must be considered.

Classic Combinations

A few combinations of particular coffees are so successful that they have become standards through the years. Mocha (either from Yemen or a

reasonable second from Ethiopia) and Mysore from India are the most famous coffee marriage. Mocha-Java will be a bit earthier and heavy, but still winey, and wild (or gamey) from the Mocha. A very particular Mocha-Brazil combination is that favoured by Middle-Eastern roasters for the traditional "Turkish" coffee flavour: the Brazilian coffee is the famous, or infamous, rio-y flavour. A good Brazilian Santos will smooth out an average robusta to make a strong, smooth blend, while a blend requiring some lightness can be illuminated by the addition of some Kenyan coffee, or a high-grown Central American. A Haiti or a Peruvian adds some decent flavour without being too expensive. An aged coffee adds sweetness, and a Colombian can add aroma as well as body and flavour.

In America, a "New Orleans Blend", and in Britain a "French Blend", neither to be confused with any degree of roast, is a blend of coffee and the roots of the chicory plant, just as a "Viennese" blend in Britain contains roasted fig or fig-seasoning ground in with the coffee. Of these two "economy" blends, the Viennese is cheaper, being the least expensive coffee blend of the average British supermarket range.

STORAGE

No matter how carefully coffee is grown, processed, blended, roasted, ground and brewed, the ultimate quality depends on one overall factor: freshness. Considering the ready availability of ground coffee, there would never be any real reason to grind coffee beans at all – except, crucially, to obtain the freshest possible taste. When coffee is roasted, carbon dioxide develops within the beans; it escapes from the coffee for several hours, and does so with a force that ruptures seams in tin cans and causes softer packages to "balloon". Many roasters, therefore, allow the roasted beans or ground coffee to stand for hours before packing. Of course, while standing, the coffee goes stale, losing its volatile aromas and absorbing tasteless oxygen.

Given the practicalities of coffee packaging (which can be vacuum-sealed tins (cans), brick packs, one-way valve-lock bags, or gas-flushed packs, all trying to let the gas out and keep the freshness in), no coffee is ever 100 per cent fresh. It's no good trying to roast, grind and brew coffee within a few minutes because, until the coffee has degassed, it will not taste good.

However, the fact is that roasted beans do retain their freshness longer than ground coffee, as there is less cell surface exposed to the air. Assuming that the roasting company and the retailer have just roasted the beans and maintained their freshness, the obvious next question is how best to store them at home.

Experts differ widely in advice on storing coffee, particularly beans. Certainly coffee can absorb odours easily, and will taste of those odours when brewed. Therefore some people advise against keeping coffee in the fridge. Others advocate using an airtight container, which will keep out oxygen, but what about the oxygen sealed inside with the beans? The solution would be to keep the surface of the beans very high in the jar, but then one could never use the beans further down in the jar.

Even the freezing of beans has its opponents, who say that after freezing, the coffee will never taste the same. Certainly, freezing darker-roasted beans, which have an oily surface, is definitely not a good idea, as the oils congeal and never regain their original consistency and distribution throughout the coffee.

Above: Coffee pods for certain espresso machines are factory produced.

The ideal solution to the problem of keeping coffee fresh is to purchase smaller amounts more frequently. In Italy, for example, many people buy small amounts, perhaps 100-200g/ $3\frac{1}{2}$-7oz of coffee several times a week from their local coffee bar; they choose a blend of roasted beans, and the *barista* (barman) grinds them. The ground coffee is then placed in a grease-lined paper bag. Similarly, a person who shops infrequently could still maximize the freshness of the coffee by buying several smaller packs of factory-sealed coffee instead of one or two large packs, as unopened factory-sealed containers will stay fresh for many months.

Helpful hints for keeping whole beans and ground coffee as fresh as possible

• Never pour dry coffee out of one container into another, as that is deliberate exposure.

• Keep the smallest air space between the top of the coffee and the lid, or top, of the container.

• If kept in the refrigerator, seal the original bag or packet as tightly around the coffee as possible, place a clip on it or a rubber band around it, and place it in a similar-sized airtight container.

• If the beans will not be used within a couple of weeks, pack them as for the refrigerator and store in the freezer. It is not a good idea to freeze ground coffee.

• Store small amounts of freshly-ground coffee in resealable bags, pressing down gently to trap as little oxygen as possible in the bag to maximize freshness.

THE ART OF COFFEE DRINKING

Many people derive as much pleasure from brewing coffee as from drinking it. For some, making coffee is a time-honoured traditional ritual, and the satisfaction is even greater with the knowledge that one is using the same equipment that yielded cups of the much-loved liquid to past generations. Other people delight in acquiring and using the latest trendy gadgets, and certainly coffee brewing and serving offer scope for constant design innovations, be they practical or aesthetic, or both. The following pages show you all you need to know to be able to select, grind and brew coffee with a range of different equipment — all part of the quest for the perfect cup.

HOME GRINDING

When purchasing a grinder, the choices may not be many, but the price range is wide, and it is best to bear in mind a particular brewing method when choosing a grinder, as the degree of grind required is dictated by this.

Hand Mills

For hundreds of years, coffee to be used at home was ground by hand with a box-type mill that held only a small amount of coffee. Anyone who uses one of these, and they are still available, realizes immediately that a greater storage capacity is not required; it takes so long to grind the beans that any ground coffee would be drunk before the little box could ever be full. Still, the hand mill can grind well, and with a surprising degree of uniformity in the particles. The grind is adjustable within a range that would qualify as "coarse", to a "medium" or even "fine", but it cannot grind fine enough for espresso. These are inexpensive, but it is an extremely time consuming method of grinding.

Below: Hand grinders have changed little for hundreds of years.

Using a hand mill

1 Rotating the lid reveals the aperture through which the beans are poured.

2 The coffee grounds, which fall into the drawer below, should be of a fairly consistent size, whether coarse, medium or fine.

Turkish Grinders

The prince of hand mills is the genuine Turkish grinder. The tall, heavy copper or brass mills are still used today throughout Turkey and other Middle Eastern countries for home grinding. The dome-like top pulls off to reveal the space where the whole beans go. The handle on the top is used to turn the mill; this detaches and fits over the grind adjustment screw which is revealed in the middle of the cylinder when the bottom half is removed. At the end of grinding – the range of which is all degrees of "extremely fine" – the bottom part of the cylinder holds the ground coffee. Middle Eastern coffee must be ground to the consistency of talcum powder, something no other type of domestic grinder can achieve. The difficulty in serving an authentic Middle Eastern coffee is not in getting the grind right; rather, it is in finding the right blend of coffee roasted to the right degree. (It is far easier just to buy a commercial brand, such as People's, imported from Nicosia, or Kurukahveçi, from Istanbul.)

Below: Turkish grinder.

Using a Turkish grinder

1 Remove the handle and dome top and insert the whole beans into the upper cylinder. Use the handle to adjust the grind screw to achieve the desired grind size.

2 After obtaining the desired grind consistency, replace the dome top and handle. Turn the handle to grind the beans. Remove the coffee from the bottom cylinder.

Electric Grinders

There is a wide range of electric coffee grinders available for the domestic market, most with some sort of receptacle or space for catching the ground coffee, which never needs to hold more than enough coffee for a day or two. There are two general designs for domestic grinders – those which simply cut the beans with a propeller-type blade, and those which truly grind the beans between metal discs.

Blade, or propeller, grinder The most common kind of home coffee grinder is the rotating blade, or propeller, grinder. This type, which sometimes comes as an accessory for a blender or some other food processor, is almost useless when it comes to coffee. The first problem is that it is nearly impossible to get uniformity of grind, which means that the coffee liquid will be very unevenly extracted. The larger chunks are wasted if they are too coarse for the water to penetrate; the fine powder particles will quickly saturate and yield bitterness, and can also clog a filter basket and create sediment in cups of plunger-pot coffee.

With a blade grinder it is best to grind small amounts of beans, shaking them up and down in the hope that the propellers will get to all the particles. Running the machine in short bursts will help you avoid scorching the beans from overheating. At least it is relatively easy to keep a blade-type grinder clean and avoid contamination with rancid coffee oils. With the machine unplugged, use a damp cloth or sponge to wipe the chamber and the blades. The plastic lid is washable, but must be carefully rinsed, so as not to leave a soapy taste for the beans to absorb.

Below: Electric grinder.

Using an electric blade grinder

Always ensure the grinder is un-plugged when adding or removing coffee, or when cleaning.

Burr Mills By far the best all-round domestic grinder is a burr mill, which is the closest thing to a commercial grinder in that two metal discs perform the grinding. The uniformity of particles is amazingly precise considering the fairly compact size of the machines. The costs vary widely between brands, but even the cheapest will do a decent job. In fact, it is probably better to invest in a good burr mill than in an expensive coffee-maker, if the object is a good cup of freshly-ground coffee.

Burr mills are noisy and slow, but easy to operate, as the grind choice is made by selecting a number or degree on a knob. Manufacturers' instructions, which indicate certain settings for

desired grinds, may not be entirely accurate, but once the desired grind is discovered, it is easy to get consistent results. Certain brands of burr mills are better at one range of grind, although all are adjustable. Some also have a timer, and will switch off automatically.

Never grind more coffee than will be used within a day or two. Before grinding, clear the discs of any old coffee remains, or of any coffee of a different origin or blend, by running the grinder with just a few beans of the new batch, before grinding in earnest.

For those that need an espresso grind, it is possible to buy a burr mill that specializes in very fine espresso grinds. They are precise and quick, but tend to cost more than those intended

for a more general range of grinds; even so, in the espresso grinder category there are some models that can do an adequate job without requiring a bank loan. The price can be daunting, but it may be worth paying a higher price for a model with a measured espresso dose-dispenser, which makes the task of loading the filter-holder infinitely simpler and less messy, as the proper amount of coffee required is dispensed straight into the filter-holder. Espresso brewing, generally, benefits from buying proper equipment; a good grinder is just as important as the brewing machine, if not more so.

Below left and right: Two electric mills intended for espresso grind. The one on the right has a convenient dose-dispenser.

Degrees of Grind

Commercial coffee grinds vary from brand to brand. Coffee companies set and monitor coffee grinds by using mesh sieves stacked in a series with the coarsest mesh at the top. The level at which the particles of a grind stop falling, as well as the percentage of particles arrested in other sieves of the stacks, gauges not only the basic degree of grind, but also indicates the uniformity of particle size. If, for example, a coffee company wanted to check its medium-grind coffee, intended for a cafetière or percolator, it would expect that a high percentage of particles from a sample of ground coffee would stop at Gauge 9. If too many particles were to fall too far, or perhaps never even drop through to the Gauge 9 sieve, the company would know that the grind was faulty, and that the grinder might need re-calibrating.

Also, beans grind differently depending on the degree of roast. For example, darker-roasted beans become more brittle with moisture loss and are more prone to break into various sized pieces and powder. The grinder might need some adjustment in order to produce the same degree of grind as that obtained with a different roast.

An excellent way to determine the correct degree of grind to suit the brewing method, is to obtain a small sample of commercially ground coffee. Rubbed between thumb and forefinger, the degree of grind is relatively easy to judge. Commercial grinds are specifically designated as Turkish, espresso, filter fine, and medium grinds. Grinds coarser than medium are practically non-existent commercially. They are generally used only in *al fresco* or jug (carafe) brewing, and are not very economical, since the same amount of beans ground coarsely produces less volume, less extraction and therefore less flavour than if it were ground finer.

In recent years, certain coffee companies have attempted to gain a larger share of the market by producing in-between grinds, promising consumers of filter and cafetière coffee alike that the same "omnigrind" works for both. Another grind (which defies the laws of physics) is one that supposedly satisfies the requirements of both filter and espresso machines. Not only does the production of such grinds result in the wrong extraction in one or the other of the brewing methods, it also confuses people who want to understand why coffee is ground to different degrees.

One good result of the "omnigrind" for machines requiring a fine- or a medium-ground coffee, is that it provides the perfect alternative grind for the Neapolitan flip machine and the Cona vacuum machine. Both of these methods of brewing benefit from the greater extraction rate of a near-filter grind, and the fact that the very slightly larger particles of the "omnigrind" are not as prone to fall into the coffee liquid because of the machine design.

One tip for espresso perfectionists: in Italy, to maintain the production of a perfect espresso, the barman (barista) will alter his grinder to produce a very slightly coarser grind on a day of high humidity.

Turkish grind

Espresso grind

Fine (filter) grind

Omnigrind

Medium grind

BEFORE BEGINNING TO BREW

A coffee lover, setting out to make the best possible coffee, or at least a very enjoyable cup of coffee, should ponder several things before investing in any equipment. He or she must first consider which type of coffee is the preferred taste. It can be anything from the rich flavour of espresso or a mellow, high-grown arabica blend, whose acidity is softened by a touch of cream. Perhaps a full-bodied cup, providing pleasure in both taste and stimulation, is what is required. It is important to have the freedom to experiment with all sorts of blends and roasts.

Second, the time of day and how the choice of coffee is brewed needs to be taken into account. At breakfast, when time is short, volume and caffeine content are perhaps most welcome. After dinner, however, a small cup of pure flavour is more appropriate, ensuring that both the conversation continues and the palate is cleared of any lingering flavours of the meal still clinging to the taste-buds. At a quiet, reflective moment or when seeking to unwind, slowly savouring a deep, smoky, velvety black coffee transports the mind into another place and time.

The volume and strength of the coffee should also be considered. Is a small amount of coffee likely to be drunk all at once or are several cups required immediately? Perhaps one person may want to drink several cups over an extended period. Texture, too, is important. The liquid could slip down better if it were clean and clear of sediment, or one might prefer the roughness of a brew steeped in the particles from which it comes. Weak or strong, clear or thick, morning or evening, all of the requirements of coffee can be met by one or the other method of brewing.

Ensuring Lasting Flavour

Once the brewing method is decided, the question of "to grind or not to grind, and if so, what grind is necessary?" can be answered. The ultimate question is then "Can the magic of the moment last, can the coffee be maintained as fresh as it was brewed, until it is finished?" This question is perhaps the easiest to answer because it has been discovered that hot coffee stored in a preheated vacuum flask will taste good far longer than that kept hot by any other method. Nothing lasts forever, and the fresh flavour may very gradually deteriorate, but the coffee is not being heated up and cooled down and heated up again, which is what happens to the coffee molecules in a jug (carafe) on a hotplate.

Left: From elegant serving styles to tough durability, vacuum (or insulated) jugs and flasks can provide the solution to almost any situation where coffee quality needs to be maintained more than half an hour.

THE PRINCIPLES OF COFFEE BREWING

The beverage called coffee is the result of mixing dry coffee with water. The combination can be done by one of many methods – ranging from the very simple, with the minimum of equipment – to the use of complex machines which can cost thousands of pounds. Understanding a few facts about coffee brewing can help answer some of the questions which arise when wondering which brewing method to use.

Extracting the Flavour

A single coffee bean is an extremely complex entity, being composed of literally hundreds of substances, many of which are water-soluble. Nearly one-third of these water-soluble compounds can be removed in normal extraction processes. The goal of brewing coffee, however, is not to extract the greatest number of elements from ground coffee, because not all of them are desirable. Expert tasters generally agree that the overall coffee flavour, which consists of colour, aroma, taste and body, is best when about 18–22 per cent of the flavour components have left the solid coffee and infused into the water. When more than 22 per cent of the extractable materials permeate into the water, over-extraction occurs and harsh flavours are added to the brew, as the last substances to leave the grounds are unpleasant and bitter.

A second technical consideration is that, even if only the best flavoured components have been extracted from the coffee, the cup flavour can be too concentrated or too diluted, depending on how much water is used. Again, most expert tasters generally agree that a cup of coffee tastes best when the liquid consists of between 98.4–98.7 per cent water and 1.3–1.6 per cent "soluble solids", the latter being what

Above: From the coffee cherry spills two beans: the object of universal interest.

would be left if a cup of liquid coffee was reduced back to dry ingredients by an evaporation process. This ideal coffee strength is easily achieved by controlling the proportion of ground coffee to water, which for European tastes ranges between 50–75g/2–3oz/ per 1 litre/33fl oz/4 cups of water. Many would consider normal strength coffee as one brewed at about 55g/ 10 tbsp per litre of water. Much of North America drinks a weaker cup.

The most beautiful and expensive coffee machines do not always produce the most satisfying cup of coffee, and when choosing coffee-brewing equipment, consideration must be given to whether the design allows for a correct balance of brewing factors, as well as taking into account various safety aspects.

Water Condition

People often buy coffee from a particular place where they have enjoyed an excellent cup. They take the coffee home, brew it correctly and wonder why it doesn't taste the same. As a cup of coffee is more than 98 per cent water, the condition and taste of the water are at least as important as the coffee used, and only water from the same source will recreate an exact taste. Coffee experts tend to agree that the best water for brewing coffee is slightly hard; a few minerals will

---

Key brewing factors

Correct coffee brewing depends on a balance of several factors, and each coffee will react differently and uniquely to exactly the same balance of factors. When brewing, consider the following factors:
• The degree of grind of the ground coffee.
• The ratio of coffee to water.
• The condition of the water.
• The water temperature.
• The contact time between the coffee and the water.

Above: These two glasses show the difference in strength when coffee is made with 50g/2oz of coffee per litre, left, and when made with only 75g/3oz, right.

The importance of having the right grind

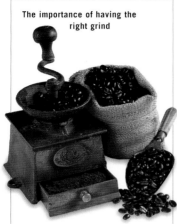

The finer the grind, the greater the surface area exposed to the water and the faster the extraction of soluble solids. Finely-ground particles of coffee are thus required for brewing methods where the contact time between the coffee and the water is shorter.

Conversely, a coarser grind will help to delay the extraction when grounds are left in the container from which the coffee will be served. A good grinder, whether manual or electric, will reduce the coffee beans to particles of a consistent size, so as to ensure an even extraction.

enhance the coffee flavour, hence the old custom of adding a pinch of salt to "bring out the flavour". If the brewing water is very hard, however, the calcium and magnesium ions can actually get between the water molecules and the coffee particles, interfering with the extraction process, and the resulting brew will have little flavour.

When considering the effect of soft water in brewing coffee, it is interesting to examine the softest water possible, which is distilled or de-ionized; as water it has virtually no taste, and no one would dream of making coffee with it. It could therefore be assumed that

coffee made with distilled water would also be tasteless and would need a "pinch of salt to bring out the flavour". Wrong! Because it contains nothing to interfere with the extraction, coffee brewed with tasteless, distilled water has a very strong coffee flavour, which in the course of normal brewing, especially with a cheap blend, could easily be far too strong. Very soft water requires less coffee per brew, or a slightly coarser grind, or less contact time – any of which work to ensure that over-extraction does not occur. The old wives' habit of adding a pinch of salt may have worked not in "bringing out the flavour", but rather in toning it down, modifying the flavour for the better, if the original water was very soft.

Chlorinated or other chemically treated water, or water polluted by old pipes, rust or other tastes can affect the flavour of coffee. Filtering devices, which remove objectionable tastes, are available both in jug (carafe) form and in more permanent systems that attach to the kitchen main water pipe.

Generally, experts agree that fresh, cold water, which presumably has a higher oxygen content, makes the best coffee. Somewhat confusingly, however, it is oxygen that causes ground coffee to go stale, and it is from oxygen that vacuum flasks protect liquid coffee. Thus the need to have oxygen in the brewing water seems surprising, especially as convincing scientific explanations are rather scarce. (This calls for the challenge of a taste test: try brewing the same coffee with stale, warm water and with fresh, cold water and observe the difference.) Remember that most electric coffee-makers are equipped with thermostats which expect to start with cold water, and may not function very well if hot water is used.

Water Temperature

Water of any temperature will extract coffee, but hot water extracts faster than cold. Never pour boiling water on coffee, even on instant, as it brings out a harsh flavour. The optimum temperature range for coffee preparation is between 92–96°C/

Comparing water types

You can easily do a few comparative tests for yourself on the effect different types of water have on the flavour of a cup of coffee. Try different waters, such as tap and distilled, and also add a pinch of salt to some distilled water to see if salt does in fact "bring out the flavour".

197–205°F. Conversely, if cooler water is used, the brew will be under-extracted. When coffee is intentionally boiled, as with Turkish brewing, sweetening offsets any bitterness.

Contact Time

When ground coffee and water are combined, a certain amount of time is needed for the water to saturate the coffee grounds and extract the various soluble solids, some of which take longer than others to pass into the water. For the first few minutes of the brewing cycle, the "blend" of the flavour compounds in the liquid is changing continuously. If the contact time is to be limited, the particles must be finer for the water to penetrate them and extract the flavour compounds. If the contact time is very long, the grounds should be coarser so as to slow the rate of extraction. In certain methods of brewing, such as those in which cold water drips very slowly through coffee grounds for several hours, the resulting brew will be extremely bitter, which is to be expected with such over-extraction, but will be offset later by dilution and sweetening.

Helpful Hints

• When using coffee equipment for the first time, follow the manufacturer's instructions. The following pages give recommended measures of coffee for each method of brewing. A good idea is to take one coffee scoop, and, having filled and weighed its capacity content, use it all the time for ease of measuring.

• If all the same equipment is to be used regularly and for the same amounts of coffee, note the number and size of the scoops of dry coffee required as well as the level of water in the measuring jug (cup). If it should happen that the first coffee brewed turns out to be weaker or stronger than preferred – all coffee is a matter of personal taste – make a note to adjust either the coffee, the water or perhaps the brewing time.

• Many coffee makers have indicators for the level of water required for a specific number of cups, but this rarely seems to correspond to the actual number of cups poured, no matter what size cup is being used. If in doubt about the ratio of coffee to water, it is far better to use more coffee than may be required; if the brew is too strong, it can be diluted after brewing. Coffee made too weak, that is, with too little dry coffee, cannot be "undone".

• Remember that coffee grounds absorb some water, so the yield of liquid coffee will always be less than the amount of water used in the brew; 600g of coffee will absorb 1.2 litres of water, which means that 1g of dry coffee will absorb 2ml of water.

• As much as possible, never reheat coffee and never use the same coffee grounds more than once.

• Any time a small amount of coffee (one or two cups) is being brewed, and the amount of coffee is not dictated by the size of the machine (as it is with the espresso pot, for example), use proportionally more dry coffee per cup. Approximately 50g coffee per litre of water is almost exactly 1oz per pint; this makes a slightly weakish "normal" brew and is a good starting point for determining preferred strength.

Above: The key to a good espresso machine is a mix of fine-tuning of the machine's pressure by the manufacturer, the skills of the roaster and blender, and the careful grinding and brewing of the barista (barman).

Some useful conversions

DRY MEASURES

28g = 1oz
440g = 1lb
5.7g coffee = 1 rounded tbsp
2.5g coffee = 1 heaped tsp
55g coffee = 10 tbsp/generous $^2/_3$ cup

LIQUID MEASURES

50ml = 2fl oz/$^1/_4$ cup
1 litre = 33fl oz/4 cups
600ml = 20fl oz/2$^1/_2$ cups

1 espresso
cup (empty) =
2$^1/_2$fl oz

Liquid
coffee for
1 espresso cup =
1$^1/_2$fl oz coffee
(about 44ml)

Below: The basic equipment for brewing coffee couldn't be simpler – a scoop, measuring jug, saucepan and coffee – the trick is to familiarize yourself with your equipment and what amount and type of coffee and water best suit your equipment and tastes. Whatever the brewing method, measuring the coffee and water, noting the levels of each and the resulting flavour, makes successive brews easy.

COFFEE AND HEALTH

Caffeine (C8H10N4O2) is a white, slightly bitter alkaloid, sometimes also called "theine". It is a natural ingredient in coffee, where it comprises two to three per cent of the weight of each bean, or from about 60–90mg in an average cup of coffee. Robusta coffee has a much higher caffeine content than does arabica. As well as in coffee, caffeine is found in about 60 other plants, such as tea, cocoa, guarana and kola, and in products made from them, such as chocolate and cola-based soft drinks.

Because caffeine, as a stimulant of the central nervous system and cerebral circulation, imparts a feeling of energy and can often alleviate headaches, it is an ingredient in many pharmaceutical products, particularly those for headaches and colds. It is also a diuretic.

Tests have proved that caffeine increases mental alertness and the ability to concentrate, but the idea that strong coffee can offset the effects of too great a consumption of alcohol is a fallacy. Coffee does not "sober up" a truly inebriated person. Rather, it wakes one up, and as a sleepy drunk is preferable to a lively one, administering strong coffee to counter the alcohol is probably not a good idea. Also, the ensuing hangover seems to be worsened by the added complication of large doses of caffeine.

Excess Coffee

In general, too much caffeine consumption can cause palpitations, shaky hands, a feeling of anxiety and an inability to sleep. "Too much", however, varies enormously among caffeine consumers; for some people a single cup of coffee causes ill effects, while others thrive on ten cups a day. Coffee is one of the most widely-researched substances on earth, and yet scientific and medical opinions are still extremely divided. There is every reason to believe that the individual coffee drinker, exercising some degree of moderation according to his or her level of caffeine tolerance, can probably look forward to many years of "safe" coffee enjoyment.

Coffee is an acidic drink, especially if it is high-grown arabica, and many people, who find that coffee upsets their stomach, blame the caffeine content instead of the acidity. Decaffeination does not remove acidity, so drinking decaffeinated coffee is not the solution for stomach upset. Acid-neutralized coffees are difficult to find, but they are available in North America and the United Kingdom, in France (café allégé) and Germany (reizarmer Kaffee). They may not, however, be particularly tasty, as it is acidity that contributes so crucially to the flavours of high-grown arabicas and their blends.

Above: To many people, the difference in flavour between decaffeinated and regular coffee beans, will be slight. When market research indicated a growing niche for decaffeinated coffee, better quality beans were used by coffee companies.

Coffee and Medical Research

It has been proven that pregnancy greatly increases the time required for a woman's body to metabolize caffeine, and, as caffeine can be transferred to a foetus (fetus), it is recommended that a pregnant woman reduce her regular coffee intake by at least 50 per cent, with greater spaces of time between cups. If concerned, eliminate all caffeine from the diet during pregnancy.

For years, many thorough and exhaustive studies have been conducted to try to link coffee consumption with cancer or heart disease, but to no avail; nor does caffeine cause high blood pressure. One study indicating a definite link between coffee and high blood cholesterol (which in itself may cause cardiovascular problems), found that cholesterol was increased only in certain subjects who drank large amounts of coffee prepared by a particular Scandinavian method of excessive boiling and steeping of coffee. Filtering the boiled coffee before consumption, however, seemed to eliminate the cholesterol-raising oils. Other tests which link boiled coffee to an increase in cholesterol have proved that it is some other substance, and not caffeine which raises the cholesterol levels, as decaffeinated coffee – but only that which has been boiled and is consumed unfiltered – seems to contribute to higher cholesterol. Of course, if one suffers from low caffeine tolerance, is concerned about the safety of caffeine consumption, or simply wants to enjoy the taste of a late-night coffee drink without losing any sleep, a decaffeinated or even one brewed half-and-half, provides a perfectly acceptable alternative.

Decaffeinated Coffee

It is a fairly accurate statement that, although decaffeinated coffee has been produced since the early years of the 20th century, most of it was rather tasteless, at best, before about 1980. During the mid-80s, most likely due to numerous unfounded health scares about caffeine, there was an unprecedented interest in decaffeinated coffee. Almost immediately the flavour of decaffeinated coffee improved immensely, and all the major brands of supermarket coffee offered such a version. The decaffeination processes were changed very little, if at all. The Swiss Water Process, patented by

Coffex SA in 1979, needed several years to acquire a wide following, and many coffee companies are still producing decaffeinated beans that are not water-processed. So why did decaffeinated coffee start tasting good? The answer is that suddenly there was a market for it. For years only the very committed health enthusiast had drunk decaffeinated coffee, and coffee companies did not bother to use good beans for such a low-profile product. By about 1987, when decaffeinated sales represented around 25 per cent of the massive United States coffee market, coffee companies, in order to cash in on the phenomenal demand, started using higher quality beans for decaf products, and the flavour improved as quickly as the market grew.

Since caffeine is almost tasteless, except for a slight bitterness, its removal should not interfere with the coffee flavour at all, unless the decaffeination process inadvertently extracts flavour compounds as well as the caffeine. The goal of all decaf processors has been to remove only the caffeine, not the flavour. It is the quality of the beans that will ultimately determine the flavour of the coffee.

For around 200 years it has been known that, while caffeine survives roasting, retaining its properties through temperatures as high as 240°C/475°F, it is completely vulnerable to liquid, and will pass from green (unroasted) coffee beans into any liquid in which they are soaked. Some liquids extract the caffeine faster than others.

Left: Hide the package and most people would not know from taste alone if a coffee was decaffeinated.

The Decaffeination Process

The oldest method of decaffeinating coffee is that used by Kaffee Hag, among others, in which carbon dioxide, pressurized to a supercritical nearly-fluid state, is forced through steamed green beans, removing the caffeine. Many companies do not use this method simply because the equipment and facilities required are so expensive.

The most widespread means of decaffeination occurs when warmed or steamed green beans are soaked in a solution containing a chemical solvent, usually methylene chloride, which is selective in its target: all but about three per cent of the caffeine, and practically none of the flavour, passes into the solvent. The beans, rinsed and dried, go on to be roasted, and almost any trace of the solvent remaining with the beans is destroyed in the high roasting temperatures. In 1995 this method was banned in Europe because methylene chloride vapours, particularly in aerosol form, destroy the ozone layer. The United States Food and Drug Administration has limited methylene chloride residues in brewed coffee to ten parts per million, a figure which does not worry most coffee processors, who insist the actual residue is already less than one-millionth part anyway.

The slowest, and therefore most expensive, form of decaffeination is the patented Swiss Water Method, which uses only steamed beans, hot water and carbon filters to remove the caffeine. Unfortunately, some of the volatile flavour compounds also go with the caffeine, so the water is evaporated, and the remaining flavour concentrate is then sprayed on to the decaffeinated beans.

Although coffee lovers and experts alike are still convinced that decaffeination destroys the taste of coffee, many would find it extremely difficult to differentiate between a "regular" coffee and its "unleaded" version. In an exhaustive tasting project carried out over a period of several weeks at the International Coffee Organization, United Kingdom, a panel of trained tasters compared three cups of coffee, each made from beans from the same crop and same plantation; one cup was coffee decaffeinated with a solvent, one was water-processed decaffeinated, and the third was regular un-decaffeinated coffee. The tests were carried out time and again, not just with one set of coffee samples, but with coffees from Kenya, Colombia and Brazil. The results showed that often tasters could not tell which cups contained decaffeinated coffee, and, further, when tasters thought they could distinguish a difference, if asked for a preference, they often preferred the taste of the chemically decaffeinated coffee to the "regular" version of the same coffee.

Anyone who loves the taste of coffee, but is concerned about the effects of caffeine, should realize that today there are some fabulous decaffeinated coffees available, particularly from specialist shops. Cover the label, hide the box, and enjoy one of the luxuries of life: a cup of good coffee.

Left: Good beans make good flavour – decaf or not.

BREWING EQUIPMENT

Considering that there are a limited number of ways that coffee and water can be combined, it is amazing how many factors there are in brewing that make a difference to the resulting coffee flavour. But then it seems rather miraculous that anyone ever thought of combining the two substances anyway. Almost certainly, the first means of brewing coffee (probably only a few steps removed from the earliest practice of chewing on the fruit) was based on boiling the beans in water, although it was probably the entire coffee cherry that was first boiled.

The Turkish method of brewing coffee soon became the common way to prepare coffee, though Europeans did not take up the same means of brewing it. The first Europeans undoubtedly boiled the coffee, but not in a device like that retained throughout Islam for perhaps 600 years. We can only wonder why Europeans and their colonial descendants throughout the world have felt the need to constantly modify their coffee-makers. Museums around the world are filled with strange-looking pieces, such as beakers and tubes suspended above a flame, ceramic locomotives, complicated cylinders forcing water upwards, machines with pistons of near horse-power proportions which eke out tiny streams of coffee, cloth bags that could double as dirty socks and slow-drip devices like some form of water torture. The following brewing methods, perhaps less creative than the above, but generally more gratifying, are only some of those available to coffee lovers seeking the perfect cup.

Above: It is quite likely that very soon after coffee began to be used in Yemen, the brewing method we today call the Turkish became the common way to prepare coffee.

TURKISH IBRIK

The only real difficulty in making Turkish coffee is obtaining the right blend. The traditional Middle Eastern concoction has a very distinctive taste, due primarily to a penchant for rio-y flavoured Brazilian beans, which are usually blended with Ethiopian ones. Many people erroneously believe that Turkish coffee is dark-roasted, but the pulverized coffee is usually a reddish-brown shade, not dark at all.

The traditional brewing vessel, the *ibrik* (or Greek *briki*), is a small, long-handled copper- or brass-plated pan with a narrow neck. *Ibriks* come in different sizes, and usually each one has a tiny number underneath, which indicates how many cups it holds.

If an *ibrik* is not available, a small straight-sided pan for heating milk will do, although the coffee may not boil as easily. This is the only method which insists on breaking the "never boil coffee" rule, but as the coffee actually boils with sugar, the bitterness from boiling never affects the flavour. Adding spices to the brew, further adds to the flavour.

Left: Turkish coffee is usually served with a small glass of water and/or a piece of Turkish Delight. Turkish coffee is never served with milk or cream.

Using a Turkish *ibrik*

1 Remembering the proportions for Turkish coffee is simple: one of everything for each cup the *ibrik* holds. If it is a two-cup *ibrik*, place two very heaped teaspoons of Turkish coffee in the *ibrik*. (The coffee will heap high on the spoon very easily because of its fine consistency.)

3 Lastly, using one of the tiny Turkish cups from which the coffee will be drunk, measure two cups of water into the *ibrik*. At this point possibilities for variations from the basic Turkish taste can be obtained by adding cardamom pods, a stick of cinnamon or aniseed to the brew.

5 When the froth rises to the top the third time, carefully remove the *ibrik* from the heat and alternate pouring the contents of the *ibrik* between the two small Turkish cups, being careful to give some of the all-important froth to each.

COOK'S TIP

Returning the *ibrik* to boil the third time ensures the roundness of flavour and thorough blending of coffee and sugar.

Below: A number on the under-side of an ibrik indicates how many cups it holds.

2 Next, place two very heaped teaspoons of sugar in the *ibrik*. (The sugar will not heap quite as easily as the coffee, but it really needs to be somewhere between heaped and very heaped anyway, to achieve the "medium" sweet specification favoured by most Westerners.)

4 Place the *ibrik* over a lowish heat and wait for it to boil. When the seething mixture threatens to run over the rim of the *ibrik*, quickly remove it from the heat, stir it, and return it to the heat. In a moment it will again start to boil over, so it must be instantly removed from the heat. Don't bother to stir again.

AL FRESCO

This is a simple method of making coffee when no proper serving jug (carafe) is available, or when the source

Above: Al fresco *coffee requires only a saucepan, measuring jug and strainer.*

Making coffee al fresco

1 Measure the amount of cold water needed into a saucepan. If no measuring jug is available, use a coffee cup (multiplied by the number of cups to be served plus a little extra for absorption). Place the saucepan over the heat.

2 Measure out the amount of dry medium-to-coarse grind coffee needed. When the water is just beginning to boil, quickly add all the coffee to the water.

3 Immediately remove the saucepan from the heat, stirring well. Set aside for about four minutes. Strain the coffee into each cup.

of heat is a cooker or even an open fire. Any blend or roast of coffee is suitable, and brew for normal strength at 55g/10 tbsp per 1 litre/33fl oz/4 cups of water.

As *al fresco* brewing is useful in Spartan conditions, it is possible that the correct grind of coffee – medium

if it is a commercial grind, slightly coarser if home-ground – may not always be available. If fine-grind coffee is used, shorten the brewing time to no more than three minutes and expect some sediment to remain in the bottom of each cup served.

JUG (CARAFE)

As with *al fresco* brewing, this infusion method is simple and requires little equipment. Any blend or roast of coffee is acceptable – though a medium grind is best, it can be a bit coarser, too.

Above: Earthenware jugs are ideal for this method of brewing coffee.

Making coffee with a jug or pot

1 Warm the jug by filling it with hot water, mentally noting the desired water level in the jug. Meanwhile, heat enough water for another jugful. Pour the first hot water out of the jug. (Measure the water capacity of the jug by pouring the water into a measuring jug.) Dry the jug and place medium-grind coffee in the bottom. Normal strength coffee for the jug would be about 55g/10 tbsp per 1 litre/1¾ pints/4 cups of water.

2 When the water being heated is below boiling point – either just before or after it has boiled – pour the water over the coffee. Stir well, preferably with a wooden spoon, and wait about four minutes before straining the coffee into the cups.

COOK'S TIP

Do not try to keep jug coffee hot. If it is not to be drunk immediately, strain it into a preheated vacuum flask.

THE CAFETIÈRE (THE PRESS POT)

Making coffee in a cafetière (press pot) is almost exactly like making coffee in a simple jug (carafe). In fact, it is easier than using a jug in that it requires no separate strainer, and once one is accustomed to using it, it is easier to judge the correct water level. (It is not easier to clean, however.) The correct grind of coffee is medium, but if for some reason only finely ground is available, the brewing time should be reduced to no more than three minutes. Using a fine grind may make the plunging difficult – take care when pressing down, so that there is no danger of breaking the glass. Also, if using a fine grind, there will be more sediment in the bottom of the cup.

Cafetières, also called French presses, come in a variety of sizes, and there are various styles of "cosies" available to fit most; although cafetière coffee cannot be kept hot, its warmth can be slightly prolonged by wrapping a cosy around it. If the coffee is not to be drunk immediately, pour it into a preheated vacuum flask (thermos) directly after plunging.

There are many different sizes and brands of cafetières available, and the prices vary enormously. The more expensive ones, however, are generally better made, and the mesh sieve will last longer. In cheaper models the mesh may fray and curl around the edges, letting coffee grounds escape into the brew, and replacement meshes may not be available.

General Care and Maintenance

The cafetière is not as easy to clean as an ordinary jug because coffee grounds get trapped in the mesh and the metal disks on either side of it. These should be separated and cleaned after every use, as coffee grounds are oily and can go rancid, ruining the flavour of successive brews. When pressing the plunger pot down, be sure to press straight down and not at an angle, thus minimizing the risk of breaking the glass.

Above: Mesh sieves and also the strong glass jugs (carafes) can be replaced in the more expensive models, so it is worth enquiring about availability of spare parts when purchasing a cafetière (press pot).

Using a plunger pot

1 Preheat the glass cylinder by filling it with hot water; and while more water is heating for brewing, pour the water from the glass cylinder into a measuring jug and calculate the amount of coffee needed, working at 55g/10 tbsp per1 litre/33fl oz/4 cups of water.

2 Dry the glass and place the dry coffee in it. When the water for brewing is almost at boiling point (just before it boils or just after), pour it over the dry coffee.

3 Stir it very well with a large spoon. The more freshly ground the coffee, the more it has a tendency to float and seems more resistant to saturation by the water, so stir thoroughly to incorporate all the dry coffee.

4 Prop the sieve device, with the lid above it, just inside the top of the cylinder for about four minutes. When the brewing time is up, hold the lid down with one hand to stabilize the plunger shaft and, with the other hand, slowly push down the plunger. Serve the coffee as soon as possible.

THE NEAPOLITAN

Like the earliest large espresso machines, the Napoletana was claimed by Italians but was actually invented in France, where it is called the "café filtre", and indeed it is a form of filter machine, as the hot water, after the "flip", filters down through the ground coffee. Using a Neapolitan is a wonderful way of making a relatively small amount of coffee.

These unusual-looking pots are not particularly common, however, and well-made ones, in stainless steel, are even harder to come by, so no one quibbles about whether it's a two-cup or three-cup machine. Once a good Neapolitan

is purchased, however, it should practically last forever, as long as the handle doesn't break. There are no glass parts to break, no disposable requirements to run short of, no seals or washers to wear out, and no electric coils to burn out.

Getting to Know Your Neapolitan

The trick when using this type of machine is getting the right grind, as all the aspects of brewing would indicate that the grind should be filter fine. The top and bottom of the coffee compartment, however, are both perforated, and the size of the holes

Choosing your Neapolitan

When purchasing a Neapolitan, look for sturdy, preferably stainless steel, construction, and an extremely welcome safety feature is a wooden or plastic-coated handle for holding when flipping over. The perforations in the top and bottom of the coffee basket can often vary in size from one manufacturer to the next, and generally speaking, the smaller the holes, the easier the operation of the machine, as fewer grounds will fall through and a finer grind is more desirable.

Above: Quirky and distinctive, the Neapolitan is a fun way to brew coffee.

can vary depending on the nationality of the manufacturer. The coffee must therefore be somewhere between medium and fine, so if a commercial grind is used, perhaps this method is one for "omnigrind".

Ascertaining that the water is the right temperature for flipping is not always easy. Some people therefore heat the water cylinder without attaching the coffee basket or the spouted cylinder until the water is hot, and ready for flipping. If the machine (or "macchinetta", as it is sometimes called in North America) is not assembled until the water is hot, care must be taken not to burn oneself; again, a non-metal handle is strongly recommended.

Occasionally, when the "flip" is done with a particular Neapolitan model, a small stream of water may arch out of the tiny steam vent, which at this stage is now towards the bottom of the top compartment. If this happens, it is only for a second or two, as it is just a few drops which get free before the coffee basket inside blocks the hole. Having the steam vent aligned with the spout below may ensure that the drops are caught by the spout. After the coffee is brewed and served, it is a good idea to let the apparatus cool down before attempting to separate the two halves for cleaning, and they usually fit together very tightly. When cooler, they contract and are less likely to burn anyone attempting the separation.

Using a Neapolitan

1 When using the machine for the first time, measure the capacity of the unspouted cylinder. To make the coffee, fill this cylinder with water, then place the ground coffee in the coffee container, observing whether the grounds are falling through the bottom perforations; if they are, the grind is too fine and should not be used. Be generous with the coffee, especially if only one or two cups are being made; too few grounds will let the water zip through instead of holding it long enough for good extraction to take place.

2 If the grind is all right, place the coffee compartment on top of the pot with the water, and attach the spouted top in an upside-down position. The attachment varies depending on the manufacturer, but it should lock securely.

3 Place the Neapolitan over a low to medium heat and wait for the water to boil. It is not always easy to tell when the water in the lower chamber starts boiling. (Of course, by the time a bit of steam comes from the hole near the top of the lower chamber, it is definitely boiling.)

4 Remove the machine from the heat and wait a few seconds for the water to drop to just off the boil. Flip the machine over, being careful not to touch any hot parts, and set it on a heat-proof surface. The water will filter through the coffee for about three minutes, passing to the bottom cylinder, which now has a spout.

5 If the spout is set fairly low in its cylinder, the brew will not need stirring, as the first cup will get good-strength coffee and serving it will mix the remainder of the brew. If the spout is higher up the cylinder, remove the top half of the apparatus and the coffee compartment and stir the pot before serving the coffee.

COOK'S TIP
Although the Neapolitan is designed to sit on a burner, do not be tempted to try to keep the coffee hot over a low heat; it never works and the flavour will be ruined.

Above: Omnigrind coffee is best for Neapolitan brewing.

FILTER COFFEE MACHINES

Manual and One-Cup Filter Machines

For many years people have been letting water run through coffee grounds to extract the flavour instead of leaving the coffee to steep in the water. In a sense the electric percolator is a form of filtering, but the term "filter" (or filtre, as the French invented it) is understood by most people to mean some form of drip mechanism.

With filter coffee, the brew is clear and clean (although admittedly this can make the body seem thinner), and a stopwatch is no longer necessary, as the timing is all down to gravity, once the correct grind is obtained. Because the contact time between the ground coffee and the water is limited, a fine degree of grind is required for the proper amount of extraction to take place, but take care not to use too fine a grind or use too much coffee in the brew basket, lest the filter clog, causing over-extraction.

The invention of the electric drip machine about forty years ago meant that filter lovers were no longer required to stand over a filter device. However, the manual filter is cheaper to buy and maintain, easier to clean, requires less space and is far easier to control. Even its one disadvantage is actually another benefit: there is no hotplate on which to stew the coffee. The only equipment necessary is a kettle; a filter and filter paper, or a metal or synthetic filter which requires no paper; a jug for catching the liquid (a thermal jug (carafe) or vacuum flask (thermos) solves the problem of keeping the brew hot); and a spoon (wooden is best) with which to stir.

Plastic filter cones or baskets come in various sizes, and it is important to have a brew basket that corresponds to the number of cups to be brewed; the

Left and above: Manual filter cups come in a variety of sizes and shapes.

Making filter coffee using a manual filter machine

1 First, preheat the jug (carafe) or flask with hot water. It helps to know the desired level of the brewed coffee in the jug, in order to assess the amount of dry coffee to be used.

A good amount for normal strength filter coffee is about 55g/10 tbsp per 1 litre/33fl oz/4 cups, but if in doubt, use more coffee, as filter coffee can be diluted very successfully with a little hot water after the brewing is completed.

2 While the brewing water is heating, place the filter cone or brew basket on the jug. Measure the coffee into the cone.

3 Give the filter a gentle shake to level out the bed of coffee; this will help to ensure even extraction.

4 When the water has boiled, count to ten to let the temperature drop to about 95 C/203°F.

5 Pour a small amount of the water as widely as possible over the grounds just to moisten the surface, and pause a few seconds while the grounds form into a harder bed.

6 Continue slowly pouring the rest of the water over the grounds in a circular motion. If any grounds remain dry, or if the drip flow stops, stir the mixture in the filter basket.

7 When the water has all run through the grounds, remove the basket from the top of the jug, stir the coffee and serve, or seal the flask if the coffee is not to be drunk immediately.

Below: Individual-sized manual filter.

bed of coffee will be too shallow if less than 50 per cent of the basket capacity is used. A wedge-shaped filter is better for brewing smaller amounts of coffee (one to three cups) as it concentrates the grounds and provides a deeper bed of coffee to keep the water from rushing through too quickly. Flat-bottomed baskets work better for larger brews.

Commercial Products

For several years commercial coffee companies have produced individual one-cup or on-cup coffee filters. These are pre-measured, pre-packaged doses of filter coffee and a plastic holder with a lid, designed to sit on almost any-sized coffee cup or mug. Most companies offer these in both regular and decaffeinated versions. Some companies sell "sleeves" of usually ten of these filters, each designed to be disposed of entirely after using once; this seems a terrible waste of materials

and packaging and space. Other companies sell boxes supplying two plastic filter-holders and lids, and ten individually vacuum-sealed pods of coffee, which fit neatly into a recess in the filter-holder. The same company will also sell boxes of just the ten pods of coffee without the filter-holders at a cheaper price, for regular return customers who have retained the plastic filter-holders from a previous purchase.

Commercial on-cup filters are extremely easy to use, requiring only a kettle or some other source of hot water, and a cup or mug for drinking. The coffee is good, well-packaged and correctly ground, and by simply filling the filter holder with hot water as it holds the coffee pod over the cup, there is little mess to clear up. In situations where two people require two vacuum flasks, if, for example one preferred decaffeinated coffee, or perhaps tea, to the other person's

"regular" coffee, one good vacuum flask of extremely hot water could satisfy the demands of both people with the use of one or two on-cup filters.

There are only two drawbacks to on-cup disposable filters. One is that they are more expensive than an equivalent cup of just ground coffee, but, as they eliminate the need for any equipment other than a hot-water source, and as they are clean and convenient to use, the extra cost can be easily justified by many happy consumers.

The other negative aspect of on-cup commercial filters for the coffee "gourmet" is that one has very little choice or information about the origins of the coffee itself, although this aspect could be eliminated somewhat if a coffee company were to market a package containing perhaps two pods each of five different blends or coffees from five different countries of origin, with accompanying labelling.

Automatic Filter Machines

The many brands of electric filter machines vary as much in quality as they do in price, but there are a few points to consider when purchasing one. The first factor in choosing a machine is the capacity, which is critical in filter machines, as the filter cone or brew basket is of a particular size to accommodate a certain amount of coffee. Use too little coffee for the design (less than 50 per cent of the machine's capacity) and the water will rush through, not having time to extract the coffee flavour. Use too much coffee and the bed of coffee will be too deep, the water will be held too long in the basket and the coffee will be over-extracted. Even worse, brewing the full capacity of a badly-designed filter machine can easily result in the water/coffee mixture overflowing the sides of the brew basket, because there is not enough headroom at the top of the brew basket. Coffee grounds swell to nearly double their original volume during brewing, especially when freshly roasted and ground.

Another consideration is whether to buy a filter machine that comes with a permanent filter, which is probably made of metal mesh coated with gold (or of some sort of synthetic mesh), or a machine that requires paper liners for the filter basket. Generally, paper filters, easily disposed of, produce a cleaner, clearer cup of coffee, than do permanent filters, but what a nuisance to discover – at an inconvenient time of day or night – a lack of filter papers. Care must be taken to keep a permanent filter clean, however – a stiff brush is recommended – as its mesh can easily become clogged with old coffee grounds, causing a rancid taste and uneven extraction.

The importance of power Possibly the most important consideration in the choice of a filter machine will be the electrical power, as the greatest complaint against filter machines is a cold cup of coffee. The machine should take no longer than six minutes total to brew coffee, and should start the brewing cycle with a burst of water, which hits the grounds at a minimum temperature of 92°C/198°F. Whatever the wattage of the available machines, the higher the power, the better.

Many filter machines offer welcome options, such as a timer, so that the machine can be loaded with coffee and water at night to produce a morning brew at a specific time. However, any filter machine can be set to brew with the kind of timer that simply plugs into an electrical socket. The option of interrupting the brewing cycle by removing the jug (carafe) from the hotplate can be very convenient, but the coffee poured from the first half of an interrupted cycle will not be evenly extracted, and may be extremely strong and rather unpleasant. The best option possible on an electric filter machine is having a thermal vacuum jug to brew into instead of a conventional glass jug and hotplate.

Right: Permanent filters, besides eliminating the need to keep buying paper filters, allow more flavour (and a tiny bit of sediment) to come through.

General Care and Maintenance

An automatic filter machine needs to be descaled regularly to prevent calcium build-up in its internal tubes that can slow down the flow of water, extending the brewing time and causing over-extraction. Calcium scale can also shorten the life of the machine. Undiluted vinegar can be just as effective as a commercial descaler in cleaning a machine if the scale build-up is not excessive.

1 Keeping an electric machine clean is also important, as coffee is oily and can leave an invisible film which can turn rancid. Clean and rinse the jug (carafe) after every use.

2 Do not allow the spray head to become clogged with old coffee grounds that will spoil the flavour of successive brews, as well as cause uneven extraction. Clean regularly with a soft cloth. Also, a hotplate will heat more efficiently and evenly if it is cleaned of liquid coffee residues.

Using domestic electric filter machines

It is always best to follow the manufacturer's instructions, which can vary from model to model. Most filter machines have markers on the side of the water reservoir indicating how many cups of coffee are made by certain water levels. These cups never seem to correspond to any exact cup size, so again, a trial-and-error system is best when getting used to a new machine. If in doubt about the number of cups and the amount of dry coffee required, use more coffee than may be correct, in the knowledge that the stronger coffee liquid can be diluted quite easily and successfully with hot water afterwards.

1 Begin with loading the electric filter machine with cold water and a level bed of dry, fine-grind coffee, at a ratio of about 55g/10 tbsp per 1 litre/33fl oz/4 cups of water.

It is not a good idea to try to hasten the brewing process by pouring preheated water into the machine, as it has a thermostat set to operate with cooler water. The time saved will be slight at any rate.

COOK'S TIP

Never re-use coffee grounds; after one brew cycle the flavour is completely extracted and the grounds produce only a weak and bitter liquid.

2 If it is a good machine, the brewing cycle will begin with a burst of water (which a thermometer will show to be between 92–96°C/198–205°F) wetting the grounds. Look at the coffee bed in mid-brew to check that all the grounds are wet and the surface of the mixture is fairly even; if it isn't, stir it.

3 When the brew is finished, stir the jug and serve. The hotplate should hold any remaining coffee at 80–85°C/176–185°F, but do not leave the jug on the hotplate longer than half an hour.

If the coffee is not to be drunk within this time, it should be stored in a preheated vacuum flask. Some machines supply jugs with funnel lids, which fill from the bottom, but by far the best optional feature of an electric filter machine is a thermal flask jug into which the coffee is brewed and which can be sealed.

MANUAL AND ELECTRIC PERCOLATORS

For many years, the "modern" means of making coffee was the percolator, which sat on a burner of the cooker (stove). It consisted of a metal jug (carafe), inside which was a central tube topped with a perforated metal brewing basket and its cover. The lid to the entire jug often had a glass knob through which coffee could be seen to be "perking".

Today's percolators are electric, but are still based on the same brewing principles: fresh, cold water in the bottom of the jug is brought to the boil, and passes up the hollow tube and out of the top, overflowing the perforated cover of the brew basket. It then filters through the dry coffee in the basket and drops back down into the bottom of the jug in the form of liquid coffee.

Contrary to the opinion of many connoisseurs, percolators can make excellent coffee, but the brewing cycle must occur only once. Better brands of electric percolators achieve this by switching to a lower heat after one cycle, which usually takes six to seven minutes. Remove the brew basket after one cycle. Even so, some, but hopefully not much, of the first coffee brewed is going to be boiled and re-passed through the grounds, which breaks all the rules. In spite of percolator brewing being basically a filter-drip method, a medium grind of coffee is required, to keep potentially disastrous over-extraction to a minimum. Again the ratio of coffee to water should be about 55g/10tbsp per 1 litre/33fl oz/4 cups.

Right: Today's electric percolators still rely on the same principles implemented by the original percolators first invented earlier this century.

Russell Hobbs

Using electric percolators

1 Pour the fresh, cold water (allowing a bit extra for absorption by the grounds) into the pot. The water level should not be so high as to make contact with the bottom of the brew basket when the water boils.

2 Fill the brew basket with medium-grind coffee. Slide the brew basket on to the central tube and cover with the perforated lid.

As with the filter, even though the electric percolator can keep coffee warm, it is better to hold it in a preheated vacuum flask (thermos) if it is not for immediate drinking.

General Care and Maintenance

Cleaning the jug of an electric percolator is not easy, as most are not submersible, but it must be done. The invisible film left by coffee liquid can ruin the flavour of successive brews. Any surfaces touched by the grounds or the liquid should be washed with a mild detergent and well rinsed to avoid tainting future brews with a soapy taste.

CONA VACUUM POT

The vacuum pot, invented before 1840 by the Scottish engineer Robert Napier, is best known today by the name Cona, the principal manufacturer of these elegant and amazing machines. The method of brewing is actually steeping, or infusion, as the grounds are inundated by water for a few minutes before the natural law of cool air contraction takes over and separates the grounds from the brew. The Cona company supplies not only the machines (and replacement parts) and very good instructions for operating them, but also the choice of apparatus for one of two methods of heat: a spirit lamp and an electric coil. In addition to the source of heat, the vacuum mechanism consists of a glass jug (carafe), a glass bowl, a funnel, a plug and a holder frame. A large spoon will also be needed.

This is another machine that works best when the coffee is a grind somewhere between filter fine and medium, and the best choice of commercial grinds is "omnigrind". The ratio of coffee to water is the usual 55g/10 tbsp per 1 litre/33fl oz/4 cups, but as the machine works best at full capacity, it is not difficult to calculate, if the size of the model is known.

General Care and Maintenance

The Cona vacuum machine provides a science lesson by way of a fascinating visual experience, and it can be an interesting topic of conversation at the end of a dining table, but its greatest feat is producing an excellent pot of coffee. The disadvantages of this method of brewing are that it is definitely not fast and the delicacy and fragility of the glass parts, particularly the funnel, mean that it must be treated with great care during cleaning and handling to avoid breakage (although replacement parts are available from the Cona company).

Right: Perhaps one of the most striking designs for a domestic coffee machine, the Cona is perfect for making coffee at the table after dinner, as it is both beautiful and interesting to watch.

Using a Cona vacuum pot

1 As the glass jug (carafe) must be filled with hot water, it is quicker to heat the water in a kettle and add it to the jug. (The alternative is to let the water heat from cold in the jug, but it will take much longer, as neither the spirit lamp nor the electric coil can boil water quickly.)

2 Carefully insert the funnel plug into the funnel, place the glass bowl on top of the jug with the funnel in the water, and join the bowl and the jug by gently but firmly twisting together.

3 Light the spirit lamp or turn on the electric coil. Measure the dry coffee into the upper bowl and place the entire structure in the frame that will suspend it above the heat.

4 After the water boils, it will begin to move up the funnel into the upper bowl. When most of the water has risen, extinguish the spirit lamp or turn off the electric coil. The water will continue to rise. (Waiting a bit longer before reducing the heat will slightly prolong the brewing time, as the cooling of the air in the jug will be delayed.)

5 When enough water has risen to wet the ground coffee thoroughly, stir the mixture in the upper bowl, making sure that all the coffee is saturated. (Some water will remain below in the jug, as the funnel does not reach to the very bottom.)

6 When the temperature in the jug has dropped sufficiently, a partial vacuum will be created that will suck the liquid coffee back down into the jug, leaving the spent grounds above.

7 Very carefully detach the bowl and funnel, placing it in the hole provided over a small drip tray in the frame.

8 Serve the coffee immediately, or pour it into a preheated vacuum flask (thermos) if it is not to be drunk within a few minutes of brewing.

ALL ABOUT ESPRESSO

The simplest and most accurate definition of espresso is "hot water being forced under pressure through very finely ground, dark-roasted coffee". The idea of using steam to propel the brewing water for coffee was the brainchild of a Frenchman, Louis Bernard Rabaut, in the early 1820s. Another Frenchman, Edward Loysel de Santais, used the same principle to produce a machine that could make larger amounts of coffee; he exhibited it at the Paris Exposition of 1855. In Italy, around the turn of the century, changes were made that enabled several

Below: Manual espresso pots come in a wide variety of shapes and sizes, convenient for individual use or by two or more people.

individual cups – instead of one large pot of coffee – to be brewed by steam pressure at a speed which gave rise to the name "espresso".

The improvements culminated in Luigi Bezzera's patented machine of 1902. Another milestone towards the perfection of the commercial espresso machine was Giovanni Achille Gaggia's 1948 use of a spring-powered piston to increase the amount of pressure on the brewing water, so that it no longer needed to be at such a high temperature, potentially scalding the coffee. Eventually the spring-powered pistons gave way to electric pumps, and today's *barista*, Italian barman, needs only to press a button to harness nine bars of pressure for a few sips of pure liquid energy.

Espresso *crema*

Making espresso to compare with that of a commercial machine is sometimes still beyond the limits of those espresso devices used domestically, many of which lack the capacity to produce that indication of espresso perfection, the *crema*. This is simply the light-brown foam on the espresso surface that results from the exact combination of fresh coffee and the correct degrees of grind, water temperature and pressure.

There are also definite differences between espresso made with a manual espresso pot and that produced by an electric domestic espresso machine. It is reassuring to remember, however, that probably 90 per cent of all Italian homes are still content to rely on the simple pot, which will never show signs of any *crema*, to provide the breakfast brew, consisting of half coffee and half milk, the latter heated in a saucepan. After a marathon midday Italian meal,

the same simple pot will brew the small cups of black "caffè" (as many Italians call an espresso) which provide caffeine stimulation while the human body is trying to concentrate on digestion. (In Italy, evening coffee is often taken in a bar or restaurant.)

Making cappuccino at home

Electric home espresso machines can cost a fair amount of money and still do not guarantee a commercial-type cup of espresso, *crema* included. As for cappuccino, even if the little electric machine is capable of frothing cold milk – and not all are – the number of cups of cappuccino that can be produced in succession is directly dependent on the steam power and the price tag.

For owners of espresso pots and electric machines incapable of steaming milk, it is worth remembering that some electric machines offer accessory devices for frothing milk, and there are separate machines available which only steam and froth milk. Some of the latter are electric and others, are made to produce steam on the stove-top.

Above: There are a number of devices capable of frothing milk for home users.

MANUAL ESPRESSO POTS

There are numerous manufacturers of manual espresso pots, which vary in size and materials of construction as well as in price, although most operate in exactly the same way. As an espresso pot must be used to its full capacity, buying the right size is probably the most important priority. Bear in mind that the smallest pots may not balance over an average-size gas burner, so an adapter frame may be necessary to make the pot stable.

For more than 60 years, the most popular and affordable brand has been the Moka Express, but these, unfortunately, are made of aluminium, which can interact with coffee acids, producing off-flavours, and they conduct heat so well that they can burn the coffee. More expensive and reassuringly heavier are those models made of stainless steel, but even so, a high price does not guarantee the best results. Certain stainless steel designer models are disastrous when it comes to usage, as the handles are not heat resistant and are red-hot if touched during or after brewing. The lids, as well as being too hot to touch, have no hinge and are too tight to remove easily, which is a problem if one wants to check the level of the coffee in the upper half of the pot.

Safety and Hygiene

A few safety and hygiene tips for the espresso pot include:
• Never leave an espresso pot unattended on a hot stove top.
• Never let an espresso pot remain on heat with no water in the bottom.
• Wash the espresso pot after every use.
• Check to make sure that the rubber seal underneath the upper half does not need replacing.
• Make sure the inside of the bottom chamber is thoroughly dry before storing it.

Using a manual espresso pot

1 To make coffee in an espresso pot, fill the lower chamber with fresh water up to the bottom of the safety valve.

2 Fill the filter funnel basket with very finely ground dark-roasted coffee, using the back and edge of a spoon to eliminate any possible air pockets in the coffee and any gaps around the rim of the basket.

3 The ground coffee should always be level with the top of the basket. (The coffee should be very slightly compressed and any space in the top of the coffee basket filled; this holds the water longer in the coffee grounds and prevents the coffee being too watery.)

4 Using your finger, remove any loose coffee grounds from the outside of the basket rim, and place the coffee basket into the top of the lower chamber.

5 Very firmly screw the top half of the pot on to the bottom, keeping the bottom chamber containing the water upright, to avoid wetting the coffee grounds too soon.

6 Place the espresso pot on low to medium heat. After the water boils, its steam will start to push the remainder of the water up the funnel and into the coffee.

7 Immediately reduce the heat to very low. (If the heat remains too high, the coffee liquid will be acidic and thin, as the water will have passed through it too quickly.)

8 When most of the water has left the lower chamber the bubbling sound will become more intermittent, and it is very important to remove the pot from the heat at this time. Wait for the bubbling to ease before serving.

Above: Stove-top manual espresso.

ELECTRIC DOMESTIC ESPRESSO MACHINES

Choosing an electric espresso machine for home use is not an easy matter, as there are many brands and the price range is wide. If money is no object, a few companies that make commercial machines offer models that are nearly more commercial than domestic. Sadly, only the most serious espresso lovers can justify paying several hundred pounds for this type of machine.

Looking at machines at a more average price level, the pump machines (not the piston) are the easiest to operate, although all may take some getting used to. Also, making espresso with an electric machine is always a bit messy, so it is a good idea to opt for the added accessory of a "knock-out"

drawer as a means of clearing the filter holder of used grounds. When making a choice, consider weight and solidity an indication of strength; if the apparatus for holding the coffee filter (the "group") feels lightweight, it may reflect the flimsiness of the metal used overall. The newer thermal block machines have the advantage of being quieter, but a common complaint is that they lack pressure; as this is a prime consideration, a wiser choice might be to go for a noisy machine with normal boiler-generated pressure.

The machines which are made to brew only a particular pre-packaged "pod" or cartridge of espresso coffee can provide a temptingly easy solution

to messy brewing, and worrying about the roast, the blend and the grind. The machine, however, is expensive and the cost of the coffee is also very high. Also, no real espresso lover wants to be tied to drinking the same coffee day after day, denied the opportunity to experiment with other tastes.

Another relatively recent addition is the filter holder with a valve that enables even cheaper machines to produce espresso with surface *crema* and good body. This is a very desirable feature, and obviously an important factor to consider when choosing a machine. Previously, the lack of *crema* highlighted the inferiority of a smaller machine to a commercial one.

Using electric espresso machines

1 To use an electric domestic espresso, follow the manufacturer's instructions, which, with most machines, will incorporate the following points. Assuming that the right roast and grind are being used, place a sufficient amount of water in the reservoir, and turn on the espresso machine.

2 Wait for a light to come on or go off indicating that steam is available, then decide on whether to brew one cup or two and, with the appropriate filter holder in place, use the "brew" mechanism to run some water through the filter to warm it.

3 Remove the filter holder, shaking out any water, and load it with espresso-grind coffee, allowing approximately 6g/1 tbsp per cup.

4 Press the coffee down evenly and firmly with the tamper supplied.

5 Clear any remaining coffee grounds from around the rim of the filter holder (or group). Position the filter holder under the water (brewing) aperture by holding the filter holder level, with the handle on the far left side (usually). Raise the filter holder to the brewing aperture until it feels securely in place.

6 Lock the filter holder into place by pulling the handle to the far right.

7 Place the cup(s) under the filter and press the brew button (with a valve-filter option), then open the valve by pulling the filter handle back to the left.

8 Stop the brew when the cups are slightly more than half-full (about 40ml/1$\frac{1}{2}$fl oz).

Below: Choose from a range of sugars; clockwise from back left: soft brown, demerara, dark muscovado, sugar cubes, cane sugar, caster (superfine) sugar.

Chocolate

In any form and any colour, chocolate provides a superb accompanying flavour for coffee, so much so that many coffee drinks include the word "mocha", which can imply a combination with chocolate. Also, as the Aztecs seem to have been the first chocolate drinkers, many coffee-chocolate recipes contain "Mexican" in their title. Powdered chocolate or cocoa powder (which is slightly bitter) can be sprinkled on top of any foamy, milky coffee surface. Chocolate syrup or melted chocolate of any type can be added to coffee to produce a happy combination. Chocolate mints or plain chocolate (milk, dark or white) wafers make a lovely garnish, as do chocolate-covered whole coffee beans.

Sugar

Sugar is an ingredient in many coffee drinks, not only to stabilize milk, but also to off-set the bitterness, which is almost always present to some degree in recipes using cold coffee. There are many types of sugar available, and a lot of people assume that one must be better for use in coffee than others.

Various sugars have different tastes depending on whether they are refined (all white sugars) or unrefined ("raw") cane sugar. Unrefined sugar has more flavour because of the molasses content, which varies from low in demerara to higher amounts in dark muscovado and darker soft brown sugar. Other brown sugars are made from white refined sugar to which molasses is added. The truth is that, like many aspects of coffee drinking, the choice of sugar is purely a matter of taste. Caster (superfine) sugar is excellent in recipes because it is quick-dissolving. Chunky rock

sugar crystals, marketed specifically for coffee, are simply lumps of amber-coloured refined (white) sugar. Used in small cups of espresso, which is not normally brewed at a particularly high temperature, rock sugar has little chance of dissolving before the coffee is consumed, and it contributes little flavour. It could therefore be considered a waste of time, although admittedly, it looks good in a sugar bowl.

Right: Chocolate powder and chocolate garnishes.

Essences and Flavourings

Vanilla, in the form of syrup, powder or even vanilla sugar, goes well with coffee. A drop of vanilla essence (extract) can convert an ordinary drink into an addictive elixir.

Many people consider cinnamon, either in the natural stick form, as an essence, or more commonly as a sprinkling powder, a suitable coffee accompaniment. Sometimes coffee concoctions containing cinnamon have the word "Viennese" somewhere in their title – these are not to be confused with coffee marketed in Britain as "Viennese style", which is normal coffee bulked out with no more than 4 per cent fig or fig seasoning. The addition of fig makes the blend less expensive, as well as altering the coffee taste slightly.

The early 1980s saw a widening of flavours considered suitable coffee companions with the development of "flavoured" coffees. Just after roasting, flavour concentrates in the form of oil or powder are mixed with the hot coffee beans to produce combinations of fruit, nut and liqueur tastes in the brewed coffee. These are still very popular, particularly in North America, and perhaps also with people who prefer another taste than that of coffee. They can, however, provide a welcome change or round off a special meal. Any coffee equipment which touches a flavoured coffee must be thoroughly washed and

Left: Adding a drop of essence (extract) or a flavouring can greatly change the taste of an ordinary coffee drink.

rinsed afterwards, as the flavourings can cling persistently and influence the taste of future brews adversely.

Just as all coffee is a matter of taste, there are no hard and fast rules concerning combinations of other flavours with that of coffee. Somehow the "gourmet" coffee craze which began in the United States has led to all sorts of taste combinations, many of which are obtained by the use of simple syrups, essences, or liqueurs, as well as the natural product itself. If a cold coffee recipe calls for milk or cream, as most do, a scoop of flavoured ice cream can be substituted (with amendments to the proportions, of course).

Above: Fruit and nuts make versatile flavourings and garnishes.

Left: Cinnamon sticks, nutmeg, star anise, and ground ginger all combine well with coffee.

as does mint, and a mint leaf or a dollop of whipped cream makes a lovely garnish.

Ginger, cardamom, cinnamon, nutmeg and cumin are spices which might be overlooked as coffee companions, but those flavours, if used in small proportions, provide a subtle difference to a coffee drink. The best way to add a ginger or nutmeg flavour is to grind small amounts of the fresh spice. A single cracked cardamom seed or a stick of cinnamon work particularly well in hot coffee drinks. A few cumin seeds or a sprinkle of ground cumin can provide a delicate undertone to a cold, milky coffee drink.

Fruit, Nuts and Spices

Fruit flavour possibilities include banana, blackcurrant, blueberry, cherry, coconut, lemon, orange, peach, pineapple, raspberry and strawberry. These can be combined with coffee in various ways, depending on the desired texture and length of the concoction. The use of a blender can provide a smooth mélange of coffee and fresh fruit. Alternatively, fruit pieces or slices can be used in the drink or as a garnish. Fruit syrups, concentrates and essences are easy ways of obtaining a coffee and fruit flavour mix.

Nuts seem to provide a more indisputably happy marriage with coffee, and the tastes of hazelnut, almond, pecan and even peanut, obtained from powders, essences (extracts), or the nuts themselves used as garnish, work very well in coffee drinks.

Caramel and maple are flavours that enhance coffee well,

Right: Alcohol and coffee have made many classic combinations.

Alcohol

Coffee and alcohol can be a delightful combination. In general, orange-based liqueurs, such as Cointreau, curaçao and orange-flavoured brandy, are wonderful coffee partners. "Normal" brandy, Armagnac, cognac, Calvados and poire each individually blend well with the flavour of coffee, as do grappa, marc and raki.

More individual tastes are achieved with Benedictine, Galliano, kirsch, Strega, Southern Comfort, crème de menthe, Drambuie, vodka, or, of course, the classic Caribbean standard, rum. Numerous variations on the established Irish coffee are possible with Scotch whiskey or American bourbon. In fact, used in the right proportions with usually quite strong coffee, there are few alcoholic beverages that would not make a suitable addition to a coffee-based concoction.

HOT NON-ALCOHOLIC DRINKS

Be it a classic cappuccino with snowy-white frothed milk on top or a Spanish combination of coffee and molasses, there can be nothing more enjoyable than a steaming hot cup of coffee on a cold winter's day.

Cappuccino

The classic espresso and milk drink.

SERVES TWO

INGREDIENTS
   160–250ml/generous 5–8fl oz/
   ¹/₂–1 cup very cold whole milk
   about 15g/¹/₂oz/2 tbsp dark-roast
   espresso finely-ground coffee
   chocolate or cocoa powder (optional)

1 Pour very cold milk into a metal jug or frothing device, steam until a fine, smooth foam has formed, and set aside.

2 Next, brew two cups of espresso into cappuccino or regular 150ml/6fl oz/
²/₃ cup coffee cups.

3 Pour the steamed milk over the coffee, holding back the froth with a spoon until last, when it can be spooned on to the surface.

4 The ideal cappuccino should be about one-third each espresso coffee, steamed milk and frothed milk. (After brewing the coffee you may need to re-steam the milk for just a moment if it has begun to "fall" or lose the froth.) If the milk has boiled or has been too aerated, throw the milk away and start again.

5 Top with a sprinkle of chocolate or cocoa powder, if desired.

Caffè Latte (Café au Lait)

The is a very basic breakfast drink, as served in homes and bars throughout Italy and France. It can be made with only a manual espresso pot and a saucepan to heat the milk.

SERVES TWO

INGREDIENTS
   2 parts espresso or very strong coffee
   6 parts boiled milk
   sugar (optional)
   steamed, frothed milk for
      topping (optional)

1 Pour the brewed coffee into glasses or large French coffee bowl. Add the hot milk and sugar, if using, and stir well.

2 Top each glass with a spoonful of steamed, frothed milk if desired.

VANILLA VARIATION

1 Pour 700ml/24fl oz/scant 3 cups milk into a saucepan. Add a vanilla pod and place over a low heat until hot. Set aside to infuse for about 10 minutes, then remove the vanilla pod.

2 Mix strong coffee with 500ml/ 16fl oz/2 cups milk in a large heatproof jug. Add sugar to taste.

3 Return the saucepan of milk to the heat and add 45ml/3 tbsp vanilla sugar. Bring to the boil, then reduce the heat. Add 115g/4 oz dark chocolate. Heat until melted. Pour the chocolate milk into the jug and whisk. Serve in tall mugs with whipped cream and a cinnamon stick.

Normandy Coffee

Normandy, like Washington State in the United States of America, is known for its apple orchards, and gives it name to many dishes made with apple juice or apple sauce. This recipe blends the flavour of apples with spices for a delicious, tangy coffee drink.

SERVES FOUR

INGREDIENTS

    475ml/16fl oz/2 cups strong black coffee (espresso strength, or filter/plunger brewed at 75g/ 13 tbsp/scant 1 cup coffee per 1 litre/33fl oz/4 cups of water)
    475ml/16fl oz/2 cups apple juice
    30ml/2 tbsp brown sugar, to taste
    3 oranges, thinly sliced
    2 small cinnamon sticks
    pinch of ground allspice
    pinch of ground cloves
    cinnamon stick, to serve

1 Bring all the ingredients to the boil over a moderate heat, then reduce the heat and simmer for 10 minutes.

COOK'S TIP

This recipe could be made into an alcoholic drink if one-fourth of the apple juice were replaced with Calvados, added when the heat is reduced to simmer in step 1. Do not allow the Calvados to boil.

2 Strain the liquid into a preheated flask or serving jug. Pour into cappuccino-style cups, adding a cinnamon stick to each, if you wish.

Georgia 'n Ginger

This is named after the US state of Georgia, famous for its peaches.

SERVES SIX

INGREDIENTS

    1 can (450–500g/1–1$^{1}\!/_{4}$lb) sliced peaches in syrup
    750ml/26fl oz/3 cups strong coffee
    120ml/4fl oz/$^{1}\!/_{2}$ cup whipping cream
    25ml/1$^{1}\!/_{2}$ tbsp brown sugar
    1.5ml/$^{1}\!/_{4}$ tsp ground cinnamon
    $^{1}\!/_{8}$ tsp (generous pinch) ground ginger
    zest of orange rind, to decorate

1 Drain the peaches, retaining the syrup. In a blender, process half of the coffee and the peaches for 1 minute.

2 In a clean bowl, whip the cream, taking care not to over whip.

3 Place 250ml/8fl oz/1 cup cold water, the sugar, cinnamon, ginger and peach syrup in a saucepan and bring to the boil over a moderate heat; reduce the heat and simmer for 1 minute.

4 Add the blended peaches and the remaining coffee to the pan and stir well. Serve topped with whipped cream and decorated with orange zest.

Mexican Coffee

The Aztec Indians were the first known chocolate addicts, and chocolate is an ingredient in many Mexican recipes. Combined with coffee, it makes a rich, smooth drink.

SERVES FOUR

INGREDIENTS
  30ml/2 tbsp chocolate syrup
  120ml/4fl oz/½ cup whipping cream
  1.5ml/¼ tsp ground cinnamon
  30ml/2 tbsp brown sugar
  pinch of ground nutmeg
  475ml/16fl oz/2 cups strong
    black coffee
  whipped cream and cinnamon
    shavings, to decorate

1 Whip together the chocolate syrup, cream, cinnamon, sugar and nutmeg.

2 Pour the hot coffee into the mixture and stir well, before dividing between four mugs. Top with a generous dollop of whipped cream and decorate with a few shavings of cinnamon.

COOK'S TIP
This recipe can be made with filter or plunger brewed coffee using 40g/ 7 tbsp/½ cup coffee per 475ml/16fl oz/ 2 cups of water, to taste.

Café de Olla

This recipe is traditionally brewed in large quantities over a wood fire in a heavy earthenware Mexican cooking pot, called an "olla".

SERVES FOUR

INGREDIENTS
  1 litre/33fl oz/4 cups water
  150g/5oz/⅔ cup dark
    brown sugar
  5ml/1 tsp molasses
  1 small cinnamon stick
  aniseeds (optional)
  50g/9 tbsp/⅔ cup darker-roasted
    coffee, medium grind

1 Place the water, sugar, molasses, cinnamon and aniseeds, if using, in a saucepan and slowly bring to the boil.

2 Stir thoroughly to dissolve the sugar and molasses.

3 When the mixture reaches boiling point, stir in the dry coffee, remove from the heat, cover, and steep for 5 minutes. Strain into earthenware mugs and serve immediately. Add a few of the aniseeds, if you wish.

COOK'S TIP
Use a French or Viennese roast coffee, dark but not as dark as that for espresso, so that the spice and molasses flavours aren't overwhelmed.

HOT ALCOHOLIC DRINKS

There are any number of combinations of alcohol with hot brewed coffee, some more successful than others. The following recipes include six of the classic mixes, and provide the perfect starting place for discovering your own personal favourite blends and flavours.

Jamaican Black Coffee

This delicious version of black coffee is only slightly alcoholic.

SERVES ABOUT EIGHT

INGREDIENTS
    1 lemon and 2 oranges, finely sliced
    1.5 litres/50fl oz/6¼ cups black coffee (filter/plunger brewed using 55g/10 tbsp/generous ²⁄₃ cup coffee per 1 litre/33fl oz/4 cup of water)
    45ml/3 tbsp rum
    85g/14 tbsp/⅓ cup caster (superfine) sugar
    8 lemon slices, for serving

1 Place the lemon and orange slices in a saucepan. Add the coffee and heat.

2 When the mixture is about to boil, pour in the rum and sugar, stirring well until the sugar is dissolved, and immediately remove from the heat.

3 While the coffee is still very hot, pour or ladle into glasses, and decorate with a lemon slice.

COOK'S TIP
This recipe uses hot normal-strength coffee. Any degree of roast is suitable, but a medium-to-darker roast will allow more perception of the citrus and rum flavours than would a dark roast.

French Toddy

This is a variation of a very old French recipe – said to have been a favourite of Flaubert – to which coffee and sugar have been added.

SERVES TWO

INGREDIENTS
    120ml/4fl oz/½ cup Calvados
    50ml/2fl oz/¼ cup apricot brandy
    20–30ml/4–6 tsp sugar, to taste
    300ml/10fl oz/1¼ cups very strong coffee (filter brewed at about 45g/ 8 tbsp/generous ½ cup coffee per 500ml/17fl oz/2 cups of water)
    25ml/1½ tbsp double (heavy) cream

1 Very gently warm the Calvados and brandy together over a low heat, and transfer to large balloon glasses.

2 Dissolve the sugar in the coffee and add to the liqueurs. Stir.

3 While the contents are still rotating from the stirring, pour the cream over the surface in a circular motion. Do not stir, just sip and savour.

COOK'S TIP
This French Toddy can be drunk without cream and/or with poire (pear *eau de vie*) substituted for the Calvados, if you would prefer.

Café à l'Orange

This is one of numerous drink possibilities in which the flavours of orange and coffee are combined.

SERVES FOUR

INGREDIENTS

120ml/4fl oz/½ cup whipping cream
30ml/2 tbsp icing
 (confectioner's) sugar
5ml/1 tsp orange zest
600ml/20fl oz/2½ cups hot coffee
150ml/5fl oz/⅔ cup any orange-
 flavoured liqueur, such as Grand
 Marnier, Filfar, Cointreau, triple sec
4 orange wedges, to decorate

1 In a clean bowl, whip the cream until stiff. Fold in the icing sugar and zest.

2 Chill for 30 minutes, or until the cream mixture is firm enough to hold a wedge of orange on top.

3 Divide the black coffee equally between tall glass mugs and stir about 30ml/2 tbsp of the liqueur into each. Top with chilled whipped cream and place an orange wedge on the cream. Serve immediately.

COOK'S TIP
The flavour of this drink will vary depending on which orange liqueur is used, as some are quite subtle.

Hot Mint Julep

Instead of a long cool sip on a shady Southern veranda, here the bourbon and mint are combined with coffee to produce something comforting for colder weather as well.

SERVES TWO

INGREDIENTS

100–150ml/4–5fl oz Bourbon
30ml/2 tbsp sugar
450ml/15fl oz/scant 2 cups hot
 strong black coffee
30ml/2 tbsp double (heavy) cream
2 sprigs mint leaf, to decorate

1 Put the bourbon and sugar into two warmed large wine glasses. Add the hot coffee and stir to dissolve the sugar.

2 Top with cream by pouring it over the back of a spoon. Do not stir. Decorate with the chopped mint leaf.

VARIATION
This simple recipe can be adapted for use with any one of the many different forms of alcohol available. For example, Southern Comfort or Wild Turkey will certainly add different flavour from that of ordinary bourbon.

Grasshopper Coffee

This drink is named for the crème de menthe flavour suggestive of a green grasshopper colour.

SERVES TWO

INGREDIENTS
dark and white chocolate "after-dinner" style chocolate mints
50ml/2fl oz/¼ cup green crème de menthe
50ml/2fl oz/¼ cup coffee liqueur, such as Tia Maria, Sangster's
350ml/12fl oz /1½ cups hot strong coffee
50ml/2fl oz/¼ cup whipping cream

1 Cut the dark and white chocolate mints diagonally in half.

2 Divide the two liqueurs equally between two tall, strong latte glasses. Combine well.

3 Fill each glass with the hot coffee and top them with whipped cream. Decorate with the chocolate mint triangles, dividing the white and dark chocolate evenly between the drinks.

COOK'S TIP
Use coffee strong enough so as not to taste watery or be too diluted by the liqueurs, though weaker than espresso.

Easy Café Brûlot

This is a traditional coffee drink from New Orleans, where all the ingredients except the coffee are heated by being "flamed" in a heat-proof bowl at the table; the flame is extinguished by pouring the coffee into the bowl. Except for the dramatic visual effects, this recipe achieves the same flavour with less fuss.

SERVES THREE TO FOUR

INGREDIENTS
80ml/3fl oz/6 tbsp brandy or rum
50ml/2fl oz/¼ cup Cointreau or other orange-flavoured liqueur
30ml/2 tbsp sugar
6–8 cloves
2 sticks cinnamon
1 strip of lemon peel and/or 1 strip of orange peel
700ml/24fl oz/3 cups strong hot coffee
cinnamon sticks and orange rind, to decorate (optional)

1 Gently heat the brandy or rum, Cointreau, sugar, cloves, cinnamon sticks and lemon or orange peel in a large saucepan. Stir continuously to dissolve the sugar.

2 Pour the black coffee, brewed at about 65g/11½ tbsp/¾ cup per 1 litre/ 33fl oz/4 cups of water by the filter or cafetière method, into the mixture. (A slightly darker-roast is best, as espresso would be too overwhelming.) Stir and serve, ladling the mixture into coffee cups. Garnish with a cinnamon stick and orange rind, if you wish.

COOK'S TIP
For greater visual impact, ignite the brandy mixture just before the coffee is added. Slowly add the coffee in a continuous stream, extinguishing the brandy mixture.

COLD NON-ALCOHOLIC DRINKS

Perhaps one reason for coffee's enduring popularity is its sheer versatility. Drunk cold, and mixed with a variety of flavourings, nothing could be more refreshing.

Coffee Milk-shake

This is a cold coffee drink that does not require an electric blender, as any closed container used as a shaker will work equally well.

SERVES TWO

INGREDIENTS

> 200ml/7fl oz/scant 1 cup chilled
> strong coffee (about 4 generous
> cups of espresso, or filter/plunger
> brewed using 70g/12 tbsp/generous
> ¾ cup coffee per 1 litre/33fl oz/
> 4 cups of water)
> 2 eggs, well-beaten
> 450ml/¾ pint/scant 2 cups cold milk
> 100ml/3½fl oz/½ cup single (light)
> or double (heavy) cream
> 15ml/1 tbsp sugar
> pinch of salt
> 4 drops of vanilla or almond
> essence (extract)
> ginger bisuits, crumbled, to decorate

1 Combine all the ingredients in a shaker or blender until well-mixed.

2 Serve at once, sprinkled with biscuit.

Coffee Frappé

Similar to a milk-shake, this frappé recipe is another long, cold coffee drink that is both refreshing and uplifting.

SERVES TWO

INGREDIENTS

> 450ml/15fl oz/scant 2 cups cold
> strong coffee (brewed using about
> 80g/14 tbsp/1 cup coffee per
> 1 litre/33 fl oz/4 cups of water)
> 8 drops vanilla essence (extract)
> 300ml/10fl oz/1¼ cups crushed ice
> 60ml/4 tbsp condensed milk
> whipped cream and sliced banana,
> to decorate (optional)

1 Add the cold brewed coffee to a large blender.

2 Next, add the vanilla essence (extract), crushed ice and condensed milk. Blend well until a smooth texture is obtained.

3 Pour into tall, clear glasses and stir in sugar to taste. Decorate with some whipped cream and banana slices, if you wish.

VARIATION

There are countless variations on the classic frappé. Any of the following essences would be suitable: try almond, banana, maple and peppermint.

Coffee Yogurt

This is really a variation on a "lassi", the refreshing yogurt drink of Indian restaurants. It can be made as either a sweet drink (traditionally with sugar and ground cinnamon) or salty (using salt and a little cumin).

SERVES TWO

INGREDIENTS
350ml/12fl oz/1 ½ cups cold black coffee (filter/plunger brewed using about 65g/11 ½ tbsp/³⁄4 cups coffee per 475ml/16fl oz/2 cups of water)
350ml/12fl oz/1 ½ cups natural (plain) yogurt
20ml/4 tsp sugar
a pinch of ground cinnamon, to taste

VARIATION
For a salty version, use 5ml/1 tsp salt and a pinch of ground cumin, instead of the cinnamon, possibly with some sugar to taste, if desired.

1 Combine all the ingredients in a blender. Mix until creamy.

2 Serve sprinkled with cinnamon.

Chilled Coffee Caribbean

Use coffee that is not too strong; filter coffee gives a clean, clear texture.

SERVES TWO

INGREDIENTS
600ml/20 fl oz/2 ½ cups strong filter coffee, cooled for about 20 minutes
½ orange and ½ lemon, thinly sliced
1 pineapple slice
sugar, to taste
1–2 drops Angostura bitters, optional
3 ice cubes per serving
slice of orange or lemon, to decorate

1 Add the cooled coffee to the fruit slices in a large bowl.

2 Stir and chill in the freezer for about 1 hour or until very cold.

3 Remove from the freezer and stir again. Remove the fruit slices from the liquid. Add sugar to taste, and stir in the bitters, if using.

4 Add three ice cubes per drink to tall glasses, or whisky tumblers, then pour over the chilled coffee drink. Decorate with a half-slice of orange or lemon on the rim or add to the drink, if preferred.

Granita di Caffè

This is basically coffee ice, or slush.
Makes just over 1 litre/33fl oz/4 cups.

SERVES FOUR

INGREDIENTS
200ml/7fl oz/scant 1 cup strong
   coffee (about 5 generous cups of
   espresso or filter/plunger brewed
   using 80g/14 tbsp/1 cup coffee per
   1 litre/33fl oz/4 cups of water)
400ml/14fl oz/1²/₃ cups water
140g/5oz/³/₄ cup sugar
2.5ml/¹/₂ tsp vanilla essence (extract)
   (optional)
1 egg white (optional)
120ml/4fl oz/¹/₂ cup whipped cream,
   to decorate

1 Pour the brewed coffee into a large
bowl or blender and set aside.

2 Boil half the water with the sugar,
stirring to dissolve the sugar. Place in
the refrigerator.

3 When the sugar syrup is cold, add it,
the remaining water, and the vanilla to
the coffee. Stir until well-blended.

4 If using, whisk the egg white and fold
it into the mixture; it will make the
granita much smoother.

5 Pour the mixture into a shallow
freezer-proof tin (pan), such as an ice
cube tray or baking tin (sheet), and
place in the freezer.

6 About every 30 minutes, break the
freezing mixture up with a fork to create
the traditional grainy shaved-ice
consistency. When it is well-frozen serve
it in individual cups, and top them with
a little whipped cream.

Coffee-chocolate Soda

This is a fun, refreshing drink that looks
as good as it tastes.

SERVES TWO

INGREDIENTS
250ml/8fl oz/1 cup strong cold
   coffee (4 espresso cups of coffee)
60ml/4 tbsp double (heavy) cream or
   30ml/2 tbsp evaporated milk
   (optional)
250ml/8fl oz/1 cup cold soda water
2 scoops chocolate ice cream
chocolate-covered coffee beans,
   roughly chopped, to decorate

1 Pour the coffee into tall glasses. Add
the cream or evaporated milk if desired.

2 Add the soda water and stir. Gently
place a scoop of ice cream into the
mixture. Decorate with some of the
roughly chopped chocolate-covered
coffee beans. Serve with a long spoon
or a straw.

VARIATION

Try also chocolate mint, vanilla,
hazelnut or banana ice cream and
sprinkle with chocolate shavings, fruit
slices or even a few roughly chopped
up pieces of hazelnut.

COLD ALCOHOLIC DRINKS

Chilled and served in pretty glasses, coffee and alcohol make delicious and simple desserts.

Coffee Egg Nog

This is a rather special coffee drink, particularly suitable for daytime summer holiday festivities.

SERVES SIX TO EIGHT

INGREDIENTS
8 eggs, separated
225g/8oz/generous 1 cup sugar
250ml/8fl oz/1 cup cold strong coffee (espresso strength or filter/ plunger brewed at 75g/13 tbsp/ scant 1 cup coffee per 1 litre/ 33fl oz/4 cups of water)
220ml/7½fl oz/scant 1 cup whisky, Bourbon, rum or brandy, or combination of these
220ml/7½fl oz/scant 1 cup cold double (heavy) cream
120ml/4fl oz/½ cup whipped cream
ground nutmeg, to decorate

1 In a clean bowl, thoroughly beat the egg yolks, then slowly add the sugar, mixing well.

2 Place in a large saucepan, and heat gently over a low heat, stirring all the time with a wooden spoon.

3 Remove the saucepan from the heat, allow to cool a few minutes, stir in the coffee and whisky, and then slowly add the cream, stirring well.

4 Beat the egg whites until stiff and stir into the egg nog, mixing well. Pour into punch (small round) cups, top each with a small dollop of whipped cream and sprinkle nutmeg on top.

COOK'S TIP
Use a little more sugar, if necessary, to avoid the cream and alcohol separating and curdling.

African Coffee

In parts of Africa, coffee is often drunk with condensed milk. This recipe is an adaptation of an African brew with a luxurious liqueur finish.

SERVES ONE

INGREDIENTS
250ml/8fl oz/1 cup strong coffee (4 generous *espressi* or cafetière coffee brewed using 70g/ 12 tbsp/generous ¾ cup coffee per 1 litre/33fl oz/4 cups of water)
40ml/8 tsp condensed milk
20ml/4 tsp crème de cacao
ice cubes, to serve, optional

1 Add the coffee, condensed milk and liqueur to a shaker and mix well.

COOK'S TIP
Other chocolate- and coconut-based liqueurs, such as Malibu, work equally well in this recipe.

2 Serve over ice-cubes in tall glasses.

Caffè Vermouth

Vermouth is not an obvious choice to partner coffee, but the resulting flavour is good; different and sophisticated. Use a little less if unsure of the flavour.

SERVES TWO

INGREDIENTS
    120ml/4fl oz/$\frac{1}{2}$ cup red vermouth
    60ml/4 tbsp very strong cold
       coffee (espresso strength or filter/
       plunger brewed at 75g/13 tbsp/
       scant 1 cup coffee per 1 litre/
       33fl oz/4 cups of water)
    250ml/8fl oz/1 cup milk
    30ml/2 tbsp crushed ice
    10ml/2 tsp sugar
    coffee beans, to decorate

COOK'S TIP
This is another combination in which the milk product may have a tendency to separate in some cases. The use of a slightly higher sugar content can prevent this.

1 In a cocktail shaker, combine all the ingredients and shake well.

2 Serve immediately in cocktail glasses or glass tumblers. Decorate with a few roasted coffee beans.

VARIATION
Different flavours and textures can be obtained by varying the type of milk used, or by using a little cream instead of milk for a richer version.

Lisbon Flip Coffee

Here the coffee is not so much a main ingredient; rather it provides a flavourful undertone in an interesting and satisfying cocktail.

SERVES TWO

INGREDIENTS
    120ml/4fl oz/$\frac{1}{2}$ cup port
    45ml/3 tbsp curaçao
    20ml/4 tsp very strong coffee
    10ml/2 tsp icing (confectioner's) sugar
    2 eggs
    20ml/4 tsp condensed milk
    60ml/4 tbsp crushed ice
    grated chocolate and orange rind
       shavings, to decorate

1 Place all the ingredients in a cocktail shaker, including the crushed ice.

2 Shake vigorously and serve immediately in cocktail glasses. Top with the finely grated chocolate and orange rind.

COOK'S TIPS
• To make this drink, espresso ristretto is the strength required.
• Most orange-based liqueurs, such as Grand Marnier, Cointreau, Orange Nassau and triple sec, could be used in place of the curaçao, if not available.

Coffee Colada

This coffee cocktail is a riot of bold Caribbean flavours. A jug can be made up a couple of hours in advance, then allowed to partially freeze, like a frozen margarita, before topping with plenty of whipped cream.

SERVES FOUR

INGREDIENTS

450ml/15fl oz/scant 2 cups cold,
 very strong coffee (filter or cafetière
 brewed using 80g/14 tbsp/1 cup
 coffee per 1 litre/33fl oz/4 cups
 of water)
50ml/2fl oz/¼ cup tequila
 (or white rum)
50ml/2fl oz/¼ cup Malibu
100ml/3½fl oz/½ cup cream
 of coconut
2.5ml/½ tsp vanilla essence (extract)
350ml/12fl oz/1½ cups crushed ice
60ml/4 tbsp whipped cream and
 toasted coconut shavings,
 to decorate

1 In a blender, combine all the ingredients and blend on high.

2 Serve in tall wine glasses.

3 Decorate with whipped cream, and top with toasted coconut shavings.

Coffee Cognac Cooler

This drink is unabashedly decadent – not for those counting calories!

SERVES TWO

INGREDIENTS

250ml/8fl oz/1 cup cold strong
 darker-roast coffee
80ml/3fl oz/6 tbsp cognac or brandy
50ml/2fl oz/¼ cup coffee liqueur
50ml/2fl oz/¼ cup double cream
10ml/2 tsp sugar
250ml/8fl oz/1 cup crushed ice
2 scoops coffee ice cream
 chocolate shavings, to decorate

1 Shake or blend all the ingredients except the ice cream together.

2 Pour into tall glasses and gently add a scoop of ice cream to each. Decorate with chocolate shavings and serve with a long-handled spoon.

COOK'S TIP

The coffee liqueur can be either a cream-based one, such as Kahlua, or a non-cream based liqueur, such as Tia Maria.

THE
RECIPES

This section contains over 70 recipes presented in a beautifully

illustrated step-by-step format. All the classic coffee recipes are

included, such as Tiramisu, Coffee Coeurs `a la Crème, Mocha

Sponge Cake and Cappuccino Torte. There are also recipes for

all occasions, from fruit and frozen desserts, sumptuous tortes,

rich pies and pastries and irresistible biscuits and breads.

All of the recipes demonstrate just how versatile an ingredient

coffee is; it combines effortlessly with so many other flavours,

such as alcohol, fruit, chocolate and cream. Always use good-

quality coffee, and experimenting with coffees from around the

world will make each dish a delicious culinary adventure.

CREAM DESSERTS AND HOT PUDDINGS

*Smooth creamy custards form the
base of many cold desserts, such as
Coffee Crème Caramel and Petits
Pots de Cappuccino, as well as hot
ones such as Apricot Panettone
Pudding. Served in tall elegant
glasses, light airy mousses feature
frequently among the most
memorable desserts. Many are also
blissfully simple; such as Coffee
Cardamom Zabaglione and
Chocolate and Espresso Mousse.*

CLASSIC COFFEE CRÈME CARAMEL

THESE LIGHTLY SET COFFEE CUSTARDS ARE SERVED IN A POOL OF CARAMEL SAUCE. FOR A RICHER FLAVOUR, MAKE THEM WITH HALF SINGLE CREAM, HALF MILK.

SERVES SIX

INGREDIENTS
   600ml/1 pint/2½ cups milk
   45ml/3 tbsp ground coffee
   50g/2oz/¼ cup caster sugar
   4 eggs
   4 egg yolks
   spun sugar, to decorate (optional)
For the caramel sauce
   150g/5oz/¾ cup caster sugar
   60ml/4 tbsp water

1 Preheat the oven to 160°C/325°F/Gas 3. To make the caramel sauce, gently heat the sugar in a small heavy-based pan with the water, until the sugar has dissolved. Bring to the boil and boil rapidly until the syrup turns a rich golden brown.

5 Put the ramekins in a roasting tin and pour in enough hot water to come two-thirds of the way up the sides of the dishes. Bake for 30–35 minutes or until just set. Test by gently shaking one of the custards; it should wobble like a jelly. Remove the custards from the hot water and leave to cool.

6 Chill the coffee custards for at least 3 hours. To turn out, carefully loosen the sides with a palette knife then invert on to serving plates. Decorate with spun sugar, if using.

COOK'S TIP
To make spun sugar, gently heat 75g/3oz/scant ½ cup caster sugar, 5ml/1 tsp liquid glucose and 30ml/2 tbsp water in a heavy-based pan until the sugar dissolves. Boil the syrup to 160°C/325°F, then briefly dip the base of the pan into cold water. Put a sheet of greaseproof paper on the work surface to protect it. Holding two forks together, dip them into the syrup and flick them rapidly backwards and forwards over an oiled rolling pin. Store in an airtight container until ready to use.

2 Quickly and carefully, pour the hot syrup into six warmed 150ml/¼ pint/⅔ cup ramekins.

3 To make the coffee custard, heat the milk until almost boiling. Pour over the ground coffee and leave to infuse for about 5 minutes. Strain through a fine sieve into a jug.

4 In a bowl, whisk the caster sugar, eggs and yolks until light and creamy. Whisk the coffee-flavoured milk into the egg mixture. Pour into the ramekins.

TIRAMISU

THE NAME OF THIS CLASSIC DESSERT TRANSLATES AS "PICK ME UP", WHICH IS SAID TO DERIVE FROM THE FACT THAT IT IS SO GOOD THAT IT LITERALLY MAKES YOU SWOON WHEN YOU EAT IT.

SERVES FOUR

INGREDIENTS
    225g/8oz/1 cup mascarpone
    25g/1oz/¼ cup icing sugar, sifted
    150ml/¼ pint/⅔ cup strong brewed
        coffee, chilled
    300ml/½ pint/1¼ cups double cream
    45ml/3 tbsp coffee liqueur such as
        Tia Maria, Kahlúa or Toussaint
    115g/4oz Savoiardi (sponge
        finger) biscuits
    50g/2oz bittersweet or plain
        chocolate, coarsely grated
    cocoa powder, for dusting

1 Lightly grease and line a 900g/2lb loaf tin with clear film. Put the mascarpone and icing sugar in a large bowl and beat for 1 minute. Stir in 30ml/2 tbsp of the chilled coffee. Mix thoroughly.

2 Whip the cream with 15ml/1 tbsp of the liqueur until it forms soft peaks. Stir a spoonful into the mascarpone mixture, then fold in the rest. Spoon half the mascarpone mixture into the loaf tin and smooth the top.

3 Put the remaining strong brewed coffee and liqueur in a shallow dish just wider than the Savoiardi biscuits. Using half the biscuits, dip one side of each biscuit into the coffee mixture, then arrange on top of the mascarpone mixture in a single layer.

4 Spoon the rest of the mascarpone mixture over the biscuit layer and smooth the top.

5 Dip the remaining biscuits in the coffee mixture, and arrange on top. Drizzle any remaining coffee mixture over the top. Cover the dish with clear film and chill for at least 4 hours. Carefully turn the tiramisu out of the loaf tin and sprinkle with grated chocolate and cocoa powder; serve cut into slices.

COOK'S TIP
Mascarpone is a silky-textured, soft, thick cream cheese, originally from Lombardy, and made with cows' milk.

COFFEE CARDAMOM ZABAGLIONE

THIS WARM ITALIAN DESSERT IS USUALLY MADE WITH ITALIAN MARSALA WINE. IN THIS RECIPE COFFEE LIQUEUR IS USED ALONG WITH FRESHLY CRUSHED CARDAMOM.

SERVES FOUR

INGREDIENTS
    4 cardamom pods
    8 egg yolks
    50g/2oz/4 tbsp golden caster sugar
    30ml/2 tbsp strong brewed coffee
    50ml/2fl oz/¼ cup coffee liqueur
        such as Tia Maria, Kahlúa
        or Toussaint
    a few crushed roasted coffee beans,
        to decorate

1 Peel away the pale green outer husks from the cardamom pods and remove the black seeds. Crush these to a fine powder using a pestle and mortar.

2 Put the egg yolks, caster sugar and crushed cardamom seeds in a large bowl and whisk with an electric hand whisk for 1–2 minutes, or until the mixture is pale and creamy.

3 Gradually whisk the coffee and the liqueur into the egg yolk mixture.

4 Place the bowl over a saucepan of near-boiling water and continue whisking for about 10 minutes.

5 Continue whisking until the mixture is very thick and fluffy and has doubled in volume, making sure the water doesn't boil – if it does the mixture will curdle. Remove the bowl from the heat and carefully pour the zabaglione into four warmed glasses or dishes. Sprinkle with a few crushed roasted coffee beans and serve immediately.

COOK'S TIP
Cardamom is a fragrant spice from northern India. It may be bought ready-ground, but freshly crushed cardamom is much sweeter.

PETITS POTS DE CAPPUCCINO

THESE VERY RICH COFFEE CUSTARDS, WITH A CREAM TOPPING AND A LIGHT DUSTING OF DRINKING CHOCOLATE, LOOK WONDERFUL PRESENTED IN FINE CHINA COFFEE CUPS.

SERVES SIX TO EIGHT

INGREDIENTS
75g/3oz/1 cup roasted coffee beans
300ml/½ pint/1¼ cups milk
300ml/½ pint/1¼ cups single cream
1 whole egg
4 egg yolks
50g/2oz/4 tbsp caster sugar
2.5ml/½ tsp vanilla extract
For the topping
120ml/4fl oz/½ cup whipping cream
45ml/3 tbsp iced water
10ml/2 tsp drinking chocolate

1 Preheat the oven to 160°C/325°F/ Gas 3. Put the roasted coffee beans in a saucepan over a low heat for about 3 minutes, shaking the pan frequently.

2 Pour the milk and cream over the beans. Heat until almost boiling; cover and leave to infuse for 30 minutes.

3 Whisk the egg, the egg yolks, sugar and vanilla together. Return the milk to boiling and pour through a sieve on to the egg mixture. Discard the beans.

4 Pour the mixture into eight 75ml/ 5 tbsp coffee cups or six 120ml/4fl oz/ ½ cup ramekins. Cover each with a small piece of foil.

5 Put in a roasting tin with hot water reaching about two-thirds of the way up the sides of the dishes. Bake them for 30–35 minutes, or until lightly set. Let cool. Chill in the fridge for at least 2 hours.

6 Whisk the whipping cream and iced water until thick and frothy and spoon on top of the custards. Dust with drinking chocolate before serving.

COOK'S TIPS
These petits pots may also be served warm, topped with a spoonful of clotted cream. Serve straight away, with the clotted cream just starting to melt.

COFFEE AND BRANDY SYLLABUB

THIS HEAVENLY DESSERT COULDN'T BE EASIER — A FROTH OF WHIPPED COFFEE AND BRANDY CREAM TOPS JUICY GRAPES. CRISP BISCUITS ARE A DELICIOUS CONTRAST.

SERVES SIX

INGREDIENTS
  75g/3oz/6 tbsp soft light
    brown sugar
  finely grated rind of ½ orange
  120ml/4fl oz/½ cup brandy
  120ml/4fl oz/½ cup cold strong
    brewed coffee
  400ml/14fl oz/1⅔ cups double cream
  225g/8oz white seedless grapes
  sugared grapes, to decorate
  crisp biscuits, to serve

COOK'S TIP
For sugared grapes, wash and dry the
fruit, then snip into small clusters. Use
a fine brush to paint lightly beaten egg
white evenly on to the grapes, then dust
with caster sugar. Shake off excess sugar
and leave to dry before using.

1 Put the brown sugar, orange rind and
brandy into a small bowl. Stir well, then
cover with clear film and leave to stand
for 1 hour.

2 Strain the mixture through a fine
sieve into a clean bowl. Stir in the
coffee. Slowly pour in the cream,
whisking all the time.

3 Continue whisking for 3–4 minutes,
until the mixture thickens enough to
stand in soft peaks.

4 Divide the grapes between the glasses.
Pour or spoon the syllabub over the grapes.
Chill in the fridge for 1 hour. Decorate the
glasses with clusters of sugared grapes
and serve with crisp biscuits.

COFFEE JELLIES

SERVE THESE SPARKLING COFFEE JELLIES AS A LIGHT AND REFRESHING END TO A RICH MEAL.

SERVES FOUR

INGREDIENTS
  20ml/4 tsp powdered gelatine
  75ml/5 tbsp cold water
  600ml/1 pint/2½ cups very hot strong
    brewed coffee
  40g/1½oz/3 tbsp caster sugar
For the bay cream
  300ml/½ pint/1¼ cups
    whipping cream
  15ml/1 tbsp bay-scented caster sugar
  fresh bay leaves, to decorate

VARIATION
For a creamy version of these jellies,
make the coffee with hot milk and serve
with fresh fruit instead of bay cream.

COOK'S TIP
To make bay-scented caster sugar, add
2–3 dried bay leaves to caster sugar.
Leave for at least a week before using.

1 To make the jellies, sprinkle the
gelatine over the cold water. Leave to
soak for 2–3 minutes. Add to the hot
strong brewed coffee with the sugar and
stir to dissolve.

2 Allow the coffee to cool, then pour
into four 150ml/¼ pint/⅔ cup metal
moulds. Chill in the fridge for 3 hours or
until set.

3 To make the bay cream, lightly whisk
the cream and bay scented caster sugar
until very soft peaks form. Spoon into a
serving bowl.

4 To serve, dip the moulds in a bowl of
hot water for a few seconds, then invert
on to individual serving plates. Serve
with the bay cream and decorate with
fresh bay leaves.

COFFEE COEUR À LA CRÈME

THESE PRETTY HEART-SHAPED CREAMS, SPECKLED WITH ESPRESSO-ROASTED COFFEE BEANS, ARE SERVED WITH A FRESH FRUIT SAUCE. USE WILD STRAWBERRIES, IF AVAILABLE, FOR THEIR WONDERFUL PERFUME.

SERVES SIX

INGREDIENTS

    25g/1oz/generous ¼ cup espresso-
      roasted coffee beans
    225g/8oz/1 cup ricotta or
      curd cheese
    300ml/½ pint/1¼ cups crème fraîche
    25g/1oz/2 tbsp caster sugar
    finely grated rind of ½ orange
    2 egg whites
For the red fruit coulis
    175g/6oz/1 cup raspberries
    30ml/2 tbsp icing sugar, sifted
    115g/4oz/⅔ cup small strawberries,
      (or wild ones, if available), halved

1 Preheat the oven to 180°C/350°F/ Gas 4. Evenly spread the espresso-roasted coffee beans on to a baking sheet and toast for about 10 minutes. Allow to cool, then put in a large plastic bag and crush into tiny pieces with a rolling pin.

2 Thoroughly rinse 12 pieces of muslin in cold water and squeeze dry. Use to line six coeur à la crème moulds with a double layer, allowing the muslin to overhang the edges.

3 Press the ricotta or curd cheese through a fine sieve into a bowl. Stir the crème fraîche, sugar, orange rind and crushed roasted coffee beans together. Add to the cheese and mix well.

4 Whisk the egg whites until stiff and fold into the mixture. Spoon into the prepared moulds, then bring the muslin up and over the filling. Leave in the fridge overnight to drain and chill.

5 To make the red fruit coulis, put the raspberries and icing sugar in a food processor and blend until smooth. Push through a fine sieve to remove the pips. Stir in the strawberries. Chill until ready to serve.

6 Unmould the hearts on to individual serving plates and carefully remove the muslin. Spoon the red fruit coulis over before serving.

COOK'S TIP
Muslin has a fine weave which allows the liquid from the cheese to drain through. If you haven't got any muslin, use a new all-purpose disposable cloth instead.

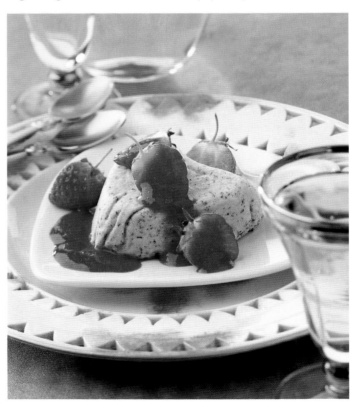

CHILLED CHOCOLATE AND ESPRESSO MOUSSE

HEADY, AROMATIC ESPRESSO COFFEE ADDS A DISTINCTIVE FLAVOUR TO THIS SMOOTH, RICH MOUSSE.
SERVE IT IN STYLISH CHOCOLATE CUPS FOR A SPECIAL OCCASION.

SERVES FOUR

INGREDIENTS
225g/8oz plain chocolate
45ml/3 tbsp brewed espresso
25g/1oz/2 tbsp unsalted butter
4 eggs, separated
sprigs of fresh mint,
 to decorate (optional)
mascarpone or clotted cream,
 to serve (optional)
For the chocolate cups
225g/8oz plain chocolate

1 For each chocolate cup, cut a double thickness 15cm/6in square of foil. Mould it around a small orange, leaving the edges and corners loose to make a cup shape. Remove the orange and press the bottom of the foil case gently on a surface to make a flat base. Repeat to make four foil cups.

2 Break the plain chocolate into small pieces and place in a bowl set over a pan of very hot water. Stir occasionally until the chocolate has melted.

3 Spoon the chocolate into the foil cups, spreading it up the sides with the back of a spoon to give a ragged edge. Refrigerate for 30 minutes or until set hard. Gently peel away the foil, starting at the top edge.

4 To make the chocolate mousse, put the plain chocolate and brewed espresso into a bowl set over a pan of hot water and melt as before. When it is smooth and liquid, add the unsalted butter, a little at a time. Remove the pan from the heat then stir in the egg yolks.

5 Whisk the egg whites in a bowl until stiff, but not dry, then fold them into the chocolate mixture. Pour into a bowl and refrigerate for at least 3 hours.

6 To serve, scoop the chilled mousse into the chocolate cups. Add a scoop of mascarpone or clotted cream and decorate with a sprig of fresh mint, if you wish.

APRICOT PANETTONE PUDDING

SLICES OF LIGHT-TEXTURED PANETTONE ARE LAYERED WITH DRIED APRICOTS AND COOKED IN A CREAMY COFFEE CUSTARD FOR A SATISFYINGLY WARMING DESSERT.

SERVES FOUR

INGREDIENTS

50g/2oz/4 tbsp unsalted
   butter, softened
6 x 1cm/½in thick slices (about
   400g/14oz) panettone containing
   candied fruit
175g/6oz/¾ cup ready-to-eat dried
   apricots, chopped
400ml/14fl oz/1⅔ cups milk
250ml/8fl oz/1 cup double cream
60ml/4 tbsp mild-flavoured
   ground coffee
90g/3½oz/½ cup caster sugar
3 eggs
30ml/2 tbsp demerara sugar
pouring cream or crème fraîche,
   to serve

1 Preheat the oven to 160°C/325°F/ Gas 3. Brush a 2 litre/3½ pint/8 cup oval baking dish with 15g/½oz/1 tbsp of the butter. Spread the panettone with the remaining butter and arrange in the baking dish. Cut to fit and scatter the apricots among and over the layers.

2 Pour the milk and cream into a pan and heat until almost boiling. Pour the milk mixture over the coffee and leave to infuse for 10 minutes. Strain through a fine sieve, discarding the coffee grounds.

3 Lightly beat the caster sugar and eggs together, then whisk in the warm coffee-flavoured milk. Slowly pour the mixture over the panettone. Leave to soak for 15 minutes.

4 Sprinkle the top of the pudding with demerara sugar and place the dish in a large roasting tin. Pour in enough boiling water to come halfway up the sides of the baking dish.

5 Bake for 40–45 minutes until the top is golden and crusty, but the middle still slightly wobbly. Remove from the oven, but leave the dish in the hot water for 10 minutes. Serve warm with pouring cream or crème fraîche.

COOK'S TIP
This recipe works equally well with plain or chocolate-flavoured panettone.

STICKY COFFEE AND GINGER PUDDING

THIS COFFEE-CAPPED FEATHER-LIGHT SPONGE IS MADE WITH BREADCRUMBS AND GROUND ALMONDS.
SERVE WITH CREAMY CUSTARD OR SCOOPS OF VANILLA ICE CREAM.

SERVES FOUR

INGREDIENTS
- 30ml/2 tbsp soft light brown sugar
- 25g/1oz/2 tbsp stem ginger, chopped
- 30ml/2 tbsp mild-flavoured
  ground coffee
- 75ml/5 tbsp stem ginger syrup (from
  a jar of stem ginger)
- 115g/4oz/generous ½ cup
  caster sugar
- 3 eggs, separated
- 25g/1oz/¼ cup plain flour
- 5ml/1 tsp ground ginger
- 65g/2½oz/generous 1 cup fresh
  white breadcrumbs
- 25g/1oz/¼ cup ground almonds

1 Preheat the oven to 180°C/350°F/
Gas 4. Grease and line the base of a
750ml/1¼ pint/3 cup pudding basin,
then sprinkle in the soft light brown
sugar and chopped stem ginger.

2 Put the ground coffee in a small
bowl. Heat the ginger syrup until almost
boiling; pour into the coffee. Stir well
and leave for 4 minutes. Pour through
a fine sieve into the pudding basin.

3 Beat half the caster sugar and egg
yolks until light and fluffy. Sift the flour
and ground ginger together and fold
into the egg mixture with the
breadcrumbs and ground almonds.

4 Whisk the egg whites until stiff, then
gradually whisk in the remaining caster
sugar. Fold into the mixture, half at a
time. Spoon into the pudding basin and
smooth the top.

5 Cover the basin with a piece of
pleated greased greaseproof paper and
secure with string. Bake for 40 minutes,
or until the sponge is firm to the touch.
Turn out and serve immediately.

COOK'S TIP
This pudding can also be baked in a
900ml/1½ pint/3¾ cup loaf tin and
served thickly sliced.

SOUFFLES

AND

MERINGUES

Fluffy soufflés that rise to the occasion and melt-in-the-mouth meringues — these are coffee desserts to tempt your eye and your palate. The basic ingredients for meringues couldn't be simpler — just egg whites and sugar, to which coffee lends a sophisticated touch. For the perfect finish to a meal, try spicy Floating Islands, or the tropical taste of Mango and Coffee Meringue Roll.

CHILLED COFFEE AND PRALINE SOUFFLÉ

A SMOOTH COFFEE SOUFFLÉ WITH A CRUSHED PRALINE TOPPING THAT IS SPECTACULAR AND EASY.

<u>SERVES SIX</u>

INGREDIENTS
150g/5oz/¾ cup caster sugar
75ml/5 tbsp water
150g/5oz/generous 1 cup blanched
    almonds, plus extra, for decoration
120ml/4fl oz/½ cup strong brewed
    coffee, e.g. hazelnut-flavoured
15ml/1 tbsp powdered gelatine
3 eggs, separated
75g/3oz/scant ½ cup soft light
    brown sugar
15ml/1 tbsp coffee liqueur, such as
    Tia Maria, Kahlúa or Toussaint
150ml/¼ pint/⅔ cup double cream
about 150ml/¼ pint/⅔ cup double
    cream, for decoration (optional)

1 Cut a paper collar from a double
layer of greaseproof paper, 5cm/2in
deeper than a 900ml/1½ pint/3¾ cup
soufflé dish. Wrap around the dish and
tie in place with string. Refrigerate.

2 Oil a baking sheet. Put the caster
sugar in a small heavy-based pan with
the water and heat gently until the
sugar dissolves. Boil rapidly until the
syrup becomes pale golden. Add the
almonds and boil until dark golden.

3 Pour the mixture on to the baking
sheet and leave to set. When hard,
transfer to a plastic bag and break into
pieces with a rolling pin. Reserve 50g/
2oz/½ cup and crush the remainder.

4 Pour half the coffee into a small bowl;
sprinkle over the gelatine. Leave to soak
for 5 minutes, then place the bowl over
a pan of hot water; stir until dissolved.

5 Put the egg yolks, soft light brown
sugar, remaining coffee and liqueur in
a bowl over a pan of simmering water.
Whisk until thick and foamy, then whisk
in the dissolved gelatine.

6 Whip the cream until soft peaks form,
then whisk the egg whites until stiff.
Fold the crushed praline into the cream,
then fold into the coffee mixture. Finally,
fold in the egg whites, half at a time.

7 Spoon into the soufflé dish and
smooth the top; chill for at least 2 hours
or until set. Put in the freezer for
15–20 minutes before serving. Remove
the paper collar by running a warmed
palette knife between the set soufflé
and the paper. Whisk the cream for
decoration, if using, and place large
spoonfuls on top. Decorate with the
reserved praline pieces and whole
blanched almonds.

TWICE-BAKED MOCHA SOUFFLÉ

*THE PERFECT WAY TO END A MEAL, THESE MINI MOCHA SOUFFLÉS CAN BE MADE UP TO 3 HOURS
AHEAD, THEN REHEATED JUST BEFORE YOU SERVE THEM.*

SERVES SIX

INGREDIENTS
  75g/3oz/6 tbsp unsalted
    butter, softened
  90g/3½ oz bittersweet or
    plain chocolate, grated
  30ml/2 tbsp ground coffee
  400ml/14fl oz/1⅔ cup milk
  40g/1½oz/⅓ cup plain flour, sifted
  15g/½ oz/2 tbsp cocoa, sifted
  3 eggs, separated
  50g/2oz/¼ cup caster sugar
  175ml/6fl oz/¾ cup creamy
    chocolate or coffee liqueur, such as
    Crème de Caçao, Sheridans

1 Preheat the oven to 200°C/400°F/
Gas 6. Thickly brush six 150ml/¼ pint/
⅔ cup dariole moulds or mini pudding
basins with 25g/1oz/2 tbsp of the butter.
Coat with 50g/2oz of the grated chocolate.

2 Put the ground coffee in a small bowl.
Heat the milk until almost boiling and pour
over the coffee. Infuse for 4 minutes
and strain, discarding the grounds.

3 Melt the remaining butter in a small
pan. Stir in the flour and cocoa to make
a roux. Cook for about 1 minute, then
gradually add the coffee milk, stirring
all the time to make a very thick sauce.
Simmer for 2 minutes. Remove from the
heat and stir in the egg yolks.

VARIATION
Good quality white or milk cooking
chocolate can be use instead of plain,
if preferred.

4 Cool for 5 minutes, then stir in the
remaining chocolate. Whisk the egg
whites until stiff, then gradually whisk
in the sugar. Stir half into the sauce to
loosen, then fold in the remainder.

5 Spoon the mixture into the dariole
moulds and place in a roasting tin. Pour
in enough hot water to come two-thirds
of the way up the sides of the tins.

6 Bake the soufflés for 15 minutes.
Turn them out on to a baking tray and
leave to cool completely.

7 Before serving, spoon 15ml/1 tbsp
chocolate or coffee liqueur over each
pudding and reheat in the oven for
6–7 minutes. Serve on individual plates
with the remaining liqueur poured over.

CLASSIC CHOCOLATE AND COFFEE ROULADE

THIS RICH, SQUIDGY CHOCOLATE ROLL SHOULD BE MADE AT LEAST 12 HOURS BEFORE SERVING, TO ALLOW IT TO SOFTEN. EXPECT THE ROULADE TO CRACK A LITTLE WHEN YOU ROLL IT UP.

SERVES EIGHT

INGREDIENTS
    200g/7oz plain chocolate
    200g/7oz/1 cup caster sugar
    7 eggs, separated
For the filling
    300ml/½ pint/1¼ cups double cream
    30ml/2 tbsp cold strong brewed
        coffee, e.g. mocha-flavoured
    15ml/1 tbsp coffee liqueur, such as
        Tia Maria, Kahlúa or Toussaint
    60ml/4 tbsp icing sugar, for dusting
    little grated chocolate, for sprinkling

1 Preheat the oven to 180°C/350°F/ Gas 4. Grease and line a 33 x 23cm/ 13 x 9in Swiss roll tin with non-stick baking parchment.

2 Break the chocolate into squares and melt in a bowl over a pan of barely simmering water. Remove from the heat and leave to cool for 5 minutes.

3 In a large bowl, whisk the sugar and egg yolks until light and fluffy. Stir in the melted chocolate.

4 Whisk the egg whites until stiff, but not dry, and then gently fold into the chocolate mixture.

5 Pour the chocolate mixture into the prepared tin, spreading it level with a spatula. Bake for about 25 minutes until firm. Leave the cake in the tin and cover with a cooling rack, making sure it doesn't touch the cake.

6 Cover the rack with a damp tea towel, then wrap in clear film. Leave in a cool place for at least 8 hours or overnight, if possible.

7 Dust a large sheet of greaseproof paper with icing sugar and turn out the roulade on to it. Peel off the lining.

8 To make the filling, whip the double cream with the coffee and liqueur until soft peaks form. Spread the cream over the roulade. Starting from one of the short ends, carefully roll it up, using the paper to help.

9 Place the roulade, seam-side down, on to a serving plate; dust generously with icing sugar and sprinkle with a little grated chocolate before serving.

COOK'S TIP
If liked, decorate the roulade with swirls of whipped cream and chocolate coffee beans or with clusters of raspberries and mint leaves.

MANGO AND COFFEE MERINGUE ROLL

A LIGHT AND FLUFFY ROLL OF MERINGUE IS THE IDEAL CONTRAST TO THE UNSWEETENED FILLING OF COFFEE, MASCARPONE AND JUICY RIPE MANGO.

SERVES SIX TO EIGHT

INGREDIENTS
    4 egg whites
    225g/8oz/generous 1 cup
        caster sugar
For the filling
    45ml/3 tbsp strong-flavoured
        ground coffee
    75ml/5 tbsp milk
    350g/12oz/1½ cups mascarpone
    1 ripe mango, cut into
        1cm/½in cubes

COOK'S TIP

If you like, the meringue can be sprinkled with 50g/2oz/½ cup of skinned chopped hazelnuts before baking.

1 Preheat the oven to 190°C/375°F/ Gas 5. Line a 33 x 23cm/13 x 9in Swiss roll tin with lightly greased non-stick baking parchment. Whisk the egg whites until stiff. Gradually add the sugar, whisking after each addition until thick and glossy.

2 When the meringue is thick and glossy, spoon it into the prepared tin and smooth the surface. Bake for 15 minutes or until firm and golden.

3 Turn the meringue out on to a sheet of non-stick baking parchment. Remove the lining paper and leave until cold.

4 To make the filling, put the coffee in a small bowl. Heat the milk until it is nearly boiling and pour over the coffee. Leave to infuse for 4 minutes, then strain through a fine sieve, discarding the coffee grounds.

5 Beat the mascarpone until soft, then gradually beat in the coffee. Spread over the meringue, then scatter with the chopped mango.

6 Gently roll up the meringue from one of the short ends, with the help of the baking parchment. Transfer to a serving plate seam-side down. Chill for at least 30 minutes before serving.

GINGERED COFFEE MERINGUES

WHAT COULD BE MORE ENTICING THAN TO BREAK THROUGH THE COATING OF CRISP MERINGUE TO REVEAL JUST-MELTING COFFEE ICE CREAM ON A MOIST GINGER SPONGE?

SERVES SIX

INGREDIENTS
275g/10oz bought ginger cake
600ml/1 pint/2½ cups coffee
 ice cream
4 egg whites
1.5ml/¼ tsp cream of tartar
150g/5oz/¾ cup caster sugar
25g/1oz/2 tbsp preserved ginger,
 finely chopped

1 Preheat the oven to 230°C/450°F/ Gas 8. Cut the ginger cake lengthways into three slices. Stamp out two rounds from each slice, using a 5cm/2in cutter, and put on a baking tray.

2 Top each cake round with a large scoop of coffee ice cream, then place the baking tray in the freezer for at least 30 minutes.

3 Whisk the egg whites and cream of tartar until soft peaks form. Gradually add the sugar and continue whisking until the mixture forms stiff peaks. Fold in the preserved ginger.

4 Carefully spoon the meringue and ginger mixture into a piping bag fitted with a large plain nozzle.

COOK'S TIP
The ice cream is insulated in the oven by the tiny bubbles of air in the meringue, so ensure it is completely covered. Once coated, the ice cream cakes could be frozen until ready to cook.

5 Quickly pipe the meringue over the ice cream, starting from the base and working up to the top.

6 Bake in the oven for 3–4 minutes, until the outside of the meringue is crisp and lightly tinged with brown. Serve immediately.

FLOATING ISLANDS

THIS WELL-KNOWN DESSERT GETS ITS NAME FROM THE POACHED MERINGUES SURROUNDED BY A "SEA" OF CRÈME ANGLAISE. THIS VERSION IS GIVEN A TOUCH OF THE EXOTIC THROUGH THE ADDITION OF STAR ANISE AND IS SERVED WITH A RICH COFFEE SAUCE.

SERVES SIX

INGREDIENTS
For the coffee crème Anglaise
  150ml/¼ pint/⅔ cup milk
  150ml/¼ pint/⅔ cup single cream
  120ml/4fl oz/½ cup strong
    brewed coffee
  4 egg yolks
  25g/1oz/2 tbsp soft light
    brown sugar
  5ml/1 tsp cornflour
For the caramel sauce
  90g/3½oz/½ cup caster sugar
For the poached meringues
  2 egg whites
  50g/2oz/¼ cup caster sugar
  1.5ml/¼ tsp ground star anise
  pinch of salt

1 To make the coffee crème Anglaise, pour the milk, cream and coffee into a pan and heat to boiling point.

2 In a large bowl, whisk the egg yolks, brown sugar and cornflour together until creamy. Whisk in the hot coffee mixture, then pour the entire mixture back into the pan.

3 Heat for 1–2 minutes, stirring until the sauce thickens. Take off the heat and allow to cool, stirring occasionally.

COOK'S TIP
Once poached, the meringues will keep their shape for up to 2 hours.

4 Cover the bowl containing the sauce with clear film and place in the fridge.

5 For the caramel, put the sugar in a small heavy-based pan with 45ml/3 tbsp water and heat very gently until dissolved. Boil rapidly until the syrup turns a rich golden colour. Off the heat, carefully add 45ml/3 tbsp hot water – it will splutter. Leave to cool.

6 To make the meringues, whisk the egg whites until stiff. Combine the sugar and star anise; add to the egg whites.

7 Pour 2.5cm/1in of boiling water into a large frying pan. Add the salt and bring to a gentle simmer. Shape the meringue into small ovals, using two spoons, and add to the water. Poach four or five of the meringues at a time for about 3 minutes, until firm.

8 Remove with a slotted spoon and drain on kitchen paper. Repeat with the remaining mixture.

9 To serve, spoon a little coffee crème Anglaise on to each serving plate. Float two or three "islands" on top, then drizzle with caramel sauce.

COFFEE MERINGUES <u>WITH</u> ROSE CREAM

THESE SUGARY MERINGUES, WITH CRUSHED ESPRESSO-ROASTED COFFEE BEANS, ARE FILLED WITH A DELICATE ROSE-SCENTED CREAM. LIGHTLY SPRINKLE ROSE PETALS FOR A ROMANTIC FINISH.

MAKES TWENTY PAIRS OF MERINGUES

INGREDIENTS
    25g/1oz/generous ¼ cup espresso-
      roasted coffee beans
    3 egg whites
    175g/6oz/scant 1 cup caster sugar
    25g/1oz/¼ cup pistachio nuts,
      roughly chopped
    few rose petals, for decoration
For the rose cream
    300ml/½ pint/1¼ cups double cream
    15ml/1 tbsp icing sugar, sifted
    10ml/2 tsp rose water

1 Preheat the oven to 180°C/350°F/
Gas 4. Spread the coffee beans on a
baking sheet and toast for 8 minutes.
Allow to cool, then put in a plastic bag
and crush with a rolling pin. Turn the
oven to 140°C/275°F/Gas 1.

2 Whisk the egg whites and sugar in a
bowl over a pan of hot water until thick.

3 Remove from the heat and continue
whisking until the meringue holds stiff
peaks. Whisk in the crushed beans.

4 Fill a piping bag fitted with a large
star nozzle with the mixture and pipe
about 40 small swirls on to two baking
sheets lined with non-stick baking
parchment. Leave some space between
each swirl.

5 Sprinkle with the pistachio nuts.
Bake the meringues for 2–2½ hours, or
until dry and crisp, swapping the
position of the baking trays halfway
through the cooking time. Leave to cool,
then remove from the paper.

6 To make the rose cream, whip the
cream, icing sugar and rose water until
soft peaks form. Use to sandwich the
meringues together in pairs. Arrange on
a serving plate and serve scattered with
rose petals for decoration.

VARIATION
Orange-flower water may be used instead
of rose water in the cream and a drop of
pink food colouring added, if you like.

COFFEE PAVLOVA <u>WITH</u> EXOTIC FRUITS

BOTH AUSTRALIA AND NEW ZEALAND CLAIM TO HAVE INVENTED THIS FLUFFY MERINGUE NAMED AFTER THE BALLERINA ANNA PAVLOVA. THE SECRET OF SUCCESS IS TO LEAVE THE MERINGUE IN THE OVEN UNTIL COMPLETELY COOLED, AS A SUDDEN CHANGE IN TEMPERATURE WILL MAKE IT CRACK.

SERVES SIX TO EIGHT

INGREDIENTS
   30ml/2 tbsp ground coffee,
     e.g. mocha orange-flavoured
   30ml/2 tbsp near-boiling water
   3 egg whites
   2.5ml/½ tsp cream of tartar
   175g/6oz/scant 1 cup caster sugar
   5ml/1 tsp cornflour, sifted
For the filling
   150ml/¼ pint/⅔ cup double cream
   5ml/1 tsp vanilla orange-flower water
   150ml/¼ pint/⅔ cup crème fraîche
   500g/1¼lb sliced exotic fruits, such
     as mango, papaya and kiwi
   15ml/1 tbsp icing sugar

4 Using a long knife or spatula, spoon the meringue mixture on to the baking sheet, spreading to an even 20cm/8in circle. Make a slight hollow in the middle. Bake in the oven for 1 hour, then turn off the heat and leave in the oven until cool.

5 Transfer the meringue to a plate, peeling off the lining. To make the filling, whip the cream with the orange-flower water until soft peaks form. Fold in the crème fraîche. Spoon into the meringue. Arrange the fruits over the cream and dust with icing sugar.

1 Preheat the oven to 140°C/275°F/ Gas 1. Draw a 20cm/8in circle on non-stick baking parchment. Place pencil-side down on a baking sheet.

2 Put the coffee in a small bowl and pour the hot water over. Leave to infuse for 4 minutes, then strain through a very fine sieve.

3 Whisk the egg whites with the cream of tartar until stiff, but not dry. Gradually whisk in the sugar until the meringue is stiff and shiny, then quickly whisk in the cornflour and coffee.

VARIATION
450g/1lb soft fruit, such as wild or cultivated strawberries, raspberries and blueberries, may be used instead of the exotic fruits, if you wish.

FRUIT
DESSERTS

*If you're looking for colour, flavour
and freshness and something
a little out of the ordinary, opt for
one of these fruit and coffee combinations. Fruit always makes the
perfect pudding, no matter how simple or grand the meal, but it doesn't
have to be chilled. Try steeping
oranges in a hot coffee syrup or
serve a slice of Sticky Pear Pudding
for pure indulgence.*

ORANGES IN HOT COFFEE SYRUP

THIS RECIPE WORKS WELL WITH MOST CITRUS FRUITS; TRY PINK GRAPEFRUIT OR SWEET, PERFUMED CLEMENTINES, PEELED BUT LEFT WHOLE, FOR A CHANGE.

SERVES SIX

INGREDIENTS
    6 medium oranges
    200g/7oz/1 cup sugar
    50ml/2fl oz/¼ cup cold water
    100ml/3½fl oz/scant ½ cup
        boiling water
    100ml/3½fl oz/scant ½ cup fresh
        strong brewed coffee
    50g/2oz/½ cup pistachio nuts,
        chopped (optional)

COOK'S TIP
Choose a pan in which the oranges will just fit in a single layer.

1 Finely pare the rind from one orange, shred and reserve the rind. Peel the remaining oranges. Cut each one crosswise into slices, then re-form with a cocktail stick through the centre.

2 Put the sugar and cold water in a heavy-based pan. Heat gently until the sugar dissolves, then bring to the boil and cook until the syrup turns pale gold.

3 Remove from the heat and carefully pour the boiling water into the pan. Return to the heat until the syrup has dissolved in the water. Stir in the coffee.

4 Add the oranges and the shredded rind to the coffee syrup. Simmer for 15–20 minutes, turning the oranges once during cooking. Sprinkle with pistachio nuts, if using, and serve hot.

FRESH FIG COMPOTE

LIGHTLY POACHING FIGS IN A VANILLA AND COFFEE SYRUP BRINGS OUT THEIR WONDERFUL FLAVOUR.

SERVES FOUR TO SIX

INGREDIENTS
    400ml/14fl oz/1⅔ cups
        brewed coffee
    115g/4oz/½ cup clear honey
    1 vanilla pod
    12 slightly under-ripe
        fresh figs
    Greek yogurt, to serve (optional)

COOK'S TIPS
• Rinse and dry the vanilla pod; it can be used several times.
• Figs come in three main varieties – red, white and black – and all three are suitable for cooking. Naturally high in sugar, they are sweet and succulent and complement well the stronger flavours of coffee and vanilla.

1 Choose a frying pan with a lid, large enough to hold the figs in a single layer. Pour in the coffee and add the honey.

2 Split the vanilla pod lengthways and scrape the seeds into the pan. Add the vanilla pod, then bring to the boil. Bring the syrup to a rapid boil and cook until reduced to about 175ml/6fl oz/¾ cup. Leave to cool.

3 Wash the figs and pierce the skins several times with a sharp skewer. Cut in half and add to the syrup. Lower the heat, cover and simmer for 5 minutes. Remove the figs from the syrup with a slotted spoon and set aside to cool.

4 Strain the syrup over the figs. Allow to stand at room temperature for 1 hour before serving with yogurt, if liked.

STICKY PEAR PUDDING

CLOVES ADD A DISTINCTIVE FRAGRANT FLAVOUR TO THIS HAZELNUT, PEAR AND COFFEE PUDDING.

SERVES SIX

INGREDIENTS

30ml/2 tbsp ground coffee,
  e.g. hazelnut-flavoured
15ml/1 tbsp near-boiling water
50g/2oz/½ cup toasted
  skinned hazelnuts
4 ripe pears
juice of ½ orange
115g/4oz/8 tbsp butter, softened
115g/4oz/generous ½ cup golden
  caster sugar, plus an extra 15ml/
  1 tbsp, for baking
2 eggs, beaten
50g/2oz/½ cup self-raising
  flour, sifted
pinch of ground cloves
8 whole cloves, optional
45ml/3 tbsp maple syrup
fine strips of orange rind,
  to decorate
For the orange cream
  300ml/½ pint/1¼ cups
    whipping cream
  15ml/1 tbsp icing sugar, sifted
  finely grated rind of ½ orange

1 Preheat the oven to 180°C/350°F/
Gas 4. Lightly grease a 20cm/8in loose-
based sandwich tin. Put the ground
coffee in a small bowl and pour the
water over. Leave to infuse for 4 minutes,
then strain through a fine sieve.

COOK'S TIP
If you can't find ready-toasted skinned
hazelnuts, prepare your own. Toast under
a hot grill for 3–4 minutes, turning
frequently until well browned. Rub off
the skins and cool before grinding.

2 Grind the hazelnuts in a coffee
grinder until fine. Peel, halve and core
the pears. Thinly slice across the pear
halves part of the way through. Brush
with orange juice.

3 Beat the butter and the 115g/4oz/
generous ½ cup caster sugar together
in a large bowl until very light and fluffy.
Gradually beat in the eggs, then fold in
the flour, ground cloves, hazelnuts and
coffee. Spoon the mixture into the tin
and level the surface.

4 Pat the pears dry on kitchen paper,
then arrange in the sponge mixture, flat
side down.

5 Lightly press 2 whole cloves into
each pear half, if using. Brush the
pears with 15ml/1 tbsp maple syrup.

6 Sprinkle the pears with the 15ml/
1 tbsp caster sugar. Bake for 45–50
minutes or until firm and well-risen.

7 While the sponge is cooking, make
the orange cream. Whip the cream,
icing sugar and orange rind until soft
peaks form. Spoon into a serving dish
and chill until needed.

8 Allow the sponge to cool for about
10 minutes in the tin, then remove and
place on a serving plate. Lightly brush
with the remaining maple syrup before
decorating with orange rind and serving
warm with the orange cream.

COFFEE CRÊPES WITH PEACHES AND CREAM

JUICY GOLDEN PEACHES AND CREAM CONJURE UP THE SWEET TASTE OF SUMMER. HERE THEY ARE DELICIOUS AS THE FILLING FOR THESE LIGHT COFFEE CRÊPES.

SERVES SIX

INGREDIENTS
    75g/3oz/²⁄₃ cup plain flour
    25g/1oz/¼ cup buckwheat flour
    1.5ml/¼ tsp salt
    1 egg, beaten
    200ml/7fl oz/scant 1 cup milk
    15g/½oz/1 tbsp butter, melted
    100ml/3½ oz/scant ½ cup strong
      brewed coffee
    sunflower oil, for frying
For the filling
    6 ripe peaches
    300ml/½ pint/1¼ cups double cream
    15ml/1 tbsp Amaretto liqueur
    225g/8oz/1 cup mascarpone
    65g/2½oz/generous ¼ cup
      caster sugar
    30ml/2 tbsp icing sugar, for dusting

1 Sift the flours and salt into a mixing bowl. Make a well in the middle and add the egg, half the milk and the melted butter. Gradually mix in the flour, beating until smooth, then beat in the remaining milk and coffee.

2 Heat a drizzle of oil in a 15–20cm/ 6–8in crêpe pan. Pour in just enough batter to thinly cover the base of the pan. Cook for 2–3 minutes, until the underneath is golden brown, then flip over and cook the other side.

COOK'S TIP
To keep the pancakes warm while you make the rest, cover them with foil and place the plate over a pan of barely simmering water.

3 Slide the crêpe out of the pan on to a plate. Continue making crêpes until all the mixture is used, stacking and interleaving with greaseproof paper.

4 To make the filling, halve the peaches and remove the stones. Cut into thick slices. Whip the cream and Amaretto liqueur until soft peaks form. Beat the mascarpone with the sugar until smooth. Beat 30ml/2 tbsp of the cream into the mascarpone, then fold in the remainder.

5 Spoon a little of the Amaretto cream on to one half of each pancake and top with peach slices. Gently fold the pancake over and dust with icing sugar. Serve immediately.

PLUM AND RUM BABAS

A POLISH KING THOUGHT UP THESE SPONGY YEAST CAKES AFTER HEARING THE STORY OF ALI BABA.
SOAKED IN A COFFEE AND RUM SYRUP, THEIR MIDDLES ARE FILLED WITH JUICY PLUMS.

SERVES SIX

INGREDIENTS
 65g/2½oz/5 tbsp unsalted
  butter, softened
 115g/4oz/1 cup strong plain flour
 pinch of salt
 7.5ml/1½ tsp easy-blend dried yeast
 25g/1oz/2 tbsp soft light
  brown sugar
 2 eggs, beaten
 45ml/3 tbsp warm milk
 crème fraîche, to serve
For the syrup
 115g/4oz/generous ½ cup
  granulated sugar
 120ml/4fl oz/½ cup water
 450g/1lb plums, halved, stoned and
  thickly sliced
 120ml/4fl oz/½ cup brewed coffee
 45ml/3 tbsp dark rum

4 Cover with clear film and leave to rise for 40 minutes.Cut the remaining butter into cubes and mix into the dough. Put the tins on a baking tray and drop the dough into the moulds. Cover with oiled clear film and leave until the dough has almost risen to the top. Remove the film and bake for 15–20 minutes.

5 Meanwhile make the syrup. Put 25g/1oz/2 tbsp of the sugar in a pan with the water. Add the plums and cook over a low heat until barely tender; remove with a slotted spoon. Add the remaining sugar and coffee to the pan. Heat gently until dissolved, but do not boil. Remove from the heat and stir in the rum.

6 Turn out the babas on to a wire rack and leave to cool for 5 minutes. Dunk them in the warm syrup until well soaked. Return them to the wire rack with a plate underneath to catch any drips. Leave to cool completely.

7 Put the babas on a serving plate and fill the middles with the sliced plums. Spoon a little extra syrup over each and serve with crème fraîche.

1 Preheat the oven to 190°C/375°F/Gas 5. Thickly brush six 9cm/3½in ring tins with 15g/½oz/1 tbsp of the butter.

2 Sift the flour and salt into a mixing bowl and stir in the yeast and soft light brown sugar.

3 Make a well in the middle and add the eggs and warm milk. Beat for about 5 minutes with a wooden spoon to make a very sticky dough that is fairly smooth and elastic.

COOK'S TIP
The babas may also be split in half horizontally, filled with whipped cream and sandwiched back together.

COCONUT AND COFFEE TRIFLE

DARK COFFEE SPONGE, LACED WITH LIQUEUR, COCONUT CUSTARD AND A COFFEE CREAM TOPPING MAKES THIS A LAVISH DESSERT. SERVE IN A LARGE GLASS BOWL FOR MAXIMUM IMPACT.

SERVES SIX TO EIGHT

INGREDIENTS
For the coffee sponge
    45ml/3 tbsp strong-flavoured
      ground coffee
    45ml/3 tbsp near-boiling water
    2 eggs
    50g/2oz/¼ cup soft dark brown sugar
    40g/1½oz/⅓ cup self-raising
      flour, sifted
    25ml/1½ tbsp hazelnut or
      sunflower oil
For the coconut custard
    400ml/14fl oz/1⅔ cup canned
      coconut milk
    3 eggs
    40g/1½oz/3 tbsp caster sugar
    10ml/2 tsp cornflour
For the filling and topping
    2 medium bananas
    60ml/4 tbsp coffee liqueur, such as
      Tia Maria, Kahlúa or Toussaint
    300ml/½ pint/1¼ cups double cream
    30ml/2 tbsp icing sugar, sifted
    ribbons of fresh coconut, to decorate

1 Preheat the oven to 160°C/325°F/ Gas 3. Grease and line an 18cm/7in square tin with greaseproof paper.

2 Put the coffee in a small bowl. Pour the hot water over and leave to infuse for 4 minutes. Strain through a fine sieve, discarding the grounds.

3 Whisk the eggs and soft dark brown sugar in a large bowl until the whisk leaves a trail when lifted.

4 Gently fold in the flour, followed by 15ml/1 tbsp of the coffee and the oil. Spoon the mixture into the tin and bake for 20 minutes, until firm. Turn out on to a wire rack, remove the lining paper and leave to cool.

5 To make the coconut custard, heat the coconut milk in a saucepan until it is almost boiling.

6 Whisk the eggs, sugar and cornflour together until frothy. Pour on the hot coconut milk, whisking all the time. Add to the pan and heat gently, stirring for 1–2 minutes, until the custard thickens, but do not boil. Set aside to cool for about 10 minutes, stirring occasionally.

7 Cut the coffee sponge into 5cm/2in squares and arrange in the base of a large glass bowl. Slice the bananas and arrange on top of the sponge. Drizzle the coffee liqueur on top. Pour the custard over and leave until cold.

8 Whip the cream with the remaining coffee and icing sugar until soft peaks form. Spoon the cream over the custard. Cover and chill for several hours. Sprinkle with ribbons of fresh coconut before serving.

COOK'S TIP
To make coconut ribbons, use a vegetable peeler to cut thin ribbons from the flesh of a fresh coconut, or buy shredded coconut and toast until it is pale golden.

FLAMBÉED BANANAS WITH CARIBBEAN COFFEE SAUCE

THIS DESSERT HAS ALL THE FLAVOUR OF THE CARIBBEAN; BANANAS, DARK SUGAR, COFFEE AND RUM.

SERVES FOUR TO SIX

INGREDIENTS
  6 bananas
  40g/1½oz/3 tbsp butter
  50g/2oz/¼ cup soft dark brown sugar
  50ml/2fl oz/¼ cup strong
    brewed coffee
  60ml/4 tbsp dark rum
  vanilla ice cream, to serve

1 Peel the bananas and cut in half lengthways. Melt the butter in a large frying pan over a medium heat. Add the bananas and cook for 3 minutes, turning halfway through cooking time.

COOK'S TIP
These hot bananas taste equally good served with coconut or coffee ice cream.

2 Sprinkle the sugar over the bananas, then add the coffee. Continue cooking, stirring occasionally, for 2–3 minutes, or until the bananas are tender.

3 Pour the rum into the pan and bring to the boil. With a long match or taper and tilting the pan, ignite the rum. As soon as the flames subside, serve the bananas with vanilla ice cream.

GRILLED NECTARINES WITH COFFEE MASCARPONE FILLING

THIS SIMPLE DESSERT IS PERFECT FOR NECTARINES THAT ARE STILL SLIGHTLY HARD, AS THEY'RE GRILLED WITH A DELICIOUS HONEY AND BUTTER GLAZE AND FILLED WITH CHILLED COFFEE CREAM.

SERVES FOUR

INGREDIENTS
  115g/4oz/½ cup mascarpone
  45ml/3 tbsp cold very strong
    brewed coffee
  4 nectarines
  15g/½oz/1 tbsp butter, melted
    and cooled
  45ml/3 tbsp clear honey
  pinch of ground mixed spice
  25g/1oz/¼ cup slivered brazil nuts

1 Beat the mascarpone until softened, then gradually mix in the cold brewed coffee. Cover with clear film and chill for 20 minutes.

2 Cut the nectarines in half and remove the stones. In a small bowl, mix the butter, 30ml/2 tbsp of the honey and ground mixed spice. Brush the spicy butter all over the cut surfaces.

3 Arrange the nectarines, cut-side up on a foil-lined grill pan. Cook under a hot grill for 2–3 minutes. Add the brazil nuts to the grill pan for the last minute of cooking and toast until golden.

4 Put a spoonful of the chilled cheese mixture in the centre of each hot nectarine. Drizzle with the remaining honey and sprinkle with the toasted brazil nuts before serving.

COOK'S TIP
If possible, choose a scented honey for this dessert: orange blossom and rosemary are both delicious.

VANILLA POACHED PEARS WITH FROTHY CAPPUCCINO SAUCE

VANILLA-SCENTED PEARS ARE SERVED WITH A BUBBLY ESPRESSO SAUCE AND FINISHED WITH A FAINT DUSTING OF SPICY CHOCOLATE FOR A LIGHT, ELEGANT DESSERT.

SERVES SIX

INGREDIENTS
    1 vanilla pod
    150g/5oz/¾ cup granulated sugar
    400ml/14fl oz/1⅔ cups water
    6 slightly under-ripe pears
    juice of ½ lemon
For the frothy cappuccino sauce
    3 egg yolks
    25g/1oz/2 tbsp caster sugar
    50ml/2fl oz/¼ cup brewed
      espresso coffee
    50ml/2fl oz/¼ cup single cream
    10ml/2 tsp drinking chocolate
    2.5ml/½ tsp ground cinnamon

1 Split the vanilla pod lengthways and scrape out the black seeds into a large saucepan. Add the split pod, sugar and water. Heat gently until the sugar has completely dissolved.

2 Meanwhile, peel and halve the pears, then rub with lemon juice. Scoop out the cores with a melon baller or teaspoon. Add the cored pears to the syrup and pour in extra water to cover.

3 Cut out a circle of greaseproof paper and cover the top of the pears. Bring to a light boil, cover the pan with a lid and simmer for 15 minutes, or until tender.

4 Using a slotted spoon, transfer the pears to a serving bowl. Bring the syrup to a rapid boil and cook for 15 minutes, or until reduced by half.

5 Strain over the pears and leave to cool. Cover with clear film and chill for several hours. Allow to come back to room temperature before serving.

6 To make the sauce, put the egg yolks, sugar, coffee and cream into a heatproof bowl over a pan of barely simmering water. With a balloon whisk, beat until the mixture is very thick and frothy. Remove from the heat and continue beating for 2–3 minutes.

7 Arrange the pears on individual plates and pour a little sauce over each. Mix together the drinking chocolate and cinnamon and sprinkle over the sauce. Serve immediately.

FRAGRANT FRUIT SALAD

THE SYRUP OF THIS EXOTIC FRUIT SALAD IS FLAVOURED AND SWEETENED WITH LIME AND COFFEE LIQUEUR. IT CAN BE PREPARED UP TO A DAY BEFORE SERVING.

SERVES SIX

INGREDIENTS

130g/4½oz/½ cup sugar
thinly pared rind and juice of 1 lime
60ml/4 tbsp coffee liqueur, such as
   Tia Maria, Kahlúa or Toussaint
1 small pineapple
1 medium mango
1 papaya
2 pomegranates
2 passion fruits
fine strips of lime peel, to decorate

1 Put the sugar and lime rind in a small saucepan with 150ml/¼ pint ⅔ cup water. Heat gently until the sugar dissolves, then bring to the boil and simmer for 5 minutes. Leave to cool, then strain into a large serving bowl, discarding the lime rind. Stir in the lime juice and liqueur.

2 Using a sharp knife, cut the plume and stalk end from the pineapple. Peel thickly and cut the flesh into bite-sized pieces, discarding the woody central core. Add to the bowl.

3 Cut the papaya in half and scoop out the seeds. Cut away the skin, then cut into slices. Cut the pomegranates in half and scoop out the seeds. Break into clusters and add to the bowl.

COOK'S TIP
To maximise the flavour of the fruit, allow the salad to stand at room temperature for an hour before serving.

4 Cut the mango lengthways, along each side of the stone. Peel the skin off the flesh. Add with the rest of the fruit to the bowl. Stir well.

5 Halve the passion fruits and scoop out the flesh using a teaspoon. Spoon over the salad and serve, decorated with fine strips of lime peel.

CARAMELIZED APPLES

A TRADITIONAL DESSERT WITH A DIFFERENCE — BAKED APPLES BATHED IN A RICH COFFEE SYRUP.

SERVES SIX

INGREDIENTS
  6 eating apples, peeled, but
    left whole
  50g/2oz/4 tbsp unsalted butter,
    melted and cooled
  90g/3½oz/½ cup caster sugar
  1.5ml/¼ tsp ground cinnamon
  90ml/6 tbsp strong brewed coffee
  whipped or clotted cream,
    to serve

COOK'S TIP
This recipe is equally good made with
pears, but reduce the cooking time by
10–15 minutes and use mixed spice in
place of the cinnamon.

1 Preheat the oven to 180°C/350°F/
Gas 4. Cut a thin slice from the bottom
of each apple to give them a flat base.
Using a pastry brush, thickly coat each
apple with melted butter.

2 Mix the caster sugar and cinnamon
in a shallow dish. Holding each apple
by its stalk, roll in the mixture to coat.

3 Arrange the apples in a shallow
baking dish into which they just fit.
Stand them upright.

4 Pour the coffee into the dish then
sprinkle over any remaining sugar
mixture. Bake the apples for 40 minutes,
basting with the coffee two or three
times throughout. Baste a last time,
then pour the juices into a small pan,
returning the apples to the oven.

5 Boil the juices rapidly until syrupy
and reduced to about 60ml/4 tbsp. Pour
over the apples and cook for 10 more
minutes, or until the apples are tender.
Serve hot with a spoonful of cream.

SUMMER BERRIES WITH COFFEE SABAYON

FOR A LIGHT AND DELICIOUSLY REFRESHING FINALE, SERVE A PLATTER OF FRESH SUMMER FRUIT WITH
A FLUFFY COFFEE SAUCE, WHICH HAS THE ADDED ADVANTAGE OF BEING DELIGHTFULLY EASY TO MAKE.

SERVES SIX

INGREDIENTS
  900g/2lb/6–8 cups mixed summer
    berries such as raspberries,
    blueberries and strawberries (hulled
    and halved, if large)
  5 egg yolks
  75g/3oz/scant ½ cup caster sugar
  50ml/2fl oz/¼ cup brewed coffee
  30ml/2 tbsp coffee liqueur, such as
    Tia Maria, Kahlúa or Toussaint
  strawberry or mint leaves,
    to decorate (optional)
  30ml/2 tbsp icing sugar, to dust

COOK'S TIP
Ensure that the water doesn't get too hot
when making the sauce, or it may curdle.

1 Arrange the fruit on a serving platter
and decorate with strawberry or mint
leaves, if you like. Dust with icing sugar.

2 Whisk the egg yolks and caster sugar
in a bowl over a pan of simmering water
until the mixture begins to thicken.

3 Gradually add the coffee and liqueur,
pouring in a thin, continuous stream
and whisking all the time. Continue
whisking until the sauce is thick and
fluffy. Serve warm, or allow to cool,
whisking occasionally, and serve cold
with the fruit.

FROZEN DESSERTS

Frozen desserts are an ideal choice for all occasions as they can be made in advance, then stored in the freezer. In this chapter, you'll find smooth, velvety ice cream and refreshing sorbets. Some ices are only part of the dessert, such as in Dark Chocolate and Coffee Mousse Cake, a rich chocolate sponge with an ice cream centre.

CINNAMON AND COFFEE SWIRL ICE CREAM

LIGHT ICE CREAM SUBTLY SPICED WITH CINNAMON AND RIPPLED WITH A SWEET COFFEE SYRUP.

SERVES SIX

INGREDIENTS
    300ml/½ pint/1¼ cups single cream
    1 cinnamon stick
    4 egg yolks
    150g/5oz/¾ cup caster sugar
    300ml/½ pint/1¼ cups
        double cream
For the coffee syrup
    45ml/3 tbsp ground coffee
    45ml/3 tbsp near-boiling water
    90g/3½oz/½ cup caster sugar
    50ml/2fl oz/¼ cup water

1 Pour the single cream into a small pan and add the cinnamon stick. Slowly bring to the boil. Turn off the heat, cover with a lid and leave to infuse for 30 minutes. Bring back to the boil and remove the cinnamon stick.

2 Whisk the yolks and sugar until light. Pour the hot cream over the egg mixture, whisking. Return to the pan and stir over low heat for 1–2 minutes, until it thickens. Allow to cool.

3 Whip the double cream until peaks form and fold into the custard. Pour into a container and freeze for 3 hours.

4 Meanwhile, to make the syrup, put the coffee in a bowl and pour the hot water over. Leave to infuse for 4 minutes, then strain through a sieve.

COOK'S TIP
Make sure that the cinnamon ice cream is sufficiently frozen before adding the coffee syrup.

5 Gently heat the sugar and cold water in a pan until completely dissolved. Bring to the boil and gently simmer for 5 minutes. Cool, then stir in the coffee.

6 Turn the cinnamon ice cream into a chilled bowl and briefly whisk to break down the ice crystals.

7 Spoon a third back into the container and drizzle some of the coffee syrup over. Repeat in this way until all is used.

8 Drag a skewer through the mixture a few times to achieve a marbled effect. Freeze for 4 hours, or until solid. Allow to soften slightly before serving.

TOASTED NUT AND COFFEE ICE CREAM IN BRANDY SNAP BASKETS

SCOOPS OF CRUSHED CARAMEL AND TOASTED NUT ICE CREAM ARE SERVED IN CRISP CASES, THEN DRIZZLED WITH A WARM COFFEE AND COGNAC SAUCE.

SERVES SIX

INGREDIENTS
  75g/3oz/½ cup whole nuts, such as
    blanched almonds and hazelnuts
  90g/3½oz/½ cup caster sugar
  1 vanilla pod, split
  30ml/2 tbsp ground coffee
  200ml/7fl oz/scant 1 cup
    double cream
  300ml/½ pint/1¼ cups Greek yogurt
  6 brandy snap baskets, to serve
For the coffee and cognac sauce
  115g/4oz/½ cup soft light
    brown sugar
  50ml/2fl oz/¼ cup hot water
  100ml/3½fl oz/½ cup strong
    brewed coffee
  60ml/4 tbsp cognac

2 Pour on to an oiled baking sheet to cool and harden. Crush to a fine powder. Put the vanilla, coffee and cream in a pan. Heat almost to boiling, turn off the heat, cover and infuse.

3 After 15 minutes, strain through a sieve and leave to cool. Stir the coffee cream into the yogurt with the crushed nut mixture. Transfer to a freezerproof container and freeze for 4 hours.

4 To make the sauce, heat the sugar and water in a small heavy-based pan over a gentle heat until melted. Simmer for 3 minutes. Cool slightly, then stir in the coffee and cognac.

5 Meanwhile, allow the ice cream to soften in the fridge for 15 minutes. Scoop into the brandy snap baskets and serve immediately with the warm coffee and cognac sauce.

1 Put the whole nuts and caster sugar in a large heavy-based pan and heat gently until the sugar caramelizes to a light golden brown, shaking the pan only occasionally.

COOK'S TIP
To make brandy snap baskets, in a bowl, gently melt 50g/2oz/4 tbsp butter, 50g/2oz/¼ cup demerara sugar and 50g/2oz/¼ cup golden syrup. Stir in 50g/2oz/½ cup sifted plain flour and 5ml/1 tsp brandy. Drop well-spaced teaspoons on to oiled baking trays. Bake in a preheated oven at 160°C/325°F/Gas 3 for about 8 minutes. Cool for 1 minute, then lift with a palette knife and mould over the base of an inverted glass.

COFFEE ICE CREAM

FRESHLY GROUND COFFEE GIVES THIS CLASSIC ICE CREAM A DISTINCTIVE AND SOPHISTICATED FLAVOUR. CHOOSE A DARK-ROASTED BEAN TO ENSURE A RICH, GLOSSY COLOUR TO THE ICE CREAM.

<u>SERVES EIGHT TO TEN</u>

INGREDIENTS
    60ml/4 tbsp dark-roasted
        ground coffee
    600ml/1 pint/2½ cups milk
    200g/7oz/scant 1 cup soft light
        brown sugar
    6 egg yolks
    475ml/16fl oz/2 cups
        whipping cream

1 Put the coffee in a jug. Heat the milk in a saucepan to near-boiling point and pour over the coffee. Leave to stand for 4 minutes.

2 Meanwhile, in a large bowl, beat the sugar and egg yolks until light. Pour the milk over, whisking all the time. Strain the mixture back into the pan through a fine sieve.

3 Cook the custard over a low heat for 1–2 minutes, stirring until it coats the back of a wooden spoon. Do not boil. Pour into a shallow freezer container and leave to cool, stirring occasionally.

COOK'S TIP
If using an ice cream maker, do not whip the cream: stir it into the coffee custard before adding to the machine.

4 Freeze for about 2 hours, then tip into a bowl and whisk with a fork until smooth. Whip the cream until peaks form and fold into the frozen mixture.

5 Return to the freezer for 1 more hour, then turn out and whisk again. Finally, freeze for 3–4 hours, until solid. Transfer to the fridge for 20 minutes, before scooping and serving.

CAPPUCCINO CONES

PRETTY WHITE AND DARK CHOCOLATE CONES ARE FILLED WITH SWIRLS OF CAPPUCCINO CREAM AND TOPPED WITH A LIGHT DUSTING OF COCOA POWDER.

<u>SERVES SIX</u>

INGREDIENTS
    115g/4oz each good quality plain and
        white cooking chocolate
For the cappuccino cream
    30ml/2 tbsp ground espresso or other
        strong-flavoured coffee
    30ml/2 tbsp near-boiling water
    300ml/½ pint/1¼ cups double cream
    45ml/3 tbsp icing sugar, sifted
    15ml/1 tbsp cocoa powder,
        for dusting

1 Cut nine 13 x 10cm/5 x 4in rectangles from non-stick baking parchment, then cut each rectangle in half diagonally to make 18 triangles. Roll up each to make a cone and secure with sticky tape.

2 Heat the plain chocolate in a bowl over a pan of hot water until melted. Using a small pastry brush, thickly brush the insides of half the paper cones with chocolate. Chill until set. Repeat with the white chocolate. Carefully peel away the paper and keep the cones in the fridge until needed.

3 To make the cappuccino cream, put the coffee in a small bowl. Pour the hot water over. Leave to infuse for 4 minutes, then strain though a fine sieve into a bowl. Leave to cool. Add the cream and sugar and whisk until soft peaks form. Spoon into an icing bag fitted with a medium star nozzle.

4 Pipe the cream into the chocolate cones. Put on a baking sheet and freeze for at least 2 hours or until solid. Arrange on individual plates, allowing three cones per person and dusting with cocoa powder before serving.

COOK'S TIP
Make sure, when melting the chocolate, that the water doesn't boil or the chocolate will overheat and stiffen.

MAPLE COFFEE AND PISTACHIO BOMBES

REAL MAPLE SYRUP TASTES INFINITELY BETTER THAN THE SYNTHETIC VARIETIES AND IS WELL WORTH SEARCHING FOR. HERE IT SWEETENS THE DARK COFFEE CENTRE OF THESE PRETTY PISTACHIO BOMBES.

SERVES SIX

INGREDIENTS
For the pistachio ice cream
    50g/2oz/¼ cup caster sugar
    50ml/2 fl oz/¼ cup water
    175g/6oz can evaporated
      milk, chilled
    50g/2oz/½ cup shelled and skinned
      pistachio nuts, finely chopped
    drop of green food colouring
      (optional)
    200ml/7fl oz/scant 1 cup
      whipping cream
For the maple coffee centres
    30ml/2 tbsp ground coffee
    150ml/¼ pint/⅔ cup single cream
    50ml/2fl oz/¼ cup maple syrup
    2 egg yolks
    5ml/1 tsp cornflour
    150ml/¼ pint/⅔ cup whipping cream

1 Put six 175ml/6fl oz/¾ cup mini pudding basins or dariole moulds into the freezer to chill. Put the sugar and water in a heavy-based saucepan and heat gently until dissolved. Bring to the boil and simmer for 3 minutes.

2 Cool, then stir in the chilled evaporated milk, pistachio nuts and colouring, if using. Lightly whip the cream until it forms soft peaks and blend into the mixture.

3 Pour the mixture into a freezerproof container and freeze for at least 2 hours. Whisk the ice cream until smooth, then freeze for a further 2 hours or until frozen, but not solid.

4 To make the centres, put the ground coffee in a jug. Heat the single cream to near-boiling point and pour over the coffee. Leave to infuse for 4 minutes. Whisk the maple syrup, egg yolks and cornflour together. Strain the hot coffee cream over the egg mixture, whisking continuously. Return to the pan and cook gently for 1–2 minutes, until the custard thickens. Leave to cool, stirring occasionally.

5 Meanwhile, line the moulds with the ice cream, keeping the thickness as even as possible right up to the rim. Freeze until the ice cream is firm again.

6 Beat the cream until peaks form, then fold into the custard. Spoon into the middle of the moulds. Cover and freeze for 2 hours. Serve immediately.

FROSTED RASPBERRY <u>AND</u> COFFEE TERRINE

*A WHITE CHOCOLATE AND RASPBERRY LAYER AND A CONTRASTING SMOOTH COFFEE LAYER MAKE THIS
ATTRACTIVE LOOKING DESSERT DOUBLY DELICIOUS.*

SERVES SIX TO EIGHT

INGREDIENTS
    30ml/2 tbsp ground coffee,
      e.g. mocha orange-flavoured
    250ml/8fl oz/1 cup milk
    4 eggs, separated
    50g/2oz/¼ cup caster sugar
    30ml/2 tbsp cornflour
    150ml/¼ pint/⅔ cup double cream
    150g/5oz white chocolate,
      roughly chopped
    115g/4oz/⅔ cup raspberries
    shavings of white chocolate and
      cocoa powder, to decorate

1 Line a 1.5 litre/2½ pint/6¼ cup loaf
tin with clear film and put in the freezer
to chill. Put the ground coffee in a jug.
Heat 100ml/3½fl oz/scant ½ cup of the
milk to near-boiling point and pour over
the coffee. Leave to infuse.

2 Blend the egg yolks, sugar and
cornflour together in a saucepan and
whisk in the remaining milk and the
cream. Bring to the boil, stirring all the
time, until thickened.

3 Divide the hot mixture between two
bowls and add the white chocolate to
one, stirring until melted. Strain the
coffee through a fine sieve into the
other bowl and mix well. Leave until
cool, stirring occasionally.

COOK'S TIP
After decorating, allow the terrine to
soften in the fridge for 20 minutes
before slicing and serving.

4 Whisk two of the egg whites until stiff.
Fold into the coffee custard. Spoon into
the tin and freeze for 30 minutes. Whisk
remaining whites and fold into the
chocolate mixture with the raspberries.

5 Spoon into the tin and level before
freezing for 4 hours. Turn the terrine out
on to a flat serving plate and peel off
the clear film. Cover with chocolate
shavings and dust with cocoa powder.

COFFEE AND MINTY-LEMON SORBET

THE FLAVOURS OF FRESH MINT, SHARP LEMON AND AROMATIC COFFEE ARE COMBINED IN THIS DELICIOUS ICY SORBET. THE LEMON SHELLS ARE AN EASY, BUT PRETTY, SUMMERY DECORATIVE TOUCH.

SERVES SIX

INGREDIENTS
115g/4oz/generous ½ cup sugar
400ml/14fl oz/1⅔ cups water
15g/½oz fresh mint leaves
30ml/2 tbsp coffee liqueur, such as
  Tia Maria, Kahlúa or Toussaint
6 lemons
1 egg white
sprigs of fresh mint, to decorate

1 Put the sugar in a large heavy-based saucepan with the water and heat gently until dissolved, stirring occasionally. Bring to the boil, and simmer for 5 minutes.

COOK'S TIP
Fresh fruit sorbets will keep in the freezer for up to 2 months, but are best eaten within several days of making.

2 Remove from the heat, add the mint leaves, stir and leave to cool. Strain into a jug and stir in the liqueur.

3 Cut a thin slice from the base of each lemon so that they will stand upright, being careful not to cut through the pith. Cut the tops off the lemons and keep for lids. Scrape out the lemon flesh and squeeze the juice. Strain the juice into the mint and coffee syrup.

4 Pour into a freezerproof container and freeze for 3 hours. Whisk to break down the ice crystals, then freeze for 1 more hour. Whisk the egg white until stiff, then whisk into the ice. Scoop into the lemon shells and replace the lids.

5 Place upright on a tray and freeze for 2 hours, until solid. Transfer to the fridge 5 minutes before serving, to soften. Decorate with sprigs of mint.

ESPRESSO GRANITA

THIS FAMOUS FROZEN ITALIAN ICE MAKES A REFRESHING FINISH TO A RICH MEAL.

SERVES SIX

INGREDIENTS
90g/3½oz/½ cup sugar
600ml/1 pint/2½ cups espresso or
  other strong-flavoured coffee
whipped cream, to serve
  (optional)

COOK'S TIPS
• Don't whisk the granita too vigorously – it should have a rough granular texture, rather than a smooth one like a sorbet.
• After step 3, the granita can either be served at that stage or covered and stored in the freezer for up to 2 weeks.

1 Add the sugar to the hot coffee and stir until dissolved. Leave to cool, then pour into a 900ml/1½ pint/3¾ cup shallow freezer container.

2 Freeze for at least 3 hours, or until ice crystals form around the edges. Whisk with a fork, then return to the freezer for another hour.

3 Whisk the mixture again with a fork and re-freeze. Repeat until the mixture is frozen and there is no liquid.

4 Transfer the granita to the fridge 20 minutes before serving. Break up the ice crystals with a strong fork and serve in glasses, topped with whipped cream, if you like.

ICED COFFEE MOUSSE IN A CHOCOLATE CASE

A DARK CHOCOLATE BOWL IS FILLED WITH A LIGHT, ICED COFFEE MOUSSE. IT LOOKS A DRAMATIC DESSERT, BUT ISN'T DIFFICULT TO MAKE.

SERVES EIGHT

INGREDIENTS
  1 sachet powdered gelatine
  60ml/4 tbsp very strong
    brewed coffee
  30ml/2 tbsp coffee liqueur, such as
    Tia Maria, Kahlúa or Toussaint
  3 eggs, separated
  75g/3oz/scant ½ cup caster sugar
  150ml/¼ pint/⅔ cup whipping cream,
    lightly whipped
For the chocolate bowl
  225g/8oz plain chocolate squares,
    plus extra for decoration

1 Grease and line a deep 18cm/7in loose-based cake tin with non-stick baking parchment.

2 Melt the chocolate in a bowl over a pan of simmering water. Using a pastry brush, brush a layer of chocolate over the base of the tin and about 7.5cm/3in up the sides, finishing with a ragged edge. Allow the chocolate to set before repeating. Put in the freezer to harden.

3 Sprinkle the gelatine over the coffee in a bowl and leave to soften for 5 minutes. Put the bowl over a pan of simmering water, stirring until dissolved. Remove from the heat and stir in the liqueur. Whisk the egg yolks and sugar in a bowl over the simmering water until thick enough to leave a trail. Remove from the pan and whisk until cool. Whisk the egg whites until stiff.

4 Pour the dissolved gelatine into the egg yolk mixture in a thin stream, stirring gently. Chill in the fridge for 20 minutes, or until just beginning to set, then fold in the cream, followed by the whisked egg whites.

5 Remove the chocolate case from the freezer and peel away the lining. Put it back in the tin, then pour in the mousse. Return to the freezer for at least 3 hours. To serve, remove from the tin and place on a plate. Allow to soften in the fridge for 40 minutes before serving. Decorate with grated chocolate. Use a knife dipped in hot water and wiped dry to cut into slices to serve.

DARK CHOCOLATE <u>AND</u> COFFEE MOUSSE CAKE

THIS DOUBLE TREAT WILL PROVE IRRESISTIBLE — RICH SPONGE FILLED WITH CREAMY COFFEE MOUSSE.

<u>SERVES EIGHT</u>

INGREDIENTS
  4 eggs
  115g/4oz/generous ½ cup
    caster sugar
  75g/3oz/⅔ cup plain flour, sifted
  25g/1oz/¼ cup cocoa powder, sifted
  60ml/4 tbsp coffee liqueur, such as
    Tia Maria, Kahlúa or Toussaint
  icing sugar, to dust
For the coffee mousse
  30ml/2 tbsp dark-roasted
    ground coffee beans
  350ml/12fl oz/1½ cups double cream
  115g/4oz/generous ½ cup
    granulated sugar
  120ml/4fl oz/½ cup water
  4 egg yolks

1 Preheat the oven to 180°C/350°F/ Gas 4. Grease and line the bases of a 20cm/8in square and a 23cm/9in round cake tin with non-stick baking parchment. Put the eggs and sugar in a bowl over a pan of hot water and whisk until thick.

2 Remove from the heat and whisk until thick enough to leave a trail when the whisk is lifted. Gently fold in the flour and cocoa. Pour a third of the mixture into the square tin and the remainder into the round tin. Bake the square sponge for 15 minutes and the round for 30 minutes, until firm.

3 Cool on a wire rack before slicing the round cake in half horizontally. Place the bottom half back in the tin. Sprinkle with half the liqueur.

4 Trim the edges of the square sponge, cut into 4 equal strips and use to line the sides of the tin.

5 To make the mousse, put the coffee in a bowl. Heat 50ml/2fl oz/¼ cup of the cream to near-boiling and pour over the coffee. Leave to infuse for 4 minutes, then strain through a fine sieve.

6 Gently heat the sugar and water until dissolved. Increase the heat and boil steadily until the syrup reaches 107°C/ 225°F. Cool for 5 minutes, then pour on to the egg yolks, whisking until the mixture is very thick.

7 Add the coffee cream to the remaining cream and whip until soft peaks form. Fold into the egg mixture. Spoon into the sponge case and freeze for 20 minutes. Sprinkle the remaining liqueur over the second sponge half and place on top of the mousse. Cover and freeze for 4 hours. Remove from the tin and dust with icing sugar.

COOK'S TIP
Cover the seams of the cake with swirls of piped whipped cream and decorate with chocolate coffee beans, if you like.

CAKE AND TORTE RECIPES

From simple sponges to elaborate tortes and velvety cheesecakes, these are cakes to rival any shop-bought confection. Some, such as Coffee Almond Marsala Slice, are perfect with mid-morning coffee. Others, like Coffee Chocolate Mousse Cake and Cappuccino Torte, make unforgettable dinner party desserts.

COCONUT COFFEE CAKE

COCONUT AND COFFEE ARE NATURAL PARTNERS, AS THESE LITTLE SQUARES OF ICED CAKE PROVE.

SERVES NINE

INGREDIENTS
   45ml/3 tbsp ground coffee
   75ml/5 tbsp near-boiling milk
   25g/1oz/2 tbsp caster sugar
   175g/6oz/²⁄₃ cup golden syrup
   75g/3oz/6 tbsp butter
   40g/1½oz/½ cup desiccated coconut
   175g/6oz/1½ cups plain flour
   2.5ml/½ tsp bicarbonate of soda
   2 eggs, lightly beaten
For the icing
   115g/4oz/8 tbsp butter, softened
   225g/8oz/2 cups icing sugar, sifted
   25g/1oz/⅓ cup shredded or flaked
      coconut, toasted

1   Preheat the oven to 160°C/325°F/
Gas 3. Grease and line the base of a
20cm/8in square tin.

2   Put the ground coffee in a small
bowl and pour the hot milk over. Leave
to infuse for 4 minutes, then strain
through a fine sieve.

3   Heat the caster sugar, golden syrup,
butter and desiccated coconut in a pan,
stirring with a wooden spoon, until
completely melted.

4   Sift the flour and bicarbonate of soda
together and stir into the mixture, along
with the eggs and 45ml/3 tbsp of the
coffee-flavoured milk.

5   Spoon the mixture into the prepared
tin and level the top. Bake in the oven
for 40–50 minutes until well-risen and
firm. Allow the cake to cool in the tin for
about 10 minutes, before running a
knife around the edges to loosen. Turn
out and cool on a wire rack.

6   To make the icing, beat the softened
butter until smooth then gradually beat
in the icing sugar and remaining coffee
milk to give a soft consistency. Spread
over the top of the cake and decorate
with toasted coconut. Cut into 5cm/2in
squares to serve.

VARIATION
Substitute 50g/2oz/½ cup chopped
pecan nuts for the desiccated coconut
and decorate the squares with pecan
halves dusted with icing sugar.

MOCHA SPONGE CAKE

THE YEMENI CITY OF MOCHA WAS ONCE CONSIDERED TO BE THE COFFEE CAPITAL OF THE WORLD, AND STILL PRODUCES A COFFEE THAT TASTES A LITTLE LIKE CHOCOLATE. TODAY "MOCHA" MAY REFER TO THE VARIETY OF COFFEE OR MEAN A COMBINATION OF COFFEE OR CHOCOLATE, AS IN THIS RECIPE.

SERVES TEN

INGREDIENTS
    25ml/1½ tbsp strong-flavoured
        ground coffee
    175ml/6fl oz/¾ cup milk
    115g/4oz/8 tbsp butter
    115g/4oz/½ cup soft light
        brown sugar
    1 egg, lightly beaten
    185g/6½oz/1⅔ cups self-raising flour
    5ml/1 tsp bicarbonate of soda
    60ml/4 tbsp creamy liqueur, such as
        Baileys or Irish Velvet
For the glossy chocolate icing
    200g/7oz plain chocolate, broken
        into pieces
    75g/3oz/6 tbsp unsalted
        butter, cubed
    120ml/4fl oz/½ cup double cream

1 Preheat the oven to 180°C/350°F/ Gas 4. Grease and line a 18cm/7in round fixed-base cake tin with greaseproof paper.

2 To make the cake, put the coffee in a jug. Heat the milk to near-boiling and pour over. Leave to infuse for 4 minutes, then strain through a sieve and cool.

3 Gently melt the butter and sugar until dissolved. Pour into a bowl and cool for 2 minutes, then stir in the egg.

4 Sift the flour over the mixture and fold in. Blend the bicarbonate of soda with the coffee-flavoured milk and gradually stir into the mixture.

5 Pour into the tin, smooth the surface, and bake for 40 minutes, until well-risen and firm. Cool in the tin for about 10 minutes. Spoon the liqueur over the cake and leave until cold. Loosen the edges with a palette knife and turn out on to a wire rack.

6 To make the icing, place the broken chocolate in a bowl over a pan of barely simmering water until melted. Remove from the heat and stir in the butter and cream until smooth. Allow to cool before coating the top and sides of the cake, using a palette knife. Leave until set.

COFFEE ALMOND MARSALA SLICE

ROASTED AND CRUSHED COFFEE BEANS ARE SPECKLED THROUGHOUT THIS DELICIOUS ALMOND CAKE, DISTINCTLY FLAVOURED WITH ITALIAN MARSALA WINE.

SERVES TEN TO TWELVE

INGREDIENTS
    25g/1oz/⅓ cup roasted coffee beans
    5 eggs, separated
    175g/6oz/scant 1 cup caster sugar
    120ml/4fl oz/½ cup Marsala wine
    75g/3oz/6 tbsp butter, melted
      and cooled
    115g/4oz/1 cup ground almonds
    115g/4oz/1 cup plain flour, sifted
    25g/1oz/¼ cup flaked almonds
    icing sugar, to dust
    crème fraîche, to serve

1 Preheat the oven to 180°C/350°F/ Gas 4. Grease and line the base of a 23cm/9in round loose-based tin with greaseproof paper. Put the coffee beans on a baking sheet and roast for about 10 minutes. Cool, then place in a large plastic bag and gently crush with a rolling pin.

2 Beat the yolks and 115g/4oz/ generous ½ cup of the caster sugar until very pale and thick.

3 Stir in the crushed coffee, Marsala, butter and almonds. Sift the flour over, then carefully fold in.

4 Whisk the egg whites until they are stiff, then gradually incorporate the remaining caster sugar.

5 Fold into the almond mixture, a third at a time. Spoon into the tin and sprinkle the top with flaked almonds.

6 Bake for 10 minutes, then reduce the oven to 160°C/325°F/Gas 3 and cook for a further 40 minutes, or until a skewer inserted into the centre comes out clean. After 5 minutes, turn out and cool on a wire rack. Dust with icing sugar and serve with crème fraîche.

SOUR CHERRY COFFEE LOAF

DRIED SOUR CHERRIES HAVE A WONDERFULLY CONCENTRATED FRUIT FLAVOUR AND CAN BE BOUGHT IN SUPERMARKETS AND HEALTH FOOD SHOPS.

SERVES EIGHT

INGREDIENTS
    175g/6oz/12 tbsp butter, softened
    175g/6oz/scant 1 cup golden
      caster sugar
    5ml/1 tsp vanilla extract
    2 eggs, lightly beaten
    225g/8oz/2 cups plain flour
    1.5ml/¼ tsp baking powder
    75ml/5 tbsp strong brewed coffee
    175g/6oz/1 cup dried sour cherries
For the icing
    50g/2oz/½ cup icing sugar, sifted
    20ml/4 tsp strong brewed coffee

1 Preheat the oven to 180°C/350°F/ Gas 4. Grease and line a 900g/2lb loaf tin with greaseproof paper. Cream the butter, sugar and vanilla until fluffy.

2 Gradually add the eggs, beating well after each addition. Sift the flour and baking powder together.

3 Fold into the mixture with the coffee and 115g/4oz/⅔ cup of the sour cherries. Spoon the mixture into the prepared tin and level the top.

4 Bake for 1¼ hours or until firm to the touch. Cool in the tin for 5 minutes, then turn out and cool on a wire rack.

5 To make the icing, mix together the icing sugar and coffee and the remaining cherries. Spoon over the top and sides. Leave to set before slicing.

COFFEE AND MINT CREAM CAKE

GROUND ALMONDS GIVE THIS BUTTERY COFFEE SPONGE A MOIST TEXTURE AND DELICATE FLAVOUR. IT'S SANDWICHED TOGETHER WITH A GENEROUS FILLING OF CRÈME DE MENTHE BUTTERCREAM.

SERVES EIGHT

INGREDIENTS
 15ml/1 tbsp ground coffee
 25ml/1½ tbsp near-boiling water
 175g/6oz/12 tbsp unsalted
  butter, softened
 175g/6oz/scant 1 cup
  caster sugar
 225g/8oz/2 cups self-raising
  flour, sifted
 50g/2oz/½ cup ground almonds
 3 eggs
 small sprigs of fresh mint,
  to decorate
For the filling
 50g/2oz/4 tbsp unsalted butter
 115g/4oz/1 cup icing sugar, sifted,
  plus extra for dusting
 30ml/2 tbsp crème de
  menthe liqueur

1 Preheat the oven to 180°C/350°F/ Gas 4. Lightly grease and base line two 18cm/7in sandwich tins with greaseproof paper.

2 Put the coffee in a bowl and pour the hot water over. Leave to infuse for about 4 minutes, then strain through a sieve.

3 Put the butter, sugar, flour, almonds, eggs and coffee in a large bowl. Beat well for 1 minute until blended. Divide the mixture evenly between the tins and level off. Bake for 25 minutes until well-risen and firm to the touch. Leave in the tins for 5 minutes, then turn out on to a wire rack to cool.

4 To make the filling, cream the unsalted butter, icing sugar and crème de menthe liqueur together in a bowl until light and fluffy.

COOK'S TIP
Make sure the butter is really soft and creamy before starting to mix the cake.

5 Remove the lining paper from the sponges and sandwich together with the filling.

6 Generously dust the top with icing sugar and place on a serving plate. Scatter with the fresh mint leaves just before serving.

COFFEE AND WALNUT SWISS ROLL WITH COINTREAU CREAM

COFFEE AND WALNUTS HAVE A NATURAL AFFINITY. HERE THEY APPEAR TOGETHER IN A LIGHT AND FLUFFY SPONGE ENCLOSING A SMOOTH ORANGE CREAM.

SERVES SIX

INGREDIENTS
10ml/2 tsp ground coffee,
  e.g. mocha orange-flavoured
15ml/1 tbsp near-boiling water
3 eggs
75g/3oz/scant ½ cup caster sugar,
  plus extra for dusting
75g/3oz/⅔ cup self-raising flour
50g/2oz/½ cup toasted walnuts,
  finely chopped
For the Cointreau cream
115g/4oz/generous ½ cup
  caster sugar
50ml/2fl oz/¼ cup cold water
2 egg yolks
115g/4oz/8 tbsp unsalted
  butter, softened
15ml/1 tbsp Cointreau

1 Preheat the oven to 200°C/400°F/Gas 6. Grease and line a 33 x 23cm/13 x 9in Swiss roll tin with non-stick baking parchment.

2 Put the coffee in a bowl and pour the hot water over. Leave to infuse for about 4 minutes, then strain through a sieve.

3 Whisk the eggs and sugar together in a large bowl until pale and thick. Sift the flour over the mixture and fold in with the coffee and walnuts. Turn into the tin and bake for 10–12 minutes, until springy to the touch.

4 Turn out on a piece of greaseproof paper sprinkled with caster sugar, peel off the lining paper and cool for about 2 minutes. Trim the edges then roll up from one of the short ends, with the greaseproof paper where the filling will be. Leave to cool.

5 To make the filling, heat the sugar in the water over a low heat until dissolved. Boil rapidly until the syrup reaches 105°C/220°F on a sugar thermometer. Pour the syrup over the egg yolks, whisking all the time, until thick and mousse-like. Gradually add the butter, then whisk in the orange liqueur. Leave to cool and thicken.

6 Unroll the sponge and spread with the Cointreau cream. Re-roll and place on a serving plate seam-side down. Dust with extra caster sugar and chill in the fridge until ready to serve.

COOK'S TIP
Decorate the roll with swirls of piped whipped cream and walnuts, if you like.

COFFEE CHOCOLATE MOUSSE CAKE

SERVE THIS DENSE, DARK CHOCOLATE CAKE IN SMALL PORTIONS AS IT IS VERY RICH.

SERVES SIX

INGREDIENTS
175g/6oz plain chocolate
30ml/2 tbsp strong brewed coffee
150g/5oz/10 tbsp butter, cubed
50g/2oz/¼ cup caster sugar
3 eggs
25g/1oz/¼ cup ground almonds
about 25ml/1½ tbsp icing sugar,
   for dusting
For the mascarpone and coffee cream
250g/9oz/generous 1 cup mascarpone
30ml/2 tbsp icing sugar, sifted
30ml/2 tbsp strong brewed coffee

1 Preheat the oven to 200°C/400°F/
Gas 6. Lightly grease and line the
base of a 15cm/6in square tin with
greaseproof paper.

2 Put the chocolate and coffee in a
small heavy-based pan and heat very
gently until melted, stirring occasionally.

3 Add the butter and sugar to the pan
and stir until dissolved. Whisk the eggs
until frothy and stir into the chocolate
mixture with the ground almonds.

4 Pour into the prepared tin, then put
in a large roasting tin and pour in
enough hot water to come two-thirds up
the cake tin. Bake for 50 minutes, or
until the top feels springy to the touch.
Leave to cool in the tin for 5 minutes,
then turn the cake out upside-down on
to a board and leave to cool.

5 Meanwhile, beat the mascarpone
with the icing sugar and coffee. Dust
the cake generously with icing sugar,
then cut into slices. Serve on individual
plates with the mascarpone and coffee
cream alongside.

COOK'S TIP
The top of this flourless cake, with its
moist mousse-like texture, will crack
slightly as it cooks.

CAPPUCCINO TORTE

THE FAMOUS AND MUCH LOVED BEVERAGE OF FRESHLY BREWED COFFEE, WHIPPED CREAM, CHOCOLATE
AND CINNAMON IS TRANSFORMED INTO A SENSATIONAL DESSERT.

SERVES SIX TO EIGHT

INGREDIENTS
75g/3oz/6 tbsp butter, melted
275g/10oz shortbread
   biscuits, crushed
1.5ml/¼ tsp ground cinnamon
25ml/1½ tbsp powdered gelatine
45ml/3 tbsp cold water
2 eggs, separated
115g/4oz/½ cup soft light
   brown sugar
115g/4oz plain chocolate, chopped
175ml/6fl oz/¾ cup brewed espresso
400ml/14fl oz/1⅔ cups
   whipping cream
chocolate curls and ground
   cinnamon, to decorate

1 Mix the butter with the biscuits and
cinnamon. Spoon into the base of a
20cm/8in loose-based tin and press
down well. Chill in the fridge while
making the filling.

2 Sprinkle the gelatine over the cold
water. Leave to soften for 5 minutes,
then place the bowl over a pan of hot
water and stir to dissolve.

3 Whisk the egg yolks and sugar until
thick. Put the chocolate in a bowl with
the coffee and stir until melted. Add
to the egg mixture, then cook gently in
a pan for 1–2 minutes until thickened.
Stir in the gelatine. Leave until just
beginning to set, stirring occasionally.

4 Whip 150ml/¼ pint/⅔ cup of the
cream until soft peaks form. Whisk the
egg whites until stiff. Fold the cream
into the coffee mixture, followed by the
egg whites. Pour the mixture over the
biscuit base and chill for 2 hours.

5 When ready to serve, remove the torte
from the tin and transfer to a serving
plate. Whip the remaining cream and
place a dollop on top. Decorate with
chocolate curls and a little cinnamon.

BAKED COFFEE CHEESECAKE

THIS RICH, COOKED AND CHILLED CHEESECAKE, FLAVOURED WITH COFFEE AND ORANGE LIQUEUR, HAS A WONDERFULLY DENSE, VELVETY TEXTURE.

<u>SERVES EIGHT</u>

INGREDIENTS
    45ml/3 tbsp near-boiling water
    30ml/2 tbsp ground coffee
    4 eggs
    225g/8oz/generous 1 cup
        caster sugar
    450g/1lb/2 cups cream cheese,
        at room temperature
    30ml/2 tbsp orange liqueur, such
        as Curaçao
    40g/1½oz/⅓ cup plain flour, sifted
    300ml/½ pint/1¼ cups
        whipping cream
    30ml/2 tbsp icing sugar, to dust
    single cream, to serve
For the base
    115g/4oz/1 cup plain flour
    5ml/1 tsp baking powder
    75g/3oz/6 tbsp butter
    50g/2oz/¼ cup caster sugar
    1 egg, lightly beaten
    30ml/2 tbsp cold water

1 Preheat the oven to 160°C/325°F/ Gas 3. Lightly grease and line a 20cm/8in loose-based tin with greaseproof paper.

2 Sift the flour and baking powder into a bowl. Rub in the butter until the mixture resembles fine breadcrumbs. Stir in the sugar, then add the egg and water and mix to a dough. Press the mixture into the base of the tin.

3 To make the filling, pour the water over the coffee and leave to infuse for 4 minutes. Strain through a fine sieve.

4 Whisk the eggs and sugar until thick. Using a wooden spoon, beat the cream cheese until softened, then beat in the liqueur, a spoonful at a time.

5 Gradually mix in the whisked eggs. Fold in the flour. Finally, stir in the whipping cream and coffee.

6 Pour the mixture over the base and bake in the oven for 1½ hours. Turn off the heat and leave in the oven to cool with the door ajar. Chill the cheesecake in the fridge for 1 hour. Dust the top with the icing sugar. Remove from the tin and place on a serving plate, Serve with single cream.

IRISH COFFEE CHEESECAKE

THE FLAVOURS OF WHISKEY, COFFEE AND GINGER GO WELL TOGETHER, BUT YOU CAN RING THE CHANGES BY USING ALMOND OR DIGESTIVE BISCUITS FOR THE BASE OF THIS CHEESECAKE.

SERVES EIGHT

INGREDIENTS
    45ml/3 tbsp ground coffee
    1 vanilla pod
    250ml/8fl oz/1 cup single cream
    15ml/1 tbsp powdered gelatine
    45ml/3 tbsp cold water
    450g/1lb/2 cups curd cheese, at
        room temperature
    60ml/4 tbsp Irish whiskey liqueur,
        such as Millars or Irish Velvet
    115g/4oz/½ cup soft light brown
        sugar
    150ml/¼ pint/⅔ cup whipping cream
To decorate
    150ml/¼ pint/⅔ cup whipping cream
    chocolate-covered coffee beans
    cocoa, for dusting
For the base
    150g/5oz gingernut biscuits,
        finely crushed
    25g/1oz/¼ cup toasted
        almonds, chopped
    75g/3oz/6 tbsp butter, melted

1 To make the base, mix together the crushed gingernut biscuits, toasted almonds and melted butter and press firmly into the base of a 20cm/8in loose-based tin. Chill in the fridge.

2 Heat the coffee, vanilla and single cream in a pan to near-boiling point. Cover and leave to infuse for 15 minutes. Strain through a fine sieve. Sprinkle the gelatine over the water in a bowl and leave for 5 minutes. Place over a pan of simmering water until dissolved. Stir into the coffee cream.

3 Mix the curd cheese, liqueur and sugar together, then gradually blend in the coffee cream. Leave until just beginning to set.

4 Beat the whipping cream until soft peaks form, and fold into the coffee mixture. Spoon into the tin and chill for 3 hours, until set.

5 To decorate, whisk the whipping cream until soft peaks form and spread lightly over the top. Chill for at least 30 minutes, then transfer to a serving plate. Decorate with chocolate-covered coffee beans and cocoa.

VARIATION
Instead of a smooth layer of cream on top of the cheesecake, pipe swirls of cream around the edge of the cake.

PIES, TARTS AND PASTRIES

The flavour and aroma of real

coffee transforms perennial family

favourites into something special,

as you'll discover when you taste a

slice of Coffee Custard Tart or

Crunchy Topped Coffee Meringue

Pie. Along with these much-loved

pies and tarts are classic pastries

from around the world.

WALNUT PIE

SWEETENED WITH COFFEE-FLAVOURED MAPLE SYRUP, THIS PIE HAS A RICH AND STICKY TEXTURE. THE WALNUTS CAN BE REPLACED BY PECANS FOR AN AUTHENTIC AMERICAN PIE.

SERVES EIGHT

INGREDIENTS
30ml/2 tbsp ground coffee
175ml/6 fl oz/³/₄ cup maple syrup
25g/1oz/2 tbsp butter, softened
175g/6oz/³/₄ cup soft light brown sugar
3 eggs, beaten
5ml/1 tsp vanilla extract
115g/4oz/1 cup walnut halves
crème fraîche or vanilla ice cream,
   to serve
For the pastry
150g/5oz/1¼ cups plain flour
pinch of salt
25g/1oz/¼ cup golden icing sugar
75g/3oz/6 tbsp butter, cubed
   and cubed
2 egg yolks

1 Preheat the oven to 200°C/400°F/ Gas 6. To make the pastry, sift the flour, salt and icing sugar into a bowl. Rub in the butter until the mixture resembles fine breadcrumbs.

2 Add the egg yolks and mix to a dough. Turn out and knead on a lightly floured surface for a few seconds until smooth. Wrap in clear film and chill for 20 minutes.

3 Roll out the pastry and use to line a 20cm/8in fluted flan tin. Line with greaseproof paper and baking beans and bake for 10 minutes. Remove the paper and beans and bake for a further 5 minutes. Take out the pastry case and turn the oven to 180°C/350°F/Gas 4.

4 To make the filling, put the coffee and maple syrup in a small pan and heat until almost boiling. Remove from the heat and leave until just warm. Mix together the butter and sugar, then gradually beat in the eggs. Strain the maple syrup mixture through a fine sieve into the bowl and stir in with the vanilla extract.

5 Arrange the walnuts in the pastry case, then carefully pour in the filling. Bake for 30–35 minutes or until lightly browned and firm. Serve warm with crème fraîche or vanilla ice cream.

MISSISSIPPI PIE

THIS AMERICAN FAVOURITE WAS NAMED AFTER THE MUDDY BANKS OF THE MISSISSIPPI RIVER. IT HAS A DENSE LAYER OF CHOCOLATE MOUSSE, TOPPED WITH A MURKY COFFEE TOFFEE LAYER AND, FLOATING ON TOP, LOTS OF LOVELY FRESHLY WHIPPED CREAM.

SERVES EIGHT

INGREDIENTS
For the base
    275g/10oz digestive biscuits, crushed
    150g/5oz/10 tbsp butter, melted
For the chocolate layer
    10ml/2 tsp powdered gelatine
    30ml/2 tbsp cold water
    175g/6oz plain chocolate, broken
      into squares
    2 eggs, separated
    150ml/¼ pint/⅔ cup double cream
For the coffee toffee layer
    30ml/2 tbsp ground coffee
    300ml/½ pint/1¼ cups double cream
    200g/7oz/1 cup caster sugar
    25g/1oz/4 tbsp cornflour
    2 eggs, beaten
    15g/½oz/1 tbsp butter
    150ml/¼ pint/⅔ cup whipping cream
      and chocolate curls, to decorate

1 Grease a 21cm/8½in loose-based tin. Mix together the biscuit crumbs and butter and press over the base and sides of the tin. Chill for 30 minutes.

2 To make the chocolate layer, sprinkle the gelatine over the cold water and leave for 5 minutes. Put the bowl over a pan of hot water and stir until dissolved. Melt the chocolate in a bowl over hot water. Stir in the gelatine.

3 Blend the egg yolks and cream and stir into the chocolate. Whisk the egg whites and fold into the mixture. Pour into the biscuit case and chill for 2 hours.

4 To make the coffee layer, put the coffee in a bowl. Reserve 60ml/4 tbsp of cream. Heat the remaining cream to near-boiling and pour over. Leave to infuse for 4 minutes. Strain through a sieve back into the pan. Add the sugar and heat gently until dissolved.

5 Mix the cornflour with the reserved cream and the eggs. Add to the coffee and cream mixture and simmer gently for 2–3 minutes, stirring.

6 Stir in the butter and leave to cool for 30 minutes, stirring occasionally. Spoon over the chocolate layer. Chill in the fridge for 2 hours.

7 To make the topping, whip the cream until soft peaks form and spread thickly over the coffee toffee layer. Decorate with chocolate curls and chill until ready to serve.

CRUNCHY TOPPED COFFEE MERINGUE PIE

A SWEET PASTRY CASE IS FILLED WITH A COFFEE CUSTARD AND A MERINGUE TOPPING – CRISP AND GOLDEN ON THE OUTSIDE AND SOFT AND "MARSHMALLOWY" UNDERNEATH.

SERVES SIX TO EIGHT

INGREDIENTS
For the pastry
    175g/6oz/1½ cups plain flour
    15ml/1 tbsp icing sugar
    75g/3oz/6 tbsp butter
    1 egg yolk
    finely grated rind of ½ orange
    15ml/1 tbsp orange juice
For the filling
    30ml/2 tbsp ground coffee
    350ml/12fl oz/1½ cups milk
    25g/1oz/4 tbsp cornflour
    130g/4½ oz/⅔ cup caster sugar
    4 egg yolks
    15g/½ oz/1 tbsp butter
For the meringue
    3 egg whites
    1.5ml/¼ tsp cream of tartar
    150g/5oz/¾ cup caster sugar
    25g/1oz/¼ cup skinned hazelnuts
    15ml/1 tbsp demerara sugar

1 Preheat the oven to 200°C/400°F/Gas 6. Sift the flour and icing sugar into a bowl. Rub in the butter until the mixture resembles breadcrumbs. Add the egg yolk, orange rind and juice and mix to a firm dough. Wrap in clear film and chill for 20 minutes. Roll out and use to line a 23cm/9in loose-based fluted flan tin. Cover with clear film and chill for 30 minutes.

COOK'S TIP
The pastry case can be made up to 36 hours in advance, but once filled and baked the pie should be eaten on the day of making.

2 Prick the pastry all over, line with greaseproof paper and baking beans and bake for 15 minutes, removing the paper and beans for the last 5 minutes. Turn the oven to 160°C/325°F/Gas 3.

3 To make the filling, put the coffee in a bowl. Heat 250ml/8fl oz/1 cup of the milk until near-boiling and pour over the coffee. Leave to infuse for 4 minutes, then strain. Blend the cornflour and sugar with the remaining milk in a pan and whisk in the coffee-flavoured milk.

4 Bring the mixture to the boil, stirring until thickened. Remove from the heat.

5 Beat the egg yolks. Stir in a little of the hot coffee mixture into the egg yolks, then add to the remaining coffee mixture with the butter. Cook the filling over a low heat for 3–4 minutes, until very thick. Pour into the pastry case.

6 To make the meringue, whisk the egg whites and cream of tartar until stiff. Whisk in the caster sugar a spoonful at a time.

7 Spoon the meringue over the filling and spread right to the edge of the pastry, swirling into peaks. Sprinkle with hazelnuts and demerara sugar and bake for 30–35 minutes, or until golden brown and crisp. Serve warm, or cool on a wire rack and serve cold.

COFFEE CUSTARD TART

A CRISP WALNUT PASTRY CASE, FLAVOURED WITH VANILLA, IS FILLED WITH A SMOOTH CREAMY COFFEE CUSTARD, BAKED UNTIL LIGHTLY SET AND TOPPED WITH CREAM.

SERVES SIX TO EIGHT

INGREDIENTS
  1 vanilla pod
  30ml/2 tbsp ground coffee
  300ml/½ pint/1¼ cups single cream
  150ml/¼ pint/⅔ cup milk
  2 eggs, plus 2 egg yolks
  50g/2oz/¼ cup caster sugar
  icing sugar, for dusting
  lightly whipped double cream,
    to serve
For the pastry
  175g/6oz/1½ cups plain flour
  30ml/2 tbsp icing sugar
  115g/4oz/8 tbsp butter, cubed
  75g/3oz/½ cup walnuts,
    finely chopped
  1 egg yolk
  5ml/1 tsp vanilla extract
  10ml/2 tsp iced water

1 Preheat the oven to 200°C/400°F/ Gas 6. Put a baking sheet in the oven. Sift the flour and sugar into a bowl. Rub in the butter until the mixture resembles breadcrumbs. Stir in the walnuts. Mix together the egg yolk, vanilla and water. Add to the dry ingredients and mix to a dough. Wrap in clear film and chill for 20 minutes.

2 Roll out the dough and use to line a deep plain or fluted 20cm/8in flan ring, using a knife to smooth the edges. Chill again for 20 minutes. Prick the base with a fork. Fill with greaseproof paper and baking beans and bake on the hot baking sheet for 10 minutes. Remove the paper and beans and bake for a further 10 minutes. Turn the oven to 150°C/300°F/Gas 2.

3 Meanwhile, split the vanilla pod and scrape out the seeds. Put both in a pan with the coffee, cream and milk. Heat until near-boiling point, cover and infuse for 10 minutes. Whisk the eggs, egg yolks and caster sugar together.

4 Bring the cream back to boiling point and pour on to the egg mixture, stirring. Strain into the pastry case.

5 Bake the tart for 40–45 minutes or until lightly set. Take out of the oven and leave on a wire rack to cool. Remove the tart from the tin, pipe cream rosettes around the edge and dust with icing sugar to serve.

BLUEBERRY FRANGIPANE FLAN

A TANGY LEMON PASTRY CASE IS FILLED WITH A SWEET ALMOND FILLING DOTTED WITH RIPE BLUEBERRIES. THE JAM AND LIQUEUR GLAZE ADDS AN INDULGENT FINISH.

SERVES SIX

INGREDIENTS
30ml/2 tbsp ground coffee
45ml/3 tbsp near-boiling milk
50g/2oz/4 tbsp unsalted butter
50g/2oz/¼ cup caster sugar
1 egg
115g/4oz/1 cup ground almonds
15ml/1 tbsp plain flour, sifted
225g/8oz/2 cups blueberries
30ml/2 tbsp seedless
  blackberry jam
15ml/1 tbsp liqueur, such as
  Amaretto or Cointreau
mascarpone, crème fraîche or
  soured cream, to serve
For the pastry
175g/6oz/1½ cups plain flour
115g/4oz/8 tbsp unsalted butter
25g/1oz/2 tbsp caster sugar
finely grated rind of ½ lemon
15ml/1 tbsp chilled water

1 Preheat the oven to 190°C/375°F/ Gas 5. Sift the flour into a bowl and rub in the butter. Stir in the sugar and lemon rind, then add the water and mix to a firm dough. Wrap in clear film and chill for 20 minutes.

2 Roll out the pastry on a lightly floured surface and use to line a 23cm/9in loose-based flan tin. Line the pastry with greaseproof paper and baking beans and bake for 10 minutes. Remove the paper and beans and bake for a further 10 minutes. Remove from the oven.

3 Meanwhile, to make the filling, put the coffee in a bowl. Pour the milk over and leave to infuse for 4 minutes. Cream the butter and sugar until pale. Beat in the egg, then add the almonds and flour. Strain in the coffee through a fine sieve and fold in.

COOK'S TIP
This flan can also be made in individual tartlets. Use six 10cm/4in tartlet tins and bake for 25 minutes.

4 Spoon the coffee mixture into the pastry case and spread evenly. Scatter the blueberries over the top and push them down slightly into the mixture. Bake for 30 minutes, until firm, covering with foil after 20 minutes.

5 Remove from the oven and allow to cool slightly. Heat the jam and liqueur in a small pan until melted. Brush over the flan and remove from the tin. Serve warm with a scoop of mascarpone or with crème fraîche or soured cream.

TIA MARIA TRUFFLE TARTS

THE IDEAL DESSERT FOR A TEA OR COFFEE BREAK, THESE MINI COFFEE PASTRY CASES ARE FILLED WITH A CHOCOLATE LIQUEUR TRUFFLE CENTRE AND TOPPED WITH FRESH RIPE BERRIES.

SERVES SIX

INGREDIENTS
  300ml/½ pint/1¼ cups double cream
  225g/8oz/generous ¾ cup seedless
    bramble or raspberry jam
  150g/5oz plain chocolate, broken
    into squares
  45ml/3 tbsp Tia Maria liqueur
  450g/1lb mixed berries, such as
    raspberries, small strawberries
    or blackberries
For the pastry
  225g/8oz/2 cups plain flour
  15ml/1 tbsp caster sugar
  150g/5oz/10 tbsp butter, cubed
  1 egg yolk
  30ml/2 tbsp very strong brewed
    coffee, chilled

1 Preheat the oven to 200°C/400°F/
Gas 6. Put a baking sheet in the oven
to heat. To make the pastry, sift the
flour and sugar into a large bowl. Rub
in the butter. Stir the egg yolk and
coffee together, add to the bowl and mix
to a stiff dough. Knead lightly on a
floured surface for a few seconds until
smooth. Wrap in clear film and chill for
about 20 minutes.

2 Use the pastry to line six 10cm/4in
fluted tartlet tins. Prick the bases with a
fork and line with greaseproof paper
and baking beans. Put on the hot
baking sheet and bake for 10 minutes.
Remove paper and beans and bake for
8–10 minutes longer, until cooked. Cool
on a wire rack.

3 To make the filling, slowly bring the
cream and 175g/6oz/generous ½ cup of
the jam to the boil, stirring continuously
until dissolved.

COOK'S TIP
When making the pastry, blend the egg
yolk and coffee together until well mixed
to ensure an evenly coloured pastry.

4 Remove from the heat, add the
chocolate and 30ml/2 tbsp of the
liqueur. Stir until melted. Cool, then
spoon into the pastry cases, and
smooth the tops. Chill for 40 minutes.

5 Heat the remaining jam and liqueur
until smooth. Arrange the fruit on top of
the tarts, then brush the jam glaze over
it. Chill until ready to serve.

COFFEE CREAM PROFITEROLES

*CRISP-TEXTURED COFFEE CHOUX PASTRY PUFFS ARE FILLED WITH CREAM AND DRIZZLED WITH A
WHITE CHOCOLATE SAUCE. FOR THOSE WITH A SWEET TOOTH, THERE IS PLENTY OF EXTRA SAUCE.*

SERVES SIX

INGREDIENTS
  65g/2½oz/9 tbsp plain white flour
  pinch of salt
  50g/2oz/4 tbsp butter
  150ml/¼ pint/⅔ cup brewed coffee
  2 eggs, lightly beaten
For the white chocolate sauce
  50g/2oz/¼ cup sugar
  100ml/3½fl oz/scant ½ cup water
  150g/5oz good quality white dessert
    chocolate, broken into pieces
  25g/1oz/2 tbsp unsalted butter
  45ml/3 tbsp double cream
  30ml/2 tbsp coffee liqueur, such as
    Tia Maria, Kahlúa or Toussaint
To assemble
  250ml/8fl oz/1 cup double cream

1 Preheat the oven to 220°C/425°F/
Gas 7. Sift the flour and salt on to a piece
of greaseproof paper. Cut the butter into
pieces and put in a pan with the coffee.

2 Bring to a rolling boil, then remove
from the heat and tip in all the flour.
Beat until the mixture leaves the sides
of the pan. Leave to cool for 2 minutes.

3 Gradually add the eggs, beating well
between each addition. Spoon the
mixture into a piping bag fitted with a
1cm/½in plain nozzle.

4 Pipe about 24 small buns on to a
dampened baking sheet. Bake for
20 minutes, until well risen and crisp.

5 Remove the buns from the oven and
pierce the side of each with a sharp
knife to let out the steam.

6 To make the sauce, put the sugar
and water in a heavy-based pan and
heat gently until dissolved. Bring to the
boil and simmer for 3 minutes. Remove
from the heat. Add the chocolate and
butter, stirring until smooth. Stir in the
cream and liqueur.

7 To assemble, whip the cream until
soft peaks form. Using a piping bag, fill
the choux buns through the slits in the
sides. Arrange on plates and pour a
little of the sauce over, either warm or at
room temperature. Serve the remaining
sauce separately.

DANISH COFFEE PASTRIES

THESE WORLD FAMOUS CRISP PASTRIES ARE TIME-CONSUMING TO MAKE, BUT WELL WORTH THE EFFORT.

MAKES SIXTEEN

INGREDIENTS
   45ml/3 tbsp near-boiling water
   30ml/2 tbsp ground coffee
   115g/4oz/generous ½ cup
      caster sugar
   40g/1½ oz/3 tbsp unsalted butter
   1 egg yolk
   115g/4oz/1 cup ground almonds
   beaten egg, to glaze
   275g/10oz/1 cup apricot jam
   30ml/2 tbsp water
   175g/6oz/1½ cups icing sugar
   50g/2oz/½ cup flaked
      almonds, toasted
   50g/2oz/¼ cup glacé cherries
For the pastry
   275g/10oz/2½ cups plain flour
   1.5ml/¼ tsp salt
   15g/½oz/1 tbsp caster sugar
   225g/8oz/1 cup butter, softened
   10ml/2 tsp easy-blend dried yeast
   1 egg, beaten
   100ml/3½fl oz/scant ½ cup cold water

1 Sift the flour, salt and sugar into a bowl. Rub in 25g/1oz/2 tbsp butter. Stir in the yeast. Stir the egg and water, add to the bowl and mix to a soft dough. Lightly knead for 4–5 minutes. Put in a plastic bag and chill for 15 minutes.

2 Put the remaining butter between 2 sheets of greaseproof paper and beat with a rolling pin to make a 18cm/7in square. Roll out the dough to about 25cm/10in square. Put the butter in the middle, like a diamond, then bring up each corner of dough to fully enclose it.

3 Roll out the pastry to about 35cm/14in long. Turn up the bottom third of the pastry, then fold down the top third. Seal the edges together with a rolling pin. Return the pastry to the plastic bag and chill for 15 minutes.

4 Repeat the rolling and folding three more times, each time turning the pastry so that the short ends are at the top and bottom. Allow a 15 minute rest between each turn.

5 To make the filling, pour the hot water over the coffee and infuse for 4 minutes. Strain through a fine sieve. Cream the sugar and butter together. Beat in the egg yolk, ground almonds and 15ml/1 tbsp of the coffee.

6 Divide the dough and filling equally into three. Roll one dough portion to an 18 x 35cm/7 x 14in rectangle. Spread with filling and roll up from a short end. Cut into six equal slices. Roll another portion into a 25cm/10in square; cut into a 25cm/10in round, remove the trimmings and cut into six segments.

7 Put a spoonful of filling at the widest end of each triangle, then roll up towards the point into a crescent.

8 Roll out the remaining dough into a 20cm/8in square; cut into four. Put some filling into the centre of each. Make cuts from each corner almost to the centre and fold four alternate points to the centre.

9 Preheat the oven to 220°C/425°F/ Gas 7. Put the pastries on greased baking sheets, spaced apart. Cover loosely with oiled clear film and leave to rise for 20 minutes, until almost doubled in size. Brush with beaten egg and bake for 15–20 minutes, until lightly browned and crisp. Cool on wire racks.

10 Put the jam in a pan with the water; bring to the boil, then sieve. Brush the jam over the warm pastries. Mix the icing sugar with the remaining coffee, adding more water if necessary to make a thick icing. Drizzle the icing over some of the pastries and decorate some with flaked almonds or chopped glacé cherries. Leave to set before serving.

GREEK FRUIT AND NUT PASTRIES

AROMATIC SWEET PASTRY CRESCENTS, KNOWN AS "MOSHOPOUNGIA" IN GREECE, ARE PACKED WITH CANDIED CITRUS PEEL AND WALNUTS, SOAKED IN A COFFEE SYRUP.

MAKES SIXTEEN

INGREDIENTS
    60ml/4 tbsp clear honey
    60ml/4 tbsp strong brewed coffee
    75g/3oz/½ cup mixed candied citrus
        peel, finely chopped
    175g/6oz/1 cup walnuts,
        chopped
    1.5ml/¼ tsp freshly grated nutmeg
    milk, to glaze
    caster sugar, for sprinkling
For the pastry
    450g/1lb/4 cups plain flour
    2.5ml/½ tsp ground cinnamon
    2.5ml/½ tsp baking powder
    pinch of salt
    150g/5oz/10 tbsp unsalted butter
    30ml/2 tbsp caster sugar
    1 egg
    120ml/4fl oz/½ cup chilled milk

1 Preheat the oven to 180°C/350°F/
Gas 4. To make the pastry, sift the flour,
ground cinnamon, baking powder and
salt into a bowl. Rub in the butter until
the mixture resembles fine breadcrumbs. Stir in the sugar. Make a well
in the middle.

2 Beat the egg and milk together and
add to the well in the dry ingredients.
Mix to a soft dough. Divide the dough
into two and wrap each in clear film.
Chill in the fridge for 30 minutes.

3 Meanwhile, to make the filling, mix
the honey and coffee. Add the peel,
walnuts and nutmeg. Stir well, cover
and leave to soak for at least 20 minutes.

4 Roll out a portion of dough on a
lightly floured surface until about
3mm/⅛in thick. Stamp out rounds using
a 10cm/4in round cutter.

5 Place a heaped teaspoonful of filling
on one side of each round. Brush the
edges with a little milk, then fold over
and press the edges together to seal.
Repeat with remaining pastry until all
the filling is used.

6 Put the pastries on lightly greased
baking sheets, brush with milk and
sprinkle with caster sugar.

7 Make a steam hole in each with a
skewer. Bake for 35 minutes, or until
lightly browned. Cool on a wire rack.

BAKLAVA

TURKISH COFFEE IS BLACK, THICK, VERY SWEET AND OFTEN SPICED. HERE IT IS USED IN THIS FAMOUS PASTRY CONFECTION, TRADITIONALLY SERVED ON RELIGIOUS FESTIVAL DAYS IN TURKEY.

MAKES SIXTEEN

INGREDIENTS
50g/2oz/½ cup blanched
  almonds, chopped
50g/2oz/½ cup pistachio
  nuts, chopped
75g/3oz/scant ½ cup caster sugar
115g/4oz filo pastry
75g/3oz/6 tbsp unsalted butter,
  melted and cooled
For the syrup
115g/4oz/generous ½ cup
  caster sugar
7.5cm/3in piece cinnamon stick
1 whole clove
2 cardamom pods, crushed
75ml/5 tbsp strong brewed coffee

1 Preheat the oven to 180°C/350°F/ Gas 4. Mix the nuts and sugar together. Cut the pastry to fit a tin measuring 18 x 28cm/7 x 11in. Brush the tin with a little butter. Lay a sheet of pastry in the tin and brush with melted butter.

2 Repeat with three more sheets and spread with half the nut mixture.

3 Layer up three more sheets of pastry, lightly brushing butter between the layers, then spread the remaining nut mixture over them, smoothing it over the entire surface. Top with the remaining pastry and butter. Gently press down the edges to seal.

4 With a sharp knife, mark the top into diamonds. Bake for 20–25 minutes until golden brown and crisp. Meanwhile, put the syrup ingredients in a small pan and heat gently until the sugar has dissolved. Cover with a lid and leave to infuse for 20 minutes.

5 Remove the baklava from the oven. Re-heat the syrup and strain over the pastry. Leave to cool in the tin. Cut into diamonds, remove from the tin and serve.

COOK'S TIP
While assembling the baklava, keep the pile of filo pastry covered with a damp cloth to stop it drying out and becoming brittle, which makes it difficult to use.

SWEETS,
BISCUITS
AND BREADS

Few people can resist the

tantalizing display of biscuits and

breads in the baker's shop window,

but it's easy to recreate those

delectable bakes at home. Here,

you'll find a selection of

traditional and Continental recipes

from rich and gooey truffles to a

stunning candied fruit plait.

STUFFED PRUNES

CHOCOLATE-COVERED PRUNES, SOAKED IN LIQUEUR, HIDE A MELT-IN-THE-MOUTH COFFEE FILLING.

MAKES APPROXIMATELY THIRTY

INGREDIENTS
    225g/8oz/1 cup unstoned prunes
    50ml/2fl oz/¼ cup Armagnac
    30ml/2 tbsp ground coffee
    150ml/¼ pint/⅔ cup double cream
    350g/12oz plain chocolate, broken
        into squares
    10g/¼oz/½ tbsp vegetable fat
    30ml/2 tbsp cocoa powder,
        for dusting

1 Put the unstoned prunes in a bowl and pour the Armagnac over. Stir, then cover with clear film and set aside for 2 hours, or until the prunes have absorbed the liquid.

COOK'S TIP
Fresh dates can be used instead of prunes, if preferred.

2 Make a slit along each prune to remove the stone, making a hollow for the filling, but leaving the fruit intact.

3 Put the coffee and cream in a pan and heat almost to boiling point. Cover, infuse for 4 minutes, then heat again until almost boiling. Put 115g/4oz of the chocolate into a bowl and pour over the coffee cream through a sieve.

4 Stir until the chocolate has melted and the mixture is smooth. Leave to cool, until it has the consistency of softened butter.

5 Fill a piping bag with a small plain nozzle with the chocolate mixture. Pipe into the cavities of the prunes. Chill in the fridge for 20 minutes.

6 Melt the remaining chocolate in a bowl over a pan of hot water. Using a fork, dip the prunes one at a time into the chocolate to give them a generous coating. Place on non-stick baking parchment to harden. Dust each with a little cocoa powder.

COFFEE CHOCOLATE TRUFFLES

BECAUSE THESE CLASSIC CHOCOLATES CONTAIN FRESH CREAM, THEY SHOULD BE STORED IN THE FRIDGE AND EATEN WITHIN A FEW DAYS.

MAKES TWENTY-FOUR

INGREDIENTS
  350g/12oz plain chocolate
  75ml/5 tbsp double cream
  30ml/2 tbsp coffee liqueur, such as
    Tia Maria, Kahlúa or Toussaint
  115g/4oz good quality white
    dessert chocolate
  115g/4oz good quality milk
    dessert chocolate

1 Melt 225g/8oz of the plain chocolate in a bowl over a pan of barely simmering water. Stir in the cream and liqueur, then chill the mixture in the fridge for 4 hours, until firm.

2 Divide the mixture into 24 equal pieces and quickly roll each into a ball. Chill for one more hour, or until they are firm again.

3 Melt the remaining plain, white and milk chocolate in separate small bowls. Using two forks, carefully dip eight of the truffles, one at a time, into the melted milk chocolate.

4 Repeat with the white and plain chocolate. Place the truffles on a board, covered with wax paper or foil. Leave to set before removing and placing in a serving bowl or individual paper cases.

VARIATIONS
Ring the changes by adding one of the following to the truffle mixture:
Ginger – Stir in 40g/1½oz/¼ cup finely chopped crystallized ginger.
Candied fruit – Stir in 50g/2oz/⅓ cup finely chopped candied fruit, such as pineapple and orange.
Pistachio – Stir in 25g/1oz/¼ cup, chopped skinned pistachio nuts.
Hazelnut – Roll each ball of chilled truffle mixture around a whole skinned hazelnut.
Raisin – Soak 40g/1½oz/generous ¼ cup raisins overnight in 15ml/1 tbsp coffee liqueur, such as Tia Maria or Kahlúa and stir into the truffle mixture.

CHOCOLATE AND COFFEE MINT THINS

*THESE COFFEE-FLAVOURED CHOCOLATE SQUARES CONTAIN PIECES OF CRISP MINTY CARAMEL AND ARE
IDEAL FOR SERVING WITH AFTER-DINNER COFFEE.*

MAKES SIXTEEN

INGREDIENTS
  75g/3oz/scant ½ cup sugar
  75ml/5 tbsp water
  3 drops oil of peppermint
  15ml/1 tbsp strong-flavoured
    ground coffee
  75ml/5 tbsp near-boiling
    double cream
  225g/8oz plain chocolate
  10g/¼oz/½ tbsp unsalted butter

COOK'S TIP
Don't put the chocolate in the fridge to
set, or it may loose its glossy appearance
and become too brittle to cut easily into
neat squares.

1 Line a 18cm/7in square tin with non-
stick baking parchment. Gently heat the
sugar and water in a heavy-based pan
until dissolved. Add the peppermint,
and boil until a light caramel colour.

2 Pour the caramel on to an oiled
baking sheet and leave to harden, then
crush into small pieces.

3 Put the coffee in a small bowl and
pour the hot cream over. Leave to
infuse for about 4 minutes, then strain
through a fine sieve. Melt the chocolate
and unsalted butter in a bowl over
barely simmering water. Remove from
the heat and beat in the hot coffee
cream. Stir in the mint caramel.

4 Pour the mixture into the prepared
tin and smooth the surface level. Leave
in a cool place to set for at least
4 hours, preferably overnight.

5 Carefully turn out the chocolate on to
a board and peel off the lining paper.
Cut the chocolate into squares with a
sharp knife and store in an airtight
container until needed.

COFFEE AND HAZELNUT MACAROONS

*MACAROONS ARE TRADITIONALLY MADE WITH GROUND ALMONDS. THIS RECIPE USES HAZELNUTS,
WHICH ARE LIGHTLY ROASTED BEFORE GRINDING, BUT YOU CAN USE WALNUTS INSTEAD, IF PREFERRED.*

MAKES TWENTY

INGREDIENTS
  edible rice paper
  115g/4oz/⅔ cup skinned hazelnuts
  225g/8oz/generous 1 cup
    caster sugar
  15ml/1 tbsp ground rice
  10ml/2 tsp ground coffee,
    e.g. hazelnut-flavoured
  2 egg whites
  caster sugar, for sprinkling

1 Preheat the oven to 180°C/350°F/
Gas 4. Line two baking sheets with rice
paper. Place the skinned hazelnuts on a
baking sheet and cook for 5 minutes.
Cool, then place in a food processor
and grind until fine.

2 Mix the ground nuts with the sugar,
ground rice and coffee. Stir in the egg
whites to make a fairly stiff paste.

3 Spoon into a piping bag fitted with a
1cm/½in plain nozzle. Pipe rounds on
the rice paper, leaving room to spread.

4 Sprinkle each macaroon with a little
caster sugar then bake for 20 minutes,
or until pale golden in colour. Transfer
to a wire rack to cool. Remove excess
rice paper when completely cold. Serve
immediately or store in an airtight tin
for up to 2–3 days.

VIENNESE WHIRLS

THESE CRISP, MELT-IN-THE-MOUTH PIPED BISCUITS ARE FILLED WITH A CREAMY COFFEE BUTTERCREAM.

MAKES TWENTY

INGREDIENTS
175g/6oz/12 tbsp butter
50g/2oz/½ cup icing sugar
2.5ml/½ tsp vanilla essence
115g/4oz/1 cup plain flour
50g/2oz/½ cup cornflour
icing sugar and cocoa powder,
    to dust
For the filling
15ml/1 tbsp ground coffee
60ml/4 tbsp single cream
75g/3oz/6 tbsp butter, softened
115g/4oz/1 cup icing
    sugar, sifted

1 Preheat the oven to 180°C/350°F/
Gas 4. Cream together the butter, icing
sugar and vanilla essence until light.
Sift in the flour and cornflour and mix
in until smooth.

2 Using two tablespoons, spoon the
mixture into a piping bag fitted with
a 1cm/½in fluted nozzle.

3 Pipe small rosettes well apart on
greased baking sheets. Bake in the
oven for 12–15 minutes until golden.
Transfer to a wire rack to cool.

4 To make the filling, put the coffee in
a bowl. Heat the cream to near-boiling
and pour it over. Infuse for 4 minutes,
then strain through a fine sieve.

5 Beat the butter, icing sugar and
coffee-flavoured cream until light. Use
to sandwich the biscuits in pairs. Dust
with icing sugar and cocoa powder.

VARIATION
For mocha Viennese whirls, substitute
25g/1oz/¼ cup cocoa powder for 25g/
1oz/¼ cup of the flour.

BLACK RUSSIAN COOKIES

THE INGREDIENTS OF THE FAMOUS COCKTAIL — COFFEE AND VODKA — FLAVOUR THESE FABULOUS COOKIES.

MAKES SIXTEEN

INGREDIENTS
30ml/2 tbsp ground espresso or other
    strong-flavoured coffee
60ml/4 tbsp near-boiling milk
115g/4oz/8 tbsp butter
115g/4oz/½ cup soft light
    brown sugar
1 egg
225g/8oz/2 cups plain flour
5ml/1 tsp baking powder
pinch of salt
For the icing
115g/4oz/1 cup icing sugar
about 25ml/1½ tbsp vodka

1 Preheat the oven to 180°C/350°F/
Gas 4. Put the coffee in a small bowl
and pour the hot milk over. Leave to
infuse for 4 minutes, then strain
through a fine sieve and leave to cool.

2 Cream the butter and sugar together
until light and fluffy. Gradually beat in
the egg. Sift the flour, baking powder
and salt together and fold in with the
coffee-flavoured milk to make a fairly
stiff mixture.

3 Place dessertspoonfuls of the mixture
on greased baking sheets, spacing them
slightly apart to allow room for a little
spreading. Bake the cookies for about
15 minutes, until lightly browned. Cool
on a wire rack.

4 To make the icing, mix the icing
sugar and enough vodka together to
make a thick icing. Spoon into a small
greaseproof paper piping bag.

5 Snip off the end of the piping bag
and lightly drizzle the icing over the
top of each cookie. Allow the icing to
set before serving.

COFFEE AND MACADEMIA MUFFINS

THESE MUFFINS ARE DELICIOUS EATEN COLD, BUT ARE BEST SERVED STILL WARM FROM THE OVEN.

MAKES TWELVE

INGREDIENTS
   25ml/1½ tbsp ground coffee
   250ml/8fl oz/1 cup milk
   50g/2oz/4 tbsp butter
   275g/10oz/2½ cups plain flour
   10ml/2 tsp baking powder
   150g/5oz/10 tbsp light
    muscovado sugar
   75g/3oz/½ cup macadamia nuts
   1 egg, lightly beaten

1 Preheat the oven to 200°C/400°F/ Gas 6. Lightly grease a 12-hole muffin or a deep-bun tray with oil. Alternatively, line with paper muffin cases.

2 Put the coffee in a jug or bowl. Heat the milk to near-boiling and pour it over. Leave to infuse for 4 minutes, then strain through a sieve.

3 Add the butter to the coffee-flavoured milk mixture and stir until melted. Leave until cold.

4 Sift the flour and baking powder into a large mixing bowl. Stir in the sugar and macadamia nuts. Add the egg to the coffee-flavoured milk mixture, pour into the dry ingredients and stir until just combined – do not over-mix.

5 Divide the coffee mixture between the prepared muffin tins and bake for about 15 minutes until well risen and firm. Transfer to a wire rack and serve warm or cold.

COOK'S TIP
To cool the coffee-flavoured milk quickly, place the jug in a large bowl of iced or cold water.

CHUNKY WHITE CHOCOLATE AND COFFEE BROWNIES

BROWNIES SHOULD HAVE A GOOEY TEXTURE, SO TAKE CARE NOT TO OVERCOOK THEM — WHEN READY, THE MIXTURE WILL STILL BE SLIGHTLY SOFT UNDER THE CRUST, BUT WILL FIRM AS IT COOLS.

MAKES TWELVE

INGREDIENTS
   25ml/1½ tbsp ground coffee
   45ml/3 tbsp near-boiling water
   300g/11oz plain chocolate, broken
    into pieces
   225g/8oz/1 cup butter
   225g/8oz/1 cup caster sugar
   3 eggs
   75g/3oz/⅔ cup self-raising
    flour, sifted
   225g/8oz white chocolate, chopped

1 Preheat the oven to 190°C/375°F/ Gas 5. Grease and line the base of a 18 x 28cm/7 x 11in tin with greaseproof paper. Put the coffee in a bowl and pour the water over. Leave to infuse for 4 minutes, then strain through a sieve.

2 Put the plain chocolate and butter in a bowl over a pan of hot water and stir occasionally until melted. Remove from the heat and cool for 5 minutes.

3 Mix the sugar and eggs together. Stir in the chocolate and butter mixture and the coffee. Stir in the sifted flour.

4 Fold in the white chocolate pieces. Pour into the prepared tin.

5 Bake for 45–50 minutes, or until firm and the top is crusty. Leave to cool in the tin. When completely cold, cut into squares and remove from the tin.

PECAN TOFFEE SHORTBREAD

COFFEE SHORTBREAD IS TOPPED WITH PECAN-STUDDED TOFFEE. CORNFLOUR GIVES IT A CRUMBLY LIGHT TEXTURE, BUT ALL PLAIN FLOUR CAN BE USED IF YOU LIKE.

MAKES TWENTY

INGREDIENTS
    15ml/1 tbsp ground coffee
    15ml/1 tbsp near-boiling water
    115g/4oz/8 tbsp butter, softened
    30ml/2 tbsp smooth peanut butter
    75g/3oz/scant ½ cup caster sugar
    75g/3oz/⅔ cup cornflour
    185g/6½oz/1⅔ cups plain flour
For the topping
    175g/6oz/12 tbsp butter
    175g/6oz/¾ cup soft light
      brown sugar
    30ml/2 tbsp golden syrup
    175g/6oz/1 cup shelled pecan nuts,
      roughly chopped

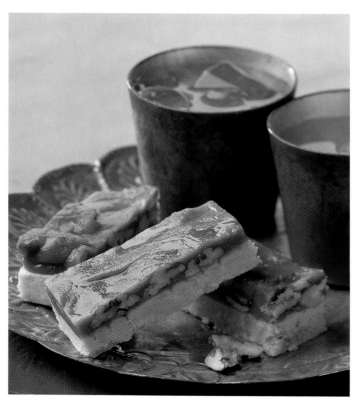

1 Preheat the oven to 180°C/350°F/ Gas 4. Lightly grease and line the base of a 18 x 28cm/7 x 11in tin with greaseproof paper.

2 Put the ground coffee in a small bowl and pour the hot water over. Leave to infuse for 4 minutes, then strain through a fine sieve.

3 Cream the butter, peanut butter, sugar and coffee together until light. Sift the cornflour and flour together and mix in to make a smooth dough.

4 Press into the base of the tin and prick all over with a fork. Bake for 20 minutes. To make the topping, put the butter, sugar and syrup in a pan and heat until melted. Bring to the boil.

5 Allow to simmer for 5 minutes, then stir in the chopped nuts. Spread the topping over the base. Leave in the tin until cold, then cut into fingers. Remove from the tin and serve.

COFFEE BISCOTTI

THESE CRISP BISCUITS ARE MADE TWICE AS DELICIOUS WITH BOTH FRESHLY ROASTED GROUND COFFEE
BEANS AND STRONG AROMATIC BREWED COFFEE IN THE MIXTURE.

MAKES ABOUT THIRTY

INGREDIENTS
   25g/1oz/⅓ cup espresso-roasted
     coffee beans
   115g/4oz/⅔ cup blanched almonds
   200g/7oz/scant 2 cups plain flour
   7.5ml/1½ tsp baking powder
   1.5ml/¼ tsp salt
   75g/3oz/6 tbsp unsalted butter, cubed
   150g/5oz/¾ cup caster sugar
   2 eggs, beaten
   25–30ml/1½–2 tbsp strong
     brewed coffee
   5ml/1 tsp ground cinnamon,
     for dusting

1 Preheat the oven to 180°C/350°F/
Gas 4. Put the espresso coffee beans in
a single layer on one side of a large
baking sheet and the almonds on the
other. Roast in the oven for 10 minutes.
Leave to cool.

2 Put the coffee beans in a blender or
food processor and process until fairly
fine. Tip out and set aside. Process the
almonds until finely ground.

3 Sift the flour, baking powder and salt
into a bowl. Rub in the butter until the
mixture resembles fine breadcrumbs.
Stir in the caster sugar, ground coffee
and almonds. Add the beaten eggs and
enough brewed coffee to make a fairly
firm dough.

COOK'S TIP
Store the biscotti in an airtight tin for at
least a day before serving.

4 Lightly knead for a few seconds until
smooth and shape into two rolls about
7.5cm/3in in diameter. Place on a
greased baking sheet and dust with
cinnamon. Bake for 20 minutes.

5 Using a sharp knife, cut the rolls into
4cm/1½in slices on the diagonal.
Arrange the slices on the baking tray
and bake for a further 10 minutes, or
until lightly browned. Cool on a rack.

CAPPUCCINO PANETTONE

THIS LIGHT BREAD IS SERVED IN ITALY AS PART OF THEIR CHRISTMAS FARE. IT'S TRADITIONALLY A TALL LOAF WITH A DOME ON THE TOP, FORMED BY THE RICH YEASTED DOUGH AS IT RISES.

SERVES EIGHT

INGREDIENTS
  450g/1lb/4 cups strong plain flour
  2.5ml/½ tsp salt
  75g/3oz/scant ½ cup caster sugar
  7g/¼oz sachet easy-blend
    dried yeast
  115g/4oz/8 tbsp butter
  100ml/3½fl oz/scant ½ cup very hot
    strong brewed espresso coffee
  100ml/3½fl oz/½ cup milk
  4 egg yolks
  115g/4oz/⅔ cup plain
    chocolate chips
  beaten egg, to glaze

1 Preheat the oven to 190°C/375°F/ Gas 5. Lightly grease and line a deep 14–15cm/5½–6in cake tin with greaseproof paper. Sift the flour and salt into a large bowl. Stir in the sugar and yeast.

2 Add the butter to the coffee and stir until melted. Stir in the milk, then add to the dry ingredients with the egg yolks. Mix together to make a dough.

COOK'S TIP
Unlike commercial varieties, home-made panettone should be eaten within a day or two of baking.

3 Turn the dough out on to a lightly floured surface and knead for 10 minutes, until smooth and elastic. Knead in the chocolate chips.

4 Shape into a ball, place in the tin and cover with oiled clear film. Leave to rise in a warm place for 1 hour or until the dough reaches the top of the tin. Lightly brush with beaten egg and bake for 35 minutes.

5 Turn down the oven to 180°C/350°F/ Gas 4 and cover the panettone with foil if it has browned enough. Cook for a further 10–15 minutes, or until done.

6 Allow the panettone to cool in the tin for 10 minutes, then transfer to a wire rack. Remove the lining paper just before slicing and serving.

CANDIED FRUIT BREAD

THE CENTRE OF THIS COFFEE-FLAVOURED YEASTED PLAIT CONTAINS BRIGHTLY COLOURED CANDIED FRUITS, MOISTENED BY SOAKING IN RICH COFFEE LIQUEUR.

SERVES SIX TO EIGHT

INGREDIENTS

175g/6oz/1 cup mixed candied fruit,
    such as pineapple, orange and
    cherries, chopped
60ml/4 tbsp coffee liqueur, such as
    Tia Maria, Kahlúa or Toussaint
30ml/2 tbsp ground coffee
100ml/3½fl oz/½ cup
    near-boiling milk
225g/8oz/2 cups strong plain flour
1.5ml/¼ tsp salt
25g/1oz/2 tbsp soft light brown sugar
½ x 7g/¼oz sachet easy-blend
    dried yeast
1 egg, beaten
50g/2oz white almond paste, grated
65g/2½oz/¼ cup apricot jam
15g/½oz/1 tbsp unsalted butter
15ml/1 tbsp caster sugar
15ml/1 tbsp clear honey

1 Put the candied fruit in a small bowl and spoon the coffee liqueur over. Stir to coat the fruit, then cover with clear film and leave to soak overnight.

2 Preheat the oven to 200°C/400°F/ Gas 6. Put the coffee in a bowl; pour the hot milk over and leave until tepid. Strain through a fine sieve. Sift the flour and salt into a bowl. Stir in the brown sugar and yeast. Make a well in the centre, add the coffee-flavoured milk and the egg and mix to a soft dough.

4 Meanwhile, mix the soaked fruit, almond paste and jam together. Lightly knead the dough again for 1 minute, then roll out to a rectangle 35 x 30cm/ 14 x 12in.

5 Spread the filling in a 7.5cm/3in strip lengthways down the middle to within 5cm/2in of each end. Make 14 diagonal cuts about 2cm/¾in wide in the dough either side of the filling.

6 Fold the ends of the dough up over the filling, overlapping alternate strips, Tuck in the last two strips neatly. Place on a greased baking tray.

7 Cover with clear film and leave to rise for 20 minutes. Melt the butter, sugar and honey in a small pan, then brush over the braid. Bake for 20–25 minutes. Allow to cool before slicing and serving.

3 Knead for 10 minutes. Put the dough in a clean bowl, cover with clear film and leave to rise for 1 hour.

USEFUL ADDRESSES

Good coffee is sold in countless places all over the world. The following addresses are intended as a starting point for those in search of quality coffee – either in coffee houses or as freshly roasted beans to brew at home.

Australia

Coffee suppliers:
Arabicas Coffee Australia Pty Ltd
136 Mason St
Mareeba QLD 4880
Tel: (07) 4092 4101
North Queensland's original boutique coffee roasters

Aromas Pty Ltd
427 Montague Rd
West End QLD 4101
Tel: (07) 3846 2594

Aromas Tea and Coffee Merchants
191 Margaret St
Toowoomba QLD 4350
Tel: (07) 4632 4533

Australian Estate Coffee Direct Mail Order
Tel: (1800) 043 611
Chemical-free coffee, low in caffeine, stocks Plateau Gold

Exporters:
Web: www.australiancoffee-exporters.com.au
Email: sales@australiancoffee-exporters.com.au
7 Lena Close,
Clifton Beach QLD 4879
Tel: (07) 40 553315

Skybury Coffee Estate
Atherton Tablelands, QLD
Tel: (07) 4093 2194

Coffee tree supplier:
Coffee Pot Nursery
179 Tintenbar Road
Tintenbar NSW 2478
Tel: (02) 6687 8430
Specializes in Byron Red coffee trees suited to Australian conditions – frost and disease resistant

Coffee equipment suppliers:
Coffee & Tea Supplies of W.A.
93 Pavers Circle
Malaga WA 6090
Tel: (08) 9248 1500
Fax: (08) 9248 1499

Segafredo Zanetti Australia Pty Ltd
4 Huntley St
Alexandria 2015 NSW
Tel: (02) 9310 3664
Fax: (02) 9310 3751
Email:
segafred@ozemail.com.au

Tasman Coffee Company Pty Ltd
Depot Road
Mornington 7018 TAS
Tel: (03) 6245 9330
Fax: (03) 6245 9331

The Short Black Company
25 Burwood Rd
Hawthorn 3122 VIC
Tel: (03) 9818 0667
Fax: (03) 9819 0843

Art Deco Coffee Repairs & Sales
123 Holden St
Ashfield 2131 NSW
Tel: 0412 45 5994

Auto Cappuccino Machines
6 South Boulivard
Tea Tree Gully 5091 SA
Tel: (08) 8264 7751

Belaroma
75 Kenneth Rd
Manly Vale 2093 NSW
Tel: (02) 9948 0221
Equipment and coffee shop

Classic Coffee Company Cairns
126 Sheridan St
Cairns 4870 QLD
Tel: (07) 4051 8966

Five Star Gourmet Foods Sydney
13 Willoughby Road
Crows Nest NSW 2065
Tel: (02) 9438 5666
Equipment and coffee shop

Coffee houses and cafés:
Grinder's Coffee House
1 Taylor St
Darlinghurst NSW 2010
Tel: (02) 9360 3255
http://www.grinderscoffee.com.au/
Grinds coffee daily, and is also distributor of espresso coffee and coffee-making equipment

Forsyth Coffee
284 Willoughby Road
Naremburn NSW 2065
Tel: (02) 9906 7388
www.netorder.com.au/forsyth/coffee

La Buvette
Shop 2, 65 Macleay Street
Potts Point NSW 2011
Tel: 02 9358 5113

Caffee e'Cucina
581 Chapel Street
South Yarra Victoria 3141
Tel: (03) 9827 4139
Fax: (03) 9826 8355

Internet Sites:
Coffee from Oz Coffee
http://www.ozcoffee.com.au/
Supplier of fine coffee via the web

Coast Roast Coffee Co,
Cairns QLD Australia
http://www.coastroast.com.au/
Supplier of fine coffee via the web

Boema
http://www.boema.com.au/CoffeeRecipes.htm
Coffee machine supplier for domestic and office use

Kona Coffee Company
Offices in all states
http://www.kona.com.au/default.htm
Supplier of fine coffee via the web

Bay Coffee Roasters
Neutral Bay
email:
http://www.baycoffee.com.au/

England

Coffee suppliers:
Algerian Coffee Stores
52 Old Compton St
London W1V 6PB
Tel: (0171) 437 2480

The Drury Tea and Coffee Company
37 Drury Lane
London WC2B 5RR
Tel: (0171) 836 2607

Fern's Coffee Specialists and Tea Merchants
27 Rathbone Place
Oxford Street
London W1P 2EP
Tel: (0171) 636 2237

Fortnum & Mason
181 Piccadilly
London W1A 1ER
Tel: (0171) 734 8040

Harrods
Knightsbridge
London, SW1X 7XL
Tel: (0171) 730 1234

Harvey Nichols
Knightsbridge
London SW1
Tel: (0171) 235 5000

H.R. Higgins
79 Duke Street
London W11M 6AS
Tel: (0171) 629 3913

The Monmouth Coffee
Company
27 Monmouth Street
London WC2H 9DD
Tel: (0171) 836 5272

Selfridges
400 Oxford Street
London W1A 1AB
Tel: (0171) 629 1234

Wilkinson's Tea and Coffee
Merchants
5 Lobster Lane
Norwich NR2 1DQ
Tel: (01603) 625121
Fax: (01603) 789016

Wittard of Chelsea
Head Office:
Union Court,
22 Union Road
London SW4 6JQ
Tel: (0171) 627 8885

Coffee houses and cafés:
Aroma
273 Regent Street
London W1
Tel: (0171) 495 4911

Bar Italia
22 Frith Street
London W1
Tel: (0171) 437 4520

Café Mezzo
100 Wardour Street
London W1
Tel: (0171) 314 4000

Café Minema
43 Knightsbridge
London SW1
Tel: (0171) 201 1618

Café Nero
43 Frith Street
London W1V 5CE
Tel: (0171) 434 3887

Coffee Republic
2 South Molton Street
London W1
Tel: (0171) 629 4567

Maison Bertaux
28 Greek Street
London W1V 5LL
Tel: (0171) 437 6007

Pret à Manger
Head office:
Old Mitre Court
43 Fleet Street
London EC4Y 1BT
Tel: (0171) 827 6300

Seattle Coffee Company
Head office: 51/54 Long Acre,
Covent Garden
London WC2 9JR
Tel: (0171) 836 2100

Maison Bertaux
28 Greek Street
London W1V 5LL
Tel: (1071) 437 6007

Museums and Organizations:
Bramah Tea and Coffee
Museum
The Clove Building,
Maguire Street, Butlers Wharf
London SE1 2NQ
Tel: (0171) 378 0222

International Coffee
Organization
22 Berners Street
London W1P 4DD
Tel: (0171) 580 8591

Europe

Coffee suppliers and cafés:
Austria:
Café Central
Palais Ferstel, Herrengasse
and Strauchgasse

Vienna, Austria
Tel: (1) 53 33 76 30

Café Museum
Friedrichstrasse 6
Vienna, Austria
Tel: (1) 586 52 02

Café Sacher
Philharmonikerstrasse 4
Vienna, Austria
Tel: (1) 512 14 87

Demel's
Kohlmarkt 14
Vienna, Austria
Tel: (1) 53 51 71 70

Belgium:
Cafés Knopes
Grand Place 24
Aron, Belguim 6700
Tel: (63) 22 7407

Corica
49 rue du Marché aux Puces
Brussels, Belguim 1000
Tel: (2) 511 88 52

Czech Republic:
Café Savoy
Vitezna, 1, Prague,

France:
Brûlerie de L'Odeon
6 rue de Crébillon
Paris, France 75006
Tel: (01) 43 26 39 32

Café Beaubourg
45 rue Saint-Merri
Paris, France, 75004
Tel: (01) 48 87 63 96

Cafés Estrella
34 rue Saint-Sulpice
Paris, France 75006
Tel: (01) 46 33 16 37

Café de Flore
172 boulevard Saint-Germain
Paris, France 75006
Tel: (01) 45 48 55 26

Café de La Paix
Place de l'Opera
Paris, France 75009
Tel: (01) 40 07 30 20

Café Richelieu
Place Carrousel
(part of Louvre Museum's
Richelieu wing)
Paris, France 75001
Tel: (01) 47 03 99 68

Couleur Café
34 rue de Ponthieu
Paris, France 75008
Tel: (01) 42 56 00 15

Les Deux Magots
6 place Saint-Germain-
des-Prés
Paris, France 75006
Tel: (01) 45 48 55 25

La Grande Épicerie de Paris
(Le Bon Marché)
38 rue de Sèvres
Paris, France 75007
Tel: (01) 44 39 81 00

Cathy et Pascal Guraud
21 Boulevard de Reuilly
Paris, France 75012
Tel: (01) 43 43 39 27

Lapeyronie
3 rue Brantôme
Paris, France 75003
Tel: (01) 40 27 97 57

Verlet
256 rue Saint-Honoré
Paris, France 75001
Tel: (01) 42 60 67 39

Whittard of Chelsea
22 rue de Buci
Paris, France 75006

Germany:
Café Einstein
Kurfürstendamm 58

Berlin, Germany
Tel: (30) 261 50 96

Eduscho
Head office:
Lloydstrasse 4
Bremen, Germany 28217
Tel: (421) 3 89 30

Alois Dallmayr
Dienerstrasse 14–15
Munich, Germany 80331
Tel: (89) 21 35 0

Eilles
Residenzstrasse 13
Munich, Germany 80333
Tel: (89) 22 61 84

Italy:
Caffè Tazza D'Oro
Via degli Orfani 84
Rome. Italy
Tel (6) 6678 97 92

Caffè Florian
Piazza San Marco 56–59
Venice, Italy
Tel: (41) 528 53 38

Caffè Paskowski
Piazza della Republica
Florence 122
Italy
Tel: (55) 21 02 36

Caffè Perocchi
Via Otto Febbraio 15
Padua, Italy
Tel: (49) 876 25 76

Caffè Ristorante Torino
Piazza San Carlo 204
Turin
Italy
Tel: (11) 547 356

Caffè Rivoire
Piazza della Signoria 4R
Florence, Italy
Tel: (55) 21 44 12

Caffè San Carlo
Piazza San Carlo 156
Turin, Italy
Tel: (11) 561 77 48

Caffè degli Specchi
Piazza Unità d'Italia 7
Trieste, Italy
Tel: (40) 36 57 77

Caffè Tommaseo
Riva Tre Novembre 5
Trieste, Italy
Tel: (40) 36 57 77

Sant'Eustachio
Piazza Sant'Eustachio 82
Rome, Italy
Tel: (6) 688 02 048

New Zealand

Coffee roasters and suppliers:
Allpress Espresso Coffee
Roasters
Tel: (09) 358 3121

Altura Coffee Company Ltd
3/11 Colway Place
Tel:(09) 443 4111

Atomic Coffee Roasters
420 New North Road
Kingsland
Tel: 846 5883

Burton Hollis Coffee
6 Mepai Place
Auckland
Tel: (09) 277 6375

Chiasso Coffee Co. Ltd
71b Lake Road
Devonport, Auckland
Tel: (09) 445 1816

Columbus Coffee
Head Office:
43 High Street, Auckland
Tel: (09) 309 2845

Robert Harris Coffee &
Equipment
Direct mail order
Tel: (0800) 426 3333

Santos Coffee Roasting Co. Ltd
14 Adelaide Street
P.O. Box 91-723
Freeman's Bay, Auckland
Tel: (09) 309 8977
email: santos@xtra.co.nz

Starbucks Coffee
305 Parnell Road
Auckland
Tel: (09) 336 1599

Sweet Inspirations
143 Williamson Ave
Auckland
Tel: (09) 378 7261

Vinotica
Unit D, 3 Henry Rose Place
Albany, Auckland
Tel: (09) 415 5942

Vittoria Coffee and Equipment
Cntarella Bros Pty Ltd
8 Goodman Place
Onehunga
Tel: (09) 622 2409

United States

Coffee roasters and suppliers:
Ancora Coffee Roasters
112 King Street
Madison, WI 53703
Tel: (800) 666 4869

Armeno Coffee Roasters, Ltd
75 Otis Street
Northborough, MA 01532
Tel: (800) ARMENO-1

Bainbridge Coffee Company
584 Winslow Way East
Bainbridge Island, WA 98110
Tel: (888) 472 6333

Bean Central
2817 West End Avenue
Nashville, TN 37200
1800 JAVA BEAN

Beans and Machines
1121 First Avenue
Seattle, WA 98100

Bunn Coffee Service Inc.
51 Alpha Plaza
Hicksville, NY 11801
Tel: (800) 542 0566

Caribou Coffee
55 West Monroe
Chicago, IL 60602
Tel: (888) 227 4268
www.caribou-coffee.com

Coffee Concepts
10836 Grissom Suite 110
Dallas, TX 75229
Tel: (972) 241 1618
www.coffeeconcepts.com

The Coffee Mill Roastery
161 East Franklin Street
Chapel Hill, NC 27514
Tel: (919) 929 1727
www.coffeeroastery.com

Daybreak Coffee Roasters, Inc.
2377 Main Street
Glastonbury, CT 06033
Tel: (860) 657 4466
www.daybreakcoffee.com

Greene Brothers Specialty
Coffee Roasters
313 High Street
Hackettstown, NJ 07840
Tel: (888) 665 2626

The Kona Coffee Council
P.O. Box 2077
Kealakekua, HI 96750
www.kona-coffee-council.com

Maui Coffee Roasters
444 Hana Highway
Kahului, Maui, HI 96732
Tel: (800) 645 2877
www.nicbeans@maui.net

The Original San Juan Coffee
Roasting Company
18 Cannery Landing
Friday Harbor, WA 98250
Tel: (800) 624 4119

Ozzies Coffee & Tea
57 Seventh Avenue
Brooklyn, NY 11215
Tel: (888) 699 4371
www.ozziescoffee.com

Peet's Coffee & Tea
P.O. Box 12509
Berkeley, CA 94712-3509
Tel: (800) 999 2132
Email: www.peets.com

Roast Your Own
P.O. Box 198
Genoa, NY 13071
Tel: (800) 784 7117

Royal Blend Coffee Company
P.O. Box 7066
Bend, OR 97708
Tel: (541) 388 8164
www.royalblend.com

San Francisco Bay Gourmet
Coffee
1933 Davis Street, Suite 308
San Leandro, CA 94577
Tel: (800) 732 2948

Spinelli Coffee Company 495
Barneveld Avenue
San Francisco, CA 94124
Tel: (800) 421 5282
Fax: (415) 821 7199

Starbucks
Consumer Relations
P.O. Box 3717
Seattle, WA 98124 3717
Tel: (206 447 1575 x2900
www.starbucks.com

Wilderness Coffee Company
13541 Grove Drive North
Maple Grove, MN 55311
Tel: (612) 420 4830
Fax: (612) 420 7510

Internet sites and cybercafés
Alt.Coffee
139 Avenue A
New York, NY 10009
Tel: (215) 529-CAFE
www.altdotcoffee.com

Café and Internet of America
12536 S.W. 88th Street
Miami, FL 33280

Café Cyberway
25 High Street Ellsworth,
ME 04605
Tel: (207) 667 0718
www.cyberway.com

Cafe Internet
133 SW Century Drive
Suite 204
Bend, OR
Tel: (541) 318 8802
www.cafeinternet-band.com

Coffee & @ BYTE Cyber Café
235 West Cocoa Beach
Causeway
Cocoa Beach, FL 32931
Tel: (407) 453 2233
www.coffeeandabyte.com

The Connection C@fe, Inc.
149 Emerald Street
Keene, NH 03431
Tel: (603) 352 1500

The Cyber Shop
2227 Lake Tahoe Boulevard
Suite E
South Lake Tahoe,
CA 96150
Tel: (800) 618 2463
www.cyberstop.com

Cybercafé of St. Augustine
31 Orange Street
St. Augustine, FL
Tel: (904) 824 6121
www.tepee.com/cybercafe

CyberHawk's Internet Cafe and
Gaming Center
153 West Wilson Street
Batavia, IL 60510
Tel: (630) 761 4440
www.cyberhawkscafe.com

Cybersmith
Harvard Square
42 Church Street
Cambridge, MA 02138
Tel: (617) 492 5857
email: sryherd@cybersmith.com

CyberSTOP Café
1513 17th Street NW
Washington, DC 20036
Tel: (202) 234 2470
cyberstopcafe.com

Gold Rush Coffee
251 West Riverside Drive
Estes Park,
CO 80517
Tel: (970) 586 7874
www.goldrushcoffee.com

Gypsy Java
3321 East Bell Road
Phoenix, AZ 85000
Tel: (602) 404 9779

Java Java
860 Fifth Avenue South
Naples, FL 34102
Tel: (941) 435 1180

Java Net Cafe
241 Main Street
Northampton, MA 01060
email: support@javanet.com

Jeremy's Cybercafé & Beer
Haus
29 Palm Highway
Joshua Tree,
CA 92252
Tel: (760) 366 9799

New Hope Cybernet
1 West Bridge Street
New Hope, PA 18938
Tel: (215) 862 9550
email: info@newhopecyber.net

Realm of Delirium
941 Rue Decatur
New Orlean, LA 70100
www.realmofdelirium.com

Soapy's Station@Sockeye
Sam's
425 Water Street,
Ketchikan AK 99901
Tel: (907) 247 9191

Soho's Cyber Café
273 Lafayette Street
New York,
NY 10009
Tel: (212) 334 5140
www.cyber-cafe.com

Speakeasy Cafe
2304 Second Avenue
Seattle,
WA 98028
Tel: (206) 728 9770
www.speakeasy.net

PICTURE CREDITS

All pictures are by William
Lingwood, Louisa Dare and
Janine Hosegood, except for
the following: p11b, p29 and
p53, Advertising Archives;
p10, p11t, p14, p28, p32,
p33, p35, p35b, p36t, p37,
p38b, p39, p44, p45, p46
and p49 AKG Photographic
Library; p12, p36, p95t,
p100b, p116t Cephas; p12t
and b, p17, p18 and p19
Charmet; p21 p23, p25, p26,

p30, p34b, p40t and b, p42t
and p43b E.T. Archive; p22,
p43t, p46, p47, p48 and p50
Hulton Getty; p31 and p42b
Museum of London; p41
Lloyds; p24 Workers on a
Coffee Plantation (engraving)
by F.M. Reynolds (19th
century) and p27 Coffee
Roasting, 1870 (engraving)
(b&w photo), English school
(19th century), private collection, Bridgeman Art Library.

THE FACTS ABOUT COFFEE

The following information is provided by the International Coffee Organization, *Coffee Statistics, September 1998.*

Total production of exporting members. Crop year commencing (000 bags)	1993	1998
Angola	33	160
Benin	0	1
Brazil	26 787	34 547
Burundi	394	278
Cameroon	682	1 333
Central African Republic	165	150
Colombia	11 320	12 500
Congo, Democratic Rep. of	980	1 000
Congo, Rep of	3	25
Costa Rica	2 259	2 223
Cote d'Ivoire	2 293	2 742
Cuba	285	350
Dominican Republic	604	454
Ecuador	2 069	1 584
El Salvador	2 378	1 840
Equatorial Guinea	0	5
Ethiopia	2 865	3 867
Gabon	3	4
Ghana	46	51
Guatemala	3 536	2 800
Guinea	64	145
Haiti	459	420
Honduras	1 829	2 300
India	3 448	3 833
Indonesia	7 301	6 600
Jamaica	35	40
Kenya	1 328	1 133
Liberia	5	10
Madagascar	442	950
Malawi	62	65
Mexico	4 285	4 400
Nicaragua	706	1 147
Nigeria	45	55
Panama	142	173
Papua New Guinea	1 019	1 255
Paraguay	70	60
Peru	665	1 930
Philippines	875	685
Rwanda	443	250
Sierra Leone	37	50
Sri Lanka	54	40
Tanzania	736	700
Thailand	1275	1 000
Togo	195	334
Trinidad and Tobago	16	20
Uganda	3 142	3 600
Venezuela	1 307	1 400
Vietnam	3 020	6 200
Zambia	27	50
Zimbabwe	12	167

Imports of all forms of coffee from all sources Country (000 bags)	1993	1996
Algeria	1 470	888
Argentina	649	712
Australia	802	845
Austria	1 310	1 544
Belgium/Luxembourg	2 310	2 618
Canada	2 489	2 763
Chile	187	248
China	242	384
Denmark	1 071	1 000
Fiji	2	4
Finland	1 359	1 090
France	6 550	7 019
Germany	13 844	13 871
Greece	598	636
Hungary	668	603
Ireland	124	111
Israel	466	450
Italy	5 609	5 768
Japan	6 239	6 371
Lebanon	250	300
Malaysia	212	432
Morocco	343	377
Netherlands	3 366	3 056
New Zealand	150	157
Norway	819	710
Portugal	650	757
Saudi Arabia	144	281
Singapore	1 917	968
South Africa	403	328
Spain	3 055	3 807
Sudan	150	107
Sweden	1 913	1 599
Switzerland	1 068	1 009
Taiwan	157	210
Turkey	171	252
United Kingdom	3 488	2 959
United States of America	16 720	20 873
Former U.S.S.R	1 919	1 493

BIBLIOGRAPHY

Adler C., Ramsay A., *Told in the Coffee House* (Macmillan Co. NY, 1898)

Alcott, Dr W.A., *Tea and Coffee: their physical, intellectual and moral effects on the human system* (Stoke-upon-Trent, UK, 1859)

Angell, John. *Health Lectures 8-10 Tea, Coffee and Cocoa.* (John Heywood, London, 1886)

Beeton, Isabella. *The Book of Household Management* (Facsimile), (Jonathan Cape, London, 1968)

Bradshaw, Steve. *Café Society Bohemian Life from Swift to Bob Dylan* (Wiedenfeld & Nicholson, London 1978)

Boettcher, Jürgen (ed.). *Coffee Houses of Europe* (Thames and Hudson, London, 1980)

Bramah, Edward. *Tea & Coffee* (Hutchinson, London, 1972)

Campbell, Dawn and Smith, Janet. *The Coffee Book* (Pelican Publishing Company, Louisiana, USA, 1995)

Chamberlain, Lesley. *The Food and Cooking of Eastern Europe* (Penguin Books, London, 1989)

Chamberlayne, John (trans.). *The Manner of Making Coffee, Tea and Chocolate* (London, 1685)

Coffee Bar and Coffee Lounge, (Periodical Publications, London, 1959–60)

Coptic Press. *Coffee Houses of Old London* (London, 1965)

Davids, Kenneth. *The Coffee Book* (Whittet Books, Weybridge, UK, 1976)

Debry, Gérard. *Coffee and Health* (John Libbey Eurotext, Paris, 1994)

Douglas, Dr James. *Yemensis fructum Coté ferens; or, a description and history of the Coffee tree* (London, 1727)

Food and Agriculture Organization of the United Nations. *Traditional Foods in the Near East* (Rome, 1991)

Food and Agriculture Organization of the United Nations, *Utilization of tropical foods: sugars, spices and stimulants* (Rome, 1989)

Harleian Miscellany, vol.8. *The Character of a Coffee-House.* (London, 1673)

Harleian Miscellany, vol.8. *Coffee Houses Vindicated* (London,1673)

Hattox, Ralph S. *Coffee and Coffee Houses: The origin of a Social Beverage in the Medieval Near East* (University of Washington Press, USA, 1985)

Heise, Ulla. *Coffee and Coffee Houses* (Schiffer Publishing, Pennsylvania, 1987)

Jobin, P., *Les Cafés produits dans le monde* (P. Jobin et Cie, Le Havre, 4th ed.)

Joel, G.C.W. (compiler). *One Hundred Years of Coffee* (London, 1942)

Kolpas, Norman. *Coffee* (John Murray, London, 1979)

Kummer, Corby, *The Joy of Coffee* (Houghton Mifflin

UK, 1985)

Company, New York, 1997)

Law, William. *History of Coffee* (London, 1850)

Librairie Larousse. *Larousse Gastronomique* (Hamlyn, London, 1988)

McCoy, Elin and Walker, John Frederick. *Coffee and Tea* (Signet, New York, 1976)

Mennell, Stephen. *All Manners of Food* (Blackwell, Oxford,

Porter, Roy and Teich, Mikulás (eds.). *Drugs and Narcotics in History* (Cambridge University Press, UK, 1995)

Renner, H.D. *The Origin of Food Habits* (Faber and Faber, London, 1954)

Roden, Claudia. *Coffee* (Faber, London, 1977)

Roden, Claudia. *The Book of Jewish Food* (Viking, London, 1997)

Roland, Paul. *Revelations: The Wisdom of the Ages* (Carlton Books, London, 1995)

Shaida, Margaret. *The Legendary Cuisine of Persia* (Penguin Books, London, 1994)

Schapira, Joel, David and Karl.

The Book of Coffee and Tea (St Martin's Press, New York, 1975)

Simmonds, P.L. *Coffee as It Is, and As It Ought To Be* (London, 1850)

Stein, Stanley J. *Vassouras, a Brazilian Coffee County 1850-1900* (Princeton University Press, USA, 1985)

Stella, Alain. *The Book of Coffee* (Flammarion, Paris, 1997)

Stobart, Tom. *Herbs, Spices and Flavourings* (Penguin Books, London, 1977)

The Men's Answer to the Women's Petition Against Coffee... (London, 1674)

The Times Atlas of World History (Times Books, London, 1981)

The Vertues of Coffee (London, 1663)

The Women's Petition Against Coffee... (London, 1674)

Thorn, Jon, *The Coffee Companion* (Quintet, London, 1995)

Toussaint-Samat, Maguelonne. *History of Food* (Blackwell, Oxford, UK. 1994)

Trager, James. *The Food Chronology* (Henry Holt and Company, New York, 1995)

Ukers, W. *The Romance of Coffee* (Tea and Coffee Trade Journal Co., New York, 1948)

Uribe, C.Andres. *Brown Gold* (Random House, New York, 1954)

Wrigley, Gordon, *Coffee* (Longman Scientific & Technical)

ACKNOWLEDGEMENTS

The publishers would like to thank the following people for their generous assistance with the preparation of this book: Tony Higgins of H.R. Higgins Ltd., London; Mehmet Kurukaveçi of Istanbul; Frank Neale; Celcius Lodder, Martin Wattam and the library staff of

the International Coffee Organization, Coffee Information Centre, London.

The following companies provided helpful assistance, equipment and coffee bean samples: Algerian Coffee Company; Andronicus;

Bramah Tea and Coffee Museum; Ecom; Fairfax Kitchens; Gala Tea and Coffee company; Heals Café, Tottenham Court Road London, UK; Master Roasts; Monmouth Coffee Company and The Priory Tea and Coffee Company.

INDEX

NOTES

Notes

NOTES

NOTES

NOTES

NOTES

NOTES

NOTES

CHOCOLATE

CHOCOLATE

CHRISTINE McFADDEN AND CHRISTINE FRANCE

HERMES HOUSE

This edition is published by Hermes House

Hermes House is an imprint of Anness Publishing Ltd
Hermes House, 88–89 Blackfriars Road, London SE1 8HA
tel. 020 7401 2077; fax 020 7633 9499
info@anness.com

© Anness Publishing Ltd 1997, 2002

Published in the USA by Hermes House, Anness Publishing Inc.
27 West 20th Street, New York, NY 10011; fax 212 807 6813

A CIP catalogue record for this book is available from the British Library.

Publisher: Joanna Lorenz
Text by: Christine McFadden
Recipes by: Christine France
Project Editor: Joanne Rippin
Assistant Editor: Emma Gray
Designer: Nigel Partridge
Special Photography: Don Last
Picture Researcher: Vanessa Miles
Handcrafted dishes on pp:58, 206, 231, 237 by Sue Shaw 01252 726684
Production Controller: Don Campaniello

Previously published as *The Ultimate Encyclopedia of Chocolate* and
as *The Cook's Encyclopedia of Chocolate*

Printed and bound in China
1 3 5 7 9 10 8 6 4 2

CONTENTS

INTRODUCTION

O ne of the greatest treasures ever discovered was the bean from the tree *Theobroma cacao,* the original source of chocolate. Smooth in texture, intense in taste, subtly perfumed and elegant to behold, chocolate is a rich source of sensory pleasure, adored by almost everyone.

The Ultimate Encyclopedia of Chocolate is a celebration of this divine food, and divine it really is – translated from the Greek, *theobroma* literally means "food of the gods". In the first chapter chocolate's journey is traced from the land of the Maya in Central America to Spain and the rest of Europe, and then back across the Atlantic to the United States. Through doing so, it is evident that since the earliest days of its discovery chocolate has woven intricate links among people on every imaginable level – national, cultural, social, economic and spiritual. Chocolate has never failed to make an impact, initiating comment from the church, the medical profession, scientists, social reformers and royalty. Over the centuries it has been eagerly consumed in one form or another by all levels of society.

The chapter on Cultivation and Processing outlines where and how cacao is grown and harvested, and describes the different types of bean. The book follows the American, and less confusing, convention of using the term "cacao" for the plant and all

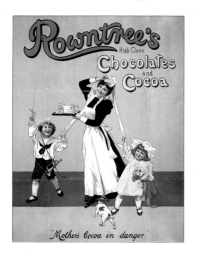

its products before processing; and the term "chocolate" for the processed beans, regardless of whether they are ground, liquid or in solid form. The word "cocoa" refers only to the concentrated cocoa powder invented by the Dutch.

The chapter goes on to trace the transformation from bean to beverage and from beverage to confectionery, and describes how this was made possible on a commercial scale. The industry's founding fathers, from the Quaker families in Britain – the Frys, the Terrys, the Cadburys and the Rowntrees – to the colourful Domingo Ghirardelli in San Francisco, and the persistent Dutch chemist Coenraad Van Houten, were all acutely aware of chocolate's popular appeal and commercial potential and went on to establish businesses that in most cases are still providing the world with chocolate today.

The taste and quality of chocolate is examined as we look at the specialist world of quality chocolate, demystifying terms such as couverture and cacao solids, praline and ganache. There is also a guide on how to taste chocolate properly – in the same way that wine-tasters evaluate a fine wine – for it is only by doing so that we learn to appreciate the alchemy that takes place during manufacture.

The international world of chocolate, including the characteristics of each country's chocolate, is also investigated. Flavourings and sweetness may vary, but what unites them is that smooth, sensuous, melt-in-the-mouth quality that is so hard and so pointless to resist. The book then delves into the physiology and psychology of chocolate, covering nutritional aspects, craving and addiction, passion and pleasure.

With this wealth of background knowledge, chocolate is then taken into the kitchen. The book's recipe section covers essential techniques to help you make the most of the two hundred tempting recipes that follow. You will find mouthwatering ideas for every kind of chocolate cake imaginable, from homely Chocolate Chip Walnut Loaf to the decadent White Chocolate Cappuccino Gâteau. A chapter on hot desserts will devastate you with Hot Chocolate Zabaglione, Hot Mocha Rum Soufflés and Chocolate Pecan Pie. Recipes for chocolate tarts and chilled desserts include classics such as luscious Mississippi Mud Pie and Tiramisu; and there are plenty of recipes for biscuits and little cakes. You will also see how to make your own chocolates and truffles, and the most deeply indulgent chocolate drinks. The recipes finish with a section on sauces, frostings and icings.

The *Ultimate Encyclopedia of Chocolate* is not only a celebration of a wonderful food, it will also fascinate, inform and instruct you in the history and production of this unique gastronomic treasure. Indulge yourself in a visual chocolate feast and accept the fact that if chocolate is not already an intrinsic part of your life, this book will make sure that it becomes so.

The History of Chocolate

Drink of the Gods

The origins of the solid, sensuous and, to some, addictive substance we know as chocolate are rooted in New World prehistory in the mysterious realm of the Olmec and the Maya. It was these ancient Mesoamerican civilizations living in the heart of equatorial Central America who were responsible for cultivating the tree from which chocolate is derived.

The Olmec

Three thousand years ago the Olmec people, one of the earliest Mesoamerican civilizations, occupied an area of tropical forests south of Veracruz on the Gulf of Mexico. Modern linguists have managed to reconstruct the ancient Olmec vocabulary and have found that it includes the word "cacao". Given the cacao tree's requirement for hot, humid and shady conditions, such as the land of the Olmecs, many historians are certain that the first civilization to cultivate the tree was the Olmec, and not the Aztecs, as is commonly believed.

The Maya

Around the fourth century AD, several centuries after the demise of the Olmec, the Maya had established themselves in a large region just south of present-day Mexico, stretching from the Yucatán peninsula in Central America across to the Chiapas and the Pacific coast of Guatemala. The humid climate there was perfect for the cacao tree, and it flourished happily in the shade of the tropical forest.

The Maya called the tree *cacahuaquchtl* – "tree" – as far as they were concerned, there was no other tree worth naming. They believed that the tree belonged to the gods and that the pods growing from its trunk were an offering from the gods to man.

LEFT: The Maya wrote their books on folding screens of bark paper. These two pages show a black-faced merchant god with cacao growers.

BELOW: Fifteenth-century Aztec stone figure holding a cacao pod.

ABOVE: This pre-Columbian codex shows Theobroma cacao, *with its pods, growing in a soil-filled sink-hole.*

The period around AD 300, known as the Classic Mayan civilization, was a time of great artistic, intellectual and spiritual development. The Maya built magnificent stone palaces and temples, carving into the sacred walls images of cacao pods – for them the symbol of life and fertility.

Known as "the people of the book", the Maya also devised a system of hieroglyphics, which were written down on fragile sheets of bark paper. Today only four of the Maya's books

— THEOBROMA CACAO —

The eighteenth-century Swedish botanist Linnaeus, who invented the binomial system of classification for all living things, later named the tree *Theobroma cacao,* meaning "drink of the gods", from the Greek *theos* (god) and *broma* (beverage). He felt it deserved a name that reflected the Mayan belief that the tree belonged to the gods, rather than the New World name of cacao or chocolate tree.

survive, and these are all from the post-Classic period. The books are full of drawings of gods who are depicted performing various religious rituals in which cacao pods frequently appear, and the text often refers to cacao as the god's food.

The Maya were the originators of a bitter brew made from cacao beans. This was a luxury drink enjoyed by kings and noblemen, and also used to solemnize sacred rituals. In their books the Maya describe several ways of making and flavouring the brew. It could be anything from porridge thickened with ground maize meal, to a thinner concoction for drinking. An early picture shows the dark brown liquid being poured from one vessel to another to produce an all-important froth. Various spices were used as flavourings, the favourite being hot chilli.

More evidence of Maya use of cacao survives on the many painted vessels that have been unearthed from their burial grounds. A tomb excavated in Guatemala in 1984 contained several vessels obviously used for chocolate drinking. One exotic and beautiful specimen bears the Mayan symbol for chocolate on its lid and was found still to contain residues of the drink.

THE TOLTECS AND AZTECS

After the mysterious fall of the Mayan empire around AD 900, the gifted and supremely civilized Toltecs, later followed by the Aztecs from Mexico, settled in former Mayan territory. Quetzalcoatl, the Toltec king, was also believed to be the god of air, whose mission was to bring the seeds of the cacao tree from Eden to man and to teach mortals how to cultivate various crops.

Because of political uprisings, Quetzalcoatl and his followers left the capital and fled south to the Yucatan. During a period of ill health he was persuaded to drink a mysterious cure, which, in fact, drove him insane. Convinced he must leave his kingdom, Quetzalcoatl sailed away on a small raft, promising to return in a preordained year to reclaim his kingdom. The legend of his exile became part of Aztec mythology, and astrologers predicted that in 1519 a white-faced king would return to release his people. This belief was to influence the whole future of the New World.

RIGHT: Aztecs greeting the white-skinned explorers landing on the coast of Tabasco. The Aztecs believed they were gods returning to recover their kingdom.

THE SPANISH ADVENTURERS

Although the Spanish explorer Hernán Cortés is generally considered to be the first European to recognize the potential of Aztec chocolate, the initial discovery must be attributed to Christopher Columbus. In 1502, on his fourth and final voyage to the Caribbean, Columbus reached the island of Guanaja off the Honduran coast. The story goes that he was greeted by Aztecs who offered him a sackful of what looked like large almonds in exchange for some of his own merchandise. Noticing his puzzlement, the Aztecs explained that a very special drink, *tchocolatl* (or *xocolatl)*, could be made with these beans. Their chief demonstrated by having his servants prepare some on the spot. Columbus and his crew found the resulting dark and bitter concoction repellent but nevertheless took some cacao beans back to Spain for curiosity value, little realizing their future economic worth.

ABOVE: Hernán Cortés, the Conquistador.

CACAO AS CURRENCY

When Hernán Cortés arrived in the New World seventeen years later, Montezuma II, the then Aztec Emperor, believed Cortés to be a reincarnation of Quetzalcoatl, the exiled Toltec god-king whose return had been predicted to take place in the same year. The confusion made it easy for Cortés to gain access to Tenochtitlán, the Aztec capital, where Montezuma received him and his men with a royal welcome. The emperor offered them numerous gifts, including a cacao plantation, and an extravagant banquet was prepared in their honour.

Despite the overwhelming welcome, Montezuma eventually realized that he had made a mistake and had wrongly identified the Spaniard. Immediately recognizing the insecurity of his position, Cortés enlisted the help of sympathetic natives and managed to take Montezuma prisoner. Within the space of two or three years he brought about the downfall of the Aztec kingdom. Unlike Columbus, Cortés quickly realized the enormous economic value of the cacao bean, both as food and a form of currency. A contemporary of Cortés reported that a slave could be bought for one hundred cacao beans, the services of a prostitute for ten, and a rabbit for four. The Jesuit, Pedro Martyre de Angleria, called the beans "pecuniary almonds" and described them as "blessed money, which exempts its

ABOVE: A painting showing Montezuma giving a royal welcome to Cortés.

RIGHT: Aztecs greeting Columbus and his fleet with welcoming gifts as he lands on Guanaja.

possessors from avarice, since it cannot be hoarded or hidden underground". It is presumed that he was referring to the fact that the beans could not be stored for long without rotting.

The writings of Thomas Gage, a seventeenth-century English Dominican friar, are a rich source of information on chocolate. Visiting the City of Mexico, Gage describes how the cacao bean is used as "both meat and current money". Basing the exchange rate on the Spanish real, which at that time (1625) was worth sixpence (2½p), he explained that two hundred small cacao beans were worth one Spanish real, and "with these the Indians buy what they list, for five, nay for two cacaos, which is a very small part of a real, they do buy fruits and the like".

THE CACAO PLANTATIONS

When Cortés set out on his voyage to the New World, his primary goal was to find El Dorado – Aztec gold. When he failed to unearth the dreamed-of riches, his attention turned to cacao beans. Having seen them used as currency, and noticing the importance attached to them, Cortés soon realized that money could literally be made to grow on trees. He devoted the next few years to exploiting the commercial potential of this "liquid gold" by setting up cacao plantations around the Caribbean.

Cacao was cheap to cultivate and reasonably profitable, and the prospect of easy riches attracted plenty of Spanish colonists. Before long, the Spanish had established plantations in Mexico, Ecuador, Venezuela, Peru, and the islands of Jamaica and Hispaniola (now called Haiti and the Dominican Republic). Cacao production has since spread all over the world, but the plantations in these original regions still produce the most highly prized varieties of bean.

THE SPANISH SECRET

The Spanish colonists had tried to keep the secret of cultivating and preparing cacao to themselves, and with good reason – they were making fat profits out of processing the beans in Latin America before shipping them to Europe. However, the colonists did not remain in sole possession of their secret forever. In 1580, the first ever chocolate-processing plant was set up in Spain. From then on the popularity of chocolate gradually spread to other European countries.

LEFT: An early illustration showing cacao pods drying and a cacao tree growing under a shade-creating "mother" tree.

ABOVE: This lithograph, produced by the Empire Marketing Board, shows cacao pods being gathered.

These, in turn, established their own plantations, trade routes and processing facilities.

The Dutch transplanted the tree to their East Indian states of Java and Sumatra in the early seventeenth century, and from there it spread to the Philippines, New Guinea, Samoa and Indonesia with a degree of financial success made possible by the exploitation of hundreds of thousands of African slaves. The French settled in Martinique in 1660, and in Brazil in 1677, along with the Portuguese. Trinidad was fought over by the Dutch, the French and the British for years; it eventually went to the British in 1802. In the early nineteenth century, the Portuguese successfully transplanted Brazilian cacao saplings to the island of São Tomé off the African coast, and later to the island of Fernando Póo (now called Bioko) and West Africa. By the end of the nineteenth century, the Germans had settled in the Cameroons and the British in Sri Lanka. Plantations have since spread to South-East Asia, and Malaysia is now one of the world's leading producers.

> #### — CACAO FEVER —
>
> It was no easy job for the early planters to clear the jungle, but their fierce determination spurred them on. A Brazilian writer, Jorge Amado, described the vision of those early planters gripped by "cacao fever": "He does not see the forest … choked with dense creepers and century-old trees, inhabited by wild animals and apparitions. He sees fields planted with cacao trees, straight rows of trees bearing golden fruit, ripe and yellow. He sees plantations pushing the forest back and stretching as far as the horizon."

THE POWER OF CHOCOLATE

To the Aztecs, chocolate was a source of spiritual wisdom, tremendous energy and enhanced sexual powers. The drink was highly prized as a nuptial aid, and, predictably, was the favourite beverage at wedding ceremonies. The Emperor Montezuma was reputed to get through fifty flagons of chocolate a day, always fortifying himself with a cup before entering his harem.

Although drunk on a daily basis, chocolate was still considered an exotic luxury and consumed primarily by kings, noblemen and the upper ranks of the priesthood. (Some historians say that priests would not have drunk chocolate, arguing that it would have been the equivalent of a priest quaffing champagne every day.)

Because of its renowned energy-boosting properties, chocolate was also given to Aztec warriors to fortify them on military campaigns. The chocolate was compressed into conveniently travel-sized tablets and wafers. Perhaps as a kind of incentive scheme a special law was instated declaring that unless a warrior went to war, he was forbidden to drink chocolate or eat luxury meats, or wear cotton, flowers or feathers – even if he was a royal prince or nobleman.

The Spanish colonists, too, became infatuated by the chocolate mystique. Once they had become accustomed to the strangeness of the drink, they took to it with enthusiasm. The Jesuit, José de Acosta, wrote "The Spaniards, both men and women, that are accustomed to the country, are very greedy of this chocolaté. They say they make diverse sortes of it, some hote, some colde, and put therein much of that chili."

Increasingly aware of its restorative values, Cortés convinced Carlos I of Spain of the enormous potential of this New World health food: "... the divine drink which builds up resistance and

---

— THE MIDAS TOUCH —

Chocolate has always been associated with gold, possibly originating from Montezuma's ritual of drinking chocolate from a golden goblet, which, immediately after use, was thrown into the lake beside his palace. The lake turned out to be quite literally a gold mine for the Spanish after the conquest. Evidence of the association with gold can still be seen today with chocolate manufacturers, especially the Swiss, selling fake gold bars and chocolate coins encased in gold wrapping.

---

fights fatigue. A cup of this precious drink enables a man to walk for a whole day without food".

Thomas Gage was heavily reliant on it too. He wrote: "Two or three hours after a good meal of three or four dishes of mutton, veal or beef, kid, turkeys or other fowles, our stomackes would bee ready to faint, and so wee were fain to support them with a cup of chocolatte".

RIGHTS, RITUALS AND CEREMONIES

The writings of New World travellers give us fascinating insights into the strange and sometimes barbaric rites, rituals and ceremonies attached to the cacao bean and the drinking of chocolate.

Religious rituals took place at different stages during cultivation. The Maya always held a planting festival in honour of the gods during which they sacrificed a dog with a cacao-coloured spot in its hair. Another practice, calling for a certain amount of commitment, required the planters to remain celibate for thirteen nights. They were allowed to return to their wives on the fourteenth night, and then the beans were sown. Another somewhat gory planting ceremony involved placing the seeds in small

LEFT: Chocolate was drunk by Aztec warriors in military campaigns, but it didn't win them victory over the Spanish.

RIGHT: An Aztec with his chocolate pot and molinillo. The molinillo has shaped paddles for making the drink frothy.

— *CHOCOLATE AND CUISINE* —

Contrary to what some cookery writers would have us believe, the Aztecs did not use chocolate as an ingredient in cooking. To do so would have been considered sacrilegious – rather like devout Christians using communion wine to make gravy. What possibly causes confusion is a classic Mexican recipe called *Mole Poblano*, turkey or chicken in a chilli sauce flavoured with chocolate. The recipe is often assumed to have Aztec origins, but the ingredients include several items – onions, tomatoes and garlic, for instance – that would not have been available then. This is a recipe for Mole Poblano:

8 dried mulato chillies; 4 dried ancho chillies; 4 dried pasilla chillies; 2 dried chipotle chillies; 1 small turkey; 50g/2oz/ 4 tbsp lard (or vegetable oil); 60ml/4 tbsp sesame seeds; 115g/4oz/1 cup blanched almonds; 1 corn tortilla; 2 crushed garlic cloves; 1 chopped onion; ¼ tsp each of ground cloves; cinnamon and anise; 6 black peppercorns; 50g/2oz/⅓ cup raisins; 3 peeled tomatoes; 5ml/1 tsp salt; 50g/2oz/2 squares unsweetened chocolate; chicken or turkey stock

Arrange the dried chillies in a single layer in a roasting tin and soften in a hot oven for 2–3 minutes, taking care not to let them burn. Discard the stems and seeds and put the chillies in a bowl. Cover with barely boiling water. Leave to soak for 20–30 minutes.

Divide the turkey into portions. Heat the lard or oil in a heavy-based flameproof casserole and fry the turkey until golden brown. Using a slotted spoon, remove the turkey portions from the casserole and set aside.

Roast the sesame seeds and almonds in a dry frying pan over a medium heat until golden. Remove from the pan. Cut the tortilla into strips and heat in the pan until brittle.

Put the almonds, tortilla and all but 5ml/1 tsp sesame seeds into a food processor. Add the garlic, onion, spices, raisins, tomatoes and salt. Drain the chillies, reserving the soaking water, add them to the processor and purée until smooth, adding some of the chilli soaking water if necessary. Add this purée to the fat remaining in the casserole. Fry gently for about 5 minutes, stirring constantly.

Return the turkey to the casserole, with the chocolate and enough stock to just cover. Bring to the boil, then lower the heat, cover and simmer gently for 45–60 minutes until the turkey is tender and cooked through and the sauce has thickened. Garnish with the reserved sesame seeds and serve with rice and tortillas.

NOTE: If you have difficulty in finding Mexican dried chillies, use 115g/4oz fresh green chillies and 2 small dried red chillies, and do not preheat them in the oven. Simply remove the seeds, tear the chillies into shreds and soak as above.

LEFT: *A Mexican* metate *was used for grinding cacao beans to a paste.*

LEFT: *A mosaic of Quetzalcoatl, the Toltec king and god who, according to legend, brought the cacao bean as a gift to human kind.*

bowls before performing secret rites in the presence of an idol. Blood was then drawn from different parts of the human body and used to anoint the idol. Other practices include sprinkling "the blood of slain fowls" over the land to be sown. There were also tales of frenzied dancing, orgiastic rituals and bloody sacrifices. The sixteenth-century Italian historian and traveller, Girolamo Benzoni, recorded that during festivals "they used to spend all the day and half the night in dancing with only cacao for nourishment". Another legend tells of how, as a prize, the winner of a type of ball game would be offered as a sacrifice. The unfortunate man was first fed vast quantities of chocolate in order "to colour his blood" before his heart was cut out and presented to the gods, who, it was believed, would be honoured by the chocolate-rich blood.

Another use of chocolate was as a face paint with which the Aztecs adorned themselves in religious ceremonies. Even the early Spanish planters believed that secret rites were necessary for a successful crop and performed planting ceremonies. From its earliest days, then, chocolate was regarded as a substance of power, a gift from the gods, a source of vitality and life.

BELOW: *Cacao beans laid out to dry on plantain leaves.*

FROM BEAN TO BEVERAGE

ABOVE: A seventeenth-century lithograph showing an imaginary scene on a plantation, with Aztecs harvesting, preparing and cooking chocolate.

The Aztec drink bore little resemblance to the deliciously smooth, rich and creamy beverage we know today; it was bitter, greasy and served cold. Early travellers give differing accounts of how it was made. Giramolo Benzoni, a sixteenth-century Italian botanist, described the method used in rural areas: "They take as many fruits as they need and put them in an earthenware pot and dry them over the fire. Then they break them between two stones and reduce them to flour just as they do when they make bread. They then transfer this flour into vessels made of gourd halves ..., moisten the flour gradually with water, often adding their 'long pepper' [chilli]."

Still on the subject of ingredients, Thomas Gage described additions other than chilli: "But the meaner set of people, as Blackamoors and Indians, commonly put nothing in it, but Cacao, Achiotte, Maize, and a few Chillies with a little Aniseed". Maize was used to blot up the cacao butter which floated to the top, and also to bind and thicken the drink.

It seems that the grinding stone, or *metate,* was an important part of the production process. One writer describes the process in some detail: "For this purpose they have a broad, smooth stone, well polished and glazed very hard, and being made fit in all respects for their use, they grind the cacaos thereon very small, and when they have so done, they have another broad stone ready, under which they keep a gentle fire". Because of the crude manual processing, all sorts of undesirable bits and pieces – shells, husks and pith – were allowed to remain in the resulting

RIGHT: Aztec chocolate-making equipment: chocolate pot, drinking goblet, whisk and rolling pin.

liquor. In Benzoni's opinion: "This mixture looks more fit for the pigs than like a beverage for human beings".

A FROTHY BREW

The Jesuit José de Acosta wrote: "The chief use of this cacao is in a drincke which they call chocolaté, whereof they make great account, foolishly and without reason: for it is loathsome to such as are not acquainted with it, having a skumme or frothe that is very unpleasant to taste, if they be not well conceited thereof."

For the Maya and Aztecs the froth was an all-important and most delicious part of the drink. One historian pointed out the importance "of opening the mouth wide, in order to facilitate deglutition, that the foam may dissolve gradually and descend imperceptibly, as it were, into the stomach". The Maya made the drink frothy by pouring it from one bowl to another from a height. Later, the Aztecs invented a device that the Spanish called a *molinillo* – a wooden swizzle stick with specially shaped paddles at one end, which fitted into the hole in the lid of the chocolate pot.

The eighteenth-century missionary, Father Jean-Baptiste Labat, described this indispensable item in one of his books: "A stick is about ten inches longer than the chocolate pot, thus enabling it to be freely twirled between the palms of the hand." The *molinillo* is still in use today and can be found in Latin American shops and markets. The design of the basic wooden stick remains unchanged, but there are also beautiful antique pots and swizzle sticks in silver and other decorative materials, which have become collectors' items.

There is evidence of yet more ingredients than those

— CHAMPURRADO (CHOCOLATE ATOLE) —

The addition of maize would have turned the Aztec drink into a thin gruel or porridge known as *atole.* This is a type of fortified drink, not necessarily flavoured with chocolate, still served at meals or used as a pick-me-up by workers in the fields in Latin America today. The chocolate-flavoured version is always referred to as *champurrado,* from *champurrar,* meaning to mix one drink with another:

Put 65g / 2½oz / ½ cup masa harina (treated maize flour) or finely ground tortillas in a large pan with 750ml / 1¼ pints / 3 cups water. Stir over low heat until thickened. Remove from the heat and stir in 175g / 6oz / 1 cup soft light brown sugar (or to taste), and 750ml / 1¼ pints / 3 cups milk. Grate three 25g / 1oz squares unsweetened chocolate and add to the pan. Beat well with a molinillo and serve steaming hot.

> ### A MEXICAN RECIPE FOR HAND-MADE CHOCOLATE
> *Take 6 pounds [2.75kg] of good quality cacao beans, at least*
> *three different types, in equal quantities. Roast in a metal*
> *pan studded with holes just until they begin to give off their*
> *oil. Take care not to remove the beans from the heat too soon,*
> *or the resulting chocolate will be discoloured and indigestible.*
> *If the beans are allowed to burn, the chocolate will be bitter*
> *and acrid.*
> *Rub the roasted beans through a fine hair sieve to remove the*
> *husks. Next, place your metate (grinding stone) on a flat pan*
> *containing hot coals. Once the stone is warm begin to grind*
> *the chocolate. Grind the chocolate with 4 to 6 pounds*
> *[1.75–2.75kg] of sugar, depending on desired sweetness,*
> *pounding it with a large mallet.*
> *Shape the resulting paste into tablets as preferred – round,*
> *hexagonal or oblong – and place on a rack to air. If you wish,*
> *make dividing lines on the surface of the chocolate with the*
> *tip of a sharp knife.*

mentioned by Thomas Gage. The Spanish historian, Sahagún, describing a menu of chocolate drinks to be served to lords, tells us that there were "ruddy cacao; brilliant red cacao; orange cacao; black cacao; and white cacao". Many of the very early recipes for chocolate share common ingredients, and from these we can tell that the likely flavourings for the lords' impressive choice of cacao were chilli, allspice, cloves, vanilla, a type of black pepper, various flower petals, nuts and annatto.

BELOW: A modern chocolate pot, whisk and chocolate from Colombia. The design of the whisk has not changed since the days of the Aztecs.

ABOVE: Aztecs poured chocolate from a height to make it frothy.

Sugar was not added until much later. There is a story that the nuns of Oaxaca, an Aztec town occupied by the Spanish until 1522, developed new recipes in deference to the Spanish sweet tooth. They added sugar and sweet spices such as cinnamon and aniseed, and so the bitter beverage of the Aztecs began its transformation to the delicious drink that we know today.

THE SPANISH VERSION

In 1701 an Englishman travelling in Spain gave a detailed and lengthy account of the manufacturing process developed by the Spanish. After the preliminary roasting, dehusking and grinding, the cacao mass was ground again to a fine paste with plenty of sugar, cinnamon, vanilla, musk and annatto. The chocolate was formed into blocks, along the lines of modern block chocolate, but even so, these were still used only for making the beverage, rather than as confectionery.

As far as we know, this is the recipe that was used throughout Spain and the rest of Europe until the process was revolutionized in the nineteenth century by the technological achievements of the Dutchman Van Houten.

FROM BEVERAGE TO CONFECTIONERY

ABOVE: A 1893 poster with a background of cacao pods and leaves.

VAN HOUTEN'S PRESS

In its early days chocolate was an extremely rich beverage. It contained a fatty substance known as cacao butter, which tended to rise to the top, where it would float in unappetizing greasy pools. Manufacturers overcame this to some extent by adding starchy substances to absorb the fat – a process similar to the Aztec tradition of adding ground maize.

Manufacturers had also tried unsuccessfully for years to devise a way of separating out the greasy cacao butter. Breakthrough came in 1828 when, after years of trial and error, a Dutch chemist named Coenraad Van Houten patented a new and extremely efficient hydraulic press. His machine was able to extract about fifty per cent of the cacao butter present in the "liquor" (the paste produced after grinding the beans), leaving behind a refined, brittle, cake-like residue that could then be pulverized to a fine powder.

Not satisfied, Van Houten went one step further. He treated the powder with alkaline salts in order to improve the ease with which it could be mixed with water. The process, which came to be known as "Dutching", also darkened the colour of the chocolate and lightened the flavour – a curious anomaly since plain chocolate is usually assumed to have a stronger flavour. Today many people believe they prefer Dutch chocolate because of its strong flavour, but it may simply be the colour that attracts them.

Van Houten's inexhaustible patience revolutionized the chocolate industry. It led to the manufacture of what we now know as cocoa powder, which in Van Houten's time was called "cocoa essence". It also led to an all-round improvement within the industry. Van Houten sold his rights ten years after he took out the patent, and the machine came into general use. Among the first customers were the Frys and the Cadburys, ever eager to outdo

RIGHT: Modern packaging based on the art nouveau style.

ABOVE: An early advertisement for Van Houten's cocoa powder – "the best liquid drinking chocolate".

each other. Both firms were quick to enter the cocoa essence market, actively promoting the product's purity and ease of preparation. The old-style starch-based products were classified as adulterated, resulting in several fierce legal battles between rival firms. Van Houten's press also initiated the industry's next step in gearing up – the large-scale production of chocolate as confectionery.

EATING CHOCOLATE

Having separated out the butter from the bean, the industry was left with the question of what to do with it – it was certainly too good to waste. What happened was that somehow one of the cocoa manufacturers – and there are conflicting claims as to who was the first – hit upon the idea of melting the cacao butter and combining it with a blend of ground cacao beans and sugar. The resulting mixture was a smooth and malleable paste

ABOVE: A charming poster for Bovril's nourishing new chocolate bars, or cakes. The lettering on the box refers to them as "the perfect food".

caught on in a big way. Not to be outdone Cadburys introduced the first box of small individual chocolates, followed by a Valentine's Day presentation box. Other companies, such as Bovril, began producing eating chocolate, and the new confectionery was firmly established.

As a result of the new craze the price of cacao butter rocketed and, predictably, eating chocolate became an expensive sought-after product popular with society's élite. Meanwhile, cocoa was relegated to the masses.

The United States developed their version of chocolate bars a little later on. After experimenting with cream and chocolate – time and time again, the mixture scorched or failed to set – Milton Hershey's milk chocolate bars finally appeared on the market in 1900. His world-famous Kisses followed in 1907. Over on the west coast, Ghirardelli was making use of new chocolate-moulding technology, and soon added chocolate bars to their lines too. Specialist chocolate shops began to spring up all over the country and most towns had at least one well-respected establishment producing hand-made chocolates. The early chocolatiers were too small to import cacao beans or invest in expensive processing machinery. Instead, they bought indus-trial-sized blocks of coating chocolate from large companies such as Guittard and melted them down to use as "couverture" for their own hand -dipped fillings. Alice Bradley's 1917 *Candy Cook Book*, published in America, devoted a whole chapter to "Assorted Chocolates" with over sixty recipes for fillings. Bradley stated: "More than one hundred different chocolates may be found in the price lists of some manufacturers." The American chocolate industry got its biggest boost during the Second World War, when millions of chocolate bars were issued to the American armed forces in Europe. By this time both Ghirardelli and Hershey were well-equipped for the chal-lenge of supplying them.

ABOVE: Modern packaging with old-fashioned appeal.

ABOVE: Ghirardelli's first chocolate bars were "full of toasted almonds".

that tolerated the added sugar without becoming gritty; the fat helped to dissolve it. The paste was also thin enough to be poured into a mould and cast, and it is from this concept that "eating chocolate" was developed.

The Fry family claim to have been the first to market the new product. Reflecting the current popularity of French-style products, they named the bars "Chocolat Délicieux à Manger" and exhibited them at a trade fair in Birmingham in 1849. The bars were an imme-diate success, and eating chocolate

RIGHT: Hershey's famous little Kisses were introduced in 1907.

CHOCOLATE TRAVELS THE WORLD

During the sixteenth century chocolate began its journey into the countries of Europe as colonialists exploited their new world discoveries. Reaching Spain first, then following trade routes to Northern Europe and Great Britain, chocolate eventually made its way back across the Atlantic to North America.

SPAIN

It was probably through merchants and also through contact between New World convents and monasteries and their Spanish counterparts, that chocolate found its way to Spain.

Once the first commercial cargo of beans from Veracruz had been unloaded in 1585 and the official trade routes established, chocolate quickly became part of the Spanish way of life, especially among society's élite. However, a French noblewoman visiting Spain was unimpressed. She says of the drink: "They take it with so much pepper and so many spices, that it is impossible they don't burn themselves up." Nor was she impressed by their dental care and personal habits: "Their teeth are good, and would be white if they took care of them, but they neglect them. Besides the sugar and the chocolate which spoil them, they have the bad habit, men and women alike, of cleaning them with a toothpick, in whatever company they are."

Chocolaterías, chocolate houses, sprang up in cities all over the country, and it became the fashion to visit them in the afternoons to drink a cup of the foaming fragrant brew, accompanied by *picatoste,* fried bread, to dip it in. Today, the chocolate drinking habit remains strong in Spain, and there are still many *chocolaterías*. A traditional time to take the beverage is in the

RIGHT: The chambermaid model for "The Beautiful Chocolate Girl" married a wealthy aristocrat and so got to drink chocolate herself.

BELOW: This early eighteenth-century Spanish tiled panel shows gentlemen serving chocolate to their ladies.

The Spanish like their chocolate thick — so thick that a spoon will stand up in it, and it can almost be classified as a food rather than a drink. Cornflour is used as a thickener, or sometimes eggs, which practically turn the drink into chocolate mousse.

— *SPANISH EGG CHOCOLATE* —

In a double boiler, melt 50g/2oz/2 squares unsweetened chocolate in 475ml/16fl oz/2 cups milk until thick and smooth. Keep stirring and add 115g/4oz/½ cup sugar, pinch of salt, 10ml/2 tsp ground cinnamon and 5ml/1 tsp vanilla essence. Beat 1 egg in the bottom of a jug with a molinillo, pour over the hot chocolate mixture, whisk until frothy and serve immediately.

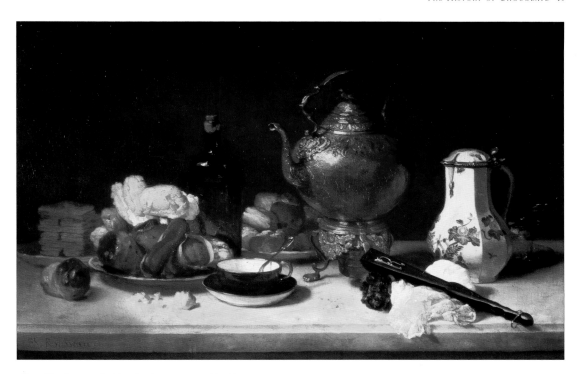

ABOVE: The pleasures of taking chocolate are captured in this seventeenth-century still life by Philippe Rousseau.

morning with freshly cooked *churros* (piped strips of deep-fried choux pastry), which replaced the *picatoste*.

In Spain, as in the rest of Europe, chocolate was always associated with stimulating foods such as spices, coffee and tea; it was a long while before chocolate was used as an ingredient for confectionery and desserts. Although its first use was as a beverage, chocolate was also a flavouring ingredient in savoury dishes. Both the Spanish and the Mexicans traditionally add chocolate to sauces for meat and game, and even fish.

THE NETHERLANDS

The Netherlands became part of the Spanish territories in the fourteenth century. Because of this, the Dutch were familiar with chocolate from an early stage.

The Dutch West India Company eventually defied the Spanish ban on foreign traders and started shipping cacao beans in bulk to Amsterdam during the seventeenth century. They then re-exported the beans in small lots to foreign buyers, as well as setting up their own processing plants in the Netherlands. Until the end of the eighteenth century, production was limited and chocolate was only seen in the homes of a few wealthy merchants and financiers.

ITALY

There are conflicting theories as to how and when chocolate reached Italy. Some historians believe it was around the middle of the sixteenth century when the exiled duke Emmanuel-Philibert returned to power, having experienced the delights of chocolate in Spain. The popular theory is that chocolate was imported by a Florentine merchant, Antonio Carletti, who discovered it while travelling the world in search of new products to sell. The most likely theory is that chocolate was brought in as a medicine through the convents and monasteries.

By the seventeenth century a growing number of chocolate companies had become established in northern Italy, particularly around the towns of Perugia and Turin. These companies in turn began to export their newly developed products to other European countries.

A collection of recipes by an eighteenth-century Italian priest shows the imagination of the Italians in their use of chocolate compared with other countries. Recipes included such dishes as: Liver dipped in chocolate and fried, Chocolate soup, Chocolate pudding with veal, marrow and candied fruit, and Chocolate polenta.

FRANCE

France was also quick to fall under chocolate's spell. As with Spain and Italy, there are conflicting theories about the circumstances surrounding its first appearance. Some say it was a result of networking between Spanish and French monasteries. Another theory states that chocolate entered France as a medicine. There is certainly some evidence from the French historian Bonaventure d'Argonne that the Cardinal of Lyons drank chocolate "to calm his spleen and appease his rage and foul temper", and that he may have "had the secret from

ABOVE: Cardinal Mazarin travelled with a chocolate-maker.

some Spanish monks who brought it to France". However, there is also no doubt that the trend was largely set by nobility and the royal court as it was in other European countries.

The most popular theory is that the drink made its first appearance in 1615 when Louis XIII married Anne of Austria, the young daughter of Philip II of Spain. The new queen loved her chocolate with a passion and introduced it to members of the court. There were plenty of devotees: the king's personal adviser, the formidable Cardinal Mazarin, absolutely refused to travel anywhere without his personal chocolate-maker; and later

BELOW: A tapestry depicting the marriage of María Teresa, the Spanish princess, to Louis XIV. Chocolate and the king were her only passions.

Marie Antoinette, also very fond of chocolate, created the prestigious "Charge of chocolate-maker of the Queen". Chocolate parties held by royalty, *chocolat du roi,* became a fashionable social ritual to which it was the ultimate in chic to be invited.

The many anecdotes include the story of the Spanish princess María Theresa, who married Louis XIV in 1660. She is said to have declared: "Chocolate and the King are my only passions." (Note the order.) The princess brought with her a Spanish maid, who prepared chocolate each morning for her queen. The ladies of the French court were intrigued by this new drink, especially as word had got round that it was an aphrodisiac. Chocolate sales in France apparently sky-rocketed around that time. Another often-repeated story about the princess is that her passion for chocolate was so excessive that she developed a horrendous complexion, and that her teeth were black and riddled with cavities.

Throughout France, chocolate never failed to evoke strong feelings. In 1664 learned academics praised its food value, presumably because of the fat content, but at the same time it was violently attacked by other writers, who accused those who drank it of moral depravity. Even Madame de Sévigné, a French courtesan and a great devotee of chocolate, turned against it for a while. In one of her letters to her daughter she wrote: "Chocolate is no longer for me what it was, fashion has led me astray, as it always does … it is the source of vapors and palpitations; it flatters you for a while, and then suddenly lights a continuous fever in you that leads to death … In the name of God, don't keep it up …" In another letter she told a horrendous tale of the Marquise de

ABOVE: Chocolate consumption was often depicted as being risqué.

Coëtlogon who "took so much chocolate during her pregnancy last year that she produced a small boy as black as the devil, who died". Eventually Madame de Sévigné regained her enthusiasm, and in a wonderful letter she neatly got round the issue of fasting and chocolate: "I took some chocolate night before last to digest my dinner, in order to have a good supper. I had some yesterday for sustenance so that I could fast until the evening. What I find most pleasant about chocolate is that it acts according to one's wishes."

SWITZERLAND

After the mid-seventeenth century, chocolate was making an appearance in all the principal cities of Europe. Although

ABOVE: The elegant refreshment room where chocolate was served at Confiserie Sprüngli in Zurich.

Switzerland was later to become a major producer of chocolate as confectionery, chocolate as a beverage was relatively late in arriving. It was first noticed in Zurich in 1697 after the Mayor had enjoyed drinking chocolate on a trip to Brussels. By the mid-eighteenth century, chocolate was more widely available and was often brought into the country by travelling Italian merchants, known as *cioccolatieri*, who sold it at fairs and markets.

GERMANY AND AUSTRIA

Like Switzerland, Germany was also relatively late to take up chocolate. For years the Germans regarded it as medicine, and it was sold only by apothecaries. But by the middle of the seventeenth century, chocolate had become accepted among fashionable society, although enthusiasm varied from city to city. Berliners still looked on it as an unpleasant tonic, but the drink was a hit in Dresden and in Leipzig, where the city's *glitterati*

took to drinking it at the fashionable Felsche café, one of the earliest German *schokoladestuben* (chocolate houses).

Among Germany's confirmed chocoholics were the famous poets Goethe (1749–1832) and Schiller (1759–1805). Goethe was reputed to have found the beverage a deep source of inspiration and drank it well into ripe old age. During his travels he often wrote to his wife asking her to send supplies from his favourite chocolate-maker, Riquet, in Leipzig.

Germany started producing its own chocolate on a large scale in 1756 when Prince Wilhelm von der Lippe erected a factory at Steinhude and brought over Portuguese workers especially skilled in the art of chocolate-making.

In Austria, Viennese aristocracy were quick to take up the new drink, especially after the Emperor Charles VI had moved his court and his chocolate from Madrid to Vienna in 1711. Since Austria did not impose such punishing taxes on chocolate as Germany, it was drunk not just by the aristocracy but also by lesser mortals who could afford it. There is a story of a German traveller in Vienna who was horrified to see someone as common as a tailor drinking a cup of best quality chocolate.

Both the Germans and the Austrians were accomplished pastry-cooks. Indeed, in the Austrian imperial court it seemed that the head pâtisserie chef was on a par with the most senior general. Like the Italians, the German and Austrian pastry-cooks took a while to start using chocolate as an ingredient in their baking rather than just as a beverage. It was worth the wait their most wickedly delicious creations, the rich Black Forest Cake from Germany and the Viennese Sachertorte, are now celebrated forms of indulgence the world over.

BELOW: "Goethe in the Campagna" (1787) by German painter Johann Tischbein. Goethe was a lifelong drinker of chocolate.

The popularity of chocolate spawned a whole new industry for the famous china factories in both Austria and Germany, and in France too. At the beginning of the eighteenth century, European factories from Vienna to Berlin to Sèvres started producing the most exquisite chocolate services in porcelain; before that earthenware or metal, including gold and silver, were the materials used. As well as the traditionally shaped serving pots, the new range included elegant cups known as *trembleuse*. These new porcelain wares were specially designed to protect the aristocracy from the embarrassment of accidental spills. They featured double-handled cups which fitted into a holder or a very deep saucer.

ABOVE: The interior of a typical seventeenth-century London chocolate house – hotbeds of gossip, frequented by politicians and the literary set.

GREAT BRITAIN

In the sixteenth century, when the Spanish were shifting cacao as if there were no tomorrow, the British couldn't have cared less about it. Even the pirates who plagued the Spanish ports and shipping routes seemed unaware of its economic and cultural importance, for they showed no interest in the valuable cargo. Like their Dutch counterparts, they are reputed to have thrown boatloads of it overboard in disgust.

When chocolate finally arrived in Britain, it did so more or less simultaneously with two other stimulants, tea from Asia and coffee from Africa. Coffee was the first to catch on in British society – it was relatively cheaper – but chocolate soon followed.

Documentary evidence of the first chocolate house in London appeared in *The Public Advertiser* in 1657, followed two years later by a paragraph in *Needham's Mercurius Politicus* that drew attention to "an excellent West India drink, sold in Queen's-Head alley, in Bishopsgate-street, by a Frenchman".

The most famous establishment was White's Chocolate House, near St James's Palace, opened by an Italian immigrant. A rival establishment was The Cocoa Tree in St James's Street.

LEFT: Sacks of cacao beans from the tropics arriving at an English warehouse.

RIGHT: "A Cup of Chocolate" by Sir John Lavery. Drinking chocolate in the new chocolate houses was a fashionable pastime for ladies of society.

By chance rather than design the two establishments catered to different political loyalties – The Cocoa Tree was the favourite haunt of members of the Tory party, while the Whig aristocrats and the literary set frequented White's. White's was the inspiration for some of the scenes from William Hogarth's famous series of paintings *The Rake's Progress.*

For the wealthy upper classes, both the coffee and chocolate houses were *the* place to be seen. They were hotbeds of vicious gossip and political intrigue, as well as popular gambling venues where vast fortunes were won and lost. In 1675, Charles II tried in vain to have both types of establishment closed down on the grounds that politicians and businessmen were frequenting them too often and were in danger of neglecting their families. It is also possible that he was trying to suppress the kind of talk that could potentially lead to a rebellion similar to the one that caused his father's execution in 1649.

The diarist Samuel Pepys (1633–1703) was an ardent fan of chocolate, or "jocolatte", and a regular frequenter of the chocolate houses. One entry in his diary records a horrendous hangover the morning after the king's coronation: "Waked in the morning with my head in a sad taking through last night's drink, which I am very sorry for; so rose, and went with Mr Creed to drink our morning draught, which he did give me in Chocolate to settle my stomach."

In England, as in other countries, the government seized on chocolate as a potential source of revenue. Importers were

LEFT: Examples of early packaging for Domingo Ghirardelli's revolutionary instant cocoa powder.

given a somewhat different reception to the one it had received in Europe. Although the wealthy east coast society enjoyed chocolate, they drank it at home – chocolate houses did not exist. Another difference was that chocolate was generally marketed to the masses rather than the elite (as in Europe), with the emphasis on wholesomeness rather than sophistication, so it consequently reached a far broader segment of society than it had in Spain, France and England.

The first chocolate factory was set up in 1765 in Massachusetts by Dr James Baker and John Hannon. The Walter Baker Company was established in 1780 by Baker's grandson and is still synonymous with quality chocolate. By 1884, Milton Hershey, of the Hershey Chocolate Company, was producing baking chocolate, cocoa and sweet chocolate coatings for his famous caramels; and by 1885, Domingo Ghirardelli had set up his California Chocolate Manufactory in San Francisco. Right from the start, chocolate was big business in North America.

BELOW: Nineteenth-century advertising poster for curious chocolate products from the Walter Baker Company.

obliged to pay a hefty duty on every sack of cacao beans brought into the country, and in 1660 a tax of 8d (about 3p) a gallon was imposed on all chocolate made and sold in England.

These penalties led to an inevitable increase in smuggling cacao beans, as well as adulteration of the chocolate, for which anything from brick dust to red lead was used. Brandon Head in *The Food of the Gods* refers to "the reprehensible practice (strongly condemned)" of padding out chocolate with husks and shells. He goes on: "To prevent this practice it was enacted in 1770 that the shells or husks should be seized or destroyed." Some of these husks did not go to waste, however. Head tells us: "From these a light, but not unpalatable, table decoction is still prepared in Ireland and elsewhere, under the designation of 'miserables'."

By the mid-1800s, the high levels of taxation had come down, thanks to the vast volume of imports, as well as the influence of respected Quaker industrialists who had convinced the government of chocolate's nourishing virtues. Chocolate was now affordable by all and had become big business.

UNITED STATES OF AMERICA

The first chocolate found its way back across the Atlantic to North America around 1765, probably in the pockets of high-ranking English officials going to their posts in the east coast colonies. We also know that Domingo Ghirardelli, an Italian confectioner then trading in Lima in Peru, exported cacao beans and other essential commodities from South America to San Francisco to supply the needs of the gold rush hordes. Another possible route for cacao beans was directly from Jamaica after the Spanish had given up control there.

Thomas Jefferson (1743–1826), third president of the United States, is quoted as saying: "The superiority of chocolate, both for health and nourishment, will soon give it the preference over tea and coffee in America which it has in Spain." Because of the pioneering nature of North American society, chocolate was

CHOCOLATE AND THE CHURCH

The Church played an important role, directly and indirectly, in the early history of chocolate. The bitter and bloody religious wars raging between Catholics and Protestants in the sixteenth and seventeenth centuries, were, in a way, the cause of chocolate's appearance and gradual dispersal through Europe. The Jesuits, actively involved in the religious wars and fiercely committed to empowering the Catholic Church, were a driving political force both in Europe and Latin America. It was almost certainly the Jesuit missionaries, rather than New World explorers, who were responsible for bringing the first chocolate into Spain, Italy and France; it would have passed through an international network of monasteries and convents. It was also thanks to the pressure of Jesuit missionaries that raw, rather than processed, cacao beans were eventually shipped to Europe. Before this, the Spanish colonists had had a monopoly on processing the beans in Latin America, making fat profits by doing so.

In Italy, the religious wars resulted in a great many high-level marriages between aristocratic families and the ruling powers.

ABOVE: Friar Drinking Chocolate *by Jose M. Oropeza.*

Until its unification in 1879, Italy was a collection of self-governing states, and it was felt that marriages of this kind were the best way of cementing diplomatic relationships and consolidating the states' collective power. The aristocratic brides liked to take their maids, cooks and favourite foods with them when they moved from one Italian state or foreign country to another, and so through them chocolate began to appear in all sorts of places.

Until the eighteenth century, chocolate was made by monks and nuns, both in Europe and Latin America, using the methods handed down from the Aztecs. Thomas Gage, in his book *The English-American, His Travail by Sea and Land, or a New Survey of the West Indies* (published 1648), wrote of "cloister churches" run by nuns and friars. He said these were "talked off far and near, not for their religious practices, but for their skill in making drinkes which are used in those parts, the one called

BELOW: Part of Columbus's mission was to conquer new lands in the name of the Catholic Church. This picture illustrates that religious fervour.

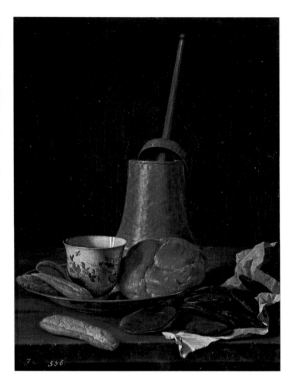

ABOVE: This seventeenth-century Spanish still-life shows tablets of chocolate, which were often made by monks and nuns.

chocolatte, another atolle. Chocolatte is (also) made up in boxes, and sent not only to Mexico, but much of it yearly transported into Spain".

In the New World, the Church generally took a pragmatic view of chocolate. It was popular with nuns and monks because it sustained them through the lengthy fasts they had to endure, and they were convinced of its health-promoting properties. There was an occasional difference of opinion in the Old World, however. A Spanish monk was said to have declared the drink diabolical, claiming its invigorating properties were the work of evil spirits, but his views went unheard. In 1650 the Society of Jesus (the Jesuit school) issued an act outlawing the drink to Jesuits, but this was impossible to enforce, especially when students started to abandon the school because of it.

THE CHOCOLATE OF CHIAPA
One major objection to chocolate appears to have been raised by the Bishop of Chiapa whose Mass was continually disturbed by its use. A famous and rather lengthy story told by Thomas Gage is worth repeating. The upper-class white ladies of Chiapa Real claimed "much weakness and squeamishness of stomacke, which they say is so great that they are not able to continue in church ... unless they drinke a cup of hot chocolatte .... For this purpose it was much used by them to make their maids bring them to church ... a cup of chocolatte, which could not be done to all without a great confusion and interrupting both mass and sermon".

Driven to distraction by the endless disturbances, the Bishop posted a notice stating that anyone who ate or drank in church would be excommunicated. The scornful women carried on their chocolate drinking regardless, and eventually the situation exploded into an uproar in which swords were drawn against the priests as they tried to remove the cups of chocolate from the women's maids.

The women retaliated by refusing to attend the Bishop's services, and attending Mass at the convents instead. The local priest warned the Bishop that if the women "cannot have their wills, they will surely work revenge either by chocolate or conserves, or some fair present, which shall surely carry death along with it!" Lo and behold, the Bishop fell ill and died a most unpleasant death eight days later. Gage wrote: "His head and face, did so swell that the least touch upon any part of him caused the skin to break and cast out white matter, which had corrupted and overflown all his body." Rumour had it that a gentlewoman "noted to be somewhat too familiar with one of the Bishop's pages" had persuaded the innocent young man to administer a cup of poisoned chocolate to "him who so rigorously had forbidden chocolate to be drunk in Church". A popular proverb in the region thereafter was "Beware of the chocolate of Chiapa".

DANGEROUS STIMULANTS
At the time that chocolate was becoming all the rage in Europe, there was a similar rise in the consumption of other tropical commodities such as coffee, tea, tobacco, rum and sugar; it seems that the Europeans were developing a taste for stimulants. The Church took a strong position and, with the exception of sugar, denounced the new foods as potentially dangerous. Even so, there was a certain amount of rule-bending when it came to chocolate.

RIGHT: Detail from a diorama based on a seventeenth-century engraving of monks drinking chocolate.

CHOCOLATE AS MEDICINE

Chocolate was used therapeutically as long ago as the fourth century, when the Maya first started cultivating the cacao tree. Sorcerers, the predecessors of priests and doctors, prescribed cacao both as a stimulant and as a soothing balm. Warriors took it as an energy-boosting drink, and cacao butter was used as a dressing for wounds.

Later on, the Aztecs prescribed a potion of cacao mixed with the ground exhumed bones of their ancestors as a cure for diarrhoea. The Spanish colonists, too, were aware of cacao's healing properties. A traveller reported of his countrymen: "They make paste thereof, the which they say is good for the stomacke, and against the catarre."

However, chocolate was given a mixed reception by the scientific and medical community, who were just as vociferous as the Church when it came to debating the rights and wrongs of this mysterious new substance. In the sixteenth century, when medicine was in its infancy, many of the theories were based on the principle of "hot" and "cold" humours, or body energies, which, if not kept in balance, would cause illness. The Spanish classified chocolate as "cold" and tried to neutralize its effect by

ABOVE: Utensils needed "to make cocoa to perfection".

drinking it hot, flavoured with "hot" spices. They found it hard to understand why the Aztecs drank unheated chocolate when it was already a "cold" food.

By the seventeenth century, chocolate had been given the seal of approval by several botanists and medical men, who discovered that it contained all kinds of beneficial substances. Henry Stubbe (1632–72), the English court physician, visited the West Indies to investigate the physical effects of chocolate. On his return, he published *The Indian Nectar*, in which he had nothing but praise for the beverage, with the proviso that adding too much sugar or spice was unwise.

Among the many others who sang the praises of chocolate was Stephani Blancardi (1650–1702), an Italian physician. He commented: "Chocolate is not only pleasant of taste, but it is also a veritable balm of the mouth, for the maintaining of all glands and humours in a good state of health. Thus it is, that all who drink it, possess a sweet breath."

The French faculty of medicine officially approved its use in 1661. The magistrate and gastronome, Brillat-Savarin (1755–1826), summed up in *Physiologie du Gout*: "Chocolate, when carefully prepared, is a wholesome and agreeable form of food … is very suitable for persons of great mental exertion, preachers, lawyers, and above all travellers … it agrees with the feeblest stomachs, has proved beneficial in cases of chronic illness and remains the last resource in the diseases of the pylorus." Some of his contemporaries claimed that chocolate cured tuberculosis. A French doctor, probably sensing chocolate's ability to lift the spirits, was convinced of its merits as an antidote to a broken heart. He wrote "Those who love, and are unfortunate enough to suffer from the most universal of all gallant illnesses, will find [in chocolate] the most enlightening consolation."

Praise was by no means universal. An eighteenth-century physician to the Tuscan court threw a spanner in the works by declaring that chocolate was "hot" and that it was madness to add "hot drugs" to it. He obviously noticed the effects of caffeine for he lists as ill effects incessant chatter, insomnia, irritability and hyperactivity in children. The French, too, became disenamoured for a short period, blaming chocolate for "vapours", palpitations, wind and constipation.

In general, however, the medicinal and nutritional benefits

BELOW: French doctors believed chocolate was beneficial for chronic illnesses and broken hearts.

— *A MEXICAN RECIPE FOR LIP SALVE* —
Take half a teaspoon [2.5ml] of cocoa butter from freshly roasted beans and mix to an ointment with sweet almond oil.

RIGHT: This eighteenth-century painting shows how chocolate was adopted by well-to-do households as a nutritious breakfast drink.

BELOW: This engraving from "Physiologie du Gout ou Méditations de Gastronomie Transcendante" (1848) depicts chocolate being served to uplift the spirits.

BELOW: This nineteenth-century advertisement shows British children enjoying cocoa. Medical experts in Britain proclaimed cocoa as "the drink par excellence for children, with whom it is a universal favourite".

of chocolate were well accepted. An early English writer described it as "incomparable as a family drink for breakfast or supper, when both tea and coffee are really out of place unless the latter is nearly all milk". Brillat-Savarin commented on digestion: "When you have breakfasted well and copiously, if you swallow a generous cup of good chocolate at the end of the meal, you will have digested everything perfectly three hours later."

By the 1800s charlatans were beginning to cash in on chocolate's seal of approval by the medical profession. Various forms of "medicinal" chocolate started to appear including sinister-sounding products such as "pectoral chocolate" made with Indian tapioca, recommended for people suffering from consumption, and "analeptic" chocolate made with a mysterious "Persian tonic".

By the end of the century, the genuine article was approved of by hospitals and sanatoria, as well as by the navy, the army and various public institutions.

THE FOUNDING FATHERS

ABOVE: Nineteenth-century British cocoa manufacturers were keen to wean the poor off their favourite tipple of gin.

GREAT BRITAIN

The manufacture of drinking chocolate in Britain was transformed by the Industrial Revolution and the cultural, social and economic changes that followed in its wake. During the eighteenth century the pioneering chocolate manufacturers were still using primitive manufacturing methods, similar to those used by the Aztecs. Technology gradually entered the scene with two key developments: a hydraulic grinding press, invented in 1728 by Walter Churchman, and, in 1765, James Watt's steam engine, which changed the food industry overnight. Another crucial development in chocolate manufacture was a revolutionary type of chocolate press invented in 1828 by a Dutch chemist, Coenraad Van Houten.

In 1853 the taxes on drinking chocolate were reduced because the volume of imports had grown enormously. By then the new railways had made transport easier, and power-driven machinery had largely replaced the old slow method of making chocolate by hand. These changes radically brought down the price, meaning that drinking chocolate could potentially be enjoyed by all.

It was during this era that several

RIGHT: Cadburys printed endorsements from the medical press on their packaging.

eminent Quaker families – the Frys, the Cadburys, the Rowntrees and the Terrys – became involved in chocolate manufacturing. These families established themselves as the main producers in Britain and succeeded in transforming chocolate from the drink of the aristocracy to the drink of the people.

It was undoubtedly the Quakers' evangelical outlook which was behind their decision to choose chocolate as a commercial venture. Because the beverage was so wholesome, the Quakers hoped it would provide a means of weaning the poor off beer and gin, their favourite tipples, and improving the quality of their lives in general. The Quakers were also concerned for their employees' welfare. They created exemplary working conditions and built model villages where education, healthcare and community services were provided for the workers, both active and retired, without charge. Cadbury's Bournville village near Birmingham and Rowntree in York are famous examples.

The Frys were the sole suppliers of chocolate to the navy, making them the largest chocolate manufacturer in the world. Not to be outdone, the rival Cadbury family gained the privileged title of purveyors of chocolate to Queen Victoria.

ITALY

The Italians have always been accomplished sweet-makers. They started using chocolate as an ingredient very early on and thus established themselves as leading experts in the art of making fine chocolates. In 1884, when the Russian Czar commissioned from the jeweller Fabergé his first golden egg with its surprise filling of precious stones, Italian producers introduced what may have been the

ABOVE: Military-style packaging.

first chocolate Easter eggs containing a surprise gift.

The Italian chocolate industry is centred around Turin in Piedmont and Perugia in Umbria. Production on a commercial level developed in the early nineteenth century when Bozelli, an engineer from Genoa, designed a machine capable of producing over 300kg/660lb of chocolate per day. By the end of the century the industry was booming.

There are several long-established firms in northern Italy. These include Caffarel, from whom the Italians learned to make chocolate, and Baratti & Milano, from the Turin area; Perugina (now owned by Nestlé) from Perugia, makers of the famous "Baci" (kisses) chocolates with the memorable pack; and Majani in Bologna, who now produce the ultimate in designer chocolates.

SWITZERLAND

Unsurprisingly, Switzerland boasts an incredible list of founding fathers. The first, an enterprising young man named François Cailler, travelled to Turin in 1815, learned the tricks of the trade from Caffarel, then opened the first Swiss chocolate factory four years later. Next to set up was Philippe Suchard, inventor of the world's first chocolate mixing machine. In 1845 Richard Sprüngli opened his world-famous shop in Zurich, followed by a factory in 1900. Henri Nestlé, a chemist, invented a type of evaporated milk powder, which was used by Daniel Peter, a chocolate-maker, to produce the first milk chocolate bars in 1879. In the same year Rodolphe Lindt invented the "conching" process, which revolutionized forever the texture and flavour of solid chocolate bars. Richard Sprüngli's grandson, David, bought out Lindt in 1899; five generations later, Lindt-Sprüngli is Switzerland's largest independent chocolate manufacturer. Finally, in 1908 Jean Tobler produced the famous "Toblerone" bar, now marketed by Suchard. Its distinctive triangular shape was designed to represent the Swiss Alps.

FRANCE

The first chocolate factories appeared in the mid-seventeenth century, and, as in England, production was a slow and primitive process. Life became easier in 1732, when a Frenchman named Dubuisson invented a grinding table. This allowed the workers to grind the beans standing up, instead of kneeling in front of a floor-level stone, which they had done until then.

France's most famous mass-producers were Auguste Poulain and Jean-Antoine Menier. Poulain set up shop in Blois in 1848, making chocolate in a back room. By 1878 he was producing chocolate by the ton from five different factories. In 1884 his son Albert developed a chocolate breakfast drink, now known as Grand Arôme and still loved by French children. Meanwhile, Menier, a pharmacist famous for his "medicinal powders", bought a small chocolate factory near the River Marne, intending simply to produce chocolate to coat his pills. When he died in 1853, his son Émile-Justin stepped in, concentrating on full-scale chocolate manufacture. A man of capitalist vision, Émile built a new factory in France, opened a factory in

LEFT: Menier cooking chocolate is widely used today.

RIGHT: As this 1893 poster shows, Menier chocolate has always been popular with French children.

LEFT: Established for over a hundred years, Weiss still produces quality drinking chocolate.

London, a warehouse in New York, bought cacao plantations in Nicaragua, and built a Bournville-like model village for his workers. When he died Émile's son, Henri, continued in the same expansionary spirit. In 1889 he arranged for electricity lines and telephones to be installed in the workers' homes, and, many years before the rest of the French working population, gave them the right to retire at sixty.

France's chocolatiers also include a strong contingent of smaller specialist firms that played an important role in forming the character of France's present-day chocolate industry. Debauve & Gallais was established in Paris in 1800 and are the oldest producers of hand-made chocolates in the city today. Another prestigious company is Weiss, based in Saint-Étienne for over a hundred years, and famous for its delicious drinking chocolate and hefty foil-wrapped chocolate drops.

ABOVE: The electronic automobile bought by Hershey in 1900.

UNITED STATES OF AMERICA
Chocolate arrived relatively late in North America, around the middle of the eighteenth century. The first industrial producers were Dr James Baker and his partner John Hannon, who built a chocolate factory in 1765 on the banks of the River Neponset in Massachusetts. In 1780 the company was renamed the Walter Baker Company, after John Hannon's grandson, and is still a household name today, producing baker's (a confusing generic term) chocolate as well as better quality varieties under their own name of Baker's.

Over a century later Milton Hershey, a successful caramel manufacturer from Pennsylvania, visited the 1893 Chicago World's Fair and was overwhelmingly impressed by German chocolate production machinery on display. With a shrewd sense of timing, he decided that chocolate was going to be a runaway success; and his company has never looked back. Milton sold his first milk chocolate bar in 1895, and since then Hershey Bars and Hershey Kisses have become part of the American way of life – just as he predicted.

Like his Quaker counterparts in Britain, Milton had a social conscience. He enlisted nutritionists to vouch for the sanctity of his product, set up a squeaky-clean working environment, and built the factory town of Hershey in Pennsylvania. The main thoroughfares are East Chocolate Avenue and Cocoa Avenue, while the tree-lined side streets are named after places where cacao is grown, or by types of bean – Java, Caracas, Arriba and so on. Milton went one better than the Quaker factory villages in England and provided very generous out-of-town facilities for his employees such as an amusement park, a zoo, sporting facilities and a theatre. Milton also made it clear that no "taverns, piggeries, glue, soap, candle, lamp-black factories" were allowed, making sure that his model working communities stayed as wholesome as possible.

It is interesting that the early North American and British manufacturers of a product that was, and still is, associated with sensory enjoyment and indulgence, should have had quite a puritanical outlook. A cynical view might be that their social philanthropy was a clever marketing ploy, but these businessmen did have a genuine social conscience, and it is perhaps another illustration that chocolate is all things to all people – both a luxurious treat and a wholesome daily food.

Milton Hershey was not the only American producer

pushing the wholesomeness of chocolate. Like-minded but rather more extreme companies included the Taylor brothers, who entered the market with their Natural Hygienist Practitioners, and Dr William Hay, of the still-popular Hay System of food-combining. Taylor's selling point was the curative, homeopathic nature of chocolate. This shows a continuity with the earliest European marketeers, who sold their chocolate

ABOVE: Street signs to the main thoroughfares in Hershey.

through the apothecaries, monasteries and convents of the sixteenth and seventeenth centuries, and had much to say on the beneficial properties of the cacao bean and its products.

A much more colourful American chocolate producer was

BELOW: Early publicity for Taylor Brothers demonstrating their social conscience, while promoting the nourishing powers of chocolate.

ABOVE: A picture of the original Guittard building surrounded by scenes showing early chocolate manufacture.

Domingo Ghirardelli, an Italian confectioner with South American links who was originally in business in Lima, Peru. Ghirardelli befriended an American cabinetmaker named James Lick, who, in 1847 just before the discovery of gold at Sutter's Mill, moved from Lima to San Francisco, taking with him a large quantity of Ghirardelli's chocolate. Lured by reports of a lucrative market, Ghirardelli followed Lick to California. As astute and entrepreneurial as his fellow chocolate producers, both in

BELOW: The Ghirardelli company was the first in America to make easily dissolvable powdered cocoa.

the United States and worldwide, Ghirardelli foresaw the potential in satisfying the day-to-day needs of the goldrush pioneers, who by then were arriving in hordes. He set up a business in San Francisco importing and selling commodities such as sugar, coffee and, of course, chocolate.

There were various disasters over the years, including devastating bankruptcy and a serious fire, but business continued despite the inevitable setbacks in a volatile period of American history. By 1856 the company was known as Ghirardelli's California Chocolate Manufactory. The company was to make its mark on the chocolate industry in the 1860s when, by sheer accident, a way of making a low-fat powdered cocoa was discovered. The new product was known as Sweet Ground Chocolate and Cocoa and is still sold today.

The original factory buildings have become a well-known San Francisco landmark in Ghirardelli Square, and the company continues to flourish. It was bought by the Golden Grain Macaroni Company in 1963, which in turn was acquired as a subsidiary of the Quaker Oats Company in 1983.

Another chocolate maker, Etienne Guittard from France, set off for the gold fields of San Francisco in 1860. After three years, he hadn't found any gold, but the supply of fine chocolate he had brought with him to barter for prospecting gear had been enthusiastically received. The shopkeepers he traded with assured him that there was a future for him and his wonderful chocolate in San Francisco. Guittard went back to France, where he worked and saved to buy the equipment he would need. In 1868 he returned to San Francisco and opened the business that developed into one of the important American manufacturers of top-grade chocolate for wholesale customers. Some of the country's best confectioners, bakers and ice-cream makers (Baskin-Robbins, for one) use Guittard.

— GHIRARDELLI'S ACCIDENT —

Cacao beans have a high fat content and because of this do not combine easily with liquids when ground to a powder. Ghirardelli's most important contribution to the chocolate industry was the accidental discovery of a way of making a virtually fat-free powder.

A worker left some ground cacao beans hanging from a hook in a cloth bag overnight. By the morning, the floor was covered in cacao butter that had dripped from the bag. The ground chocolate left behind was almost fat-free and was found to combine with liquids much more smoothly. Ghirardelli's ever-popular Sweet Ground Chocolate and Cocoa was developed from this.

CULTIVATION AND PROCESSING

GROWING AND HARVESTING

Above: Cacao tree and seedling.

There are many stages in the processing of chocolate, and there has been a corresponding amount of development in its history as it has grown from a cold drink to the complex and adaptable substance it is today. This chapter traces the most important steps in the production of chocolate.

GROWING

The cacao bean grows in large pods on the cacao tree, *Theobroma cacao*, an evergreen which thrives in tropical areas lying between 20° north and 20° south of the equator. The tree is an exacting specimen, for it refuses to grow where it is too high, too cold or too dry, and it demands shelter from wind and sun. It also needs protection from wild animals which delight in picking its pods, and it easily succumbs to various rots, wilts and fungal diseases.

It is traditional for the cacao tree to be grown under the protection of taller shade-creating trees, the conditions resembling its natural jungle habitat. In areas such as Grenada and parts of Jamaica, cacao trees grow successfully without additional shade, as long as there are sufficient moisture and nutrients in the soil. The cacao tree grows to about the size of an apple tree and starts

Below: A shady cacao plantation in the garden island of Grenada, where cacao production is a staple industry.

CACAO is essentially the botanical name and refers to the tree, the pods and, at one time, the unfermented beans from the pods. The term is now also used for beans that have been fermented.

COCOA refers to the manufactured powder sold for drinking or food manufacturing purposes.

bearing fruit in its third year. With luck, it will continue to do so until at least its twentieth year, and it is not unknown for a tree to live to be a hundred years old. The glossy dark green leaves, similar to those of the laurel, grow to nearly 30 cm/ 12 in long. The small pale pink flowers grow in dense clusters straight out of the trunk and main branches on little raised cushions, a feature technically known as "cauliflory".

After pollination, the flowers take about five months to develop into cacao pods. It's a colourful crop – the pods range from bright red, green, purple or yellow, changing hue as they ripen. Ripe pods are about 20 cm/8 in long, oval and pointed, each containing 20 to 40 beans, embedded in a soft white pulp.

HARVESTING

It is by assessing the colour of the pod and the sound it makes when tapped that the picker can be sure it is ready for picking. To be absolutely certain that the pod is ripe requires years of practice, and experienced pickers are highly valued.

The pods are removed from the tree by cutting through their stalks, those within reach with a cutlass, and those on higher branches with a curved knife fixed to a long pole. Cutting must be done with extreme care so as not to damage the "cauliflory", as this continually produces the flowers and therefore the fruit.

In some countries, harvesting takes place all year round, although most heavily from May to December. In other parts of the world, West Africa for instance, the main crop is harvested from September to February.

FERMENTING

The next stage is to split the pods with a cutlass, taking care not to damage the precious beans. These are scooped out, together with their surrounding pulp, and formed into a conical heap on a carefully arranged mat of banana leaves. When the heap is complete the leaves are folded over, and yet more of these giant

ABOVE: Early lithograph issued by the Empire Marketing Board in Britain showing cacao beans being scooped from the pods.

— TYPES OF CACAO BEAN —

There are two distinct species of cacao bean used in the manufacture of chocolate: the criollo (meaning "native") and the forastero (meaning "foreign").

The criollo, the Rolls Royce of beans and the most delicate, is in a way a "limited edition", representing only 10 to 15 per cent of the world's production. It is cultivated mainly in the countries where cacao originated, namely Nicaragua, Guatemala, Mexico, Venezuela and Colombia, as well as Trinidad, Jamaica and Grenada. The criollo's exceptional flavour and aroma are prized by chocolate manufacturers the world over. Not surprisingly, the bean is always used in combination with other varieties.

The much hardier and higher-yielding forastero bean is grown mainly in Brazil and Africa, and it accounts for about 80 per cent of the production. It has a stronger, more bitter flavour than the criollo and is mainly used for blending.

The one exception is the amenolado variety, known as the "Arriba" bean, grown in Ecuador. Its delicate flavour and fine aroma considered equal to the world's best beans.

Finally, there are also several hybrid beans, of which the trinitario is the best known. As the name suggests, it began life in Trinidad where, following a hurricane in 1727 that all but destroyed the plantations, it was a result of cross-breeding. It has inherited the robustness of the forastero and the delicate flavour of the criollo, and it is used mainly for blending.

leaves are added to enclose the heap completely. This is the start of the fermentation process, which lasts for up to six days.

The chemical processes involved are complicated, but, basically, bacteria and yeasts present in the air multiply on the sugary pulp surrounding the beans, causing it to decompose to an acidic juice. The process raises the temperature of the heap and under these conditions magical changes take place within the bean itself. The colour changes from purple to chocolate brown and the familiar cacao smell begins to emerge – the first crucial stage in developing beans of superior quality. That said, the fermentation process is sometimes omitted, with planters and manufacturers arguing both for and against.

DRYING

After fermentation, the beans are spread out on bamboo mats or wooden drying floors. During the ten to twenty days needed for drying, the beans are regularly turned to keep them well aired and to prevent moulds forming. In some places, where rainfall and humidity are high, the beans are dried in commercial drying plants. However, the best quality cacao comes from beans that have been dried naturally in the warm tropical sun.

BELOW: The large and beautiful cacao pods grow directly from the tree branches and change colour as they ripen.

MODERN MANUFACTURING

ABOVE: A chocolate manufacturer inspects a shipment of beans.

CLEANING AND GRADING

Cacao beans arrive at a chocolate factory in the condition in which they leave the plantations in cacao-growing countries. They have been fermented and dried but are still a raw material with the edible part enclosed inside the hard skin, which is dusty with the remains of the dried pulp.

The beans are given a preliminary cleaning, during which any stones or other objects that may have arrived in the sacks are removed by sieving. The beans pass on a moving belt to storage hoppers, and from there they travel on another conveyor belt to the cleaning and grading machines. The beans are carefully inspected, and any shrivelled or double beans are discarded, as is any undesirable material still clinging to the beans. Next, the cleaned and graded beans are collected either in containers or passed on another continuous conveyor belt to the roasting machines.

ROASTING FOR FLAVOUR

Roasting is a crucial part of the process and serves several functions. First, it develops the flavour and aroma, and it enriches the colour. Roasting also dries the husk surrounding the "nib", or edible inner part of the bean, making its removal easier, and dries the nib itself so that it is ready for grinding.

The degree of roasting is extremely important. Overdoing

BELOW: The beans are cleaned and sifted through a mesh to get rid of small or shrivelled beans and foreign bodies.

ABOVE: A contemporaneous picture of Richard Sprüngli's famous factory, which opened in Switzerland in 1900.

it destroys the natural flavour of the bean and produces a bitter product, while under-roasting makes the removal of the husk more difficult and also fails to eradicate the natural bitterness of the raw bean. Some manufacturers who want their chocolate to have a strong flavour, but who are not prepared to increase the cacao content, attempt to achieve the required intensity by roasting the beans longer.

Different types of bean need different roasting temperatures, depending on their texture and flavour; the mild varieties are usually roasted at lower temperatures than the stronger types.

After roasting, the beans are cooled as quickly as possible to prevent further internal roasting.

BELOW: The beans are gently roasted to develop the aroma, enrich the colour and to dehydrate them prior to grinding.

WINNOWING

During the next stage the beans are passed through the husking and winnowing machine, which cracks open the roasted beans, and blows the lighter husks away from the heavier pieces of nib.

Manufacturers send the husks off for recycling as garden mulch, or use them to make low-quality soft "shell" butter.

THE CRUCIAL BLEND

During the blending process, specified quantities of different varieties of cacao nibs are weighed and transferred to a cylindrical blender before they are fed into the grinding machines.

The blending of beans for cocoa powder is generally less exacting than for eating chocolate. The latter requires the utmost skill from the chocolatier since knowledge of the characteristic flavours imparted by different beans is only acquired by years of experience. There are subtle differences of flavour in each type of bean, and the final flavour is obtained by blending two, three or more types of bean after roasting. In the same way that the winemaker blends his grapes, the chocolatier needs to determine the proportion of strong and mild cacao beans necessary

ABOVE: A picture of the grinding hall in the Sprüngli factory. The rollers can be seen on the left.

to produce a blend that will result in a satisfying chocolate, and the formulae are jealously guarded secrets.

GRINDING

Once in the grinding mill, the nibs pass through a series of rollers, resulting in coarse particles that eventually turn into a warm paste because of the frictional heat of the grinding action. Then follows a second grinding to bring the particles down to the required size, usually between 25 and 50 microns (about 0.001in). Large particles result in coarse grainy chocolate, while very finely ground particles will produce a pasty and slightly sticky chocolate. After grinding, the cacao mass or "liquor" flows out of the machine into shallow metal containers.

THE PARTING OF THE WAYS

At this stage, further treatment of the liquor depends on whether it is to be made into cocoa powder or eating chocolate. For cocoa powder the next step is the extraction of a large proportion of the cacao butter. This is pressed out of the liquor, and the residue is formed into cakes, which go through one more grinding. Some cocoa is "dutched", which helps to make cocoa powder easier to mix with water. It also improves the colour and lightens the flavour. Sometimes a wetting agent is added, especially to the "instant" varieties of cocoa intended for use as a cold drink; it makes the powder easier to mix with cold water or milk. The wetting agent is usually lecithin, a vegetable fat found in egg yolks and soy beans. Chocolate destined for eating is treated very differently from cocoa powder.

RIGHT: Two types of instant drinking chocolate.

— BEAN BLENDS —

The final flavour of chocolate depends largely on the chocolatier's skill and experience in selecting and blending various types of beans. Availability of supplies and cost also have to be taken into account.

Types of cacao beans may be divided into strong and mild varieties:

STRONG VARIETIES	MILD VARIETIES
Accra	Caracas
St Lucia	Mauritius
Para	Sri Lanka
Trinidad	Arriba
Grenada	Java
Surinam	Madras
Cuba	Jamaica
Dominica	Seychelles

If made only with Accra beans, for example, chocolate will have a very strong, harsh flavour, whereas Caracas beans make mild but excellently flavoured chocolate. Superb chocolate can be made with a blend of 42 per cent Trinidad beans (strong), 21 per cent Accra beans (strong) and 37 per cent Caracas (mild).

THE MANUFACTURE OF EATING CHOCOLATE

ABOVE: Rolls of ground chocolate paste (foreground) are moulded into bars and various shapes in the moulding hall.

ABOVE: Prolonged conching transforms the chocolate paste into velvety smoothness.

MIXING

Cacao beans used for manufacturing eating chocolate are processed in a different way from beans used in cocoa manufacture. First, a carefully selected blend of roasted and ground nibs, the edible centre of the bean, is mixed with pulverized sugar and enriched with cacao butter, not necessarily extracted from the same batch of nibs. The mass producers in the chocolate industry are very keen on adding lecithin, a vegetable fat, to replace some or all of the cacao butter. This means they can sell the valuable butter at a profit.

The mixture then goes to the *mélangeur,* a round machine with a horizontal rotating base on which run heavy rollers. After mixing, the chocolate paste that is discharged from the *mélangeur* resembles well-kneaded dough.

When manufacturing milk chocolate, powdered milk or evaporated sweetened milk is added to the rest of the ingredients in the mixer.

REFINING

Next, the chocolate paste is ground between a series of five rollers, each succeeding roller rotating faster than the previous one. The paste enters the first pair of rollers as a thin film, which is then taken up by the next pair, through a carefully adjusted gap – rather like making pasta with a machine. By the time the paste emerges from the fifth roller it is wafer-thin.

As far as some mass-producers are concerned this is the end of the process, but the finest quality chocolate needs further treatment known as "conching".

CONCHING

The conching machine was invented in 1880 by the Swiss chocolatier, Rodolfe Lindt. The name comes from the French (*conche,* meaning "shell") and is derived from the shape of the machine, a large shell-shaped container.

The function of the machine is to agitate the liquid chocolate gently over a period that may be as long as seven days. It is a vital process in which the flavour of the chocolate is developed and mellowed, any residual bitterness is removed, and the texture reaches that essential stage of velvety smoothness.

Manufacturers of cheaper chocolate give as little as twelve hours to the process. Quality producers will continue conching for up to a week, sometimes adding extra cacao butter to make the chocolate smoother still.

During conching, various flavours are added, such as vanilla, cloves or cinnamon.

LEFT: Luscious slices of crystallized fruit are enrobed with smooth, dark chocolate.

Vanilla is almost always used and dates back to the days of the Aztecs. Our palates have become so accustomed to its flavour in chocolate that leaving it out would be like making bread without salt. Pure vanilla extract is used for the best quality chocolate, but cheaper varieties are likely to contain vanillin, a synthetic substitute.

TEMPERING

Once the conching stage is complete, the chocolate is fed into tempering kettles, where it is stirred and carefully cooled but still remains liquid. This is a tricky process since cacao butter contains various types of fat, all with different melting and setting points. If the chocolate mass is cooled too slowly, some fats will remain liquid and separate from the mass, creating a bloom on the surface when the chocolate finally solidifies. Tempering causes rapid cooling resulting in a more even distribution of the various fats.

After tempering, chocolate to be made into bars is pumped into moulding machines, while chocolate to be used as coating is pumped into enrobing machines.

BELOW: Hollow Easter eggs, filled with small chocolates, are a classic example of chocolate moulding.

Mr R. Whymper in *Cocoa and Chocolate* (1921) told an interesting story of how, in the early 1900s, the popularity of milk chocolate "raised hopes in the breasts of manufacturers that a similar demand might be created among the masses for such articles as Date Chocolate, Egg Chocolate, Malt Chocolate". A number of patents were taken out, one of which was for mixing cacao beans and dates to a pulp, and covered the use of apples, pears and apricots for the same purpose. There was apparently a shortage of cane sugar at the time, and the fruit pulp was intended to be a sweetener.

Another patent was for "dietetic and laxative" chocolate. As Mr Whymper pointed out: "Such preparations must have only a very limited sale, so long as the chocolate-consuming public does not seek to find cures in its confections."

MOULDING

Liquid chocolate is also moulded into hollowed-out shapes which are sometimes filled with small chocolates. These products are often marketed as gifts for children, and specialist chocolate-makers give full rein to their creativity here, producing not simply exquisite Easter eggs, bunnies and hearts, but also pigs, fish, lions, hippos, crocodiles and

ABOVE: 1930's metal moulds for producing novelty chocolates.

cars. Because of the contact with the smooth tinned surfaces of the mould, good quality hollow chocolate has a high degree of gloss, which adds to its attraction.

ENROBING

Enrobing is the tricky process of coating confectionery centres. Liquid chocolate of a slightly "thin" consistency is pumped into the enrobing machine, where it is agitated once more and maintained at a temperature just high enough to keep it liquid. The centres themselves have to be warm when they enter the coating chamber, but not so warm that they lose their shape. The danger of a cold centre is that it is likely to expand when it comes in contact with the warm coating, resulting in burst chocolates. Enrobing is the process used not only for top quality chocolates in their luxury packaging, but also for the mass-produced candy bars that are bought as snacks around the world.

TASTE, QUALITY AND PRESENTATION

TYPES OF EATING CHOCOLATE

There is a wealth of wonderful chocolate products available, with an often confusing array of types, qualities, fillings and flavourings. Here is a brief guide on what you should look for and how to enjoy chocolate at its best.

PLAIN CHOCOLATE (ALSO KNOWN AS BITTERSWEET)

Plain or bittersweet chocolate must contain a minimum of 34 per cent cacao solids, but generally speaking, the higher the proportion the better the chocolate. Not so long ago, plain chocolate containing just 30 per cent cacao solids was considered high quality. Nowadays, as our taste and awareness of chocolate grows, 60 per cent is the preferred minimum, while for chocoholics 70-80 per cent is even more desirable.

High quality dark chocolate contains a correspondingly small proportion of sugar. Adding sugar to chocolate has been compared with adding salt to food. You need just enough to enhance the flavour but not so much that the flavour is destroyed. Quality chocolate contains pure vanilla, an expensive flavouring sometimes called Bourbon Vanilla, extracted from a type of orchid grown in Madagascar. It also contains the minutest amount of lecithin, a harmless vegetable stabilizer. In unsweetened chocolate, which is found only in specialist shops, cacao solids are as high as 98 per cent.

ABOVE: Quality white, milk and dark chocolate.

COUVERTURE

This is high-quality chocolate in the professional league, used mainly for coating and in baking. Couverture usually has a minimum of 32 per cent cacao butter, which enables it to form a much thinner shell than ordinary chocolate.

LEFT: Couverture chocolate, which has a very high proportion of cacao solids.

RIGHT: Best quality couverture with a good sheen. Blocks of this size are supplied to chocolatiers.

> ### — FORMULA FOR QUALITY CHOCOLATE —
> 56-70% cacao solids, to include 31% cacao butter
> 29-43% finely ground sugar
> 1% lecithin and pure vanilla extract
>
> ### — FORMULA FOR MASS-PRODUCED MILK CHOCOLATE —
> 11% cacao solids
> 3% vegetable fat
> 20% milk solids
> 65% sugar
> 1% lecithin and synthetic vanillin

MILK CHOCOLATE

To some *aficionados,* milk chocolate is not really chocolate, but, increasingly, there are good brands around even though they may be difficult to find. A good brand will have a cacao solid content of around 40 per cent, but most mass-produced milk chocolate contains only 20 per cent. Mass-produced milk chocolate has a high sugar content, often up to 50 per cent. It can also contain up to 5 per cent vegetable fat, used as a substitute for expensive cacao butter, and artificial flavouring.

WHITE CHOCOLATE

This is basically cacao butter without any cacao solids, with some added sugar, flavouring and milk. White chocolate does not have the same depth of flavour as plain chocolate. It is mainly sold for its novelty value or to provide an attractive colour contrast

Left: A layered bar of plain, white and milk chocolate.

in chocolates and chocolate desserts. The best quality brands tend to be French and Swiss. British brands usually contain vegetable oil instead of cacao butter, as well as synthetic flavourings.

Assessing Quality

All our senses – sight, smell, sound, touch and taste – come into play when assessing the quality of plain chocolate. There are several points to watch out for:

APPEARANCE: The chocolate should be smooth, brilliantly shiny and pure mahogany-black in colour.

SMELL: The chocolate should not smell excessively sweet.

SOUND: The chocolate should be crisp and make a distinct "snap" when broken in two. If the chocolate splinters, it is too dry; if it resists breaking, it is too waxy.

TOUCH: Chocolate with a high cacao butter content should quickly start to melt when held in the hand – this is a good sign. In the mouth, it should feel ultra-smooth with no hint of graininess, and it should melt instantly.

TASTE: Chocolate contains a kaleidoscope of flavours and aromas which continue to develop in the mouth. The basic flavours are bitterness with a hint of acidity, sweetness with a suggestion of sourness, and just a touch of saltiness which helps release the aromas of cocoa, pineapple, banana, vanilla and cinnamon.

Storage

Humidity and heat are chocolate's greatest enemies; both can cause a "bloom" to appear on the surface. Heat-induced bloom

---

— Tasting Techniques —

It is best to taste chocolate on an empty stomach. If your chocolate is correctly stored, you will need to allow an hour or so for it to reach the recommended temperature of 19–25°C/66–77°F.

PLAIN CHOCOLATE: Allow the chocolate to sit in your mouth for a few moments to release its primary flavours and aromas. Then chew it five to ten times to release the secondary aromas. Let it rest lightly against the roof of your mouth so that you experience the full range of flavours. Finally, enjoy the lingering tastes in your mouth.

FILLED CHOCOLATE: Allow the chocolate to sit in your mouth for a few moments to release its primary flavours and aromas. Then chew it three to five times to mix the chocolate and the filling. Let the mixture melt slowly in your mouth so that you experience a new range of flavours. Enjoy the lingering tastes.

Left: The perfect bar of chocolate has a glossy sheen and a rich dark colour.

is the result of cacao butter crystals rising to the surface and recrystallizing. The flavour is unaffected but the appearance is spoiled.

Humidity-induced bloom is more damaging. It is a result of sugar crystals being drawn to the surface, where they dissolve in the moist atmosphere and eventually recrystallize to form an unpleasant grey coating. As the texture and taste of the chocolate deteriorate, too, the dustbin is the best place for chocolate that has suffered in this way. The ideal temperature for storage is 10–15°C (50–60°F), slightly warmer than the refrigerator, and the humidity should be 60–70 per cent. Chocolate also absorbs surrounding odours easily and should be kept in an airtight container.

Below: A bloom has formed on the surface of the chocolate on the right. An unaffected piece on the left shows the difference in appearance.

— What to Drink with Chocolate —

Generally speaking, chocolate and wine do not mix. The lingering intensity of the chocolate competes with the aroma of the wine, and chocolate's bitterness can mask the tannins essential to the wine's flavour. White wine or champagne drunk with chocolate is a particularly uneasy combination. At the end of a meal, coffee, perhaps accompanied by a fine cognac, whisky or bourbon, is the best choice. Professional chocolate tasters swear by a glass of cold, fresh water; as it not only quenches the thirst but also cleanses the palate.

FLAVOURINGS AND FILLINGS

Every chocolate manufacturer has a secret condiment or blend of flavourings that he or she claims gives their product a unique character. Fillings and flavourings from the same tropical latitude as the cacao bean itself – vanilla, cinnamon, cardamom, coffee, rum, ginger, even pepper and chilli – are the ones most commonly used. Even in this age of "culinary fusion", when we happily mix and match cuisines in our never-ending quest for novelty, flavouring chocolate with spices from a more northerly latitude simply seems wrong – it is hard to imagine fennel or caraway-flavoured chocolate, for instance – but perhaps it is merely a matter of time before it happens.

SECRET FLAVOURS

Every chocolate-consuming country has its favourite flavourings. Italy prefers its chocolate mixed with hazelnuts, almonds or chestnuts. France likes a nutty flavour too, but strongly flavoured dark bitter chocolate is also popular there. Spain likes spiced chocolate, and fillings such as almonds and dried fruits, America consumes mostly milk chocolate, often with whole peanuts or almonds embedded in it, while Britain

LEFT: Spanish chocolate packed with plump almonds.

ABOVE: Handmade "tartufini" from southern Italy – whole almonds coated in praline and dusted with dark cocoa and powdered sugar.

likes vanilla. Not only that, every country uses different blends of beans, and, as already mentioned, the subtle variations in the flavour of different bean varieties play their part in determining the final flavour of the chocolate. If we also take into account different processing methods used by individual factories, the number of flavour combinations is almost endless.

Within the scientific community, the complexity of chocolate's flavour is a source of enormous fascination to the flavour scientists who are regularly producing learned papers on the subject. Daniel Querici, speaking at the 1992 Oxford Symposium on Food & Cookery, summed up the subject of chocolate's flavour in a delightful way: "Its complex flavour profile looks like a royal peacock tail, although not fully deployed, as food scientists keep discovering new components."

BELOW: Plump and glistening, these unusual, luscious chocolate-covered figs come from Italy.

— FILLINGS —

BOILED: based on sugar and glucose and including caramels, butterscotch and fudge.

CREAMS AND FONDANTS: a mixture of sugar crystals in a sugar syrup, with fruit or other flavourings, coated with tempered chocolate.

CROQUET (OR BRITTLE): molten sugar with crushed nuts.

GANACHE: a mixture of chocolate, cream and butter, either rolled in cocoa powder to make a truffle or enrobed in tempered chocolate.

GIANDUJA: finely ground nuts and sugar mixed with plain or milk chocolate.

MARZIPAN: molten sugar mixed with ground almonds, coated with plain or milk chocolate.

NOUGAT: a mixture of beaten egg white, boiled sugar, nuts and/or candied fruit. Known as *Montélimar* in France (after the town where it is made), *torrone* in Italy, and *turrón* in Spain.

PRALINE: similar to *gianduja* but with a coarser texture and usually coated with plain or milk chocolate.

ABOVE: Italian chocolates with succulent fillings of walnuts, dried fruit and pistachio marzipan.

FANTASTIC FILLINGS

Chocolate has been used as a coating for anything from almonds and dried fruit to bizarre ingredients such as ants, and a look at the contents of a global box of chocolates will reveal many more.

In the United States, chillies and chocolate come together once more in the whacky confectionery range created by two chocolatiers from Oregon. Their products, which won an award at the Fiery Foods Show at Albuquerque, New Mexico, include Mexican Zingers, a creamy, green jalapeño salsa encased in a white chocolate shell, and Southwest Coyote Kickers, a red jalapeño salsa cream covered in light milk chocolate.

Although chilli-filled chocolates are legal in the United States, alcoholic fillings are not universally acceptable. As recently as 1986, only one American state permitted the manufacture of alcoholic chocolates, only eleven states permitted their sale, and

BELOW: Handmade British chocolates with melt-in-the-mouth fondant fillings, delicately flavoured with violet and rose.

> ### — A FILLING STORY —
>
> In 1987, Ethel M Chocolates owned by 82-year-old Forrest Mars and named after his mother, attempted to introduce liqueur-filled chocolates to Las Vegas, Nevada. The chocolates were spiked with crème de menthe, brandy, Scotch and bourbon.
>
> Mr Mars found that the sale and/or manufacture of alcoholic chocolates was illegal in most American states. Things were not looking good, especially as an appeal to legalize alcoholic chocolates had recently been rejected in Pennsylvania, home of Hersheyville. As was to be expected, the squeaky-clean Hershey Company added their support to the rejection on the grounds that "liquor-laced chocolates are inconsistent with values emphasized by religious and medical communities".
>
> Not one to give up easily, the determined Mr Mars successfully petitioned the sale and manufacture of alcoholic chocolates in his home state of Nevada. This meant he could sell his chocolates there but not across the border, and so he had to content himself with selling to the twenty million tourists who visit Las Vegas each year. Ethel M Chocolates are still to be found at Las Vegas airport and in many of the city's luxury hotels.

even then the permitted alcohol levels were severely restricted.

Move on to Europe, however, and it is a different story. In Italy smooth dark chocolates are filled with decadent liqueur-soaked fruits – cherries, kumquats, slices of dried peach, pear, apricots and oranges. There are also plump prunes, dates and walnuts filled with marzipan and covered with dark chocolate.

In Britain, chocolate lovers can enjoy delicate fondant fillings such as violet and rose creams or marzipan; truffle fillings laced with champagne, Cointreau or Drambuie; or chunks of stem ginger, and whole Brazil nuts. France is the birthplace of the dusky chocolate truffle created in the late nineteenth century by the Duc de Praslin, one of Louis XIV's ministers. At that time it was considered amusing to create a food resembling something totally unrelated. *Truffes au chocolat* were deeply rich, buttery chocolate balls that were then rolled in dark cocoa powder to resemble the savoury black fungi from Périgord.

The dragée is a French confectionery classic that in its original form, almonds coated with sugar and honey, dates back to the thirteenth century. The dragée adapted well to the introduction of chocolate and now consists of praline or nuts covered in chocolate and a hard sugar coating.

CHOCOLATE WRAPPERS AND BOXES

Wrapping and packaging tell a great deal about what kind of chocolate is inside. Much can be learnt from the nutritional information on a bar, while the style of its presentation says much about who is expected to buy it.

WORDING ON WRAPPERS

As with the label on a bottle of fine wine or virgin olive oil, the wording on a chocolate wrapper can provide significant clues as to the quality of the product, so for a chocolate lover it is worth becoming familiar with the terminology.

An area of confusion arises over the terms "cacao liquor" and "cacao solids". Liquor is the term used in the United States, while Europe favours solids, but both refer to the same thing – the entire cacao content including the butter. This is usually expressed as a percentage of the net weight of the end product. Cacao content ranges from 15 per cent, which hardly comes into the category of chocolate, to an incredible 99 per cent, which is an almost inedible but interesting experience.

ABOVE: A wrapper that makes a feature of the high cacao content.

Since the setting up of the European Union, legislation on the labelling of food has become much more regulated, and the classification of chocolate has become an issue. Some chocolate-producing countries feel that Britain's product should be classified as "vegolate" because of its use of vegetable fat and low cacao content. Happily for British chocolate producers this has as yet remained a discussion point only.

WHAT TO LOOK FOR

The key indicator of quality is the cacao content – the combined total of cacao solids (liquor) and cacao butter. In some cases, couverture for instance, the cacao

LEFT: As well as listing the ingredients, some wrappers are packed with other interesting information.

butter content is itemized separately. In the case of plain chocolate, a minimum of 50 per cent total cacao is an indicator of quality. Quality milk chocolate should have a minimum of 30 per cent. Since sugar makes up the balance of the ingredients, a high sugar content is a warning of a correspondingly low cacao content.

Unlike wine labels, which mention the grape variety, chocolate wrappers rarely divulge the type of cacao bean used and are not obliged to do so. An exception is in France, where the words *fine cocoa* mean that the superior varieties of bean, such as the criollo, have been used.

Vegetable or animal fats are used as a cheap substitute for some or all of the cacao butter, so if either is listed as an ingredient, the chocolate is not going to come up to scratch. The fact that they are not listed, however, does not always necessarily mean they are not present. In Britain, for example, up to 5 per cent cacao butter substitutes can be included without mentioning them on the wrapper.

Lecithin, an emulsifier derived from egg yolk and soya beans, is used in all types of chocolate, and at 1 per cent or less is not an indicator of inferior quality. Its function is to stabilize the chocolate and to absorb any moisture.

As far as flavourings are concerned, look for the words "pure vanilla extract". If "vanillin", a synthetic substitute, or simply the word "flavouring" is listed, the chocolate is likely to be of inferior quality.

The Americans outdo any other nation in the world when it comes to providing information on the ingredients that go into their chocolate; the wrappers and packaging often read like a book. There are very precise

LEFT AND BELOW: Early chocolate boxes often featured inlaid metal decorations and intricate decorative painting.

LEFT: The ultimate in kitsch packaging, this opulent white plastic "grand piano" chocolate box comes from Germany.

specifications for the quantity of cacao solids in different types of chocolate; all flavouring ingredients must be fully declared; there are additional lists of sugars, such as dextrose and glucose, which all have maximum permitted levels; and there is always a detailed panel of nutritional information.

CHOCOLATE BOXES

Chocolate-makers have been strongly aware of the value of shelf-appeal since the industry's early days. In France the most exquisitely designed chocolate boxes came into vogue as early as 1780, featuring beautiful paintings, intricately embossed plaques and inlaid semi-precious stones. Britain's chocolate boxes were not so ostentatious; they featured sentimental images that were very much the fashion when boxed chocolates came on the market. The first was produced in 1868 by Cadbury and featured a painting of a young girl cuddling a kitten; the model was Richard Cadbury's daughter Jessica.

Also part of the appeal are the beautiful papers used to line boxes and separate layers of chocolate. Although grease-resistant, the types of paper used have always had a special quality. They may be elaborately padded or embossed with gold or silver, or mysteriously translucent, like crisp tracing paper, with a swirly hammered finish. Another type of paper is known as glasine. It has a waxy feel and comes in wonderfully glossy, dark colours, almost smelling of chocolate in its own right.

Nowadays, packaging design veers from one extreme of style to another. Reminiscent of the glamourous thirties, there are amazingly lavish fabric-covered boxes trimmed with satiny ribbons and roses. In the kitsch category there is a large, white grand-piano-shaped box from Germany with chocolates hidden beneath the lid, and at the other end of the spectrum there is the ultimate in modern minimalist designer chocolates and packaging with slim chocolates wrapped in gold leaf.

BELOW: The packaging room at Cadbury's factory in 1932. Cadbury were the first manufacturer in Britain to produce boxed chocolates.

BELOW: Espresso-infused dark chocolate truffle fingers from the United States, end-wrapped with delicate gold foil.

A WORLD OF CHOCOLATE

In the next few pages of the book we survey some of the world's highest quality chocolate products. This is not a comprehensive selection, and it includes some of the most familiar quality brands as well as the more exclusive. Some products, such as the famous Toblerone bars, are internationally popular and universally available, and others, such as the exquisite chocolates made by the small specialist companies in America, are known to a much smaller market, but their first-class products are available by mail order and their market will increase as our appreciation of chocolate becomes more discerning.

BELGIUM

Belgium is renowned for its *ballotins,* chocolate-covered pralines, invented by Jean Neuhaus who, in 1912, developed coating chocolate capable of containing liquid fillings. Today NEUHAUS is well known for its flavoured Côte d'Or bars.

Of all Belgian chocolate companies, GODIVA must be the most recognized internationally. Established in 1929 by the Drap family, the company has 14-year old Joseph Drap to thank for its success. Realising people needed a little luxury in the austere post-war years Joseph created the chocolate truffle. They were marketed under the name of Godiva and were an instant success. Belgium also boasts many smaller specialists producing their own excellent chocolates.

ABOVE: *A selection of Kim's Cachet chocolates, exported worldwide.*

CHARLEMAGNE produces superior quality thin squares of plain and white chocolate with exotic flavours such as spiced ginger,

cardamom and coffee, and spiced Earl Grey tea.

KIM'S, established in 1987 and manufacturer of the widely available luxury Cachet brand, specializes in handmade fillings. Kim's range includes white, milk and plain chocolate bars with luscious cream fillings such as hazelnut, coconut truffle, mocha and vanilla.

PIERRE COLAS specializes in unusual bars of plain and milk chocolate that are set in antique moulds and flavoured with esoteric combinations of cardamom, juniper, pink peppercorns and lavender. The company supplies specialist retailers in Belgium, Spain, France and the London chocolate shop Rococo.

WITTAMER probably ranks highest with connoisseurs. The range includes unusual seasonal specialities and Wittamer's famous Samba cake made with two contrasting chocolate mousses.

THE NETHERLANDS

The Netherlands is the birthplace of Coenraad Van Houten who revolutionized the chocolate industry with his cocoa press. With this background, it is not surprising that the Dutch chocolate industry today concentrates largely on cocoa rather than eating chocolate. The four biggest companies, VAN HOUTEN, BENSDORP, DE ZAAN and GERKENS, were all set up in the nineteenth century and continue to supply the world with fine-quality unsweetened cocoa powder. Van Houten is now based in Germany, having undergone several takeovers

and mergers, and trades in Europe, the United States, Hong Kong and Singapore.

The Netherlands do produce a certain amount of eating chocolate, however, and enthusiasts enjoy Dutch chocolate for its dark colour and distinctive flavour. DROSTE, of the distinctive "Droste man" logotype, makes delicious chocolate discs, or pastilles, from which the logotype is derived. Bensdorp and Van Houten also make quality chocolate.

LEFT: *Droste are famous for their chocolate pastilles.*

GERMANY

The Germans are one of the largest consumers of chocolate in Europe. Faced with this demanding clientele, German chocolate manufacturers pride themselves on producing fresh, quality chocolates made with the very best ingredients.

CONFISERIE HEINEMANN, based in München-Gladbach and run by master chocolatier Heinz Heinemann, makes over sixty varieties of freshly made chocolates every day, including exceptional champagne truffles. Heinemann also offers an interesting range of moulded chocolate-filled seasonal specialities.

DREIMEISTER is a long-established family enterprise set up by the father of Hans Wilhelm Schröder, the present owner, and originally known as Café Schröder. Although the company has a large turnover and supplies to hotels, restaurants and airlines, Dreimeister produces the freshest of chocolates and truffles, made only with top-quality ingredients.

FEODORA is probably Germany's best-known brand

BELOW: Feodora's elegant range produced for the international market.

RIGHT: Leysieffer's freshly made seasonal chocolate.

internationally. Their chocolate is wonderfully smooth due to lengthy conching. The elegantly packaged quality chocolates include champagne truffles, bitter milk chocolate wafers, espresso Brazil chocolates and luxury pralines.

HACHEZ, based in Bremen since 1890, makes chocolates exclusively with rare cacao beans from Venezuela and Ecuador. Loved by generations of chocolate connoisseurs, the range includes melt-in-the-mouth cat's tongues, gold-covered nut sticks, ginger sticks, chocolate leaves and fruit cream-filled chocolate pastilles.

LEYSIEFFER has produced handmade chocolates in its Osnabrück bakery since 1909. In order to guarantee absolute freshness, the company starts manufacture only on receipt of an order. Its products include good quality white and milk chocolate, flavoured with a tempting range of ingredients — cinnamon, ginger, orange, pistachio and a mouthwatering combination of mocca and Jamaica rum.

STOLLWERCK in Cologne began as a bakery in 1839 and is now an international group with impressive headquarters on the banks of the River Elbe. The Imhoff-Stollwerck Museum boasts a fascinating collection of chocolate-related exhibits, including a collection of vending machines resembling grandfather clocks, porcelain chocolate services and printed ephemera, as well as a tropical greenhouse planted with young cacao trees. The company produces a wide range of chocolates for all levels of the market.

AUSTRIA

Austria's chocolate delicacies include both pâtisserie and confectionery. World-famous pâtisserie establishments are the palatial HOTEL IMPERIAL, Vienna's grandest, and home of Imperial Torte, an unbelievably rich layered square chocolate cake; and the HOTEL SACHER, famous for its delectable Sachertorte, a moist apricot-glazed rich chocolate cake; and DEMEL, the celebrated Viennese pâtisserie, which produces a rival version of Sachertorte based on a recipe said to have been given to Anna Demel by Franz Sacher's son. Demel also

produces whole roasted cacao beans coated with fine chocolate.

ALTMANN & KÜHNE, established in Vienna for more than eighty years, produce exquisite hand-dipped miniature chocolates, appropriately called Liliputconfekte, in the most unusual shapes. The chocolates are beautifully packaged in miniature chests of drawers and treasure chests.

MIRABELL in Salzburg produces traditional Mozartkugeln, an Austrian speciality consisting of creamy marzipan and hazelnut-nougat balls with a delicate chocolate coating.

ITALY

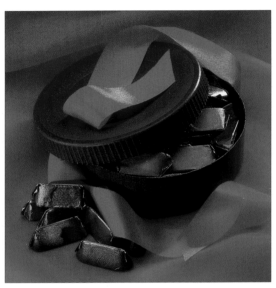

ABOVE: Gianduja are Italy's favorite chocolate.
RIGHT: Italians prefer chocolate in bite-size pieces.

An ancient culture of confectionery lives on in Italy's far south, and it was here in Salantino, in Italy's heel, that MAGLIO opened their factory in 1875. The business has passed from father to son and is now run by brothers Massimo and Maurizio. The Maglio range is based on plump, dark chocolates with inspirational fillings, including liqueur-infused dried kumquats, peaches, pears and oranges, marzipan-stuffed dates and prunes, and lemon-zest-coated figs stuffed with a whole almond.

Founded in 1796, MAJANI in Bologna is one of Italy's most creative chocolate makers. Their specialties are *scorze,* deliciously bittersweet chocolate sticks still made from the same ancient recipe, and *"Fiat" Cremino,* launched in 1911 as a publicity stunt to celebrate the Fiat Tipo 4 car. The car has since gone out of production but *"Fiat" Cremino* live on. These stunning miniature squares are made with four types of layered chocolate, something like a brown striped licorice allsort.

PERUGINA, based in the medieval city of Perugia, Umbria, was set up in 1907 by Francesco Buitoni, a descendant of the well known pasta-making family. From its humble beginnings making sugared almonds, Perugina is now one of Italy's largest chocolate manufacturers. The most popular brand in their extensive range is *Baci* (kisses), introduced in 1922 and still going strong. Lovers still like to discover the romantic messages hidden under the wrapper.

PEYRANO, an exclusive chocolatier in Turin, is almost unique in grinding their own cacao beans — very, very few chocolatiers do so. The chocolates are superb, especially their *gianduja.* Peyrano also sell *bicerin,* a very rare paste of bitter chocolate, cocoa, hazelnuts and honey used for sweetening coffee.

Hazelnuts, chestnuts, almonds and honey have always been an integral part of Italian cuisine. It comes as no surprise therefore, that Italians like their chocolate nutty and sweet. They also like their chocolate small, so bars are often sold in single serving sizes — handy for a quick fix, should the need arise. Neapolitans, which look exactly like miniature chocolate bars, complete with individual wrappers, are well known throughout Europe.

The Italians are creative chocolate makers, and they excel at presentation too; Italian packaging is stunning, whether the design is traditionally ornate or 1990s minimalist.

CAFFAREL in Turin is one of Italy's oldest chocolate makers. Established in 1826, the company purchased a chocolate-making machine designed by Bozelli, a Genoese engineer, and so became the pioneers in setting out on the route to industrialization. In 1865 Caffarel developed Italy's favorite confection, *gianduja,* a rectangle of luscious chocolate and hazelnut paste, instantly recognizable by its triangular profile and rounded ends. Nowadays most Italian chocolate makers produce their own special version of *gianduja* using jealously guarded recipes. There is a glorious giant-sized version, *grangianduja,* as well as miniature *gianduiotti.*

BELOW: Romantically packaged Baci conceal a lover's message.

SWITZERLAND

ABOVE: The Confiserie Sprüngli in Zurich, around 1895.

Three key developments undoubtedly contribute to Switzerland's national preference for its very delicate, melt-in-the-mouth milk chocolate. Switzerland is the birthplace of Rodolphe Lindt, inventor of the conching machine which transforms chocolate from a rough gritty paste to a state of silky-smooth perfection. Lindt also created soft, creamy fondant chocolate by adding cacao butter to the paste before conching. We have the Swiss to thank, too, for the invention of milk chocolate.

SPRÜNGLI in Zurich is one of the most famous chocolate establishments in the world. The shop in Bahnhofstrasse is renowned for its freshest of fresh *Truffes du Jour*, a heart-stopping mixture of finest chocolate, cream and butter, made to the highest possible standards. The company operates a worldwide delivery service which guarantees that the longed-for parcel will arrive within 24 hours of despatch.

Set up by master confectioner Rudolf Sprüngli in 1845, the company has been handed down through six generations of Sprünglis. When Rudolf retired, he divided his empire between his two sons. The younger, David, received the confectionery shops. The elder brother, Johann, became the owner of the

ABOVE: A 1935 street poster.

chocolate factory. In the same year he retired, Rudolf Sprüngli also decided to purchase Rodolphe Lindt's chocolate factory in Berne. Overnight, the company acquired all Lindt's manufacturing secrets, and it was this transaction that was the foundation for the success of the now world-famous Lindt & Sprüngli company.

LINDT & SPRÜNGLI operates entirely independently from Sprüngli. The company produces an enormous range of excellent quality chocolates sold in supermarkets and specialist shops world-wide. One of their best products is the tastefully thin Excellence bar, a sublime blend of finest cacao beans with a hint of pure

vanilla, and a cacao solid content of 70 per cent. This is closely followed in quality by Excellence Milk, possibly one of the best milk chocolate bars available. Another Lindt bar, called Swiss Bittersweet Chocolate, which is easily recognized by its traditional wrapper design, is also good.

ABOVE: Bars of superior chocolate.

SUCHARD in Berne is another long-established and respected company, now owned by the American multinational Philip Morris. Suchard was a gold medallist several times over at the 1855 Exposition Universelle in Paris, and their milk chocolate bar, Milka, produced in 1901, is well-known all over Europe. Since 1970, Suchard have been the manufacturer of the famous Toblerone bars, although these were originally produced by their inventor Jean Tobler. The bars were designed with a triangular profile representing the Swiss Alps. The name is derived from merging that of the inventor, Tobler, together with the word *torrone*, the Italian word for nougat. Toblerone is made with a blend of chocolate, nougat, almonds and egg white, and the bar is one of Switzerland's most popular products – outside the country at least. Enthusiasts can enjoy giant bars weighing more than 4kg/8.8lb, miniature bars and a whole range in between.

ABOVE: Lindt's mini chocolate bars.

ABOVE: The famous Toblerone bars.

FRANCE

ABOVE: Early poster for the French Chocolate and Tea Company.

A large part of the French chocolate industry is made up of small, independent firms making ever more innovative *grand cru* chocolates to jealously guarded recipes. The French, who prefer dark, intensely flavoured chocolate, have a wide choice at their disposal.

BERNACHON, a greatly respected family of artisan chocolatiers, set up in 1955 in Lyon. Sharing the caring attitude of the Quakers, the company provides daily lunch for the workers and, until recently, housed them in dormitories above the workshop. The Bernachons travel the world in search of the rarest cacao beans and the best nuts and fruit. Their chocolates are the very best. The range includes unusually flavoured chocolate bars, truffles, pralines, *giandujas* and marzipans.

BONNAT in Voiron near Grenoble is one of the few companies that roasts its own beans. A purist at heart, master chocolatier Raymond Bonnat uses a single *grand cru* bean, rather than a blend, for each of the chocolates in his range. Bonnat's choice of seven *crus,* which consist of Côte d'Ivoire, Madagascar, Ceylon, Trinité, Chuao, Maragnan and Puerto Cabellois, is selected from the world's finest cacao plantations. Bonnat chocolates are available from specialist outlets in France, and from Mortimer and Bennett's shop in London, which is the sole British importer.

RIGHT: The ultimate dark chocolate.

CLUIZEL, in Paris, is a family-run business set up in 1947, producing excellent chocolate with rare South American and African beans ground and roasted on the premises. It is perhaps best known for a small and rather sinister chocolate bar containing 99 per cent cacao solids. Cluizel's chocolates are available throughout Europe.

ABOVE: Chocolate almonds.

CHRISTIAN CONSTANT, set up in 1970 in Paris, produces matchless ganache-filled chocolates. The flavourings read like an exotic travel brochure: Malabar cardamom, Yemeni jasmine, Chinese ginger and Tahitian vanilla.

The famous FAUCHON shop in Paris was established in 1925 by August Fauchon, whose passion was for collecting unusual merchandise. The company was taken over after his death by Joseph Pilosoff, whose granddaughter runs the business today. Fauchon specialities are the very best quality chocolate *marrons glacés,* truffles, pralines and ganaches, all exquisitely packaged.

LA MAISON DU CHOCOLAT in Paris was opened in 1977 by Robert Linxe, master chocolate-maker *extraordinaire.* Linxe's rigorous training and deep understanding of chocolate's complexities have played a major part in furthering the reputation

ABOVE: One of Bonnat's superb grand cru *bars.*

of France's chocolate-makers. It was Linxe's collaboration with Valrhona which set the quality of their *grand cru* couvertures, which they in turn supply to smaller chocolate-makers. Linxe's specialities are exquisitely shaped squares, pyramids and lozenges of the very best plain and milk chocolate, filled with praline, buttery caramel or the lightest and creamiest ganache. The chocolates are sold in Paris and by leading specialist outlets in New York, Houston and Dallas.

LE ROUX, founded in 1977 in Quiberon, Brittany, is renowned for *Caramel au Beurre Salé* (salted butter caramel), and for rare chocolate truffles containing fragments of Périgord truffle.

MICHEL CHAUDUN set up shop in Paris in 1986. His award-winning work includes not only the highest quality chocolates but ambitious chocolate sculptures. Only the rarest cacao beans are used together with top quality fruit and nuts. His chocolates are available in Paris and Tokyo.

RICHART DESIGN ET CHOCOLAT started life in 1925 in the laboratory of Lyon-based master chocolatier Joseph Richart. Using

BELOW: A Chocolat Carpentier poster from 1895.

ABOVE: Elegant chocolates and packaging from Richart Design et Chocolat.

only the finest cacao beans, Richart produces exquisite, smoother than smooth, miniature chocolate squares silk-screened with designs in cacao butter. Fillings and flavourings are equally inspired. The choice includes pure malt Scotch, green tea, blackcurrants, pineapple, clementines, the very best Andalucian almonds, chestnuts from the Ardèche, and pralines and ganaches flavoured with thyme, curry, bergamot, anise or nutmeg. Beautifully packaged in slim trays, Richart's chocolates are sold in boutiques in Paris, Lyon and New York.

VALRHONA, set up in 1922 and based in the Rhône valley, is the leading supplier of couverture chocolate for smaller chocolate-makers. The beans are all of superior quality and include guanaja, pur caraibe, manjari and jivara. Each shipment is tested by a panel of experts. Its products include *Carré*, small chocolate squares made from individual bean varieties, packed in beautiful tins; *BonBons de Chocolat,* individual chocolates packed in gift boxes with a guide recommending the order in which they should be eaten; and the well-known Valrhona bars in their distinctive black wrappers. The cacao content of the bars ranges from 71 per cent for *Noir Amer* (bitter) to a relatively high 40 per cent for *Le Lacté* (milk).

RIGHT: Valrhona Lacté has a high cacao content.

SPAIN

As recently as 1920, chocolate-makers in Spain were still using the curved granite metate for grinding cacao beans. The *chocolateros* would travel around with the *metate* strapped to their backs and bags of cacao beans under their arms. They would kneel on a little cushion in front of the stone and grind the beans in full public view so that the buyer could be sure he was getting unadulterated stone-ground chocolate. Nowadays chocolate-making in Spain is a fully industrialized process, but, even so, the tradition of quality craftsmanship is very much alive and well.

In some ways Spanish chocolate is indistinguishable from quality chocolate made in the rest of Europe. What sets it apart is the creativity and imagination of the chocolate-makers, and their use of the very best quality Mediterranean fruits and nuts. Spain grows some of the best nuts in the world, so there is no shortage of supply. Plump almonds, hazelnuts, pine kernels and mouth-puckeringly bitter Seville oranges are all used by the chocolate-makers with excellent results.

BLANXART, set up in 1954 in Barcelona, is one of Spain's smaller specialist firms, producing handmade high-quality chocolates from the very best cacao beans. The company prides itself on roasting and grinding the beans itself to achieve the desired perfection of flavour and aroma. The mouthwatering range includes a delicate curl of candied Seville orange dipped in bitter chocolate, clusters of chocolate-covered pine nuts, as well as liqueur-filled chocolates and several types of praline.

LUDOMAR, in Barcelona, specializes in superior, made-to-order chocolates, which they sell to pâtisserie shops in Spain, France, Germany and Britain. Specialities are plump, chocolate-smothered cherries; *postre de músico*, a chocolate-covered cluster of fresh almonds, hazelnuts and raisins; and *grageas*, almonds or hazelnuts drenched in dark chocolate, white chocolate or toffee.

RAMÓN ROCA is a large company set up in Gerona in 1928 by the Roca family. Roca chocolates are said to be a favourite of former US Secretary of State Henry Kissinger, and they certainly grace the tables of Spain's society élite, as well as finding their way on to first class intercontinental flights and the pillows of Spain's grandest hotels. Roca has always been imaginative in a showy type of way, producing masterpieces such as a 500g/1¼lb chocolate sculpture of the Statue of Liberty, and a hand-painted chocolate reproduction of the twelfth-century tapestry that hangs in Gerona cathedral. The company also

ABOVE: The Spanish love chocolate "a la taza" (in the cup).

produces a unique range of edible board games, particularly popular with the Japanese, which includes a draughts set in luxury dark and white chocolate. Their Victoria Bonbons (named after Ramón Roca's mother) – an elegant wafer of dark chocolate decorated with a perfectly positioned almond, a hazelnut, a walnut and four raisins – won first prize at the 1988 Chicago Fancy Food Fair.

RIGHT: The Valor range of chocolates.
LEFT: Chocolate croquettes from Roca.

VALOR in Villajoyosa, Alicante, was founded in 1881 by López Lloret, one of Spain's itinerant *chocolateros*. The fledgling enterprise has been handed down through three generations and is now one of Spain's largest and most technologically advanced chocolate companies with a gleaming stainless-steel fully computerized factory. Even though Valor has an enormous turnover and a vast range of products, the company prides itself on maintaining traditional quality, creativity and attention to detail.

Drinking chocolate is still widely enjoyed

RIGHT: Chunks of chocolate in tablet form, used in Spain for making thick, dark drinking chocolate.

in Spain, and Valor is the country's leading producer. It is sold both in powdered form and, more commonly, as a solid bar to be broken off as required and dissolved in foaming hot milk.

On the confectionery side, Valor's specialities are Chocolate Pearls – chocolate-covered almonds gathered from local almond groves; *doblones* – individually wrapped chocolate wafers; foil-wrapped hazelnut pralines; exquisite miniature four-piece gift boxes of chocolates; and luxury chocolate bars filled with toffee, cream caramel or *tiramisu*. Eye-catching and attractive packaging is a crucial part of the presentation, particularly as Valor's luxury chocolates are exported to speciality shops all over the world.

MEXICO

Chocolate as confectionery never really caught on in Mexico. The most important use of chocolate is still as a beverage, and as a flavouring in some of the special *moles* – rich, savoury sauces thickened with ground nuts and seeds. Chocolate is sold in rough, grainy tablets made with cacao, sugar, ground almonds and cinnamon – not so very different from the tablets made by the Spanish in the days of the conquistadors.

The most widely available brand outside Mexico is Ibarra, manufactured by CHOCOLATERA DE JALISCO in Guadalajara, and packaged in a striking red and yellow striped hexagonal box. The individually wrapped tablets are delicious whipped to a froth in hot milk and served with freshly baked *churros* (fried pastries).

RIGHT: Coarse, grainy tablets of Ibarra chocolate in traditional wrappers.
BELOW: The melted tablets make a delicious sauce for vanilla ice-cream.

They can be used in baking to give a unique spicy flavour to chocolate cake. The tablets can also be melted to make a wonderfully fudgey chocolate sauce that goes particularly well with good quality vanilla ice-cream.

GREAT BRITAIN

ABOVE: Ackermans chocolates, a favourite of the Royal family.

During the last few years British taste in chocolate has been undergoing a quiet revolution. Following the establishment of The Chocolate Society, a sort of sub-culture of chocolytes has emerged. Perhaps as a result of this new-found fervour, superior varieties of chocolate are increasingly finding their way into supermarkets, where they provide much-needed competition for the old-style sweet British milk chocolate.

ACKERMANS, a small family firm founded fifty years ago by German-born Werner Ackerman and his wife, is one of the major producers of handmade chocolates in Britain. Ackermans has a shop in north London, and also supplies leading supermarkets and specialist outlets in Britain, mainland Europe and the United States. Its chocolates are a favourite with Queen Elizabeth The Queen Mother, who awarded the firm her Royal Warrant in 1969. Ackermans offers a range of fresh cream truffles, chocolate-coated whole nuts, ginger wafers, hand-dipped crystallized fruits, and rose and violet fondant creams. It also produces a wonderful chocolate menagerie of hollow moulded hippos, crocodiles, bears and bunnies.

BENDICKS OF MAYFAIR, founded in the late 1920s by Colonel Benson and Mr Dickson, was granted a Royal Warrant by Elizabeth II in 1962. Bendicks are famous for their excellent peppermint chocolates – an essentially British taste not shared by other European countries. Best-loved by connoisseurs are Bendicks Bittermints, a powerful mint fondant disc drenched with smooth, dark unsweetened chocolate – a devastating combination. As well as the mint collection, Bendicks produces delicious truffles, chocolate-coated stem ginger, and the delightfully named Sporting & Military Chocolate.

CHARBONNEL ET WALKER, founded in 1825, is one of Britain's earliest producers of chocolates. With the encouragement of

BELOW: Bendicks are the premier supplier of superior mint chocolates.

BELOW: Exquisite chocolates from the Charbonnel et Walker range.

LEFT: *Organic chocolate made with Maya beans.*

Edward VII, the company began life as a partnership between Mrs Walker and Madame Charbonnel from the Maison Boissier chocolate house in Paris. Tempting items from the magnificent range include truffles flavoured with chartreuse, muscat or port and cranberry; chocolate-covered espresso beans; and cointreau-flavoured marzipan. The packaging is superb and caters for styles ranging from elegant navy-trimmed white boxes, nostalgic boxes with a faded pink floral pattern, and outrageously lavish, ruched red satin boxes.

GERARD RONAY is one of Britain's most highly respected private chocolatiers. A former psychiatric nurse, Ronay set up in 1989 having trained with the very best teachers – Linxe, Constant and Bernachon in France, Wittamer in Belgium and Charbonnel et Walker in Britain. His highly secretive recipes include geranium chocolate and superb hand-painted eggs.

GREEN AND BLACK'S, set up in the 1980s by Josephine Fairly, sells organic chocolate endorsed by The Soil Association. The company launched with its Organic Dark Chocolate, soon followed by its latest brain child, the "ethically correct" Maya Gold Organic Dark Chocolate, made with beans grown by the Kechi Maya in Belize. This product was the first in Britain to be awarded the Fairtrade mark which guarantees that small farmers are not exploited. Maya Gold contains 70 per cent cacao solids, but no cacao butter, and is described on the wrapper as having "the authentic Maya taste of rain forest spices and

ABOVE: A tempting and imaginative range from The Chocolate Society.

orange". Even though oranges were unknown to the Maya in pre-Conquest days, the chocolate still tastes pretty good.

ROCOCO, in London's King's Road, is an Aladdin's cave of a shop founded in 1983 by chocolate enthusiast Chantal Coady. Using cacao from the world's finest plantations, Rococo specialize in *grand cru* single bean bars; artisan bars with exotic flavourings such as pink pepper and juniper, lavender, petitgrain and cardamom; stunning chocolate dragées – try the dark green *Olives de Nyons;* and handmade boxed chocolates moulded into the most beautiful shapes.

SARA JAYNE, a London-based private chocolate-maker, is also public relations manager of the Académie Culinaire de France. She learnt her chocolate-making skills first hand from leading experts, including the Roux brothers. Blackberry and calvados, ginger and spice, and champagne are among the tempting flavourings used in her celebrated handmade truffles.

TERRYS OF YORK, founded in 1797, is perhaps alone among the mass-producers in manufacturing plain chocolate with a reasonable flavour. Their famous chocolate orange has been tucked in the toe of British children's Christmas stockings for generations, while their individually wrapped miniature Neapolitans have always been a welcome gift.

THE CHOCOLATE SOCIETY was formed in 1990 to promote the consumption of the finest chocolate. The society manufactures a range of products under its own label, as well as selling quality brands made by other companies. Its own range includes the most delicious chocolate-dipped candied citrus fruits; imaginative moulded items such as pigs, egg-filled nests, fish, hens and hearts; fresh handmade truffles with luscious flavourings such as raspberry, whisky or champagne; and elegant tins of drinking-chocolate flakes, cocoa powder and cooking chocolate.

BELOW: Rococo's grand cru *single bean bars with distinctive wrappers.*

THE UNITED STATES OF AMERICA

Chocolate consumers in the United States share the British liking for sweet milk chocolate, and the American chocolate industry is therefore dominated by a small number of very large mass-producers who satisfy this national need. However, in the same way that British consumers have become aware of and learned to appreciate quality handmade plain chocolate, American taste has been changing too. A number of small but sophisticated chocolate-makers have appeared on the scene and are taking advantage of the increasing popularity of European-style chocolate.

Above and right: Ghirardelli, new and old.

Above: Glossy sugar-coated dragées from Dilettante.

DILETTANTE, in Seattle, was established in 1976 by Dana Davenport, a third-generation chocolatier and descendant of Hungarian master chocolatier Julius Franzen. Franzen emigrated to the USA in 1910, after studying in Paris, and won prestigious appointments in Vienna as Master Pâtissier to Emperor Franz Joseph, and later in St Petersburg as Master Chocolatier to Czar Nicholas II. Franzen passed on his skills to his brother-in-law Earl Remington Davenport, whose grandson Dana carries on the business today. Dilettante's signature product is its Aristocrat range of chocolate truffles, flavoured with ginger, raspberries, hazelnuts, pecans or coffee. Dilettante also makes intensely rich buttercream fondant, beautiful chocolate dragées with various coatings, and slim bars of good quality milk or dark chocolate.

FRAN'S, set up in Seattle by ex-accountant Fran Bigelow, is at the forefront of America's new generation of chocolatiers. She trained in cookery under

Josephine Araldo, a 1921 graduate of the Cordon Bleu school in Paris, and later enrolled at the California Culinary Academy, where desserts became her passion. Bigelow opened a tiny dessert shop in 1982, supplying local restaurants with speciality cakes. Her reputation went from strength to strength, and, soon after, she started making the European-style chocolates on which her business is now founded. An award-winning speciality are Fran's baton-shaped Fixations – individual sticks of Belgian chocolate with soft, creamy centres, flavoured with espresso, peanut butter, orange or mint. Her range also includes rich dark truffles, hand-dipped fruit and nuts covered in smooth dark Belgian chocolate, GoldBars studded with macadamia nuts, and the smaller GoldBites with almonds, as well as chocolate and caramel sauces, and various seasonal items.

GHIRARDELLI, founded in 1856 in San Francisco and one of

Above: Irresistible luxury from Fran's.

RIGHT: Joseph Schmidt's stunning truffles.

America's pioneering chocolate-makers, produces quality eating chocolate, chocolate products for use in baking, and powdered drinking chocolate. Ghirardelli's Sweet Ground Chocolate with Cocoa has been a signature product for over a century. Although a mass producer, Ghirardelli uses methods based on European traditions, producing bittersweet eating chocolate as well as the popular sweet milk varieties. Ghirardelli still grinds and roasts its own cacao beans shipped from quality plantations in Central and South America, and West Africa. Its range includes milk, white and plain chocolate squares and attractively wrapped bars with tempting flavours such as raspberry, white mocha and biscotti, and double chocolate mocha.

JOSEPH SCHMIDT CONFECTIONS was opened in San Francisco in 1983 by master chocolatier Joseph Schmidt and partner Audrey Ryan. Born in 1939 and raised in what was formerly known as Palestine, Schmidt looks to his Austrian roots for his skills. He was trained as a baker, but his supremely imaginative and sometimes outrageous creations show no evidence of this conventional background. Unusual in the chocolate world for his bold use of colour, and the large size of the individual chocolates, Schmidt's truffles gleam with perfect hand-painted spots of bright red or green, and his Slicks, thin chocolate discs, are beautifully painted in various colours. Special commissions include amazingly opulent sculpted creations for visiting dignitaries from abroad – including a giant panda for Prince Philip and a white dove for Nelson Mandela. Schmidt's chocolates are available from department stores in the United States and Harrods in London.

RICHARD DONNELLY, in Santa Cruz, California, is another of America's new breed of young, inspired artisan chocolate-makers.

Donnelly trained with several renowned chocolatiers both in Europe and the United States before setting up on his own in 1988. Donnelly uses French couverture chocolate to which he adds flavourings and fillings geared to the American market – coffee buttercream, and roasted salted macadamia nuts, for instance. His speciality is very slim, smooth chocolate bars which, in terms of quality, are among the very best chocolate in the world. The bars are beautifully wrapped in handmade Japanese papers.

MOONSTRUCK CHOCOLATIER in Portland, Oregon, is a young company set up by an impressive consortium of live-wire marketing experts. With more then a hundred outlets in the United States and a thriving mail order business they look set to make their name in the world of chocolate.

Moonstruck's chocolates are inspired creations from master chocolatier Robert Hammond, who served his apprenticeship in America and France, and who is now thought to be one of the leading experts in modern chocolate-making. Moonstruck's signature product is a moon-shaped, metallic blue box containing a stunning selection of beautifully designed chocolates. Flavourings include wine, brandy, coffee, *sake* and various fruits, often using award-winning local products. Favourites are wild huckleberry truffles made with white chocolate ganache and Clear Creek apple brandy truffles. There is also an impressive *gianduja* almond praline tower of crisp buttery toffee and toasted almonds.

RIGHT: Elegance from Richard Donnelly.

PHYSIOLOGY AND PSYCHOLOGY

CHOCOLATE'S THERAPEUTIC POWERS

The therapeutic properties of chocolate were much written about in the seventeenth and eighteenth centuries. The Aztec beliefs in the power of chocolate travelled with it, and great claims were made by manufacturers and converts alike for its powers as an antidote to exhaustion and weakness. Soldiers, scholars and clerics used it to keep them going during prolonged periods of physical, intellectual or spiritual endurance.

We now know that it is the fat and carbohydrate in chocolate which provide fuel for the body, and the fat content means that chocolate is digested slowly, thus maintaining a feeling of fullness and satiety. Even the iron content, which helps transport oxygen to the brain, may result in greater mental alertness, although this has yet to be proven.

(PER 100G)	PLAIN CHOCOLATE	MILK CHOCOLATE	WHITE CHOCOLATE
Protein (g)	4.7	8.4	8.0
Fat (g)	29.2	30.3	30.9
Calories	525	529	529
Carbohydrate (g)	64.8	59.4	58.3
Calcium (mg)	38	220	270
Magnesium (mg)	100	55	26
Iron (mg)	2.4	1.6	0.2
Zinc (mg)	0.2	0.2	0.9
Carotene (vitamin A) (mcg)	40	40	75
Vitamin E (mg)	0.85	0.74	1.14
Thiamin (vitamin B1) (mg)	0.07	0.10	0.08
Riboflavin (vitamin B2) (mg)	0.08	0.23	0.49
Niacin (vitamin B3) (mg)	0.4	0.2	0.2
Vitamin B6 (mg)	0.07	0.07	0.07
Vitamin B12 (mcg)	—	trace	trace
Folate (mcg)	10	10	10
Vitamin C	0	0	0

Source: McCance and Widdowson's The Composition of Foods, fifth edition.

NUTRITIONAL ANALYSIS

Although the relevance of nutritional analysis is questionable if the level of cacao solids or brand of chocolate used is not known, we can see from the comparative table above that plain chocolate, considered by the chocolate fraternity as infinitely superior, does not fare as well as might be expected.

Containing no milk, plain chocolate provides roughly half the protein of white and milk chocolate, and much less calcium. Protein is vital for the growth, repair and maintenance of the body; calcium is essential for muscle contraction, including the muscles which make the heart beat, and for healthy nerve function, enzyme activity and clotting of blood.

LEFT: Early publicity material depicted cocoa as wholesome.
RIGHT: Chocolate fortified the army in the First World War.

ABOVE: Carbohydrate in chocolate provides fuel for vigorous activity.

Plain chocolate contains slightly less fat, something we are advised to cut down on, and comes out on top in terms of carbohydrate, magnesium (an essential constituent of our body cells and involved with releasing energy from the food we eat), iron (essential for the production of red blood cells, and for transporting oxygen around the body) and niacin (also involved in energy release from food). Plain chocolate also contains slightly fewer calories. White chocolate, sometimes dismissed by chocolate experts, contains more calcium, zinc, carotene and riboflavin (vitamin B2) than plain chocolate.

A NATURAL STIMULANT

As well as the more well-known nutrients, chocolate contains certain alkaloids – organic substances found in plants – which have a potent effect on the body. The most important is theobromine, which stimulates the kidneys as a mild diuretic. Chocolate is also a stimulant of the central nervous system, with an effect similar to caffeine, which is also present in chocolate. Theobromine makes up about 2 per cent of the cacao bean and about 200 mg finds its way into an average-sized bar. The caffeine content is much smaller – about 25 mg per bar, roughly one quarter the amount found in a fresh cup of coffee.

BELOW RIGHT: Many manufacturers depicted chocolate as providing growing children with plenty of energy for healthy activity.

— HOMEOPATHIC "PROVING" OF CHOCOLATE —

Experimental "provings" of chocolate by homeopaths clearly indicate its stimulating effect. One experiment conducted with a decoction of roasted ground cacao beans in boiling water produced "an excitement of the nervous system similar to that caused by a strong infusion of black coffee" and "an excited state of the circulation, shown by an accelerated pulse". Interestingly, when the same decoction was made with unroasted beans neither effect was noticeable, leading the provers to conclude that the physiological changes were caused by aromatic substances released during roasting.

— MYTHS AND PREJUDICES —

Claims that chocolate is bad for you are almost certainly based on the excess sugar and added vegetable fat in poor grade, mass-produced chocolate. Quality chocolate contains pure cacao butter with no added fat, as well as a high percentage of cacao solids and correspondingly less sugar – in some cases hardly any. Specific claims that chocolate causes migraine, obesity, acne, tooth decay and allergies have also been refuted by several medical experts:

MIGRAINE Cheese and chocolate have been cited as the cause of migraine, which can be set off by large doses of tyramine. Chocolate, however, contains only a very small quantity of tyramine, far less than cheese.

OBESITY Good quality plain chocolate is unlikely to be the cause of obesity because it contains far less sugar than junk chocolate and, because it is more expensive, is less likely to be eaten to excess.

ACNE American surveys show no correlation between chocolate consumption and acne in teenagers. Likely culprits are hormonal imbalances and a lack of fresh fruit and vegetables in the diet.

TOOTH DECAY Chocolate melts in the mouth and is therefore in contact with the teeth for a relatively short time. While the sugar content will contribute to tooth decay, the risk is far less than that associated with sticky sweets or toffee, which remain in the mouth for longer.

ALLERGY Less than 2 per cent of the population have a genuine food allergy, and an allergy to chocolate is extremely rare. It is more likely to be the nuts and milk in chocolate that are the cause, so check the ingredients.

CHOCOLATE AND THE MIND

The question of whether or not chocolate is an addictive substance always raises spirited discussion. Some social historians have even reported tales of chocolate addiction and associated crimes committed in order to satisfy an ever-increasing need. And as recently as 1991, the French dietary expert Michel Montignac advised in his book *Dine Out and Lose Weight*: "Be sure to limit yourself, since chocolate is of an addictive nature. To control your 'chocoholism', drink a tall glass of water."

LEFT: A deeply indulgent chocolate experience.

Linda Henly, a contemporary American writer, positively recommends that addictive personalities should use chocolate to satisfy their needs, stating that its advantages vastly outweigh those of other substances: "Chocolate doesn't make you stupid and clumsy. It doesn't render you incapable of operating heavy machinery… You don't have to smuggle chocolate across the border…Possession, even possession with intent to sell, is perfectly legal."

Some medical experts believe that the theobromine and caffeine in chocolate are the cause of its so-called addictive properties, but it may well be the presence of another substance called phenylethylamine. This is one of a group of chemicals known as endorphins, which have an effect similar to amphetamine, to which phenylethylamine is related. When released into the bloodstream, endorphins lift the mood, creating positive energy and feelings ranging from happiness to euphoria, as experienced in the runner's "high" or the aerobic exerciser's "burn". Phenylethylamine is also naturally present in the human body. Levels in the brain have even been found to increase when we experience the state we refer to as "falling in love", which is no doubt why we experience that heady feeling when we eat good chocolate.

CRAVING AND ADDICTION

Chocolate lovers would do well to be aware of the wealth of difference there is between craving and addiction. Craving is an unmet desire for a pleasurable substance, whether it be chocolate, hot buttered toast, or a cup of coffee. The craving is usually brought on by stress, and the desired substance usually diffuses the stress more effectively than any other means, and may actually, as a result, enhance a person's performance by increasing concentration and reducing fatigue.

Addiction, on the other hand, is defined as the habitual use of a substance, such as alcohol or drugs, which becomes less and less effective at satisfying the need and results in unpleasant withdrawal symptoms should any attempt be made to give up the substance in question.

Chocolate hardly comes into the addictive category, although it has been said that the glucose in chocolate triggers a release in the production of endorphins – the body's natural opiates – which in turn can lead to a cycle of craving.

LEFT: A silver platter of gorgeous, high quality, hand-made chocolates is every chocolate lover's fantasy.

BELOW: An advertisement showing two French ladies sharing a bottle of chocolate as if it were wine. The initial effect can be very similar.

RIGHT: Dark, rich and irresistible, a slice of moist chocolate cake is both pleasure and temptation.

BELOW: French courtesan and famous chocolyte, Madame Du Barry, was well aware of the stimulating effect chocolate had on her lovers.

WOMEN'S CRAVING AND CHOCOLATE

Women are the greatest consumers of chocolate, and several studies have sought to explain why. Although some women may enjoy chocolate as a guilt-free treat or as an energy-boost, others seem almost obsessed by it. While researching her 1995 book *Why Women Need Chocolate*, Debra Waterhouse conducted a survey which revealed that of the women surveyed:

- 97 per cent reported cravings, 68 per cent of which are for chocolate
- 50 per cent would choose chocolate in preference to sex
- 22 per cent were more likely than men to choose chocolate as a mood elevator

Psychiatrists have suggested that the mechanism that regulates body levels of phenylethylamine may be faulty in some women. This may explain a tendency to binge on chocolate after an emotional upset – it is an instinctive form of self-medication to treat the imbalance of mood-controlling chemicals.

Waterhouse states that the foods we crave are defined by a multitude of factors that may include cultural influences, emotional attachments, taste and habit as well as biological, chemical and physiological factors. In the case of chocolate, the "prozac of plants", Waterhouse adds to its mood-changing components a substance called seratonin, known for its calming properties.

It must be said, however, that although statistically it may be the case that more women buy chocolate than men, it is also true that for both sexes, and for people of all ages, chocolate can be many things. There are probably many women who could instantly name a man whose chocolate consumption is more regular and compulsive than hers, and it is perhaps one of the many cultural myths that women are more addicted to it than men. What we can say is that the seduction of chocolate, and its comforting allure, is as strong in the present as it was for the Maya warrior princes and princesses of the fourth century.

CHOCOLATE AND LOVE

Chocolate has long been associated with passion and its reputation as an aphrodisiac can be traced back to the days of the Aztecs and the Spanish conquistadors. Conclusions were obviously drawn from the Emperor Montezuma's liking for copious flagons of chocolate before retiring to his harem. However, as observer Bernal Díaz del Castillo was careful to point out in his memoirs: "It [chocolate] was said to have aphrodisiac properties, but we did not pay any attention to this detail."

In *The True History of Chocolate* authors Sophie and Michael Coe state that the idea that Montezuma needed sexual stimulants was a Spanish obsession for which there was no factual basis. The conquistadors apparently suffered from constipation and "searched for native Mexican laxatives as avidly as they did for aphrodisiacs". However, once the rumour that chocolate was an aphrodisiac had taken root, there was no stopping it. When chocolate eventually appeared in Europe, eighteenth-century society took to it with suspicious enthusiasm.

Historical sources abound with tales of chocolate being used as an aphrodisiac. Casanova thought that hot chocolate was "the elixir of love", and drank it instead of champagne! It may well be that the unshakeable belief of the Spanish had something to do with chocolate being an ingredient in that notorious aphrodisiac "Spanish Fly". In the following tale, the Marquis de Sade uses both chocolate and Spanish fly to amuse his guests at a ball: "Into the dessert he slipped chocolate pastilles so good that a number of people devoured them ... but he had mixed in some Spanish fly ... those who ate the pastilles began to burn with unchaste ardor ... Even the most respectable of women were unable to resist the uterine rage that stirred within them. And so it was that M. de Sade enjoyed the favors of his sister-in-law."

RIGHT: An early Cadbury chocolate tin uses sensual imagery.

THE GREAT INFLAMER

Brandon Head, in *The Food of the Gods,* reported that even after chocolate had become widely accepted as a nourishing beverage, it was still regarded by some "as a violent inflamer of passions, which should be prohibited to the monks". In 1905 a journalist writing in the British Spectator magazine issued dire warnings: 'I shall also advise my fair readers to be in a particular manner careful how they meddle with romances, chocolates, novels, and the like inflamers, which I look upon as very dangerous to be made use of...'

SENSUAL ASSOCIATIONS

Although contemporary scientific research suggests that chocolate does not contain substances of a directly aphrodisiac nature, modern advertising clearly links chocolate with sensuality and sexuality. With the exception of chunky "macho" chocolate products, or situations in which the product is being used as a healthy, energy-boosting snack, chocolate is invariably depicted as a "naughty" indulgence, appearing in scenes heavy with sexual innuendo.

Advertising also demonstrates a definite gender bias by specifically targeting women as the primary users. Most advertisements show chocolate being enjoyed by beautiful

LEFT AND RIGHT: The images may not be as explicit as today, but advertising has always used chocolate's link with sensuality to sell its products.

ABOVE: A poster illustrating the link between lovers and chocolate.

advertising made much of the wholesomeness of chocolate with posters of healthy, lively children enjoying cups of chocolate in the fresh air. The first chocolate boxes showed sentimental images of pretty young girls, flowers and kittens. Chocolate plays a large part in childhood the world over. Christmas treats, Easter eggs, birthday presents, party gifts, rewards or bribes from parents coaxing their offspring to behave well. Encouraged as most of us are to be passionate about chocolate from an early age, it is no wonder we carry that ardour with us through childhood and beyond.

RIGHT: The famous Rowntree advertisement.

BELOW: A loving mother offers chocolate to her daughter.

women, or gifts of chocolate being offered to them by a man.

The association between women, sensuality and chocolate was reinforced by the cinema, too. A common image in the 1930s was the glamorous *femme fatale*, usually blonde and usually draped on satin sheets, languorously working her way through a lavish box of chocolates.

This association between chocolate and women perpetuated the association between chocolate and romantic love, as shown on Perugina's classic Baci box. *Baci* means "kisses" in Italian, and since the chocolates first appeared in 1922 they have been exchanged as gifts between lovers who look for the romantic message hidden beneath the foil wrapper of each chocolate.

CHOCOLATE AND CHILDHOOD

This association with love and nurture, but not necessarily passion, was also exploited by manufacturers. Chocolate cake mix packets carry homely scenes of mother in the kitchen; the earliest cocoa tins portrayed nursemaids or even parents serving nourishing mugs of chocolate to young children, and

THE PLEASURE OF CHOCOLATE

Research carried out by ARISE (Associates for Research Into the Science of Enjoyment) suggests that pleasure, far from being an emotion of indeterminate nature, is a distinct neuro-chemical process with its own pathway through the nervous system. Laboratory tests have shown that when we are experiencing pleasure, the body's defence system is more effective; and when we are unhappy, depressed or stressed, the system becomes less efficient, leaving us less resistant to infection.

So it seems that pleasure is good for us even if it means we indulge in "forbidden fruits" such as chocolate. The secret, it would seem, is to indulge in our "naughty" craving without feeling guilty or anxious. That said, ARISE make it clear that they are not advocating orgies of over-indulgence; the secret is to eat better chocolate, not more chocolate.

SENSORY PLEASURE

One of the reasons we love chocolate so much is the pure unmatched physical pleasure we get not just from eating it, but also from unwrapping it, smelling it, looking at it and feeling it. When we slip the wrapper off a slim bar of dark chocolate or open up the softly padded papers of a luxury box, our sense of anticipation is already at work. The pure chocolatey smell is like perfume and the chocolate looks so smooth and glossy we want to stroke it. Breaking off a piece, it snaps cleanly with a pleasing crack. When it finally passes the lips, chocolate melts instantly in the mouth – an exquisitely pleasurable sensation. Then the flavours come flooding through – overwhelming our taste buds with over five hundred of them, two-and-a-half times more than any other food. With such a wealth of sensory pleasure in store, no wonder chocolate should be eaten slowly.

Whether or not we choose to share our pleasure with others by attempting to describe the complex flavours is another matter. The current passion for chocolate indicates that perhaps a tasting language will evolve along the same lines as that used for wine and, more recently, olive oil. At the moment, fellow chocolate lovers get by without a specialized vocabulary – they just know when it is good and a roll of the eyes or a deep sigh is enough to communicate this.

Elaine Sherman, a twentieth-century American writer, more than adequately sums up: "Chocolate is heavenly, mellow, sensual, deep, dark, sumptuous, gratifying, potent, dense, creamy,

BELOW: Chocolate provides unmatched sensory pleasure – a delight to look at, a pleasure to touch, wonderful to smell and pleasurable to eat.

ABOVE: Chocolate has been used as a gift since the days of the Aztecs. It speaks a thousand words and feelings.

seductive, suggestive, rich, excessive, silky, smooth, luxurious, celestial. Chocolate is downfall, happiness, pleasure, love, ecstasy, fantasy … chocolate makes us wicked, guilty, sinful, healthy, chic, happy."

A CULTURAL AND SOCIAL LUBRICANT

Chocolate has always been used as a gift. As Michel Richart, an inspired chocolate-maker in Lyon, rightly states, when we share good quality chocolate it weaves links between people on many, many levels. Chocolate also creates valuable cultural, social and even spiritual awareness.

A small box of luxury chocolates says a thousand "thank-you's" to a hostess, a mother or a lover. Chocolate also says "good luck", "congratulations", "bon voyage" and "sorry". Queen Victoria symbolically sent 5,000 lbs/2,268 kg chocolate to her loyal troops at Christmas. Sales of chocolate rocket on Mother's Day and Valentine's Day. We use it in one form or another to celebrate Easter, Christmas and weddings.

There is hardly a country in the western world that does not have chocolate as part of its culinary culture, whether it be a moist chocolate brownie from America, a chocolate-covered pancake from Hungary, a velvety square of Swiss milk fondant chocolate, or a foaming cup of thick Spanish drinking chocolate. It is these chocolate "experiences" that unite chocolate lovers throughout the world in celebration of the food of the gods.

THE RECIPES

TYPES OF CHOCOLATE

COUVERTURE (LEFT)

The professionals' choice, this is a fine-quality pure chocolate with a high percentage of cocoa butter, which gives it a high gloss. It is suitable for decorative use and for making handmade chocolates. It must generally be tempered.

PLAIN DARK CHOCOLATE (BELOW)

Often called "luxury", "bitter" or "continental" chocolate, this has a high percentage of cocoa solids — around 75 per cent — with little or no added sugar. Its rich, intense flavour and good dark colour make it an ideal ingredient in desserts and cakes.

MILK CHOCOLATE (RIGHT)

This contains powdered or condensed milk and generally around 20 per cent cocoa solids. The flavour is mild and sweet. Although this is the most popular eating chocolate, it is not as suitable as plain chocolate for melting and cooking.

PLAIN CHOCOLATE (ABOVE)

Ordinary plain chocolate is the most widely available chocolate to use in cooking. It contains anywhere between 30 per cent and 70 per cent cocoa solids, so check the label before you buy. The higher the cocoa solids, the better the chocolate flavour will be.

COCOA (LEFT)

This is made from the pure cocoa mass after most of the cocoa butter has been extracted. The mass is roasted, then ground to make a powder. It is probably the most economical way of giving puddings and baked goods a chocolate flavour.

ORGANIC CHOCOLATE (ABOVE)
This is slightly more expensive than other types of chocolate but is a quality product, high in cocoa solids, produced without pesticides and with consideration for the environment.

CHOCOLATE CHIPS (ABOVE)
These are small pieces of chocolate of uniform size. They contain fewer cocoa solids than ordinary chocolate and are available in plain dark, milk and white flavours.

CHOCOLATE-FLAVOURED CAKE COVERING (LEFT)
This is a blend of sugar, vegetable oil, cocoa and flavourings. The flavour is poor, but the high fat content makes it suitable for chocolate curls – to improve the flavour, add some plain chocolate.

CHOCOLATE POWDER (BELOW)
Chocolate powder is used in baking and for making drinks. It has lower cocoa solids than pure cocoa and has a much milder, sweeter taste.

WHITE CHOCOLATE (BELOW LEFT)
This does not contain any cocoa solids but gets its flavour from cocoa butter. It is sweet, and the better quality white chocolate is quite rich and smooth. White chocolate must be melted with care, as it does not withstand heat as well as plain chocolate.

TECHNIQUES

MELTING CHOCOLATE

If chocolate is being melted on its own, all the equipment must be completely dry, as water may cause the chocolate to thicken and become a stiff paste. For this reason, do not cover chocolate during or after melting it, as condensation could form. If chocolate does thicken, add a little pure white vegetable fat (not butter or margarine) and mix well. If this does not work, start again. Do not discard the thickened chocolate; melt it with cream to make a sauce.

With or without liquid, chocolate should be melted very slowly. It is easily burned or scorched, and then develops a bad flavour. If any steam gets into the chocolate, it can turn into a solid mass. If this happens, stir in a little pure white vegetable fat. Dark chocolate should not be heated above 50°C/120°F. Milk and white chocolate should not be heated above 45°C/110°F. Take particular care when melting white chocolate, which clogs very easily when subjected to heat.

MELTING CHOCOLATE OVER SIMMERING WATER

1 Chop or cut the chocolate into small pieces with a sharp knife to enable it to melt quickly and evenly.

2 Put the chocolate in the top of a double boiler or in a heatproof bowl over a saucepan of barely simmering water. The bowl should not touch the water.

3 Heat gently until the chocolate is melted and smooth, stirring occasionally. Remove from the heat and stir.

MELTING CHOCOLATE OVER DIRECT HEAT

When a recipe recommends melting chocolate with a liquid such as milk, cream or even butter, this can be done over direct heat in a saucepan.

1 Choose a heavy-based saucepan. Add the chocolate and liquid and melt over a low heat, stirring frequently, until the chocolate is melted and the mixture is smooth. Remove from heat immediately. This method is also used for making sauces, icings and some sweets.

2 Chocolate can also be melted in a very low oven. Preheat oven to 110°C/225°F/Gas ¼. Put the chocolate in an ovenproof bowl and place in the oven for a few minutes. Remove the chocolate before it is completely melted and stir until smooth.

MELTING CHOCOLATE IN THE MICROWAVE

Check the chocolate at frequent intervals during the cooking time. These times are for a 650–700 W oven and are approximate, as microwave ovens vary.

1 Place 115g/4oz chopped or broken dark, bittersweet or semi-sweet chocolate in a microwave-safe bowl and microwave on Medium for about 2 minutes. The same quantity of milk or white chocolate should be melted on Low for about 2 minutes.

2 Check the chocolate frequently during the cooking time. The chocolate will not change shape, but will start to look shiny. It must then be removed from the microwave and stirred until completely melted and smooth.

TEMPERING CHOCOLATE

TEMPERING CHOCOLATE

Tempering is the process of gently heating and cooling chocolate to stabilize the emulsification of cocoa solids and butterfat. This technique is generally used by professionals handling couverture chocolate. It allows the chocolate to shrink quickly (to allow easy release from a mould, for example with Easter eggs) or to be kept at room temperature for several weeks or months without losing its crispness and shiny surface. All solid chocolate is tempered in production, but once melted loses its "temper" and must be tempered again unless it is to be used immediately. Untempered chocolate tends to "bloom" or becomes dull and streaky or takes on a cloudy appearance. This can be avoided if the melted chocolate is put in the fridge immediately: chilling the chocolate solidifies the cocoa butter and prevents it from rising to the surface and "blooming". General baking and dessert-making do not require tempering, which is a fussy procedure and takes practice. However, it is useful to be aware of the technique when preparing sophisticated decorations, moulded chocolates or coatings. Most shapes can be made without tempering if they are chilled immediately.

EQUIPMENT

To temper chocolate successfully, you will need a marble slab or similar cool, smooth surface, such as an upturned baking sheet. A flexible plastic scraper is ideal for spreading the chocolate, but you can use a palette knife. As the temperature is crucial, you will need a chocolate thermometer. Look for this at a specialist kitchen supply shop, where you may also find blocks of tempered chocolate, ready for immediate use.

1 Break up the chocolate into small pieces and place it in the top of a double boiler or a heatproof bowl over a saucepan of hot water. Heat gently until just melted.

2 Remove from the heat. Spoon about three-quarters of the melted chocolate on to a marble slab or other cool, smooth, non-porous work surface.

3 With a flexible plastic scraper or palette knife, spread the chocolate thinly, then scoop it up before spreading it again. Repeat the sequence, keeping the chocolate constantly on the move, for about 5 minutes.

4 Using a chocolate thermometer, check the temperature of the chocolate as you work it. As soon as the temperature registers 28°C/82°F, tip the chocolate back into the bowl and stir into the remaining chocolate.

5 With the addition of the hot chocolate, the temperature should now be 32°C/90°F, making the chocolate ready for use. To test, drop a little of the chocolate from a spoon on to the marble; it should set very quickly.

STORING CHOCOLATE

Chocolate can be stored successfully for up to a year if the conditions are favourable. This means a dry place with a temperature of around 20°C/68°F. At higher temperatures, the chocolate may develop white streaks as the fat comes to the surface. Although this will not spoil the flavour, it will mar the appearance of the chocolate, making it unsuitable for use as a decoration. When storing chocolate, keep it cool and dry. Place inside an airtight container, away from strong smelling foods. Check the "best before" dates on the pack.

PIPING WITH CHOCOLATE

Pipe chocolate directly on to a cake, or on to non-stick baking paper to make run-outs, small outlined shapes or irregular designs. After melting the chocolate, allow it to cool slightly so it just coats the back of a spoon. If it still flows freely it will be too runny to hold its shape when piped. When it is the right consistency, you then need to work fast as the chocolate will set quickly. Use a paper piping bag and keep the pressure very tight, as the chocolate will flow readily without encouragement.

MAKING A PAPER PIPING BAG
A non-stick paper cone is ideal for piping small amounts of messy liquids like chocolate as it is small, easy to handle and disposable, unlike a conventional piping bag, which will need cleaning.

1 Fold a square of non-stick baking paper in half to form a triangle. With the triangle point facing you, fold the left corner down to the centre.

2 Fold the right corner down and wrap it around the folded left corner to form a cone. Fold the ends into the cone.

3 Spoon the melted chocolate into the cone and fold the top edges over. When ready to pipe, snip off the end of the point neatly to make a tiny hole, about 3 mm/⅛ in in diameter.

4 Another method is to use a small heavy-duty freezer or plastic bag. Place a piping nozzle in one corner of the bag, so that it is in the correct position for piping. Fill as above, squeezing the filling into one corner and twisting the top to seal. Snip off the corner of the bag, if necessary, so that the tip of the nozzle emerges, and squeeze gently to pipe the design.

CHOCOLATE DRIZZLES
You can have great fun making random shapes or, with a steady hand, special designs that will look great on cakes or biscuits.

1 Melt the chocolate and pour it into a paper cone or small piping bag fitted with a very small plain nozzle. Drizzle the chocolate on to a baking sheet lined with non-stick baking paper to make small, self-contained lattice shapes, such as circles or squares. Allow to set for 30 minutes then peel off the paper.

2 Chocolate can be used in many designs, such as flowers or butterflies. Use non-stick baking paper as tracing paper and pipe the chocolate over the chosen design or decorative shape.

3 For butterflies, pipe chocolate on to individually cut squares and leave until just beginning to set. Use a long, thin box (such as an egg carton) and place the butterfly shape in the box or between the cups so it is bent in the centre, creating the butterfly shape. Chill until needed.

PIPING ON TO CAKES
This looks effective on top of a cake iced with coffee glacé icing.

1 Melt 50g/2oz each of white and plain dark chocolate in separate bowls, and allow to cool slightly. Place the chocolates in separate paper piping bags. Cut a small piece off the pointed end of each bag in a straight line.

2 Hold each piping bag in turn above the surface of the cake and pipe the chocolates all over as shown in the picture. Alternatively, pipe a freehand design in one continuous curvy line, first with one bag of chocolate, then the other.

PIPING CURLS

Make lots of these curly shapes and store them in a cool place ready for using as cake decorations. Try piping the lines in contrasting colours of chocolate to vary the effect.

1 Melt 115g/4oz chocolate and allow to cool slightly. Cover a rolling pin with baking parchment and attach it with tape. Fill a paper piping bag with the chocolate and cut a small piece off the pointed end in a straight line.

2 Pipe lines of chocolate backwards and forwards over the baking parchment.

3 Leave the piped curls to set in a cool place, then carefully peel off the baking parchment. Use a palette knife to lift the curls on to the cake.

FEATHERING OR MARBLING CHOCOLATE

These two related techniques provide some of the easiest and most effective ways of decorating the top of a cake, and they are also used when making a swirled mixture for cut-outs. Chocolate sauce and double cream can also be feathered or marbled to decorate a dessert.

1 Melt two contrasting colours of chocolate and spread one over the cake or surface to be decorated.

2 Spoon the contrasting chocolate into a piping bag and pipe lines or swirls over the chocolate base.

3 Working quickly before the chocolate sets, draw a skewer or cocktail stick through the swirls to create a feathered or marbled effect.

CHOCOLATE RUN-OUTS

Try piping the outline in one colour of chocolate and filling in the middle with another. The effect can be dramatic.

1 Tape a piece of greaseproof paper to a baking sheet or flat board. Draw around a shaped biscuit cutter on to the paper several times. Secure a piece of non-stick baking paper over the top.

2 Pipe over the outline of your design in a continuous thread.

3 Cut the end off the other bag, making the hole slightly wider than before, and pipe the chocolate to fill in the outline so it looks slightly rounded. Leave the shapes to set in a cool place, then carefully lift them off the non-stick baking paper with a palette knife.

CHOCOLATE DECORATIONS

GRATED CHOCOLATE

Chocolate can be grated by hand or in a food processor. Make sure you grate it at the correct temperature.

1 Chill the chocolate and hold it with a piece of folded foil or paper towel to prevent the heat of your hand melting it. Hold a hand- or box-grater over a large plate and grate with an even pressure.

2 A food processor fitted with the metal blade can also be used to grate chocolate, but be sure the chocolate is soft enough to be pierced with a sharp knife. Cut the chocolate into small pieces and, with the machine running, drop the chocolate pieces through the feeder tube until very fine shavings are produced. Use the grater attachment and pusher to feed the chocolate through the processor for larger shavings.

COOK'S TIPS

The chocolate you use for decorating should not be too cold or it will splinter; warm chocolate will give a softer, looser curl, but do not allow it to become too soft or warm or it will be difficult to handle and may bloom. Use tempered chocolate for the best results.

COOK'S TIPS

If using a metal grater for grating chocolate, chill it in the freezer before use and the chocolate will be less likely to melt.
Experiment with different utensils when making chocolate curls. Metal palette knives, paint scrapers, tablespoons and even wide, straight pastry scrapers can be used.

MINI CHOCOLATE CURLS

Chocolate curls make an ideal decoration for many desserts and cakes, whether these are made from plain, bittersweet or white chocolate. These curls can be made very quickly using a vegetable peeler, and can be stored for several weeks in an airtight container in a cool, dry place.

1 Bring a thick piece or bar of chocolate to room temperature. (Chocolate that is too cold will "grate", or if too warm will slice.) With a swivel-bladed peeler held over a plate or baking sheet, pull the blade firmly along the edge of the chocolate and allow curls to fall on to the plate or baking sheet in a single layer.

2 Use a skewer or cocktail stick to transfer curls to the dessert or cake.

CHUNKY CHOCOLATE CURLS

These curls are best made with dark chocolate that has been melted with pure white vegetable fat (about 5ml/1tsp per 25g/1oz of chocolate), which keeps the chocolate from hardening completely.

1 Melt 175g/6oz plain or bittersweet chocolate with 30ml/2tbsp pure white vegetable fat, stirring until smooth. Pour into a small rectangular or square tin lined with foil or non-stick baking paper to produce a block about 2.5cm/1in thick. Chill until set.

2 Allow the block to come to room temperature, remove it from the tin, then hold it with a piece of folded foil or paper towel (to stop it melting) and use a swivel-bladed peeler to produce short chunky curls. The block of chocolate can also be grated.

COOK'S TIPS

The decorations on this page are useful for all kinds of cakes and desserts. When you have mastered the techniques, try marbling dark and white chocolate together for a special effect.

CHOCOLATE SCROLLS OR SHORT ROUND CURLS

Temper dark or white chocolate, or use chocolate prepared for Chunky Chocolate Curls to produce these scrolls.

1 Pour the prepared chocolate evenly on to a marble slab or the back of a baking sheet. Using a metal palette knife, spread to about 3mm/⅛in thick and allow to set for about 30 minutes until just firm.

2 To make long scrolls, use the blade of a long, sharp knife on the surface of the chocolate, and, with both hands, push away from your body at a 25–45° angle to scrape off a thin layer of chocolate. Twist the handle of the knife about a quarter of a circle to make a slightly wider scroll. Use a teaspoon to make cup-shaped curls.

3 A variety of shapes and sizes can be produced, depending on the temperature of the chocolate and the tool used.

CHOCOLATE SQUIGGLES

Melt a quantity of chocolate and spread fairly thinly over a cool, smooth surface, leave until just set, then draw a citrus zester firmly across the surface to remove curls or "squiggles" of the chocolate.

CHOCOLATE CUT-OUTS

You can make abstract shapes, or circles, squares and diamonds, by cutting them out free-hand with a sharp knife.

1 Cover a baking sheet with baking parchment and tape down at each corner. Melt 115g/4 oz dark, milk or white chocolate. Pour the chocolate on to the baking parchment.

2 Spread the chocolate evenly with a palette knife. Allow to stand until the surface is firm enough to cut, but not so hard that it will break. It should no longer feel sticky when touched lightly with your finger.

3 Press the cutter firmly through the chocolate and lift off the paper with a palette knife. Try not to touch the surface of the chocolate or you will leave marks on it and spoil its appearance.

4 The finished shapes can be left plain or piped with a contrasting chocolate for a decorative effect.

5 Abstract shapes can be cut with a knife free-hand. They look particularly effective pressed on to the sides of a cake iced with plain or chocolate buttercream.

COOK'S TIPS
If you do not feel confident about cutting chocolate cut-outs freehand, use biscuit or aspic cutters. Cut-outs look good around the sides of cakes or gâteaux. Space them at regular intervals or allow them to overlap.

CHOCOLATE LEAVES

You can use any fresh, non-toxic leaf with distinct veins, to make these decorations. Rose, bay or lemon leaves work well. If small leaves are required, for decorating petits fours, for instance, use mint or lemon balm leaves.

1 Wash and dry the leaves thoroughly. Melt plain or white chocolate and use a pastry brush or spoon to coat the veined side of each leaf completely.

2 Place the coated leaves chocolate-side up on a baking sheet lined with non-stick baking paper to set.

3 Starting at the stem end, gently peel away each leaf in turn. Store the chocolate leaves in a cool place until needed.

CHOCOLATE BASKETS

These impressive baskets make pretty, edible containers for mousse, or ice cream.

MAKES 6

175g/6oz plain, milk or white chocolate
25g/1oz/2 tbsp butter

1 Cut out six 15cm/6in rounds from non-stick baking paper.

2 Melt the chocolate with the butter in a heatproof bowl over barely simmering water. Stir until smooth. Spoon one-sixth of the chocolate over each round, using a teaspoon to spread it to within 2cm/¾in of the edge.

BELOW: Chocolate baskets can be used to hold many kinds of delicious desserts, such as mousse, ice cream and tiramisu.

3 Carefully lift each covered paper round and drape it over an upturned cup or ramekin, curving the edges to create a frilled effect.

4 Leave until completely set, then carefully lift off the chocolate shape and peel away the paper.

5 For a different effect, brush the chocolate over, leaving the edges jagged. Invert chocolate baskets on individual dessert plates and gently peel off the paper. Add your chosen filling, taking care not to break the chocolate.
6 For a simple filling, whip cream with a little orange-flavoured liqueur, pipe the mixture in swirls in the chocolate cups and top with mandarin segments, half-dipped in chocolate.

CHOCOLATE CUPS

Large or small cupcake papers or sweet cases can be used to make chocolate cups to fill with ice cream, mousse or liqueur. Use double liners inside each other for extra support.

1 Melt the chocolate. Using a paintbrush or pastry brush, completely coat the bottom and sides of the paper cases. Allow to set, then repeat once or twice to build up the layers. Allow to set for several hours or overnight.

2 Carefully peel off the paper case, set the chocolate cups on a baking sheet and fill as desired.

CHOCOLATE SHORTCRUST PASTRY (1)

Suitable for sweet flans and tarts, this quantity will line a 23cm/9in flan tin.

*115g/4oz plain chocolate, broken into
squares
225g/8oz/2 cups plain flour
115g/4oz/¹/₂ cup unsalted butter
15–30ml/1–2 tbsp cold water*

1 Melt the chocolate in a heatproof bowl over hot water. Remove from the heat and allow to cool, but not set.

2 Place the flour in a mixing bowl. Rub in the butter until the mixture resembles fine breadcrumbs.

3 Make a well in the centre of the rubbed-in mixture. Add the cooled chocolate and mix in together with just enough cold water to mix to a firm dough. Knead lightly, then wrap in clear film and chill before rolling out. Once you have chilled the flan tin, chill again before baking.

LEFT: These tiny chocolate cups are ideal as a container for sweets. You can also fill them with nuts and fruit for petits fours. Look out for different sizes of cases for these little cups.

CHOCOLATE SHORTCRUST PASTRY (2)

An alternative sweet chocolate pastry, this time made with cocoa. Use a 23cm/9in flan tin.

*175g/6oz/1¹/₂ cups plain flour
30ml/2 tbsp cocoa powder
30ml/2 tbsp icing sugar
115g/4oz/¹/₂ cup butter
15–30ml/1–2 tbsp cold water*

1 Sift the flour, cocoa powder and icing sugar into a mixing bowl.
2 Place the butter in a pan with the water and heat gently until just melted. Cool.
3 Stir into the flour to make a smooth dough. Chill until firm, then roll out and use as required.

TIPS FOR COOKING WITH CHOCOLATE

Melt chocolate slowly, as overheating will spoil both the flavour and texture.
Avoid overheating – dark chocolate should not be heated above 49°C/120°F; milk and white chocolate should not be heated above 43°C/110°F.
Never allow water or steam to come into contact with melting chocolate, as this may cause it to stiffen. If the chocolate comes into contact with steam, and forms a solid mass, add a small amount of pure vegetable oil and mix in. If this does not work you will have to start again. Don't discard spoiled chocolate, it will probably melt when added to another ingredient such as milk, butter or cream.
Remember to use high quality chocolate for the best results.
Look for the cocoa solid content on the back of the wrapper.
Do not cover chocolate after melting, as condensation could cause it to stiffen.

TEA-TIME CHOCOLATE TREATS

SIMPLE CHOCOLATE CAKE

2 Cream the butter or margarine with the sugar in a mixing bowl until pale and fluffy. Add the eggs one at a time, beating well after each addition. Stir in the chocolate mixture until well combined.

3 Sift the flour and cocoa over the mixture and fold in with a metal spoon until evenly mixed. Scrape into the prepared tins, smooth level and bake for 35–40 minutes or until well risen and firm. Turn out on to wire racks to cool.

SERVES 6–8

115g / 4oz plain chocolate, chopped into small pieces
45ml / 3 tbsp milk
150g / 5oz / ⅔ cup unsalted butter or margarine, softened
150g / 5oz / scant 1 cup light muscovado sugar
3 eggs
200g / 7oz / 1¾ cups self-raising flour
15ml / 1 tbsp cocoa powder
1 quantity Chocolate Buttercream, for the filling
icing sugar and cocoa powder, for dusting

1 Preheat oven to 180°C / 350°F / Gas 4. Grease two 18 cm / 7 in round sandwich cake tins and line the base of each with non-stick baking paper. Select a small saucepan and a heatproof bowl that will fit over it. Place the chocolate and the milk in the bowl. Bring a small saucepan of water to just below simmering point. Place the bowl containing the chocolate mixture on top. Leave for about 5 minutes, until the chocolate softens, then stir until smooth. Leave the bowl over the saucepan, but remove from the heat.

4 Sandwich the cake layers together with a thick, even layer of chocolate buttercream. Dust with a mixture of icing sugar and cocoa just before serving.

ONE-MIX CHOCOLATE SPONGE

SERVES 8–10

*175g / 6oz / ¾ cup soft margarine, at room
temperature*
115g / 4oz / ½ cup caster sugar
60ml / 4 tbsp golden syrup
175g / 6oz / 1½ cups self-raising flour, sifted
30ml / 2 tbsp cocoa powder, sifted
2.5ml / ½ tsp salt
3 eggs, beaten
little milk (optional)
150ml / ¼ pint / ⅔ cup whipping cream
15–30ml / 1–2 tbsp finely shredded marmalade
sifted icing sugar, to decorate

1 Preheat the oven to 180°C / 350°F / Gas 4.
Grease two 18 mm / 7 in sandwich cake
tins. Cream the margarine, sugar, syrup,
flour, cocoa, salt and eggs in a bowl.

2 If the mixture seems a little thick, stir
in enough milk to give a soft dropping
consistency. Spoon the mixture into the
prepared tins, and bake for about 30
minutes, changing shelves if necessary
after 15 minutes, until just firm and
springy to the touch.

3 Leave the cakes to cool for 5 minutes,
then remove from the tins and leave to
cool completely on a wire rack.

4 Whip the cream and fold in the
marmalade. Use the mixture to sandwich
the two cakes together. Sprinkle the top
with sifted icing sugar.

CHOCOLATE AND BEETROOT LAYER CAKE

SERVES 10–12

cocoa powder, for dusting
225g/8oz can cooked whole beetroot, drained and juice reserved
115g/4oz/½ cup unsalted butter, softened
425g/15oz/2½ cups soft light brown sugar
3 eggs
15ml/1 tbsp vanilla essence
75g/3oz bittersweet chocolate, melted
225g/8oz/2 cups plain flour
10ml/2 tsp baking powder
2.5ml/½ tsp salt
120ml/4fl oz/½ cup buttermilk
chocolate curls (optional)

CHOCOLATE GANACHE FROSTING

475ml/16fl oz/2 cups whipping cream or double cream
500g/1¼lb fine quality, bittersweet or plain chocolate, chopped into small pieces
15ml/1 tbsp vanilla essence

1 Preheat the oven to 180°C/350°F/ Gas 4. Grease two 23 cm/9 in cake tins and dust the base and sides with cocoa. Grate the beetroot and add to the juice. Set aside. With a hand-held electric mixer, beat the butter, brown sugar, eggs and vanilla essence in a mixing bowl until pale. Reduce the speed and beat in the melted chocolate. Sift the flour, baking powder and salt into a bowl.

2 With the mixer on low speed gradually beat the flour mixture into the butter mixture, alternately with the buttermilk. Add the beetroot and juice and beat for 1 minute. Divide between the tins and bake for 30–35 minutes or until a cake tester inserted in the centre of each cake comes out clean. Cool for 10 minutes, then turn the cakes out on a wire rack and cool completely.

3 To make the ganache frosting, heat the cream in a heavy-based saucepan over medium heat, until it just begins to boil, stirring occasionally to prevent it from scorching. Remove from the heat and stir in the chocolate, stirring constantly until melted and smooth. Stir in the vanilla essence. Strain into a bowl. Cool, then chill, stirring every 10 minutes for about 1 hour, until spreadable.

4 Assemble the cake. Place one layer on a serving plate and spread with one-third of the ganache frosting. Place the second layer on top and spread the remaining ganache over the cake, taking it down the sides. Decorate with the chocolate curls, if using. Allow the ganache frosting to set for 20–30 minutes, then chill the cake before serving.

FRENCH CHOCOLATE CAKE

SERVES 10

250g / 9oz bittersweet chocolate, chopped into
small pieces
225g / 8oz / 1 cup unsalted butter, cut into
small pieces
90g / 3½oz / scant ½ cup granulated sugar
30ml / 2 tbsp brandy or orange-flavoured
liqueur
5 eggs
15ml / 1tbsp plain flour
icing sugar, for dusting
whipped or soured cream, for serving

1 Preheat oven to 180°C/350°F/Gas 4.
Generously grease a 23 x 5 cm / 9 x 2 in
springform tin. Line the base with non-
stick baking paper and grease. Wrap the
bottom and sides of the tin in foil to
prevent water from seeping through into
the cake.

2 In a saucepan, over a low heat, melt the
chocolate, butter and sugar, stirring
frequently until smooth. Remove from
the heat, cool slightly and stir in the
brandy or liqueur.

3 In a large bowl beat the eggs lightly for
1 minute. Beat in the flour, then slowly
beat in the chocolate mixture until well
blended. Pour into the tin.

4 Place the springform tin in a large
roasting tin. Add enough boiling water to
come 2 cm / ¾ in up the side of the
springform tin. Bake for 25–30 minutes,
until the edge of the cake is set but the
centre is still soft. Remove the
springform tin from the roasting tin and
remove the foil. Cool on a wire rack. The
cake will sink in the centre and become
its classic slim shape as it cools. Don't
worry if the surface cracks slightly.

5 Remove the side of the springform tin
and turn the cake on to a wire rack. Lift
off the springform tin base and then
carefully peel back the paper, so the base
of the cake is now the top. Leave the cake
on the rack until it is quite cold.

6 Cut 6–8 strips of non-stick baking
paper 2.5 cm / 1 in wide and place
randomly over the cake. Dust the cake
with icing sugar, then carefully remove
the paper. Slide the cake on to a plate and
serve with whipped or soured cream.

Hazelnut and Chocolate Cake

Serves 10

115g/4oz/½ cup unsalted butter, softened
150g/5oz plain chocolate
115g/4oz/½ cup caster sugar
4 eggs, separated
115g/4oz/1 cup ground lightly toasted hazelnuts
50g/2oz/1 cup fresh breadcrumbs
grated rind of 1½ oranges
30ml/2 tbsp sieved marmalade, warmed
60ml/4 tbsp chopped hazelnuts, to decorate

For the Icing

150g/5oz plain chocolate, chopped into small pieces
50g/2oz/¼ cup butter, diced

1 Preheat oven to 180°C/350°F/Gas 4. Butter a 23 cm/9 in round cake tin and line the base with greaseproof paper.

2 Melt the chocolate and set aside. Beat the butter and sugar together, then gradually add the egg yolks, beating well. The mixture may curdle slightly. Beat in the melted chocolate, then the hazelnuts, breadcrumbs and orange rind. Whisk the egg whites until stiff, then fold into the chocolate mixture. Transfer to the cake tin. Bake for 40–45 minutes, until set.

3 Remove from the oven, cover with a damp dish towel for 5 minutes, then transfer to a wire rack until cold.

4 Make the icing. Place the chocolate and butter in a heatproof bowl over a pan of simmering water and stir until smooth. Leave until cool and thick. Spread the cake with the marmalade, then the icing. Scatter over the nuts, then leave to set.

CHOCOLATE AND ORANGE ANGEL CAKE

SERVES 10

25g / 1oz / ¼ cup plain flour
30ml / 2 tbsp cocoa powder
30ml / 2 tbsp cornflour
pinch of salt
5 egg whites
2.5ml / ½ tsp cream of tartar
115g / 4oz / ½ cup caster sugar
blanched and shredded rind of 1 orange,
to decorate

FOR THE ICING

200g / 7oz / scant 1 cup caster sugar
75ml / 5 tbsp cold water
1 egg white

1 Preheat oven to 180°C / 350°F / Gas 4. Sift the flour, cocoa, cornflour and salt together three times. Beat the egg whites in a large bowl until foamy. Add the cream of tartar to the egg whites and whisk until soft peaks form.

2 Add the caster sugar to the egg whites a spoonful at a time, whisking after each addition. Add, by sifting, a third of the flour and cocoa mixture, and gently fold in. Repeat, sifting and folding in the flour and cocoa two more times. Spoon the mixture into a 20 cm / 8 in non-stick ring tin and level the top. Bake for 35 minutes or until springy when lightly pressed. When cooled, turn upside-down on to a wire rack and leave to cool in the tin.

3 Make the icing. Put the sugar in a pan with the water. Stir over a low heat until dissolved. Boil until the syrup reaches a temperature of 120°C / 250°F on a sugar thermometer, or when a drop of the syrup makes a soft ball when dropped into a cup of cold water. Remove the pan from the heat. Ease the cake out of the tin.

4 Whisk the egg white until stiff. Add the syrup in a thin stream, whisking all the time. Continue to whisk until the mixture is very thick and fluffy. Spread the icing over the top and sides of the cooled cake. Sprinkle the orange rind over the top of the cake and transfer it to a platter. Serve.

CHOCOLATE AND CHERRY POLENTA CAKE

SERVES 8

50g/2oz/⅓ cup quick-cook polenta
200g/7oz plain chocolate, chopped into
small pieces
5 eggs, separated
175g/6oz/¾ cup caster sugar
115g/4oz/1 cup ground almonds
75ml/5 tbsp plain flour
finely grated rind of 1 orange
115g/4oz/1 cup glacé cherries, halved
icing sugar, for dusting

__1__ Place the polenta in a heatproof bowl and pour over just enough boiling water to cover (about 120ml/4 fl oz/½ cup). Stir well, then cover the bowl and leave to stand for about 30 minutes, until the quick-cook polenta has absorbed all the excess moisture.

__2__ Preheat oven to 190°C/375°F/Gas 5. Grease a deep 22 cm/8½ in round cake tin and line the base with non-stick baking paper. Melt the chocolate.

__3__ Whisk the egg yolks with the sugar in a bowl until thick and pale. Beat in the chocolate, then fold in the polenta, ground almonds, flour and orange rind.

__4__ Whisk the egg whites in a grease-free bowl until stiff. Stir about 15ml/1 tbsp of the whites into the chocolate mixture to lighten it, then fold in the rest. Finally, fold in the cherries. Scrape the mixture into the prepared tin and bake for 45–55 minutes or until well risen and firm. Turn out and cool on a wire rack, then dust with icing sugar to serve.

MARBLED CHOCOLATE-PEANUT BUTTER CAKE

SERVES 12–14

115g/4oz bittersweet chocolate, chopped into
small pieces
225g/8oz/1 cup unsalted butter, softened
225g/8oz/⅔ cup smooth or chunky
peanut butter
200g/7oz/scant 1 cup granulated sugar
225g/8 oz/1¼ cups soft light brown sugar
5 eggs
225g/8 oz/2 cups plain flour
10ml/2 tsp baking powder
2.5ml/½ tsp salt
120ml/4fl oz/½ cup milk
50g/2oz/⅓ cup chocolate chips

CHOCOLATE PEANUT BUTTER GLAZE

25g/1oz/2 tbsp butter, cut up
30ml/2 tbsp smooth peanut butter
45ml/3 tbsp golden syrup
5ml/1 tsp vanilla essence
175g/6oz plain chocolate, chopped into
small pieces
15ml/1 tbsp water

1 Preheat oven to 180°C/350°F/Gas 4.
Generously grease and flour a 3 litre/
5 pint/12 cup tube or ring tin. Melt
the chocolate. In a large mixing bowl beat
the butter, peanut butter and sugars until
light and creamy. Add the eggs one at a
time, beating well after each addition.
2 In a medium bowl, sift together the
flour, baking powder and salt. Add to the
butter mixture alternately with the milk
until just blended. Pour half the mixture
into another bowl. Stir the melted
chocolate into one bowl of batter until
well blended. Stir the chocolate chips
into the other bowl of batter.

3 Using a large spoon, drop alternate
spoonfuls of chocolate mixture and
peanut butter mixture into the prepared
tin. Using a knife, pull through the
batters to create a swirled marbled effect.
Bake for 50–60 minutes, until the top
springs back when touched. Cool the
cake in the tin for 10 minutes. Turn out
on to a rack to cool completely.

4 Make the glaze. Combine all the
ingredients in a small saucepan. Melt over
a low heat, stirring until well blended and
smooth. Cool slightly. When slightly
thickened, drizzle the glaze over the cake,
allowing it to run down the sides.

CHOCOLATE-ORANGE BATTENBURG

3 Fold the rest of the flour and the cocoa into the remaining bowl of mixture, with sufficient milk to give a soft dropping consistency. Fill one half of the tin with the orange mixture and the second half with the chocolate. Flatten the top with a wetted spoon. Bake for 15 minutes, then reduce the heat to 160°C/325°F/Gas 3, and bake the cake for a further 20–30 minutes or until the top is just firm. Leave to cool in the tin for a few minutes. Turn out the cakes on to a board and cut each one into two identical strips. Trim so that they are even, then leave to cool.

4 Using the chocolate and nut spread, sandwich the cakes together, chocolate and orange side by side, then orange and chocolate on top. Spread the sides with more of the chocolate and nut spread. On a board lightly dusted with cornflour, roll out the white almond paste to a rectangle 18 cm/7 in wide and long enough to wrap all around the cake. Wrap the almond paste carefully around the cake, making the join underneath. Press to seal. Mark a criss-cross pattern on the almond paste with a knife, then pinch together the corners if desired. Store in a cool place. Cut with a sharp knife into chequered slices to serve.

SERVES 8

115g/4oz/½ cup soft margarine
115g/4oz/½ cup caster sugar
2 eggs, beaten
few drops of vanilla essence
115g/4oz/1 cup ground almonds
115g/4oz/1 cup self-raising flour, sifted
grated rind and juice of ½ orange
30ml/2 tbsp cocoa powder, sifted
30–45ml/2–3 tbsp milk
1 jar chocolate and nut spread
cornflour, to dust
225g/8oz white almond paste

1 Preheat oven to 180°C/350°F/Gas 4. Grease and line an 18 cm/7 in square cake tin. Arrange a double piece of foil across the middle of the tin, to divide it into two equal rectangles.

2 Cream the margarine and sugar in a mixing bowl, then beat in the eggs, vanilla essence and ground almonds. Divide the mixture evenly between two bowls. Fold half the flour into one bowl, then stir in the orange rind and sufficient juice to give a soft dropping consistency. Set the orange-flavoured mixture aside.

CHOCOLATE CHIP WALNUT LOAF

MAKES 1 LOAF

115g / 4 oz / ½ cup caster sugar
115g / 4 oz / 1 cup plain flour
5ml / 1 tsp baking powder
60ml / 4 tbsp cornflour
115g / 4 oz / ½ cup butter, softened
2 eggs, beaten
5ml / 1 tsp vanilla essence
30ml / 2 tbsp currants or raisins
25g / 1 oz / ¼ cup walnuts, finely chopped
grated rind of ½ lemon
45ml / 3 tbsp plain chocolate chips
icing sugar, for dusting

1 Preheat oven to 180°C/350°F/Gas 4. Grease and line a 22 x 12 cm/8½ x 4½ in loaf tin. Sprinkle 25ml/1½ tbsp of the caster sugar into the pan and tilt to distribute the sugar in an even layer over the bottom and sides. Shake out any excess sugar.

2 Sift the flour, baking powder and cornflour into a mixing bowl. Repeat this twice more. Set aside.

3 With an electric mixer, cream the butter until soft. Add the remaining sugar and continue beating until light and fluffy. Add the eggs, one at a time, beating after each addition.

4 Gently fold the dry ingredients into the butter mixture, in three batches; do not overmix.

5 Fold in the vanilla essence, currants or raisins, walnuts, lemon rind and chocolate chips until just blended.

6 Pour the mixture into the prepared tin and bake for 45–50 minutes. Cool in the tin for 5 minutes before transferring to a rack to cool completely. Place on a serving plate and dust over an even layer of icing sugar before serving. Alternatively, top with glacé icing and decorate with walnut halves.

Bitter Marmalade Chocolate Loaf

Serves 8

*115g/4oz plain chocolate, chopped into
small pieces*
3 eggs
200g/7oz/scant 1 cup caster sugar
175ml/6fl oz/¾ cup soured cream
200g/7oz/1¾ cups self-raising flour
For the Filling and Glaze
175g/6oz/⅔ cup bitter orange marmalade
*115g/4oz plain chocolate, chopped into
small pieces*
60ml/4 tbsp soured cream
shredded orange rind, to decorate

<u>1</u> Preheat oven to 180°C/350°F/Gas 4.
Grease a 900g/2lb loaf tin lightly, then
line it with non-stick baking paper. Melt
the chocolate.

<u>2</u> Combine the eggs and sugar in a mixing
bowl. Using a hand-held electric mixer,
whisk the mixture until it is thick and
creamy, then stir in the soured cream and
chocolate. Fold in the self-raising flour
evenly, using a metal spoon and a figure-
of-eight action.

<u>3</u> Scrape the mixture into the prepared
tin and bake for about 1 hour or until
well risen and firm to the touch. Cool for
a few minutes in the tin, then turn out on
to a wire rack and leave the loaf to cool
completely.

<u>4</u> Make the filling. Spoon two-thirds of
the marmalade into a small saucepan and
melt over a gentle heat. Melt the
chocolate and stir it into the marmalade
with the soured cream.

<u>5</u> Slice the cake across into three layers
and sandwich back together with about
half the marmalade filling. Spread the rest
over the top of the cake and leave to set.
Spoon the remaining marmalade over the
cake and scatter with shredded orange
rind, to decorate.

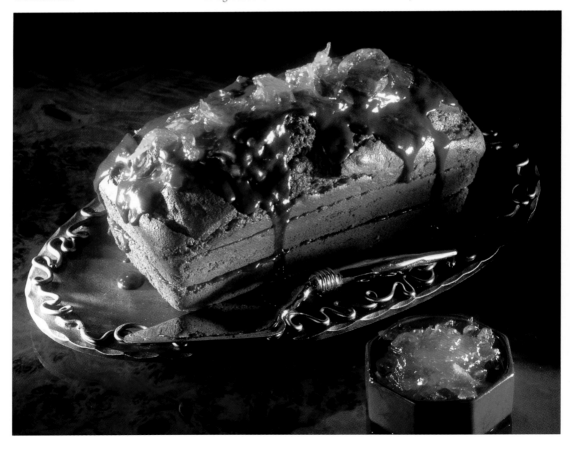

CHOCOLATE CHIP MARZIPAN LOAF

MAKES 1 LOAF

115g/4oz/½ cup unsalted butter, softened
150g/5oz/scant 1 cup light muscovado sugar
2 eggs, beaten
45ml/3 tbsp cocoa powder
150g/5oz/1¼ cups self-raising flour
130g/3½ oz marzipan
60ml/4 tbsp plain chocolate chips

1 Preheat oven to 180°C/350°F/Gas 4. Grease a 900g/2lb loaf tin and line the base with non-stick baking paper. Cream the butter and sugar in a mixing bowl until light and fluffy.

2 Add the eggs to the creamed mixture one at a time, beating well after each addition to combine.

3 Sift the cocoa and flour over the mixture and fold in evenly.

4 Chop the marzipan into small pieces with a sharp knife. Tip into a bowl and mix with the chocolate chips. Set aside about 60ml/4 tbsp and fold the rest evenly into the cake mixture.

5 Scrape the mixture into the prepared tin, level the top and scatter with the reserved marzipan and chocolate chips.

6 Bake for 45–50 minutes or until the loaf is risen and firm. Cool for a few minutes in the tin, then turn out on to a wire rack to cool completely.

CHOCOLATE COCONUT ROULADE

4 Scrape the mixture into the prepared tin, taking it right into the corners. Smooth the surface with a palette knife, then bake for 20–25 minutes or until well risen and springy to the touch.

5 Turn the cooked roulade out on to the sugar-dusted greaseproof paper and carefully peel off the lining paper. Cover with a damp, clean dish towel and leave to cool completely.

6 Make the filling. Whisk the cream with the whisky in a bowl until the mixture just holds it shape, grate the creamed coconut and stir in with the sugar.

SERVES 8

115g / 4oz / ½ cup caster sugar
5 eggs, separated
50g / 2oz / ½ cup cocoa powder
FOR THE FILLING
300ml / ½ pint / 1¼ cups double cream
45ml / 3 tbsp whisky
or brandy
50g / 2oz piece solid creamed
coconut
30ml / 2 tbsp caster sugar
FOR THE TOPPING
a piece of fresh coconut
dark chocolate for curls

1 Preheat oven to 180°C/350°F/Gas 4. Grease a 33 x 23 cm/13 x 9 in Swiss roll tin. Lay a large sheet of greaseproof paper or non-stick baking paper on the work surface and dust it evenly with 30ml/ 2 tbsp of the caster sugar.

2 Place the egg yolks in a heatproof bowl. Add the remaining caster sugar and whisk with a hand-held electric mixer until the mixture is thick enough to leave a trail. Sift the cocoa over, then fold in carefully and evenly with a metal spoon.

3 Whisk the egg whites in a clean, grease-free bowl until they form soft peaks. Fold about 15ml/1 tbsp of the whites into the chocolate mixture to lighten it, then fold in the rest evenly.

7 Uncover the sponge and spread about three-quarters of the cream mixture to the edges. Roll up carefully from a long side. Transfer to a plate, pipe or spoon the remaining cream mixture on top. Use a vegetable peeler to make coconut and chocolate curls and pile on the cake.

CHOCOLATE CHESTNUT ROULADE

SERVES 10–12

175g/6oz bittersweet chocolate, chopped into
small pieces
30ml/2 tbsp cocoa powder, sifted
60ml/4 tbsp hot strong coffee or espresso
6 eggs, separated
75g/3oz/6 tbsp caster sugar
pinch of cream of tartar
5ml/1 tsp pure vanilla essence
cocoa powder, for dusting
glacé chestnuts, to decorate

CHESTNUT CREAM FILLING

475ml/16fl oz/2 cups double cream
30ml/2 tbsp rum or coffee-flavoured liqueur
350g/12oz/1½ cups canned sweetened
chestnut purée
115g/4oz bittersweet chocolate, grated

4 Dust a dish towel with cocoa. Turn the cake out on to the towel immediately and remove the paper. Trim off any crisp edges. Starting at a narrow end, roll the cake and towel together Swiss roll fashion. Cool completely.

1 Preheat oven to 180°C/350°F/Gas 4. Lightly grease the base and sides of a 39 x 27 x 2.5 cm/15½ x 10½ x 1 in Swiss roll tin. Line with non-stick baking paper, allowing a 2.5 cm/1 in overhang. Melt the chocolate. Dissolve the cocoa in the hot coffee to make a paste. Set aside.

2 Using a hand-held mixer, beat the egg yolks with half the sugar in a mixing bowl until pale and thick. Slowly beat in the melted chocolate and cocoa-coffee paste until just blended. In a separate bowl, beat the egg whites and cream of tartar until stiff peaks form. Sprinkle the remaining sugar over the whites in two batches and beat until the whites are stiff and glossy, then beat in the vanilla essence.

3 Stir a spoonful of the whites into the chocolate mixture to lighten it, then fold in the rest. Spoon into the tin. Bake for 20–25 minutes or until the cake springs back when touched with a fingertip.

5 Make the filling. Whip the cream and rum or liqueur until soft peaks form. Beat a spoonful of cream into the chestnut purée to lighten it, then fold in the remaining cream and grated chocolate. Set aside a quarter of this mixture for the decoration. Unroll the cake and spread chestnut cream to within 2.5 cm/1 in of the edge.

6 Using a dish towel to lift the cake, carefully roll it up again. Place seam-side down on a serving plate. Spread some of the reserved chestnut cream over the top and use the rest for piped rosettes. Decorate with the glacé chestnuts.

MARBLED SWISS ROLL

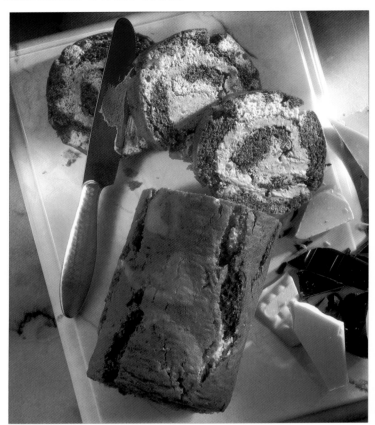

SERVES 6–8

90g / 3½oz / scant 1 cup plain flour
15ml / 1 tbsp cocoa powder
25g / 1oz plain chocolate, grated
25g / 1oz white chocolate, grated
3 eggs
115g / 4oz / ½ cup caster sugar
30ml / 2 tbsp boiling water

FOR THE FILLING
1 quantity Chocolate Buttercream
45ml / 3 tbsp chopped walnuts

1 Preheat oven to 200°C/400°F/Gas 6. Grease a 30 x 20 cm/12 x 8 in Swiss roll tin and line with non-stick baking paper. Sift half the flour with the cocoa into a bowl. Stir in the grated plain chocolate. Sift the remaining flour into another bowl. Stir in the grated white chocolate.

2 Whisk the eggs and sugar in a heatproof bowl set over a saucepan of hot water until it holds its shape when the whisk is lifted and a ribbon trail remains.
3 Remove the bowl from the heat and tip half the mixture into a separate bowl. Fold the plain chocolate mixture into one portion, then fold the white chocolate mixture into the other. Stir 15ml/1 tbsp boiling water into each half to soften.

BAKED ALASKA

For a delicious dessert that takes only minutes to prepare, make individual Baked Alaskas by topping slices of the roll with chocolate ice cream, covering both cake and ice cream thickly with meringue mixture and baking at 230°C/450°F/Gas 8 for 2–3 minutes, watching carefully, until the meringue is tinged with brown.

4 Place alternate spoonfuls of mixture in the prepared tin and swirl lightly together with a knife or slim metal skewer for a marbled effect. Bake for about 12–15 minutes or until the cake is firm and the surface springs back when touched with a fingertip. Turn the cake out on to a sheet of non-stick baking paper placed flat on the work surface.

5 Trim the edges to neaten and cover with a damp, clean dish towel. Cool.
6 For the filling, mix the chocolate buttercream and walnuts in a bowl. Uncover the sponge, lift off the lining paper and spread the surface with the buttercream. Roll up carefully from a long side and place on a serving plate. Slice to serve, and store in an airtight container.

CHOCOLATE CHRISTMAS LOG

SERVES 12–14

1 chocolate Swiss roll, see Chocolate Chestnut Roulade
1 quantity of Chocolate Ganache or Buttercream

FOR THE WHITE CHOCOLATE CREAM FILLING

200g/7oz fine quality white chocolate, chopped into small pieces
475ml/16fl oz/2 cups double cream
30ml/2 tbsp brandy or chocolate-flavoured liqueur (optional)

FOR THE CRANBERRY SAUCE

450g/1lb fresh or frozen cranberries, rinsed and picked over
275g/10oz/1 cup seedless raspberry preserve, melted
115g/4oz/1½ cup granulated sugar, or to taste

1 Make the cranberry sauce. Process the cranberries in a food processor fitted with a metal blade, until liquid. Press through a sieve into a small bowl, and discard pulp. Stir in the melted raspberry preserve and the sugar to taste. If the sauce is too thick, add a little water to thin. Cover and place in the fridge.

2 Make the filling. In a small pan, heat the chocolate with 120ml/4 fl oz/½ cup of the cream until melted, stirring. Strain into a bowl and cool to room temperature. In a separate bowl, beat the remaining cream with the brandy or liqueur until soft peaks form; fold into the chocolate mixture.

3 Unroll the Swiss roll, spread with the mixture and roll up again from a long end. Cut off a quarter of the roll at an angle and arrange both pieces on a cake board to resemble a log.

4 If using chocolate ganache for the topping, allow it to soften to room temperature, then beat to a soft, spreading consistency. Cover the log with ganache or buttercream and mark it with a fork to resemble bark. Dust lightly with icing sugar and top with a sprig of holly or similar Christmas decoration. Serve with the cranberry sauce.

MERINGUE MUSHROOMS
Small, decorative mushrooms are traditionally used to decorate the yule log. Using meringue mix, pipe the "caps" and "stems" separately, dry out in a low oven, then sandwich together with ganache or chocolate buttercream. Dust with cocoa, if you like. Alternatively, shape mushrooms from marzipan.

RICH CAKES AND GATEAUX

CHOCOLATE DATE TORTE

SERVES 8

4 egg whites
115g/4oz/½ cup caster sugar
200g/7oz plain chocolate
*175g/6oz/scant 1 cup Medjool dates, pitted
and finely chopped*
*175g/6oz/1½ cups walnuts or pecan
nuts, chopped*
5ml/1 tsp vanilla essence
FOR THE FROSTING
200g/7oz/scant 1 cup fromage frais
200g/7oz/scant 1 cup mascarpone
few drops of vanilla essence
icing sugar, to taste

1 Preheat oven to 180°C/350°F/Gas 4.
Grease a round 20 cm/8 in springform
cake tin. Line the base of the tin with
non-stick baking paper.

2 Make the frosting. Mix together the
fromage frais and mascarpone, add a few
drops of vanilla essence and icing sugar to
taste, then set aside.

3 Whisk the egg whites in a bowl until
they form stiff peaks. Whisk in 30ml/
2 tbsp of the caster sugar until the
meringue is thick and glossy, then fold in
the remainder.

4 Chop 175g/6 oz of the chocolate, then
carefully fold into the meringue with the
dates, nuts and vanilla essence. Pour into
the prepared tin, spread level and bake
for about 45 minutes, until risen around
the edges.

5 Allow the cake to cool in the tin for
10 minutes, then invert on a wire rack.
Peel off the lining paper and leave until
completely cold.

6 Swirl the frosting over the top of the
torte. Melt the remaining chocolate. Use
a small paper piping bag to drizzle the
chocolate over the torte. Work quickly
and keep up an even pressure on the
piping bag. Chill the torte before serving,
then cut into wedges. This torte is best
eaten on the day it is made.

CHOCOLATE REDCURRANT TORTE

SERVES 8–10

115g/4oz/½ cup unsalted butter, softened
115g/4oz/⅔ cup dark muscovado sugar
2 eggs
150ml/¼ pint/⅔ cup soured cream
150g/5oz/1¼ cups self-raising flour
5ml/1 tsp baking powder
50g/2oz/½ cup cocoa powder
75g/3oz/¾ cup stemmed redcurrants, plus
115g/4oz/1 cup redcurrant sprigs, to decorate

FOR THE ICING

150g/5oz plain chocolate, chopped into small pieces
45ml/3 tbsp redcurrant jelly
30ml/2 tbsp dark rum
120ml/4fl oz/½ cup double cream

1 Preheat oven to 180°C/350°F/Gas 4. Grease a 1.2 litre/2 pint/5 cup ring tin and dust lightly with flour. Cream the butter with the sugar in a mixing bowl until pale and fluffy. Beat in the eggs and soured cream until thoroughly mixed.

2 Sift the flour, baking powder and cocoa over the mixture, then fold in lightly and evenly. Fold in the stemmed redcurrants. Spoon the mixture into the prepared tin and smooth the surface level. Bake for 40–50 minutes or until well risen and firm. Turn out on to a wire rack and leave to cool completely.

3 Make the icing. Mix the chocolate, redcurrant jelly and rum in a heatproof bowl. Set the bowl over simmering water and heat gently, stirring occasionally, until melted. Remove from the heat and cool to room temperature, then add the double cream, a little at a time. Mix well.
4 Transfer the cooked cake to a serving plate. Spoon the icing evenly over the cake, allowing it to drizzle down the sides. Decorate with redcurrant sprigs just before serving.

COOK'S TIP
Use a decorative gugelhupf tin or mould, if you have one. When preparing it, add a little cocoa powder to the flour used for dusting the greased tin, as this will prevent the cooked chocolate cake from being streaked with white.

SACHERTORTE

SERVES 10–12

225g/8oz plain dark chocolate, chopped into
small pieces
150g/5oz/⅔ cup butter, softened
115g/4oz/½ cup caster sugar
8 eggs, separated
115g/4oz/1 cup plain flour
FOR THE GLAZE
225g/8oz/scant 1 cup apricot jam
15ml/1 tbsp lemon juice
FOR THE ICING
225g/8oz plain dark chocolate, cut into
small pieces
200g/7oz/scant 1 cup caster sugar
15ml/1 tbsp golden syrup
250ml/8fl oz/1 cup double cream
5ml/1 tsp vanilla essence
plain chocolate leaves, to decorate

1 Preheat oven to 180°C/350°F/Gas 4.
Grease a 23 cm/9 in round springform
cake tin and line with non-stick baking
paper. Melt the chocolate in a heatproof
bowl over barely simmering water, then
set the bowl aside.

2 Cream the butter with the sugar in a
mixing bowl until pale and fluffy, then
add the egg yolks, one at a time, beating
after each addition. Beat in the melted
chocolate, then sift the flour over the
mixture and fold it in evenly.

3 Whisk the egg whites in a clean, grease-
free bowl until stiff, then stir about a
quarter of the whites into the chocolate
mixture to lighten it. Fold in the
remaining whites.

4 Tip the chocolate mixture into the
prepared cake tin and smooth level. Bake
for about 50–55 minutes or until firm.
Cool in the tin for 5 minutes, then turn
out carefully on to a wire rack and leave
to cool completely.

5 Make the glaze. Heat the apricot jam
with the lemon juice in a small saucepan
until melted, then strain through a sieve
into a bowl. Once the cake is cold, slice
in half across the middle to make two
even-size layers.

6 Brush the top and sides of each layer
with the apricot glaze, then sandwich
them together. Place on a wire rack.

7 Make the icing. Mix the chocolate,
sugar, golden syrup, cream and vanilla
essence in a heavy saucepan. Heat gently,
stirring constantly, until the mixture is
thick and smooth. Simmer gently for 3–5
minutes, without stirring, until the
mixture registers 95°C/200°F on a sugar
thermometer. Pour the icing quickly over
the cake, spreading to cover the top and
sides completely. Leave to set, decorate
with chocolate leaves, then serve with
whipped cream, if wished.

QUEEN OF SHEBA CAKE

SERVES 8–10

*100g / 3½oz / scant 1 cup whole blanched
almonds, lightly toasted
115g / 4oz / ½ cup caster sugar
40g / 1½oz / ⅓ cup plain flour
115g / 4oz / ½ cup unsalted butter, softened
150g / 5oz plain chocolate, melted
3 eggs, separated
30ml / 2 tbsp almond liqueur (optional)
chopped toasted almonds, to decorate*

FOR THE CHOCOLATE GLAZE

*175ml / 6fl oz / ¾ cup whipping cream
225g / 8oz plain chocolate, chopped
25g / 1oz / 2 tbsp unsalted butter
30ml / 2 tbsp almond liqueur (optional)*

1 Preheat oven to 180°C / 350°F / Gas 4.
Grease and base-line a 20–23 cm / 8–9 in
springform cake tin. Dust the tin lightly
with flour.

2 In the bowl of a food processor fitted
with a metal blade, process the almonds
and 30ml / 2 tbsp of the sugar until very
fine. Transfer to a bowl and sift over the
flour. Stir to mix, then set aside.

3 Beat the butter until creamy, then add
half of the remaining sugar and beat for
about 1–2 minutes until very light.
Gradually beat in the melted chocolate,
then add the egg yolks one at a time,
beating well after each addition. Beat in
the liqueur, if using.

4 In another bowl, beat the egg whites
until soft peaks form. Add the remaining
sugar and beat until the whites are stiff
and glossy, but not dry. Fold a quarter of
the whites into the chocolate mixture to
lighten it, then alternately fold in the
almond mixture and the remaining whites
in three batches. Spoon the mixture into
the prepared tin and spread evenly.

5 Bake for 30–35 minutes, until the edges
are puffed but the centre is still soft. Cool
in the tin for 15 minutes, then remove
the sides and invert the cake on a wire
rack. When quite cold, lift off the base of
the tin and the paper.

6 To make the chocolate glaze, bring the
cream to the boil in a saucepan. Remove
from the heat and add the chocolate,
stirring gently until it has melted and the
mixture is smooth. Beat in the butter and
almond liqueur, if using. Cool for about
20–30 minutes, until slightly thickened,
stirring occasionally.

7 Place the cake on the wire rack over a
baking sheet and pour over most of the
warm glaze to cover completely. Cool
slightly, then press the nuts on to the
sides of the cake. Use the remaining glaze
for a piped decoration. Transfer to a plate
and chill until ready to serve.

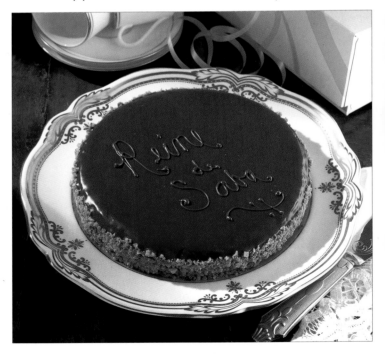

STICKY CHOCOLATE, MAPLE AND WALNUT SWIRLS

SERVES 12

450g / 1lb / 4 cups strong white flour
2.5m / ½ tsp ground cinnamon
50g / 2oz / ¼ cup unsalted butter, cut into small pieces
50g / 2oz / ¼ cup caster sugar
1 sachet easy-blend dried yeast
1 egg yolk
120ml / 4fl oz / ½ cup water
60ml / 4 tbsp milk
45ml / 3 tbsp maple syrup, to finish

FOR THE FILLING

40g / 1½oz / 3 tbsp unsalted butter, melted
50g / 2oz / ⅓ cup light muscovado sugar
175g / 6oz / 1 cup plain chocolate chips
75g / 3oz / ¾ cup chopped walnuts

1 Grease a deep 23 cm / 9 in springform cake tin. Sift the flour and cinnamon into a bowl, then rub in the butter until the mixture resembles coarse breadcrumbs.

2 Stir in the sugar and yeast. In a jug or bowl, beat the egg yolk with the water and milk, then stir into the dry ingredients to make a soft dough.

3 Knead the dough on a lightly floured surface until smooth, then roll out to a rectangle measuring about 40 x 30 cm / 16 x 12 in.

4 For the filling, brush the dough with the melted butter and sprinkle with the sugar, chocolate chips and nuts.

5 Roll up the dough from one long side like a Swiss roll, then cut into 12 thick even-size slices. Pack close together in the tin, cut sides up. Cover and leave in a warm place for about 1½ hours, until well risen and springy. Meanwhile, preheat oven to 220°C / 425°F / Gas 7.

6 Bake for 30–35 minutes, until golden brown. Remove from the tin and cool on a wire rack. Brush with maple syrup while still warm. Pull swirls apart to serve.

WHITE CHOCOLATE MOUSSE AND STRAWBERRY LAYER CAKE

4 Make the mousse filling. In a medium saucepan over a low heat, melt the chocolate and cream until smooth, stirring frequently. Stir in the rum or strawberry-flavoured liqueur and pour into a bowl. Chill until just set. With a wire whisk, whip lightly.

SERVES 10

115g/4oz fine white chocolate, chopped into small pieces
120ml/4fl oz/½ cup double cream
120ml/4fl oz/½ cup milk
15ml/1 tbsp rum or vanilla essence
115g/4oz/½ cup unsalted butter, softened
175g/6oz/¾ cup granulated sugar
3 eggs
225g/8oz/2 cups plain flour
10ml/2 tsp baking powder
pinch of salt
675g/1½lb fresh strawberries, sliced, plus extra for decoration
750ml/1¼ pints/3 cups whipping cream
30ml/2 tbsp rum or strawberry-flavoured liqueur

WHITE CHOCOLATE MOUSSE FILLING

250g/9oz white chocolate, chopped into small pieces
350ml/12fl oz/1½ cups double cream
30ml/2 tbsp rum or strawberry-flavoured liqueur

1 Preheat oven to 180°C/350°F/Gas 4. Grease and flour two 23 x 5 cm/9 x 2 in cake tins. Line the base of the tins with non-stick baking paper. Melt the chocolate and cream in a double boiler over a low heat, stirring until smooth. Stir in the milk and rum or vanilla essence, and set aside to cool.

2 In a large mixing bowl, beat the butter and sugar with a hand-held electric mixer for 3–5 minutes, until light and creamy, scraping the sides of the bowl occasionally. Add the eggs one at a time, beating well after each addition. In a small bowl, stir together the flour, baking powder and salt. Alternately add flour and melted chocolate to the egg mixture in batches, until just blended. Pour the mixture into the tins and spread evenly.

3 Bake for 20–25 minutes, until a skewer inserted in the cake comes out clean. Cool in the tin for 10 minutes, then turn cakes out on to a wire rack, peel off the paper and cool completely.

5 Assemble the cake. With a serrated knife, slice both cake layers in half, making four layers. Place one layer on the plate and spread one third of the mousse on top. Arrange one third of the sliced strawberries over the mousse. Place the second layer on top and spread with another third of the mousse. Arrange another third of the sliced strawberries over the mousse. Place the third layer on top and spread with the remaining mousse. Cover with the remaining sliced strawberries. Top with the last cake layer.

6 Whip the cream with the rum or liqueur until firm peaks form. Spread about half the whipped cream over the top and the sides of the cake. Spoon the remaining cream into a decorating bag fitted with a medium star tip and pipe scrolls on top of the cake. Decorate with the remaining sliced strawberries, pressing half of them into the cream on the side of the cake and arranging the rest on top.

CHOCOLATE GINGER CRUNCH CAKE

SERVES 6

150g / 5oz plain chocolate, chopped into small pieces
50g / 2oz / ¼ cup unsalted butter
115g / 4oz ginger nut biscuits
4 pieces of preserved stem ginger
30ml / 2 tbsp stem ginger syrup
45ml / 3 tbsp desiccated coconut

TO DECORATE

25g / 1oz milk chocolate, chopped into small pieces
pieces of crystallized ginger

1 Grease a 15 cm / 6 in flan ring and place it on a sheet of non-stick baking paper. Melt the plain chocolate with the butter in a heatproof bowl over barely simmering water. Remove from the heat and set aside.

2 Crush the biscuits into small pieces. Tip them into a bowl.

3 Chop the stem ginger fairly finely and mix with the crushed ginger nut biscuits.

4 Stir the biscuit mixture, ginger syrup and coconut into the melted chocolate and butter, mixing well until evenly combined.

5 Tip the mixture into the prepared flan ring and press down firmly and evenly. Chill in the fridge until set.

6 Remove the flan ring and slide the cake on to a plate. Melt the milk chocolate, drizzle it over the top and decorate with the pieces of crystallized ginger.

FROSTED CHOCOLATE FUDGE CAKE

SERVES 6–8

115g / 4oz plain chocolate, chopped into small pieces
175g / 6oz / ¾ cup unsalted butter or margarine, softened
200g / 7oz / generous 1 cup light muscovado sugar
5ml / 1 tsp vanilla essence
3 eggs, beaten
150ml / ¼ pint / ⅔ cup Greek-style yogurt
150g / 5oz / 1¼ cups self-raising flour
icing sugar and chocolate curls, to decorate

FOR THE FROSTING

115g / 4 oz plain dark chocolate, chopped into small pieces
50g / 2oz / ¼ cup unsalted butter
350g / 12oz / 2¼ cups icing sugar
90ml / 6 tbsp Greek-style yogurt

1 Preheat oven to 190°C / 375°F / Gas 5. Lightly grease two 20 cm / 8 in round sandwich cake tins and line the base of each with non-stick baking paper. Melt the chocolate.

2 In a mixing bowl, cream the butter or margarine with the sugar until light and fluffy. Beat in the vanilla essence, then gradually add the beaten eggs, beating well after each addition.

3 Stir in the melted plain chocolate and yogurt evenly. Fold in the flour with a metal spoon.

4 Divide the mixture between the prepared tins. Bake for 25–30 minutes or until the cakes are firm to the touch. Turn out and cool on a wire rack.

5 Make the frosting. Melt the chocolate and butter in a saucepan over a low heat. Remove from the heat and stir in the icing sugar and yogurt. Mix with a rubber spatula until smooth, then beat until the frosting begins to cool and thicken slightly. Use about a third of the mixture to sandwich the cakes together.

6 Working quickly, spread the remainder over the top and sides. Sprinkle with icing sugar and decorate with chocolate curls.

RICH CHOCOLATE LEAF GATEAU

SERVES 8

*75g / 3oz plain dark chocolate, broken
into squares
150ml / ¼ pint / ⅔ cup milk
175g / 6oz / ¾ cup unsalted butter, softened
250g / 9oz / 1⅓ cups light muscovado sugar
3 eggs
250g / 9oz / 2¼ cups plain flour
10ml / 2 tsp baking powder
75ml / 5 tbsp single cream*

FOR THE FILLING AND TOPPING

*60ml / 4 tbsp raspberry conserve
1 quantity Chocolate Ganache
dark and white chocolate leaves*

1 Preheat oven to 190°C/375°F/Gas 5.
Grease and base-line two 22 cm / 8½ in
sandwich cake tins. Melt the chocolate
with the milk over a low heat and allow
to cool slightly.

2 Cream the butter with the light
muscovado sugar in a mixing bowl until
light and fluffy. Add the eggs, one at a
time, beating well after each addition.
3 Sift the flour and baking powder over
the mixture and fold in gently but
thoroughly. Stir in the chocolate mixture
and the cream, mixing until smooth.
Divide between the prepared tins and
level the tops.

4 Bake the cakes for 30–35 minutes or
until they are well risen and firm to the
touch. Cool in the tins for a few minutes,
then turn out on to wire racks.

5 Sandwich the cake layers together with
the raspberry conserve. Spread the
chocolate ganache over the cake and
swirl with a knife. Place the cake on a
serving plate, then decorate with the
chocolate leaves.

CHOCOLATE ALMOND MOUSSE CAKE

SERVES 8

50g / 2oz plain dark chocolate, broken
into squares
200g / 7oz marzipan, grated or chopped
200ml / 7fl oz / scant 1 cup milk
115g / 4oz / 1 cup self-raising flour
2 eggs, separated
75g / 3oz / ⅓ cup light muscovado
sugar

FOR THE MOUSSE FILLING

115g / 4oz plain chocolate, chopped into
small pieces
50g / 2oz / ¼ cup unsalted butter
2 eggs, separated
30ml / 2 tbsp Amaretto di Saronno
liqueur

FOR THE TOPPING

1 quantity Chocolate Ganache
toasted flaked almonds, to decorate

__1__ Preheat oven to 190°C / 375°F / Gas 5.
Grease a deep 17 cm / 6½ in square cake
tin and line with non-stick baking paper.
Combine the chocolate, marzipan and
milk in a saucepan and heat gently
without boiling, stirring until smooth.
__2__ Sift the flour into a bowl and add the
chocolate mixture and egg yolks, beating
until evenly mixed.

__3__ Whisk the egg whites in a clean, grease-
free bowl until stiff enough to hold firm
peaks. Whisk in the sugar gradually. Stir
about 15ml / 1 tbsp of the whites into the
chocolate mixture to lighten it, then fold
in the rest.
__4__ Spoon the mixture into the tin,
spreading it evenly. Bake for 45–50
minutes, until well risen, firm and
springy to the touch. Leave to cool on a
wire rack.
__5__ Make the mousse filling. Melt the
chocolate with the butter in a small
saucepan over a low heat, then remove
from the heat and beat in the egg yolks
and Amaretto. Whisk the egg whites in a
clean, grease-free bowl until stiff, then
fold into the chocolate mixture.

__6__ Slice the cold cake in half across the
middle to make two even layers. Return
one half to the clean cake tin and pour
over the chocolate mousse. Top with the
second layer of cake and press down
lightly. Chill until set.

__7__ Turn the cake out on to a serving plate.
Allow the chocolate ganache to soften to
room temperature, then beat it to a soft,
spreading consistency. Spread the
chocolate ganache over the top and sides
of the cake, then press toasted flaked
almonds over the sides. Serve chilled.

DEATH BY CHOCOLATE

SERVES 16–20

225g/8oz plain dark chocolate, chopped into
small pieces
115g/4 oz/½ cup unsalted butter
150ml/¼ pint/⅔ cup milk
225g/8oz/1¼ cups light muscovado sugar
10ml/2 tsp vanilla essence
2 eggs, separated
150ml/¼ pint/⅔ cup soured cream
225g/8oz/2 cups self-raising flour
5ml/1 tsp baking powder

FOR THE FILLING AND TOPPING

60ml/4 tbsp seedless raspberry jam
60ml/4 tbsp brandy
400g/14oz plain dark chocolate, chopped
into small pieces
200g/7oz/scant 1 cup unsalted butter
1 quantity Chocolate Ganache
plain chocolate curls, to decorate

1 Preheat oven to 180°C/350°F/Gas 4.
Grease and base-line a deep 23 cm/9 in
springform cake tin. Place the chocolate,
butter and milk in a saucepan. Stir over a
low heat until smooth. Remove from the
heat, beat in the sugar and vanilla essence,
then leave to cool slightly.
2 Beat the egg yolks and cream in a bowl,
then beat into the chocolate mixture. Sift
the flour and baking powder over the
surface and fold in.
3 Whisk the egg whites in a grease-free
bowl until stiff. Stir about 30ml/2 tbsp of
the whites into the chocolate cake
mixture, to lighten it. Fold in the
remaining whites, using a metal spoon.
4 Scrape the mixture into the prepared
tin and bake for about 45–55 minutes or
until firm to the touch. Cool in the tin for
15 minutes, then invert the cake on to a
wire rack, remove the tin and set aside
until completely cold.

5 Slice the cold cake across the middle to
make three even layers. Make the filling.
In a small saucepan, warm the raspberry
jam with 15ml/1 tbsp of the brandy, then
brush over two of the layers. Leave to set.
6 Place the remaining brandy in a
saucepan with the chocolate and butter.
Heat gently, stirring, until the mixture is
smooth. Pour into a bowl and cool until it
begins to thicken.

7 Spread the bottom layer of the cake
with half the chocolate filling, taking care
not to disturb the jam. Top with a second
layer, jam side up, and spread with the
remaining filling. Top with the final layer
and press lightly.

8 Leave to set, then spread the top and
sides of the cake with the chocolate
ganache. Decorate with chocolate curls
and then dust the top of the cake with
cocoa powder.

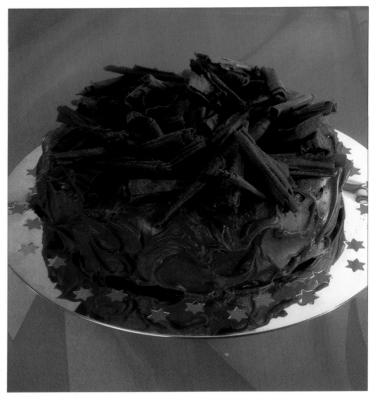

VEGAN CHOCOLATE GATEAU

SERVES 8–10

275g / 10oz / 2½ cups self-raising
wholemeal flour
50g / 2oz / ½ cup cocoa powder
45ml / 3 tbsp baking powder
225g / 8oz / 1¼ cups caster sugar
few drops of vanilla essence
135ml / 9 tbsp sunflower oil
350ml / 12fl oz / 1½ cups water
sifted cocoa powder, for sprinkling
25g / 1oz / ¼ cup chopped nuts, to decorate
FOR THE CHOCOLATE FUDGE
50g / 2oz / ¼ cup vegan (soya) margarine
45ml / 3 tbsp water
250g / 9oz / 2 cups icing sugar
30ml / 2 tbsp cocoa powder
15–30ml / 1–2 tbsp hot water

1 Preheat oven to 160°C / 325°F / Gas 3.
Grease a deep 20 cm / 8 in round cake tin,
line with non-stick baking paper and
grease the paper lightly with a little
sunflower oil.

2 Sift the flour, cocoa and baking powder
into a large mixing bowl. Add the caster
sugar and vanilla essence, then gradually
beat in the sunflower oil. Add the water
in the same way, beating constantly to
produce a smooth mixture with the
consistency of a thick batter.

3 Pour the cake mixture into the
prepared tin and smooth the surface with
the back of a spoon.

4 Bake the cake for about 45 minutes or
until a cake tester or fine metal skewer
inserted in the centre comes out clean.
Remove from the oven but leave in the tin
for about 5 minutes, before turning out
on to a wire rack. Peel off the lining
paper and leave to cool. Cut the cake in
half to make two equal layers.

5 Make the chocolate fudge. Place the
margarine and water in a pan and heat
gently until the margarine has melted.
Remove from the heat and add the sifted
icing sugar and cocoa powder, beating
until shiny, adding more hot water if
needed. Pour into a bowl and cool until
firm enough to spread and pipe.

6 Place the bottom layer of the cake on a
serving plate and spread over two-thirds
of the chocolate fudge mixture. Top with
the other layer. Fit a piping bag with a
star nozzle, fill with the remaining
chocolate fudge and pipe stars over the
cake. Sprinkle with cocoa powder and
decorate with the chopped nuts.

BLACK FOREST GATEAU

4 Prick each layer all over with a skewer or fork, then sprinkle with Kirsch. Using a hand-held electric mixer, whip the cream in a bowl until it starts to thicken, then gradually beat in the icing sugar and vanilla essence until the mixture begins to hold its shape.

5 To assemble, spread one cake layer with a thick layer of flavoured cream and top with about half the cherries. Spread a second cake layer with cream, top with the remaining cherries, then place it on top of the first layer. Top with the final cake layer.

6 Spread the remaining cream all over the cake. Dust a plate with icing sugar, and position the cake carefully in the centre. Press grated chocolate over the sides and decorate the cake with the chocolate curls and fresh or drained cherries.

SERVES 8–10

6 eggs

200g/7oz/scant 1 cup caster sugar

5ml/1 tsp vanilla essence

50g/2oz/½ cup plain flour

50g/2oz/½ cup cocoa powder

115g/4oz/½ cup unsalted butter, melted

FOR THE FILLING AND TOPPING

60ml/4 tbsp Kirsch

600ml/1 pint/2½ cups double cream

30ml/2 tbsp icing sugar

2.5ml/½ tsp vanilla essence

675g/1½lb jar stoned morello cherries, well drained

TO DECORATE

icing sugar, for dusting

grated chocolate

Chocolate Curls

fresh or drained canned morello cherries

1 Preheat oven to 180°C/350°F/Gas 4. Grease three 19 cm/7½ in sandwich cake tins. Line the bottom of each with non-stick baking paper. Combine the eggs with the sugar and vanilla essence in a bowl and beat with a hand-held electric mixer until pale and very thick.

2 Sift the flour and cocoa powder over the mixture and fold in lightly and evenly with a metal spoon. Gently stir in the melted butter.

3 Divide the mixture among the prepared cake tins, smoothing them level. Bake for 15–18 minutes, until the cakes have risen and are springy to the touch. Leave them to cool in the tins for about 5 minutes, then turn out on to wire racks and leave to cool completely. Remove the lining paper from each cake layer.

WHITE CHOCOLATE CAPPUCCINO GATEAU

SERVES 8

4 eggs
115g/4oz/½ cup caster sugar
15ml/1 tbsp strong black coffee
2.5ml/½ tsp vanilla essence
115g/4oz/1 cup plain flour
75g/3oz white chocolate, coarsely grated

FOR THE FILLING
120ml/4fl oz/½ cup double cream or whipping cream
15ml/1 tbsp coffee liqueur

FOR THE FROSTING AND TOPPING
15ml/1 tbsp coffee liqueur
1 quantity White Chocolate Frosting
white chocolate curls
cocoa powder or ground cinnamon, for dusting

1 Preheat oven to 180°C/350°F/Gas 4. Grease two 18 cm/7 in round sandwich cake tins and line the base of each with non-stick baking paper.

2 Combine the eggs, caster sugar, coffee and vanilla essence in a large heatproof bowl. Place over a saucepan of hot water and whisk until pale and thick.

3 Sift half the flour over the mixture; fold in gently and evenly. Fold in the remaining flour with the grated white chocolate.

4 Divide the mixture between the prepared tins and smooth level. Bake for 20–25 minutes, until firm and golden brown, then turn out on wire racks and leave to cool completely.

5 Make the filling. Whip the cream with the coffee liqueur in a bowl until it holds its shape. Spread over one of the cakes, then place the second layer on top.

6 Stir the coffee liqueur into the frosting. Spread over the top and sides of the cake, swirling with a palette knife. Top with curls of white chocolate and dust with cocoa or cinnamon. Transfer the cake to a serving plate and set aside until the frosting has set. Serve the gâteau on the day it was made, if possible.

CHOCOLATE BRANDY SNAP GATEAU

SERVES 8

225g / 8oz plain dark chocolate, chopped
225g / 8oz / 1 cup unsalted butter, softened
200g / 7oz / generous 1 cup dark
muscovado sugar
6 eggs, separated
5ml / 1 tsp vanilla essence
150g / 5oz / 1¼ cups ground hazelnuts
60ml / 4 tbsp fresh white breadcrumbs
finely grated rind of 1 large orange
1 quantity Chocolate Ganache, for filling
and frosting
icing sugar, for dusting

FOR THE BRANDY SNAPS

50g / 2oz / ¼ cup unsalted butter
50g / 2oz / ¼ cup caster sugar
75g / 3oz / ⅓ cup golden syrup
50g / 2oz / ½ cup plain flour
5ml / 1 tsp brandy

1 Preheat oven to 180°C / 350°F / Gas 4. Grease two 20 cm / 8 in sandwich cake tins and line the base of each with non-stick baking paper. Melt the chocolate and set aside to cool slightly.

2 Cream the butter with the sugar in a mixing bowl until pale and fluffy. Beat in the egg yolks and vanilla essence. Add the chocolate and mix thoroughly.

3 In a clean, grease-free bowl, whisk the egg whites to soft peaks, then fold them into the chocolate mixture with the ground hazelnuts, breadcrumbs and orange rind.

4 Divide the cake mixture between the prepared tins and smooth the tops. Bake for 25–30 minutes or until well risen and firm. Turn out on to wire racks. Leave the oven on.

5 Make the brandy snaps. Line two baking sheets with non-stick baking paper. Melt the butter, sugar and syrup together.

6 Stir the butter mixture until smooth. Remove from the heat and stir in the flour and brandy.

7 Place small spoonfuls of the mixture well apart on the baking sheets and bake for 8–10 minutes, until golden. Cool for a few seconds until firm enough to lift on to a wire rack.

8 Immediately pinch the edges of each brandy snap to create a frilled effect. If the biscuits become too firm, soften them briefly in the oven.

9 Sandwich the cake layers together with half the chocolate ganache, transfer to a plate and spread the remaining ganache on the top. Arrange the brandy snaps over the gâteau and dust with icing sugar.

COOK'S TIP
To save time, you could use ready-made brandy snaps. Simply warm them for a few minutes in the oven until they are pliable enough to shape. Or use as they are, filling them with cream, and arranging them so that they fan out from the centre of the gâteau.

MERINGUE GATEAU WITH CHOCOLATE MASCARPONE

SERVES ABOUT 10

4 egg whites
pinch of salt
175g/6oz/¾ cup caster sugar
5ml/1 tsp ground cinnamon
75g/3oz plain dark chocolate, grated
icing sugar and rose petals, to decorate

FOR THE FILLING

115g/4oz plain chocolate, chopped into small pieces
5ml/1 tsp vanilla essence or rosewater
115g/4oz/½ cup mascarpone cheese

1 Preheat oven to 150°C/300°F/Gas 2. Line two large baking sheets with non-stick baking paper. Whisk the egg whites with the salt in a clean, grease-free bowl until they form stiff peaks.

2 Gradually whisk in half the sugar, then add the rest and whisk until the meringue is very stiff and glossy. Add the cinnamon and chocolate and whisk lightly to mix.

3 Draw a 20 cm/8 in circle on the lining paper on one of the baking sheets, replace it upside down and spread the marked circle evenly with about half the meringue. Spoon the remaining meringue in 28–30 small neat heaps on both baking sheets. Bake for 1½ hours, until crisp.

4 Make the filling. Melt the chocolate in a heatproof bowl over hot water. Cool slightly, then add the vanilla essence or rosewater and cheese. Cool the mixture until it holds it shape.

5 Spoon the chocolate mixture into a large piping bag and sandwich the meringues together in pairs, reserving a small amount of filling for assembling the gâteau.

6 Arrange the filled meringues on a serving platter, piling them up in a pyramid. Keep them in position with a few well-placed dabs of the reserved filling. Dust the pyramid with icing sugar, sprinkle with the rose petals and serve at once, while the meringues are crisp.

CARIBBEAN CHOCOLATE RING WITH RUM SYRUP

SERVES 8–10

115g/4oz/1/2 cup unsalted butter
115g/4oz/3/4 cup light muscovado sugar
2 eggs, beaten
2 ripe bananas, mashed
30ml/2 tbsp desiccated coconut
30ml/2 tbsp soured cream
115g/4oz/1 cup self-raising flour
45ml/3 tbsp cocoa powder
2.5ml/1/2 tsp bicarbonate of soda

FOR THE SYRUP

115g/4oz/1/2 cup caster sugar
30ml/2 tbsp dark rum
50g/2oz plain dark chocolate, chopped

TO DECORATE

mixture of tropical fruits, such as mango,
pawpaw, starfruit and cape gooseberries
chocolate shapes or curls

1 Preheat oven to 180°C/350°F/Gas 4. Grease a 1.5 litre/2½ pint/6¼ cup ring tin with butter.

2 Cream the butter and sugar in a bowl until light and fluffy. Add the eggs gradually, beating well, then mix in the bananas, coconut and soured cream.

3 Sift the flour, cocoa and bicarbonate of soda over the mixture and fold in thoroughly and evenly.

4 Tip into the prepared tin and spread evenly. Bake for 45–50 minutes, until firm to the touch. Cool for 10 minutes in the tin, then turn out to finish cooling on a wire rack.

5 For the syrup, place the sugar in a small pan. Add 60ml/4 tbsp water and heat gently, stirring occasionally until dissolved. Bring to the boil and boil rapidly, without stirring, for 2 minutes. Remove from the heat.

6 Add the rum and chocolate to the syrup and stir until the mixture is melted and smooth, then spoon evenly over the top and sides of the cake.

7 Decorate the ring with tropical fruits and chocolate shapes or curls.

SPECIAL OCCASION AND NOVELTY CAKES

STRAWBERRY CHOCOLATE VALENTINE GATEAU

SERVES 8

175g / 6oz / 1½ cups self-raising flour
10ml / 2 tsp baking powder
75ml / 5 tbsp cocoa powder
115g / 4oz / ½ cup caster sugar
2 eggs, beaten
15ml / 1 tbsp black treacle
150ml / ¼ pint / ⅔ cup sunflower oil
150ml / ¼ pint / ⅔ cup milk

FOR THE FILLING

45ml / 3 tbsp strawberry jam
150ml / ¼ pint / ⅔ cup double cream or
whipping cream
115g / 4oz strawberries, sliced

TO DECORATE

1 quantity Chocolate Fondant
chocolate hearts
icing sugar, for dusting

1 Preheat oven to 160°C/325°F/Gas 3. Grease a deep 20 cm/8 in heart-shaped cake tin and line the base with non-stick baking paper. Sift the self-raising flour, baking powder and cocoa powder into a large mixing bowl. Stir in the sugar, then make a well in the centre of the dry ingredients.

2 Add the eggs, treacle, oil and milk to the well. Mix with a spoon to incorporate the dry ingredients, then beat with a hand-held electric mixer until the mixture is smooth and creamy.

3 Spoon the mixture into the prepared cake tin and spread evenly. Bake for about 45 minutes, until well risen and firm to the touch. Cool in the tin for a few minutes, then turn out on to a wire rack to cool completely.

4 Using a sharp knife, slice the cake neatly into two layers. Place the bottom layer on a board or plate. Spread with the strawberry jam.

5 Whip the cream in a bowl. Stir in the strawberries, then spread over the jam. Top with the remaining cake layer.

6 Roll out the chocolate fondant and cover the cake. Decorate with chocolate hearts and dust with icing sugar.

COOK'S TIP

If you do not have a heart-shaped cake tin, consider hiring one from a kitchen shop. All sorts of sizes are available, often for a modest fee.

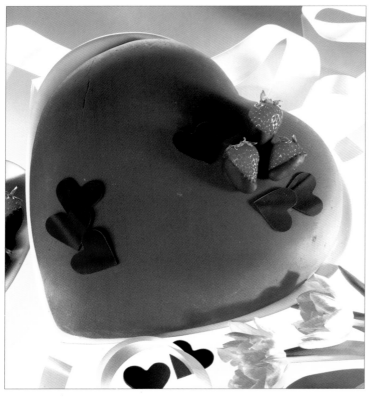

DOUBLE HEART ENGAGEMENT CAKE

SERVES 20

*double quantity One-Mix Chocolate
Sponge mixture
double quantity Chocolate Buttercream
icing sugar, for sifting
chocolate curls and fresh raspberries,
to decorate*

VARIATIONS

Use plain buttercream, tinted to a
delicate shade of rose. Decorate with
strawberries, half-dipped in melted
chocolate.
Cover the cakes with Chocolate
Ganache and drizzle melted
chocolate over the top. Arrange
chocolate-dipped fruit on top.
Cover both the cakes with Chocolate
Fondant and top with pale apricot or
cream sugar roses and chocolate
leaves. Trim each cake with a narrow
apricot or cream ribbon.

1 Preheat oven to 160°C/325°F/Gas 3.
Grease and base-line with greaseproof
paper two 20 cm/8 in heart-shaped cake
tins. Divide the one-mix chocolate
sponge cake mixture evenly between the
tins and smooth the surfaces. Bake for 30
minutes. Turn on to a wire rack, peel off
the lining paper and leave to cool.

2 Cut each cake in half horizontally. Use
about one-third of the buttercream to fill
both cakes, then sandwich them together
to make two. Cover the tops of the cakes
with buttercream.

3 Arrange on a cake board. Use the
remaining icing to coat the sides of the
cakes. Make sure it is thickly covered.

4 Generously cover the tops and sides
of both the cakes with the chocolate
curls, beginning from the top of the heart
and arranging them as shown, and
pressing them gently into the
buttercream as you go.
5 Dust a little icing sugar over the top of
each cake and decorate with raspberries.
Chill until ready to serve.

WHITE CHOCOLATE CELEBRATION CAKE

SERVES 40–50

900g / 2lb / 8 cups plain flour
2.5ml / ½ tsp salt
20ml / 4 tsp bicarbonate of soda
450g / 1lb white chocolate, chopped
475ml / 16fl oz / 2 cups whipping cream
450g / 1lb / 2 cups unsalted butter, softened
900g / 2lb / 4 cups caster sugar
12 eggs
20ml / 4 tsp lemon essence
grated rind of 2 lemons
335ml / 11fl oz / 1⅓ cups buttermilk
lemon curd, for filling
chocolate leaves, to decorate

FOR THE LEMON SYRUP

200g / 7oz / scant 1 cup granulated sugar
250ml / 8fl oz / 1 cup water
60ml / 4 tbsp lemon juice

FOR THE BUTTERCREAM

675g / 1½lb white chocolate chopped
1kg / 2¼lb cream cheese, softened
500g / 1¼lb / 2½ cups unsalted butter, at room temperature
60ml / 4 tbsp lemon juice
5ml / 1 tsp lemon essence

1 Divide all the ingredients into two equal batches, so that the quantities are more manageable. Use each batch to make one cake. Preheat oven to 180°C / 350°F / Gas 4. Grease a 30 cm / 12 in round cake tin. Base-line with non-stick baking paper. Sift the flour, salt and bicarbonate of soda into a bowl and set aside. Melt the chocolate and cream in a saucepan over a medium heat, stirring until smooth. Set aside to cool to room temperature.

VARIATION

For a summer celebration, decorate the cake with raspberries and white chocolate petals. To make the petals, you will need about 20 x 7.5 cm / 3 in foil squares. Spread melted white chocolate thinly over each piece of foil, so that it resembles a rose petal. Before the chocolate sets, bend the foil up to emphasize the petal shape. When set, peel away the foil.

2 Beat the butter until creamy, then add the sugar and beat for 2–3 minutes. Beat in the eggs, then slowly beat in the melted chocolate, lemon essence and rind. Gradually add the flour mixture, alternately with the buttermilk, to make a smooth pouring mixture. Pour into the tin and bake for 1 hour or until a skewer inserted in the cake comes out clean.

3 Cool in the tin for 10 minutes, then invert the cake on a wire rack and cool completely. Wrap in clear film until ready to assemble. Using the second batch of ingredients, make another cake in the same way.

4 Make the lemon syrup. In a small saucepan, combine the sugar and water. Over a medium heat, bring to the boil, stirring until the sugar dissolves. Remove from the heat, stir in the lemon juice and cool completely. Store in an airtight container until required.

5 Make the buttercream. Melt the chocolate. Cool slightly. Beat the cream cheese in a bowl until smooth. Gradually beat in the cooled white chocolate, then the butter, lemon juice and essence. Chill.

6 Split each cake in half. Spoon syrup over each layer, let it soak in, then repeat. Spread the bottom half of each cake with lemon curd and replace the tops.

7 Gently beat the buttercream in a bowl until creamy. Spread a quarter over the top of one of the filled cakes. Place the second filled cake on top. Spread a small amount of softened butter over the top and sides of the cake to create a smooth, crumb-free surface. Chill for 15 minutes, so that the buttercream sets a little.

8 Place the cake on a serving plate. Set aside a quarter of the remaining buttercream for piping, then spread the rest evenly over the top and sides of the filled cake.

9 Spoon the reserved buttercream into a large icing bag fitted with a small star tip. Pipe a shell pattern around the rim of the cake. Decorate with chocolate leaves, made with dark or white chocolate (or a mixture) and fresh flowers.

CHOCOLATE BOX WITH CARAMEL MOUSSE AND BERRIES

SERVES 8–10

275g/10oz plain chocolate, chopped into
small pieces

FOR THE CARAMEL MOUSSE

4 x 50g/2oz chocolate-coated caramel bars,
coarsely chopped
25ml/1½ tbsp milk or water
350ml/12fl oz/1½ cups double cream
1 egg white

FOR THE CARAMEL SHARDS

115g/4oz/½ cup granulated sugar
60ml/4 tbsp water

FOR THE TOPPING

115g/4oz fine quality white chocolate,
chopped into small pieces
350ml/12fl oz/1½ cups double cream
450g/1lb mixed berries or cut up fruits such
as raspberries, strawberries, blackberries or
sliced nectarine and orange segments

1 Prepare the chocolate box. Turn a 23 cm/9 in square baking tin bottom-side up. Mould a piece of foil around the tin, then turn it right side up and line it with the foil, pressing against the edges to make the foil as smooth as possible.

2 Place the plain chocolate in a heatproof bowl over a saucepan of simmering water. Stir until the chocolate has melted and is smooth. Immediately pour the melted chocolate into the lined tin. Tilt to coat the bottom and sides evenly, keeping the top edges of the sides as straight as possible. As the chocolate coats the sides, tilt the pan again to coat the corners and sides once more. Chill until firm.

3 Place the caramel bars and milk or water in a heatproof bowl. Place over a pan of simmering water and stir until melted. Remove the bowl from the heat and cool for 10 minutes, stirring occasionally.

4 Using a hand-held electric mixer, whip the cream in a bowl until soft peaks form. Stir a spoonful of the whipped cream into the caramel mixture to lighten it, then fold in the remaining cream. In another bowl beat the egg white until just stiff. Fold the egg white into the mousse mixture. Pour into the box. Chill for several hours or overnight, until set.

5 Meanwhile, make the caramel shards. Lightly oil a baking sheet. In a small pan over a low heat, dissolve the sugar in the water, swirling the pan gently. Increase the heat and boil the mixture for 4–5 minutes, until the sugar begins to turn a pale golden colour. Protecting your hand with an oven glove, immediately pour the mixture on to the oiled sheet. Tilt the sheet to distribute the caramel in an even layer. (*Do not touch – caramel is dangerously hot.*) Cool completely, then using a metal palette knife, lift the caramel off the baking sheet and break into pieces.

6 Make the topping. Combine the white chocolate and 120ml/4fl oz/½ cup of the cream in a small pan and melt over a low heat until smooth, stirring frequently. Strain into a medium bowl and cool to room temperature, stirring occasionally. In another bowl, beat the remaining cream with a hand-held electric mixer, until firm peaks form. Stir a spoonful of cream into the white chocolate mixture, then gently fold in the remaining whipped cream.

7 Using the foil as a guide, remove the mousse-filled box from the tin and peel the foil carefully from the sides, then the bottom. Slide the box gently on to a serving plate.

8 Spoon the chocolate-cream mixture into a piping bag fitted with a medium star tip. Pipe a decorative design of rosettes or shells over the surface of the set mousse. Decorate the cream-topped box with the mixed berries or cut up fruits and the caramel shards.

PUPPIES IN LOVE

SERVES 8–10

1 chocolate Swiss roll
115g/4oz yellow marzipan
60ml/4 tbsp Chocolate Buttercream
115g/4oz/1⅓ cups desiccated coconut
green, brown, pink and red food colourings
450g/1lb bought sugarpaste
icing sugar, for dusting
60ml/4 tbsp apricot jam, warmed and sieved

1 Cut the Swiss roll in half. Each half will form the body of one of the puppies. To make the faces, cut the marzipan in half and roll each portion into a ball, then into a squat cone shape. Use the buttercream to stick the faces on to the bodies.

2 Place the desiccated coconut in a bowl. Add a few drops of green food colouring and a few drops of water and stir until the coconut is flecked with green and white. Scatter it over a cake board, then position the two puppy shapes on the board.

3 Cut off about 25g/1oz of the sugarpaste and set aside, wrapped in clear film. Colour half the remaining icing brown and half pink. Cut off about 50g/2oz from each colour, wrap in clear film and set aside.

4 Lightly dust the work surface with icing sugar and roll out the larger portions of brown and pink paste into rectangles large enough to wrap each piece of Swiss roll. Cut each portion of paste in half widthways and trim the edges. Cover all four sections with clear film and set aside.

5 Roll out the reserved pieces of brown and white paste, then use a small round cutter to stamp out several circles. Gather up the paste trimmings and set aside, wrapped in clear film. Stick the white circles on to one of the brown rectangles, then the brown circles on to one of the pink rectangles, using a little water. Use a rolling pin to press them in slightly.

6 Use a sharp knife to slash all four paste rectangles along the two short edges. Brush each half of Swiss roll with jam, then lay the brown paste without spots over one body, and the pink paste without spots over the other. Place a little water on the back of each, then put the brown spotty paste over the brown dog and the pink spotty paste over the pink dog.

7 Roll half of the reserved trimmings, pink and brown, in your hands to make the tails. Stick them in place with a little jam. Make a fringe from the brown icing for the brown puppy, and tie a few strands of pink icing together with ribbon to make a fringe for the pink puppy. Stick them in place with a dab of water.

8 Use the remaining pieces of sugarpaste to shape eyes, a nose and a mouth for each puppy. Stick them on to the faces.

PORCUPINE

SERVES 15

1 quantity One-mix Chocolate Sponge Cake
1½ quantity Chocolate Buttercream
5–6 chocolate flake bars
60g / 2oz white marzipan
cream, black, green, red, brown food
colourings
9 cocktail sticks

<u>1</u> Preheat the oven to 180°C/350°F/
Gas 4. Grease and line the bottoms of a
900ml/1½ pint/3¾ cup and a 600ml/
1 pint/2½ cup pudding basin (deep bowl).
Spoon the cake mixture into both basins
(bowls) to two-thirds full. Bake in a
preheated oven allowing 55 mins–1 hour
for the larger basin (bowl) and 35–40
mins for the smaller basin (bowl). Turn
out and allow to cool on a wire rack.

<u>2</u> When they are completely cool, place
both cakes on a surface so the widest ends
are underneath. Take the smaller cake
and, holding a sharp knife at an angle,
slice off a piece from one side, cutting
down towards the middle of the cake.
Then make a corresponding cut on the
other side to make a pointed nose shape
at one end.

<u>3</u> Place the larger cake on the cake board
behind the smaller one. Cut one of the
cut-off slices in half and position either
side, between the larger and smaller cake,
to fill in the side gaps. Place the other
cut-off piece on top to fill in the top gap,
securing all with a little buttercream.

<u>4</u> Spread the remaining buttercream over
the cake. On the pointed face part, make
markings with a cocktail stick.
<u>5</u> Break or cut the flake bars into thin
strips and stick at an angle into the
buttercream over the body of the
porcupine to represent spikes.
<u>6</u> Reserve a small portion of marzipan.
Divide the remainder into three and
colour one portion black, one green and
one cream. Colour a tiny portion of the
reserved, white marzipan brown for the
apple stems.
<u>7</u> With the cream coloured marzipan,
shape the ears and feet, using black and
white make the eyes, and with the rest of
the black shape the nose and the claws for
the feet. With the green marzipan make
the apples, painting on red markings with
a fine paintbrush. Position the stems.
Place everything except the apples in its
proper place on the porcupine cake.
Finally, place the apples on the board by
the front of the porcupine.

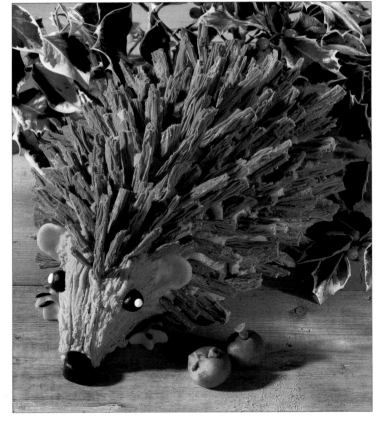

APPLE TREE

SERVES 10–12

1 chocolate Swiss Roll
225g / 8oz / 1 cup Buttercream, tinted with
pale green food colouring
½ quantity Chocolate Buttercream
One-mix Chocolate Sponge Cake, baked in a
450g / 1lb fluted round cake tin
225g / 8oz marzipan
red and green food colouring
florist's tape and florist's wire, for the apples
green-coloured desiccated coconut (see Puppies
in Love, step 2)
tiny fresh flowers, to decorate (optional)

3 Twist the florist's tape around the florist's wire, then cut it into 7.5 cm / 3 in lengths. Press the lengths of wire through most of the apples, bending the ends so the apples cannot fall off when hanging. Press the hanging apples into the tree, reserving the remaining apples.

4 Fill a piping bag with the remaining green buttercream. Pipe leaves all over the tree top. Scatter the green coconut around the base of the tree and pipe a few extra leaves. Add a few tiny fresh flowers for effect, if liked. Remove the wires from the cake before serving.

1 Stand the Swiss roll upright on a cake board, trimming it, if necessary. Anchor it on the board with a dab of the buttercream. Spread with chocolate buttercream, swirling the icing. Using about three-quarters of the green buttercream, thickly cover the round sponge cake. Draw the icing into peaks and swirls. Position the cake on top of the trunk to make the top of the tree.

2 Colour about 25g / 1oz of the marzipan green. Colour the remainder red, then roll it into cherry-size apples. Roll the green marzipan into tiny sausage shapes and shape the stalks and leaves. Use a cocktail stick to make tiny holes in the tops of the apples, then insert a stalk and leaf into each.

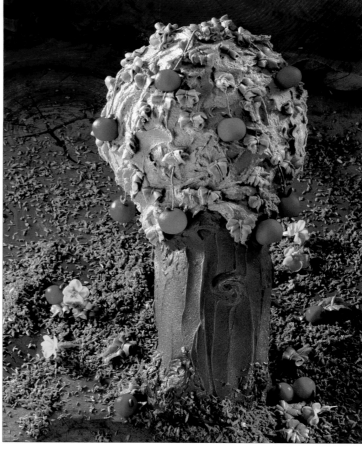

HOT DESSERTS

CHOCOLATE CINNAMON CAKE WITH BANANA SAUCE

6 Fold a dollop of whites into the chocolate mixture to lighten it. Fold in the remaining whites in three batches, alternating with the sifted flour mixture.

7 Pour the mixture into the prepared tin. Bake for 40-50 minutes or until a skewer inserted in the centre comes out clean. Turn the cake out on to a wire rack. Preheat the grill.

8 Make the sauce. Slice the bananas into a shallow, flameproof dish. Stir in the brown sugar and lemon juice. Place under the grill for 8 minutes, stirring occasionally, until caramelized.
9 Mash the banana mixture until almost smooth. Tip into a bowl and stir in the cream and rum, if using. Slice the cake and serve with the sauce.

SERVES 6
25g/1oz plain chocolate, chopped into
small pieces
115g/4oz/½ cup unsalted butter, at room
temperature
15ml/1 tbsp instant coffee powder
5 eggs, separated
225g/8oz/1 cup granulated sugar
115g/4oz/1 cup plain flour
10ml/2 tsp ground cinnamon
FOR THE SAUCE
4 ripe bananas
45ml/3 tbsp soft light brown sugar
15ml/8oz/1 tbsp fresh lemon juice
175ml/6fl oz/¾ cup whipping cream
15ml/1 tbsp rum (optional)

1 Preheat oven to 180°C/350°F/Gas 4. Grease a 20 cm/8 in round cake tin.
2 Combine the chocolate and butter in the top of a double boiler or in a heatproof bowl set over a saucepan of simmering water. Stir until melted. Remove from the heat and stir in the coffee. Set aside.
3 Beat the egg yolks with the granulated sugar until thick and lemon-coloured. Add the chocolate mixture and beat on low speed until just blended.
4 Stir the flour and cinnamon together in a bowl.
5 In another bowl, beat the egg whites until they hold stiff peaks.

RICH CHOCOLATE AND COFFEE PUDDING

SERVES 6

75g / 3oz / ¾ cup plain flour
10ml / 2 tsp baking powder
pinch of salt
50g / 2oz / ¼ cup butter or margarine
25g / 1oz plain chocolate, chopped into
small pieces
115g / 4oz / ½ cup caster sugar
75ml / 3fl oz / 5 tbsp milk
1.5ml / ¼ tsp vanilla essence
whipped cream, for serving

FOR THE TOPPING

30ml / 2 tbsp instant coffee powder
325ml / 11fl oz / generous ½ pint hot water
90g / 3½oz / 7 tbsp soft dark brown sugar
65g / 2½oz / 5 tbsp caster sugar
30ml / 2 tbsp unsweetened cocoa powder

1 Preheat oven to 180°C/350°F/Gas 4. Grease a 23 cm/9 in square non-stick baking tin.

2 Sift the flour, baking powder and salt into a small bowl. Set aside.

3 Melt the butter or margarine, chocolate and caster sugar in a heatproof bowl set over a saucepan of simmering water, or in a double boiler, stirring occasionally. Remove the bowl from the heat.

4 Add the flour mixture and stir well. Stir in the milk and vanilla essence. Mix with a wooden spoon, then pour the mixture into the prepared baking tin.

5 Make the topping. Dissolve the coffee in the water in a bowl. Allow to cool.

6 Mix the brown sugar, caster sugar and cocoa powder in a bowl. Sprinkle the mixture over the pudding mixture.

7 Pour the coffee evenly over the surface. Bake for 40 minutes or until the pudding is risen and set on top. The coffee mixture will have formed a delicious creamy sauce underneath. Serve immediately with whipped cream.

Hot Chocolate Cake

Makes 10–12 slices

200g / 7oz / 1¾ cups self-raising wholemeal
flour
25g / 1oz / ¼ cup cocoa powder
pinch of salt
175g / 6oz / ¾ cup soft margarine
175g / 6oz / 1 cup soft light brown sugar
few drops of vanilla essence
4 eggs
75g / 3oz white chocolate, roughly chopped
chocolate leaves and curls, to decorate

For the White Chocolate Sauce

75g / 3oz white chocolate chopped into
small pieces
150ml / ¼ pint / ⅔ cup single cream
30–45ml / 2–3 tbsp milk

1 Preheat oven to 160°C/325°F/Gas 3. Sift the flour, cocoa and salt into a bowl, then tip in the bran remaining in the sieve. Cream the margarine, sugar and vanilla essence until fluffy, then gently beat in 1 egg.

2 Gradually stir in the remaining eggs, one at a time, alternately with the flour mixture, to make a smooth mixture.
3 Stir in the white chocolate and spoon into a 675–900g/1½–2lb loaf tin or a 18 cm/7 in greased cake tin. Bake for 30–40 minutes or until just firm to the touch and shrinking away from the sides of the tin.
4 To make the sauce, heat the chocolate and cream very gently in a pan until the chocolate is melted. Add the milk and stir until cool. Spoon a little sauce on to each plate and add a slice of cake. Decorate with chocolate leaves and curls. Do this just before you are ready to serve.

STEAMED CHOCOLATE AND FRUIT PUDDINGS WITH CHOCOLATE SYRUP

SERVES 4

115g/4oz/⅔ cup dark muscovado sugar
1 eating apple
75g/3oz/¾ cup cranberries, thawed if frozen
115g/4oz/½ cup soft margarine
2 eggs
115g/4oz/½ cup self-raising flour
45ml/3 tbsp cocoa powder

FOR THE CHOCOLATE SYRUP

115g/4oz plain chocolate, chopped
30ml/2 tbsp clear honey
15ml/½oz/1 tbsp unsalted butter
2.5ml/½ tsp vanilla essence

1 Prepare a steamer or half fill a saucepan with water and bring it to the boil. Grease four individual pudding basins and sprinkle each one with a little of the muscovado sugar to coat well all over.

2 Peel and core the apple. Dice it into a bowl, add the cranberries and mix well. Divide the fruit among the prepared pudding basins.

3 Place the remaining muscovado sugar in a mixing bowl. Add the margarine, eggs, flour and cocoa. Beat until combined and smooth.

4 Spoon the mixture into the basins and cover each with a double thickness of foil. Steam for about 45 minutes, topping up the boiling water as required, until the puddings are well risen and firm.

5 Make the syrup. Mix the chocolate, honey, butter and vanilla essence in a small saucepan. Heat gently, stirring until melted and smooth.

6 Run a knife around the edge of each pudding to loosen it, then turn out on to individual plates. Serve at once, with the chocolate syrup.

CHOCOLATE, DATE AND WALNUT PUDDING

SERVES 4

25g / 1oz / ¼ cup chopped walnuts
25g / 1oz / 2 tbsp chopped dates
2 eggs
5ml / 1 tsp vanilla essence
30ml / 2 tbsp golden caster sugar
45ml / 3 tbsp plain wholemeal flour
15ml / 1 tbsp cocoa powder
30ml / 2 tbsp skimmed milk

1 Preheat oven to 180°C/350°F/Gas 4. Grease and base-line with greaseproof paper a 1.2 litre/2 pint/5 cup pudding basin. Spoon in the walnuts and dates.
2 Combine the egg yolks, vanilla essence and sugar in a heatproof bowl. Place over a pan of hot water.

3 Whisk the egg whites to soft peaks. Whisk the egg yolk mixture until it is thick and pale, then remove the bowl from the heat. Sift the flour and cocoa over the mixture and fold them in with a metal spoon. Stir in the milk, to soften the mixture, then fold in the egg whites.

4 Spoon the mixture over the walnuts and dates in the basin and bake for 40–45 minutes or until the pudding is well risen and firm to the touch. Run a knife around the pudding to loosen it from the basin, and then turn it out on to a plate and serve immediately.

MAGIC CHOCOLATE MUD PUDDING

SERVES 4

50g / 2oz / 4 tbsp butter, plus extra for greasing
90g / 3½oz / scant 1 cup self-raising flour
5ml / 1 tsp ground cinnamon
75ml / 5 tbsp cocoa powder
200g / 7oz / generous 1 cup light muscovado or demerara sugar
475ml / 16fl oz / 2 cups milk
crème fraîche, Greek-style yogurt or vanilla ice cream, to serve

1 Preheat oven to 180°C/350°F/Gas 4. Prepare the dish: use the extra butter to grease a 1.5 litre/2½ pint/6¼ cup ovenproof dish. Place the dish on a baking sheet and set aside.

2 Sift the flour and ground cinnamon into a bowl. Sift in 15ml/1 tbsp of the cocoa and mix well.

3 Place the butter in a saucepan. Add 115g/4oz/½ cup of the sugar and 150ml/¼ pint/⅔ cup of the milk. Heat gently without boiling, stirring from time to time, until the butter has melted and all the sugar has dissolved. Remove the pan from the heat.

4 Stir in the flour mixture, mixing evenly. Pour the mixture into the prepared dish and level the surface.

5 Mix the remaining sugar and cocoa in a bowl, then sprinkle over the pudding mixture.

6 Pour the remaining milk evenly over the pudding.

7 Bake for 45–50 minutes or until the sponge has risen to the top and is firm to the touch. Serve hot, with the crème fraîche, yogurt or ice cream.

Chocolate Chip and Banana Pudding

Serves 4

200g/7oz/1¼ cups self-raising flour
75g/3oz/6 tbsp unsalted butter or margarine
2 ripe bananas
75g/3oz/6 tbsp caster sugar
60ml/4 tbsp milk
1 egg, beaten
60ml/4 tbsp plain chocolate chips or chopped chocolate
Glossy Chocolate Sauce, to serve

1 Prepare a steamer or half fill a saucepan with water and bring it to the boil. Grease a 1 litre/1¼ pint/4 cup pudding basin. Sift the flour into a bowl and rub in the unsalted butter or margarine until the mixture resembles coarse breadcrumbs.

2 Mash the bananas in a bowl. Stir them into the flour and butter mixture, then add the caster sugar and mix well.
3 Whisk the milk with the egg in a jug or small bowl, then beat into the pudding mixture. Stir in the chocolate chips or chopped chocolate.

4 Spoon the mixture into the prepared basin, cover closely with a double thickness of foil, and steam for 2 hours, topping up the water as required.
5 Run a knife around the top of the pudding to loosen it, then turn it out on to a serving dish. Serve hot, with the sauce.

DARK CHOCOLATE RAVIOLI WITH WHITE CHOCOLATE AND CREAM CHEESE FILLING

SERVES 4

175g/6oz/1½ cups plain flour
25g/1oz/¼ cup cocoa powder
salt
30ml/2 tbsp icing sugar
2 large eggs, beaten
15ml/1tbsp olive oil
single cream and grated chocolate, to serve

FOR THE FILLING

175g/6oz white chocolate, chopped
350g/12oz/3 cups cream cheese
1 egg, plus 1 beaten egg to seal

1 Make the pasta. Sift the flour with the cocoa, salt and icing sugar on to a work surface. Make a well in the centre and pour the eggs and oil in. Mix together with your fingers. Knead until smooth. Alternatively, make the dough in a food processor, then knead by hand. Cover and rest for at least 30 minutes.

2 To make the filling, melt the white chocolate in a heatproof bowl placed over a pan of simmering water. Cool slightly. Beat the cream cheese in a bowl, then beat in the chocolate and eggs. Spoon into a piping bag fitted with a plain nozzle.

3 Cut the dough in half and wrap one portion in clear film. Roll the pasta out thinly to a rectangle on a lightly floured surface, or use a pasta machine. Cover with a clean damp dish towel and repeat with the remaining pasta.

4 Pipe small mounds (about 5ml/1 tsp) of filling in even rows, spacing them at 4 cm/1½ in intervals across one piece of the dough. Using a pastry brush, brush the spaces of dough between the mounds with beaten egg.

5 Using a rolling pin, lift the remaining sheet of pasta over the dough with the filling. Press down firmly between the pockets of filling, pushing out any trapped air. Cut the filled chocolate pasta into rounds with a serrated ravioli cutter or sharp knife. Transfer to a floured dish towel. Leave for 1 hour to dry out, ready for cooking.

6 Bring a frying pan of water to the boil and add the ravioli a few at a time, stirring to prevent them sticking together. (Adding a few drops of a bland oil to the water will help, too.) Simmer gently for 3–5 minutes, remove with a perforated spoon and serve with a generous splash of single cream and grated chocolate.

HOT MOCHA RUM SOUFFLES

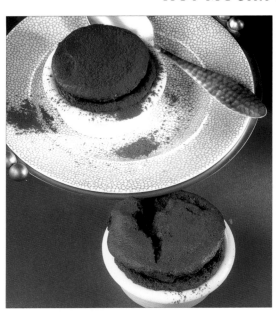

SERVES 6

25g/1oz/2 tbsp unsalted butter, melted
65g/2½ oz/generous ½ cup cocoa powder
75g/3oz/6 tbsp caster sugar
60ml/4 tbsp strong black coffee
30ml/2 tbsp dark rum
6 egg whites
icing sugar, for dusting

1 Preheat oven to 190°C/375°F/Gas 5. Grease six 250ml/
8fl oz/1 cup soufflé dishes with melted butter.
2 Mix 15ml/1 tbsp of the cocoa powder with 15ml/1 tbsp of
the caster sugar in a bowl. Tip the mixture into each of the
dishes in turn, rotating them so that they are evenly coated.
3 Mix the remaining cocoa powder with the coffee and rum in a
medium bowl.
4 Whisk the egg whites in a clean, grease-free bowl until they
form firm peaks. Whisk in the remaining caster sugar. Stir a
generous spoonful of the whites into the cocoa mixture to
lighten it, then fold in the remaining whites.
5 Spoon the mixture into the prepared dishes, smoothing the
tops. Place on the hot baking sheet, and bake for 12–15 minutes
or until well risen. Serve immediately, dusted with icing sugar.

EASY CHOCOLATE AND ORANGE SOUFFLES

SERVES 4

600ml/1 pint/2½ cups milk
50g/2oz/generous ¼ cup semolina
50g/2oz/⅓ cup soft light brown sugar
grated rind of 1 orange
90ml/6 tbsp fresh orange juice
3 eggs, separated
65g/2½ oz plain chocolate, grated
icing sugar, for sprinkling
single cream, to serve

1 Preheat oven to 200°C/400°F/Gas 6. Butter a shallow
1.75 litre/3 pint/7½ cup ovenproof dish. Place a baking sheet
in the oven to heat up.
2 Pour the milk into a heavy-based saucepan, sprinkle over the
semolina and brown sugar, then heat, stirring the mixture all the
time, until boiling and thickened. Remove the pan from the
heat. Cool slightly, then beat in the orange rind and juice, egg
yolks and all but 15ml/1 tbsp of the grated chocolate.
3 In a clean, grease-free bowl, whisk the egg whites until stiff
but not dry, then lightly fold into the semolina mixture in three
batches. Spoon the mixture into the dish. Place the dish on the
baking sheet and bake for about 30 minutes, until just set in the
centre and risen. Sprinkle the top with the reserved chocolate
and dust with the icing sugar. Serve with cream.

CHOCOLATE AMARETTI PEACHES

SERVES 4

115g/4oz amaretti biscuits, crushed
50g/2oz plain chocolate, chopped
grated rind of ½ orange
15ml/1 tbsp clear honey
1.5ml/¼ tsp ground cinnamon
1 egg white, lightly beaten
4 firm ripe peaches
150ml/¼ pint/⅔ cup white wine
15ml/1 tbsp caster sugar
whipped cream, to serve

1 Preheat oven to 190°C/375°F/Gas 5. Mix together the crushed amaretti biscuits, chocolate, orange rind, honey and cinnamon in a bowl. Add the beaten egg white and mix to bind the mixture.

2 Halve and stone the peaches and fill the cavities with the chocolate mixture, mounding it up slightly.

3 Arrange the stuffed peaches in a lightly buttered, shallow ovenproof dish, which will just hold the peaches comfortably. Mix the wine and sugar in a jug.

4 Pour the wine mixture around the peaches. Bake for 30–40 minutes, until the peaches are tender when tested with a slim metal skewer and the filling is golden. Serve at once with a little of the cooking juices spooned over. Offer the whipped cream separately.

Peachy Chocolate Bake

Serves 6
200g/7oz plain dark chocolate, chopped into
small pieces
115g/4oz/½ cup unsalted butter
4 eggs, separated
115g/4oz/½ cup caster sugar
425g/15oz can peach slices, drained
whipped cream or Greek-style yogurt,
to serve

1 Preheat oven to 160°C/325°F/Gas 3. Butter a wide ovenproof dish. Melt the chocolate with the butter in a heatproof bowl over barely simmering water. Remove from the heat.

2 Whisk the egg yolks with the sugar until thick and pale. In a clean, grease-free bowl, whisk the whites until stiff.

3 Beat the chocolate into the egg yolk mixture. Fold in the whites lightly.

4 Fold the peach slices into the mixture, then tip into the prepared dish. Bake for 35–40 minutes or until risen and just firm. Serve hot, with cream or Greek-style yogurt if liked.

PUFFY PEARS

SERVES 4

225g / 8oz puff pastry, thawed if frozen
2 pears, peeled
2 squares plain chocolate, roughly chopped
15ml / 1 tbsp lemon juice
1 egg, beaten
15ml / 1 tbsp caster sugar

1 Roll the pastry into a 25 cm / 10 in square on a lightly floured surface. Trim the edges, then cut it into four equal smaller squares. Cover with clear film and set aside.
2 Remove the core from each pear half and pack the gap with the chopped chocolate. Place a pear half, cut-side down, on each piece of pastry and brush them with the lemon juice, to prevent them from going brown.
3 Preheat oven to 190°C / 375°F / Gas 5. Cut the pastry into a pear shape, by following the lines of the fruit, leaving a 2.5 cm / 1 in border. Use the trimmings to make leaves and brush the pastry border with the beaten egg.
4 Arrange the pastry and pears on a baking sheet. Make deep cuts in the pears, taking care not to cut right through the fruit, and sprinkle them with the sugar. Cook for 20–25 minutes, until lightly browned. Serve hot or cold.

VARIATION
Use apples instead of pears, if preferred. Cut the pastry into 10 cm / 4 in rounds. Slice 2 peeled and cored eating apples. Toss with a little lemon juice, drain and arrange on the pastry. Dot with 25g / 1oz / 2 tbsp butter and chopped milk chocolate. Bake as for Puffy Pears. While still hot, brush the apple slices with warmed redcurrant jelly.

PEARS IN CHOCOLATE FUDGE BLANKETS

SERVES 6

6 ripe eating pears
30ml / 2 tbsp lemon juice
75g / 3oz / 6 tbsp caster sugar
300ml / ½ pint / 1¼ cups water
1 cinnamon stick
FOR THE SAUCE
200ml / 7fl oz / scant 1 cup double cream
150g / 5oz / scant 1 cup light muscovado sugar
25g / 1oz / 2tbsp unsalted butter
25g / 1oz / 2 tbsp golden syrup
120ml / 4fl oz / ½ cup milk
200g / 7oz plain dark chocolate, broken into squares

1 Peel the pears thinly, leaving the stalks on. Scoop out the cores from the base. Brush the cut surfaces with lemon juice to prevent them from browning.
2 Place the sugar and water in a large saucepan. Heat gently until the sugar dissolves. Add the pears and cinnamon stick with any remaining lemon juice, and, if necessary, a little more water, so that the pears are almost covered.
3 Bring to the boil, then lower the heat, cover the pan and simmer the pears gently for 15–20 minutes or until they are just tender when pierced with a slim skewer.
4 Meanwhile, make the sauce. Place the cream, sugar, butter, golden syrup and milk in a heavy-based saucepan. Heat gently until the sugar has dissolved and the butter and syrup have melted, then bring to the boil. Boil, stirring constantly, for about 5 minutes or until the sauce is thick. Remove from the heat and stir in the chocolate, a few squares at a time, until melted.
5 Using a slotted spoon, transfer the poached pears to a dish. Keep hot. Boil the syrup rapidly to reduce to about 45–60ml / 3–4 tbsp. Remove the cinnamon stick and stir the syrup into the chocolate sauce. Serve poured over the pears in individual bowls.

PRUNE BEIGNETS IN CHOCOLATE ARMAGNAC SAUCE

SERVES 4

75g/3oz/¾ cup plain flour
45ml/3 tbsp ground almonds
45ml/3 tbsp oil or melted butter
1 egg white
60ml/4 tbsp water
oil, for deep frying
175g/6oz/1 cup ready-to-eat
stoned prunes
45ml/3 tbsp vanilla sugar
15ml/1 tbsp cocoa powder

FOR THE SAUCE

200g/7oz milk chocolate, chopped into
small pieces
120ml/4fl oz/½ cup crème fraîche
30ml/2 tbsp Armagnac or brandy

1 Start by making the sauce. Melt the chocolate, remove from the heat, stir in the crème fraîche until smooth, then add the Armagnac or brandy. Replace the bowl over the water, off the heat, so that the sauce stays warm.

2 Beat the flour, almonds, oil or butter and egg white in a bowl, then beat in enough of the water to make a smooth thick batter.

3 Heat the oil for deep frying to 180°C/350°F or until a cube of dried bread browns in 30–45 seconds. Dip the prunes into the batter and fry a few at a time until the beignets rise to the surface of the oil and are golden brown and crisp.

4 Remove each successive batch of beignets with a slotted spoon, drain on kitchen paper and keep hot. Mix the vanilla sugar and cocoa in a bowl or stout paper bag, add the drained beignets and toss well to coat.

5 Serve in individual bowls, with the chocolate sauce poured over the top of each serving.

COOK'S TIPS

Vanilla sugar is sold commercially in many European countries but is very easy to make. Simply store a vanilla pod in a jar of granulated or caster sugar for a few weeks, until the sugar has taken on the vanilla flavour. Shake the jar occasionally. Used in cakes, biscuits and puddings, vanilla sugar imparts a delicate flavour. If you do not have any vanilla sugar for tossing the beignets, use plain granulated or caster sugar and add a pinch of ground cinnamon, if you like.

Serve the beignets as soon as possible after cooking, as they do not keep well. Use stoned dates or dried apricots as a substitute for the prunes if you prefer.

CHOCOLATE, DATE AND ALMOND FILO COIL

SERVES 6

275g / 10oz pack filo pastry, thawed if frozen
50g / 2oz / 4 tbsp unsalted butter, melted
icing sugar, cocoa powder and ground
cinnamon, for dusting

FOR THE FILLING

75g / 3oz / 6 tbsp unsalted butter
115g / 4oz plain dark chocolate, chopped into small pieces
115g / 4oz / 1 cup ground almonds
115g / 4oz / ⅔ cup chopped dates
75g / 3oz / ½ cup icing sugar
10ml / 2 tsp rosewater
2.5ml / 1½ tsp ground cinnamon

<u>1</u> Preheat oven to 180°C / 350°F / Gas 4. Grease a 22 cm / 8½ in round cake tin. Make the filling. Melt the butter with the chocolate, then stir in the other ingredients to make a paste. Leave to cool.

<u>2</u> Lay one sheet of filo on a clean work surface. Brush it lightly with melted butter, then lay a second sheet on top and brush that with melted butter too.

<u>3</u> Roll a handful of the chocolate almond mixture into a long sausage shape and place along one long edge of the layered filo. Roll the pastry tightly around the filling to make a roll. Keep the roll even, shaping it with your hands.

<u>4</u> Place the roll in the tin, coiling it around against the sides. Make enough rolls to fill the tin and fit them in place.

<u>5</u> Brush the coil with the remaining melted butter. Bake in the oven for 30–35 minutes, until the pastry is golden brown and crisp.

<u>6</u> Remove the coil from the tin, and place it on a plate. Serve warm, dusted with icing sugar, cocoa and cinnamon.

CHOCOLATE ALMOND MERINGUE PIE

SERVES 6

175g / 6oz / 1½ cups plain flour
50g / 2oz / ½ cup ground rice
150g / 5oz / ⅔ cup unsalted butter
finely grated rind of 1 orange
1 egg yolk
flaked almonds and melted plain dark
chocolate, to decorate

FOR THE FILLING

150g / 5oz plain dark chocolate, chopped into
small pieces
50g / 2oz / 4 tbsp unsalted butter, softened
75g / 3oz / 6 tbsp caster sugar
10ml / 2 tsp cornflour
4 egg yolks
75g / 3oz / ¾ cup ground almonds

FOR THE MERINGUE

3 egg whites
150g / 5oz / ⅔ cup caster sugar

1 Sift the flour and ground rice into a bowl. Rub in the butter until the mixture resembles breadcrumbs. Stir in the orange rind. Add the egg yolks; bring the dough together. Roll out and use to line a 23 cm / 9 in round flan tin. Chill.

2 Preheat oven to 190°C / 375°F / Gas 5. Prick the pastry base, cover with grease-proof paper weighed down with baking beans and bake blind for 10 minutes.

3 Make the filling. Melt the chocolate, then cream the butter with the sugar in a bowl, and beat in the cornflour and egg yolks. Fold in the almonds, then the melted chocolate. Remove the paper and beans from the pastry case and add the filling. Bake for a further 10 minutes.

4 Make the meringue. Whisk the egg whites in a clean, grease-free bowl until stiff, then gradually whisk in about half the caster sugar. Fold in the remaining sugar with a metal spoon.

5 Spoon the meringue over the chocolate filling, lifting it up with the back of the spoon to form peaks. Reduce the oven temperature to 180°C / 350°F / Gas 4 and bake the pie for 15–20 minutes or until the topping is pale gold. Serve warm, scattered with the almonds and drizzled with the melted chocolate.

CHOCOLATE PECAN PIE

SERVES 6

200g / 7oz / 1¾ cups plain flour
75ml / 5 tbsp caster sugar
90g / 3½oz / scant ½ cup unsalted butter,
softened
1 egg, beaten
finely grated rind of 1 orange

FOR THE FILLING

200g / 7oz / ¾ cup golden syrup
45ml / 3 tbsp soft light muscovado sugar
150g / 5oz plain chocolate, chopped into
small pieces
50g / 2oz / ¼ cup butter
3 eggs, beaten
5ml / 1 tsp vanilla essence
175g / 6oz / 1½ cups pecan nuts

1 Sift the flour into a bowl and stir in the sugar. Work in the butter evenly with your fingertips until combined.

2 Beat the egg and orange rind in a bowl, then stir into the mixture to make a firm dough. Add a little water if the mixture is too dry, and knead briefly.

3 Roll out the pastry on a lightly floured surface and use to line a deep, 20 cm / 8 in loose-based flan tin. Chill for 30 minutes.

4 Preheat oven to 180°C / 350°F / Gas 4. Make the filling. Melt the syrup, sugar, chocolate and butter in a small saucepan.

5 Remove the saucepan from the heat and beat in the eggs and vanilla essence. Sprinkle the pecan nuts into the pastry case and carefully pour over the chocolate mixture.

6 Place the tin on a baking sheet and bake the pie for 50–60 minutes or until the filling is set. Leave in the tin for 10 minutes, then remove the sides to serve. Serve plain, or with a little single cream.

BAKED CHOCOLATE AND RAISIN CHEESECAKE

SERVES 8–10

75g / 3oz / ¾ cup plain flour
45ml / 3 tbsp cocoa powder
75g / 3oz / ½ cup semolina
50g / 2oz / ¼ cup caster sugar
115g / 4oz / ½ cup unsalted butter, softened

FOR THE FILLING

225g / 8oz / 1 cup cream cheese
120ml / 4fl oz / ½ cup natural yogurt
2 eggs, beaten
75g / 3oz / 6 tbsp caster sugar
finely grated rind of 1 lemon
75g / 3oz / ½ cup raisins
45ml / 3 tbsp plain chocolate chips

FOR THE TOPPING

75g / 3oz plain chocolate, chopped into
small pieces
30ml / 2 tbsp golden syrup
40g / 1½oz / 3 tbsp butter

1 Preheat oven to 150°C / 300°F / Gas 2. Sift the flour and cocoa into a mixing bowl and stir in the semolina and sugar. Using your fingertips, work the butter into the flour mixture until it makes a firm dough.

2 Press the dough into the base of a 22 cm / 8½ in springform tin. Prick all over with a fork and bake in the oven for 15 minutes. Remove the tin but leave the oven on.

RUM AND RICOTTA CHEESECAKE

Use ricotta instead of cream cheese in the filling. Omit the lemon rind. Soak the raisins in 30ml / 2 tbsp rum before stirring them in with the chocolate chips. Add 5ml / 1 tsp rum to the topping.

3 Make the filling. In a large bowl, beat the cream cheese with the yogurt, eggs and sugar until evenly mixed. Stir in the lemon rind, raisins and chocolate chips.

4 Smooth the cream cheese mixture over the chocolate shortbread base and bake for a further 35–45 minutes or until the filling is pale gold and just set. Cool in the tin on a wire rack.

5 To make the topping, combine the chocolate, syrup and butter in a heatproof bowl. Set over a saucepan of simmering water and heat gently, stirring occasionally, until melted. Pour the topping over the cheesecake and leave until set. Remove the sides of the tin and carefully slide the chocolate and raisin cheesecake on to a serving plate. Serve sliced, with single cream, if you like.

CHOCOLATE AND ORANGE SCOTCH PANCAKES

SERVES 4

115g/4oz/1 cup self-raising flour
30ml/2 tbsp cocoa powder
2 eggs
50g/2oz plain chocolate, chopped into
small pieces
200ml/7fl oz/scant 1 cup milk
finely grated rind of 1 orange
30ml/2 tbsp orange juice
butter or oil, for frying
chocolate curls, to decorate

FOR THE SAUCE

2 large oranges
25g/1oz/2 tbsp unsalted butter
45ml/3 tbsp light muscovado sugar
250ml/8fl oz/1 cup crème fraîche
30ml/2 tbsp Grand Marnier or
Cointreau

1 Sift the flour and cocoa into a bowl and make a well in the centre. Add the eggs and beat well, gradually incorporating the surrounding dry ingredients to make a smooth mixture.

2 Mix the chocolate and milk in a saucepan. Heat gently until the chocolate has melted, then beat into the mixture until smooth and bubbly. Stir in the orange rind and juice to make a batter.

3 Heat a large heavy-based frying pan or griddle. Grease with a little butter or oil. Drop large spoonfuls of batter on to the hot surface, leaving room for spreading. Cook over a moderate heat. When the pancakes are lightly browned underneath and bubbly on top, flip over to cook the other side. Slide on to a plate and keep hot, then make more in the same way.

4 Make the sauce. Grate the rind of 1 orange into a bowl and set aside. Peel both oranges, taking care to remove all the pith, then slice the flesh fairly thinly.

5 Heat the butter and sugar in a wide, shallow pan over a low heat, stirring until the sugar dissolves. Stir in the crème fraîche and heat gently.

6 Add the pancakes and orange slices to the sauce, heat gently for 1–2 minutes, then spoon over the liqueur. Sprinkle with the reserved orange rind. Scatter over the chocolate curls and serve the pancakes at once.

CHOCOLATE CHIP BANANA PANCAKES

MAKES 16

2 ripe bananas
2 eggs
200ml / 7fl oz / scant 1 cup milk
150g / 5oz / 1¼ cups self-raising flour, sifted
25g / 1oz / ⅓ cup ground almonds
15ml / 1tbsp caster sugar
pinch of salt
15ml / 1tbsp plain chocolate chips
butter, for frying
50g / 2oz / ½ cup toasted flaked almonds

FOR THE TOPPING

150ml / ¼ pint / ⅔ cup double cream
15ml / 1 tbsp icing sugar

1 Mash the bananas in a bowl. Beat in the eggs and half the milk. Mix in the flour, ground almonds, sugar and salt. Add the remaining milk and the chocolate chips.

2 Stir the mixture well until it makes a thick batter. Heat a knob of butter in a non-stick frying pan. Spoon the pancake mixture into heaps, allowing room for them to spread. When the pancakes are lightly browned underneath, flip them over to cook the other side. Slide on to a plate and keep hot, then make more pancakes in the same way.

3 Make the topping. Pour the cream into a bowl. Add the icing sugar, to sweeten it slightly, and whip to soft peaks. Spoon the cream on to the pancakes and decorate with flaked almonds. Serve at once.

CHOCOLATE CREPES WITH PLUMS AND PORT

2 Meanwhile, make the filling. Halve and stone the plums. Place them in a saucepan and add the sugar and water. Bring to the boil, then lower the heat, cover, and simmer for about 10 minutes or until the plums are tender. Stir in the port, taking care not to break up the plums, then simmer for a further 30 seconds. Remove from the heat and keep warm.

3 Have ready a sheet of non-stick baking paper. Heat a crêpe pan, grease it lightly with a little oil, then pour in just enough batter to cover the base of the pan, swirling to coat evenly. Cook until the crêpe has set, then flip it over to cook the other side. Slide the crêpe out on to the sheet of paper, then cook 9–11 more crêpes in the same way. It should not be necessary to add more oil to the pan, but if the crêpes start to stick, add a very light coating.

4 Make the sauce. Combine the chocolate and cream in a saucepan. Heat gently, stirring until smooth. Add the port and heat gently, stirring, for 1 minute.

SERVES 6

50g/2oz plain chocolate, chopped into
small pieces
200ml/7fl oz/scant 1 cup milk
120ml/4fl oz/½ cup single cream
30ml/2 tbsp cocoa powder
115g/4oz/1 cup plain flour
2 eggs
oil, for frying

FOR THE FILLING

500g/1¼lb red or golden plums
50g/2oz/¼ cup caster sugar
30ml/2 tbsp water
30ml/2 tbsp port
150g/5oz/¾ cup crème fraîche or
Greek-style yogurt

FOR THE SAUCE

150g/5oz plain chocolate, chopped into
small pieces
175ml/6fl oz/¾ cup double cream
15ml/1 tbsp port

1 Make the crêpe batter. Place the chocolate in a saucepan with the milk. Heat gently, stirring occasionally, until the chocolate has dissolved. Pour the chocolate and milk mixture into a blender or food processor and add the cream, cocoa, flour and eggs. (If the blender or food processor is a small one, it may be necessary to do this in batches.) Process until smooth, then tip into a jug and chill for 30 minutes.

5 Divide the plum filling among the crêpes, add a dollop of crème fraîche or Greek-style yogurt to each and roll them up carefully. Serve in individual bowls, with the chocolate sauce spooned over the top of each portion.

RICH CHOCOLATE BRIOCHE BAKE

SERVES 4

40g / 1½oz / 3 tbsp unsalted butter, plus extra for greasing
200g / 7oz plain chocolate, chopped into small pieces
60ml / 4 tbsp bitter marmalade
4 individual brioches, cut into halves, or 1 large brioche loaf, cut into thick slices
3 eggs
300ml / ½ pint / 1¼ cups milk
300ml / ½ pint / 1¼ cups single cream
30ml / 2 tbsp demerara sugar

1 Preheat oven to 180°C / 350°F / Gas 4. Using the extra butter, lightly grease a shallow ovenproof dish.

2 Melt the chocolate with the marmalade and butter in a heatproof bowl over just simmering water, stirring the mixture occasionally, until smooth.

3 Spread the melted chocolate mixture over the brioche slices. Arrange them in the dish so that the slices overlap.

4 Beat the eggs in a large bowl, then add the milk and cream and mix well. Transfer to a jug and pour evenly over the slices. Sprinkle with the demerara sugar and bake for 40–50 minutes, until the custard has set lightly and the brioche slices are golden brown. Serve hot.

CHOCOLATE SOUFFLE CREPES

MAKES 12 CREPES

75g / 3oz / ¾ cup plain flour
15ml / 1 tbsp cocoa powder
5ml / 1 tsp caster sugar
pinch of salt
5ml / 1 tsp ground cinnamon
2 eggs
175ml / 6fl oz / ¾ cup milk
5ml / 1 tsp vanilla essence
50g / 2oz / 4 tbsp unsalted butter,
melted
raspberries, pineapple and mint sprigs,
to decorate

FOR THE PINEAPPLE SYRUP

½ medium pineapple, peeled, cored and
finely chopped
120ml / 4fl oz / ½ cup water
30ml / 2 tbsp natural maple syrup
5ml / 1 tsp cornflour
½ cinnamon stick
30ml / 2 tbsp rum

FOR THE SOUFFLE FILLING

250g / 9oz bittersweet chocolate, chopped into
small pieces
75ml / 3fl oz / ⅓ cup double cream
3 eggs, separated
25g / 1oz / 2 tbsp caster sugar

1 Prepare the syrup. In a saucepan over a medium heat, bring the pineapple, water, maple syrup, cornflour and cinnamon stick to the boil. Simmer for 2–3 minutes, until the sauce thickens, whisking frequently. Remove from the heat and discard the cinnamon. Pour into a bowl, and stir in the rum. Cool, then chill.

COOK'S TIP

You might be able to find ready-made crêpes in the shops, which will save time.

2 Prepare the crêpes. Sift the flour, cocoa, sugar, salt and cinnamon into a bowl. Stir, then make a well in the centre. In a bowl, beat the eggs, milk and vanilla. Gradually add to the well in the flour mixture, whisking in flour from the side of the bowl to form a smooth batter. Stir in half the melted butter and pour into a jug. Allow to stand for 1 hour.

3 Heat an 18–20 cm / 7–8 in crêpe pan. Brush with butter. Stir the batter. Pour 45ml / 3 tbsp batter into the pan; swirl the pan to cover the bottom. Cook over a medium-high heat for 1–2 minutes until the bottom is golden. Turn over and cook for 30–45 seconds, then turn on to a plate. Stack between sheets of non-stick baking paper and set aside.

4 Prepare the filling. In a saucepan over a medium heat, melt the chocolate and cream until smooth, stirring frequently.

5 In a bowl, with a hand-held electric mixer, beat the yolks with half the sugar for 3–5 minutes, until light and creamy. Gradually beat in the chocolate mixture. Allow to cool. In a separate bowl with cleaned beaters, beat the egg whites until soft peaks form. Gradually beat in the remaining sugar until stiff peaks form. Beat a large spoonful of whites in to the chocolate mixture to lighten it, then fold in the remaining whites.

6 Preheat oven to 200°C / 400°F / Gas 6. Lay a crêpe on a plate, bottom side up. Spoon a little soufflé mixture on to the crêpe, spreading it to the edge. Fold the bottom half over the soufflé mixture, then fold in half again to form a filled triangle. Place on a buttered baking sheet. Repeat with the remaining crêpes. Brush the tops with melted butter and bake for 15–20 minutes, until the filling has souffléd. Decorate with raspberries, pineapple pieces and mint and serve with the syrup.

VARIATION

For a simpler version of the crêpes, just serve with a spoonful of maple syrup rather than making the pineapple syrup.

Chocolate Orange Marquise

Serves 6–8

200g / 7oz / scant 1 cup caster sugar
60ml / 4 tbsp freshly squeezed orange juice
*350g / 12oz plain dark chocolate, chopped
into small pieces*
225g / 8oz / 1 cup unsalted butter, cubed
5 eggs
finely grated rind of 1 orange
45ml / 3 tbsp plain flour
*icing sugar and finely pared strips of orange
rind, to decorate*

1 Preheat oven to 180°C / 350°F / Gas 4.
Grease a 23 cm / 9 in round cake tin with
a depth of 6 cm / 2½ in. Line the base
with non-stick baking paper.
2 Place 115g / 4oz / ½ cup of the sugar in a
saucepan. Add the orange juice and stir
over a gentle heat until the sugar has
dissolved completely.

3 Remove from the heat and stir in the
chocolate until melted, then add the
butter, cube by cube, until thoroughly
melted and evenly mixed.
4 Whisk the eggs with the remaining
sugar in a large bowl until pale and very
thick. Add the orange rind. Then, using a
metal spoon, fold the chocolate mixture
lightly and evenly into the egg mixture.
Sift the flour over the top and fold in.

5 Scrape the mixture into the prepared
tin. Place in a roasting pan, transfer to
the oven, then carefully pour hot water
into the roasting pan to come about
halfway up the sides of the cake tin.
6 Bake for about 1 hour or until the cake
is firm to the touch. Remove the cake tin
from the water bath and place on a wire
rack to cool for 15–20 minutes. To turn
out, invert the cake on a baking sheet,
place a serving plate upside down on top,
then turn plate and baking sheet over
together so that the cake is transferred to
the plate.
7 Dust with icing sugar, decorate with
strips of pared orange rind and serve still
warm. This cake is wonderfully rich and
moist and really doesn't need an
accompaniment, but you could offer
single cream, if you wish.

HOT CHOCOLATE ZABAGLIONE

SERVES 6
6 egg yolks
150g / 5oz / ⅔ cup caster sugar
45ml / 3 tbsp cocoa powder
200ml / 7fl oz / scant 1 cup Marsala
cocoa powder or icing sugar, for dusting

1 Half fill a medium saucepan with water and bring to simmering point. Select a heatproof bowl that will fit over the pan, place the egg yolks and sugar in it, and whisk until the mixture is pale and all the sugar has dissolved.

2 Add the cocoa and Marsala, then place the bowl over the simmering water. Whisk with a hand-held electric mixer until the mixture is thick and foamy.

3 Pour quickly into tall heatproof glasses, dust lightly with cocoa or icing sugar and serve immediately with chocolate cinnamon tuiles or amaretti biscuits.

CHOCOLATE FONDUE
SERVES 4-6
225g / 8oz plain chocolate, chopped into small pieces
300ml / ½ pint / 1¼ cups double cream
30ml / 2 tbsp Grand Marnier (optional)
25g / 1oz / 2 tbsp butter, diced
cherries, strawberries, sliced bananas,
mandarin segments and cubes of sponge
cake, for dipping

1 Combine the chocolate, cream and Grand Marnier (if using) in a fondue pan or small heavy-based saucepan. Heat gently until melted, stirring frequently.

2 Arrange the fruit and cake for dipping on a large platter. Stir the butter into the fondue until melted. Place the fondue pot or pan over a lighted spirit burner.

3 Guests spear the items of their choice on fondue forks and swirl them in the dip until coated. Anyone who loses his or her dipper pays a forfeit.

CHOCOLATE TARTS, PIES AND CHEESECAKES

GREEK CHOCOLATE MOUSSE TARTLETS

SERVES 6

1 quantity Chocolate Shortcrust Pastry
chocolate shapes, to decorate
FOR THE FILLING
200g/7oz white chocolate, chopped into
small pieces
120ml/4fl oz/½ cup milk
10ml/2 tsp powdered gelatine
30ml/2 tbsp caster sugar
5ml/1 tsp vanilla essence
2 eggs, separated
250ml/8fl oz/1 cup Greek-style yogurt

1 Preheat oven to 190°C/375°F/Gas 5. Roll out the pastry and line six deep 10 cm/4 in loose-based flan tins.

2 Prick the pastry with a fork, cover with greaseproof paper weighed down with baking beans and bake blind for 10 minutes. Remove the baking beans and paper, return to the oven and bake a further 15 minutes. Cool in the tins.

3 Make the filling. Melt the chocolate. Pour the milk into a saucepan, sprinkle over the powdered gelatine and heat gently, stirring until the gelatine has dissolved completely. Remove from the heat and stir in the chocolate.

4 Whisk the sugar, vanilla essence and egg yolks in a large bowl, then beat in the chocolate mixture. Beat in the yogurt until evenly mixed.

5 Whisk the egg whites in a clean, grease-free bowl until stiff, then fold into the mixture. Divide among the pastry cases and chill for 2–3 hours, until set. Decorate with chocolate shapes, and dust with icing sugar if wished.

CHOCOLATE AND PINE NUT TART

SERVES 8

200g/7oz/1¾ cups plain flour
50g/2oz/¼ cup caster sugar
pinch of salt
grated rind of ½ orange
115g/4oz/½ cup unsalted butter, cut into small pieces
3 egg yolks, lightly beaten
15–30 ml/1–2 tbsp iced water

FOR THE FILLING

2 eggs
45ml/3 tbsp caster sugar
grated rind of 1 orange
15ml/1 tbsp orange-flavoured liqueur
250ml/8fl oz/1 cup whipping cream
115g/4oz plain chocolate, chopped into small pieces
75g/3oz/1 cup pine nuts, toasted

FOR THE DECORATION

1 orange
50g/2oz/¼ cup granulated sugar
120ml/4fl oz/½ cup water

1 In a food processor fitted with a metal blade, process the flour, sugar, salt and orange rind. Add the butter and process for 20–30 seconds, until the mixture looks like coarse crumbs. Add the yolks and pulse until the dough begins to stick together. If the dough appears dry, add the iced water, little by little, until the mixture just holds together. Knead the dough gently, then wrap in clear film. Chill for 2–3 hours or overnight.

2 Lightly grease a 23 cm/9 in tart tin with a removable base. Let the dough soften briefly, then roll out on a well-floured surface into a 28 cm/11 in round. Ease the dough into the tin and press the overhang down slightly with floured fingers, to make the top edge thicker.

3 Roll a rolling pin over the top edge to cut off excess dough. Press the thicker top edge against the sides of the tin to form a raised rim. Prick the base with a fork. Chill for 1 hour. Preheat oven to 200°C/400°F/Gas 6. Line the tart shell with greaseproof paper; fill with baking beans and bake blind for 5 minutes. Lift out the foil and beans, then return the tart shell to the oven and bake for 5 minutes more, until set. Cool in the tin on a wire rack. Lower the oven temperature to 180°C/350°F/Gas 4.

4 Prepare the filling. Beat the eggs, sugar, orange rind and liqueur in a bowl. Stir in the cream. Sprinkle the chocolate evenly over the base of the tart shell, then sprinkle with the pine nuts.

5 Gently pour the filling into the tart shell. Bake for 20–30 minutes, until the pastry is golden and the custard is set. Cool slightly in the tin on a wire rack.

6 Prepare the decoration. Peel the orange thinly, avoiding the pith, then cut the rind into thin strips. Dissolve the sugar in the water in a pan over a medium heat, then add the orange rind strips. Boil for about 5 minutes, until the syrup is thick and has begun to caramelize. Off the heat, stir in about 15ml/1 tbsp cold water to prevent the mixture from darkening further.

7 Brush the orange syrup over the tart and decorate with the caramelized strips. Remove the side of the tin and slide the tart on to a plate. Serve warm.

CHOCOLATE TRUFFLE TART

SERVES 12

115g/4oz/1 cup plain flour
30g/1¼oz/⅓ cup cocoa powder
50g/2oz/¼ cup caster sugar
2.5ml/½ tsp salt
115g/4oz/½ cup unsalted butter, cut into pieces
1 egg yolk
15–30ml/1–2 tbsp iced water
25g/1oz fine quality white or milk chocolate, melted
whipped cream for serving (optional)

FOR THE TRUFFLE FILLING

350ml/12fl oz/1½ cups double cream
350g/12oz couverture or fine quality bittersweet chocolate, chopped
50g/2oz/4 tbsp unsalted butter, cut into small pieces
30ml/2 tbsp brandy or liqueur

1 Prepare the pastry. Sift the flour and cocoa into a bowl. In a food processor fitted with a metal blade, process the flour mixture with the sugar and salt. Add the butter and process for 15–20 seconds, until the mixture resembles coarse breadcrumbs.

2 In a bowl, lightly beat the yolk with the iced water. Add to the flour mixture and pulse until the dough begins to stick together. Turn out the dough on to a sheet of clear film. Use the film to help shape the dough into a flat disc. Wrap tightly. Chill for 1–2 hours, until firm.

3 Lightly grease a 23 cm/9 in tart tin with a removable base. Let the dough soften briefly, then roll it out between sheets of waxed paper or clear film to a 28 cm/11 in round, about 5 mm/¼ in thick. Peel off the top sheet and invert the dough into a tart tin. Remove the bottom sheet. Ease the dough into the tin. Prick with a fork. Chill for 1 hour.

4 Preheat oven to 180°C/350°F/Gas 4. Line the tart with foil or non-stick baking paper; fill with baking beans. Bake blind for 5–7 minutes. Lift out the foil with the beans, return the pastry case to the oven and bake for a further 5–7 minutes, until the pastry is just set. Cool completely in the tin on a rack.

5 Prepare the filling. In a medium pan over a medium heat, bring the cream to the boil. Remove the pan from the heat and stir in the chocolate until melted and smooth. Stir in the butter and brandy or liqueur. Strain into the prepared tart shell, tilting the tin slightly to level the surface. Do not touch the surface of the filling or it will spoil the glossy finish.

6 Spoon the melted chocolate into a paper piping bag and cut off the tip. Drop rounds of chocolate over the surface of the tart and use a skewer or toothpick to draw a point gently through the chocolate to produce a marbled effect. Chill for 2–3 hours, until set. To serve, allow the tart to soften slightly at room temperature.

CHOCOLATE TIRAMISU TART

SERVES 12–16

115g/4oz/½ cup unsalted butter

15ml/1 tbsp coffee-flavoured liqueur or water

175g/6oz/1½ cups plain flour

25g/1oz/¼ cup cocoa powder

25g/1oz/¼ cup icing sugar

pinch of salt

2.5ml/½ tsp vanilla essence

cocoa powder, for dusting

FOR THE CHOCOLATE LAYER

350ml/12fl oz/1½ cups double cream

15ml/1 tbsp golden syrup

115g/4oz bittersweet chocolate, chopped into small pieces

25g/1oz/2 tbsp unsalted butter, cut into small pieces

30ml/2 tbsp coffee-flavoured liqueur

FOR THE FILLING

250ml/8fl oz/1 cup whipping cream

350g/12oz/1½ cups mascarpone cheese, at room temperature

45ml/3 tbsp icing sugar

45ml/3 tbsp cold espresso or strong black coffee

45ml/3 tbsp coffee-flavoured liqueur

90g/3½oz plain chocolate, grated

1 Make the pastry. Lightly grease a 23 cm/9 in springform tin. In a saucepan, heat the butter and liqueur or water until the butter has melted. Sift the flour, cocoa, icing sugar and salt into a bowl. Remove the butter mixture from the heat, stir in the vanilla essence and gradually stir into the flour mixture until a soft dough forms.

2 Knead lightly until smooth. Press on to the base and up the sides of the tin to within 2 cm/¾ in of the top. Prick the dough. Chill for 40 minutes. Preheat oven to 190°C/375°F/Gas 5. Bake the pastry case for 8–10 minutes. If the pastry puffs up, prick it with a fork and bake for 2–3 minutes more until set. Cool in the tin on a rack.

3 Prepare the chocolate layer. Bring the cream and syrup to a boil in a pan over a medium heat. Off the heat, add the chocolate, stirring until melted. Beat in the butter and liqueur and pour into the pastry case. Cool completely, then chill.

4 Prepare the filling. Using a hand-held electric mixer, whip the cream in a bowl until soft peaks form. In another bowl, beat the cheese until soft, then beat in the icing sugar until smooth and creamy. Gradually beat in the cold coffee and liqueur; gently fold in the whipped cream and chocolate. Spoon the filling into the pastry case, on top of the chocolate layer. Level the surface. Chill until ready to serve.

5 To serve, run a sharp knife around the side of the tin to loosen the tart shell. Remove the side of the tin and slide the tart on to a plate. Sift a layer of cocoa powder over the tart to decorate, or pipe rosettes of whipped cream around the rim and top each with a chocolate-coated coffee bean. Chocolate Tiramisu Tart is very rich, so serve it in small wedges, with cups of espresso.

WHITE CHOCOLATE AND MANGO CREAM TART

SERVES 8

175g / 6oz / 1½ cups plain flour
75g / 3oz / 1 cup sweetened, desiccated coconut
115g / 4oz / ½ cup butter, softened
30ml / 2 tbsp caster sugar
2 egg yolks
2.5ml / ½ tsp almond essence
600ml / 1 pint / 2½ cups whipping cream
1 large ripe mango
50g / 2oz / ½ cup toasted flaked almonds,
to decorate

FOR THE WHITE CHOCOLATE
CUSTARD FILLING

150g / 5oz fine quality white chocolate,
chopped into small pieces
120ml / 4fl oz / ½ cup whipping cream or
double cream
75ml / 5 tbsp cornflour
15ml / 1 tbsp plain flour
50g / 2oz / ¼ cup granulated sugar
350ml / 12fl oz / 1½ cups milk
5 egg yolks

1 Using a hand-held electric mixer at low speed, beat the flour, coconut, butter, sugar, egg yolks and almond essence in a deep bowl until the mixture forms a soft dough. Lightly grease a 23 cm/9 in tart tin with a removable base. Press the pastry on to the bottom and sides. Prick the pastry case with a fork. Chill the case for 30 minutes.

COOK'S TIP

Choose a mango that is a rich yellow in colour, with a pink or red blush. It should just yield to the touch, but should not be too soft. Peel it carefully, then cut it in half around the stone. Cut each piece in half again, then in neat slices.

---

2 Preheat oven to 180°C/350°F/Gas 4. Line the pastry case with non-stick baking paper; fill with baking beans and bake blind for 10 minutes. Remove the paper and beans and bake for a further 5–7 minutes, until golden. Cool the cooked pastry in the tin on a wire rack.

3 Prepare the custard filling. In a small saucepan over a low heat, melt the white chocolate with the cream, stirring until smooth. Set aside. Combine the cornflour, plain flour and sugar in a medium saucepan. Stir in the milk gradually. Place over a medium heat and cook, stirring constantly, until the mixture has thickened.

4 Beat the egg yolks in a small bowl. Slowly add about 250ml/8fl oz/1 cup of the hot milk mixture, stirring constantly. Return the yolk mixture to the rest of the sauce in the pan, stirring constantly.

5 Bring the custard filling to a gentle boil, stirring constantly until thickened. Stir in the melted white chocolate until well blended. Cool to room temperature, stirring frequently to prevent a skin from forming on the surface. Beat the whipping cream in a medium-sized bowl until soft peaks form. Fold approximately 120ml/4fl oz/½ cup of the whipped cream into the white chocolate custard and spoon half the custard into the base. Peel and slice the mango thinly.

6 With the aid of a slim metal spatula or palette knife, arrange the mango slices over the custard in concentric circles, starting at the rim and then filling in the centre. Try to avoid moving the mango slices once in position. Carefully pour the remaining custard over the mango slices, smoothing the surface evenly. Remove the side of the tin and slide the tart carefully on to a serving plate.

7 Spoon the remaining flavoured cream into a large piping bag fitted with a medium star tip. Pipe the cream in a scroll pattern in parallel rows on top of the tart, keeping the rows about 1 cm/½ in apart. Carefully sprinkle the toasted flaked almonds between the rows. Serve the tart chilled.

CHOCOLATE PECAN TORTE

SERVES 16

*200g / 7oz bittersweet or plain chocolate,
chopped into small pieces*
*150g / 5oz / 10 tbsp unsalted butter,
cut into pieces*
4 eggs
90g / 3½oz / scant ½ cup caster sugar
10ml / 2 tsp vanilla essence
115g / 4oz / 1 cup ground pecan nuts
10ml / 2 tsp ground cinnamon
24 toasted pecan halves, to decorate
FOR THE CHOCOLATE HONEY GLAZE
*115g / 4oz bittersweet or plain chocolate,
chopped into small pieces*
*50g / 2oz / ¼ cup unsalted butter,
cut into pieces*
30ml / 2 tbsp clear honey
pinch of ground cinnamon

1 Preheat oven to 180°C / 350°F / Gas 4.
Grease a 20 x 5 cm / 8 x 2 in springform
tin; line with non-stick baking paper.
Wrap the tin in foil to prevent water
from seeping in. Melt the chocolate and
butter, stirring until smooth. Beat the
eggs, sugar and vanilla essence in a
mixing bowl until the mixture is frothy.
Stir in the melted chocolate, ground nuts
and cinnamon. Pour into the tin.

2 Place the tin in a roasting pan. Pour in
boiling water to come 2 cm / ¾ in up the
side of the springform tin. Bake for
25–30 minutes, until the edge of the cake
is set but the centre is still soft. Remove
the tin from the water bath and lift off
the foil. Cool the cake in the tin on a
wire rack.

3 Prepare the glaze. Heat all the
ingredients in a small pan until melted,
stirring until smooth. Off the heat, half-
dip the toasted pecan halves in the glaze
and place on a baking sheet lined with
non-stick baking paper until set.

4 Remove the cake from the tin, place it
on the rack and pour the remaining glaze
over. Decorate the outside of the torte
with the chocolate-dipped pecans and
leave to set. Transfer to a plate when
ready to serve, and slice in thin wedges.

CHOCOLATE LEMON TART

SERVES 8–10

175g / 6oz / 1½ cups plain flour
10ml / 2 tsp cocoa powder
25g / 1oz / ¼ cup icing sugar
2.5ml / ½ tsp salt
115g / 4oz / ½ cup unsalted butter or
margarine
15ml / 1 tbsp water

FOR THE FILLING

225g / 8oz / 1 cup caster sugar
6 eggs
grated rind of 2 lemons
175ml / 6fl oz / ¾ cup fresh lemon juice
175ml / 6fl oz / ¾ cup double or
whipping cream
chocolate curls, for decorating

1 Grease a 25 cm / 10 in flan tin. Sift the flour, cocoa, icing sugar and salt into a bowl. Set aside. Melt the butter or margarine and water in a saucepan over a low heat. Pour over the flour mixture and stir until the flour has absorbed all the liquid and the dough is smooth.

2 Press the dough evenly over the base and side of the prepared tin. Chill the pastry case.

3 Preheat oven to 190°C / 375°F / Gas 5, and place a baking sheet inside to heat up. Prepare the filling. Whisk the sugar and eggs in a bowl until the sugar has dissolved. Add the lemon rind and juice and mix well. Stir in the cream. Taste and add more lemon juice or sugar if needed, for a sweet taste with a touch of tartness.

4 Pour the filling into the tart shell and place the tin on the hot baking sheet. Bake for 20–25 minutes or until the filling is set. Cool on a rack, then decorate with the chocolate curls.

CHOCOLATE APRICOT LINZER TART

3 Turn the dough on to a flour-dusted work surface and knead lightly until just blended. Divide the dough in half. With floured fingers, press half the dough on to the bottom and sides of the tin. Prick the base of the dough with a fork. Chill for 20 minutes. Roll out the rest of the dough between two sheets of non-stick baking paper or clear film to a 28 cm/ 11 in round; slide on to a baking sheet and chill for 30 minutes.

SERVES 10–12

50g/2oz/½ cup whole blanched almonds
115g/4oz/½ cup caster sugar
175g/6oz/1½ cups plain flour
30ml/2 tbsp cocoa powder
5ml/1 tsp ground cinnamon
2.5ml/½ tsp salt
5ml/1 tsp grated orange rind
225g/8oz/1 cup unsalted butter, cut into
small pieces
45–60ml/3–4 tbsp iced water
75g/3oz/½ cup plain mini chocolate chips
icing sugar, for dusting
FOR THE APRICOT FILLING
350g/12oz/1½ cups dried apricots
120ml/4fl oz/½ cup orange juice
175ml/6fl oz/¾ cup water
45ml/3 tbsp granulated sugar
50g/2oz/2 tbsp apricot jam
2.5ml/½ tsp almond essence

1 Prepare the filling. In a pan, simmer the apricots, orange juice and water until the liquid is absorbed, stirring often. Stir in the remaining ingredients. Strain into a bowl, cool, cover and chill.

2 Prepare the pastry. Lightly grease a 28 cm/11 in tart tin with removable base. In a food processor with a metal blade, process the almonds with half the sugar until finely ground. Into a bowl, sift the flour, cocoa, cinnamon and salt. Stir in the remaining caster sugar. Add to the food processor and process to blend. Add the rind and butter and process for 15–20 seconds until the mixture resembles coarse crumbs. Add about 30ml/2 tbsp iced water and pulse until the dough just begins to stick together. If the dough appears too dry, add 15–30ml/1–2 tbsp more iced water, little by little, until the dough just holds together.

4 Preheat oven to 180°C/350°F/Gas 4. Spread the filling on to the base of the pastry-lined tin. Sprinkle with chocolate chips. Set aside. Slide the dough round on to a lightly floured surface and cut into 1 cm/½ in strips; allow the strips to soften for 3–5 minutes so that they will be easier to work with.

5 Place half the dough strips over the filling, spacing them about 1 cm/½ in apart. Place the rest of the strips at an angle on top, as shown. With your fingertips, press down on both sides of each crossing to stress the lattice effect. Press the ends on to the side of the tart, cutting off any excess. Bake for `35–40 minutes, until the strips are golden and the filling bubbles. Cool on a rack. To serve, remove the side of the tin, then dust icing sugar over the top pastry strips.

RICH CHOCOLATE BERRY TART WITH BLACKBERRY SAUCE

SERVES 10

115g / 4oz / ½ cup unsalted butter, softened
115g / 4oz / ½ cup caster sugar
2.5ml / ½ tsp salt
15ml / 1 tbsp vanilla essence
50g / 2oz / ½ cup cocoa powder
175g / 6oz / 1½ cups plain flour
450g / 1 lb fresh berries, for topping
FOR THE CHOCOLATE GANACHE FILLING
475ml / 16fl oz / 2 cups double cream
150g / 5oz / ½ cup blackberry or raspberry jelly
225g / 8oz bittersweet chocolate, chopped into small pieces
25g / 1oz / 2 tbsp unsalted butter, cut into small pieces
FOR THE BLACKBERRY SAUCE
225g / 8oz fresh or frozen blackberries or raspberries
15ml / 1 tbsp lemon juice
30ml / 2 tbsp caster sugar
30ml / 2 tbsp blackberry- or raspberry-flavoured liqueur

1 In a food processor fitted with a metal blade, process the butter, sugar, salt and vanilla essence until creamy. Add the cocoa and process for 1 minute. Add the flour all at once, then pulse for 10–15 seconds. Place a piece of clear film on the work surface. Turn the dough out on to this, shape into a flat disc and wrap tightly. Chill for 1 hour.

2 Lightly grease a 23 cm / 9 in flan tin with a removable base. Let the dough soften for 5–10 minutes, then roll out between two sheets of clear film to a 28 cm / 11 in round, about 5 mm / ¼ in thick. Peel off the top sheet of clear film and invert the dough into the prepared tin. Ease the dough into the tin, and when in position lift off the clear film.

3 With floured fingers, press the dough on to the base and sides of the tin, then roll the rolling pin over the edge to cut off any excess dough. Prick the base of the dough with a fork. Chill for 1 hour. Preheat oven to 180°C / 350°F / Gas 4. Line the pastry case with non-stick baking paper; fill with baking beans and bake blind for 10 minutes. Remove the paper and beans and bake for 5 minutes more, until the pastry is just set. Cool in the tin on a wire rack.

4 Prepare the ganache filling. In a medium saucepan over a medium heat, bring the cream and berry jelly to the boil. Remove from the heat and add the chocolate all at once, stirring until melted and smooth. Stir in the butter until melted, then strain into the cooled tart shell, smoothing the top. Cool the tart completely.

5 Prepare the sauce. Process the berries, lemon juice and sugar in a food processor until smooth. Strain into a small bowl and add the liqueur.

6 To serve, remove the tart from the tin. Place on a serving plate and arrange the berries on top of the tart. With a pastry brush, brush the berries with a little of the blackberry sauce to glaze lightly. Serve the remaining sauce separately.

HAZELNUT CHOCOLATE MERINGUE TORTE WITH PEARS

SERVES 8–10

175g / 6oz / ¾ cup granulated sugar
1 vanilla pod, split
475ml / 6fl oz / 2 cups water
4 ripe pears, peeled, halved and cored
30ml / 2 tbsp hazelnut- or pear-flavoured
liqueur
150g / 5oz / 1¼ cups hazelnuts, toasted
6 egg whites
pinch of salt
350g / 12oz / 2¼ cups icing sugar
5ml / 1 tsp vanilla essence
50g / 2oz plain chocolate, melted

FOR THE CHOCOLATE CREAM

275g / 10oz fine quality bittersweet or plain
chocolate, chopped into small pieces
475ml / 16fl oz / 2 cups whipping cream
60ml / 4 tbsp hazelnut- or pear-flavoured
liqueur

1 In a saucepan large enough to hold the pears in a single layer combine the sugar, vanilla pod and water. Over a high heat, bring to the boil, stirring until the sugar dissolves. Lower the heat, add the pears to the syrup, cover and simmer gently for 12–15 minutes until tender. Remove the pan from the heat and allow the pears to cool in their poaching liquid. Carefully lift the pears out of the liquid and drain on kitchen paper. Transfer them to a plate, sprinkle with liqueur, cover and chill overnight.

2 Preheat oven to 180°C / 350°F / Gas 4. With a pencil draw a 23 cm / 9 in circle on each of two sheets of non-stick baking paper. Turn the paper over on to two baking sheets (so that the pencil marks are underneath). Crumb the toasted hazelnuts in a food processor fitted with a metal blade.

3 In a large bowl, beat the whites with a hand-held electric mixer until frothy. Add the salt and beat on high speed until soft peaks form. Reduce the mixer speed and gradually add the icing sugar, beating well after each addition until all the sugar has been added and the whites are stiff and glossy; this will take 12–15 minutes. Gently fold in the nuts and vanilla essence and spoon the meringue on to the circles on the baking sheets, smoothing the top and sides.

4 Bake for 1 hour until the tops are dry and firm. Turn off the oven and allow to cool in the oven for 2–3 hours or overnight, until completely dry.

5 Prepare the chocolate cream. Melt the chocolate in a heatproof bowl set over a saucepan of simmering water. Stir the chocolate until melted and smooth. Cool to room temperature. Using a hand-held electric mixer beat the cream in a bowl to form soft peaks. Quickly fold the cream into the melted chocolate; fold in the liqueur. Spoon about one third of the chocolate cream into an icing bag fitted with a star tip. Set aside.

6 Thinly slice each pear half lengthwise with a sharp knife. Place one meringue layer on a serving plate. Spread with half the chocolate cream and arrange half the sliced pears evenly over the cream. Pipe a border of rosettes around the edge.

7 Top with the second meringue layer and spread with the remaining chocolate cream. Arrange the remaining pear slices in an attractive pattern over the chocolate cream. Pipe a border of rosettes around the edge. Spoon the melted chocolate into a small paper cone and drizzle the chocolate over the pears. Chill for at least 1 hour before serving.

CHILLED CHOCOLATE AND DATE SLICE

SERVES 6–8

115g/4oz/½ cup unsalted butter, melted
225g/8oz ginger biscuits, finely crushed
50g/2oz/⅔ cup stale sponge cake crumbs
75ml/5 tbsp orange juice
115g/4oz/⅔ cup stoned dates
25g/1oz/¼ cup finely chopped nuts
175g/6oz bittersweet chocolate
300ml/½ pint/1¼ cups whipping cream
grated chocolate and icing sugar, to decorate

<u>1</u> Mix the butter and ginger biscuit crumbs in a bowl, then press the mixture on to the sides and base of an 18 cm/7 in loose-based flan tin. Chill the crust while making the filling.

<u>2</u> Put the sponge cake crumbs into a bowl. Pour over 60ml/4 tbsp of the orange juice, stir well with a wooden spoon and leave to soak. Put the dates in a saucepan and add the remaining orange juice. Warm the mixture over a low heat. Mash the warm dates thoroughly and stir in the cake crumbs, with the finely chopped nuts.

<u>3</u> Mix the chocolate with 60ml/4 tbsp of the cream in a heatproof bowl. Place the bowl over a saucepan of barely simmering water and stir occasionally until melted. In a separate bowl, whip the rest of the cream to soft peaks, then fold in the melted chocolate.

<u>4</u> Add the cooled date, crumb and nut mixture to the cream and chocolate and mix lightly but thoroughly. Pour into the crumb crust. Using a spatula, level the mixture. Chill until just set, then mark the tart into portions, using a sharp knife dipped in hot water. Return the tart to the fridge and chill until firm. To decorate, scatter the grated chocolate over the surface and dust with icing sugar. Serve in wedges, with single cream, if desired. Fresh orange segments make an excellent accompaniment.

CHOCOLATE MARSHMALLOW PIE
Make the crumb crust as for the main recipe, but add a delicious marshmallow filling. Melt 275g/10oz/3 cups white marshmallows with 30ml/2 tbsp milk or single cream in the top of a double boiler over simmering water. Alternatively, use a deep bowl and microwave the mixture on High for about 4 minutes, stirring often. Off the heat, stir in 90g/3½oz grated chocolate until melted, then add 30ml/2 tbsp brandy. Tip the mixture into a clean bowl, cool, then chill until beginning to set. Fold in 250ml/8fl oz/1 cup whipped cream, pour into the crumb crust and return to the fridge until completely set. Decorate with chocolate curls.

BAKED CHOCOLATE CHEESECAKE

SERVES 10–12

*275g / 10oz plain chocolate, chopped into
small pieces*
*1.2kg / 2½lb / 5 cups cream cheese, at room
temperature*
200g / 7oz / scant 1 cup granulated sugar
10ml / 2 tsp vanilla essence
4 eggs, at room temperature
175ml / 6fl oz / ¾ cup soured cream
15ml / 1 tbsp cocoa powder

FOR THE BASE

200g / 7oz chocolate biscuits, crushed
75g / 3oz / 6 tbsp butter, melted
2.5ml / ½ tsp ground cinnamon

1 Preheat oven to 180°C / 350°F / Gas 4.
Lightly grease the base and sides of a
23 x 7.5 cm / 9 x 3 in springform tin.

2 To make the base, mix the crushed
biscuits with the butter and cinnamon.
Press the mixture evenly on to the base of
the tin to make a crust. Melt the
chocolate and set it aside.

3 Beat the cream cheese until smooth,
then beat in the sugar and vanilla essence.
Add the eggs, one at a time.

4 Stir the soured cream into the cocoa
powder to form a paste. Add to the
cream cheese mixture. Stir in the melted
chocolate and mix until smooth.

5 Pour the filling on to the base. Bake for
1 hour. Cool in the tin, then remove the
sides of the tin and slide the cheesecake
on to a plate. Serve chilled.

MARBLED CHOCOLATE CHEESECAKE

SERVES 6

50g / 2oz / ½ cup cocoa powder
75ml / 5 tbsp hot water
900g / 2lb cream cheese, at room temperature
200g / 7oz / scant 1 cup caster sugar
4 eggs
5ml / 1 tsp vanilla essence
75g / 3oz digestive biscuits, crushed

1 Preheat oven to 180°C / 350°F / Gas 4. Line a 20 x 8 cm / 8 x 3 in cake tin with greaseproof paper. Grease the paper.
2 Sift the cocoa powder into a bowl. Pour over the hot water and stir to dissolve.
3 Beat the cheese until smooth, then beat in the sugar, followed by the eggs, one at a time. Do not overmix.
4 Divide the mixture evenly between two bowls. Stir the chocolate mixture into one bowl, then add the vanilla essence to the remaining mixture.

5 Pour a cup or ladleful of the plain mixture into the centre of the tin; it will spread out into an even layer. Slowly pour over a cupful of chocolate mixture in the centre. Continue to alternate the cake mixtures in this way until both are used up. Draw a thin metal skewer through the cake mixture for a marbled effect.
6 Set the tin in a roasting pan and pour in hot water to come 4 cm / 1½ in up the sides of the cake tin.

7 Bake the cheesecake for about 1½ hours, until the top is golden. (The cake will rise during baking but will sink later.) Cool in the tin on a wire rack.
8 Run a knife around the inside edge of the cake. Invert a flat plate over the tin and turn out the cake.

9 Sprinkle the crushed biscuits evenly over the cake, gently invert another plate on top, and turn over again. Cover and chill for 3 hours, preferably overnight.

RASPBERRY, MASCARPONE AND WHITE CHOCOLATE CHEESECAKE

SERVES 8

50g / 2oz / ¼ cup unsalted butter
225g / 8oz ginger biscuits, crushed
50g / 2oz / ½ cup chopped pecan nuts
or walnuts

FOR THE FILLING

275g / 10oz / 1¼ cups mascarpone cheese
175g / 6oz / ¾ cup fromage frais
2 eggs, beaten
45ml / 3 tbsp caster sugar
250g / 9oz white chocolate, chopped into
small pieces
225g / 8oz / 1½ cups fresh or frozen raspberries

FOR THE TOPPING

115g / 4oz / ½ cup mascarpone cheese
75g / 3oz / ⅓ cup fromage frais
white chocolate curls and fresh raspberries,
to decorate

1 Preheat oven to 150°C / 300°F / Gas 2. Melt the butter in a saucepan, then stir in the crushed biscuits and nuts. Press into the base of a 23 cm / 9 in springform cake tin. Level the surface.

2 Make the filling. Using a wooden spoon, beat the mascarpone and fromage frais in a large mixing bowl, then beat in the eggs, a little at a time. Add the caster sugar. Beat until the sugar has dissolved, and the mixture is smooth and creamy.

3 Melt the white chocolate gently in a heatproof bowl over a saucepan of simmering water, then stir into the cheese mixture. Add the fresh or frozen raspberries and mix lightly.

4 Tip into the prepared tin and spread evenly, then bake for about 1 hour or until just set. Switch off the oven, but do not remove the cheesecake. Leave it until cold and completely set.

5 Remove the sides of the tin and carefully lift the cheesecake on to a serving plate. Make the topping by mixing the mascarpone and fromage frais in a bowl and spreading the mixture over the cheesecake. Decorate with chocolate curls and raspberries.

APRICOT AND WHITE CHOCOLATE CHEESECAKE

Use 225g / 8oz / 1 cup ready-to-eat dried apricots instead of the fresh or frozen raspberries in the cheesecake mixture. Slice the apricots thinly or dice them. Omit the mascarpone and fromage frais topping and serve the cheesecake with an apricot sauce, made by poaching 225g / 8oz stoned fresh apricots in 120ml / 4fl oz / ½ cup water until tender, then rubbing the fruit and liquid through a sieve placed over a bowl. Sweeten the apricot purée with caster sugar to taste, and add enough lemon juice to sharpen the flavour. Alternatively, purée drained canned apricots with a little of their syrup, then stir in lemon juice to taste.

LUXURY WHITE CHOCOLATE CHEESECAKE

SERVES 16—20

150g / 5oz (about 16—18) digestive biscuits
50g / 2oz / ½ cup blanched hazelnuts, toasted
50g / 2oz / ¼ cup unsalted butter, melted
2.5ml / ½ tsp ground cinnamon
white chocolate curls, to decorate
cocoa powder, for dusting (optional)

FOR THE FILLING
350g / 12oz fine quality white chocolate,
chopped into small pieces
120ml / 4fl oz / ½ cup whipping cream or
double cream
675g / 1½lb / 3 x 8oz packets cream
cheese, softened
50g / 2oz / ¼ cup granulated sugar
4 eggs
30ml / 2 tbsp hazelnut-flavoured liqueur or
15ml / 1 tbsp vanilla essence

FOR THE TOPPING
450ml / ¾ pint / 1¾ cups soured cream
50g / 2oz / ¼ cup granulated sugar
15ml / 1 tbsp hazelnut-flavoured liqueur or
5ml / 1 tsp vanilla essence

3 Using a hand-held electric mixer, beat the cream cheese and sugar in a large bowl until smooth. Add the eggs one at a time, beating well. Slowly beat in the white chocolate mixture and liqueur or vanilla essence. Pour the filling into the baked crust. Place the tin on the hot baking sheet. Bake for 45—55 minutes, and do not allow the top to brown. Transfer the cheesecake to a wire rack while preparing the topping. Increase the oven temperature to 200°C/400°F/Gas 6.

4 Prepare the topping. In a small bowl whisk the soured cream, sugar and liqueur or vanilla essence until thoroughly mixed. Pour the mixture over the cheesecake, spreading it evenly, and return to the oven. Bake for a further 5—7 minutes. Turn off the oven, but do not open the door for 1 hour. Serve the cheesecake at room temperature, decorated with the white chocolate curls. Dust the surface lightly with cocoa powder, if desired.

1 Preheat oven to 180°C/350°F/Gas 4. Grease a 23 x 7.5 cm/9 x 3 in springform tin. In a food processor, process the biscuits and hazelnuts until fine crumbs form. Pour in the butter and cinnamon. Process just until blended. Using the back of a spoon, press on to the base and to within 1 cm/½ in of the top of the sides of the cake tin. Bake the crumb crust for 5—7 minutes, until just set. Cool in the tin on a wire rack. Lower the oven temperature to 150°C/300°F/ Gas 2 and place a baking sheet inside to heat up.

2 Prepare the filling. In a small saucepan over a low heat, melt the white chocolate and cream until smooth, stirring frequently. Set aside to cool slightly.

MISSISSIPPI MUD PIE

SERVES 8

175g / 6oz / 1½ cups plain flour
2.5ml / ½ tsp salt
115g / 4oz / ½ cup butter
30–45ml / 2–3 tbsp iced water

FOR THE FILLING

75g / 3oz plain chocolate, broken into
small pieces
50g / 2oz / ¼ cup butter or margarine
45ml / 3 tbsp golden syrup
3 eggs, beaten
150g / 5oz / ⅔ cup soft light brown
sugar
5ml / 1 tsp vanilla essence

TO DECORATE

115g / 4oz chocolate bar
300ml / ½ pint / 1¼ cups whipping cream

<u>1</u> Preheat oven to 220°C/425°F/Gas 7. Sift the flour and salt into a mixing bowl. Rub in the butter until the mixture resembles coarse breadcrumbs. Sprinkle in the water, about 15ml/1 tbsp at a time, and toss the mixture lightly with your fingers or a fork until the dough forms a ball.

<u>2</u> On a lightly floured surface, roll out the pastry and line a 23 cm/9 in flan tin, easing in the pastry and being careful not to stretch it. With your thumbs, make a fluted edge.

<u>3</u> Using a fork, prick the base and sides of the pastry case. Bake for 10–15 minutes, until lightly browned. Cool, in the pan.

<u>4</u> Make the filling. In a heatproof bowl set over a pan of barely simmering water, melt the plain chocolate with the butter or margarine and the golden syrup. Remove the bowl from the heat and stir in the eggs, sugar and vanilla essence.

<u>5</u> Lower the oven temperature to 180°C/350°F/Gas 4. Pour the chocolate mixture into the pastry case. Bake for 35–40 minutes, until the filling is set. Allow to cool completely in the flan tin, on a rack.

<u>6</u> Make the decoration. Use the heat of your hands to soften the chocolate bar slightly. Working over a sheet of non-stick baking paper, draw the blade of a swivel-bladed vegetable peeler across the side of the chocolate bar to shave off short, wide curls. Chill the curls until required.

<u>7</u> Before serving the pie, pour the cream into a bowl and whip to soft peaks. Spread over the top of the pie, hiding the chocolate filling completely. Decorate with the chocolate curls.

CHOCOLATE, BANANA AND TOFFEE PIE

SERVES 6

65g / 2½oz / 5 tbsp unsalted butter,
melted
250g / 9oz milk chocolate digestive biscuits,
crushed
chocolate curls, to decorate

FOR THE FILLING

397g / 13oz can condensed milk
150g / 5oz plain chocolate, chopped
120ml / 4fl oz / ½ cup crème fraîche
15ml / 1 tbsp golden syrup

FOR THE TOPPING

2 bananas
250ml / 8fl oz / 1 cup crème fraîche
10ml / 2 tsp strong black coffee

1 Mix the butter with the biscuit crumbs. Press on to the base and sides of a 23cm/9in loose-based flan tin. Chill.

2 Make the filling. Place the unopened can of condensed milk in a deep saucepan of boiling water, making sure that it is completely covered. Lower the heat and simmer, covered for 2 hours, topping up the water as necessary. The can must remain covered at all times.

3 Remove the pan from the heat and set aside, covered, until the can has cooled down completely in the water. Do not attempt to open the can until it is completely cold.

4 Gently melt the chocolate with the crème fraîche and golden syrup in a heatproof bowl over a saucepan of simmering water. Stir in the caramelized condensed milk and beat until evenly mixed. Pour the filling into the biscuit crust and spread it evenly.

5 Slice the bananas evenly and arrange them over the chocolate filling.

6 Stir the crème fraîche and coffee together in a bowl, then spoon the mixture over the bananas. Sprinkle the chocolate curls on top. Alternatively, omit the crème fraîche topping and decorate with whipped cream and extra banana slices.

CHILLED CHOCOLATE DESSERTS

DOUBLE CHOCOLATE SNOWBALL

SERVES 12–14

350g/12oz bittersweet or plain chocolate, chopped into small pieces
350g/12oz/1¾ cups caster sugar
275g/10oz/1¼ cups unsalted butter, cut into small pieces
8 eggs
60ml/4 tbsp orange-flavoured liqueur or brandy
cocoa powder, for dusting

FOR THE WHITE CHOCOLATE CREAM

200g/7oz fine quality white chocolate, chopped into small pieces
475ml/16fl oz/2 cups double or whipping cream
15ml/1 tbsp orange-flavoured liqueur (optional)

1 Preheat oven to 180°C/350°F/Gas 4. Carefully line a 1.75 litre/3 pint/7½ cup round ovenproof bowl with aluminium foil, smoothing the sides. Melt the bittersweet chocolate in a heatproof bowl over a pan of barely simmering water. Add the caster sugar and stir until the chocolate has melted and the sugar has dissolved. Strain the mixture into a medium bowl.

2 With a hand-held electric mixer at low speed, beat in the butter, then the eggs, one at a time, beating well after each addition. Stir in the liqueur or brandy and pour into the prepared bowl. Tap the sides of the bowl gently to release any large air bubbles.

3 Bake for 1¼–1½ hours until the surface is firm and slightly risen, but cracked. The centre will still be wobbly, but will set on cooling. Remove the bowl to a rack to cool to room temperature; the top will sink. Cover the surface of the cake with a dinner plate (to make an even surface for unmoulding); then wrap completely with clear film or foil and chill overnight.

4 To unmould, remove the film or foil, lift off the plate, and place an upturned serving plate over the top of the mould. Invert the mould on to the plate and shake firmly to release the cake. Carefully peel off the foil used for lining the bowl. Cover until ready to decorate.

5 In a food processor fitted with a metal blade, process the white chocolate until fine. Heat 120ml/4fl oz/½ cup of the cream in a small saucepan until just beginning to simmer. With the food processor running, pour the hot cream through the feeder tube and process until the chocolate has melted completely. Strain into a medium bowl and cool to room temperature, stirring occasionally.

6 In another bowl, beat the remaining cream with the electric mixer until soft peaks form. Add the liqueur and beat for 30 seconds or until the cream holds its shape, but is not yet stiff. Fold a spoonful of cream into the chocolate mixture to lighten it, then fold in the rest. Spoon into a piping bag fitted with a star tip and pipe rosettes over the surface of the cake. Dust lightly with cocoa powder to finish the decoration.

CHOCOLATE AMARETTO MARQUISE

SERVES 10–12

15ml/1 tbsp flavourless vegetable oil, such as groundnut or sunflower
75g/3oz/7–8 amaretti biscuits, finely crushed
25g/1oz/¼ cup unblanched almonds, toasted and finely chopped
450g/1lb fine quality bittersweet or plain chocolate, chopped into small pieces
75ml/5 tbsp Amaretto liqueur
75ml/5 tbsp golden syrup
475ml/16fl oz/2 cups double cream cocoa powder, for dusting

FOR THE AMARETTO CREAM
350ml/12fl oz/1½ cups whipping cream or double cream for serving
30–45ml/2–3 tbsp Amaretto di Soronno liqueur

1 Lightly oil a 23 cm/9 in heart-shaped or springform cake tin. Line the bottom with non-stick baking paper and oil the paper. In a small bowl, combine the crushed amaretti biscuits and the chopped almonds. Sprinkle evenly on to the base of the tin.

2 Place the chocolate, Amaretto liqueur and golden syrup in a medium saucepan over a very low heat. Stir frequently until the chocolate is melted and the mixture is smooth. Remove from the heat and allow it to cool for about 6–8 minutes, until the mixture feels just warm to the touch.

3 Pour the cream into a bowl. Whip with a hand-held electric mixer, until it just begins to hold its shape. Stir a large spoonful into the chocolate mixture, to lighten it, then quickly add the remaining cream and gently fold into the chocolate mixture. Pour into the prepared tin, on top of the amaretti and almond mixture. Level the surface. Cover the tin with clear film and chill overnight.

4 To unmould, run a thin-bladed sharp knife under hot water and dry carefully. Run the knife around the edge of the tin to loosen the dessert. Place a serving plate over the tin, then invert to unmould. Carefully peel off the paper, replacing any crust that sticks to it, and dust with cocoa powder. In a bowl, whip the cream and Amaretto liqueur to soft peaks. Serve separately.

CHOCOLATE PUFFS

SERVES 4–6

65g / 2½oz / generous ½ cup plain flour
150ml / ¼ pint / ⅔ cup water
50g / 2oz / ¼ cup butter
2 eggs, beaten

FOR THE FILLING AND ICING

150ml / ¼ pint / ⅔ cup double cream
225g / 8oz / 1½ cups icing sugar
15ml / 1 tbsp cocoa powder
30–60ml / 2–4 tbsp water

1 Preheat oven to 220°C/425°F/Gas 7. Sift the flour into a bowl. Put the water in a saucepan over a medium heat, add the butter and heat gently until it melts. Increase the heat and bring to the boil, then remove from the heat. Tip in all the flour at once and beat quickly until the mixture sticks together and becomes thick and glossy, leaving the side of the pan clean. Leave the mixture to cool slightly.

2 Add the eggs, a little at a time, to the mixture and beat by hand with a wooden spoon or with an electric whisk, until the mixture (choux pastry) is thick and glossy and drops reluctantly from a spoon. (You may not need to use all of the egg.) Spoon the choux pastry into a piping bag fitted with a 2 cm / ¾ in nozzle. Dampen two baking sheets with cold water.

3 Pipe walnut-sized spoonfuls of the choux pastry on to the dampened baking sheets. Leave some space for them to rise. Cook for 25–30 minutes, until they are golden brown and well risen. Use a palette knife to lift the puffs on to a wire rack, and make a small hole in each one with the handle of a wooden spoon to allow the steam to escape. Leave to cool.

4 Make the filling and icing. Whip the cream until thick. Put it into a piping bag fitted with a plain or star nozzle. Push the nozzle into the hole in each puff and squirt a little cream inside. Put the icing sugar and cocoa in a small bowl and stir together. Add enough water to make a thick glossy icing. Spread a little icing on each puff and serve when set.

CHOCOLATE HAZELNUT GALETTES

SERVES 4

*175g/6oz plain chocolate, chopped into small
pieces
45ml/3 tbsp single cream
30ml/2 tbsp flaked hazelnuts
115g/4oz white chocolate, chopped into small
pieces
175g/6oz/¾ cup fromage frais (8% fat)
15ml/1 tbsp dry sherry
60ml/4 tbsp finely chopped hazelnuts, toasted
physalis (Cape gooseberries), dipped in white
chocolate, to decorate*

1 Melt the plain chocolate in a heatproof
bowl over a saucepan of barely simmering
water, then remove the pan from the heat
and lift off the bowl. Stir the cream into
the melted chocolate. Draw twelve
7.5 cm/3 in circles on sheets of non-stick
baking paper.

2 Turn the baking paper over and spread
the plain chocolate over each marked
circle, covering in a thin, even layer.
Scatter flaked hazelnuts over four of the
circles, then leave until set.
3 Melt the white chocolate in a heatproof
bowl over hot water, then stir in the
fromage frais and dry sherry. Fold in the
chopped, toasted hazelnuts. Leave to cool
until the mixture holds its shape.

4 Remove the plain chocolate rounds
carefully from the paper and sandwich
them together in stacks of three,
spooning the white chocolate hazelnut
cream between the layers and using the
hazelnut-covered rounds on top. Chill
before serving.
5 To serve, place the galettes on
individual plates and decorate with
chocolate-dipped physalis.

CHOCOLATE PAVLOVA WITH PASSION FRUIT CREAM

SERVES 6

4 egg whites
200g / 7oz / scant 1 cup caster sugar
20ml / 4 tsp cornflour
45ml / 3 tbsp cocoa powder
5ml / 1 tsp vinegar
chocolate leaves, to decorate

FOR THE FILLING

150g / 5oz plain chocolate, chopped into
small pieces
250ml / 8fl oz / 1 cup double cream
150g / 5oz / ⅔ cup Greek-style yogurt
2.5ml / ½ tsp vanilla essence
4 passion fruit

<u>1</u> Preheat oven to 140°C / 275°F / Gas 1. Cut a piece of non-stick baking paper to fit a baking sheet. Draw a 23 cm / 9 in circle on the paper.

<u>2</u> Whisk the egg whites in a clean, grease-free bowl until stiff. Gradually whisk in the sugar and continue to whisk until the mixture is stiff again. Whisk in the cornflour, cocoa and vinegar.

<u>3</u> Place the baking paper upside down on the baking sheet. Spread the mixture over the marked circle, making a slight dip in the centre. Bake for 1½–2 hours.

<u>4</u> Make the filling. Melt the chocolate in a heatproof bowl over barely simmering water, then remove from the heat and cool slightly. In a separate bowl, whip the cream with the yogurt and vanilla essence until thick. Fold 60ml / 4 tbsp into the chocolate, then set both mixtures aside.

<u>5</u> Halve all the passion fruit and scoop out the pulp. Stir half into the plain cream mixture. Carefully remove the meringue shell from the baking sheet and place it on a large serving plate. Fill with the passion fruit cream, then spoon over the chocolate mixture and the remaining passion fruit pulp.

<u>6</u> Decorate with chocolate leaves and serve as soon as possible, while the meringue is still crisp on the outside and deliciously chewy within.

CHOCOLATE AND CHESTNUT POTS

SERVES 6

250g / 9oz plain chocolate
60ml / 4 tbsp Madeira
25g / 1oz / 2 tbsp butter, diced
2 eggs, separated
225g / 8oz / 1 cup unsweetened chestnut purée
crème fraîche and chocolate curls, to decorate

1 Make a few chocolate curls for decoration, then break the rest of the chocolate into squares and melt it with the Madeira in a heatproof bowl over a saucepan of barely simmering water. Remove from the heat and add the butter, a few pieces at a time, stirring until melted and smooth.
2 Beat the egg yolks quickly into the mixture, then beat in the chestnut purée, a little at a time, making sure that each addition is absorbed before you add the next, mixing until smooth.
3 Whisk the egg whites in a clean, grease-free bowl until stiff. Stir about 15ml / 1 tbsp of the whites into the chestnut mixture to lighten it, then fold in the rest evenly.
4 Spoon the mixture into six small ramekin dishes or custard cups and chill until set. Serve the pots topped with a generous spoonful of crème fraîche or whipped double cream. Decorate with the chocolate curls.

MOCHA VELVET CREAM POTS

SERVES 8

15ml / 1 tbsp instant coffee powder
475ml / 16fl oz / 2 cups milk
75g / 3oz / 6 tbsp caster sugar
225g / 8oz plain chocolate, chopped into small pieces
10ml / 2 tsp vanilla essence
30ml / 2 tbsp coffee liqueur (optional)
7 egg yolks
whipped cream and crystallized mimosa balls, to decorate

1 Preheat oven to 160°C / 325°F / Gas 3. Place eight 120ml / 4fl oz / ½ cup custard cups or ramekins in a roasting tin. Set the tin aside.
2 Put the instant coffee into a saucepan. Stir in the milk, then add the sugar and set the pan over a medium heat. Bring to the boil, stirring constantly, until both the coffee and the sugar have dissolved completely.
3 Remove the pan from the heat and add the chocolate. Stir until it has melted and the sauce is smooth. Stir in the vanilla essence and coffee liqueur, if using.
4 In a bowl, whisk the egg yolks to blend them lightly. Slowly whisk in the chocolate mixture until well mixed, then strain the mixture into a large jug and divide equally among the cups or ramekins. Pour enough boiling water into the roasting tin to come halfway up the sides of the cups or ramekins. Carefully place the roasting tin in the oven.
5 Bake for 30–35 minutes, until the custard is just set and a knife inserted into the custard comes out clean. Remove the cups or ramekins from the roasting tin and allow to cool. Place on a baking sheet, cover and chill completely. Decorate with whipped cream and crystallized mimosa balls, if desired.

CHOCOLATE VANILLA TIMBALES

SERVES 6

350ml/12fl oz/1½ cups semi-skimmed milk
30ml/2 tbsp cocoa powder
2 eggs
10ml/2 tsp vanilla essence
45ml/3 tbsp granulated sweetener
15ml/1 tbsp/1 sachet powdered gelatine
45ml/3 tbsp hot water
extra cocoa powder, to decorate

FOR THE SAUCE

115g/4oz/½ cup light Greek-style yogurt
25ml/1½ tbsp vanilla essence

1 Place the milk and cocoa powder in a saucepan and stir until the milk is boiling. Separate the eggs and beat the egg yolks with the vanilla and sweetener in a bowl, until the mixture is pale and smooth. Gradually pour in the chocolate milk, beating well.

2 Return the mixture to the pan and stir constantly over a gentle heat, without boiling, until it is slightly thickened and smooth.

3 Remove the pan from the heat. Pour the gelatine into the hot water and stir until it is completely dissolved, then quickly stir it into the milk mixture. Put this mixture aside and allow it to cool until almost setting.

4 Whisk the egg whites until they hold soft peaks. Fold the egg whites quickly into the milk mixture. Spoon the timbale mixture into six individual moulds and chill them until set.

5 To serve, run a knife around the edge, dip the moulds quickly into hot water and turn out. Dust with cocoa. For the sauce, stir together the yogurt and vanilla and spoon on to the plates.

TIRAMISU IN CHOCOLATE CUPS

SERVES 6

1 egg yolk
30ml / 2 tbsp caster sugar
2.5ml / ½ tsp vanilla essence
250g / 9oz / generous 1 cup mascarpone cheese
120ml / 4fl oz / ½ cup strong black coffee
15ml / 1 tbsp cocoa powder
30ml / 2 tbsp coffee liqueur
16 amaretti biscuits
cocoa powder, for dusting

FOR THE CHOCOLATE CUPS

175g / 6oz plain chocolate, chopped
25g / 1oz / 2 tbsp unsalted butter

1 Make the chocolate cups. Cut out six 15 cm / 6 in rounds of non-stick baking paper. Melt the chocolate with the butter in a heatproof bowl over a saucepan of simmering water. Stir until smooth, then spread a spoonful of the chocolate mixture over each circle, to within 2 cm / ¾ in of the edge.

2 Carefully lift each paper round and drape it over an upturned teacup or ramekin so that the edges curve into frills. Leave until completely set, then carefully lift off and peel away the paper to reveal the chocolate cups.

3 Make the filling. Using a hand-held electric mixer, beat the egg yolk and sugar in a bowl until smooth, then stir in the vanilla essence. Soften the mascarpone if necessary, then stir it into the egg yolk mixture. Beat until smooth.

4 In a separate bowl, mix the coffee, cocoa and liqueur. Break up the biscuits roughly, then stir them into the mixture.

5 Place the chocolate cups on individual plates. Divide half the biscuit mixture among them, then spoon over half the mascarpone mixture.

6 Spoon over the remaining biscuit mixture (including any free liquid), top with the rest of the mascarpone mixture and dust lightly with cocoa powder. Chill for about 30 minutes before serving.

DEVILISH CHOCOLATE ROULADE

SERVES 6–8

175g/6oz plain dark chocolate, chopped into small pieces
4 eggs, separated
115g/4oz/½ cup caster sugar
cocoa powder for dusting
chocolate-dipped strawberries, to decorate

FOR THE FILLING

225g/8oz plain chocolate, chopped into small pieces
45ml/3 tbsp brandy
2 eggs, separated
250g/9oz/generous 1 cup mascarpone cheese

1 Preheat oven to 180°C/350°F/Gas 4. Grease a 33 × 23 cm/13 × 9 in Swiss roll tin and line with non-stick baking paper. Melt the chocolate.

2 Whisk the egg yolks and sugar in a bowl until pale and thick, then stir in the melted chocolate. Place the egg whites in a clean, grease-free bowl. Whisk them to soft peaks, then fold lightly and evenly into the egg and chocolate mixture.

3 Scrape into the tin and spread to the corners. Bake for 15-20 minutes, until well risen and firm to the touch. Dust a sheet of non-stick baking paper with cocoa powder. Turn the sponge out on the paper, cover with a clean dish towel and leave to cool.

4 Make the filling. Melt the chocolate with the brandy in a heatproof bowl over a saucepan of simmering water. Remove from the heat. Beat the egg yolks together, then beat into the chocolate mixture. In a separate bowl whisk the whites to soft peaks, then fold them lightly and evenly into the filling.

5 Uncover the roulade, remove the lining paper and spread with the mascarpone. Spread the chocolate mixture over the top, then roll up carefully from a long side to enclose the filling. Transfer to a serving plate with the join underneath, top with fresh chocolate-dipped strawberries and chill before serving.

COOK'S TIP

Chocolate-dipped strawberries make a marvellous edible decoration for cakes and desserts. Break plain, milk or white chocolate into small pieces and place in a small deep heatproof bowl over a saucepan of barely simmering water. While the chocolate melts, line a baking sheet with non-stick baking paper and set it aside.

Stir the melted chocolate until it is completely smooth. Holding a strawberry by its stalk or stalk end, dip it partially or fully into the melted chocolate, allowing any excess chocolate to drip back into the bowl, then place the fruit on the paper-lined baking sheet. Repeat with the rest of the fruit. Leave until the chocolate has set. Use on the same day.

The same technique can be applied to other relatively firm fruits, such as cherries and orange segments.

Chocolate Cones with Apricot Sauce

Serves 6

*250g/9oz plain dark chocolate, chopped into
small pieces
350g/12oz/1½ cups ricotta cheese
45ml/3 tbsp double cream
30ml/2 tbsp brandy
30ml/2 tbsp icing sugar
finely grated rind of 1 lemon
pared strips of lemon rind, to decorate*

For the Sauce

*175g/6oz/⅔ cup apricot jam
45ml/3 tbsp lemon juice*

1 Cut twelve 10 cm/4 in double
thickness rounds from non-stick baking
paper and shape each into a cone. Secure
with masking tape.

2 Melt the chocolate over a saucepan of
simmering water. Cool slightly, then
spoon a little into each cone, swirling and
brushing it to coat the paper evenly.

3 Support each cone point downwards in
a cup or glass held on its side, to keep it
level. Leave in a cool place until the cones
are completely set. Unless it is a very hot
day, do not put the cones in the fridge, as
this may mar their appearance.

4 Make the sauce. Combine the apricot
jam and lemon juice in a small saucepan.
Melt over a gentle heat, stirring
occasionally, then press through a sieve
into a small bowl. Set aside to cool.

5 Beat the ricotta cheese in a bowl until
softened, then beat in the cream, brandy
and icing sugar. Stir in the lemon rind.
Spoon the mixture into a piping bag. Fill
the cones, then carefully peel off the non-
stick baking paper.

6 Spoon a pool of apricot sauce on to six
dessert plates. Arrange the cones in pairs
on the plates. Decorate with a scattering
of pared lemon rind strips and serve
immediately.

CHOCOLATE BLANCMANGE

SERVES 4
60ml/4 tbsp cornflour
600ml/1 pint/2½ cups milk
45ml/3 tbsp sugar
50–115g/2–4oz plain chocolate, chopped
few drops of vanilla essence
white and plain chocolate curls, to decorate

1 Rinse a 750ml/1¼ pint/3 cup fluted mould with cold water and leave it upside down to drain. Blend the cornflour to a smooth paste with a little of the milk in a medium-sized bowl.

2 Bring the remaining milk to the boil, preferably in a non-stick saucepan, then pour on to the blended mixture stirring constantly.

3 Pour all the milk back into the saucepan and bring slowly to the boil over a low heat, stirring constantly until the mixture boils and thickens. Remove the pan from the heat, then add the sugar, chocolate and vanilla essence and stir until the sauce is smooth, all the sugar has dissolved and the chocolate pieces have melted completely.

4 Pour the chocolate mixture into the mould, cover closely with dampened greaseproof paper (to prevent the formation of a skin) and leave in a cool place for several hours to set.

5 To unmould the blancmange, place a large serving plate upside down on top of the mould. Holding the plate and mould firmly together, turn them both over. Give both plate and mould a gentle but firm shake to loosen the blancmange, then lift off the mould. Scatter the chocolate curls over the top and serve.

CHOCOLATE MANDARIN TRIFLE

SERVES 6–8

4 trifle sponges
14 amaretti biscuits
60ml/4 tbsp Amaretto di Saronno or
sweet sherry
8 mandarin oranges

FOR THE CUSTARD

200g/7oz plain chocolate, chopped into
small pieces
30ml/2 tbsp cornflour or custard powder
30ml/2 tbsp caster sugar
2 egg yolks
200ml/7fl oz/scant 1 cup milk
250g/9oz/generous 1 cup mascarpone cheese

FOR THE TOPPING

250g/9oz/generous 1 cup fromage frais
chocolate shapes
mandarin slices or segments

1 Break up the trifle sponges and place them in a large glass serving dish. Crumble the amaretti biscuits over and then sprinkle with Amaretto or sherry.

2 Squeeze the juice from 2 mandarins and sprinkle into the dish. Segment the rest and put in the dish.

3 Make the custard. Melt the chocolate. In a heatproof bowl, mix the cornflour or custard powder, caster sugar and egg yolks to a smooth paste.

4 Heat the milk in a small saucepan until almost boiling, then pour on to the egg yolk mixture, stirring constantly. Return to the clean pan and stir over a low heat until the custard has thickened slightly and is smooth.

5 Stir in the mascarpone until melted, then mix in the melted chocolate. Spread over the sponge and biscuit, cool, then chill.

6 To serve, spread the fromage frais over the custard, then decorate with chocolate shapes and mandarin slices or segments.

COOK'S TIP

You can use canned mandarin oranges, if you prefer. Spoon about 30ml/2 tbsp of the juice over the sponge and biscuit mixture.

CHOCOLATE PROFITEROLES

4 Beat 1 egg in a small bowl and set aside. Add the whole eggs, one at a time, to the flour mixture, beating well after each addition. Beat in just enough of the beaten egg to make a smooth, shiny dough. It should pull away and fall slowly when dropped from a spoon.

5 Using a tablespoon, ease the dough in 12 mounds on to the prepared baking sheet. Bake for 25–30 minutes, until the puffs are golden brown.

6 Remove the puffs from the oven and cut a small slit in the side of each of them to release the steam. Return the puffs to the oven, turn off the heat and leave them to dry out, with the oven door open.

7 Remove the ice cream from the freezer and allow it to soften for about 10 minutes. Split the profiteroles in half and put a small scoop of ice cream in each. Arrange on a serving platter or divide among individual plates. Pour the sauce over the profiteroles and serve at once.

SERVES 4–6

110g / 3¾oz / scant 1 cup plain flour
1.5ml / ¼ tsp salt
pinch of freshly grated nutmeg
175ml / 6fl oz / ¾ cup water
75g / 3oz / 6 tbsp unsalted butter, cut into 6 equal pieces
3 eggs
750ml / 1¼ pints / 3 cups vanilla ice cream

FOR THE CHOCOLATE SAUCE

275g / 10oz plain chocolate, chopped into small pieces
120ml / 4fl oz / ½ cup warm water

1 Preheat oven to 200°C/400°F/Gas 6. Grease a baking sheet. Sift the flour, salt and nutmeg on to a sheet of greaseproof paper or foil.

2 Make the sauce. Melt the chocolate with the water in a heatproof bowl placed over a saucepan of barely simmering water. Stir until smooth. Keep warm until ready to serve, or reheat when required.

3 In a medium saucepan, bring the water and butter to the boil. Remove from the heat and add the dry ingredients all at once, funnelling them in from the paper or foil. Beat with a wooden spoon for about 1 minute until well blended and the mixture starts to pull away from the pan, then set the pan over a low heat and cook the mixture for about 2 minutes, beating constantly. Remove from the heat.

VARIATION

Fill the profiteroles with whipped cream, if you prefer. Spoon the cream into a piping bag and fill the slit puffs, or sandwich the halved puffs with the cream.

BITTER CHOCOLATE MOUSSE

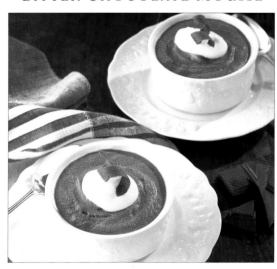

SERVES 8

225g/8oz plain chocolate, chopped into small pieces
60ml/4 tbsp water
30ml/2 tbsp orange flavoured liqueur or brandy
25g/1oz/2 tbsp unsalted butter, cut into small pieces
4 eggs, separated
90ml/6 tbsp whipping cream
1.5ml/¼ tsp cream of tartar
45ml/3 tbsp caster sugar
crème fraîche and chocolate curls, to decorate

1 Melt the chocolate with the water in a heatproof bowl over a pan of barely simmering water, stirring until smooth. Off the heat, whisk in the liqueur or brandy and butter.

2 With a hand-held electric mixer, beat the egg yolks for 2–3 minutes until thick and creamy, then slowly beat into the melted chocolate until well blended. Set aside.

3 Whip the cream until soft peaks form and stir a spoonful into the chocolate mixture to lighten it. Fold in the remaining cream.

4 In a grease free bowl, beat the egg whites slowly until frothy. Add the cream of tartar, increase the speed and continue beating until they form soft peaks. Gradually sprinkle over the sugar and continue beating until the whites are stiff and glossy.

5 Using a rubber spatula or large metal spoon, stir a quarter of the egg whites into the chocolate mixture, then gently fold in the remaining whites, cutting down to the bottom, along the sides and up to the top in a semicircular motion until they are just combined. Gently spoon into eight individual dishes. Chill for at least 2 hours or until set.

6 Spoon a little crème fraîche over each mousse and decorate with the chocolate curls.

WHITE CHOCOLATE VANILLA MOUSSE WITH DARK CHOCOLATE SAUCE

SERVES 6–8

200g/7 oz white chocolate, chopped into small pieces
2 eggs, separated
60ml/4 tbsp caster sugar
300ml/½ pint/1¼ cups double cream
1 sachet powdered gelatine
150ml/¼ pint/⅔ cup Greek-style yogurt
10ml/2 tsp vanilla essence

FOR THE SAUCE

50g/2oz plain chocolate, chopped into small pieces
30ml/2 tbsp dark rum
60ml/4 tbsp single cream

1 Line a 1 litre/1¾ pint/4 cup loaf tin with non-stick baking paper or clear film. Melt the chocolate. Whisk the egg yolks and sugar until pale and thick, then beat in the chocolate.

2 Heat the cream in a small saucepan until almost boiling, then remove from the heat. Sprinkle the powdered gelatine over, stirring until completely dissolved. Pour on to the chocolate mixture, whisking vigorously until smooth.

3 Whisk the yogurt and vanilla essence into the mixture. In a clean, grease-free bowl, whisk the egg whites until stiff, then fold them into the mixture. Tip into the prepared loaf tin, level the surface and chill until set.

4 Make the sauce. Melt the chocolate with the rum and cream in a heatproof bowl over a saucepan of simmering water, stirring occasionally, then leave to cool completely.

5 Serve the mousse in thick slices with the cooled chocolate sauce poured around.

MANGO AND CHOCOLATE CREME BRULEE

SERVES 6

2 ripe mangoes, peeled, stoned and chopped
300ml / ½ pint / 1¼ cups double cream
300ml / ½ pint / 1¼ cups crème fraîche
1 vanilla pod
115g / 4oz plain dark chocolate, chopped into
small pieces
4 egg yolks
15ml / 1 tbsp clear honey
90ml / 6 tbsp demerara sugar, for the topping

1 Divide the mangoes among six flameproof dishes set on a baking sheet.

2 Mix the cream, crème fraîche and vanilla pod in a large heatproof bowl. Place the bowl over a pan of barely simmering water.

3 Heat the cream mixture for 10 minutes. Do not let the bowl touch the water or the cream may overheat. Remove the vanilla pod and stir in the chocolate, a few pieces at a time, until melted. When smooth, remove the bowl, but leave the pan of water over the heat.

4 Whisk the egg yolks and clear honey in a second heatproof bowl, then gradually pour in the chocolate cream, whisking constantly. Place over the pan of simmering water and stir constantly until the chocolate custard thickens enough to coat the back of a wooden spoon.

5 Remove from the heat and spoon the custard over the mangoes. Cool, then chill in the fridge until set.

6 Preheat the grill to high. Sprinkle 15ml / 1 tbsp demerara sugar evenly over each dessert and spray lightly with a little water. Grill briefly, as close to the heat as possible, until the sugar melts and caramelizes. Chill again before serving the desserts.

WHITE CHOCOLATE PARFAIT

SERVES 10

*225g / 8oz white chocolate, chopped into
small pieces*
600ml / 1 pint / 2½ cups whipping cream
120ml / 4fl oz / ½ cup milk
10 egg yolks
15ml / 1 tbsp caster sugar
40g / 1½oz / ½ cup desiccated coconut
*120ml / 4fl oz / ½ cup canned sweetened
coconut milk*
*150g / 5oz / 1¼ cups unsalted macadamia nuts
curls of fresh coconut, to decorate*

FOR THE CHOCOLATE ICING

*225g / 8oz plain chocolate, chopped into
small pieces*
75g / 3oz / 6 tbsp butter
20ml / generous 1 tbsp golden syrup
175ml / 6fl oz / ¾ cup whipping cream

1 Carefully line the base and sides of a
1.4 litre / 2½ pint / 6 cup terrine mould or
loaf tin with clear film.

2 Melt the chopped white chocolate with
50ml / 2fl oz / ¼ cup of the cream in the
top of a double boiler or a heatproof bowl
set over a saucepan of simmering water.
Stir continually until the mixture is
smooth. Set aside.

3 Put the milk in a pan. Add 250ml /
8fl oz / 1 cup of the remaining cream and
bring to boiling point over a medium heat
stirring constantly.

4 Meanwhile, whisk the egg yolks and
caster sugar together in a large bowl,
until thick and pale.

5 Add the hot cream mixture to the
yolks, whisking constantly. Pour back into
the saucepan and cook over a low heat for
2–3 minutes, until thickened. Stir
constantly and do not boil. Remove the
pan from the heat.

6 Add the melted chocolate, desiccated
coconut and coconut milk, then stir well
and leave to cool. Whip the remaining
cream in a bowl until thick, then fold into
the chocolate and coconut mixture.

7 Put 475ml / 16fl oz / 2 cups of the parfait
mixture in the prepared mould or tin and
spread evenly. Cover and freeze for about
2 hours, until just firm. Cover the
remaining mixture and chill.

VARIATION

White Chocolate and Ginger Parfait:
Use sliced stem ginger instead of
macadamia nuts for the central layer
of the parfait, and substitute syrup
from the jar of ginger for the golden
syrup in the icing. Leave out the
coconut, if you prefer, and use
sweetened condensed milk instead of
the coconut milk.

8 Scatter the macadamia nuts evenly over
the frozen parfait. Spoon in the remaining
parfait mixture and level the surface.
Cover the terrine and freeze for 6–8 hours
or overnight, until the parfait is firm.

9 To make the icing, melt the chocolate
with the butter and syrup in the top of a
double boiler set over hot water. Stir
occasionally.

10 Heat the cream in a saucepan, until
just simmering, then stir into the
chocolate mixture. Remove the pan from
the heat and leave the mixture to cool
until lukewarm.

11 To turn out the parfait, wrap the
terrine or tin in a hot towel and set it
upside down on a plate. Lift off the
terrine or tin, then peel off the clear film.
Place the parfait on a rack over a baking
sheet and pour the icing evenly over the
top. Working quickly, smooth the icing
down the sides with a palette knife. Leave
to set slightly, then transfer to a freezer-
proof plate and freeze for 3–4 hours
more.

12 Remove from the freezer about 15
minutes before serving, to allow the ice
cream to soften slightly. When ready to
serve, cut into slices, using a knife dipped
in hot water between each slice. Serve,
decorated with coconut curls.

CHOCOLATE ICES AND SORBETS

WHITE CHOCOLATE RASPBERRY RIPPLE ICE CREAM

2 In a saucepan, combine the milk and 250ml/8fl oz/1 cup cream and bring to the boil. In a bowl beat the yolks and sugar with a hand-held mixer for 2–3 minutes until thick and creamy. Gradually pour the hot milk mixture over the yolks and return to the pan. Cook over a medium heat until the custard coats the back of a wooden spoon, stirring constantly.

3 Remove the pan from the heat and stir in the white chocolate until melted and smooth. Pour the remaining cream into a large bowl. Strain in the hot custard, mix well, then stir in the vanilla essence. Cool, then transfer the custard to an ice-cream maker and freeze it according to the manufacturer's instructions.

4 When the mixture is frozen, but still soft, transfer one third of the ice cream to a freezerproof bowl. Set half the raspberry sauce aside. Spoon a third of the remainder over the ice cream. Cover with another third of the ice cream and more sauce. Repeat. With a knife or spoon, lightly marble the mixture. Cover and freeze. Allow the ice cream to soften for 15 minutes before serving with the remaining raspberry sauce, and the mint.

MAKES 1 LITRE/1¾ PINTS/4 CUPS
250ml/8fl oz/1 cup milk
475ml/16fl oz/2 cups whipping cream
7 egg yolks
30ml/2 tbsp granulated sugar
225g/8oz fine quality white chocolate,
chopped into small pieces
5ml/1 tsp vanilla essence
mint sprigs to decorate

FOR THE RASPBERRY RIPPLE SAUCE
275g/10oz packet frozen raspberries in light
syrup or 275g/10oz jar reduced sugar
raspberry preserve
10ml/2 tsp golden syrup
15ml/1 tbsp lemon juice
15ml/1 tbsp cornflour mixed to a paste with
15ml/1 tbsp water

1 Prepare the sauce. Press the raspberries and their syrup through a sieve into a saucepan. Add the golden syrup, lemon juice and cornflour mixture. (If using preserve, omit cornflour, but add the water.) Bring to the boil, stirring often, then simmer for 1–2 minutes. Pour into a bowl and cool, then chill.

CHOCOLATE FUDGE SUNDAES

SERVES 4

4 scoops each vanilla and coffee ice cream
2 small ripe bananas
whipped cream
toasted flaked almonds

FOR THE SAUCE

50g / 2oz / ⅓ cup soft light brown sugar
120ml / 4fl oz / ½ cup golden syrup
45ml / 3 tbsp strong black coffee
5ml / 1 tsp ground cinnamon
150g / 5oz plain chocolate, chopped into small pieces
75ml / 3fl oz / 5 tbsp whipping cream
45ml / 3 tbsp coffee-flavoured liqueur (optional)

1 Make the sauce. Place the sugar, syrup, coffee and cinnamon in a heavy-based saucepan. Bring to the boil, then boil for about 5 minutes, stirring the mixture constantly.

2 Turn off the heat and stir in the chocolate. When the chocolate has melted and the mixture is smooth, stir in the cream and the liqueur, if using. Leave the sauce to cool slightly. If made ahead, reheat the sauce gently until just warm.

3 Fill four glasses with a scoop each of vanilla and coffee ice cream.

4 Peel the bananas and slice them thinly. Scatter the sliced bananas over the ice cream. Pour the warm fudge sauce over the bananas, then top each sundae with a generous swirl of whipped cream. Sprinkle the sundaes with toasted almonds and serve at once.

CHOCOLATE ICE CREAM

SERVES 4–6

750ml / 1¼ pints / 3 cups milk
10 cm / 4 in piece of vanilla pod
4 egg yolks
115g / 4oz / ½ cup granulated sugar
225g / 8oz plain chocolate, chopped into
small pieces

<u>1</u> Heat the milk with the vanilla pod in a small saucepan. Remove from the heat as soon as small bubbles start to form on the surface. Do not let it boil. Strain the milk into a jug and set aside.

<u>2</u> Using a wire whisk or hand-held electric mixer, beat the egg yolks in a bowl. Gradually whisk in the sugar and continue to whisk until the mixture is pale and thick. Slowly add the milk to the egg mixture, whisking after each addition. When all the milk has been added, pour the mixture into a heatproof bowl.

<u>3</u> Place the heatproof bowl over a saucepan of simmering water and add the chocolate. Stir over a low heat until the chocolate melts, then raise the heat slightly and continue to stir the chocolate-flavoured custard until it thickens enough to coat the back of a wooden spoon lightly. Remove the custard from the heat, pour into a bowl and allow to cool, stirring occasionally to prevent skin forming on the surface.

<u>4</u> Freeze the chocolate mixture in an ice-cream maker, following the manufacturer's instructions, or pour it into a suitable container for freezing. Freeze for about 3 hours, or until set. Remove from the container and chop roughly into 7.5 cm / 3 in pieces. Place in a food processor and chop until smooth. Return to the freezer container and freeze again. Repeat two or three times, until the ice cream is smooth and creamy.

CHOCOLATE FLAKE ICE CREAM

SERVES 6

300ml / ½ pint / 1¼ cups whipping cream,
chilled
90ml / 6 tbsp Greek-style yogurt
75–90ml / 5–6 tbsp caster sugar
few drops of vanilla essence
150g / 5oz / 10 tbsp flaked or roughly grated
chocolate

COOK'S TIPS

Transfer the ice cream from the freezer to the fridge about 15 minutes before serving, so that it softens, and so that the full flavour can be appreciated.
Use a metal scoop to serve the ice cream, dipping the scoop briefly in warm water between servings. If the ice cream has been made in a loaf tin, simply slice it.

1 Have ready an ice-cream maker, or use a 600–900ml / 1–1½ pint / 2½–3¾ cup freezer-proof container, preferably with a lid. Prepare a place in the freezer so you can easily reach it. If necessary, turn the freezer to the coldest setting.

2 Softly whip the cream in a large bowl then fold in the yogurt, sugar, vanilla essence and chocolate. Stir gently to mix thoroughly, and then transfer to the ice-cream maker or freezer container.

3 Smooth the surface of the ice cream, then cover and freeze. Gently stir with a fork every 30 minutes for up to 4 hours until the ice cream is too hard to stir. If using an ice-cream maker, follow the manufacturer's instructions.

CHOCOLATE SORBET

SERVES 6

150g / 5oz bittersweet chocolate, chopped
115g / 4oz plain chocolate, grated
225g / 8oz / 1¼ cups caster sugar
475ml / 16fl oz / 2 cups water
chocolate curls, to decorate

1 Put all the chocolate in a food processor, fitted with the metal blade, and process for 20–30 seconds until finely chopped.
2 In a saucepan over a medium heat, bring the sugar and water to the boil, stirring until the sugar dissolves. Boil for about 2 minutes, then remove the pan from the heat.
3 With the machine running, pour the hot syrup over the chocolate in the food processor. Keep the machine running for 1–2 minutes until the chocolate is completely melted and the mixture is smooth, scraping down the bowl once.
4 Strain the chocolate mixture into a large measuring jug or bowl. Leave to cool, then chill, stirring occasionally. Freeze the mixture in an ice-cream maker. Alternatively, pour into a container suitable for use in the freezer, freeze until slushy, whisk until smooth, then freeze again. Whisk for a second time before the mixture hardens completely. Allow the sorbet to soften for 5–10 minutes at room temperature and serve in scoops, decorated with chocolate curls.

CHOCOLATE SORBET WITH RED FRUITS

SERVES 6

475ml / 16fl oz / 2 cups water
45ml / 3 tbsp clear honey
115g / 4oz / ½ cup caster sugar
75g / 3oz / ¾ cup cocoa powder
50g / 2oz plain dark or bittersweet chocolate, chopped into
small pieces
400g / 14oz soft red fruits, such as raspberries, redcurrants
or strawberries

1 Place the water, honey, caster sugar and cocoa powder in a saucepan. Heat gently, stirring occasionally, until the sugar has completely dissolved.
2 Remove the pan from the heat, add the chocolate and stir until melted. Leave until cool.
3 Tip into an ice-cream maker and churn until frozen. Alternatively, pour into a container suitable for use in the freezer, freeze until slushy, whisk until smooth, then freeze again. Whisk for a second time before the mixture hardens completely, and cover the container.
4 Remove from the freezer 10–15 minutes before serving, so that the sorbet softens slightly. Serve in scoops in chilled dessert bowls, with the soft fruits.

ROCKY ROAD ICE CREAM

SERVES 6

*115g/4oz plain chocolate, chopped into
small pieces*
150ml/¼ pint/⅔ cup milk
300ml/½ pint/1¼ cups double cream
115g/4oz/2 cups marshmallows, chopped
115g/4oz/½ cup glacé cherries, chopped
50g/2oz/½ cup crumbled shortbread biscuits
30ml/2 tbsp chopped walnuts

1 Melt the chocolate in the milk in a saucepan over a gentle heat, stirring from time to time. Pour into a bowl and leave to cool completely.

2 Whip the cream in a separate bowl until it just holds its shape. Beat in the chocolate mixture, a little at a time, until the mixture is smooth and creamy.

3 Tip the mixture into an ice-cream maker and, following the manufacturer's instructions, churn until almost frozen. Alternatively, pour into a container suitable for use in the freezer, freeze until ice crystals form around the edges, then whisk with a strong hand whisk or hand-held electric mixer until smooth.

4 Stir the marshmallows, glacé cherries, crushed biscuits and nuts into the iced mixture, then return to the freezer container and freeze until firm.

5 Allow the ice cream to soften at room temperature for 15–20 minutes before serving in scoops. Add a wafer and chocolate sauce to each portion, if desired.

ICED CHOCOLATE NUT GATEAU

SERVES 6–8

75g / 3oz / ¾ cup shelled hazelnuts
about 32 sponge fingers
150ml / ¼ pint / ⅔ cup cold strong black coffee
30ml / 2 tbsp brandy
475ml / 16fl oz / 2 cups double cream
75g / 3oz / generous ½ cup icing sugar, sifted
150g / 5oz plain chocolate, chopped into
small pieces
icing sugar and cocoa powder, for dusting

1 Preheat oven to 200°C/400°F/Gas 6.
Spread out the hazelnuts on a baking
sheet and toast them in the oven for 5
minutes until golden. Tip the nuts on to a
clean dish towel and rub off the skins
while still warm. Cool, then chop finely.

2 Line a 1.2 litre/2 pint/5 cup loaf tin
with clear film and cut the sponge fingers
to fit the base and sides. Reserve the
remaining biscuits. Mix the coffee with
the brandy in a shallow dish. Dip the
sponge fingers briefly into the coffee
mixture and return to the tin, sugary side
down to fit neatly.

3 Whip the cream with the icing sugar
until it holds soft peaks. Fold half the
chopped chocolate into the cream with
the hazelnuts. Use a gentle figure-of-eight
action to distribute the chocolate and
nuts evenly.

4 Melt the remaining chocolate in a bowl
set over a pan of barely simmering water.
Cool, then fold into the cream mixture.
Spoon into the tin.

5 Moisten the remaining biscuits in the
coffee mixture, be careful not to soak the
biscuits, as they will collapse. Lay the
coffee-moistened biscuits over the filling.
Wrap and freeze until firm.
6 To serve, remove from the freezer
30 minutes before serving to allow the
ice cream to soften slightly. Turn out on
to a serving plate and dust with icing
sugar and cocoa.

ICED CHOCOLATE AND
MANDARIN GATEAU

Dip the sponge fingers in a mixture
of strong black coffee and mandarin
or orange liqueur. Omit the
hazelnuts from the cream filling.
About 30 minutes before serving,
remove the frozen gâteau from the
tin and place it on a serving plate.
Cover with whipped cream flavoured
with mandarin or orange liqueur.
Pipe more whipped cream around
the base of the gâteau. Decorate
with plain or chocolate-dipped
mandarin or orange segments.

ICE CREAM BOMBES

SERVES 6

1 litre / 1¾ pints / 4 cups soft-scoop chocolate ice cream

475ml / 16fl oz / 2 cups soft-scoop vanilla ice cream

50g / 2oz / ⅓ cup plain chocolate chips

115g / 4oz toffees

75ml / 5 tbsp double cream

1 Divide the chocolate ice cream equally among six small cups. Push it roughly to the base and up the sides, leaving a small cup-shaped dip in the middle. Return to the freezer and leave for 45 minutes. Take the cups out again and smooth the ice cream in each into shape, keeping the centre hollow. Return to the freezer.

2 Put the vanilla ice cream in a small bowl and break it up slightly with a spoon. Stir in the chocolate chips and use this mixture to fill the hollows in the cups of chocolate ice cream. Smooth the tops, then cover the cups with clear film, return to the freezer and leave overnight.

3 Melt the toffees with the cream in a small pan over a very low heat, stirring constantly until smooth, warm and creamy.

4 Turn out the bombes on to individual plates and pour the toffee sauce over the top. Serve immediately.

CHOCOLATE MINT ICE CREAM PIE

SERVES 8

75g / 3 oz plain chocolate chips
40g / 1½oz butter or margarine
50g / 2oz crisped rice cereal
1 litre / 1¾ pints / 4 cups mint-chocolate-chip
ice cream
chocolate curls, to decorate

1 Line a 23 cm / 9 in pie tin with foil. Place a round of greaseproof paper over the foil in the bottom of the tin.
2 In a heatproof bowl set over a saucepan of simmering water melt the chocolate chips with the butter or margarine.
3 Remove the bowl from the heat and gently stir in the cereal, a little at a time.

4 Press the chocolate-cereal mixture evenly over the base and up the sides of the prepared tin, forming a 1 cm / ½ in rim. Chill until completely hard.
5 Carefully remove the cereal base from the tin and peel off the foil and paper. Return the base to the pie tin.

6 Remove the ice cream from the freezer and allow it to soften for 10 minutes.

7 Spread the ice cream evenly in the biscuit case crust. Freeze until firm.
8 Scatter the chocolate curls over the ice cream just before serving.

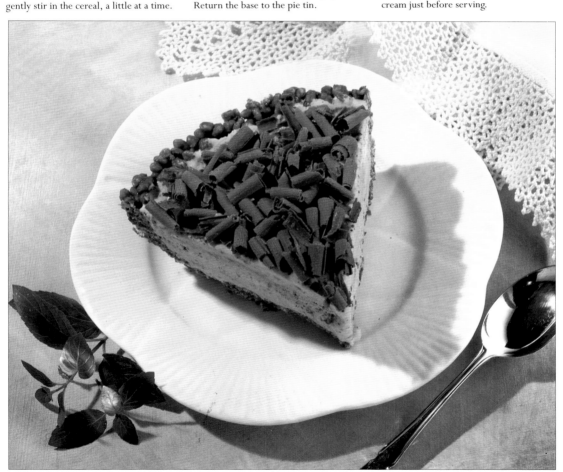

CHOCOLATE BISCUITS AND COOKIES

CHOC-CHIP NUT BISCUITS

MAKES 36

115g/4oz/1 cup plain flour
5ml/1 tsp baking powder
5ml/1 tsp salt
75g/3oz/6 tbsp butter or margarine
115g/4oz/1 cup caster sugar
50g/2oz/⅓ cup soft light brown sugar
1 egg
5ml/1 tsp vanilla essence
115g/4oz/⅔ cup plain chocolate chips
50g/2oz/½ cup hazelnuts, chopped

<u>1</u> Preheat oven to 180°C/350°F/Gas 4. Grease 2–3 baking sheets. Sift the flour, baking powder and salt into a small bowl. Set the bowl aside.
<u>2</u> With a hand-held electric mixer, cream the butter or margarine and sugars together. Beat in the egg and vanilla essence. Add the flour mixture and beat well on low speed.
<u>3</u> Stir in the chocolate chips and half of the hazelnuts. Drop teaspoonfuls of the mixture on to the prepared baking sheets, to form 2 cm/¾ in mounds. Space the biscuits about 5 cm/2 in apart to allow room for spreading.
<u>4</u> Flatten each biscuit lightly with a wet fork. Sprinkle the remaining hazelnuts on top of the biscuits and press lightly into the surface. Bake for 10–12 minutes, until golden brown. Transfer the biscuits to a wire rack and allow to cool.

CHOC-CHIP OAT BISCUITS

MAKES 60

115g/4oz/1 cup plain flour
2.5ml/½ tsp bicarbonate of soda
1.5ml/¼ tsp baking powder
1.5ml/¼ tsp salt
115g/4oz/1 cup butter or margarine, softened
115g/4oz/1 cup caster sugar
75g/3oz/½ cup light brown sugar
1 egg
1.5ml/¼ tsp vanilla essence
75g/3oz/scant 1 cup rolled oats
175g/6oz/1 cup plain chocolate chips

<u>1</u> Preheat oven to 180°C/350°F/Gas 4. Grease 3–4 baking sheets. Sift the flour, bicarbonate of soda, baking powder and salt into a mixing bowl. Set the bowl aside.
<u>2</u> With a hand-held electric mixer, cream the butter or margarine and sugars together in a bowl. Add the egg and vanilla essence and beat until light and fluffy.
<u>3</u> Add the flour mixture and beat on low speed until thoroughly blended. Stir in the rolled oats and chocolate chips, mixing well with a wooden spoon. The dough should be crumbly.
<u>4</u> Drop heaped teaspoonfuls on to the prepared baking sheets, spacing the dough about 2.5 cm/1 in apart. Bake for about 15 minutes until just firm around the edge but still soft to the touch in the centre. With a slotted spatula, transfer the biscuits to a wire rack and allow them to cool.

CHOCOLATE-DIPPED HAZELNUT CRESCENTS

MAKES ABOUT 35

275g/10oz/2 cups plain flour
pinch of salt
225g/8oz/1 cup unsalted butter, softened
75g/3oz/6 tbsp caster sugar
15ml/1 tbsp hazelnut-flavoured liqueur
or water
5ml/1 tsp vanilla essence
75g/3oz plain chocolate, chopped into
small pieces
50g/2oz/½ cup hazelnuts, toasted and
finely chopped
icing sugar, for dusting
350g/12oz plain chocolate, melted, for
dipping

1 Preheat oven to 160°C/325°F/Gas 3. Grease two large baking sheets. Sift the flour and salt into a bowl. In a separate bowl, beat the butter until creamy. Add the sugar and beat until fluffy, then beat in the hazelnut liqueur or water and the vanilla essence. Gently stir in the flour mixture, then the chocolate and hazelnuts.

2 With floured hands, shape the dough into 5 x 1 cm/2 x ½ in crescent shapes. Place on the baking sheets, 5 cm/2 in apart. Bake for 20–25 minutes until the edges are set and the biscuits slightly golden. Remove the biscuits from the oven and cool on the baking sheets for 10 minutes, then transfer the biscuits to wire racks to cool completely.

3 Have the melted chocolate ready in a small bowl. Dust the biscuits lightly with icing sugar. Using a pair of kitchen tongs or your fingers, dip half of each crescent into the melted chocolate. Place the crescents on a non-stick baking sheet until the chocolate has set.

CHUNKY DOUBLE CHOCOLATE COOKIES

MAKES 18–20

115g/4oz/½ cup unsalted butter, softened
115g/4oz/⅔ cup light muscovado sugar
1 egg
5ml/1 tsp vanilla essence
150g/5oz/1¼ cups self-raising flour
75g/3oz/¾ cup porridge oats
115g/4oz plain chocolate, roughly chopped
115g/4oz white chocolate, roughly chopped

DOUBLE-CHOC ALMOND COOKIES:
Instead of the porridge oats, use 75g/3oz/¾ cup ground almonds. Omit the chopped chocolate and use 175g/6oz/1 cup chocolate chips instead. Top each heap of cake mixture with half a glacé cherry before baking.

1 Preheat oven to 190°C/375°F/Gas 5. Lightly grease two baking sheets. Cream the butter with the sugar in a bowl until pale and fluffy. Add the egg and vanilla essence and beat well.

2 Sift the flour over the mixture and fold in lightly with a metal spoon, then add the oats and chopped plain and white chocolate and stir until evenly mixed.

3 Place small spoonfuls of the mixture in 18–20 rocky heaps on the baking sheets, leaving space for spreading.

4 Bake for 12–15 minutes or until the biscuits are beginning to turn pale golden. Cool for 2–3 minutes on the baking sheets, then lift on to wire racks. The biscuits will be soft when freshly baked but will harden on cooling.

CHOCOLATE MARZIPAN COOKIES

MAKES ABOUT 36

*200g/7oz/scant 1 cup unsalted butter,
softened*
*200g/7oz/generous 1 cup light muscovado
sugar*
1 egg, beaten
300g/11oz/2¾ cups plain flour
60ml/4 tbsp cocoa powder
200g/7oz white almond paste
*115g/4oz white chocolate, chopped into
small pieces*

<u>1</u> Preheat oven to 190°C/375°F/Gas 5.
Lightly grease two large baking sheets.
Using a hand-held electric mixer, cream
the butter with the sugar in a mixing
bowl until pale and fluffy. Add the egg
and beat well.

<u>2</u> Sift the flour and cocoa over the
mixture. Stir in with a wooden spoon
until all the flour mixture has been
smoothly incorporated, then use clean
hands to press the mixture together to
make a fairly soft dough.

<u>3</u> Using a rolling pin and keeping your
touch light, roll out about half the dough
on a lightly floured surface to a thickness
of about 5 mm/¼ in. Using a 5 cm/2 in
plain or fluted biscuit cutter, cut out 36
rounds, re-rolling the dough as required.
Wrap the remaining dough in clear film
and set it aside.

<u>4</u> Cut the almond paste into 36 equal
pieces. Roll into balls, flatten slightly and
place one on each round of dough. Roll
out the remaining dough, cut out more
rounds, then place on top of the almond
paste. Press the dough edges to seal.

<u>5</u> Bake for 10–12 minutes, or until the
cookies have risen well and are beginning
to crack on the surface. Cool on the
baking sheet for about 2–3 minutes, then
finish cooling on a wire rack.

<u>6</u> Melt the white chocolate, then either
drizzle it over the biscuits to decorate, or
spoon into a paper piping bag and quickly
pipe a design on to the biscuits.

VARIATION
Use glacé icing instead of melted
white chocolate to decorate the
cookies, if you prefer.

BLACK AND WHITE GINGER FLORENTINES

MAKES ABOUT 30

120ml/4fl oz/½ cup double cream
50g/2oz/¼ cup butter
50g/2oz/¼ cup granulated sugar
30ml/2 tbsp honey
150g/5oz/1¼ cups flaked almonds
40g/1½oz/6 tbsp plain flour
2.5ml/½ tsp ground ginger
50g/2oz/⅓ cup diced candied orange peel
75g/3oz/½ cup diced stem ginger
*50g/2oz plain chocolate, chopped into
   small pieces*
*150g/5oz bittersweet chocolate, chopped into
   small pieces*
*150g/5oz fine quality white chocolate,
   chopped into small pieces*

1 Preheat oven to 180°C/350°F/Gas 4.
Lightly grease two large baking sheets. In
a saucepan over a medium heat, stir the
cream, butter, sugar and honey until the
sugar dissolves. Bring the mixture to the
boil, stirring constantly. Remove from
the heat and stir in the almonds, flour and
ground ginger. Stir in the candied peel,
ginger and plain chocolate.

2 Drop teaspoons of the mixture on to
the baking sheets at least 7.5 cm/3 in
apart. Spread each round as thinly as
possible with the back of the spoon.

3 Bake for 8–10 minutes or until the
edges are golden brown and the biscuits
are bubbling. Do not under-bake or they
will be sticky, but be careful not to over-
bake as they burn easily. Continue baking
in batches. If you wish, use a 7.5 cm/3 in
biscuit cutter to neaten the edges of the
florentines while they are still on the
baking sheet.

4 Allow the biscuits to cool on the baking
sheets for 10 minutes, until they are firm
enough to move. Using a metal palette
knife, carefully lift the biscuits on to a
wire rack to cool completely.

5 Melt the bittersweet chocolate in a
heatproof bowl over barely simmering
water. Cool slightly. Put the white
chocolate in a separate bowl and melt in
the same way, stirring frequently.
Remove and cool for about 5 minutes,
stirring occasionally.

6 Using a small metal palette knife,
spread half the florentines with the
bittersweet chocolate and half with the
melted white chocolate. Place on a wire
rack, chocolate side up. Chill for 10–15
minutes to set completely.

CHEWY CHOCOLATE BISCUITS
MAKES 18

4 egg whites
350g/12oz/2½ cups icing sugar
115g/4oz/1 cup cocoa powder
30ml/2 tbsp plain flour
5ml/1 tsp instant coffee
15ml/1 tbsp water
115g/4oz/1 cup walnuts, finely chopped

1 Preheat oven to 180°C/350°F/
Gas 4. Line two baking sheets with
non-stick baking paper.
2 With a hand-held electric mixer,
beat the egg whites in a bowl until
frothy.
3 Sift the icing sugar, cocoa powder,
flour and coffee into the whites. Add
the water and continue beating on
low speed to blend, then on high
speed for a few minutes until the
mixture thickens. With a rubber
spatula, fold in the walnuts.
4 Place generous spoonfuls of the
mixture 2.5 cm/1 in apart on the
prepared baking sheets. Bake for
12–15 minutes, or until firm and
cracked on top but soft on the inside.
With a metal spatula, transfer the
biscuits to a wire rack to cool.

CHOCOLATE CRACKLE-TOPS

MAKES ABOUT 38

*200g / 7oz bittersweet or plain chocolate,
chopped into small pieces*
90g / 3½oz / 7 tbsp unsalted butter
115g / 4oz / ½ cup caster sugar
3 eggs
5ml / 1 tsp vanilla essence
200g / 7oz / 1¾ cups plain flour
25g / 1oz / ¼ cup cocoa powder
2.5ml / ½ tsp baking powder
pinch of salt
175g / 6oz / 1½ cups icing sugar, for coating

1 Grease two or more large baking sheets. In a heavy-based saucepan over a low heat, melt the chocolate and butter until smooth, stirring frequently. Remove from the heat. Stir in the sugar until dissolved. Add the eggs, one at a time, beating well after each addition. Stir in the vanilla essence.

2 Sift the flour, cocoa, baking powder and salt into a bowl. Gradually stir into the chocolate mixture in batches to make a soft dough. Cover in clear film and chill for at least 1 hour until the dough is firm enough to hold its shape.

3 Preheat oven to 160°C / 325°F / Gas 3. Place the icing sugar in a small, deep bowl. Using a small ice cream scoop or round teaspoon, scoop the dough into small balls and roll between your palms.

4 Drop the balls, one at a time, into the icing sugar and roll until heavily coated. Remove each ball with a slotted spoon and tap the spoon against the bowl to remove excess sugar. Place the balls on the baking sheets, about 4 cm / 1½ in apart.

5 Bake the biscuits for 10–15 minutes or until the top of each feels slightly firm when touched with a fingertip. Leave for 2–3 minutes, until just set. Transfer to wire racks and leave to cool completely.

CHUNKY CHOCOLATE DROPS

MAKES ABOUT 18

*175g/6oz bittersweet or plain chocolate,
chopped into small pieces*
115g/4oz/½ cup unsalted butter, diced
2 eggs
115g/4oz/½ cup granulated sugar
50g/2oz/⅓ cup light brown sugar
40g/1½oz/6 tbsp plain flour
25g/1oz/¼ cup cocoa powder
5ml/1 tsp baking powder
10ml/2 tsp vanilla essence
pinch of salt
*115g/4oz/1 cup pecan nuts, toasted and
coarsely chopped*
175g/6oz/1 cup plain chocolate chips
*115g/4oz fine quality white chocolate,
chopped into small pieces*
*115g/4oz fine quality milk chocolate,
chopped into small pieces*

1 Preheat oven to 160°C/325°F/Gas 3. Grease two large baking sheets. In a medium saucepan over a low heat, melt the chocolate and butter until smooth, stirring frequently. Remove from the heat and leave to cool slightly.

2 In a large mixing bowl, beat the eggs and sugars until pale and creamy. Gradually pour in the melted chocolate mixture, beating well. Beat in the flour, cocoa, baking powder and vanilla essence. Stir in the remaining ingredients.

3 Drop heaped tablespoons of the mixture on to the baking sheets, 10 cm/ 4 in apart. Flatten each to a 7.5 cm/ 3 in round. (You will only get 4–6 biscuits on each sheet.) Bake for 8–10 minutes until the tops are shiny and cracked and the edges look crisp. Do not over-bake or the biscuits will break when they are removed from the baking sheets.

4 Remove the baking sheets to wire racks to cool for 2 minutes, until the biscuits are just set, then carefully transfer them to the wire racks to cool completely. Bake the biscuits in batches, if necessary. Store in airtight containers.

CHOCOLATE AMARETTI

MAKES ABOUT 24

115g/4oz/1 cup blanched whole almonds
115g/4oz/½ cup caster sugar
15ml/1 tbsp cocoa powder
30ml/2 tbsp icing sugar
2 egg whites
pinch of cream of tartar
5ml/1 tsp almond essence
flaked almonds, to decorate

1 Preheat oven to 180°C/350°F/Gas 4. Place the almonds on a small baking sheet and bake for 10–12 minutes, turning occasionally until golden brown. Cool to room temperature. Reduce the oven temperature to 160°C/325°F/Gas 3.

2 Line a large baking sheet with non-stick baking paper. In a food processor, process the toasted almonds with half the caster sugar until the almonds are finely ground but not oily. Transfer the ground almonds to a bowl and stir in the cocoa powder and icing sugar. Set aside.

3 In a medium mixing bowl, beat the egg whites and cream of tartar with a hand-held mixer, until stiff peaks form. Sprinkle in the remaining caster sugar about 15ml/1 tbsp at a time, beating well after each addition, and continue beating until the whites are glossy and stiff. Beat in the almond essence.

4 Sprinkle over the almond-sugar mixture and gently fold into the beaten egg whites until just blended. Spoon the mixture into a large piping bag fitted with a plain 1 cm/½in nozzle. Pipe 4 cm/1½in rounds about 2.5 cm/1 in apart on the prepared baking sheet. Press a flaked almond into the centre of each biscuit.

5 Bake the biscuits for 12–15 minutes or until they are crisp. Cool on the baking sheet for 10 minutes. With a metal palette knife, transfer the biscuits to wire racks to cool completely. When cool, store in an airtight jar or biscuit tin. Serve after a dinner party with coffee, or use in trifles.

CHOCOLATE KISSES

MAKES 24

75g/3oz dark plain chocolate, chopped into small pieces
75g/3oz white chocolate, chopped into small pieces
115g/4oz/½ cup butter, softened
115g/4oz/½ cup caster sugar
2 eggs
225g/8oz/2 cups plain flour
icing sugar, to decorate

1 Melt the plain and white chocolates in separate bowls and set both aside to cool.
2 Beat the butter and caster sugar together until pale and fluffy. Beat in the eggs, one at a time. Then sift in the flour and mix well.

3 Halve the creamed mixture and divide it between the two bowls of chocolate. Mix each chocolate in thoroughly so that each forms a dough. Knead the doughs until smooth, wrap them separately in clear film and chill for 1 hour. Preheat oven to 190°C/375°F/Gas 5.

4 Shape slightly rounded teaspoonfuls of both doughs roughly into balls. Roll the balls between your palms to neaten them. Arrange the balls on greased baking sheets and bake for 10–12 minutes. Dust liberally with sifted icing sugar and cool on a wire rack.

MOCHA VIENNESE SWIRLS

MAKES ABOUT 20

*115g / 4oz plain chocolate, chopped into
small pieces*
*200g / 7oz / scant 1 cup unsalted butter,
softened*
90ml / 6 tbsp icing sugar
30ml / 2 tbsp strong black coffee
200g / 7oz / 1¾ cups plain flour
50g / 2oz / ½ cup cornflour

TO DECORATE

about 20 blanched almonds
*150g / 5oz plain chocolate, chopped into
small pieces*

1 Preheat oven to 190°C / 375°F / Gas 5.
Melt the chocolate in a bowl over barely
simmering water. Cream the butter with
the icing sugar in a bowl until smooth and
pale. Beat in the melted chocolate, then
the strong black coffee.

2 Sift the plain flour and cornflour over
the mixture. Fold in lightly and evenly to
make a soft biscuit dough.

3 Lightly grease two large baking sheets.
Spoon the dough into a piping bag fitted
with a large star nozzle. Pipe about 20
swirls on the baking sheets, allowing
room for spreading. Keep the nozzle close
to the sheet so that the swirls are flat.

4 Press an almond into the centre of each
swirl. Bake for about 15 minutes or until
the biscuits are firm and starting to
brown. Cool for about 10 minutes on the
baking sheets, then lift carefully on to a
wire rack to cool completely.

5 When cool, melt the chocolate and dip
the base of each swirl to coat. Place on a
sheet of non-stick baking paper and leave
to set completely.

CHOCOLATE MACAROONS

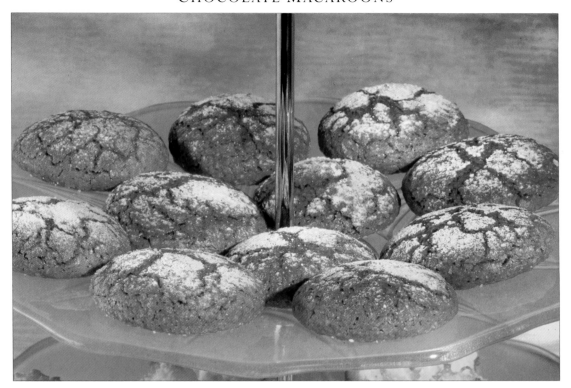

MAKES 24

*50g/2oz plain chocolate, chopped into
small pieces
115g/4oz/1 cup blanched almonds
225g/8oz/1 cup granulated sugar
3 egg whites
2.5ml/½ tsp vanilla essence
1.5ml/¼ tsp almond essence
icing sugar, for dusting*

1 Preheat oven to 160°C/325°F/Gas 3.
Line two baking sheets with non-stick
baking paper.

VARIATION

For Chocolate Pine Nut Macaroons,
spread 50g/2oz/⅔ cup toasted pine
nuts in a shallow dish. Press the balls of
chocolate macaroon dough into the nuts
to cover one side and bake as described,
nut-side up.

2 Melt the chocolate in the top of a
double boiler, or in a heatproof bowl
placed over a saucepan of barely
simmering water.
3 Grind the almonds finely in a food
processor, blender or nut grinder.
Transfer to a mixing bowl.
4 Add the sugar, egg whites, vanilla
essence and almond essence and stir to
blend. Stir in the chocolate. The mixture
should just hold its shape. If it is too soft,
chill it in the fridge for 15 minutes.

5 Use a teaspoon and your hands to shape
the dough into walnut-size balls. Place on
the baking sheets and flatten slightly.
Brush each ball with a little water and sift
over a thin layer of icing sugar. Bake for
10–12 minutes, until just firm. With a
metal spatula, transfer to a wire rack to
cool completely.

CHOCOLATE CINNAMON TUILES

3 In a separate bowl, mix together the cocoa and cinnamon. Stir into the larger quantity of mixture until well combined. Leaving room for spreading, drop spoonfuls of the chocolate-flavoured mixture on to the prepared baking sheets, then spread each gently with a palette knife to make a neat round.

4 Using a small spoon, drizzle the reserved plain mixture over the rounds, swirling it lightly to give a marbled effect.

5 Bake for 4–6 minutes, until just set. Using a palette knife, lift each biscuit and drape it over a rolling pin, to give a curved shape as it hardens. Allow the tuiles to set, then remove them and finish cooling on a wire rack. Serve on the same day.

MAKES 12
1 egg white
50g / 2oz / ¼ cup caster sugar
30ml / 2 tbsp plain flour
40g / 1½oz / 3 tbsp butter, melted
15ml / 1 tbsp cocoa powder
2.5ml / ½ tsp ground cinnamon

1 Preheat oven to 200°C/400°F/Gas 6. Lightly grease two large baking sheets. Whisk the egg white in a clean, grease-free bowl until it forms soft peaks. Gradually whisk in the sugar to make a smooth, glossy mixture.

2 Sift the flour over the meringue mixture and fold in evenly; try not to deflate the mixture. Stir in the butter. Transfer about 45ml/3 tbsp of the mixture to a small bowl and set it aside.

CHOCOLATE CUPS
Cream 150g/5oz/⅔ cup butter with 115g/4oz/½ cup caster sugar. Stir in 75g/3oz/1 cup porridge oats, 15ml/1 tbsp cocoa powder and 5ml/1 tsp vanilla essence. Roll to the size of golf balls and space well on greased baking sheets. Bake at 180°C/350°F/Gas 4 for 12–15 minutes. Cool slightly then drape over greased upturned glasses until cool and firm. Makes 8–10.

CHOCOLATE PRETZELS

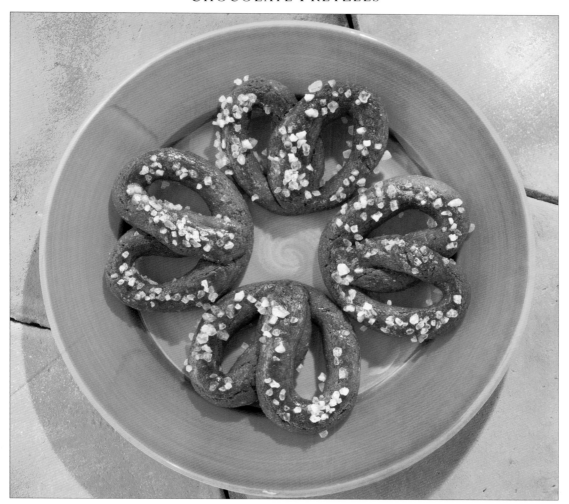

MAKES 28

150g / 5oz / 1¼ cups plain flour
pinch of salt
25g / 1oz / ¼ cup cocoa powder
115g / 4oz / ½ cup butter, softened
115g / 4oz / ½ cup caster sugar
1 egg
1 egg white, lightly beaten, for glazing
sugar crystals, for sprinkling

1 Sift the plain flour, salt and cocoa powder into a bowl. Set aside. Grease two baking sheets.

2 With a hand-held electric mixer, cream the butter. Add the caster sugar and beat until fluffy. Beat in the egg. Stir in the dry ingredients. Gather the dough into a ball and chill for 1 hour.

3 Roll the dough into 28 small balls. Preheat the oven to 190°C / 375°F / Gas 5. Roll each ball into a rope about 25 cm / 10 in long. With each rope, form a loop with the two ends facing you. Twist the ends and fold back on to the circle, pressing in to make a pretzel shape. Place on the greased baking sheets.

4 Brush the pretzels with the egg white. Sprinkle sugar crystals over the tops and bake for 10–12 minutes until firm. Transfer to a wire rack to cool.

LITTLE CAKES, SLICES AND BARS

CHOCOLATE FAIRY CAKES

MAKES 24

*115g/4oz plain chocolate, chopped into
small pieces
15ml/1 tbsp water
275g/10oz/2½ cups plain flour
5ml/1 tsp baking powder
2.5ml/½ tsp bicarbonate of soda
pinch of salt
300g/11oz/scant 1½ cups caster sugar
175g/6oz/¾ cup butter or margarine, at
room temperature
150ml/¼ pint/⅔ cup milk
5ml/1 tsp vanilla essence
3 eggs*

FOR THE ICING

*40g/1½ oz/3 tbsp butter or margarine
115g/4oz/1 cup icing sugar
2.5ml/½ tsp vanilla essence
15–30ml/1–2 tbsp milk*

1 Preheat oven to 180°C/350°F/Gas 4.
Grease 24 bun tins, about 6.5 cm/2¾ in
in diameter and line with paper cases.
2 Make the icing. Soften the butter or
margarine. Place it in a bowl and stir in
the icing sugar, a little at a time. Add the
vanilla essence, then, a drop at a time,
beat in just enough milk to make a
creamy, spreadable mixture. Cover the
surface closely with clear film and set the
bowl aside.

3 Melt the chocolate with the water in a
heatproof bowl over simmering water.
Remove from the heat. Sift the flour,
baking powder, bicarbonate of soda, salt
and sugar into a large bowl. Add the
chocolate mixture, butter or margarine,
milk and vanilla essence.

4 With a hand-held electric mixer on
medium speed, beat the mixture until
smooth. Increase the speed to high and
beat for 2 minutes. Add the eggs, one at a
time, and beat for 1 minute after each
addition. Divide the mixture evenly
among the prepared bun tins.

5 Bake for 20–25 minutes or until a
skewer inserted into the centre of a cake
comes out clean. Cool in the tins for
10 minutes, then turn out to cool
completely on a wire rack. Spread the top
of each cake with the icing, swirling it
into a peak in the centre.

CHOCOLATE MINT-FILLED CUPCAKES

MAKES 12

225g / 8oz / 2 cups plain flour
5ml / 1 tsp bicarbonate of soda
pinch of salt
50g / 2oz / ½ cup cocoa powder
150g / 5oz / 10 tbsp unsalted butter, softened
350g / 12oz / 1⅔ cups caster sugar
3 eggs
5ml / 1 tsp peppermint essence
250ml / 8 fl oz / 1 cup milk

FOR THE MINT CREAM FILLING

300ml / ½ pint / 1¼ cups double cream or whipping cream
5ml / 1 tsp peppermint essence

FOR THE CHOCOLATE MINT GLAZE

175g / 6oz plain chocolate, chopped into small pieces
115g / 4oz / ½ cup unsalted butter
5ml / 1 tsp peppermint essence

1 Preheat oven to 180°C / 350°F / Gas 4. Line a 12-hole bun tin with paper cases, using the cases double if they are thin. Sift the flour, bicarbonate of soda, salt and cocoa powder into a bowl. Set aside.

2 In a large mixing bowl, beat the butter and sugar with a hand-held electric mixer for about 3–5 minutes until light and creamy. Add the eggs, one at a time, beating well after each addition and adding a small amount of the flour mixture if the egg mixture shows signs of curdling. Beat in the peppermint essence until thoroughly mixed.

3 With the hand-held electric mixer on a low speed, beat in the flour-cocoa mixture alternately with the milk, until just blended. Spoon into the paper cases, filling them about three-quarters full.

4 Bake for 12–15 minutes, until a cake tester inserted in the centre of one of the cupcakes comes out clean.

5 Lift the cupcakes on to a wire rack to cool completely. When cool, carefully remove the paper cases.

6 Prepare the mint cream filling. In a small bowl, whip the cream and peppermint essence until stiff. Fit a small, plain nozzle into a piping bag and spoon in the flavoured cream. Gently press the nozzle into the bottom of one of the cupcakes. Squeeze gently, releasing about 15ml / 1 tbsp of the flavoured cream into the centre of the cake. Repeat with the remaining cupcakes, returning each one to the wire rack as it is filled.

7 Prepare the glaze. In a saucepan over a low heat, melt the chocolate and butter, stirring until smooth. Remove from heat and stir in the peppermint essence. Cool then spread on the top of each cake.

CHOCOLATE LEMON TARTLETS

MAKES 12 TARTLETS

1 quantity Chocolate Shortcrust Pastry
lemon twists and melted chocolate to decorate

FOR THE LEMON CUSTARD SAUCE
grated rind and juice of 1 lemon
350ml / 12fl oz / 1½ cups milk
6 egg yolks
50g / 2oz / ½ cup caster sugar

FOR THE LEMON CURD FILLING
grated rind and juice of 2 lemons
175g / 6oz / ¾ cup unsalted butter, diced
450g / 1lb / 2 cups granulated sugar
3 eggs, lightly beaten

FOR THE CHOCOLATE LAYER
175ml / 6fl oz / ¾ cup double cream
175g / 6oz bittersweet or plain chocolate,
chopped into small pieces
25g / 1oz / 2 tbsp unsalted butter, cut into
pieces

1 Prepare the custard sauce. Place the rind in a saucepan with the milk. Bring to the boil over a medium heat. Remove from the heat and allow to stand for 5 minutes to infuse. Strain the milk into a clean pan and reheat it gently.

2 In a bowl beat the yolks and sugar with a hand-held electric mixer for 2–3 minutes, until pale and thick. Pour over about 250ml / 8fl oz / 1 cup of the flavoured hot milk, beating vigorously.

3 Return the yolk mixture to the rest of the milk in the pan and cook gently, stirring constantly, over low heat until the mixture thickens and lightly coats the back of a spoon. (Do not allow sauce to boil or it will curdle.) Strain into a chilled bowl. Stir 30ml / 2 tbsp lemon juice into the sauce. Cool, stirring occasionally, then chill until ready to use.

4 Prepare the lemon curd filling. Combine the lemon rind, juice, butter and sugar in the top of a double boiler. Set over simmering water and heat gently until the butter has melted and the sugar has completely dissolved. Reduce the heat to low.

5 Stir the lightly beaten eggs into the butter mixture. Cook over a low heat, for 15 minutes, stirring constantly, until the mixture coats the back of a spoon.

6 Strain the lemon curd into a bowl and cover closely with clear film. Allow to cool, stirring occasionally, then chill to thicken, stirring occasionally.

7 Lightly butter twelve 7.5 cm / 3 in tartlet tins (if possible ones which have removable bases). On a lightly floured surface, roll out the pastry to a thickness of 3 mm / ⅛ in. Using a 10 cm / 4 in fluted cutter, cut out 12 rounds and press each one into a tartlet tin. Prick the bases with a fork. Place the tins on a baking sheet and chill for 30 minutes.

8 Preheat oven to 190°C / 375°F / Gas 5. Cut out rounds of foil and line each pastry case; fill with baking beans or rice. Bake blind for 5–8 minutes. Remove the foil with the beans and bake for 5 more minutes, until the cases are golden. Remove to rack to cool.

9 Prepare the chocolate layer. In a saucepan over a medium heat, bring the cream to the boil. Remove from the heat and add the chocolate all at once; stir until melted. Beat in the butter and cool slightly. Pour the filling into each tartlet to make a layer 5 mm / ¼ in thick. Chill for 10 minutes until set.

10 Remove the tartlets from the tins and spoon in a layer of lemon curd to come to the top of the pastry. Set aside, but do not chill. To serve, spoon a little lemon custard sauce on to a plate and place a tartlet in the centre. Decorate with a lemon twist. Dot the custard with melted chocolate. Draw a skewer through the chocolate to make heart motifs.

CHOCOLATE CREAM PUFFS

MAKES 12 LARGE CREAM PUFFS
115g/4oz/1 cup plain flour
30ml/2 tbsp cocoa powder
250ml/8fl oz/1 cup water
2.5ml/½ tsp salt
15ml/1 tbsp granulated sugar
115g/4oz/½ cup unsalted butter, diced
4 eggs

FOR THE CHOCOLATE PASTRY CREAM
450ml/¾ pint/2 cups milk
6 egg yolks
115g/4oz/½ cup granulated sugar
50g/2oz/½ cup plain flour
*150g/5oz plain chocolate, chopped into
small pieces*
115ml/4fl oz/½ cup whipping cream

FOR THE CHOCOLATE GLAZE
300ml/½ pint/1¼ cups whipping cream
50g/2oz/¼ cup unsalted butter, diced
*225g/8oz bittersweet or plain chocolate,
chopped into small pieces*
15ml/1 tbsp golden syrup
5ml/1 tsp vanilla essence

1 Preheat oven to 220°C/425°F/Gas 7. Lightly grease two large baking sheets. Sift the flour and cocoa powder into a bowl. In a saucepan over a medium heat, bring to the boil the water, salt, sugar and butter. Remove the pan from the heat and add the flour and cocoa mixture all at once, stirring vigorously until the mixture is smooth and leaves the sides of the pan clean.

2 Return the pan to the heat to cook the choux pastry for 1 minute, beating constantly. Remove from the heat.

3 With a hand-held electric mixer, beat in 4 of the eggs, one at a time, beating well after each addition, until each is well blended. The mixture should be thick and shiny and just fall from a spoon. Spoon the mixture into a large piping bag fitted with a plain nozzle. Pipe 12 mounds about 7.5 cm/3 in across at least 5 cm/ 2 in apart on the baking sheet.

4 Bake for 35–40 minutes until puffed and firm. Remove the puffs. Using a serrated knife, slice off and reserve the top third of each puff; return the opened puffs to the oven for 5–10 minutes to dry out. Remove to a wire rack to cool.

5 Prepare the pastry cream. Bring the milk to the boil in a small pan. In a bowl, heat the yolks and sugar until pale and thick. Stir in the flour. Slowly pour about 250ml/8fl oz/1 cup of the hot milk into the yolks, stirring constantly. Return the yolk mixture to the remaining milk in the pan and cook, stirring until the sauce boils for 1 minute. Remove from the heat and stir in the chocolate until smooth.

6 Strain into a bowl and cover closely with clear film. Cool to room temperature. In a bowl, whip the cream until stiff. Fold into the pastry cream.

7 Using a large piping bag, fill each puff bottom with pastry cream, then cover each puff with its top. Arrange the cream puffs on a large serving plate in a single layer or as a pile.

8 Make the glaze by heating the cream, butter, chocolate, syrup and vanilla essence in a medium saucepan over low heat until melted and smooth, stirring frequently. Cool for 20–30 minutes until slightly thickened. Pour a little glaze over each of the cream puffs to serve.

CHOCOLATE RASPBERRY MACAROON BARS

2 In a medium bowl beat the butter, sugar, cocoa powder and salt with a hand-held electric mixer for about 1 minute, until well blended and creamy. Beat in the almond essence and the flour until the mixture forms a crumbly dough.

3 Turn the dough into the prepared tin and pat firmly over the base to make an even layer. Prick the dough with a fork. Bake for 20 minutes until the pastry has just set. Remove from the oven and increase the temperature to 190°C/375°F/Gas 5.

4 Make the topping. In a small bowl, combine the raspberry jam and the liqueur. Spread the mixture evenly over the chocolate crust, then sprinkle evenly with the chocolate chips.

5 In a food processor fitted with a metal blade, process the almonds, egg whites, salt, sugar and almond essence until well blended and foamy. Gently pour over the jam layer, spreading evenly to the edges of the tin. Sprinkle with the almonds.

6 Bake for 20–25 minutes more, until the top is golden and puffed. Cool in the tin on a wire rack for 20 minutes or until firm. Using the edges of the foil, carefully remove the bake from the tin and cool completely. Peel off the foil, and, using a sharp knife, cut into bars.

MAKES 16–18 BARS
115g/4oz/½ cup unsalted butter, softened
50g/2oz/⅓ cup icing sugar
25g/1oz/¼ cup cocoa powder
pinch of salt
5ml/1 tsp almond essence
115g/4oz/1 cup plain flour
FOR THE TOPPING
150g/5oz/½ cup seedless raspberry jam
15ml/1 tbsp raspberry-flavoured liqueur
175g/6oz/1 cup mini chocolate chips
175g/6oz/1½ cups ground almonds
4 egg whites
pinch of salt
225g/8oz/1¼ cups caster sugar
2.5ml/½ tsp almond essence
50g/2oz/¼ cup flaked almonds

1 Preheat oven to 160°C/325°F/Gas 3. Invert a 33 x 23 cm/13 x 9 in baking tin. Mould a sheet of foil over the tin and smooth the foil evenly around the corners. Lift off the foil and turn the tin right side up; line with the moulded foil. Grease the foil.

CHOCOLATE BUTTERSCOTCH BARS

MAKES 24

225g/8oz/2 cups plain flour
2.5ml/½ tsp baking powder
150g/5oz plain chocolate, chopped
115g/4oz/½ cup unsalted butter, diced
50g/2oz/⅓ cup light muscovado sugar
30ml/2 tbsp ground almonds

FOR THE TOPPING

175g/6oz/¾ cup unsalted butter, diced
115g/4oz/½ cup caster sugar
30ml/2 tbsp golden syrup
175ml/6fl oz/¾ cup condensed milk
150g/5oz/1¼ cups whole toasted hazelnuts
225g/8oz plain chocolate, chopped into small pieces

1 Preheat oven to 160°C/325°F/Gas 3. Grease a shallow 30 x 20 cm/12 x 8 in tin. Sift the flour and baking powder into a large bowl. Melt the chocolate in a bowl over a saucepan of simmering water.

2 Rub the butter into the flour until the mixture resembles coarse breadcrumbs, then stir in the sugar. Work in the melted chocolate and ground almonds to make a light biscuit dough.

3 Spread the dough roughly in the tin, then use a rubber spatula to press it down evenly into the sides and the corners. Prick the surface with a fork and bake for 25–30 minutes until firm. Leave to cool in the tin.

4 Make the topping. Heat the butter, sugar, golden syrup and condensed milk in a pan, stirring until the butter and sugar have melted. Simmer until golden, then stir in the hazelnuts.

5 Pour over the cooked base. Leave to set.

6 Melt the chocolate for the topping in a heatproof bowl over barely simmering water. Spread evenly over the butterscotch layer, then leave to set again before cutting into bars to serve.

CHOCOLATE WALNUT BARS

MAKES 24

50g/2oz/½ cup walnuts
50g/2oz/¼ cup caster sugar
115g/4oz/1 cup plain flour, sifted
75g/3oz unsalted butter, cut into pieces

FOR THE TOPPING

25g/1oz/2 tbsp unsalted butter
75ml/3fl oz/5 tbsp water
25g/1oz/¼ cup cocoa powder
115g/4oz/½ cup caster sugar
5ml/1 tsp vanilla essence
pinch of salt
2 eggs
icing sugar, for dusting

1 Preheat oven to 180°C/350°F/Gas 4. Grease the base and sides of a 20 cm/8-in square baking tin.

2 Grind the walnuts with 15–30ml/ 1–2 tbsp of the sugar in a food processor, blender or coffee grinder.
3 In a bowl, combine the ground walnuts, remaining sugar and flour. With your fingertips, rub in the butter until the mixture resembles coarse breadcrumbs. Alternatively, process all the ingredients in a food processor until the mixture resembles coarse breadcrumbs.

4 Pat the walnut mixture on to the base of the prepared tin in an even layer. Bake for 25 minutes.

5 Meanwhile make the topping. Heat the butter with the water in a saucepan over a medium heat. When all the butter has melted, gradually whisk in the cocoa powder and caster sugar. Remove from the heat, stir in the vanilla essence and salt and set the mixture aside to cool for 5 minutes. Whisk in the eggs until blended.

6 Pour the topping over the baked crust, return the baking tin to the oven and bake for about 20 minutes or until set. Transfer the tin to a wire rack to cool.
7 When the bake has cooled for 5 minutes, mark it into 6 x 2.5 cm/2½ x 1 in bars. Leave until completely cold, then separate the bars and transfer them to a wire rack. Dust lightly with icing sugar. Place the bars on a plate and serve.

COOK'S TIP

Look out for walnut pieces in the supermarket or health food store. They are cheaper than walnut halves and are perfect for this recipe. Ground almonds would also work well, but because they are so fine you need to take care not to over-process the mixture or they may become oily.

CHOCOLATE, DATE AND ORANGE BARS

Make the base as in the main recipe, but substitute hazelnuts for the walnuts. Roast the hazelnuts briefly in a hot oven or under the grill, rub off the skins using a clean, dry napkin or tea towel, then grind them with the sugar in a food processor. Complete the base and bake it as described, then set it aside.
Make the topping. Mix 225g/8oz/2 cups of sugar-rolled dates, 75g/3oz/6 tbsp butter and 120ml/4fl oz/½ cup water in a saucepan. Simmer, stirring occasionally, until the butter has dissolved and the dates have broken down to form a pulp. Stir in 50g/2oz/⅓ cup soft light brown sugar until dissolved. Remove the pan from the heat and beat in the grated rind of 1 orange, with 30ml/2 tbsp orange juice. Allow to cool.
Beat 175g/6oz/1½ cups self-raising flour and 1 egg into the date mixture, then spread the topping evenly over the hazelnut base. Bake in a preheated oven at 180°C/ 350°F/Gas 4 for 30 minutes. Cool in the tin, loosen around the edges with a knife then turn out so that the hazelnut base is now uppermost. Glaze with 150g/5oz melted chocolate. Cut into bars when set.

CHOCOLATE AND TOFFEE BARS

MAKES 32

350g / 12oz / 2 cups soft light brown sugar
450g / 1lb / 2 cups butter or margarine, at room temperature
2 egg yolks
7.5ml / 1½ tsp vanilla essence
450g / 1lb / 4 cups plain or wholemeal flour
2.5ml / ½ tsp salt
175g / 6oz plain chocolate, broken into squares
115g / 4oz / 1 cup walnuts or pecan nuts, chopped

1 Preheat oven to 180°C/350°F/Gas 4. Beat the sugar and butter or margarine in a mixing bowl until light and fluffy. Beat in the egg yolks and vanilla essence, then stir in the flour and salt to make a soft dough.
2 Spread the dough in a greased 33 x 23 x 5 cm/13 x 9 x 2 in baking tin. Level the surface. Bake for 25–30 minutes, until lightly browned. The texture will be soft.
3 Remove the bake from the oven and immediately place the chocolate on top. Set aside until the chocolate is soft, then spread it out with a spatula. Sprinkle with the chopped nuts.
4 While the bake is still warm, cut it into 5 x 4 cm/2 x 1½ in bars, remove from the tin and leave to cool on a wire rack.

CHOCOLATE PECAN SQUARES

MAKES 16

2 eggs
10ml / 2 tsp vanilla essence
pinch of salt
175g / 6oz / 1½ cups pecan nuts, roughly chopped
50g / 2oz / ½ cup plain flour
50g / 2oz / ¼ cup granulated sugar
120ml / 4fl oz / ½ cup golden syrup
75g / 3oz plain chocolate, chopped into small pieces
40g / 1½oz / 3 tbsp unsalted butter
16 pecan nut halves, to decorate

1 Preheat oven to 160°C/325°F/Gas 3. Line a 20 cm/8 in square baking tin with non-stick baking paper.
2 In a bowl, whisk the eggs with the vanilla essence and salt. In another bowl, mix together the pecan nuts and flour.
3 Put the sugar in a saucepan, add the golden syrup and bring to the boil. Remove from the heat and stir in the chocolate and butter with a wooden spoon until both have dissolved and the mixture is smooth. Stir in the beaten egg mixture, then fold in the pecan nuts and flour.
4 Pour the mixture into the prepared tin and bake for about 35 minutes or until firm to the touch. Cool in the tin for 10 minutes before turning out on a wire rack. Cut into 5 cm/2 in squares and press pecan halves into the tops while still warm. Cool completely before serving.

CHUNKY CHOCOLATE BARS

MAKES 12

*350g/12oz plain chocolate, chopped into
small pieces*
115g/4oz/½ cup unsalted butter
400g/14oz can condensed milk
225g/8oz digestive biscuits, broken
50g/2oz/⅓ cup raisins
*115g/4oz ready-to-eat dried peaches,
roughly chopped*
*50g/2oz/½ cup hazelnuts or pecan nuts,
roughly chopped*

1 Line a 28 x 18 cm/11 x 7 in cake tin
with clear film.
2 Melt the chocolate and butter in a large
heatproof bowl over a pan of simmering
water. Stir until well mixed.

3 Pour the condensed milk into the
chocolate and butter mixture. Beat with a
wooden spoon until creamy.
4 Add the broken biscuits, raisins,
chopped peaches and hazelnuts or pecans.
Mix well until all the ingredients are
coated in the rich chocolate sauce.

5 Tip the mixture into the prepared tin,
making sure it is pressed well into the
corners. Leave the top craggy. Cool, then
chill until set.
6 Lift the cake out of the tin using the
clear film and then peel off the film. Cut
into 12 bars and serve at once.

CHOCOLATE AND COCONUT SLICES

MAKES 24
175g/6oz digestive biscuits
115g/4oz/1 cup walnuts
50g/2oz/¼ cup caster sugar
pinch of salt
115g/4oz/½ cup butter or margarine, melted
75g/3oz/1 cup desiccated coconut
250g/9oz/1½ cups plain chocolate chips
250ml/8fl oz/1 cup sweetened condensed milk

<u>1</u> Place the digestive biscuits in a paper bag, fold the top over so that the bag is sealed and use a rolling pin to crush the biscuits into coarse crumbs. Chop the walnuts into small pieces, and set aside.

<u>2</u> Preheat oven to 180°C/350°F/Gas 4. Put a baking sheet inside to heat up.

<u>3</u> In a bowl, combine the crushed biscuits, sugar, salt and melted butter or margarine. Press the mixture evenly over the base of an ungreased 33 x 23 cm/ 13 x 9 in baking dish.

<u>4</u> Sprinkle the coconut over the biscuit base, then scatter over the chocolate · chips. Pour the condensed milk evenly over the chocolate. Sprinkle the walnuts on top. Place on the hot baking sheet and bake for 30 minutes. Turn out on a wire rack and allow to cool. When cold, cut into slices.

WHITE CHOCOLATE MACADAMIA SLICES

MAKES 16

*150g/5oz/1¼ cups macadamia nuts,
blanched almonds or hazelnuts
400g/14oz white chocolate, broken into
squares
115g/4oz/½ cup ready-to-eat dried apricots
75g/3oz/6 tbsp unsalted butter
5ml/1 tsp vanilla essence
3 eggs
150g/5oz/scant 1 cup light muscovado sugar
115g/4oz/1 cup self-raising flour*

1 Preheat oven to 190°C/375°F/Gas 5.
Lightly grease two 20 cm/8 in round
sandwich cake tins and line the base of
each with greaseproof paper or non-stick
baking paper.

2 Roughly chop the nuts and half the
white chocolate, making sure that the
pieces are more or less the same size,
then use scissors to cut the apricots to
similar size pieces.

3 In a heatproof bowl over a saucepan of
barely simmering water, melt the
remaining white chocolate with the
butter. Remove from the heat and stir in
the vanilla essence.

4 Whisk the eggs and sugar together in a
mixing bowl until thick and pale, then
pour in the melted chocolate mixture,
whisking constantly.

5 Sift the flour over the mixture and fold
it in evenly. Finally, stir in the nuts,
chopped white chocolate and chopped
dried apricots.

6 Spoon into the tins and level the tops.
Bake for 30–35 minutes or until the top
is firm and crusty. Cool in the tins before
cutting each cake into 8 slices.

CRANBERRY AND CHOCOLATE SQUARES

MAKES 12

*150g / 5oz / 1¼ cups self-raising flour, plus
extra for dusting*
115g / 4oz / ½ cup unsalted butter
60ml / 4 tbsp cocoa powder
215g / 7½oz / 1¼ cups light muscovado sugar
2 eggs, beaten
*115g / 4oz / 1⅓ cups fresh or thawed frozen
cranberries*
*75ml / 5 tbsp coarsely grated plain chocolate,
for sprinkling*

FOR THE TOPPING
150ml / ¼ pint / ⅔ cup soured cream
75g / 3oz / 6 tbsp caster sugar
30ml / 2 tbsp self-raising flour
50g / 2oz / 4 tbsp soft margarine
1 egg, beaten
2.5ml / ½ tsp vanilla essence

1 Preheat oven to 180°C/350°F/Gas 4. Grease a 27 x 18 cm/10½ x 7 in cake tin and dust lightly with flour. Combine the butter, cocoa powder and sugar in a saucepan and stir over a low heat until melted and smooth.

2 Remove the melted mixture from the heat and stir in the flour and eggs, beating until thoroughly mixed.

3 Stir in the cranberries, then spread the mixture in the tin. Make the topping by mixing all the ingredients in a bowl. Beat until smooth, then spread over the base.

4 Sprinkle with the grated chocolate and bake for 40–45 minutes, or until risen and firm. Cool in the tin for 10 minutes. Then cut neatly into 12 squares. Remove from the tin and cool on a wire rack.

NUT AND CHOCOLATE CHIP BROWNIES

LOW-FAT BROWNIES

MAKES 9

75ml / 5 tbsp fat-reduced cocoa powder
15ml / 1 tbsp caster sugar
75ml / 5 tbsp skimmed milk
3 large bananas, mashed
175g / 6oz / 1 cup soft light brown sugar
5ml / 1 tsp vanilla essence
5 egg whites
75g / 3oz / ¾ cup self-raising flour
75g / 3oz / ¾ cup oat bran
15ml / 1 tbsp icing sugar, for dusting

1 Preheat oven to 180°C / 350°F / Gas 4. Line a 20 cm / 8 in square cake tin with non-stick baking paper. Blend the cocoa powder and caster sugar with the milk in a bowl. Add the bananas, soft brown sugar and vanilla essence.
2 In a mixing bowl, lightly beat the egg whites with a fork. Add the chocolate mixture and continue to beat well. Sift the flour over the mixture and fold in with the oat bran. Pour the mixture into the prepared cake tin.
3 Bake for 40 minutes or until the top is firm and crusty. Cool in the tin before cutting into squares. Lightly dust the brownies with icing sugar before serving.

MAKES 16

150g / 5oz plain chocolate, chopped into small pieces
120ml / 4fl oz / ½ cup sunflower oil
215g / 7½oz / 1¼ cups light muscovado sugar
2 eggs
5ml / 1 tsp vanilla essence
65g / 2½oz / generous ½ cup self-raising flour
60ml / 4 tbsp cocoa powder
75g / 3oz / ¾ cup walnuts or pecan nuts, chopped
60ml / 4 tbsp milk chocolate chips

1 Preheat oven to 180°C / 350°F / Gas 4. Lightly grease a shallow 19 cm / 7½ in square cake tin. Melt the plain chocolate in a heatproof bowl over a saucepan of barely simmering water.
2 Beat the oil, sugar, eggs and vanilla essence together in a large bowl. Stir in the melted chocolate, then beat well until evenly mixed and smooth.
3 Sift the flour and cocoa powder into the bowl and fold in thoroughly. Stir in the chopped nuts and chocolate chips, tip into the prepared tin and spread evenly to the edges.
4 Bake for 30–35 minutes, or until the top is firm and crusty. Cool in the tin before cutting into squares.

MARBLED BROWNIES

MAKES 24

225g / 8oz plain chocolate, chopped into
small pieces
75g / 3oz / 6 tbsp butter, diced
4 eggs
300g / 11oz / scant 1½ cups granulated sugar
150g / 5oz / 1¼ cups plain flour
2.5ml / ½ tsp salt
5ml / 1 tsp baking powder
10ml / 2 tsp vanilla essence
115g / 4oz / 1 cup walnuts, chopped

FOR THE PLAIN MIXTURE

50g / 2oz / ¼ cup butter, at room temperature
175g / 6oz / ¾ cup cream cheese
75g / 3oz / 6 tbsp granulated sugar
2 eggs
25g / 1oz / ¼ cup plain flour
5ml / 1 tsp vanilla essence

<u>1</u> Preheat oven to 180°C/350°F/Gas 4.
Line a 33 x 23 cm/13 x 9 in baking tin
with greaseproof paper or non-stick
baking paper. Grease the paper lightly.

<u>2</u> Melt the chocolate with the butter in a
heatproof bowl over barely simmering
water, stirring constantly until smooth.
Set the mixture aside to cool.

<u>3</u> Meanwhile, beat the eggs in a bowl
until light and fluffy. Gradually add the
sugar and continue beating until blended.
Sift over the flour, salt and baking powder
and fold in gently but thoroughly.

<u>4</u> Stir in the cooled chocolate mixture.
Add the vanilla essence and walnuts.
Measure and set aside 475ml/16fl oz/
2 cups of the chocolate mixture.

<u>5</u> For the plain mixture, cream the butter
and cream cheese in a bowl. Add the
sugar and beat well. Beat in the eggs,
flour and vanilla essence.

<u>6</u> Spread the unmeasured chocolate
mixture in the tin. Pour over the plain
mixture. Drop spoonfuls of the reserved
chocolate mixture on top.

<u>7</u> With a metal palette knife, swirl the
mixtures to marble them. Do not blend
completely. Bake for 35–45 minutes,
until just set. Turn out when cool and cut
into squares for serving.

WHITE CHOCOLATE BROWNIES WITH MILK CHOCOLATE MACADAMIA TOPPING

SERVES 12

115g/4oz/1 cup plain flour
2.5ml/½ tsp baking powder
pinch of salt
175g/6oz fine quality white chocolate,
chopped into small pieces
115g/4oz/½ cup caster sugar
115g/4oz/½ cup unsalted butter, cut into
small pieces
2 eggs, lightly beaten
5ml/1 tsp vanilla essence
175g/6oz plain chocolate chips or plain
chocolate, chopped into small pieces

FOR THE TOPPING

200g/7oz milk chocolate, chopped into
small pieces
175g/6oz/1½ cups unsalted macadamia
nuts, chopped

<u>1</u> Preheat oven to 180°C/350°F/Gas 4. Grease a 23 cm/9 in springform tin. Sift together the flour, baking powder and salt, set aside.

<u>2</u> In a medium saucepan over a low heat, melt the white chocolate, sugar and butter until smooth, stirring frequently. Cool slightly, then beat in the eggs and vanilla essence. Stir in the flour mixture until well blended. Stir in the chocolate chips or chopped chocolate. Spread evenly in the prepared tin.

<u>3</u> Bake for 20–25 minutes, until a cake tester inserted in the cake tin comes out clean; do not over-bake. Remove the cake from the oven and place the tin on a heatproof surface.

<u>4</u> Sprinkle the chopped milk chocolate evenly over the cake and return it to the oven for 1 minute.

<u>5</u> Remove the cake from the oven again and gently spread the softened chocolate evenly over the top. Sprinkle with the macadamia nuts and gently press them into the chocolate. Cool on a wire rack for 30 minutes, then chill, for about 1 hour, until set. Run a sharp knife around the side of the tin to loosen, then unclip the side of the springform tin and remove it carefully. Cut into thin wedges.

DOUBLE CHOCOLATE CHIP MUFFINS

MAKES 16

400g / 14oz / 3½ cups plain flour
15ml / 1 tbsp baking powder
30ml / 2 tbsp cocoa powder
115g / 4oz / ⅔ cup dark muscovado sugar
2 eggs
150ml / ¼ pint / ⅔ cup soured cream
150ml / ¼ pint / ⅔ cup milk
60ml / 4 tbsp sunflower oil
175g / 6oz white chocolate, chopped into
*   small pieces*
175g / 6oz plain chocolate, chopped into
*   small pieces*
cocoa powder, for dusting

1 Preheat oven to 180°C / 350°F / Gas 4. Place 16 paper muffin cases in muffin tins or deep patty tins. Sift the flour, baking powder and cocoa into a bowl and stir in the sugar. Make a well in the centre.

2 In a separate bowl, beat the eggs with the soured cream, milk and oil, then stir into the well in the dry ingredients. Beat well, gradually incorporating all the surrounding flour mixture to make a thick and creamy batter.

3 Stir the white and plain chocolate pieces into the batter mixture.

4 Spoon the chocolate mixture into the muffin cases, filling them almost to the top. Bake for 25–30 minutes, until well risen and firm to the touch. Cool on a wire rack, then dust the muffins lightly with cocoa powder.

CHOCOLATE WALNUT MUFFINS

MAKES 12

175g / 6oz / ¾ cup unsalted butter
150g / 5oz plain chocolate, chopped into
small pieces
200g / 7oz / scant 1 cup caster sugar
50g / 2oz / ⅓ cup soft dark brown sugar
4 eggs
5ml / 1 tsp vanilla essence
1.5ml / ¼ tsp almond essence
110g / 3¾oz / scant 1 cup plain flour
15ml / 1 tbsp cocoa powder
115g / 4oz / 1 cup walnuts or pecan
nuts, chopped

1 Preheat oven to 180°C / 350°F / Gas 4.
Grease a 12-cup muffin tin, or use paper
cases supported in a bun tin.

2 Melt the butter with the chocolate in
the top of a double boiler or in a
heatproof bowl set over a saucepan of
simmering water. Transfer to a large
mixing bowl.
3 Stir both the sugars into the chocolate
mixture. Mix in the eggs, one at a time,
then add the vanilla and almond essences.

4 Sift over the flour and cocoa, fold in,
then stir in the walnuts or pecan nuts.
5 Fill the muffin cups or cases almost to
the top and bake for 30–35 minutes, until
a skewer inserted in a muffin comes out
clean but slightly sticky. Leave to stand
for 5 minutes before cooling the muffins
on a rack.

CHOCOLATE CINNAMON DOUGHNUTS

MAKES 16

500g/1¼lb/5 cups strong plain flour
30ml/2 tbsp cocoa powder
2.5ml/½ tsp salt
1 sachet easy-blend dried yeast
300ml/½ pint/1¼ cups hand-hot milk
40g/1½oz/3 tbsp butter, melted
1 egg, beaten
115g/4oz plain chocolate, broken into
16 pieces
sunflower oil, for deep frying

FOR THE COATING

45ml/3 tbsp caster sugar
15ml/1 tbsp cocoa powder
5ml/1 tsp ground cinnamon

1 Sift the flour, cocoa and salt into a large bowl. Stir in the yeast. Make a well in the centre and add the milk, melted butter and egg. Stir, gradually incorporating the surrounding dry ingredients, to make a soft and pliable dough.

2 Knead the dough on a lightly floured surface for about 5 minutes, until smooth and elastic. Return to the clean bowl, cover with clear film or a clean dry dish towel and leave in a warm place until the dough has doubled in bulk.

3 Knead the dough lightly again, then divide into 16 pieces. Shape each into a round, press a piece of plain chocolate into the centre, then fold the dough over to enclose the filling, pressing firmly to make sure the edges are sealed. Re-shape the doughnuts when sealed, if necessary.

4 Heat the oil for frying to 180°C/350°F or until a cube of dried bread browns in 30–45 seconds. Deep fry the doughnuts in batches. As each doughnut rises and turns golden brown, turn it over to cook the other side. Drain the cooked doughnuts well on kitchen paper.

5 Mix the sugar, cocoa and cinnamon in a shallow bowl. Toss the doughnuts in the mixture to coat them evenly. Pile on a plate and serve warm.

VARIATION

Instead of using a square of plain chocolate to fill each doughnut, try chocolate spread instead. Use about 5ml/1 tsp of the spread for each doughnut. Seal well before frying.

CHOCOLATE ORANGE SPONGE DROPS

MAKES ABOUT 14

2 eggs
50g / 2 oz / ¼ cup caster sugar
2.5ml / ½ tsp grated orange rind
50g / 2oz / ½ cup plain flour
60ml / 4 tbsp finely shredded orange marmalade
40g / 1½oz plain chocolate, chopped into small pieces

1 Preheat oven to 200°C/400°F/Gas 6. Line three baking sheets with baking parchment. Put the eggs and sugar in a large heatproof bowl and whisk over a pan of simmering water until the mixture is thick and pale.

2 Remove the bowl from the pan of water and continue whisking until the mixture is cool. Whisk in the grated orange rind. Sift the flour over the whisked mixture and fold it in gently.

3 Put spoonfuls of the mixture on the baking sheets, spacing them well apart to allow for spreading. The mixture will make 28–30 drops. Bake for about 8 minutes or until the biscuits are golden. Allow them to cool on the baking sheets for a few minutes, then use a spatula to transfer them to a wire rack to cool completely. Sandwich the biscuits together in pairs with the marmalade.

4 Melt the chocolate in a heatproof bowl set over a pan of barely simmering water. Drizzle or pipe the chocolate over the tops of the sponge drops. Leave to set before serving.

BRIOCHES AU CHOCOLAT

MAKES 12

250g/9oz/2¼ cups strong white flour
pinch of salt
30ml/2 tbsp caster sugar
1 sachet easy-blend dried yeast
3 eggs, beaten, plus extra beaten egg,
for glazing
45ml/3 tbsp hand-hot milk
115g/4oz/½ cup unsalted butter, diced
175g/6oz plain chocolate, broken into
squares

1 Sift the flour and salt into a large mixing bowl and stir in the sugar and yeast. Make a well in the centre of the mixture and add the eggs and milk.

2 Beat the egg and milk mixture well, gradually incorporating the surrounding dry ingredients to make a fairly soft dough. Turn the dough on to a lightly floured surface and knead well for about 5 minutes, until smooth and elastic, adding a little more flour if necessary.
3 Add the butter to the dough, a few pieces at a time, kneading until each addition is absorbed before adding the next. When all the butter has been incorporated and small bubbles appear in the dough, wrap it in clear film and chill for at least 1 hour. If you intend serving the brioches for breakfast, the dough can be left overnight.

4 Lightly grease 12 individual brioche tins set on a baking sheet or a 12-hole brioche or patty tin. Divide the brioche dough into 12 pieces and shape each into a smooth round. Place a chocolate square in the centre of each round. Bring up the sides of the dough and press the edges firmly together to seal, use a little beaten egg if necessary.
5 Place the brioches, join side down, in the prepared tins. Cover and leave them in a warm place for about 30 minutes or until doubled in size. Preheat oven to 200°C/400°F/Gas 6.

6 Brush the brioches with beaten egg. Bake for 12–15 minutes, until well risen and golden brown. Place on wire racks and leave until they have cooled slightly. They should be served warm and can be made in advance and reheated if necessary. Do not serve straight from the oven, as the chocolate will be very hot.

COOK'S TIP
Brioches freeze well for up to 1 month. Thaw at room temperature, then reheat on baking sheets in a low oven and serve warm, but not hot. For a richer variation serve with melted chocolate drizzled over the top of the brioches.

Sweets, Truffles and Drinks

Chocolate and Cherry Colettes

Makes 18–20

*115g/4oz plain dark chocolate, chopped into
small pieces*
*75g/3oz white or milk chocolate, chopped
into small pieces*
25g/1oz/2 tbsp unsalted butter, melted
15ml/1 tbsp Kirsch or brandy
60ml/4 tbsp double cream
*18–20 maraschino cherries or liqueur-soaked
cherries*
milk chocolate curls, to decorate

1 Melt the dark chocolate, then remove it
from the heat. Spoon into 18–20 foil
sweet cases, spread evenly up the sides
with a small brush, then leave the cases in
a cool place until the chocolate has set.

2 Melt the white or milk chocolate with
the butter. Remove from the heat and stir
in the Kirsch or brandy, then the cream.
Cool until the mixture is thick enough to
hold its shape.

3 Carefully peel away the paper from the
chocolate cases. Place one cherry in each
chocolate case. Spoon the white or milk
chocolate cream mixture into a piping
bag fitted with a small star nozzle and
pipe over the cherries until the cases are
full. Top each colette with a generous
swirl, and decorate with milk chocolate
curls. Leave to set before serving.

COGNAC AND GINGER CREAMS

MAKES 18–20

*300g / 11oz plain dark chocolate, chopped
into small pieces*
45ml / 3 tbsp double cream
30ml / 2 tbsp cognac
*4 pieces of stem ginger, finely chopped, plus
15ml / 1 tbsp syrup from the jar*
crystallized ginger, to decorate

1 Polish the insides of 18–20 chocolate moulds carefully with cotton wool. Melt about two-thirds of the chocolate in a heatproof bowl over a saucepan of barely simmering water, then spoon a little into each mould. Reserve a little of the melted chocolate, for sealing the creams.

2 Using a small brush, sweep the chocolate up the sides of the moulds to coat them evenly, then invert them on to a sheet of greaseproof paper and set aside until the chocolate has set.

CHOCOLATE MARSHMALLOW DIPS

Have ready a large baking sheet lined with non-stick baking paper. Melt 175g / 6oz plain or bittersweet chocolate in a heatproof bowl over barely simmering water. Stir until smooth. Remove the pan from the heat, but leave the bowl in place, so that the chocolate does not solidify too soon. You will need 15–20 large or 30–35 small marshmallows. Using cocktail sticks, spear each marshmallow and coat in the chocolate. Roll in ground hazelnuts. Place on the lined baking sheet and chill until set before removing the skewers. Place each marshmallow dip in a foil sweet case.

3 Melt the remaining chopped chocolate over simmering water, then stir in the cream, cognac, stem ginger and ginger syrup, mixing well. Spoon into the chocolate-lined moulds. If the reserved chocolate has solidified, melt, then spoon a little into each mould to seal.

4 Leave the chocolates in a cool place (not the fridge) until set. To remove them from the moulds, gently press them out on to a cool surface, such as a marble slab. Decorate with small pieces of crystallized ginger. Keep the chocolates cool if not serving them immediately.

CHOCOLATE TRUFFLES

MAKES 20 LARGE OR 30 MEDIUM TRUFFLES

250ml / 8fl oz / 1 cup double cream
275g / 10oz fine quality bittersweet or plain chocolate, chopped into small pieces
40g / 1½oz / 3 tbsp unsalted butter, cut into small pieces
45ml / 3 tbsp brandy, whisky or liqueur of own choice
cocoa powder, for dusting (optional)
finely chopped pistachio nuts, to decorate (optional)
400g / 14oz bittersweet chocolate, to decorate (optional)

1 Pour the cream into a saucepan. Bring to the boil over a medium heat. Remove from the heat and add the chocolate, all at once. Stir gently until melted. Stir in the butter until melted, then stir in the brandy, whisky or liqueur. Strain into a bowl and cool to room temperature. Cover the mixture with clear film and chill for 4 hours or overnight.

2 Line a large baking sheet with non-stick baking paper. Using a small ice cream scoop, melon baller or tablespoon, scrape up the mixture into 20 large balls or 30 medium balls and place on the lined baking sheet. Dip the scoop or spoon in cold water from time to time, to prevent the mixture from sticking.

3 If dusting with cocoa powder, sift a thick layer of cocoa on to a dish or pie plate. Roll the truffles in the cocoa, rounding them between the palms of your hands. (Dust your hands with cocoa to prevent the truffles from sticking.) Do not worry if the truffles are not perfectly round as an irregular shape looks more authentic. Alternatively, roll the truffles in very finely chopped pistachios. Chill on the paper-lined baking sheet until firm. Keep in the fridge for up to 10 days or freeze for up to 2 months.

4 If coating with chocolate, do not roll the truffles in cocoa, but freeze them for 1 hour. For perfect results, temper the chocolate. Alternatively, simply melt it in a heatproof bowl over a saucepan of barely simmering water. Using a fork, dip the truffles, one at a time, into the melted chocolate, tapping the fork on the edge of the bowl to shake off excess. Place on a baking sheet, lined with non-stick baking paper. If the chocolate begins to thicken, reheat it gently until smooth. Chill the truffles until set.

MALT WHISKY TRUFFLES

MAKES 25–30

*200g / 7oz plain dark chocolate, chopped into
small pieces
150ml / ¼ pint / ⅔ cup double cream
45ml / 3 tbsp malt whisky
115g / 4oz / ¾ cup icing sugar
cocoa powder, for coating*

1 Melt the chocolate in a heatproof bowl over a saucepan of simmering water, stir until smooth, then cool slightly.

2 Using a wire whisk, whip the cream with the whisky in a bowl until thick enough to hold its shape.

3 Stir in the melted chocolate and icing sugar, mixing evenly, then leave until firm enough to handle.

4 Dust your hands with cocoa powder and shape the mixture into bite-size balls. Coat in cocoa powder and pack into pretty cases or boxes. Store in the fridge for up to 3–4 days if necessary.

TRUFFLE-FILLED EASTER EGG

MAKES 1 LARGE, HOLLOW EASTER EGG
*350g/12oz plain couverture chocolate,
tempered, or plain, milk or white chocolate,
melted*
Chocolate Truffles

1 Line a small baking sheet with non-stick baking paper. Using a small ladle or spoon, pour in enough melted chocolate to coat both halves of an Easter egg mould. Tilt the half-moulds slowly to coat the sides completely; pour any excess chocolate back into the bowl. Set the half-moulds, open side down, on the prepared baking sheet and leave for 1–2 minutes until just set.

2 Apply a second coat of chocolate and chill for 1–3 minutes more, until set. Repeat a third time, then replace the moulds on the baking sheet and chill for at least 1 hour or until the chocolate has set completely. (Work quickly to avoid having to temper the chocolate again; untempered chocolate can be reheated if it hardens.)

3 To remove the set chocolate, place a half-mould, open side up, on a board. Carefully trim any drops of chocolate from the edge of the mould. Gently insert the point of a small knife between the chocolate and the mould to break the air lock. Repeat with the second mould.

4 Holding the mould open side down, squeeze firmly to release the egg half. Repeat with the other half and chill, loosely covered. (Do not touch the chocolate surface with your fingers, as they will leave prints.) Reserve any melted chocolate to reheat for "glue".

5 To assemble the egg, hold one half of the egg with a piece of folded kitchen paper or foil and fill with small truffles. If necessary, use the remaining melted chocolate as "glue". Spread a small amount on to the rim of the egg half and, holding the empty egg half with a piece of kitchen paper or foil, press it on to the filled half, making sure the rims are aligned and carefully joined.

6 Hold for several seconds, then prop up the egg with the folded paper or foil and chill to set. If you like, decorate the egg with ribbons or Easter decorations.

CHOCOLATE CHRISTMAS CUPS

MAKES ABOUT 35 CUPS

275g/10oz plain chocolate, chopped into
small pieces
175g/6oz cold cooked Christmas pudding
75ml/2½fl oz/5 tbsp brandy or whisky
chocolate leaves and crystallized cranberries
to decorate

1 Melt the chocolate and use to coat the bottom and sides of about 35 sweet cases. Allow to set, then repeat, reheating the melted chocolate if necessary. Leave the chocolate cups to cool and set. Reserve the remaining chocolate. Crumble the Christmas pudding into a small bowl, sprinkle with brandy or whisky and allow to stand for 30–40 minutes, until the liquor is absorbed.
2 Spoon a little of the pudding mixture into each cup, smoothing the top. Reheat the remaining chocolate and spoon over the top of each cup to cover the surface. Leave to set, then peel off the cases and place in clean foil cases. Decorate with chocolate leaves and crystallized berries.

MARZIPAN LOGS

MAKES ABOUT 12

225g/8oz marzipan, at room temperature
115g/4oz/⅔ cup candied orange peel,
chopped
30ml/2 tbsp orange-flavoured liqueur
15ml/1 tbsp soft light brown sugar
edible gold powder
75g/3oz plain chocolate, melted
gold-coated sweets

1 Knead the marzipan well, then mix in the chopped peel and liqueur. Set aside for about 1 hour, to dry.
2 Break off small pieces of the mixture and roll them into log shapes.
3 Dip the tops of half of the marzipan logs in the sugar and brush them lightly with edible gold powder.
4 Dip the remaining logs in the melted chocolate. Place on non-stick baking paper and press a gold-coated sweet in the centre of each. When set, arrange all the logs on a plate.

PEPPERMINT CHOCOLATE STICKS

MAKES ABOUT 80

115g/4oz/½ cup granulated sugar
150ml/¼ pint/⅔ cup water
2.5ml/½ tsp peppermint essence
200g/7oz plain dark chocolate, chopped into
small pieces
60ml/4 tbsp toasted desiccated coconut

1 Lightly oil a large baking sheet. Place the sugar and water in a small, heavy-based saucepan and heat gently, stirring until the sugar has dissolved.
2 Bring to the boil and boil rapidly without stirring until the syrup registers 138°C/280°F on a sugar thermometer. Remove the pan from the heat and stir in the peppermint essence.

3 Pour the mixture on to the greased baking sheet and leave until set.

4 Break up the peppermint mixture into a small bowl and use the end of a rolling pin to crush it into small pieces.
5 Melt the chocolate. Remove from the heat and stir in the mint pieces and desiccated coconut.

6 Lay a 30 x 25cm/12 x 10in sheet of non-stick baking paper on a flat surface. Spread the chocolate mixture over the paper, leaving a narrow border all around, to make a rectangle measuring about 25 x 20cm/10 x 8in. Leave to set. When firm, use a sharp knife to cut into thin sticks, each about 6cm/2½in long.

Chocolate Almond Torronne

Makes about 20 slices

115g/4oz plain dark chocolate, chopped into
small pieces
50g/2oz/¼ cup unsalted butter
1 egg white
115g/4oz/½ cup caster sugar
75g/3oz/¾ cup chopped toasted almonds
50g/2oz/½ cup ground almonds
75ml/5 tbsp chopped candied peel

For the coating

175g/6oz white chocolate, chopped into small
pieces
25g/1oz/2 tbsp unsalted butter
115g/4oz/1 cup flaked almonds, toasted

1 Melt the chocolate with the butter in a
heatproof bowl over a saucepan of barely
simmering water until smooth.

2 In a clean, grease-free bowl, whisk the
egg white with the sugar until stiff.
Gradually beat in the melted chocolate
mixture, then stir in the toasted almonds,
ground almonds and peel.

3 Tip the mixture on to a large sheet of
non-stick baking paper and shape into a
thick roll.

4 As the mixture cools, use the paper to
press the roll firmly into a triangular
shape. When you are satisfied with the
shape, twist the paper over the triangular
roll and chill until completely set.

5 Make the coating. Melt the white
chocolate with the butter in a heatproof
bowl over a saucepan of simmering water.
Unwrap the chocolate roll and with a
clean knife spread the white chocolate
quickly over the surface. Press the flaked
almonds in a thin even coating over the
chocolate, working quickly before the
chocolate sets.

6 Chill the coated chocolate roll again
until firm, then cut the torronne into
fairly thin slices to serve. Torronne is
ideal to finish a dinner party.

DOUBLE CHOCOLATE-DIPPED FRUIT

MAKES 24 COATED PIECES

fruits — about 24 pieces (strawberries, cherries, orange segments, large seedless grapes, physalis (Cape gooseberries), kumquats, stoned prunes, stoned dates, dried apricots, dried peaches or dried pears)
115g/4oz white chocolate, chopped into small pieces
115g/4oz bittersweet or plain chocolate, chopped into small pieces

1 Clean and prepare fruits; wipe strawberries with a soft cloth or brush gently with pastry brush. Wash firm-skinned fruits such as cherries and grapes and dry well. Peel and leave whole or cut up any other fruits being used.

CHOCOLATE PEPPERMINT CREAMS

1 egg white
90ml/6 tbsp double cream
5ml/1 tsp peppermint essence
675g/1½lb/5½ cups icing sugar, plus extra for dusting
few drops of green food colouring
175g/6oz plain chocolate, chopped into small pieces

1 Beat the egg white lightly in a bowl. Mix in the cream and peppermint essence, then gradually add the icing sugar to make a firm, pliable dough. Work in 1–2 drops of green food colouring (apply it from a cocktail stick if you are anxious about adding too much colour) until the dough is an even, pale green.

2 On a surface dusted with icing sugar, roll out the dough to a thickness of about 1cm/½in. Stamp out 4cm/1½in rounds of squares and place on a baking sheet lined with non-stick baking paper. Leave to dry for at least 8 hours, turning once.

3 Melt the chocolate in a bowl over barely simmering water. Allow to cool slightly. Spread chocolate over the top of each peppermint cream, and place them on fresh sheets of non-stick paper. Chill until set.

2 Melt the white chocolate. Remove from the heat and cool to tepid (about 29°C/84°F), stirring frequently. Line a baking sheet with non-stick baking paper. Holding each fruit by the stem or end and at an angle, dip about two-thirds of the fruit into the chocolate. Allow the excess to drip off and place on the baking sheet. Chill the fruits for about 20 minutes until the chocolate sets.

3 Melt the bittersweet or plain chocolate, stirring frequently until smooth.

4 Remove the chocolate from the heat and cool to just below body temperature, about 30°C/86°F. Take each white chocolate-coated fruit in turn from the baking sheet and, holding by the stem or end and at the opposite angle, dip the bottom third of each piece into the dark chocolate, creating a chevron effect. Set on the baking sheet. Chill for 15 minutes or until set. Before serving, allow the fruit to stand at room temperature 10–15 minutes before serving.

CHOCOLATE-COATED NUT BRITTLE

MAKES 20–24 PIECES

*115g/4oz/1 cup mixed pecan nuts and whole
almonds
115g/4oz/½ cup caster sugar
60ml/4 tbsp water
200g/7oz plain dark chocolate, chopped into
small pieces*

<u>1</u> Lightly grease a baking sheet with
butter or oil. Mix the nuts, sugar and
water in a heavy-based saucepan. Place
the pan over a gentle heat, stirring until
all the sugar has dissolved.

<u>2</u> Bring to the boil, then lower the heat to
moderate and cook until the mixture
turns a rich golden brown and registers
155°C/310°F on a sugar thermometer. If
you do not have a sugar thermometer,
test the syrup by adding a few drops to a
cup of iced water. The mixture should
solidify to a very brittle mass.

CHOCOLATE-COATED HAZELNUTS

Roast about 225g/8oz/2 cups
hazelnuts in the oven or under the
grill. Allow to cool. Melt the
chocolate in a heatproof bowl over a
pan of barely simmering water.
Remove from the heat, but leave the
bowl over the water so that the
chocolate remains liquid. Have
ready about 30 paper sweet cases,
arranged on baking sheets. Add
the roasted hazelnuts to the
melted chocolate and stir to coat.
Using two spoons, carefully scoop
up a cluster of two or three
chocolate-coated nuts. Carefully
transfer the cluster to a paper sweet
case. Leave the nut clusters in a cool
place until set.

<u>3</u> Quickly remove the pan from the heat
and tip the mixture on to the prepared
baking sheet, spreading it evenly. Leave
until completely cold and hard.

<u>4</u> Break the nut brittle into bite-size
pieces. Melt the chocolate and dip the
pieces to half-coat them. Leave on a sheet
of non-stick baking paper to set.

CHOCOLATE NUT CLUSTERS

MAKES ABOUT 30

525ml/21fl oz/2½ cups double cream
25g/1oz/2 tbsp unsalted butter, cut into small pieces
350ml/12fl oz/1½ cups golden syrup
200g/7oz/scant 1 cup granulated sugar
75g/3oz/⅓ cup light brown sugar
pinch of salt
15ml/1 tbsp vanilla essence
350g/12oz/3 cups combination of hazelnuts, pecans, walnuts, brazil nuts and unsalted peanuts
400g/14oz plain chocolate, chopped into small pieces
15g/½oz/1 tbsp white vegetable fat

1 Lightly brush two baking sheets with vegetable oil. In a large heavy-based saucepan over a medium heat, cook the cream, butter, golden syrup, sugars and salt, stirring occasionally for about 3 minutes, until the sugars dissolve and the butter melts.

2 Bring to the boil and continue cooking, stirring frequently for about 1 hour, until the caramel reaches 119°C/238°F on a sugar thermometer, or until a small amount of caramel dropped into a cup of iced water forms a hard ball.

3 Plunge the bottom of the pan into cold water to stop cooking. Cool slightly, then stir in the vanilla essence.

4 Stir the nuts into the caramel until well coated. Using an oiled tablespoon, drop spoonfuls of nut mixture on to the prepared sheets, about 2.5cm/1in apart. If the mixture hardens, return to the heat to soften. Chill the clusters for 30 minutes until firm and cold, or leave in a cool place until hardened.

5 Using a metal palette knife, transfer the clusters to a wire rack placed over a baking sheet to catch drips. In a medium saucepan, over a low heat, melt the chocolate with the white vegetable fat, stirring until smooth. Set aside to cool slightly.

6 Spoon chocolate over each cluster, being sure to cover completely.

7 Place on a wire rack over a baking sheet. Allow to set for 2 hours until hardened. Store in an airtight container.

CHOCOLATE FUDGE TRIANGLES

MAKES ABOUT 48 TRIANGLES

600g / 1lb 5oz fine quality white chocolate, chopped into small pieces
375g / 13oz can sweetened condensed milk
15ml / 1 tbsp vanilla essence
7.5ml / 1½ tsp lemon juice
pinch of salt
175g / 6oz / 1½ cups hazelnuts or pecan nuts, chopped (optional)
175g / 6oz plain chocolate, chopped into small pieces
40g / 1½oz / 3 tbsp unsalted butter, cut into small pieces
50g / 2oz bittersweet chocolate, for drizzling

<u>1</u> Line a 20cm / 8in square baking tin with foil. Brush the foil lightly with oil. In a saucepan over low heat, melt the white chocolate and condensed milk until smooth, stirring frequently. Remove from the heat and stir in the vanilla essence, lemon juice and salt. Stir in the nuts if using. Spread half the mixture in the tin. Chill for 15 minutes.

<u>2</u> In a saucepan over low heat, melt the plain chocolate and butter until smooth, stirring frequently. Remove from the heat, cool slightly, then pour over the chilled white layer and chill for 15 minutes until set.

<u>3</u> Gently re-heat the remaining white chocolate mixture and pour over the set chocolate layer. Smooth the top, then chill for 2–4 hours until set.

<u>4</u> Using the foil as a guide, remove the fudge from the pan and turn it on to a cutting board. Lift off the foil and use a sharp knife to cut the fudge into 24 squares. Cut each square into a triangle. Melt the bittersweet chocolate in a heatproof bowl over a pan of barely simmering water. Cool slightly, then drizzle over the triangles.

EASY CHOCOLATE HAZELNUT FUDGE

MAKES 16 SQUARES
150ml / ¼ pint / ⅔ cup evaporated milk
350g / 12oz / 1½ cups sugar
large pinch of salt
50g / 2oz / ½ cup hazelnuts, halved
350g / 12oz / 2 cups plain chocolate chips

1 Generously grease a 20cm / 8in square cake tin.
2 Place the evaporated milk, sugar and salt in a heavy-based saucepan. Bring to the boil over a medium heat, stirring constantly. Lower the heat and simmer gently, stirring, for about 5 minutes.
3 Remove the pan from the heat and add the hazelnuts and chocolate chips. Stir gently with a metal spoon until the chocolate has completely melted.

4 Quickly pour the fudge mixture into the prepared tin and spread evenly. Leave to cool and set.
5 When the chocolate hazelnut fudge has set, cut it into 2.5cm / 1in squares. Store in an airtight container, separating the layers with greaseproof paper or non-stick baking paper.

TWO-TONE FUDGE
Make the Easy Chocolate Hazelnut Fudge and spread it in a 23cm / 9in square cake tin, to make a slightly thinner layer than for the main recipe. While it is cooling, make a batch of plain fudge, substituting white chocolate drops for the plain chocolate chips and leaving out the hazelnuts. Let the plain fudge cool slightly before pouring it carefully over the dark chocolate layer. Use a palette knife or slim metal spatula to spread the plain layer to the corners, then set aside to set as before. Cut into squares.

RICH CHOCOLATE PISTACHIO FUDGE

MAKES 36

250g / 9oz / generous 1 cup granulated sugar
375g / 13oz can sweetened condensed milk
50g / 2oz / ¼ cup unsalted butter
5ml / 1 tsp vanilla essence
115g / 4oz plain dark chocolate, grated
75g / 3oz / ¾ cup pistachio nuts, almonds
or hazelnuts

CHOCOLATE AND
MARSHMALLOW FUDGE
25g / 1oz / 2 tbsp butter
350g / 12oz / 1½ cups granulated sugar
175ml / 6fl oz / ¾ cup evaporated milk
pinch of salt
115g / 4oz / 2 cups white mini
marshmallows
225g / 8oz / 1¼ cups chocolate chips
5ml / 1 tsp vanilla essence
115g / 4oz / 1½ cup chopped walnuts
(optional)

1 Generously grease an 18cm / 7 in cake tin. Mix the butter, sugar, evaporated milk and salt in a heavy-based saucepan. Stir over a medium heat until the sugar has dissolved, then bring to the boil and cook for 3–5 minutes or until thickened, stirring all the time.

2 Remove the pan from the heat and beat in the marshmallows and chocolate chips until dissolved. Beat in the vanilla essence. Scrape the mixture into the prepared cake tin and press it evenly into the corners, using a metal palette knife. Level the surface.

3 If using the walnuts, sprinkle them over the fudge and press them in to the surface. Set the fudge aside to cool. Before it has set completely, mark it into squares with a sharp knife. Chill until firm before cutting the fudge up and serving it.

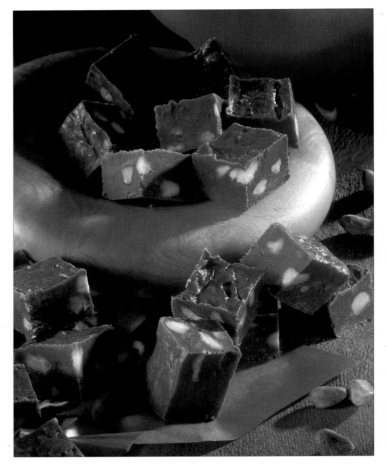

1 Grease a 19cm / 7½in square cake tin and line with non-stick baking paper. Mix the sugar, condensed milk and butter in a heavy-based pan. Heat gently, stirring occasionally, until the sugar has dissolved completely and the mixture is smooth.

2 Bring the mixture to the boil, stirring occasionally, and boil until it registers 116°C / 240°F on a sugar thermometer or until a small amount of the mixture dropped into a cup of iced water forms a soft ball.

3 Remove the pan from the heat and beat in the vanilla essence, chocolate and nuts. Beat vigorously until the mixture is smooth and creamy.

4 Pour the mixture into the prepared cake tin and spread evenly. Leave until just set, then mark into squares. Leave to set completely before cutting into squares and removing from the tin. Store in an airtight container in a cool place.

TRUFFLE-FILLED FILO CUPS

MAKES ABOUT 24 CUPS

3–6 sheets fresh or thawed frozen filo pastry,
depending on size
40g / 1½ oz / 3 tbsp unsalted butter, melted
sugar, for sprinkling
pared strips of lemon zest, to decorate

FOR THE CHOCOLATE TRUFFLE MIXTURE

250ml / 8fl oz / 1 cup double cream
225g / 8oz bittersweet or plain chocolate,
chopped into small pieces
50g / 2oz / ¼ cup unsalted butter, cut into
small pieces
30ml / 2 tbsp brandy or liqueur

1 Prepare the truffle mixture. In a saucepan over a medium heat, bring the cream to a boil. Remove from the heat and add the pieces of chocolate, stirring until melted. Beat in the butter and add the brandy or liqueur. Strain into a bowl and chill for 1 hour until thick.

2 Preheat oven to 200°C/400°F/Gas 6. Grease a 12-hole bun tray. Cut the filo sheets into 6cm/2½ in squares. Cover with a damp dish towel. Place one square on a work surface. Brush lightly with melted butter, turn over and brush the other side. Sprinkle with a pinch of sugar. Butter another square and place it over the first at an angle; sprinkle with sugar. Butter a third square and place over the first two, unevenly, so the corners form an uneven edge. Press the layered square into one of the holes in the bun tray.

3 Continue to fill the tray, working quickly so that the filo does not have time to dry out. Bake the filo cups for 4–6 minutes, until golden. Cool for 10 minutes on the bun tray then carefully transfer to a wire rack and cool completely.

4 Stir the chocolate mixture; it should be just thick enough to pipe. Spoon the mixture into a piping bag fitted with a medium star nozzle and pipe a swirl into each filo cup. Decorate each with tiny strips of lemon zest.

MEXICAN HOT CHOCOLATE

SERVES 4

1 litre / 1¾ pints / 4 cups milk
1 cinnamon stick
2 whole cloves
115g / 4oz plain dark chocolate, chopped into
small pieces
2—3 drops of almond essence

1 Heat the milk gently with the spices in a saucepan until almost boiling, then stir in the plain chocolate over a moderate heat until melted.

2 Strain into a blender, add the almond essence and whizz on high speed for about 30 seconds until frothy. Alternatively, whisk the mixture with a hand-held electric mixer or wire whisk.

3 Pour into warmed heatproof glasses and serve immediately.

WHITE HOT CHOCOLATE

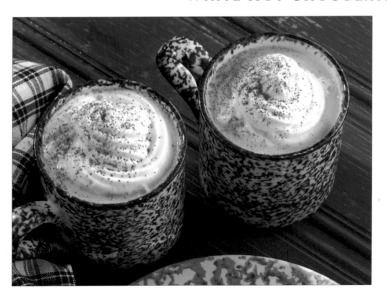

SERVES 4

1.75 litres / 3 pints / 7½ cups milk
175g / 6oz white chocolate, chopped into
small pieces
10ml / 2 tsp coffee powder
10ml / 2 tsp orange-flavoured liqueur
(optional)
whipped cream and ground cinnamon, to serve

1 Pour the milk into a large heavy-based saucepan and heat until almost boiling. As soon as bubbles form around the edge of the pan remove the milk from the heat.

2 Add the white chocolate, coffee powder and orange-flavoured liqueur, if using. Stir until all the chocolate has melted and the mixture is smooth.

3 Pour the hot chocolate into four mugs. Top each with a swirl or spoonful of whipped cream and a sprinkling of ground cinnamon. Serve immediately.

ICED MINT AND CHOCOLATE COOLER

SERVES 4

60ml/4 tbsp drinking chocolate
400ml/14fl oz/1⅔ cups chilled milk
150ml/¼ pint/⅔ cup natural yogurt
2.5ml/½ tsp peppermint essence
4 scoops of chocolate ice cream
mint leaves and chocolate shapes, to decorate

<u>1</u> Place the drinking chocolate in a small pan and stir in about 120ml/4fl oz/½ cup of the milk. Heat gently, stirring, until almost boiling, then remove the pan from the heat.

<u>2</u> Pour the hot chocolate milk into a heatproof bowl or large jug and whisk in the remaining milk. Add the natural yogurt and peppermint essence and whisk again.

<u>3</u> Pour the mixture into four tall glasses, filling them no more than three-quarters full. Top each drink with a scoop of ice cream. Decorate with mint leaves and chocolate shapes. Serve immediately.

CHOCOLATE VANILLA COOLER

Make the drink as in the main recipe, but use single cream instead of the natural yogurt and 5ml/1 tsp natural vanilla essence instead of the peppermint essence.

MOCHA COOLER

Make the drink as in the main recipe, but dissolve the chocolate in 120ml/4fl oz/½ cup strong black coffee, and reduce the milk to 300ml/½ pint/1¼ cups. Use cream instead of yogurt and leave the essence out.

IRISH CHOCOLATE VELVET

SERVES 4

250ml/8fl oz/1 cup double cream
400ml/14fl oz/1⅔ cups milk
115g/4oz milk chocolate, chopped into small pieces
30ml/2 tbsp cocoa powder
60ml/4 tbsp Irish whiskey
whipped cream, for topping
chocolate curls, to decorate

<u>1</u> Using a hand-held electric mixer, whip half the cream in a bowl until it is thick enough to hold its shape.

<u>2</u> Place the milk and chocolate in a saucepan and heat gently, stirring, until the chocolate has melted.

<u>3</u> Whisk in the cocoa, then bring to the boil. Remove from the heat and stir in the remaining cream and the Irish whiskey.

<u>4</u> Pour quickly into four warmed heatproof mugs or glasses and top each serving with a generous spoonful of the whipped cream, then the chocolate curls. Serve with Peppermint Sticks for extra indulgence.

HOT CHOCOLATE AND CHOC-TIPPED BISCUITS

SERVES 2

FOR THE CHOC-TIPPED BISCUITS

115g/4oz/1/2 cup soft margarine
15ml/3 tbsp icing sugar, sifted
150g/5oz/1¼ cups plain flour
few drops of vanilla essence
75g/3oz plain chocolate, chopped into
small pieces.

FOR THE HOT CHOCOLATE

90ml/6 tbsp drinking chocolate powder, plus
a little extra for sprinkling
30ml/2 tbsp caster sugar, or more according
to taste
600ml/1 pint/2½ cups milk
2 large squirts of cream (optional)

<u>1</u> Preheat oven to 180°C/350°F/Gas 4
and lightly grease two baking sheets.
Make the choc-tipped biscuits. Put the
margarine and icing sugar in a bowl and
beat them together until very soft. Mix in
the flour and vanilla essence.

<u>2</u> Put the mixture in a large piping bag
fitted with a large star nozzle. Pipe ten
neat lines, each 13cm/5in long, on the
baking sheets. Leave a little room
between each biscuit. They will not
spread much on cooking, but you need to
be able to remove them easily. Cook for
15–20 minutes until the biscuits are pale
golden brown. Allow to cool slightly
before lifting on to a wire rack.

<u>3</u> Put the chocolate in a heatproof bowl
over a saucepan of barely simmering
water and leave to melt. Stir until
creamy, then remove the bowl of melted
chocolate from the heat. Dip both ends of
each biscuit in the chocolate, put back on
the rack and leave to cool and set.

<u>4</u> To make the drinking chocolate, put the
drinking chocolate powder and the sugar
in a saucepan. Add the milk and bring it
to the boil, whisking all the time. Divide
between two tall mugs. Add more sugar
if needed. Top each drink with a squirt of
cream, if you like.

SAUCES, FROSTINGS AND ICINGS

SIMPLE BUTTERCREAM

MAKES ABOUT 350G/12OZ
75g/3oz butter or soft margarine
225g/8oz/1½ cups icing sugar
5ml/1 tsp vanilla essence
10–15ml/2–3 tsp milk

1 If using butter, allow it to come to room temperature so that it can easily be creamed. Sift the icing sugar. Put the butter or margarine in a bowl. Add about a quarter of the icing sugar and beat with a hand-held electric mixer until fluffy.

2 Using a metal spoon, add the remaining sifted icing sugar, a little at a time, beating well with the electric mixer after each addition. Icing sugar is so fine that if you add too much of it at one time, it tends to fly out of the bowl.

3 Beat in 5ml/1 tsp of the milk. The mixture should be light and creamy, with a spreadable consistency. Add the vanilla essence, then more milk if necessary, but not too much, or it will be too sloppy to draw into peaks. Use as a filling and/or topping on layer cakes and cupcakes.

CHOCOLATE BUTTERCREAM

ENOUGH TO FILL A 20CM/8IN ROUND LAYER CAKE
75g/3oz/6 tbsp unsalted butter or margarine, softened
175g/6oz/1 cup icing sugar
15ml/1 tbsp cocoa powder
2.5ml/½ tsp vanilla essence

1 Place all the ingredients in a large bowl.

2 Beat well to a smooth spreadable consistency.

VARIATIONS

Coffee Buttercream: Stir 10ml/2 tsp instant coffee into 15ml/1 tbsp boiling water. Beat into the icing instead of the milk.
Mocha Buttercream: Stir 5ml/1 tsp cocoa powder into 10ml/2 tsp boiling water. Beat into the icing. Add a little coffee essence.
Orange Buttercream: Use orange juice instead of the milk and vanilla essence, and add 10ml/2 tsp finely grated orange rind. Omit the rind if using the icing for piping.

WHITE CHOCOLATE FROSTING

ENOUGH TO COVER A 20CM/8IN ROUND CAKE
175g/6oz white chocolate, chopped into small pieces
75g/3oz/6 tbsp unsalted butter
115g/4oz/¾ cup icing sugar
90ml/6 tbsp double cream

1 Melt the chocolate with the butter in a heatproof bowl over a saucepan of barely simmering water. Remove the bowl from the heat and beat in the icing sugar, a little at a time, using a wire whisk.

2 Whip the cream in a separate bowl until it just holds its shape, then beat into the chocolate mixture. Allow the mixture to cool, stirring occasionally, until it begins to hold its shape. Use immediately.

COOK'S TIP
White chocolate frosting is a rich frosting suitable for a dark chocolate sponge without a filling. Use a palette knife to form peaks for an attractive finish.

FUDGE FROSTING

MAKES 350G/12OZ

50g/2oz plain chocolate, chopped into
small pieces
225g/8oz/2 cups icing sugar, sifted
50g/2oz/¼ cup butter or margarine
45ml/3 tbsp milk or single cream
15ml/1 tbsp vanilla essence

COOK'S TIP

When you have covered the cake
with the frosting, use the back of a
spoon or the tines of a fork to swirl
the fudge frosting and create an
attractive pattern on the cake, but do
this quickly, as it sets very fast.

1 Put the chocolate, icing sugar, butter or
margarine, milk or cream and vanilla
essence in a heavy-based saucepan.
2 Stir over a very low heat until the
chocolate and butter or margarine melt.
Turn off the heat, stir until smooth.

3 Beat the icing frequently as it cools until
it thickens sufficiently to use for
spreading or piping. Use immediately and
work quickly once it has reached the right
consistency. This is a popular frosting and
can be used for many kinds of cakes.

SATIN CHOCOLATE ICING

MAKES 225G/8OZ

*175g/6oz plain or bittersweet
chocolate, chopped into small pieces
150ml/¼ pint/⅔ cup double cream
2.5ml/½ tsp instant coffee powder*

COOK'S TIP

Do not touch the icing once it has
hardened or the attractive satin finish
will be spoilt. Cakes covered with
this icing need little by way of
decoration, but half-dipped cherries
look very effective.

1 Put the chocolate, cream and coffee in a
small heavy-based saucepan. Place the
cake to be iced on a wire rack over a
baking sheet or tray.

2 Place the saucepan over a very low heat
and stir the mixture with a wooden spoon
until all the pieces of plain or bittersweet
chocolate have melted and the mixture is
smooth and evenly blended.

3 Remove from the heat and immediately
pour the icing over the cake, letting it run
down the sides slowly to coat it
completely. Spread the icing with a
palette knife or slim spatula as necessary,
working quickly before the icing has time
to thicken.

CHOCOLATE FONDANT
**ENOUGH TO COVER AND DECORATE
A 23CM/9IN ROUND CAKE**

*350g/12oz plain chocolate, chopped into
small pieces
60ml/4 tbsp liquid glucose
2 egg whites
900g/2lb/7 cups icing sugar*

1 Put the chocolate and glucose in a
heatproof bowl. Place over a
saucepan of barely simmering water
and leave to melt, stirring the
mixture occasionally. When it is
smooth, remove the bowl from the
heat and cool slightly.
2 In a clean, grease-free bowl, whisk the
egg whites with a hand-held electric
mixer until soft peaks form, then stir
into the chocolate mixture with about
45ml/3 tbsp of the icing sugar.
3 Continue to beat the icing,
gradually adding enough of the
remaining icing sugar to make a stiff
paste. Wrap the fondant in clear film
if not using immediately.

BITTERSWEET CHOCOLATE SAUCE

QUICK CHOCOLATE SAUCE
MAKES 225ML/8FL OZ/1 CUP

150ml/1/4 pint/2/3 cup double cream
15ml/1 tbsp caster sugar
150g/5oz plain chocolate, chopped into
small pieces
30ml/2 tbsp dark rum or whisky
(optional)

<u>1</u> Bring the cream and sugar to the boil. Remove from the heat, add the chocolate and stir until melted. Stir in the rum or whisky.

<u>2</u> Pour the chocolate sauce into a jar. When cool, cover and store for up to 10 days. Reheat by standing the jar in a saucepan of simmering water, or remove the lid and microwave on High power for 2 minutes. Stir before serving.

MAKES ABOUT 350ML/12FL OZ

45ml/3 tbsp granulated sugar
120ml/4fl oz/1/2 cup water
175g/6oz bittersweet chocolate, chopped into
small pieces
25g/1oz/2 tbsp unsalted butter, diced
60–90ml/4–6 tbsp single cream
2.5ml/1/2 tsp vanilla essence

<u>1</u> Combine the sugar and water in a heavy-based saucepan. Bring to the boil over a medium heat, stirring constantly until all the sugar has dissolved.

<u>2</u> Add the chocolate and butter to the syrup, stir with a wooden spoon, then remove the pan from the heat and continue to stir until smooth.

<u>3</u> Stir in the single cream and vanilla essence. Serve the sauce warm, over vanilla ice cream, profiteroles, poached pears or crêpes.

GLOSSY CHOCOLATE SAUCE

SERVES 6

115g/4oz/1/2 cup caster sugar
60ml/4 tbsp water
175g/6oz plain chocolate, chopped into
small pieces
25g/1oz/2 tbsp unsalted butter
30ml/2 tbsp brandy or orange juice

COOK'S TIP
Any of these sauces would make a chocolate fondue, with fruit and dessert biscuits as dippers.

<u>1</u> Place the caster sugar and water in a heavy-based saucepan and heat gently, stirring occasionally with a wooden spoon until all the sugar has dissolved.

<u>2</u> Stir in the chocolate until melted, then add the butter in the same way. Do not allow the sauce to boil. Stir in the brandy or orange juice and serve warm.

CHOCOLATE FUDGE SAUCE

SERVES 6

150ml / ¼ pint / ⅔ cup double cream
50g / 2oz / ¼ cup butter
50g / 2oz / ¼ cup vanilla sugar
175g / 6oz plain chocolate, chopped into
small pieces
30ml / 2 tbsp brandy

1 Heat the cream with the butter and sugar in a bowl over a saucepan of barely simmering water. Stir until smooth, then leave to cool.

2 Add the chocolate to the cream mixture. Stir over simmering water until it is melted and thoroughly combined.

3 Stir in the brandy a little at a time, then cool to room temperature.

CHOCOLATE GANACHE
ENOUGH TO COVER A 23cm / 9in
ROUND CAKE

225g / 8oz plain chocolate, chopped into
small pieces
250ml / 8fl oz / 1 cup double cream

Melt the chocolate with the cream in a saucepan over a low heat. Pour into a bowl, leave to cool, then whisk until the mixture begins to hold its shape.

WHITE CHOCOLATE AND ORANGE SAUCE

SERVES 6

150ml / ¼ pint / ⅔ cup double cream
50g / 2oz / ¼ cup butter
45ml / 3 tbsp caster sugar
175g / 6oz white chocolate, chopped into
small pieces
30ml / 2 tbsp orange-flavoured liqueur
finely grated rind of 1 orange

COOK'S TIP
Serve with ice cream, or with hot waffles or fresh crêpes.

1 Pour the cream into a heavy-based saucepan. Cut the butter into cubes and add it to the pan, with the sugar. Heat gently, stirring the mixture occasionally until the butter has melted.

2 Add the chocolate to the cream. Stir over a very low heat until it is melted and thoroughly combined.
3 Stir in the orange rind, then add the liqueur a little at a time. Leave to cool.

CHOCOLATE SUPPLIERS AROUND THE WORLD

AUSTRALIA
Chocolatier Australia
224 Waterdale Road, Ivanhoe,
Victoria 3079 Tel: (3) 94 99 70 22

The Chocolate Box
761 Burke Road, Camberwell,
Victoria 3124 Tel: (3) 98 13 13 77

Darren Taylor's Handmade Chocolates
Seet Art, 96 Oxford Street, Paddington,
New South Wales 2021
Tel: (2) 93 61 66 17

Sweet William Chocolates
4 William Street, Paddington, New
South Wales 2021 Tel: (2) 93 31 54 68

Simon Johnson
181 Harris Street, Pyrmont, New South
Wales 2009 Tel: (2) 95 52 25 22

Haigh's Chocolates
Beehive Corner, 2 Rundle Mall,
Adelaide, South Australia
Tel: (8) 23 12 844

AUSTRIA
Altmann & Kühne
Graben 30, 1010 Wien
Tel: (1) 53 30 927

Demels
14 Kohlmarkt, 1010 Wien
Tel: (1) 53 51 717

Hotel Imperial
Kärtner Ring 16, A-1051 Wien
Tel: (1) 50 11 03 13
Fax: (1) 50 10 355

Mirabell Salzburger Confiserie
Hauptstrasse 14-16, A-5082 Grödig
Tel: (62) 46 20 110

BELGIUM
Charlemagne
Place Jacques Brel 8, 4040 Herstal
Tel: (41) 64 66 44

Godiva
Wapenstilstandstraat 5, 1081 Brussels
Tel: (2) 42 21 711

Kim's Chocolates
Nieuwlandlaan 12, Industriezone B-615,
B-3200 Aarschot
Tel: (16) 55 15 80

Neuhaus
Postbox 2, B - 1602 Vlenzenbeek
Tel: (2) 56 82 211

Pierre Colas
2 Rue Campagne, 4577 Modave
Tel: (2) 64 80 893

Wittamer
12 Place du Grand Sablon, Grote Zavel
12, 1000 Brussels Tel: (2) 51 28 451

FRANCE
Bonnat
8 Cours Senozan, 38500 Voiron
Tel: (76) 05 28 09

Christian Constant
26 Rue du Bac, 75007 Paris
Tel: (47) 03 30 00

Cluizel
La Fontaine au Chocolat
101 & 210 Rue Saint Honoré,
75001, Paris Tel: (1) 42 44 11 66

Fauchon
26-30 Place de la Madeleine,
75008 Paris Tel: (1) 47 42 60 11

Lalonde
59 Rue St Dizier, 54400 Nancy
Tel: 83 53 31 57

La Maison du Chocolat
225 Rue Faubourg St Honoré,
75008 Paris Tel: (1) 42 27 39 44

Le Roux
18 Rue du Port-Maria, 56170 Quiberon
Tel: 97 50 06 83

Richart Design et Chocolat
258 Bd. Saint-Germain, 75007 Paris
Tel: (1) 45 55 66 00

Chocolaterie Valrhona
BP 40, 26600 Tain L'Hermitage
Tel: 75 07 90 90

Weiss
18 Avenue Denfert-Rochereau,
42000 St Etienne
Tel: 77 49 41 41

GERMANY
Confiserie Heinemann
Krefelder Strasse 645
41066 München-Gladbach
Tel: (2161) 6930

Dreimeister
Weststrasse 47 - 49, Werl,
Westönnen Tel: 29 22 8 20 45

Feodora
Vertriebszentrale Bremen,
Postfach 105803, D28058 Bremen
Tel: (421) 59 90 61

Bremer Chocolade-Fabrik Hachez
Westerstrasse 32, D-28199 Bremen
Tel: (421) 59 50 64 62

Leysieffer
Benzstrasse 9, 49076 Osnabrück
Tel: (541) 91 420

Stollwerck
Stollwerckstrasse 27-31, 51149 Köln
Tel: (22) 03 430

Van Houten
Am Stamgleis, 22844 Norderstedt
Tel: (5) 26 020

GREAT BRITAIN
Ackermans
9 Goldhurst Terrace, Finchley Road,
London, NW6 3HX
Tel: (0171) 624 2742

Charbonnel et Walker
1 The Royal Arcade, 28 Old Bond
Street, London, W1X 4BT
Tel: (0171) 491 0939

Gerard Ronay
3 Warple Way, London, W3 0RF
Tel: (0181) 730 818

Godiva
247 Regent Street, London, W1
Tel: (0171) 409 0963

Grania & Sarni
6 Sterne Street, London, W12 8AD
Tel: (0181) 749 8274

Green & Black
Whole Earth Food, 269 Portobello
Road, London, W11 1LR
Tel: (0171) 229 7545

JB Confectionery
Unit 3, The Palmerston Centre,
Oxford Road, Harrow, Middlesex
HA3 7RG Tel: (0181) 863 0011

Mortimer & Bennett
33 Turnham Green Terrace, London,
W4 1RG Tel: (0181) 995 4145

Rococo Chocolates
321 Kings Road, London, SW3 5EP
Tel: (0171) 352 5857
Fax: (0171) 352 7360

Sara Jayne
517 Old York Road, London, SW18 1TF
Tel: (0181) 874 8500

The Chocolate Society
Clay Pit Lane, Roecliffe, Near
Boroughbridge, N. Yorks, YO5 9LS
Tel: (01423) 322 230

The Cool Chile Company
P.O. Box 5702, London, W11 2GS
Tel: (0171) 229 9360

Town & Country Chocolates
52 Oxford Road, Denham, Uxbridge,
Middlesex, UB9 4DH
Tel: (01895) 256 166

ITALY
Caffarel/Peyrano
Via Gianevello 41 - 10062 Luserna,
S. Giovanni (TO), Piedmont
Tel: (121) 90 10 86

Maglio Arte Dolciaria
73024 Maglio, La Via Gioacchino
Toma 4 Tel: (836) 25 723

Majani
Via Lunga 19/C, Crespellano (BO)
Tel: 51 96 91 57

Perugina
Nestlé Italiana
Via Pievaiola, San Sisto, PGIT
Tel: (75) 52 761

MEXICO
Chocolatera de Jalisco
Av Narianotero 1420, Apartado Postal
33121, 44510 Guadalajara, Halisco

SPAIN
Blanxart
Tambor del Bruc, 13-08970 Sant Joan
Despi, Barcelona Tel: (3) 373 3761

Ludomar
Ciudad de la Asunción 58, 08030
Barcelona Tel: (72) 203 662

Ramón Roca
Mercaders, 6 17004, Gerona
Tel: (72) 203 662

Chocolates Valor
Pianista Gonzalo Soriano, 13 Villajoyosa
Tel: (6) 589 050

SWITZERLAND
Lindt & Sprüngli
Seestrasse 204, CH-8802 Kilchberg
Tel: (1) 71 62 233

Sprüngli
Bahnhofstrasse 21, 8022 Zurich
Tel: (1) 21 15 777

THE NETHERLANDS
Bensdorp
Heerenstraat 51, Postbus 4, 1400 AA
Bussum Tel: (35) 69 74 911

Gerkens Cacao
Veerdijk 82, Postbus 82, 1530 AB
Wormer Tel: (35) 69 74 911

Cacao De Zaan
Stationsstraat 76, Postbus 2, 1540 AA
Koog aan de Zaan
Tel: (75) 62 83 601

Droste
PO Box 5, 8170AA Vaassen
Tel: (578) 57 82 00

USA
Dilettante Chocolates
416 Broadway, Seattle, WA 98102
Tel: (206) 328 1530

Fran's
2805 East Madison, Seattle, Washington,
WA 98122-4020
Tel: (206) 322 0233

Ghirardelli
900 North Point Street, San Francisco,
CA 94109 Tel: (415) 474 1414

Joseph Schmidt Confections
3489 16th Street, San Francisco,
CA 9411 Tel: (415) 861 8682

Richard Donnelly Fine Chocolates
1509 Mission Street, Santa Cruz,
CA 95060 Tel: (408) 458 4214

Moonstruck Chocolatier
6663 SW BVTN Hillsdale Highway,
STE194, Portland, Oregon, OR9 7225
Tel: (503) 283 8843

ACKNOWLEDGEMENTS
Thanks to the following companies for
supplying chocolates for photography:

Ackermans, Alfred Ritter, Bendicks
(Mayfair) Ltd, Charbonnel et Walker,
The Cool Chile Company, The
Chocolate Society, Richard Donnelly,
Feodora Chocolate, Ghirardelli
Chocolate Company, Grania & Sarni,
Green and Black, The Jenks Group, JB
Confectionery, Leonidas, Lessiters,
Nestlé Rowntree Ltd, Parsons Trading
Ltd, Perugina, Richart Design et
Chocolat, Rococo, Ryne Quality
Confectionery, Joseph Schmidt, Town &
Country Chocolates, Trustin.

Thanks also to Stefano Raimondi of the
Italian Trade Centre, Patrizia De Vito of
the Associazione Industrie Dolciarie in
Rome, Elaine Ashton of Grania and
Sarnia, Dan Mortimer of Mortimer and
Bennet, David Lyle of Town and Country
Chocolates and John Bacon of JB
Confectionery.

  Christine McFadden is particularly
indebted to the late Sophie Coe, and her
husband Michael Coe, for their book *The
True History of Chocolate*, and to Chantal
Coady for the information in *The
Chocolate Companion*.

INDEX

PICTURE ACKNOWLEDGEMENTS

Thanks to the following picture libraries for supplying additional images in the book.
AKG, London: pp9(br) *Columbus discovers the New World*, Bernhard Rode; 10(br) *First landing on Guanaja*, wood engraving; 19(b) *Goethe in the Countryside*, Johann Tischbein; 24(b) *Healing plants, cacao*, from FE Bilz; 6 (bl) & 61(tr) Poster for chocolate, *Mother's Cocoa in Danger*.

Bridgeman Art Library: 6(r) *Cacao Van Houten*, Privit Livemont, Victoria and Albert, London; 18(r) *The chocolate girl*, Jean-Etienne Liotard, Dresden Gemäldegalerie; 19 *Still life*, Philippe Rousseau, Musée des Beaux Arts, Reims, Peter Willi; 20(t) *Cardinal Mazarin*, French School, Musée Condé, Chantilly; 20(bl) *Tapestry of Louis XIV's marriage*, Gobelins, Mobilier National, Paris; 22(br) *A cup of chocolate*, Sir John Lavery, Whitford and Hughes, London; 23(r) American poster for chocolate; 26(b) *Cocoa plantation in the Isle of Grenada*, O'Shea Gallery, London; 60(bl) *Cacao Van Houten*, Privet Livemont, Victoria and Albert, London; 60(br) Box of Cadbury's assorted chocolates, c1913.

Mansell Collection: pp25(b).
Public Records Office : pp6(l);

11(t); 27(t); 28(t); 30(br); p57(br).
Visual Arts Library: pp8(l); 9(l); 10 *Montezuma offering chocolate to Herman Cortés*, PG Miguel, Artephot/Oronoz; 15(t) *Mexican making chocolate*, Codex Tuleda, Artephot/Oronoz; 20(r) *A horseman and a lady drinking chocolate*, Bonnart, Vision; 25(l) *Still Life: Chocolate set*, Luis Melendez, Museo del Prado, Madrid, Artephot/Oronoz; 26(b) *The morning cocoa*, Longhi; 25(tr) *The breakfast*, François Boucher, Musée du Louvre, Artephot/Oronoz; 25(l) *Physiologie du Goût ou Méditations de Gastronomie Transcendante*, E Baneste; 29(br) *Advertisement, Chocolat Menier*, F Bouisset, Artephot/Perrin; 16(tl) *Cacao Van Houten*, Artephot/Perrin; 16(tr) Poster for Chocolate, H Gerbault; 48(tl) Poster for French Chocolate and Tea Company, Steilen, Artephot/Perrin; 49(l) Chocolat Capentier poster; 58(br) Chocolat Mondia, Artephot/Vision; 59(l) *Portrait of Madame Du Barry*, Greuze, Artephot/Varga; 61(br) *Chocolat Masson*, Grasset, Artephot/Perrin.

Other pictures supplied courtesy of Bendick's (Mayfair) Ltd: 16(bl), Cadburys Ltd: 28(bl); 42(b); 43(bl); 60(tr). Fran's: 62. Godiva: 37(bl) 58(t). Nestlé Rowntree Ltd: 1; 27(b); 34(br) 36(tr&l), Rococo: 17(bl).

SELECTED BIBLIOGRAPHY

NATHALIE BAILLEUX, HERVÉ BIZEUL, JOHN FELTWELL, RÉGINE KOPP, CORBY KUMMER, PIERRE LABANNE, CRISTINA PAULY, ODILE PERRARD, MARIAROSA SCHIAFFINO, preface JEANNE BOURIN 1995 *The Book of Chocolate*. Paris, New York: Flammarion.
BLYTHMAN, JOANNA 1996 *The Food We Eat*. London: Michael Joseph.
COADY, CHANTAL 1993 *Chocolate: The Food of the Gods*. London: Pavilion Books.
COADY, CHANTAL 1995 *The Chocolate Companion*. London: Quintet Publishing.
COE, SOPHIE D. AND MICHAEL D. 1996 *The True History of Chocolate*. London: Thames and Hudson.
COX, CAT 1993 *Chocolate Unwrapped: The Politics of Pleasure*. London: The Women's Environmental Network.
GAGE, THOMAS 1648 *The English-American His Travail by Land and Sea, or a New Survey of the West Indies*. London.
HEAD, BRANDON 1905 *The Food of the Gods*. London: George Routledge & Sons.

McGEE, HAROLD 1984 *On Food and Cooking: The Science and Lore of the Kitchen*. London, Australia: George Allen & Unwin.
MONTIGNAC, MICHEL 1991 *Dine Out and Lose Weight*. London: Artulen UK.
RICHART DESIGN ET CHOCOLAT *Le Petit Livre Blanc du Chocolat*.
SHERR, JEREMY *The Homoeopathic Proving of Chocolate*. Dynamis School.
Spicing up the Palate: Studies of Flavourings — Ancient and Modern. Proceedings of the Oxford Symposium on Food and Cookery 1992. Totnes, Devon: Prospect Books.
STOBART, TOM 1977 *Herbs, Spices and Flavourings*. Penguin Books.
TRAGER, JAMES 1995 *The Food Chronology*. Ontario: Fitzhenry & Whiteside.
WATERHOUSE, DEBRA 1995 *Why Women Need Chocolate*. London: Vermilion.
WHYMPER, R. 1921 *Cocoa and Chocolate: Their Chemistry and Manufacture*. London: J. & A. Churchill.
WILLIAMS, C. TREVOR 1953 *Chocolate and Confectionery*. London.

NOTES

NOTES

NOTES

NOTES

NOTES

NOTES